Cotton Mather
and *Biblia Americana*
America's First Bible Commentary

Cotton Mather and *Biblia Americana*

America's First Bible Commentary

ESSAYS IN REAPPRAISAL

Edited by

Reiner Smolinski and Jan Stievermann

Baker Academic
a division of Baker Publishing Group
Grand Rapids, Michigan

© 2010 by Mohr Siebeck, Tübigen, Germany

Paperback edition published in 2011 by Baker Academic
a division of Baker Publishing Group
P.O. Box 6287, Grand Rapids, MI 49516-6287
www.bakeracademic.com

ISBN: 978-0-8010-3969-0

Originally published in 2010 in Tübigen, Germany, by Mohr Siebeck GmbH & C. KG Tübigen as
Cotton Mather and Biblia Americana—America's First Bible Commentary: Essays in Reappraisal.

Printed in the United States of America

Library of Congress Cataloging-in-Publication Data is on file at the Library of Congress, Washington, DC.

11   12   13   14   15   16   17   7   6   5   4   3   2   1

For Tanya

and

For Juliane, Ellen, and Theodor

Acknowledgments

This collection of essays constitutes one part of a larger project that revolves around the ongoing scholarly publication of Cotton Mather's "Biblia Americana," scheduled to appear in ten volumes starting in 2010 as a co-publication of Mohr Siebeck and Baker Academic. Behind the edition, to which this book serves as a kind of companion piece, is a revisionist endeavor to study afresh the work of a New England minister and polymath whose considerable intellectual achievements, as both a promoter and critic of Enlightenment ideas, as a renovator of Puritan faith in the context of the Protestant evangelical awakening, and especially as a pioneer of biblical criticism, have not been fully recognized. These essays, all of them original contributions, grew from presentations that were given at the international symposium: "Cotton Mather's 'Biblia Americana': The Early Enlightenment and the Rise of Pietism in America; Historical and Intellectual Contexts in Transatlantic Perspective," which was held at the University of Tübingen in October 2008. The conference and this volume that evolved from it are attempts to open up new perspectives on Mather, and to draw attention to the great potential his "Biblia Americana" holds as a largely untapped resource for studies in early American religion, culture and literature, church history, history of ideas, and theology.

We are very thankful to all the great scholars who made our gathering at Tübingen castle so congenial and fruitful. The conference was made possible through funding by the German Research Foundation (DFG), the American Embassy in cooperation with the German Association for American Studies (DGfA), and the *Vereinigung der Freunde der Universität Tübingen* ("Association of Friends of the University of Tübingen"). We wish to thank these organizations for their generosity in supporting this important event in launching our project, and the *Vereinigung* for contributing to the production costs of this book. For invaluable help in organizing the conference we are indebted to the Department of American Studies at the University of Tübingen, especially to Eva Rettner and Michael Dopffel. Our gratitude furthermore goes to Bernd Engler, rector of the University of Tübingen, who firmly stood behind our undertaking. Thanks are also due to Dr. Henning Ziebritzki at Mohr Siebeck, who encouraged and supported the enterprise from the beginning as well as to Paul S. Peterson and Helen K. Gelinas, who kindly helped with proofreading the essays. Finally, the editors want to thank their families for allowing Mather to intrude into their lives for so long.

Harry S. Stout

Preface

Cotton Mather was perhaps the single most influential Puritan in colonial New England, but historians have treated him with a reserved enthusiasm bordering on dismission. Two decades ago, colonial historian Edmund Morgan famously quipped that Cotton Mather is "the Puritan Americans love to hate." Part of this disrespect stemmed from Mather's infamous participation in the Salem Witch pathology (though he was not part of the court), but maybe even more from what appeared to many modern observers as a love affair with himself. Often, negative opinions of Mather's role in early American history were ultimately based on preconceptions about his moral character. There is a long line of scholars who have primarily judged Mather by his diary and found him guilty of vanity and egocentrism masquerading as Christian humility. As David Levin rightly points out, this interpretative practice of assessing by modern cultural standards Mather's typically Puritan absorption with the battle of conflicting feelings he had for himself led to gross distortions. The complex dialectic between pride and self-abasement that is at work in Mather's diary and the life writings of so many other Puritans, especially ministers, Levin argues, can only be properly understood if we remember that it was expected of the community's religious leaders to find in themselves, as the source of true Christian authority, evidence of their special calling. Insofar as such evidence had to be sought out by examining one's spiritual and practical successes, this expectation conflicted with the general duty to loath one's sins and be humble. Hence, Puritan ministers such as Mather or Jonathan Edwards inescapably ended up in a strange kind of double-bind situation with "the obligation to be at once proud and humble, distinct from counterfeit Christians and yet self-effacing" (Levin 44).

While Salem and unfair judgments about Mather's moral character are important reasons why he still suffers from a poor reputation, another, equally important, reason is the failure of historians to publish the intellectual Mather contained in the magisterial "Biblia Americana," his massive commentary on every book of the Bible. The "Biblia Americana" is the oldest comprehensive commentary on the Bible composed in British North America. Mather himself believed that the "Biblia Americana" was the best thing he had ever written, bequeathing it to posterity as his masterwork. The massive effort was in process from 1693 until his death in 1728. Over the course of a lifetime, Mather drew on his vast reservoir of knowledge to examine biblical texts from every imaginable angle – scientific, patristic, classical, historical, and geographic – in a massive undertaking totaling thousands of pages. The Mather revealed in the unpublished "Biblia Americana" is not your grandfather's Mather of witches and hysteria, but an incredibly erudite interlocutor of Enlightenment learning.

Happily, the unpublished "Biblia" will finally be made accessible in a comprehensive modern critical edition (10 vols.) under the able editorial direction of Reiner Smolinski and Jan Stievermann. The first volume covering Mather's commentary on Genesis has just come out, and the other volumes are scheduled to appear over the next ten years. A digitized edition (housed at the Jonathan Edwards Center, Yale) is also planned to accompany the letterpress edition.

To inaugurate the launch of the Mather edition, the general editors organized a major international conference held at the University of Tübingen in October 2008. This volume contains the fruits of those papers, suitably revised and prepared for publication. In these essays, readers will revel in a Mather previously unseen. At home in many worlds, the Mather contained in this volume is situated firmly in both Reformed piety and the early Enlightenment. The coverage of essays is thoroughly transatlantic, ranging from Boston to Halle. The essays deal with major themes including Mather's theology, historical criticism, international connections, ecumenism (in contrast to the rigid exclusionary stereotype), the transatlantic networks that nurtured him, the philosophical and philological dimensions of the commentary, and Mather's highly sophisticated scientific reflection grounded in the early Enlightenment. The collection also comprises cultural analysis and social history, including fascinating explorations of the place of gender, race and slavery in the commentaries.

In sum, a new scholarly Mather has been born, and the issue will grow for decades to come. What the printed edition of *The Works of Jonathan Edwards* did for Edwards scholarship over the past fifty years will now extend to Mather over the next fifty years. With this collection of essays, a better beginning to this renaissance cannot be imagined.

Works Cited

Levin, David. "Edwards, Franklin, and Cotton Mather: A Meditation on Character and Reputation." *Jonathan Edwards and the American Experience.* Ed. Nathan O. Hatch and Harry S. Stout. New York: Oxford UP, 1988. 34–50.

Contents

Section 4: Mather's Historical Method and His Approach to the History of Religions

Section 5: Aspects of Scriptural Exegesis in the "Biblia Americana"

Section 6: Gender, Race, and Slavery in the "Biblia Americana"

A Note on the Citations from "Biblia Americana":

Citations from Mather's commentaries on Genesis refer to the pagination of vol. 1 of the printed edition (*BA* 1). Citations from the still unpublished parts of the *MS* appear in square brackets and refer to the respective books, chapters, and verses of the Bible (King James Version) on which Mather comments.

Chronology of Cotton Mather

1663	Born in Boston (Febr. 12, 1662, Old Style), the eldest child of the Rev. Increase Mather and Maria (Cotton) Mather, grandson of Richard Mather and John Cotton, two of the founding Puritan clergyman of the Bay Colony
1674–78	Begins his studies at Harvard at age 11; hazed and taunted by his peers for his straight-laced behavior, but praised by his Harvard tutors; develops a stammer which threatens to render him unsuitable for a ministerial career; B.A. (with distinction)
1678–79	Admitted to church membership in his father's (Old) North Church (Second Church, Congregational); studies medicine as an alternative career path, learns to overcome his stammering, and resumes his study of theology
1680	Delivers his first sermons in Dorchester and Boston
1681	M.A., Harvard; declines call to the church in New Haven
1683–85	Chosen pastor of the North Church (ordained in 1685) as his father's colleague; ministers to his congregation for more than 42 years until his death in 1727/28
1684	Revocation of the Old Charter
1685	Appointed Overseer at Harvard; has vision of an angelic being in his study
1686	Publishes his first sermon *The Call of the Gospel*; marries Abigail Phillips of Charlestown
1687	Birth of his first child, Abigail (dies Sept. 1)
1688	Takes charge of the North Church during Increase Mather's three-year mission to England to renegotiate the Bay Charter; cures possessed Charlestown girl through prayer and fasting
1689	*Memorable Providences, Relating to Witchcraft and Possessions*; leads uprising against Governor Edmund Andros; publishes *The Declaration of the Gentlemen, Merchants, and Inhabitants of Boston*, which justifies overthrow of the governor; birth of second child, Catherine (Sept. 1)
1690	Converts and baptizes Sir William Phips; elected Fellow at Harvard

1691   Birth of third child, Mary (dies Oct. 6, 1693); publishes *Things to be Look'd for* (first of many millenarian sermons); witchcraft hysteria begins in Salem village, in the home of the Rev. Samuel Parris

1692   Increase Mather returns with controversial Second Charter (1691); Phips appointed governor; Cotton sends "Letter to John Richards" (May 31, 1692) warning him and the Salem judges against reliance on "Spectral Evidence" as grounds for conviction; Salem judges condemn Bridget Bishop June 2 (executed June 10); *The Return of Several Ministers Consulted* (June 15) repeats warnings against the court's reliance on Spectral Evidence; publishes *A Midnight Cry* and *Preparatory Meditations on the Day of Judgment* (both millenarian sermons) and *Ornaments for the Daughters of Zion* (on virtuous women)

1693   Begins work on *Magnalia Christi Americana* (publ. 1702); begins medical handbook *The Angel of Bethesda* (publ. 1974); begins Bible commentary *Biblia Americana* (publ. 2010–); Salem judges ask him to write a defense of the court's proceedings; publishes *Wonders of the Invisible World* and *Rules for the Society of Negroes*; birth of fourth child, Joseph (dies Apr. 1)

1694   Birth of fifth child, Abigail (June 14)

1695   Death of Governor William Phips, in London; birth of sixth child, Mehetabel (dies Febr. 28, 1696)

1696   Publishes *Things for Distressed People to think upon* (strong millenarian overtones)

1697   Completes *Magnalia* (sent to London in 1699); publishes *Pietas in Patriam: the Life of His Excellency Sir William Phips*; birth of seventh child, Hannah (Febr. 7)

1698   John Leverett and William Brattle organize Brattle Street Church; publishes *Eleutheria: Or, An Idea of the Reformation in England* (predicts Second Coming); becomes a commissioner of the New England Company (Society for the Propagation of the Gospel in New England) and remains active in Indian mission for the rest of his life

1699   Birth of eighth child, Increase "Cressy" (July 9); publishes *Decennium Luctuosum* (history of Indian warfare and captivities), *Faith of the Fathers* (a Catechism to convert Jews); begins autobiography *Paterna* (publ. 1976)

1700   Publishes *Indian Primer*; Robert Calef's *More Wonders of the Invisible World* accuses the Mathers and their fellow ministers of having instigated the witchcraft hysteria to regain political control; publishes *Reasonable Religion*; birth of ninth child, Samuel (dies Febr. 7, 1701)

1701   Increase Mather loses Harvard presidency; publishes *A Christian at his Calling* (work ethic)

1702   *Magnalia Christi Americana* published in London; death of his wife, Abigail (Dec. 5) of breast-cancer

1703   Appointed to Harvard presidency, but appointment is overturned; marries widow Elizabeth Clark Hubbard (Aug. 18); resigns from his position of Overseer at Harvard; composes "Problema Theologicum" (publ. 1994), his first major treatise on eschatology

1704   Birth of tenth child, Elizabeth (July 13); publishes *Eureka. The Vertuous Woman Found*

1705   Publishes *Family Religion Excited and Assisted*

1706   Finishes Stage I of "Biblia Americana" manuscript; publishes *The Negro Christianized* (advocates humane treatment of slaves and their Christianization); *Private Meetings Animated & Regulated* (encourages revivals); birth of eleventh child, Samuel (Oct. 30)

1708   Publishes *Corderius Americanus. An Essay upon The Good Education of Children* (funeral sermon for Ezekiel Cheever, Boston's Latin-School Teacher)

1709   Birth of twelfth child, Nathaniel (dies Nov. 24); publishes *The Sailours Companion and Counsellour* (encourages conversion and piety among mariners)

1710   Begins *Christian Virtuoso* (separately published as *The Christian Philosopher*, 1720/21) as an integral part of "Biblia Americana"; publishes *Bonifacius. An Essay upon the Good*, his most popular work; advertises "Biblia Americana" in an appendix to *Bonifacius*; receives Doctor of Divinity degree from the University of Glasgow; publishes *Theopolis Americana* (condemns the slave trade)

1711   Finishes Stage II of "Biblia Americana"; publishes *Orphanotrophium, or, Orphans Well-provided for* (inspired by August Hermann Francke's Halle pietism); birth of thirteenth child, Jerusha (Apr. 1)

1712   Begins *Curiosa Americana* (1712–24), a collection of scientific communications sent to the Royal Society of London; publishes *Reason Satisfied and Faith Established* (conflict between reason and revelation)

1713   Elected Fellow of the Royal Society (election confirmed in 1721); measles epidemic in Boston; birth of fourteenth and fifteenth child, twins Martha and Eleazar (Oct. 30); death of second wife (Elizabeth) of measles (Nov. 9); death of twins of measles (Nov. 17, 20); death of Jerusha of measles (Nov. 21); publishes *Letter about a Good Management under the Distemper of the Measles*; composes "Goliath

Detruncatus" (now lost), a defense of the Trinity against the Arianism of William Whiston

1714   Finishes Stage III of "Biblia Americana"; publishes *A New Offer to the Lovers of Religion and Learning* (pamphlet advertising "Biblia Americana" and to solicit subscribers); *Duodecennium Luctuosum* (enlarged history of Indian warfare and captivity narratives); *Insanabilia* (urging patience in mental illness)

1715   Marries third wife, widow Lydia (Lee) George, who develops bouts of depression and insanity; extracts *Christian Virtuoso* (*Christian Philosopher*) from "Biblia Americana," to be published separately by the Royal Society of London (1720/21)

1716   Publishes *The Stone Cut out of the Mountain* (millenarian sermon in Latin and English), also appended to "Biblia Americana"; publishes *Fair Dealing between Debtor and Creditor*; death of daughter Katherine (Dec. 16), of consumption

1717   Son Increase ("Cressy") charged with paternity suit; publishes *Malachi*, a call for toleration and union on the basis of his "Maxims of Piety"; persuades Elihu Yale to endow a college in New Haven

1718   Nearly loses his prized library to cover the ruinous debts of his third wife's inherited estate; publishes *Brethren Dwelling Together in Unity*, advocating the union of Congregationalists and Presbyterians ("United Brethren") in New and Old England; publishes *Psalterium Americanum*, his translation of the Psalms with annotations extracted from "Biblia Americana"

1720/21 Publishes *The Christian Philosopher* (formerly *Christian Virtuoso*), a collection of thirty-two essays on natural science; begins composition of "Triparadisus" (publ. 1994), his definitive study of eschatology

1721   Publishes *India Christiana*, a long essay on pietist missions in East-India and New England; advocates controversial small-pox inoculation during massive epidemic in Boston; publishes *Sentiments On the Small Pox Inoculation* and *Some Accounts of ... Inoculating ... the Small Pox*; his house is fire-bombed by an irate Bostonian, but flames are quickly extinguished; death of Abigail (Mather) Willard (Sept. 21), in childbirth

1722   Publishes several tracts in defense of inoculation: *Account of the Method and Success of Inoculating the Small-Pox*; *Account of Inoculating the Small Pox Vindicated*; *Vindication of the Ministers of Boston*

1723   Death of Increase Mather (Aug. 23); publishes *Coelestinus*; *A Father Departing*

1724   Publishes *Parentator*, a biography of his father; death of renegade son "Cressy" at sea

1726   Publishes the influential *Ratio Disciplinae Fratrum Nov-Anglorum*, an apologia for the Congregational polity in New England; publishes *Manuductio ad Ministerium*, a popular handbook for ministerial Candidates; publishes several millenarian sermons: *Diluvium Ignis*; *Terra Beata*; *The Vial Poured out upon the Sea*; death of daughter Elizabeth (Mather) Cooper (Aug. 7)

1727   Publishes *Boanerges*; *The Terror of the Lord* (sermons on earthquakes in New England presaging the Second Coming); falls seriously ill in late Autumn; his colleague Joshua Gee replaces him at the North Church

1728   Dies February 13 (the day after his 65 birthday); buried in Copp's Hill Burial Ground in Boston's North End; posthumous publication of *The Comfortable Chambers* and *Mystical Marriage* (emphasizing spiritual union with Christ)

1729   Samuel Mather, Cotton Mather's only son to join the ministry, publishes *The Life of the Very Reverend And Learned Cotton Mather*, a biography, including an updated advertisement for "Biblia Americana"

Jan Stievermann

Cotton Mather and "Biblia Americana" –
America's First Bible Commentary:
General Introduction

For the past 200 years, whenever Americans have tried to make sense of their national experience, they have regarded the Puritan movement as central. Indeed, an entire history of American culture since independence could be constructed out of the evolution of American attitudes toward and reflections about the Puritans.
David D. Hall

These critics [who argued for a Puritan origin of modern American culture] used Puritanism, however, more than they sought to understand it. They simplified it in order to make it serve as the source of everything right or wrong with twentieth-century America, typecasting the Puritans as heroes or villains in the drama of American history and identity.
Russell Reising

Probably no colonial writer except Benjamin Franklin retains among twentieth-century Americans so wide a fame and so rigidly typical a nature. Mather has been a remarkably useful emblem of puritanical meddling, self-righteousness, bigotry, credulity, pedantry, and reaction, and the efforts of several commentators during the last century to sketch a more complex, more accurate figure have had little effect on prevailing opinion either in the scholarly community or in popular lore.
David Levin

That Cotton Mather's role in American religious and intellectual history is in need of reappraisal, as the title of our collection suggests, should be plausible to any fair-minded student of these fields, even if the reasons why he still figures so poorly demand some explanations. To be sure, Mather was always of interest as a local historian, and perceived as an influential representative of New England Puritanism just before its demise. Even historians of science and medicine now customarily pay him some tribute as a mediator of new ideas and methods from Europe. For the most part, however, this Puritan theologian and prolific scholar is, as Michael Kaufmann writes, still "[b]est known for his worst moment," and serves "inside and outside the academy as the villain of the Salem witch trials." However, as Kaufmann asserts, "this greatly distorted portrayal of Mather as filiopious crank obsessively hunting the devil obscures a richly complex career" (436). We couldn't agree more. It is probably less obvious, however, even to the fair-minded, why Mather's "Biblia Americana" would serve as the impetus for a call for reassessment. This is because, outside a small circle of specialists, relatively few people know about this work that is only now being published for the very first time. So let us begin with some brief notes on the ill-fated "Biblia Americana" before we turn to the vicissitudes of Mather's reputation.

Cotton Mather and "Biblia Americana": Preliminary Observations

Born in 1663, the scion of one of New England's most powerful dynasties of ministers and church leaders – the Cottons and the Mathers – Cotton Mather received a comprehensive education in divinity, the ancient languages and liberal arts, and early on felt the urge to put these gifts to a godly use.[1] Right after he left Harvard with a B. A. in 1678 (M. A., 1681) and joined his father Increase as a minister of Boston's Old North Church (Congregational) in 1685, he began to publish. Although always busy tending one of the largest congregations in New England, during his lifetime Mather published over 400 works.[2] Learned in all fields of contemporary knowledge, he wrote on a great variety of subjects. Besides numerous works on theology, church history, and matters of practical piety, he also turned his attention to natural philosophy, medicine, zoology, astronomy, and supernatural wonders. His accomplishments were soon recognized in the wider British Empire and beyond. He received an honorary Doctor of Divinity from one of the ancient Scottish theological strongholds at the University of Glasgow (1710) and was elected a Fellow of the Royal Society of London (1713). Ironically, however, outside his family and a small group of friends, no one ever saw what Mather himself thought to be his greatest intellectual accomplishment: "Biblia Americana." It was the first comprehensive Bible commentary composed in British North America.[3] A great number of explications

---

1 Mather's life has been written many times. Most recently, he was the subject of two excellent biographies by Levin (*The Young Life*) and Silverman. An annotated bibliography of Mather's works is provided by Holmes.

2 The NAIP (North American Imprints Program), the data-base maintained by the American Antiquarian Society, identifies 3,519 authors up to the Revolution, the vast majority (2,073) represented by a single record and another 543 by two. According to the NAIP, Cotton Mather accounts for 335 records alone, making him by far the most prolific author of British North America during the entire colonial period (Hall and Martin 520). At the height of Mather's career, between 1701 and 1720, his publications account for roughly 15% of all NAIP records, and roughly 25% of all works of personal authorship (Amory 517). T. J. Holmes, Mather's bibliographer, argues that "his known printed works total 444" (1: viii).

3 Although Mather repeatedly advertized the "Biblia Americana" and described it to his many correspondents, he apparently did not circulate the manuscript beyond his immediate Boston circle. And even here he seems to have shown the manuscript to a small number of people only. We know of one instance in which Mather gave parts of the "Biblia" to Joseph

of parts or aspects of the Bible had, of course, been written by other New England Puritans, as well as by ministers and laymen of other colonies. Cotton Mather's own grandfather John Cotton, for instance, had published the widely esteemed *A Brief Exposition With Practical Observations Upon the Whole Book of Canticles* (1655), and his uncle Samuel Mather was renowned for his *Figures and Types of the Old Testament* (1683).[4] In a way, the vast majority of writings to come out of British North America, at least for the first century, were, in one way or the other, interpretations of the Holy Scriptures. However, as far as we can see, no colonial figure had previously written a continuous scholarly commentary on all of the canonical books of the Bible. And certainly no one had set for himself the goal, as Mather wrote in September 1693, to elucidate "[God's] precious Word, and [offer] learned, charming and curious *Notes* on his Word, far beyond any that had yet seen the Light" by gathering "the Treasures of *Illustrations* for the Bible, dispersed in the Volumes of this Age" so "that all the Learning in the World might bee made gloriously subservient unto the *Illustration* of the *Scripture*" (*Diary* 1: 169–70).

Mather quite understandably considered the "Biblia Americana" or, as he subtitled his work, "The Sacred Scriptures of the Old and New Testament Illustrated," to be the most important project of his entire career. Starting in 1693, just as the witch trials were brought to a close, he worked tirelessly on his "Biblia" for over thirty years until his death in 1728. During this period of time, he continually added to the manuscript, following his rule of "one gloss each morning," and so producing more than 4,500 double-spaced folio pages in six volumes. Even in 1706, when Mather began to advertise his "Biblia," in search of subscribers, the manuscript had grown to "two large Volumes in Folio" (*Diary* 1: 564). Transforming them into a printed work would have required a substantial overhead of capital that, as it turned out, was simply not to be found. The ambitious design behind the "Biblia Americana" was to produce a synoptic commentary that would satisfy the demands of specialists, biblical scholars, and theologians throughout the Atlantic world, and would simultaneously speak to the needs of a broader, popular audience looking for elucidation of difficult passages or general religious edification.[5] Mather thus combined the syn-

---

Dudley, who praised it but failed to extend his help in getting the manuscript published (Silverman 210). Especially when Mather realized that publishing the "Biblia" was increasingly unlikely, he began to recycle parts of it for other projects, including *The Christian Philosopher* and, most importantly, *Triparadisus* that, however, also never found its way into print during his lifetime.

4   In 1636, Hugh Peter had pleaded that John Cotton be given time to "go through the Bible, and raise marginal notes upon all the knotty places of the scriptures" (Hall, "Readers and Writers" 138). However, the project was never realized, and it remained for his grandson to do what Peter had desired.

5   For a detailed account of the history of "Biblia Americana," its design as well as its biographical, historical and intellectual contexts, see Smolinski's introduction to volume 1. In

optical format of other scholarly commentaries of the period – such as Bishop of Chester John Pearson's nine volume *Critici Sacri* (1660–69) or the Nonconformist Matthew Poole's five volume *Synopsis Criticorum* (1669–76) – with the format of popular, English-based annotations such as Poole's *Annotations upon the Holy Bible* (1683–85) or the Presbyterian Matthew Henry's *An Exposition of All the Books of the Old and New Testaments* (1708–10).[6] Like *Critici Sacri* or *Synopsis Criticorum*, Mather's "Biblia Americana" follows the ancient tradition of the *katena*, offering a chain, or a digest of what he perceived as the most pertinent commentaries in explicating the various meanings (historical, typological, moral) of a given scriptural verse. To these excerpted commentaries Mather then frequently adds his own original glosses as well as materials from historical or scientific literature. The result is a conceptual and linguistic hybrid – written in English but shot through with thousands of Latin, Greek and Hebrew citations – that, in the illustration of a given verse, could combine philological analysis, learned historical-contextual observations and sometimes-scientific speculations with extensive consideration of dogmatic tradition and pious applications.

Unlike most existing authors of either scholarly or popular commentaries, Mather chose not to offer elucidation on every single verse, but to concentrate on those which seemed most important, or most in need of explanation because of their centrality, their obscurity, or because of their difficulties regarding textual transmission and translation. He also abandoned the traditional chapter summaries, and reprinting of each verse, instead adopting a question-and-answer method of presentation. For each annotation, he thus devised a rhetorical question that would bring specific topics and interpretative problems into focus. Occasionally, the answers could become so long that they grew into independent essays of ten or twenty pages. With these methods, Mather aligns his "Biblia," in some ways, with Pierre Bayle's *Dictionnaire historique et critique* (1695–97) or Augustin Calmet's *Dictionnaire Historique, Critique, Chronologique, Géographique, et Littéral de la Bible* (1722). Indeed, on many of the topics it raises the "Biblia" assumes encyclopaedic dimensions, and the range of Mather's reading, from which he draws his annotations, is breathtaking. As a

---

1706 Mather sent to England "AN AMERICAN OFFER *to serve the Great Interests of Learning and Religion in Europe*" (*Diary* 1: 570) to promote his commentary in dissenting circles. Mather then advertized the work in the "General Introduction" of his 1702 *Magnalia Christi Americana* (33–34) and in an appendix to his 1710 *Bonifacius: An Essay upon the Good* (159–63). In 1714 he published a separate advertisement in a pamphlet entitled *A New Offer To the Lovers of Religion and Learning.* He also made numerous attempts through letters to solicit subscribers (See, for instance, *Selected Letters* 111–12, 148–49, 155; 170; 181, 188–90, 204, 272–73).

6 Muller and Sheppard provide good general discussions of the important developments in biblical commentaries between the sixteenth and the eighteenth century. The most successful works on the English market are surveyed in Jeffrey and Preston.

basis and framework, Mather frequently employs renowned contemporary English commentators; for example, he uses Simon Patrick's annotations for the historical books, William Lowth's for the prophets, or John Hammond's and Daniel Whitby's on the New Testament. He certainly adds to the stack, however. As his 1714 advertising pamphlet for the "Biblia," *A New Offer to the Lovers of Religion and Learning* (1714) announced, Mather made it a principle to always go beyond "the more Illustrious Literators, who are known for *Stars of the first Magnitude.*" Indeed, he drew from literally hundreds of "Books that have made no profession of serving this Cause [of illustrating the scriptures] and many of them very unsuspected ones" (5). When it came to the "very unsuspected ones," Mather was by no means just quoting English or Continental Reformed writers. His references are international, interdenominational, multilingual, historically encompassing, and, as we would say today, transdisciplinary. He not only cites the Church Fathers and medieval commentaries, rabbinic literature, ancient history, classical and modern philosophy, philology, and the natural sciences of his day, but also Reformation and post-Reformation theologians of all denominations, including Roman Catholics and Jesuits. Indeed, an ecumenical impulse to transcend old party lines is one of the "Biblia's" most conspicuous features.

Mather's *New Offer* gives us a convenient survey of the topics and issues that are addressed in the commentaries, and also of the hermeneutical approaches that are employed. The last four pages of the pamphlet, which provide a short list of these topics, issues, and hermeneutical approaches under twelve headings, are reproduced as an appendix to this introduction. As can be seen from this list, Mather's interests and methodology clearly mark him as a representative of what Brooks Holifield calls the Baconian paradigm in biblical interpretation, primarily preoccupied with the reasonableness of Christianity and, most importantly, the factuality of the scriptures. Concerned throughout with providing different kinds of proof (prophetical, historical, philological, empirical) for the Bible's factuality, Cotton Mather's "Biblia Americana," together with other works by him and his father, thus stands at the beginning of "what would become an American evidentialist tradition" (Holifield 70).[7] The list also evinces how deeply immersed Mather was in the rising tide of modern, historical-contextual criticism, which had its origin in the mid-seventeenth century and came to a climax first in the English debates between Deists and orthodox apologists

---

7 "Deeply informed by parallel patterns of thought in England and on the European continent, this evidentialist position consisted of the claim that rational evidence confirmed the uniqueness and truth of the biblical revelation. Such a claim stood behind the rise of 'evidential Christianity,' a form of theology different in important ways from either the scholastic thought of the medieval church or the theologies of revelation that came out of the Protestant reform" (Holifield 5). On the pre-eminence of evidentialism and a factual understanding of the scriptures in nineteenth-century American theology, and on the long-term consequences of this approach in defending the authority of the scriptures, see Rogers and McKim.

in the early eighteenth century.[8] The first area of concern that Mather highlights in the promotional pamphlet is, of course, biblical philology, a field that was going though a revolution during the period. All over Europe, specialists in the ancient languages worked to establish reliable texts and improve translations. In England, this communal project had produced the London polyglot Bible (*Biblia Sacra Polyglotta*, 1657), which printed scriptural texts in as many as eight different languages. Brian Walton's tomes were always open on Mather's desk, together with a host of other works by scholars such as Sebastian Münster, Johann Buxtorf the Elder, Hugo Grotius, or John Lightfoot when Mather discusses those cases in which "the most Polite and Pious masters in Philology, have expressed their Wishes to see the Common Translation Amended and Refined" (*New Offer* 11). To offer alternatives where the King James version appeared wanting or misleading, Mather examined not only the original Hebrew or Greek words, but also the Septuagint, Jerome's Vulgate, the Aramaic Targums and French and German translations.

However, Mather's philological interests extended well beyond lexical or grammatical issues. A full century before such concerns became more widespread among New England theologians (Holifield 190–95), he was dealing with questions of authorship, historical transmission, and the integrity of the biblical texts. The overriding goal of his textual criticism was to safeguard the Bible's absolute authority by affirming the general reliability of the canon and the received modern texts. Hence, the thrust of Mather's textual criticism is, for the most part, integrative; that is, he seeks to incorporate variants, and to explain lacunae, interpolations, shifts in point of view, and anachronisms in ways that ultimately affirm the overall coherence and accuracy of the biblical texts under discussion. Nevertheless, his honest engagement with the period's most astute and daring biblical critics forced him to give up many of the axiomatic assumptions then held by the Reformed and Lutheran orthodoxies.

This tendency is highlighted, for instance, by Mather's response to Richard Simon, which is especially visible in Mather's commentaries on the Pentateuch (see Smolinski "Authority and Interpretation"). In his *Histoire critique du Vieux Testament* (1678), Simon contested the Mosaic authorship of the Pentateuch as a whole by arguing that the disparities in these books suggested that multiple authors had written and re-written various parts of the five books in a long history of textual transmission (the so-called "Public Scribes" hypothesis). It is quite surprising to see how far Mather was prepared to go in meeting Simon. For example, he willingly admitted that many passages in the Pentateuch were written a long time after Moses's death and that these books, together with

---

8   For the rise of historical criticism see Scholder, Kraus (44–103), Frei, and vol. 4 of von Reventlow's *Epochen der Bibelauslegung*; von Reventlow's *The Authority of the Bible* offers an in-depth discussion of the Deist debates in Mather's time.

many of the prophetic scriptures, were compiled in the period after the Babylonian exile by Ezra and other public scribes. He vehemently maintained, however, that neither the multi-layered and heterogeneous character of the Hebrew Bible, nor its long history of textual tradition, put scriptural authority into question, because the work of the interpolators and compilers had been directed by the Holy Spirit, just as much as Moses's composition of the foundational texts. At the same time, Mather moved away from a plenary concept of verbal inspiration, arguing that only the underlying concepts had been supernaturally communicated.[9] Mather, therefore, no longer regarded the letter of the text as infallible in the sense that events or ideas were always described in a language that would satisfy modern standards of scientific accuracy. He insisted, instead, that the truths, although couched in the culturally specific language of its historical authors and accommodated to their understanding, were certain. In accordance with this accommodationist disposition, he saw it as the main task of a new kind of biblical criticism to help Christians approach the eternal truths of the Bible through the use of reasonable methods, namely by explicating and thereby making transparent its time-bound forms of expression, unveiling the universal truths they carried.

Acquiescing to such a modification of the dogma of inerrancy was one way for Mather to confront the much more radical attacks of the day against scriptural authority by the followers of Thomas Hobbes and Benedict Spinoza. Albeit in different ways, Hobbes' *Leviathan* (1651) and Spinoza's *Tractatus Theologico-Politicus* (1670) had fundamentally challenged the traditional Judeo-Christian understanding of biblical revelation by arguing that the scriptures do not offer reliable historical truths at all, but have to be understood as fanciful expressions of religious devotions, written by infant peoples according to their primitive knowledge and cultural traditions. Accordingly, the Bible needed to be subjected to rational, demystifying modes of explication to separate the wheat of valid moral teachings from the chaff of ancient customs and fantastic stories (see Preus, Frampton). Mather was very much alarmed by this kind of rationalism and attempted, in every way possible, to defend the Bible's position as supernatural revelation by proving its historical veracity.

Because Mather, like most Protestant exegetes of his time, was so invested in corroborating the *sensus historicus*, his "Biblia" gives ample space to the fields advertised under headings II, III, VII, and VIII in *A New Offer*. Mather drew

---

9   In "An Essay for further Commentary, on the Sacred Scriptures," which Mather appended to the "Biblia" he writes, "In things which only fell under *Human Prudence*, the Holy Spirit seems not immediately to have Dictated unto the Men of God; but only to have used a *Directive* or *Conductive* Power upon them; to supply them with suitable Apprehensions, & keep them in the Use of their own Rational Judgment within the Bounds of Infallible Truth, & of Expediency for the Present Occasion." In so doing, God allowed his prophets the "Use of their *own Words*, and of the *Style* that was most natural to them" (qtd. in Smolinski, "Authority and Interpretation" 198).

equally on a wide array of classical sources and the burgeoning literatures of
early modern para-theology (*historia sacra, geographia sacra* etc.). His commentaries are bustling with discussions of biblical antiquities, chronologies,
and geographies, and rarely overlook sparkling gems of Jewish and Early Christian histories, mores, customs, arcane traditions, and laws of peoples long forgotten. These preoccupations were by no means idiosyncratic, for Mather inherited them (along with many of his actual illustrations) from some of the
greatest scholars of his period such as James Ussher, Samuel Bochart, Johann
Heinrich Heidegger, or Gerard Vossius. With the help of these luminaries,
Mather worked to clear up difficulties in dating events or explaining obscure
references and to gather evidence to prove the reliability of the scriptural narratives as history and the general truthfulness of the biblical world picture. His
efforts to substantiate historic truth are directed towards the fundamentals of
the Christian faith – as, for instance, when he demonstrates the congruence of
the gospel accounts – as much as they are extended to rather trivial matters per-
taining to the history of Jerusalem or certain customs of the ancient Middle
East. Behind this urge to historicize, however, was also an anxious awareness of
how alien and often incomprehensible the world of the scriptures was to the
modern mind. In the manner of humanist philology, Mather therefore sought to
establish the linguistic, cultural, material, and biographical contexts of the biblical authors, attempting to bridge these historical differences and to decipher
the original intentions of their writings from which – according to his accom-
modatonist hermeneutics – the divine truth had to be reconstructed.

As heading VI in *A New Offer* announces, Mather's "Biblia" also undertakes frequent and extensive excursions into "Natural Philosophy" in the service of offering empirical proof of "Scriptural Religion" (see Smolinski "Natural
Science and Interpretation"). Seeking to reconcile the biblical narrative with the
findings of the new sciences, Mather's glosses offer what he calls the "fairest
Hypotheses of those Grand *Revolutions*, the *Making*, the *Drowning*, and the
Burning of the WORLD," which incorporate Copernican cosmology, Descartes's corpuscular theory, and Newtonian physics. Likewise, the countless
natural as well as the supernatural or miraculous phenomena and events mentioned in the scriptures are represented with what he calls "the *Best Thoughts of
our Times* upon them" (*New Offer* 12). Moreover, on many occasions Mather
inserts physico-theological reflections upon the natural world, in which he argues from the design of creation to show God's omnipotence and benevolence
towards humanity.

In addition to such empirical evidence, "Biblia Americana" amasses what
Mather considered historical evidence demonstrating the accuracy of scriptural
prophecies and their fulfilment in Christ's incarnation and redemptive work.
For Mather, such "prophetic proof" was central to asserting the organic coherence and symmetry of the Old and New Testaments, and to supporting the

truth of Christianity. That the Old Testament prophets really spoke of Jesus was, for Mather, a non-negotiable position, one which he everywhere defends against critics such as Hugo Grotius (*Annotationes ad Vetus Testamentum* [1644]) and the early English Deist Anthony Collins (*A Discourse of the Grounds and Reasons of the Christian Religion* [1724]), who viewed the traditional messianic readings of many Old Testament passages as unwarranted allegorizations. In this crusade, Mather joins a host of other contemporary Christian apologists, including Edward Chandler, John Edwards, Robert Jenkin, Richard Kidder, and Humphrey Prideaux. In addition to traditional intertextual arguments, Mather's commentaries present historical evidence – advertised under heading X – from secular and ecclesiastical "HISTORIES of all Ages, brought in, to show how the Prophecies of this Invaluable Book, have had their most punctual Accomplishment" (*New Offer* 13). Moreover, with the help of the most accomplished Christian Hebraists of his time, Mather frequently draws on Talmudic and other Rabbinical commentaries to back up his messianic interpretations of Old Testament prophecies. This method ties in with a more general immersion – evident everywhere in the "Biblia Americana" – in post-biblical *"Jewish writings*; not only to Illustrate the Oracles once *committed* unto the *distinguished* nation; but also to demonstrate the Truths of *Christianity"* (*New Offer* 12).

Heading X in *A New Offer* also draws attention to another important area of interest: eschatology. Throughout the "Biblia Americana," and with heightened intensity in his commentaries on the Books of Daniel and Revelation, Mather offers what he calls "strongly established *Conjectures*, (yet made with all due Modesty,)" on those prophecies which, in his opinion, *"remain to be Accomplished ..."* (*New Offer* 14) before the second coming. Heading XI of *A New Offer* reminds us that Mather was a staunch millennialist, who insisted on literalist readings of most prophecies regarding the apocalyptic tribulations and Christ's peaceable kingdom on earth (see Smolinski, Introduction and *Threefold Paradise*). He knew, however, that there were objections (which, to some extent, he himself shared) in many established Protestant churches of the early eighteenth century against chiliastic enthusiasms. Consequently, his glosses steer a middle-course between laying out in vivid descriptions such eschatological events as the global conflagration ushering in Christ's kingdom on earth (which, he conjectured, might occur in 1736), the resurrection of the saints, and the descent of the (literal, cubical) New Jerusalem. Yet he also cautioned rabid millenarians against "the more Arbitrary and less Defensible Conceits, of *overdoing Students* in the Prophecies" (*New Offer* 14). Nowhere is the peculiar Matherite mixture of rationalism, empiricism, hyperliteralism, and heightened supernaturalism more clearly on display than in his millennialist speculations.

Much more conventional is his typology (heading IV), perhaps the most conservative aspect of the "Biblia Americana." In principle, Mather remains in a patristic and orthodox Reformed framework of interpretation. While his commentaries on the books of the Hebrew Bible provide typological readings of every conceivable figure or event, even those, as heading IV puts it, "which have sometimes appeared the least Fruitful with Instruction" (*New Offer* 12), these readings never suggest anything but fulfilment in Christ. Whatever has been written about Mather's Americanization of typology (or millennialism, for that matter) is not borne out by his "Biblia."[10]

Although freighted with the learning of ages, Mather's "Biblia" again and again asserts that, at least until the return of Christ, the full meaning of God's secrets revealed in the scriptures will elude the grasp of human reason. Indeed, Mather's biblical criticism seems to have led him to the conclusion that on this side of the millennium the infallible truthfulness of the scriptures could not be irrefutably proven by rational methods of exegesis, but could only be recognized with the eyes of living faith bestowed upon those who are reborn in Christ. Thus, he came to consider the ultimate evidence of scriptural authority to be internal, rather than external. It was, he thought, something only obtained through a life of faith in Christ. The later entries in "Biblia Americana" especially reflect this Pietist inclination (expressed under heading XII), which promises the reader illustrations of "the Scriptures from EXPERIMENTAL PIETY, or the Observations of Christian Experience" (*New Offer* 14). Thus, the "Biblia Americana" develops a conceptual framework of experiential theology that promises a practical certainty even where the confidence in the absolute authority of the Bible's textual form was shaken. Influenced by Halle Pietism and the hermeneutics of August Hermann Francke (1663–1727), Mather asserted in his later years that a right way of reading of the Bible can only be established through an intimate relationship of the believer to the text that finds expression in practical devotion and good deeds. In accordance with this experiential theology, the "Biblia Americana" often puts a special emphasis on lessons of practical piety and holy living when interpreting scriptural passages.[11]

---

10   The literature on typology in early American culture and literature is extensive. See, for instance, Brumm, Bercovitch, *Typology* and *Puritan Origins*, and Lowance. Due in no small part to the formidable influence of Bercovitch, there has been a long-standing consensus amongst Americanists that the Puritans transformed typology into the central mode of their cultural imagination by extending the limits of traditional typological readings to include events and persons of New England history. In this Americanized form typology is then believed to have become an important part of U.S. national culture and art. For a critique of this interpretative paradigm, see Smolinski (*"Israel Redivivus"*). Significantly, we have so far not discovered one single instance in which Mather's "Biblia" uses typology other than in a traditional Christo-centric form.

11   Mather was familiar with Francke's most important programmatic writings on the interpretation of the Bible such as *Manuductio ad lectionem scripturae Sacrae* (1693). On Francke's Pietist hermeneutics, see the essays in Aland. For a discussion of Mather's relation with Halle and the relevant scholarly literature, see Scheiding's essay in this collection.

Woefully inadequate as such a cursory account must be, it should suffice to suggest that the "Biblia American" is a unique work not only because of its massive size (indeed, had it been printed it would have been the largest book published in British North America), but it is also with regard to its design and format, combining, as it does, scholarly, speculative, apologetic, and practical inquiries. It seems fair to say, too, that Mather's commentaries mark the beginning of historical criticism in North America and, although hidden from the eyes of the public, remained unrivalled in its engagement with modern hermeneutical concerns until the early nineteenth century when German "Higher Criticism" gained a permanent foothold in New England theological seminaries.[12] To be sure, the foundations of Mather's understanding of the Bible as the revealed and ultimately infallible word of God are still "pre-critical," to use a term suggested by Hans Frei. A wholesale historicization of the biblical texts and canon formation was yet unthinkable for Mather's generation. His commentaries, however, clearly reflect and react to those intellectual forces that were beginning to put pressure on the authority of the Bible and the literal truthfulness of its historical narrative and world picture. In Mather's sophisticated and unpublished responses to these forces, which are defensive as well as adaptive in nature, he introduced the new European exegetical methods into the British colonies of North American that would come to define modern historical criticism, even if the methods employed were intended to defend orthodoxy.

The Fate of "Biblia Americana"

Mather probably thought that the wide range of topics in his "Biblia" would attract a broad audience across denominational lines and straddle different markets, for its ecumenical orientation and hybrid format attempted to catch both the scholarly and the popular eye. Tragically, however, his "Biblia" never reached anyone and seems to have fallen in the chasm between the two markets. Perhaps it was simply a case of market saturation. When Mather rather ineptly attempted to stake his claim in the highly competitive world of the London print market, the popular and scholarly fields had been claimed by the commentaries of Matthew Poole and Matthew Henry. Or, perhaps it was just too

---

12   It has been generally assumed that historical-contextual criticism or "Higher Criticism" was only imported to New England from Germany by the generation of Moses Stuart (1780–1852), the so-called father of exegetical studies in America, and Joseph Stevens Buckminster (1785–1812), who studied the works of J.D. Michaelis, Jakob Griesbach, and Johann Gottfried Eichhorn in Göttingen. On the rise of German "Higher Criticism" in New England seminaries, see J. Brown, Giltner and Holifield. More recently, Stephen Stein and R. Brown have pointed to Jonathan Edwards's engagement with issues of biblical authorship, integrity, and historical settings. The publication of the "Biblia Americana," however, will reveal that the beginnings of historical-contextual criticism have to be pushed back another generation.

early and far too unusual for the backwater colonies to produce such massive tomes of research demanding large investments. In any case, in his lifespan, Mather failed to find patrons and publishers in the metropolitan centers (production in the colonies was impossible), and the manuscript never left Boston. Since Mather's descendants gave the six folio volumes to the Massachusetts Historical Society sometime at the beginning of the nineteenth century, they have remained in the archives, unpublished and largely unstudied.

Not that the "Biblia" was entirely forgotten. In most of the larger examinations of Mather's life or work, and sometimes in related studies, one can find brief references to his monumental Bible commentary, or a cursory account of its design and Mather's frustrated attempts to market his *magnum opus*. Except for Theodore Hornberger's lone early study, "Cotton Mather's Annotations on the First Chapter of Genesis" (1938), Cheryl Rivers' unpublished dissertation (1977), Middlekauff's brief examination of Mather's commentary on Genesis and Revelation (284–90, 344–45), Feldman's study on Mather's use of Josephus in his "Biblia" (1983), and recent articles by Smolinski and Maddux, in-depth examinations of specific aspects of the "Biblia" have not been undertaken.[13] Prior to the General Introduction to the edition (see *BA* 1: 3–210), no comprehensive assessment of the work was ever attempted. Why has the "Biblia" been overlooked for so long? And why, in light of its importance, as is here suggested, hasn't an edition been undertaken earlier?

One reason seems to be that commentaries as a genre have, unfortunately, not attracted much scholarly attention. While we have seen significant forays into the cultural history of the Bible in early America (see Hatch and Noll; Gutjahr), the history of Bible commentaries still remains, for the most part, a *terra incognita*. Another important factor was certainly the forbidding size and format of Mather's commentary. The countless (often unidentified) quotes in ancient languages surely repelled many modern scholars as well. It should be noted, moreover, that the reluctance of publishers to touch this gargantuan project – the printed edition will comprise nearly 15,000 pages – has not diminished since Mather's days, and it is no coincidence that it will take two publishing houses, in a transatlantic cooperation, to shoulder the financial burden to bring it to print. It is also no coincidence that the initiative came from a distinguished German publishing house specializing in theology, whose board of directors were not deterred by Mather's unpopular image in America, and so was uninhibited by any preconceptions in judging the significance of Mather's "Biblia Americana" as a work of biblical criticism. And here we probably get to the heart of the matter.

---

13   Another study that deals with "Biblia Americana" in a rather tangential fashion is Winship's *Seers of God* (95–98, 132–33).

Very likely, one of the main reasons why the "Biblia Americana" was so long neglected is the still prevailing negative image of Mather. Moreover, there were and still are disciplinary blinders keeping American scholars of Puritanism from looking at this work for what it is. Mather's more recent and more sympathetic biographers, as well as a number of important studies on Puritanism in which Mather played a key-role, have all suggested that his "Biblia" was of considerable importance, yet the majority of references to the "Biblia" – most of them made in passing or in footnotes – are rather dismissive. These judgments inevitably reflect popular stereotypes about Mather and were formed without careful analysis of the work in the context of contemporary Bible commentaries. A striking example of such a dismissive comment on the "Biblia" appears in a footnote of Worthington C. Ford, the editor of the *Diary of Cotton Mather*, who called the manuscript "a great indigested mass of material, drawn from many sources, and with no evidence of design or settled plan," making it the most conspicuous example of "the ill-regulated activity of Mather's labors" (*Diary* 1: 170n). Similar judgments were passed on virtually all of Mather's works, especially the *Magnalia Christi Americana*, since the early nineteenth century.[14] Had Ford (and others before or after him) been able to put aside the general anti-Puritan bias and prejudices against Mather, as well as their (post-) Romantic concern with organic expression and originality, and had they studied the "Biblia" alongside Poole, Henry or Bayle, they surely would have come to different conclusions.

Mather's Popular Reputation and Place in Academic Criticism

What, then, are the reigning prejudices about Mather that have also obscured the "Biblia"? For the vast majority of modern Americans, if they know anything about the colonial period, Cotton Mather is essentially an iconic embodiment of Puritan bigotry and what Hawthorne called the "persecuting spirit," which in the nation's collective memory found its most infamous manifestations in the witch trials at Salem village. In this view, Mather had not only inherited the religious dogmatism, intolerance, and moral self-righteousness commonly attributed to Puritan culture, but also represents the epitome of the superstition and credulity of his age. These traits were aggravated by a deeply twisted character, deformed through nagging insecurities, repressed desires and overweening pride. Predisposed in this manner and eager to assert his place, the young Mather, according to this long-prevailing narrative, put himself at the forefront of the escalating developments in Salem during the fateful summer of

---

14   For a discussion of Romantic and post-Romantic criticism of Mather's works in the context of his literary aesthetics (rather than theology), see Stievermann, "Writing."

1692. Having already contributed much to inciting the witch-craze from the pulpit and through publications, Mather, driven by zealotry and personal ambition, then assumed a leading role in the persecutions. After the first accusations were made, he lent his clerical authority to the court and urged the judges on until hundreds of people were in jail and 19 hanged. Or so it is widely believed. It makes little difference that Mather's two most recent biographies agree with much current scholarship on the witch trials that this popular narrative is a gross misrepresentation. This is not to say that Mather was fully exculpated by any of these studies, for unlike some other ministers he never called for an end to the trials, and he afterwards wrote New England's official defense of the court's procedures, the infamous *Wonders of the Invisible World* (1693). Still, there is now a general agreement that his beliefs about the invisible world were very typical of the period, that he acted as a moderating force in the context of the trials, and that he never directly participated in the proceedings. He advised the judges against using spectral evidence and offered recommendations to proceed with caution lest innocent people come to harm. In the end, Mather's role in the witchcraft episode was thus ambivalent and conflicted.[15]

In the popular imagination, however, Mather remains *the* psychopathic witch-doctor and a main culprit for the tragic events at Salem. In this role he has gained a very doubtful, but also very powerful and resilient reputation. He is probably the only figure from colonial history who ever appeared in Marvel comic books, where he briefly had a role as a cross-wielding villain fighting Spider Man. It's also not unlikely to go to a Halloween party and meet someone dressed up as Cotton Mather, complete with wig and some instrument of torture. Even in historical literature that is geared to a broader audience, in journalism or TV-documentaries, one still finds the same old "polemical stereotypes which earlier historians have built on a relatively small basis of evidence, which have an odd way of persisting and coloring the judgments of later historians even when that basis has been destroyed" (Lovelace 291).

How Mather, to borrow a phrase from Brooks Holifield's essay in this collection, came to be "trapped in Salem" in the first place is a long and complex story. There is no room and really no need here to tell that story in any detail and unravel its various strands. Skilful hands have done much of that work for us.[16] Broadly speaking, David Levin and Richard Lovelace have shown that it

---

15   For even-handed accounts of Mather's role in the witch trials, see Levin (*Cotton Mather* 195–222), Silverman (83–138), Rosenthal (esp. 135–48, 202), and Norton (esp. 203–07, 212–15, 246–52, 268–69, 284–85). The wide-spread supernatural beliefs in all segments of early modern New England society and the magical elements of both orthodox and folk religion are treated in Butler, Hall (*World of Wonder*), and Demos.

16   For anyone interested in understanding the "The Hazing of Cotton Mather" in American culture and academic discourse, David Levin's groundbreaking revisionist essay of the same title, together with Richard Lovelace's perceptive meta-historiographical study "Mather's Changing Image: A Bibliographic Inquiry" (published as an appendix to his *The Ameri-*

was polemics sparked by various socio-religious conflicts rather than careful historical inquiry that gave birth to and sustained the interpretative tradition according to which the tragedy of Salem was blamed primarily on the clergy, and in particular on Cotton Mather. Remembering Mather as the villain of Salem has always served the political and ecclesiastical needs of specific groups and helped them to define their cultural and religious identity. The origin of that tradition lies in the fierce battles over the authority of the ministers in Massachusetts's new social order, battles in which anti-clerical polemicists such as Robert Calef or William Douglass used the witch trials as a means to smear representatives of the old theocracy.

During Mather's lifetime and in the decades after his death, these attacks caused only limited damage to his overwhelmingly positive reputation as a caring pastor and renowned scholar. At the end of the eighteenth century, however, Calef's *More Wonders of the Invisible World* (1700) would then provide ammunition for quite different debates that *prima facie* had very little to do with Mather. In the intellectual debates of the early republic, America's national identity was often negotiated through a discourse about New England's history. "[M]any early republican historians," as William Van Arragon argues in this volume,

> looked to the colonial past for antecedents and icons for the new nation and found useful progenitors in the Pilgrims and Puritans, whose complex history was reduced to the famous national myth of the band of proto-democrats seeking a land of religious liberty. But the Puritan past had to be selectively purged of elements deemed incompatible with the new republican ideals. Thus Cotton Mather was found guilty by many antiquarians and scholars of fomenting the Salem witch trials and, by association, came to represent all in the Puritan past that was un-American: religious fanaticism, priestcraft, political aristocracy. (Van Arragon 61–62)

But the real blow was yet to come. As Lovelace suggested and the new research by Van Arragon and Holifield demonstrates, Mather's reputation was compromised for good in the battles over church government that followed upon the Unitarian "take-over" of Harvard and of many New England churches in the early nineteenth century. Now the old accusations about Mather's role in Salem were revived by the religious liberals to bring into disrepute the traditional Calvinistic theology for which Mather stood, and especially his ecclesiastical writings to which conservative Congregationalists liked to refer in debates over church organization. An especially acrimonious and influential product of this struggle for control over the New England churches are the *Lectures in Witchcraft* (1831) written by the Unitarian clergyman Charles W. Upham of

---

can Pietism of Cotton Mather), remain the best starting points. More recently, William Van Arragon has undertaken an extensive examination of Mather's role in American cultural memory. For a larger examination of the cultural function of the Salem witch trials in America's collective memory, see Adams.

Salem.[17] The Unitarian polemics against Mather also found their way into the
fictional literature of the American Renaissance (see Felker), the works of Romantic historians and, subsequently, into the progressive school of historiography, whose view of American history as a struggle of the common man against
undemocratic and oppressive authorities dominated the field through the first
decades of the twentieth century. One need only look at George Bancroft's account of Salem in the first volume of his 1834 *History of the United States* (1:
83–84, 95) and Vernon Parrington's treatment of Mather in the first volume
(1927) of his *Main Current's in American Thought* (93–117) to appreciate the
continuities.

Parrington's portrayal of Mather as a "crooked and diseased mind," "over-
sexed and overwrought," "an attractive subject for the psychoanalyst," whose
Diary "was a treasure-trove for the abnormal psychologist" (107, 109), bespeaks
a general resentment towards everything Puritan, which was widespread
amongst modernist theologians and intellectuals of the early twentieth century.
"By the early decades of the twentieth century," as George Marsden has written, "Puritan bashing had become widely acceptable as a way for progressive
Americans to free themselves from Victorian moralism" (501). Cotton Mather,
like Jonathan Edwards, was an easy and welcome target for cultural critics such
as H. L. Mencken and William Carlos Williams (Reising 49–53), whose vitu-
perations ultimately had very little to do with the Puritanism of the colonial
period and everything to do with the conservative Christians of their own time.
But the prevalent anti-Puritan bias of the Jazz Age very much impeded a revisionist re-assessment of Mather even when earlier controversies over church
organization had long faded, and evidence was undeniable for his rather moderate role in Salem.

As Parrington's language also demonstrates, twentieth-century judgments
on Mather and other Puritans have often been informed by a cavalier understanding of psychology and especially Freudian psychoanalysis. Even in recent
and more sympathetic studies of Mather's life and work, the language of what
Lovelace calls "psychohistorical critique" (299) frequently intrudes. In effect,
this type of critique rather bluntly pathologizes Puritan views and religious
practices, thereby obstructing more insightful consideration of the complex
theological, cultural or social contexts from which these views and practices
emerged. David Levin ("The Hazing") convincingly argued that Mather scholars were particularly prone to misconstrue – using virtually no reliable evidence
– a psychoanalytical narrative of the precocious, stuttering Puritan child-prod-
igy who is subjected to an intense religious indoctrination, stifled by an oppressive filiopietism and the expectations of an overpowering, yet frequently absent
father, at the same time that he is being bullied by his class-mates. From this

---

17   Upham reiterated his views on Mather in his *Salem Witchcraft* (1867).

unhappy boyhood, so the line of reasoning goes, grows a highly irritable and at times paranoid egomaniac who is eager to please and be subservient to his elders, but plagued by fears of impotence and brimming with pent-up (sexual) aggression and fantasies of self-importance. Needless to say, such a view reinforced existing assumptions about Mather's involvement in the witch craze even by explaining it as something for which his childhood might be to blame.

With this narrative in place, everything in Mather's adult life, from his engagement with colonial politics to his philanthropic schemes, becomes somehow symptomatic of his frenetic personality or appears as an act of overcompensation. The latter explanation has in fact been frequently cited to account for Mather's massive output as an author and even for his elaborate and hyperbolic style.[18] Explicitly or implicitly, this idea of Mather as a neurotic genius who, driven by his secret impulses, churned out dozens of works each year as compensatory acts of self-aggrandizement, belittles the stature of his works as the products of an uncontrolled, almost compulsive writing that lacked in reason and design, and were somehow deviant or unhealthy. A striking example for this would be Fords above-cited judgment on the "Biblia Americana." Much to their credit, all of our contributors refrain from putting Mather on the (amateur) psychologist's couch. They rather study his work as they would that of any other scholar of Mather's generation in which ornate styles and large œuvres were nothing out of the ordinary [19]

---

18   For all its great merits and wonderfully lucid consideration of cultural and historical contexts, even Silverman's biography frequently drifts into a rather heavy-handed psychologizing of Mather that is as speculative as it is unfair and patronizing. A particularly crude example is Silverman's treatment of Mather's famous vision (*Diary* 1: 86–87) in which an angelic being promised him – with reference to Ezekiel's prophecy (31:3–9) of the Cedar in Lebanon with its lengthening branches – a fruitful career in the service of God's church, and spoke of the many godly books he would publish not only in America but also in Europe. In Silverman's reading, "the figure whose shoulders were wings spoke Cotton Mather's own thoughts. Among other things, the angel gave expression to the 'ambitious Affectation of Praeheminencies' that had troubled him since youth, the much censored longing for applause and fame which the childlike view he maintained of himself helped restrain. Mather's need to demonstrate copious productivity appears as early as his youthful stammer, of course, and all of his writings teem with images of size. The angel merely articulated these while omitting the guilty reproofs that otherwise accompanied them, forecasting that 'a certain youth' would enjoy some enormous potency. ..." Silverman continues, "Explaining Ezekiel's prediction of the '*greatness, in the Length of his Branches*,' as referring to the books Mather would publish not only in America but also in Europe, the angel in effect promised him a transatlantic penis" (128–29). For an astute criticism of the judgmental, frequently contemptuous assessments of Mather's psychological character in recent scholarship, including Silverman's biography, see Levin, "Edwards, Franklin, and Cotton Mather."
19   How much of the perceived defects and idiosyncrasies of Mather's writings disappear when we analyze them in the context of classical literary genres, such as the Plutarchian parallel biography and the Aeniad, or in the context of certain rhetorical traditions, such as the ideal of *copia*, was demonstrated by Manierre, Van Cromphout, Bercovitch (*The Puritan Origins*), and Stievermann. See also Kennedy's essay in this volume.

It is interesting to see how the inveterate psychologizing about Mather's personality and authorship conveniently connects with the way that modern intellectual historians have often interpreted the culture of third- and fourth-generation Puritanism as a whole. In the "declension narrative" of New England Puritanism, codified in Perry Miller's *The New England Mind: From Colony to Province* (1953) and since then recast in may variants, Cotton Mather figures as the representative of a late and decadent phase. For Miller and countless others, Mather's purported propensity to shrill invectives and endless jeremiads about a backsliding populace are symptomatic of a cultural moment in which New England Puritanism had lost its earlier organic wholeness and vitality, which was fed by a robust fusion of piety and intellect. Similarly, Mather's quarrelsomeness, his fears of political plots and demonic conspiracies, is thought to indicate an anxious awareness that the traditional faith was following the old charter to its grave. With all its invocations of God's providential care for New England, its filiopious representations of an exemplary past and rhetorical affirmations of theological orthodoxy, a work like Mather's *Magnalia*, in this view, thus really bespeaks a pathetic "loss of mastery" (Peter Gay) and signals a giving in to the new order and new ideas. In this still-influential declension narrative, which ultimately is part of a larger secularization narrative,[20] Mather therefore has the rhetorical and organizational function of a typical latecomer, whose works serve as a lens of retrospection or as a telescope to look into the future of American culture.[21] By implication, the value of these works was mostly seen in either their antiquarian character as documents of what was about to be lost, or in what they anticipated and would later come to fruition.[22]

Indeed, besides his insoluble association with Salem, it seems to be Cotton Mather's historical fate, as Levin puts it, "to be considered largely as a transitional figure whose prodigious but narrow mind stretched inadequately between the zealous founding of the bible Commonwealth and the enlightened struggle for the Republic" (Levin, Introduction vii). For the Perry Miller school of American intellectual history, Mather's engagement with Enlightenment ideas, just like his turn towards European Pietism, were not part of a genuine renewal or reformulation of his ancestor's religion, but reflected the decline of New England Puritanism as it gave way to a more secular society and a this-worldly philosophy of human self-determination. Mather's perceived dabbling

---

20   For a succinct discussion of revisionist criticism of the traditional declension narrative, see Bremer (161–67 and 212–20) and the literature cited there.
21   Although well-informed and free from open hostility, Emory Elliott's portrait of Mather in *The Cambridge History of American Literature* (esp. 271–78), the most prestigious literary history at present, in many ways recasts some of the derogatory assumptions inscribed into the declension narrative.
22   For two excellent revisionist readings of Mather's *Magnalia* which challenge both the traditional declension narrative and its critical modifications at the hand of the New Americanists, see Felker (17–87) and Arch (136–89).

with natural philosophy in *The Christian Philosopher* is thus read as an inadvertent accommodation to the Deist rationalism that eventually evolved into the nature religion of Ralph Waldo Emerson, and Mather's *Bonifacius* is understood as an unconscious surrender to Arminian tendencies leading to a Franklinesque ethics of self-improvement. Thanks to Winton U. Solberg, Mather's reputation as a serious Enlightenment scientist has improved in recent years, and his *Christian Philosopher* is now more widely acknowledged as "the first comprehensive account of physical and natural sciences" (Solberg xxi) written in British North America.[23] In many respects, however, the old view persists, not least because of a general disregard of the early Enlightenment and the first half of the eighteenth century as a transitional period.

The above-cited American genealogies bring us back to another problematic tendency in interpreting Mather that has too often restricted the angle on his work and strengthened the derogatory assumptions about his character. Like many figures of the colonial era, Mather has been subject to a retrospective Americanization, that is, he has been read time and again as illustrating certain aspects or a certain developmental stage in the life of the American mind. Our habit to think of Mather as an "Early American" shows how deeply ingrained the assumption is in our minds that, in general, the Puritans formidably contributed to the making of the US and those qualities we now associate with Americanness. Indeed, the Puritans are either viewed as antagonistic forces that needed to be overcome or model forefathers bequeathing an enduring cultural legacy to the embryonic world power. As suggested above, this notion was historically born out of the search for national origins in the post-revolutionary period (see Kemmen; Hall "Puritanism"), and then became widely accepted as something of an ideological axiom by the nascent American Studies movement after WWII. With Mather in particular, the utilization of New England Puritanism as a "usable past" for the construction of a literary and cultural tradition frequently led to his reduction to an allegorical function in the ongoing processes of national self-reflection and self-definition.[24]

---

23 Earlier assessments of Mather's response to Enlightenment sciences can be found in Stearns, Beall and Shyrock. More recently, Michael P. Winship devotes much of his important book-length study to the transformation of Puritan providentialism by Cotton Mather. Winship argues that Mather's reception of early Enlightenment thought and his wish to be acknowledged in the learned culture of Britain that was moving away from the unabashed supernaturalism of the seventeenth century forced him to reformulate the Puritan belief in God's providence in the language of reason and natural philosophy that de-emphasized the importance of miracles, prodigies, and demonic forces. Mather did so, Winship argues, without being able to really resolve the fundamental contradictions between providentialism and the emerging scientific world view. Mark Noll's study ("Science, Theology, and Society") of the evangelical engagement with science portrays Mather as the American theologian who "established the main evangelical tradition with the publication in 1721 of *The Christian Philosopher*" (101).

24 In Reising's seminal study of the discipline, he discusses the "The Puritan origins theo-

"[I]n the popular panorama of the American past," as Kenneth Silverman writes, Mather is the dark forefather from whose shadow emerge the shining figures of Franklin, Jefferson and Washington to define what is quintessentially American. If the country wishes to think of its national ideology in terms of "democratic tolerance, reasonableness, individuality, and downrightness, this nebulous mythological Mather serves to symbolize what American character is not, or should not be – bigoted, superstitious, authoritarian, and devious." Hence, the "gross distortion of so complex a man into a national gargoyle" (Silverman 425) took place almost independently of Mather's actual writings or doings. Instead, as Silverman notes, it was defined by a mechanism of cultural psychology (mainly the mechanism of "Othering") at work in the construction of collective self-images. Mather's part in American "public memory" as a personification of "the worst elements of Puritanism" (Lovelace 290) that needed to be expunged or transfigured in the building of the nation has its structural parallels in the explanatory function which was assigned to him in American scholarly discourse. Here, too, one notices a long-standing obsession with Mather's meaning for America's future history and for the formation of national culture and identity. This approach to Mather is, of course, by no means singular. Indeed, as the name suggests, the entire sub-field of "Early American Studies" used to be oriented towards such nationalist mappings, searching for origins and foreshadowing, and drawing lines of continuity from Edwards to Emerson, from Bradstreet to Dickinson, and so on (see Gura). Over the past two decades, however, the discipline of American Studies has undergone an intense process of self-examination in which this nation-based paradigm of cultural and literary studies was subjected to much necessary criticism. There is now a wide-spread awareness of the ways in which the constitution of the discipline of American Studies had, from the beginning, simultaneously been informed by and reinforced ideas of American exceptionalism.[25]

In this spirit, the sub-field of Early American Studies has done much soul-searching in recent years, and has generally followed the discipline's overall "transnational turn" away from the U.S.-centered paradigm. Today most schol-

---

rists" as one of three major schools in the formative debates over what constituted a specifically American cultural and literary tradition (49–92).

25 In the preface to the collection *Shades of the Planet: American Literature as World Literature*, Wai Chee Dimock, quoting Janice Radways's 1998 presidential address to the American Studies Association, neatly sums up the drift of much recent revisionist criticism when she writes: "A field calling itself 'American' imagines that there is something exceptional about the United States, manifesting itself as a 'distinctive set of properties and themes in all things American, whether individuals, institutions, or cultural products.' This premise of exceptionalism translates into a methodology that privileges the national above all else. The field legitimizes itself as a field only because the nation does the legitimizing. The disciplinary sovereignty of the former owes everything to the territorial sovereignty of the latter" (Dimock 3).

ars of the colonial era self-consciously work not to project the conceptual framework of the nation back onto this period. The English colonies are no longer envisioned as self-contained, self-evolving cultural units that would eventually merge and come to fruition in a presumed new totality of U.S. culture. Consequently, there has been a good deal of re-evaluation of earlier scholarship, but not in all areas, and not for all key-figures. While, for instance, we had critical examinations of the retrospective Americanization of Benjamin Franklin (see Wood), unfortunately no such project has yet been undertaken with regard to Mather. Although some of the leading practitioners of contemporary Puritan studies have been champions of a transatlantic approach, this particular branch of scholarship seems, broadly speaking, most resistant to a methodological de-nationalization. This is perhaps not altogether surprising, considering how deeply entrenched Puritan origin theories are in the discipline's "field imaginary."

In the grand narratives about the formation of America's national identity construed by some of the most influential Americanists of the second half of the twentieth century, the New England Puritans figured prominently as forerunners or originators. Depending on the individual perspective, the Puritans were either celebrated or blamed for having established certain features and themes presumed to be distinctively American. Cotton Mather in particular was seen as someone foreshadowing various aspects of a presumed "American self," especially those features that were rather unlikable. We already spoke of Miller's assumption that, in Mather's later works, the Puritan notion of self-sanctification evolved into moral perfectionism and a "do gooder"-reformist mentality, which he passed down to Franklin who, after purging it of Mather's elitism and religious fanaticism, made it an essential part of the national mentality. Mather also loomed large in Sacvan Bercovitch's argument about the origins of an American exceptionalist ideology and the oppressive culture of hegemonic consensus, which he located in the Puritan transformation of a traditional Christian hermeneutics into a symbolic rhetoric of American identity. Making the *Magnalia Christi Americana* the paradigmatic text for what Bercovitch describes as the genre of representative American (auto-)biography, he turned Mather into a figurehead of US-national literature *avant la lettre*, a figurehead who anticipated many facets in the works of the American Renaissance.[26] Similarly, studies of gender and race relations in the United States have frequently traced the ideological formations of the nineteenth and twentieth centuries back to a presumed Puritan origin. As it was for the critics of exceptionalism, the study of Puritanism was, here, a way to attack aspects of American culture by

---

26 For insightful criticism of Bercovitch's master-thesis of a Puritan-derived civil theology, see Reising (74–92), Delbanco, and Harlan.

digging up the assumed historical roots of racism and oppressive gender hierarchies.[27]

We do not wish to imply that the Puritan origins theorists got it all wrong, for many of their specific findings are undoubtedly valid. Our concern is with the facets of Mather that have been obscured and sometimes distorted by the "Puritan legacy model of conceptualizing American distinctiveness" (Buell 11). Because of the search for distinctive qualities of Americanness in Mather's work, too much attention was given to a small number of texts in Mather's huge œuvre, focusing on local affairs (such as the Salem trials) or New England's history, specifically the *Magnalia*. But, more importantly, the tendency to use Puritanism and Mather as convenient shorthand for a critique of modern American culture has, in our opinion, led in many cases to a problematic, backward projection of the concepts or ideas in question. Furthermore, the guiding assumption that the meaning of Mather as a historical and transitional figure had to be primarily found in his relation to the future nation and its ideological formations, or that he himself primarily cared about the meaning of America, has all too often made scholars overlook the strong international or, more accurately, supra-regional dimensions of his thinking and writing. Because Americanists, compelled by their "field imaginary," were so busy inquiring into Mather's role in America's future history and in the creation of national culture and identity, they rarely asked other questions which we think are at least as significant, and, from a historical point of view, more appropriate: What, for instance, was his role in defining a specifically Christian Enlightenment in the Atlantic world? What was his role in the development of Protestant ecumenism, or in the rise of the international evangelical awakening in the early eighteenth century? What part did he play in contemporary world mission endeavors, transatlantic reform movements or the early attempts to abolish the slave trade? How did he position himself in the central scholarly and theological debates of his time over the authority of the Bible, the new historical-contextual approach in scriptural exegesis, and the relationship between revelation and reason?[28] Such questions are begging to be answered today.

That Mather was commonly interpreted in the framework, or measured by the standards of, a theology created by early seventeenth century American Puritanism is understandable, if not entirely accurate or satisfactory. For doing so,

---

27 The scholarly literature on the construction of gender in Mather's writings is surveyed in Gelina's essay in this collection. Mather's role in scholarly narratives of America's racial history or history of racism are discussed in Stievermann's essay.
28 Tellingly enough, those scholars of Mather's works who have begun to pursue these and similar questions in an international context are usually not Americanists. Mather's activities in the transatlantic networks of early Enlightenment science are discussed in Beall, Stearns, and Solberg. Mather's role in paving the way for the First Great Awakening is discussed in Lovelace. For a review of the literature on his ecumenical contacts and activities, see Scheiding's essay in this collection.

on the one hand, parochialized Mather and, on the other, almost inevitably lent support to some sort of declension narrative. It is even more inappropriate that Mather's works have often been read with an eye to later U.S. authors such as Ralph Waldo Emerson and their (alleged) nationalist ideas than in dialogue with his contemporary peers across the Christian world and their intellectual agendas or practical projects. However strongly he felt obliged to the Reformed tradition of the sixteenth and seventeenth centuries, Mather was very much a theologian and scholar of the early eighteenth century, and he has to be read in the context of the transatlantic debates that occupied this period if we want to understand him better. One need only look at the vast corpus of Mather's letters (of which only a small part has survived, and an even smaller fraction edited) to appreciate that he consistently looked beyond the horizon of his native province onto the broad and rapidly shifting intellectual panorama of the period. He exchanged news and debated ideas with literally hundreds of clerics, scientists and missionaries across Europe and as far away as India. Mather corresponded with Nonconformist as well as Anglican ministers across England, Scotland, and Ireland, such as John Edwards, Robert Wodrow, and William Whiston; with Richard Waller and Sir Hans Sloane, two presidents of the Royal Society; with the Lutheran Pietist August Hermann Francke in Halle, with the Lutheran missionary in Tranquebar Bartholomäus Ziegenbalgh (see Benz "Pietist and Puritan Sources"), and with the great Reformed theologian Herman Witsius at Utrecht, to name just a few examples (see Mather, *Selected Letters*).

If his network of actual correspondents was large, the cosmos of thinkers with whose works he engaged was infinitely more expansive. Mather developed his ideas and wrote his works in conversation with a vast multitude of theologians, scholars, and literary authors across the contemporary Atlantic world, but also, to borrow a phrase from Wai Chee Dimock, across "deep time." For Mather's writing continuously moves between centuries and millennia as well as between continents. Virtually everything Mather composed was either primarily exegetical, or had the Bible as its primary frame of reference, and the way he approached scripture had a strongly historical, and indeed historicist bend. Following a broad trend in Protestant theology of the era, he regarded the scriptures not simply as revelations of God's universal truth, but also as ancient documents whose full meaning could only be unlocked through rigid philological work, careful contextualization, and with the help of modern science. About the authors and cultural circumstances that brought forth these documents as well as about their textual tradition, history of reception, and history interpretation, he probably knew more than anyone in British North America at the turn of the eighteenth century. When constructing an argument, be it from the Bible or about it, he would habitually respond to the latest European studies in biblical scholarship, historiography, and the natural sciences. Consulting the original languages in which the texts were written, he draws upon

African Church Fathers, ancient Roman historians, Greek philosophers and poets, Targums, Rabbinical commentaries, and medieval scholastic works. Interpretation of Mather must therefore shift from an exclusive lens of earlier Puritans or later American writers, to a side-by-side account of his work with the authors whom he actually studied and admired and, consequently, had the greatest influence on his work. Among these, some, if by no means most, are English theologians, a very few are New English divines (mostly his father, uncle and grandfather), but the majority are either Continental or ancient figures. To really de-nationalize our approach to Mather would thus mean to study him alongside, say, his favored Church Fathers Theodoret and Chrysostom (*Manuductio* 89), the historians Eusebius and Flavius Josephus, or contemporary scholars such as Johann Buxtorf, Samuel Bochart, John Spencer, Sebastian Münster, Johann Heinrich Heidegger, or the more carefully handled Hugo Grotius.

To anyone who had eyes to see it, the broad range and historical depth of Mather's mind was evident all along in his well-known publications, but it becomes undeniable with the "Biblia Americana." His synoptic commentary shows how far removed he was from the stereotype of the provincial Puritan, and how mistaken the old clichés about his pedantry were. Belonging themselves to a discipline characterized by an inveterate monolingualism, Americanists in particular had been fond of denouncing the many quotes from the ancient languages in Mather's texts as ornamental bombast serving no purpose other than (out of some assumed inferiority complex) showing off the author's erudition. Measured against works of an American literary canon that had been constructed on the basis of a (post-) Romantic aesthetic, Mather's sprawling and multilingual writing simply appeared as bad taste. If seen in the context of early eighteenth-century scholarship, however, it appears as a perfectly normal *modus operandi*.

For one thing, Mather approached the Bible, and through it, all of nature and secular history, as a trained philologist who sought the meaning of God's truth by analyzing and comparing the linguistic forms in which it had been originally expressed (Hebrew, Aramaic, Greek) and into which it had been later translated, such as Latin (VUL), Greek (LXX) and also later Aramaic versions of the Hebrew Bible. Furthermore, he also considered the later vernaculars into which the Holy Bible was translated such as French, German and Spanish. More than any other of his works, the "Biblia Americana" also reveals that Mather did not just decorate his ideas and thoughts with foreign learning but, in accordance with the prevailing methodologies of both biblical criticism and historiography, developed them through extensive dialogues with multiple sources, most of which were in languages other than English. In an age that considered it good academic practice to quote one's sources in the original, the nineteenth- and twentieth-century complaints about the *Magnalia's* "numerous quotations in Latin, Greek and Hebrew which rise up like so many decayed, hideous stumps ... to deform the surface" (Tudor 256) would have sounded odd to any scholar's ear. Moreover, at the time Latin was still the *lingua franca* amongst the learned, and a good many of the contemporary works that Mather cites were written in that language. Seen in its proper context, Mather's citation-laden style, and especially his frequent recourse to Latin (the language in which he, out of necessity, also conducted his correspondence with Continental theologians such as Francke or Witsius), were neither marks of Mather's foppish pompousness nor of his antiquarian backwardness, as many Americanists liked to think, but the required graces of any and every serious theologian in the early eighteenth century and long before.

It is one of the central goals of this collection to demonstrate that Mather is most fruitfully studied as a figure whose thinking was not so much inward-looking as intensely transatlantic in orientation. For one thing, his publications drew on a vast array of Old World sources and often responded to European debates. Furthermore, the texts show the marks of being written for an audience beyond that of his geographical location. This is also the case with regard to his practical projects of religious revival, church reform, or mission: again and again his pen points to the world outside and ties him inextricably into the context of Protestantism both within and beyond Britain. Having said all this, we do not wish to deny that Mather, maybe more so than many of his fellow New Englanders at the time, was conscious of living in America and of being a colonial. There undoubtedly is a pronounced regionalist dimension to a lot of the things he wrote. After all, according to the *OED*, he was the first white British colonial to refer to himself as an American,[29] and he used this adjective in the titles of some of his most important works, including *Magnalia Christi Americana, Corderius Americanus, Theopolis Americana, Psalterium Americanum* and, of course, "Biblia Americana." Nevertheless, taking this regionalist dimension of his work as something like a proto-nationalist mentality would be a misinterpretation of this early eighteenth-century mind.

It is certainly no coincidence that most of the works to which he gave the epithet "American" have titles in Latin – the language of international scholarship – marking this rhetorical gesture as an intersection of regional concerns, colonial self-consciousness, and cosmopolitan aspiration. Behind this contrary gesture we sense feelings of inferiority, a dogged sense of pride, and the wish for recognition. In his biography, Silverman has given us a vivid picture of how

---

29 According to the *OED*, Cotton Mather was the first writer of English descent born in the New World who used the adjective American in the sense of "a native or inhabitant of America; especially of the British colonies in North America; of European descent." In this way the adjective was first employed in Mather's 1691 *The Triumph of the Reformed Religion in America* (88), and then in self-reference ("One poor feeble American") in the "General Introduction" of the *Magnalia* (33).

painfully self-aware Mather was of his colonial condition, of the remoteness from the metropolitan center, and how conscious he was of the dominant European perception of people in America as backward, uncouth, and incapable of cultural or scholarly accomplishments. In his many transatlantic conversations Mather thus felt "both challenged to report the uniqueness of his country and pained by the relative crudeness of its intellectual life ..." (Silverman 245). Simultaneously embarrassed about his provincialism, and determined to assert the significance of New England's religious legacy (most importantly the legacy of the Mather dynasty!), he indeed strove "to become conspicuous as an American. For he looked out eagerly from the New World on major intellectual developments abroad, aspiring to contribute to them ..." in the "hope of putting America on the cultural map" (425–26).[30]

However, Mather's hope and the undeniable wish for cultural self-assertion as an American did not relate to a "country," not even an "infant country" (245), as Silverman and others would have it. Mather's aspiration and emotional bonds related to his native New England as an outward province of the British Empire. The national framework is misleading here, since someone like Mather certainly had little sense of community with Anglican planters in Virginia or Quakers in Pennsylvania. The self-identification as American should not be interpreted as an expression of solidarity with other groups of colonials across British North America, but as the message of a Boston scholar directed at a European audience of peers from which he strove to gain recognition. The message Mather sent, however, is decidedly mixed and constitutes, on the one hand, an act of proud defiance of the "poor American" (as he liked to style himself), who could produce such wondrous works despite the circumstances in which he lived and, on the other hand, a subservient *captatio benevolentiae* intended to evoke sympathetic interest or to sequester potential criticism.[31]

Both Mather's ambition to become the first New England luminary in the intercontinental Republic of Letters and his anxious self-consciousness as a marginalized colonial are clearly on display in the rhetorical gymnastics he performs to advertise his "Biblia Americana" in *A New Offer*. Biblical scholarship was probably the most prestigious intellectual discipline at the turn of the eight-

---

30 Winship's insightful comment on this matter deserves to be quoted here: "Although he never traveled far from Boston, he always saw himself as a transatlantic figure, a person out to make his mark on a European intellectual and religious world, which he did with a respectable degree of success" (87).
31 Interestingly enough, Mather also attributed part of his difficulties to find subscribers for "Biblia Americana" to metropolitan arrogance towards the colonial provinces. In a 1715 letter to Sir William Ashurst he complained that many London Dissenters "seem to be of the opinion, that a poor American must never be allow'd capable of doing any thing worth any ones regarding; or to have ever look'd on a Book. And the Truth is, we are under such Disadvantages, that if we do any thing to purpose, it must carry in it a tacit Rebuke to the sloth of people more advantageously circumstanced" (*Diary* 2: 331).

eenth century and, as Peter N. Miller has written, comparable in status to rocket science in the second half of the twentieth century. No one knew this better than Mather, but he also knew that Britain had just recently launched such prestigious spaceships as *Biblia Sacra Polyglotta*, *Critici Sacri*, and *Synopsis Criticorum*. Thus, in his 1714 pamphlet he staked his claim in the market with considerable nervousness and trepidations. "Sometimes very mean things," he winked at potential subscribers with one of his characteristic puns, "have on the score of their being *Far-fetcht*, had a Value set upon them, and not been look'd upon as too Dear-bought, when a great Price has been given for them."

> If a Work, which is a *Tree*, that grew on the Western side of the *Atlantic*, may on *that score* hope to be valued by good Men, in the *other Hemisphere*, there will be an accession of *this peculiar Circumstance*, that, *Gentlemen*, the *Fruits* upon it, or at least, the *Seeds* that produced them, were most of them, Originally *Your own*: And it cannot but be a *Pleasure*, if not a *Surprize* unto you, to find that so many of your *Best Things*, have passed over *the great and wide Sea* unto the *American Strand*. Nor will it be New or Strange, if some Things happen to be *Meliorated*, and made more *Sweet and Fine*, by passing over this mighty Ocean. Or, to address you under *another Figure*; The Writers whom you made much of, while you had them *at Home* with you in a more *separate Condition*, certainly, will not lose your Favour, for having *Travelled Abroad*, and now *Returned Home* in *Company*; tho' with their *Habit* and *Language* having something of an *American* Change upon it. (*A New Offer* 10)[32]

You can trust the quality of this American product, Mather – in a figurative reversal of the mercantile relations between the colonies and the motherland – is telling his target audience across the British Empire, because all the wonderful intellectual raw materials that went into its production have been originally imported from Europe. Besides the insights this passage offers us into the psychology of the colonial condition, it is also highly revealing with respect to Mather's self-understanding as a New England intellectual and with respect to the question, what did he think was specifically American about his "Biblia Americana"? Obviously, Mather did not aspire for originality in the Romantic sense, and he had no notion of an autochthonous American writing. Rather, he saw his own role as that of a collector, organizer, amalgamator and, ideally, a creative emendator of European learning. The word "European" needs emphasis here because the seeds of learning, which Mather hoped to bring into fruition, were by no means predominantly English. Guided by the early modern

---

32   The trope of the towering tree on the Western side of the Atlantic recalls the imagery from the prophecy of Ezekiel (31:3–9) and the imagery with which the angel in Mather's vision spoke to him "of the books this youth should write and publish, not only in America, but in Europe" and "of the great works this youth should do for the church of Christ in the revolutions that are now at hand" (*Diary* 1: 86–87). This suggests that Mather looked at his "Biblia Americana" as the true fulfillment of his calling and expected that its publication would bring him lasting glory.

ideal of *copia*, he imagined the Americanness of his work to lie in the unprecedented breadth and abundance of accumulated knowledge. More importantly, the "American Change" of which *A New Offer* speaks points to Mather's hope of achieving a pious synthesis of biblical revelation with the various branches of contemporary knowledge in a manner that would also translate into practical lessons for holy living and evangelical renewal (see Stievermann, "Writing").

In no way, however, does the identification (either of himself or his works) as American imply an attempt to achieve a cultural "divorce from Europe" (Silverman 426). This is the agenda of other New England intellectuals a hundred years later. If Silverman repeats the old Americanist *topos* according to which Mather's works "contain an embryonic element of nationalism" (245), Silverman, without acknowledging the contradiction, corrects this misjudgment in a wonderfully perceptive commentary on the *Magnalia*. Whereas generations of Americanists have read the *Magnalia* as something of an early patriotic epic-invariably quoting its famous opening sentence, "I WRITE the WONDERS of the CHRISTIAN RELIGION, flying from the depravations of Europe to the American Strand ..." – Silverman notices that almost the entire "General Introduction" of that work is a qualification of its first paragraph. Because he wrote the book primarily for a European readership, "specifically for an English audience," Mather is indeed anxious "to exhibit New England's affection for the mother country, aware, and not distressed that New England's place in history was that of one outpost in a taut new transatlantic imperial network" (Silverman 160). The same can be said for his "Biblia" which, as he puts it in *A New Offer*, was undertaken in the hope "that AMERICA may at length, with a Benign and Smiling Aspect of her Lady-Mother upon her, come to something, for an Interest that must *have these uttermost Parts of the Earth for its Possession*" (9).

Mather was therefore eager to demonstrate the religious and cultural significance of these *"uttermost Parts of the Earth"* vis-à-vis the Old World, but never entertained any fantasies about American (cultural) autonomy. Such fantasies would have been virtually unthinkable for him. Not just because he understood himself as a loyal subject of the British crown, but because God's true Church, as the community which mattered most to him, was, like the international Republic of Letters, a global community. In fact, as he grew older, Mather's understanding of the Church became increasingly ecumenical and thus transnational. Although it has never been widely acknowledged in the field of American Studies, Mather's strong ecumenism has long been established beyond doubt by church historians such as Ernst Benz ("Ecumenical Relations") and Richard Lovelace, and shown to be an integral part of his theology, especially his eschatology (Middlekauff 227–32). Nowhere is this ecumenical spirit more clearly on display than in Mather's "Biblia Americana." In his advertisement of the "Biblia," Mather announced that the commentary was written by one "strictly adhering to the principles of the *Christian Religion*, professed in the *Reformed Churches*," but that it was "not a Work animated with the *Spirit of Party*." Ultimately, the target audience for "the Oblations which he brings from those that may be accounted *Better than himself*," he writes, is "the Church, to which we all owe our *All*" (*New Offer* 9). Spelled with a capital C, the Church here clearly signifies an international community of Protestants "who embrace the *True Religion*, tho' of different Perswasions in some lesser Points of it" (*A New Offer* 7–8).

By offering the collected fruits of his scholarship to this international and interdenominational community of "Impartial Christians, of whatever Denomination or Subdivision in Christianity" (*New Offer* 7), Mather wished to draw them together on the basis of the essential points demonstrated from the scriptures so that they could engage in worldwide co-operations for reformist and missionary work. For Mather, fostering an active Christian union of Protestant churches under the banner of Pietist renewal was "a necessary part of the preparation for the Second Coming" (Middlekauff 231) and the rise of the millennium. He hoped that New England would be allowed a place in the millennial kingdom, but never thought his native province and its churches would take center stage in Christ's reign. In his view, New England (be it as a community or as a model of church government) was neither the hub of the universe, nor the primary frame of reference; furthermore, there is no reason to claim that his eschatological hopes were invested in America as a region or special agent in redemption history (see Smolinski "*Israel Redivivus*").

Multilingual, of enormous geographical and temporal range, cosmopolitan and ecumenical in orientation, the "Biblia Americana," for all intents and purposes, was probably the closest thing to a genuine work of American world literature before the syncretistic world scriptures of the Transcendentalists. With this collection, we make an attempt to do more justice to these dimensions of Mather's work. Although completely free in their choice of topics, none of our contributors had anything to say about Mather's contributions to a presumed American character or ideology. Apart from a general weariness with this kind of approach, it seems as if working with the "Biblia Americana" makes one almost automatically gravitate away from the nation-centered paradigm of Puritan studies. This does not mean that our contributors overlook how deeply Mather was involved in regional affairs and how much his writings, by responding to these affairs, reveal about the religious, cultural and political life in British North America. Mather, Michael Kaufmann rightly says, "provides an entry into virtually every area of the colonial experience." Through his published works, we can study the gradual transformation from "colony to province," the interaction between learned theology, Enlightenment science and folk religion, the formation of the Great Awakening and rise of Evangelicalism, "gender relations and the domestic scene" or "the racial politics of the New World" (Kaufmann 437–38).

As a number of essays in this volume show, his "Biblia Americana" greatly adds to all of these areas of insight and often complicates previous findings. For example, his commentaries on the Bible shed new light on his understanding of gender hierarchies, his promotion of female education, but also on his ambiguous views of slavery and Anglo-Indian relations. However, even with a subject such as Mather's response to the spread of slavery in New England, his position is best understood as the result of intersecting local and transatlantic developments, both on the level of changing ideas and beliefs, and on the level of sociopolitical or economical shifts. When it comes to his positions on the more abstract or academic questions of natural philosophy, theology, or biblical criticism, a failure to connect them to contemporary European trends or debates inevitably leads to very serious misunderstandings and distortions. Arguably, this all-too-common failure, which is a direct outgrowth of passé Americanists' agendas and their monopolization of Mather, has done almost as much as the specter of Salem to diminish his stature as a scholar and theologian.

Towards A New Mather

In the predominant view, Cotton Mather still appears as the villain of Salem at worst and as a significant, if transitional, figure of early American cultural and religious history at best. Very rarely, however, has he been deemed a scholar or theologian of any lasting consequence. While there has been an intense revival of interest in Jonathan Edwards as a theologian since WWII, which brought his writings to the curricula of seminaries as well as philosophy or history departments, and generated a plethora of scholarly works on all aspects of Edwards's thinking, Mather did not fare so well.[33] With the exception of his eschatology, the various aspects of Mather's thinking on divinity (e.g. his Christology, his understanding of the Trinity, his interpretation of redemption history) and their philosophical foundations and implications (e.g. his metaphysics, epistemology, or moral thought) have not received an even comparable degree of systematic study.[34] Thanks in no small part to the now complete Yale edition, Edwards's writings are appreciated by academics, ministers, and many lay Christians alike. Over the last few decades, Edwards has thus been promoted to the role of the first great American theologian in the evangelical tradition; he is attributed with having successfully led Calvinism into modernity, and even granted the universal honorary title of "America's theologian." It has

---

33 On Edwards's reputation and the Edwards Renaissance since WWII see Part III in *The Cambridge Companion to Jonathan Edwards*, especially the essays by Sweeney, Lesser, and Crocco and the literature cited there.
34 For studies of Mather's eschatology, see Smolinski (*"Israel Redivivus"*; Introduction) and Erwin.

also been suggested that if one considered his many manuscript works in the field of biblical studies "Edwards may be the most prolific exegetical scholar in American history" (Sweeney, "Jonathan Edwards" 311). By contrast, Mather's theology is usually approached for purely historical reasons and with detachment, if not disdain. As a major biblical interpreter he does not figure at all, even though his unpublished exegetical work and sermons at least matches the size of the Edwardsean corpus. Of course, there have been a number of noteworthy attempts to correct this picture, efforts which have very much influenced the essays in this collection. However, so far the impact on academic culture at large (not to speak of popular culture) has been limited.

The most momentous work was probably Robert Middlekauff's *The Mathers: Three Generations of Puritan Intellectuals* (1977), in which Cotton is reassessed as "the most admirable of the three because he was the most daring (and the most driven)," and who, by the time of his death, "had refashioned, with the help of his father, much in Puritanism – ecclesiastical theory, the psychology of religious experience, covenant preaching, and the conception of Christian history and prophecy" (xvii). Contra the old declension narrative, Middlekauff convincingly argues that Cotton Mather's openness to Enlightenment ideas or ecumenical trends in international Protestantism and his emphasis on practical piety was not a symptom of intellectual surrender or weakening faith, but rather reflected his ability to incorporate new elements into the traditional tenets of Reformed orthodoxy without eroding their substance. More specifically, Mather did not give up the covenantal framework of his forebears, but rather reinterpreted it in more Christocentric terms, de-emphasizing human agency in the salvation process. Middlekauff is also able to show that the strong attention given to the emotional dimension of man's regeneration through the free gift of a saving faith in Christ gave Mather's theology an experiential orientation that in many respects anticipated the "religious style" of a Jonathan Edwards.

This vital continuity between Mather's and the new type of theology that evolved from the First Great Awakening is the central subject of Richard L. Lovelace's *The American Pietism of Cotton Mather* (1979). Lovelace's greatest merit is that he completely overturned the old perception of Mather as a latecomer, in whom a great tradition came to its end, maintaining instead that we should see him as a great innovator who stands – as the subtitle of Lovelace's study suggests – at the very beginnings of modern American Evangelicalism. Now we know that it is no coincidence that Mather was the first writer in the English language to use the term "revival" in a religious sense.[35] Lovelace also earns praise for drawing more attention to the significance of Mather's transat-

---

35   According to the *OED*, Mather was the first to use the noun "revival" (*Magnalia*, bk. 3, p. 323) in the sense of "A general reawakening of or in religion in a community or some part of one."

lantic connections with other Protestant groups, especially with Halle Pietism, and also for helping to understand why and how he sought to revitalize the Puritan faith under dramatically altered circumstances. Like Middlekauff, Lovelace stresses how central Mather's millennialism and his end-time expectations were to every aspect of his theology. Yet only through Smolinski's annotated edition of the unpublished *Triparadisus* (written 1726/27) and a series of revisionist studies has the development of Mather's eschatology emerged in all its complexity.

The findings of Middlekauff, Lovelace, and Smolinski are reflected in the best recent survey histories of theology in North America. Both Holifield and Noll (*America's God*), acknowledge Mather as a notable representative of the New England tradition of divinity who ensured the transition of the Reformed faith into the eighteenth century by recasting its essence in modernized forms.[36] Similarly, Mather is frequently mentioned now, if only in passing, as a precursor of the Great Awakening in histories of evangelicalism.[37] Yet, measured by the attention that is bestowed on Edwards, Mather the theologian still stands as a relatively minor figure. It is to be hoped that the participation of prominent Edwards scholars both in the edition and in this collection will serve as a catalyst for a theological rediscovery of Mather. Besides the preconceptions of Mather that were already discussed, one significant reason for the lack of attention given to Mather, in contrast to Edwards, is the enduring lack of a comprehensive edition of his works. Some of his publications have been reprinted, some even appeared in scholarly editions.[38] The bulk of Mather's printed books, however, including some of his most interesting theological, philosophical, and reformist treatises, are no longer easily accessible and are virtually unknown except to a very small number of specialists. In addition, the vast majority of Mather's sermons and some larger works still remain in manuscript.

Above all, of course, the "Biblia Americana," the work that he considered the crowning achievement and sum of his theological career, never saw the light of day, and even Mather scholars consulted the manuscript only sporadically and, even then, quite selectively. As our preliminary discussion of this wide-ranging, erudite, and very sophisticated commentary suggests, its availability to a wider public promises to fundamentally change the ways Mather is perceived and to foster the appreciation of his standing as a theologian, philosopher, historical thinker, reformist and, most importantly, as a philologist and

---

36 Holifield's discussion of Increase and Cotton Mather (68–78) is probably the most lucid and balanced survey.

37 See Ward, *The Protestant Evangelical Awakening* (esp. 272–75) and *Early Evangelicalism* (91–95); Noll, *The Rise of Evaneglicalism* (58).

38 Currently, we have scholarly editions of the first two books of *Magnalia Christi Americana*, of *Bonifacius*, "Problema Theologicum," *Angel of Bethesda*, *The Christian Philosopher*, and *Triparadisus*.

scriptural exegete. The first fruits of Smolinski's and Maddux's work on the "Biblia" provide a foretaste of what lies in store. Already we have learned that Mather was not afraid to venture onto dangerous water in defence of scriptural authority. He took on the radical challenges posed by the rise of historical criticism, such as "the debate about the authorship of the Pentateuch and the dispute about the divine inspiration of the scriptures" (Smolinski, "Authority and Interpretation" 178), and he was "more audacious in employing the new sciences as an exegetical tool than most of his peers who supplied American pulpits until the Revolution" (Smolinski, "Natural Science and Interpretation"). This volume is intended to continue the process of discovery in attempting to re-examine the familiar "old Mather" from different angles without claiming to have invented a definite "new Mather." The studies brought together here should be understood, quite literally, as *essays* in reappraisal, that is, as tentative attempts to sketch out new interpretative perspectives when no definitive conclusions can yet be offered. As pioneering and impressive a work we believe our contributors have done, we think that the significance of their essays lies at least as much in showing what remains to be done.

Quite likely, the ongoing edition of the "Biblia Americana" will produce insights which, in turn, demand further modification or even critical reassessment of some of the preliminary appraisals offered here. We welcome this critical reception and acknowledge that it is the risk that everybody runs who chooses to delve into fresh materials and to explore new territory. All of our contributors made that choice. Without exception, their essays look beyond Mather's well-thumbed works, such as the *Magnalia*, which come freighted with so much ideological baggage, and approach their respective subjects by a direct examination of understudied or never-before-studied sources. In most cases, these sources are the newly transcribed scriptural commentaries from various parts of the "Biblia Americana"; in others cases, they are neglected works by Mather or new contexts that shed a different light on Mather. Secondly, all of the essays seek to engage with Mather on fair terms, that is, to discuss his ideas and arguments with due consideration of their respective historical, religious, and intellectual backgrounds. Whatever methodological approach the different studies follow – most fall under the capacious rubric of intellectual and religious history; others lean towards theology or literary studies – they are consistently informed by a healthy skepticism against grand theoretical narratives (be it "secularization as progress" theories or "Puritan origin" narratives) and, as much as possible, abstain from presentist judgments about the attitudes of the early eighteenth century. Thirdly, and maybe most importantly, all of them make a conscious effort to disentangle themselves from popular prejudices and disciplinary preconceptions about Mather and Puritanism in general. For as many new insights lie buried in the manuscript pages of his "Biblia Americana," they will only show themselves to us if we uproot the recalcitrant stereotypes from our minds. The attempt to fathom the "Biblia Americana" and the revisionist endeavor to reassess its prodigious author are mutually dependent upon each other.

Summary of the Essays

If twentieth century scholars have been generally disinclined to treat Mather in a respectful, subtle, and circumspect manner and have been more prone towards unsympathetic generalizations about his questionable character or role in American history, his image in modern popular culture is even less nuanced and indeed outright cartoonish. The two essays in **Section 1 (The Vicissitudes of Mather's Reputation)** remind us that this was not always so and investigate when and how the dramatic eclipse of Mather's reputation came about.

As a kind of prequel to his book-length study on the construction of Mather in nineteenth-century historiography, WILLIAM VAN ARRAGON goes back to the year 1728 to examine both public and private responses to Mather's death. Through detailed readings not only of textual representations in funeral sermons, biographies, and unpublished diary accounts, but also of the ways in which Mather's deathbed rituals and funeral procession were performed by the Boston community, Van Arragon's essay arrives at a twofold conclusion: although Mather's immediate contemporaries acknowledged that he was a complex, sometimes perplexing and controversial character, they unanimously chose to remember him as a great man of enormous learning, deep piety, and untiring commitment to the community's well-being, as one of New England's eminent spiritual leaders. While in their essence these assessments of Mather and his death were doubtlessly heartfelt, they also fulfilled, as Van Arragon argues, a socio-political function. By creating an exemplary image of Mather, which embodied Puritan virtues as a model for self-fashioning, the mourners were at the same time contributing to the ongoing negotiations of New England's collective identity.

E. BROOKS HOLIFIELD basically takes things up where Van Arragon leaves them. How do we explain, Holifield asks, the relatively swift and steep decline of Mather's once glorious reputation from 1728 to the mid-nineteenth century, when, to many Americans, the name of Cotton Mather already signified little but "Salem"? Drawing on a vast array of primary sources and his profound knowledge of American religious history, Holifield argues that Mather's reduction to the role of the witch-doctor had only indirectly to do with his writings on the invisible world or his actual involvement with the Salem trials. In the final analysis, Mather was something like a collateral victim in the battles over church government that were waged in the early decades of the nineteenth century between the orthodox establishment of Massachusetts and its liberal opponents. Mainly because of his now almost forgotten ecclesiastical work *Ratio Disciplinae Fratrum* (1726), Mather served for both parties as a reference point for traditionalist views on church government. It was in this context that religious liberals exploited Mather's supernaturalism and the association with Salem as a means of subverting his authority on questions of church government and thereby to weaken their antagonists. While the conflicts between Unitarians and Congregationalists were soon forgotten, the damage done to Mather's image would prove more permanent.

Professional historians of American culture, of course, always knew that there was much more to Mather than his caricature in popular culture suggested. In fact, academic interest in the Puritan clergyman was consistently strong. However, in academic discourse, especially in that of the newly founded discipline of American Studies, Mather frequently suffered another abridgement: his retrospective Americanization. It has been suggested above that for a long time, Puritan studies in general and Mather scholarship in particular tended to look at their subjects with – to borrow from Lawrence Buell's astute assessment of American Studies movement as a whole – an anachronistic "nation-focusedness [that] uncritically reinforced a posture of U.S. exceptionalism even and indeed perhaps especially when," as in the case of Bercovitch, "dissent from mainstream American values has been basic to the critical orientation" (Buell 2). While the entire collection makes an attempt at deparochializing Mather, the essays in **Section 2 (Cotton Mather in the Context of International Protestantism)** do so in a pointed and programmatic manner.

In the first two essays of the section, Mather's Protestant ecumenism and his connections with continental Pietism serve as the point of departure. Drawing on the scholarship of Benz, Lovelace, and others, FRANCIS J. BREMER, a long-standing critic of Americanist insularity in Puritan studies, simply takes as a given Mather's ecumenism and his close associations with scholars all over Europe. For Bremer, Cotton Mather's outspoken internationalism and interdenominationalism serve as a springboard for a larger argument about the need to recognize the often more covert ecumenical and cosmopolitan tendencies in the generation of his father and grandfather. The essay thus sets out to demonstrate that Mather's openness to Protestants across the board and his far-flung connections were not something new that occurred only in response to the downfall of the Puritan theocracy, but actually constituted the product of a long history of Puritan contacts with Continental reform. Without studying these contacts more closely, Bremer says, we cannot properly understand New England's heavy involvement in the evangelical awakenings that began to gather momentum around the Protestant world toward the end of Cotton Mather's life. After surveying the intimate ties between England and the Continent during the Reformation age, Bremer zeroes in on the group around Samuel Hartlib, a key figure in furthering the connection of English Puritans with Continental clergy. During the great migration, the Hartlib network then also expanded across the Atlantic and included figures such John Davenport and John Winthrop, Jr., who in turn set a model for the transatlantic activities of Increase Mather.

OLIVER SCHEIDING revisits the transatlantic exchange between Cotton Mather and August Hermann Francke, the great leader of Halle Pietism. Although it is well-known that such an exchange existed, its significance, Scheiding claims, has been at least partly underestimated. While Mather undeniably showed great enthusiasm for German Pietism, most existing studies agree that this enthusiasm remained largely unrequited and ultimately did not play a decisive role for his reformulation of Puritanism into an "American Pietism" (Lovelace) or evangelicalism. However, Scheiding's essay presents fresh evidence that the religious network between Boston and Halle was characterized by much greater reciprocity in terms of mutual interest and influence than is commonly understood or acknowledged. After reviewing the extant archival record together with the current state of the scholarly debate, Scheiding focuses on the *Narratio Epistolica Ad Cott. Matherum* (1735), a historical narrative written by August Hermann Francke, in part, and completed, edited, and published by his close associate Johann Heinrich Callenberg, a Lutheran church historian and important second-generation promoter of the Pietist movement. In his reading of Callenberg, Scheiding convincingly demonstrates that this hitherto-ignored document reveals substantial new information about Halle's relationship with and impact on Mather. Published after Mather's death, the *Narratio* shows the great degree of attitudinal congruence, affections, and shared religious dispositions between both sides that formed the foundation for joined projects centering on the notion of universal religious improvement (*Universalverbesserung*).

Given their natural affinities as revitalization movements within the Reformed fold, it is surprising that we know even less about the connections that existed between New England Puritanism and the Dutch *Nadere Reformatie* than we know about the Puritan ties to Lutheran Pietism. An authority on Peter van Mastricht, ADRIAAN NEELE brings more light into this darkness. Neele offers striking proof for the great appreciation Cotton Mather had for Mastricht's *Theoretico-practica theologia* (1682–87) and for the ample use Mather made of this important work. However, the essay moves beyond a simple influence study and examines the dialogue between Mastricht and Mather not just in terms of explicit reference, but also with a view to their close similarities in their approaches to practicing and teaching theology. According to Neele, the *theoretico-practica* motif or paradigm that informs Mastricht's *opus magnum* and gives it its title is also a fruitful interpretive framework for many works of Cotton Mather as it characteristically combines scholarly biblical exegesis, speculative theology, and a deep concern for practical piety. With an eye to the future,

Neele's essay shows how much could be gained if one studied Mather side by side with some of his frequently cited authorities such as Herman Witsius.

The essays in **Section 3 (Enlightenment Rationalism, Biblical Literalism and the Supernatural)** look at another transatlantic network in which Mather participated. Like few other people in British North America at the time, Mather followed and actively involved himself in the multifarious discourses we now associate with the terms "Early Enlightenment" and "Scientific Revolution." While Mather's much-coveted membership in the Royal Society is an outward emblem of this involvement, its strongest expression through his own publications can be found in the physico-theological compendium *The Christian Philosopher* (1721). At least since Winton U. Solberg's new edition of this work, Mather has gained some recognition in academia (though the wider public still needs to take notice) as an important early representative of Enlightenment thought in America. This recognition, though, has raised a number of difficult questions which still need to be answered. Where precisely did Mather position himself in the broad spectrum of attitudes, convictions, and ideas which the Enlightenment comprised? How exactly did he reconcile (or attempted to reconcile) the methods and findings of the new sciences with his biblical literalism and the belief in the infallible authority of the scriptures? And how could he harmonize, if at all, a support for scientific empiricism with his pronounced supernaturalism, his unshakeable belief in ghosts, demons, and witches which earned him his modern reputation as a credulous witch-doctor? These are the problems which the essays in this section explore by studying sections of the "Biblia Americana" in the contexts of Mather's published works.

Building on his earlier study of *The Christian Philosopher*, WINTON U. SOLBERG attempts a reappraisal of Mather's place in the complex history of the Enlightenment. To simply say that Mather was a representative of the Enlightenment, Solberg suggests, is not saying very much. When seen in the rather conservative context of intellectual life in the British colonies, Mather certainly strikes one as an intellectual innovator and pioneer of the new sciences. However, if we view him through the lens of works by Baruch Spinoza and his European followers, who have recently attracted much attention as representatives of the so-called Radical Enlightenment, Mather appears as a defender of Christian orthodoxy. After tracing the outlines of Spinoza's fundamental critique of revealed religion in his famous *Tractatus Theologico-Politicus* (1670) and surveying the early history of Spinozism on the Continent and in Britain, Solberg gauges Mather's response to the Radical Enlightenment in the "Biblia Americana." Only on some occasions does Mather target Spinoza directly. He is more concerned with the reception of Spinoza's ideas among prominent biblical critics such as Jean LeClerc and English Deists such as Charles Blount or Anthony Collins. Attacks on these figures abound. The Mather who emerges from Solberg's essay is a champion of a moderate Enlightenment who seeks to defend the authority of the scriptural revelations and demonstrate its reconcilability with reason, while being anxiously aware of growing conflicts between traditional religion and science.

MICHAEL DOPFFEL undertakes an in-depth study of Mather's gloss on Jer. 8:7 that formed the basis for one of the first "Curiosa Americana" sent to the Royal Society and later published in its *Transactions*. In this lengthy commentary and the subsequent letter to London, which derive much of their argument from a tract by Charles Morton, a teacher at Harvard, Mather constructs the hypothesis that the migratory birds, whose whereabouts during the absences from their normal habitats was then still a mystery to science, were flying to planetoids circling between the earth and the moon. What makes this (from our point of view) rather amusing theory so interesting is that it showcases the relationship in Mather's thinking between orthodox scripturalism and a scientific approach to the world, a relationship which, despite his own rhetoric of harmonious progress, was in fact riddled by tensions and increasing problems. More specifically, Dopffel's essay throws into relief the complicated interplay between a literalist hermeneutics and an empiricist epistemology that especially marks Mather's later writings. If in many entries of the "Biblia" Mather felt either forced to abandon a traditional literalist hermeneutics or openly embrace anti-scientific supernaturalism, the various "Curiosa" developed from scriptural illustration, such as this theory about migratory birds, offer quite a different picture. In these "Curiosa," which are mostly concerned with occult phenomena of nature (i.e., phenomena that in all probability lay within the realm of nature, but could not yet be explained by man's currently still very limited knowledge), Mather was free, as it were, to engage in wishful thinking rather than having to squeeze biblical revelations into a Procrustean bed of natural laws irrefutably established by science. In so doing, Dopffel argues, Mather left us significant testimony of what he had hoped for from the marriage between science and religion. Since he was dealing with phenomena for which the sciences had as yet no convincing answer, or which were outside the reach of its methods of observation, literalism and empiricism could still be rendered as complementary, mutually reinforcing methods of interpretation. Here, Mather could offer a speculative hypothesis that was empiricist in its basic approach or rationale and, at the same time, based on a strictly literalist reading of a specific verse of the Bible.

Finally, PAUL WISE takes a shot at what is the proverbial six-hundred pound gorilla in the room whenever Mather is discussed: his belief in the wonders of the invisible world. At the most basic level, Wise's essay is a plea for careful contextualization. That Mather championed the new sciences at the same time that he vehemently affirmed the existence of ghosts and witchcraft may seem contradictory to most people today, but this belief would have been perfectly normal to the vast majority of contemporary intellectuals. Through an exten-

sive survey of English-language publications relating to the subjects of demonology and witchcraft up through the middle of the eighteenth century, Wise
comes to the conclusion that outspoken skepticism on these matters was an exceptional position during the early stages of the Enlightenment. In the broad
mainstream of the moderate Enlightenment, in which Solberg has located
Mather, there was an almost unanimous consensus that demons and witches
existed as reported in the scriptures, a consensus that was carried by the very
alliance of biblical literalism and empiricism that Dopffel's essay examines.
More specifically, Wise demonstrates that in the "Biblia," Mather's approach to
many of the scriptural passages that speak about the supernatural, whether demonic or angelic, is decidedly empiricist in orientation. He frequently argues
from personal experience that he had (often after long sessions of praying and
fasting) throughout his life. In fact, it may have been Mather's capacity for "particular faiths" and dream visions, his ability to witness visitors from the invisible world that gave his biblical interpretations such a decidedly literal cast.
"[E]ven my *Senses* have been convinced of such a World," he wrote in *The
Christian Philosopher*, "by as clear, plain, full *Proofs* as ever any Man's have had
of what is most obvious in the *sensible World*" (306). At the same time, however,
Mather's deliberations on such experiences always aim at establishing, in quasi-
scientific manner, the laws of the supernatural realm and to link these to the
known laws of the natural realm through speculations about a connecting medium or agency he termed, following the Hebrew, the *Nishmath-Chajim*
(נשמת חיים, "breath of life", cf. Gen. 2:7). Again, none of this was wholly unusual.
As Wise reminds us, many prominent members of the Royal Society at the time,
including, for instance, Joseph Glanvill, Henry More, or Robert Boyle, advocated and often undertook research both into the natural and the supernatural
worlds. For these men, as for Mather, the reality of spirits and devils could not
be separated from the reality of the spirit of God, or the immortality of the soul.
Hence, in their view, to "assert the reality of supernatural phenomena" against
the skeptical philosophers of the Radical Enlightenment, such as Spinoza or
Hobbes, was equivalent to "defending Christianity itself" (Silverman 92).

     In the introductory observations we noted our reservations about reading
Mather as an early link in a chain of distinctively American authors. To the
many other reasons that speak against such an interpretative practice, one might
add that the emphatic emphasis on the present, the desire to forget the past that
supposedly characterizes the American vein of writing, is entirely alien to
Mather. Mather's mind, we said earlier, was of a strongly historical and, indeed,
historicist bent. He lived in a period which, on the one hand, still continued in
the accustomed intellectual habit which instinctively ascribed authority to the
past, not just to the Bible as God's past revelations, but also to other traditions
of learning, accepting a historical continuum of *auctoritates* and *exempla* that
reached all the way back into Greco-Roman antiquity. On the other hand,

Mather's time was marked by a rapid growth of knowledge about bygone ages and ancient cultures, which led to an increasing awareness of historical difference, an awareness that problematized any easy recurrence to the precepts of the past. The essays in **Section 4 (Mather's Historical Method and His Approach to the History of Religions)** explore the multiple tensions that arose from this constellation. They show how Mather consistently argues from history, that is, from received opinions and ancient authorities, while he is simultaneously embroiled in arguments about history, especially about the history of religions, arguments that are preoccupied with the dynamic development of human cultures in biblical and post-biblical times, and thereby highlight the remoteness of the past.

RICK KENNEDY attends to Mather's historical method of composition which, among other things, gave the "Biblia Americana" its massive shape. Mather's working practice as an author, Kennedy states, owes much to a commonplace book tradition of history, which had its origins in Aristotelian rhetoric and pervaded all fields of learning in the early modern period. The commonplace book tradition gave rise to the ubiquitous anthologies or *florilegia* of classical writers, as well as to theological *katena*-texts, *loci communes*-collections for students of divinity, and synoptic commentaries of the Bible such as Matthew Poole's *Synopsis Criticorum*. In almost any self-description of his writing, Mather signals a deliberate continuity with this tradition through the use of certain key metaphors (most importantly, those of flower-picking and the beehive). Accordingly, he perceives the historian's or exegete's role to lie primarily in gathering, selecting, and re-organizing past opinions for improved effect and usage. It was this communal understanding of authorship that defined Mather's heavily intertextual style, piling citation upon citation. Moreover, Kennedy suggests that the Aristotelian tradition, with its roots in a forensic context, also defined the "Question and Answer" format of the "Biblia," in which Mather raises a critical issue and then allows a variety of commentators to have their say, often without forcing contradictory views into a final conclusion.

KENNETH P. MINKEMA offers the first findings from his edition of Mather's commentaries on the Historical Books. Perhaps even more than other parts, this section of the "Biblia" shows Mather following a trend in contemporary Protestant hermeneutics that Peter Miller has called the antiquarianization of biblical scholarship. Feeding this trend was, in part, the desire to establish the *sensus literalis* which, however, was frustrated in so many parts of the Bible by seemingly irresolvable obscurities or ambiguities, creating the need for ever more excessive historical contextualization. Like so many of his European colleagues, Mather thus exhibits an intense interest in the ancient Hebrew lifestyle and society, focusing on even the most minute details of the customs, practices, and language in biblical times. Moreover, the attention to historical detail, Minkema explains, is a response to the rising tide of rationalist and liberal criticism led by Thomas Hobbes, Baruch Spinoza, Richard Simon, and others. The great length to which Mather goes in locating events, in reconciling the seeming discrepancies in the historical accounts, or in explaining the dizzying genealogies of the various kings and the lengths of their reigns thus have to be seen as part of his overall effort to defend the historical veracity of the biblical texts on which the other levels of scriptural truth depended. The subject of false idols and idolatry is Minkema's prime example for how Mather builds typological, prophetical, and moral readings, as well as apologetic or polemical readings, upon a primarily historical interpretation. In numerous glosses, Mather, in the manner of a religious historian, discusses the origin and nature of false gods mentioned in the Historical Books, the worship of them, their priests, and related topics – all with the ultimate goal of authenticating the higher meanings he draws from the scriptural passages. To approach the ancient cults in a historical and comparative fashion, though, and to place Israel's relationship with Yahweh in the context of neighboring religions was not without risk for orthodox Christians such as Mather. Ultimately, the antiquarianization of biblical scholarship, as Miller observes, carried the danger of undermining the authority of the scriptures for "once the sacred was made fully and finally historical, it ceased to be sacred" (Miller 465).

In his essay, REINER SMOLINSKI discusses a scholarly *cause célèbre* of the late seventeenth century in which this danger of historicizing became especially conspicuous, causing an international debate over decades which left many traces in the "Biblia." First published in 1685, John Spencer's *De Legibus Hebræorum Ritualibus Earumque Rationibus* deeply disturbed many contemporary theologians because it presented with great erudition and persuasiveness the argument that most of the ceremonial and cultic laws of the Levites were not given to Moses by the God of the Israelites, but were indeed adapted from their Egyptian, Chaldaean, and Canaanite neighbors. After more than four-hundred years in Egyptian exile, Spencer maintained, the Israelites had completely assimilated to pagan cults, and the only way in which Moses was able to bring his people back to a worship of their ancestor's God was by indulging their penchant for heathen rituals and tangible idols while redirecting their devotions to the service of Yahweh. Since it denied an origin in supernatural revelation, Spencer's evolutionary explanation of the Mosaic laws, rites, and customs, in the final analysis, also invalidated their typological or prophetic interpretations by Christian exegetes. It is therefore rather unexpected to see how much Mather respected Spencer's scholarly work and sought to accommodate his findings. Focusing on Mather's commentaries on several cultic instruments (Aaron's golden calf, the polymorphous cherubim, and the ark of the covenant), Smolinski investigates just how far Mather is prepared to go along with Spencer's argument and where and why he departs from Spencer. As the essay demonstrates, Mather generally welcomes Spencer's historical contextualization of the Mosaic laws and their origin within the dictates of ancient Egyptian culture. Using the same ambidextrous approach that can also be observed in engagements with Richard Simon or Jean LeClerc, Mather incorporates Spencer's learned exegesis wherever it appeared relevant and acceptable to his own purposes and praises Spencer for his vast reading and erudition. Yet wherever Spencer directly threatens the divine authority of the scriptures, Mather challenges his radical conclusions.

HARRY CLARK MADDUX explores Mather's frequent use of two favored concepts amongst biblical scholars of the period for countering historical-evolutionist arguments about the Israelites and gentiles borrowing their religion from one another: *prisca theologia* (ancient theology) and Euhemerism. All over the "Biblia" Mather finds occasion to assert that the many parallels between ancient myths the world over, between pagan stories and the heroes in the Hebrew Scriptures, as well as the cultic similarities between Jewish and pagan religion, sprang from the fountainhead of their common ancestor: the Patriarch Noah. Expanding upon the research of his European peers, Mather provides ample space to demonstrating how Noah's sons, Shem, Ham, and Japheth carried the religion of their father, the ancient theology, into all the corners of the world, and how, following the dispersal of the people after Babel, the true religion that God had taught Adam and passed down to Noah became corrupted by the admixture of human inventions and errors. Within this larger framework of *prisca theologia*, Mather frequently employs the interpretative method known as Euhemerism (after the ancient Greek historian Euhemerus), attributing the origins of deities to the apotheosis of historical heroes and explained mythological stories as dimly remembered historical events. After this fashion, the "Biblia" attempts to prove that many mythologies of ancient cultures derived from the Hebrew patriarchs and from corrupted memories of God's providential interventions into history as they were recorded in the Bible. By leading all pagan religions back to an aboriginal Noachic monotheism, as Maddux makes clear, Mather thus hoped to deflate arguments such as Spencer's claim that Moses gleaned his ceremonial laws from the Egyptians.

Just as we are only beginning to understand him as an historical thinker, Mather, the biblical theologian, is still largely unknown. With some notable exceptions, Mather's exegetical work has not received much consideration. For reasons discussed above, this central aspect of his work has been eclipsed by the predominant Americanist interest in the relatively small number of his publications that deal with colonial history or seem to speak to the development of an American national ideology. Indeed, most theologians assume that Jonathan Edwards was the only biblical exegete from pre-revolutionary North America whose studies of the scriptures are still worth reading for other than antiquarian reasons. The essays in **Section 5 (Aspects of Scriptural Exegesis in the "Biblia Americana")** suggest differently, showing a Mather who not only worked directly at the forefront of contemporary developments in international biblical scholarship, but also wrestled with theological questions that are still relevant for many Christians today. All four studies demonstrate what treasures the "Biblia Americana" still holds for further inquiries into the history of biblical scholarship in America. Stein, Peterson, and Clark, moreover, give us fine examples of how fruitful a comparison of Mather's exegetical works with those of Edwards can be.

In his trailblazing essay, STEPHEN J. STEIN compares Mather's commentaries on the Epistle of James with the notes Edwards made in his recently edited "Blank Bible" on this controversial part of the New Testament canon. Stein pays special attention to the ways in which Mather and Edwards addressed issues of continuing concern to interpreters of the epistle, namely, the history as well as the early reception of the text and its views on the role of human conduct in the salvation process. The similarities regarding methods, thematic concerns, and theological judgment are as striking as the contrasts. Amongst the many fascinating findings that the essay has to offer, two of Stein's conclusions can be singled out here as particularly significant. Both exegetes are in agreement that Luther's famous condemnation of the epistle was unfounded and that the teaching of James, with its emphasis on the importance of good works, are not in irreconcilable conflict with the Pauline corpus in the New Testament where the saving grace of faith – *sola fide* – is foregrounded. Both hold that the contradiction is only apparent because Paul and James are speaking about different stages in the process of salvation. For both Mather and Edwards, good works are ultimately an essential and necessary manifestation of justifying faith. For all their closeness in terms of essential theological judgments, Stein also suggests that Mather's exegetical method might have differed from Edwards's in that it devoted more space to philological as well as to historical-contextual questions. Stein notes that Mather shows a more academic interest in the Greek text and, in contrast to Edwards, engaged critical issues concerning the epistle's authorship, time of composition, and reception within the Christian community–issues which are still debated in exegetical circles today. For instance, Mather suggests the possibility that the text was written by Jews and for Jews and, therefore, the epistle acquired its Christian character later, when this epistle was judged, in the fourth century, to be consistent with Christian teachings. Moreover, he rejects the notion that the Epistle of James was received uniformly by all Christian communities, thereby relegating the epistle to a lower status within the canon and lending support to a later time of composition than the lifetime of James, the brother of Christ, whom many interpreters still believed to be the author.

PAUL S. PETERSON opens a window onto a very important, but so far almost completely neglected dimension of Mather's thought that is evident throughout the "Biblia Americana." Mather shared with many Protestant and especially many Reformed exegetes of the period a strong interest in post-biblical Jewish traditions and Rabbinical commentaries. As one striking example of Mather's Christian Hebraism, Peterson examines the re-interpretation of the Shechinah, the ancient Jewish conception of God's visible manifestation in history. The essay shows how Mather, in conversation with other contemporary Christian Hebraists (especially John Stillingfleet and Thomas Tenison), appropriated commentaries on the Shechinah from Rabbinical commentaries and adopted them into a Christological framework, thereby turning many of the Theophanies of the Hebrew Bible into Christophanies. According to Peterson, the Christianized concept of the Shechniah helped Mather argue not only for the Christocentric unity of redemption history spanning both the Old and New covenants, but also to defend the organic wholeness and harmony of the scriptures against the rise of historical criticism by locating an interpretive center of the Old and New Testament. In his concluding observations Peterson contrasts Mather's understanding of the Shechniah with that of Jonathan Edwards, whose notion of God's indwelling has a strong neo-platonic bent and thus de-emphasizes the disruption of the natural order.

Albeit in quite different ways, the last two essays in this section both examine Mather's eschatological readings of the scriptures. MICHAEL P. CLARK starts from the observation that, throughout his life, Mather was concerned with the nature of signs. Behind this conspicuous interest, Clark suggests, was an anxiety about the capacity of material signifiers to reveal spiritual truths, an anxiety that bespeaks more general conflicts in Puritan thought, which looked back to medieval mysticism and incorporated elements of Enlightenment empiricism simultaneously. The essay argues that, as a consequence of these tensions, Mather developed what Clark calls an eschatological semiotics. Generally speaking, this semiotics was still rooted in a strictly dualistic ontology that made a sharp distinction between the world of nature and a higher realm of the spirit, and hence assumed that the spiritual significance of natural or historical referents could not be completely known to the finite mind of mortal man. More specifically, Mather thought that the full meaning of signs, including those given in the scriptures, would not be revealed on this side of the millennium. At the same time, his exegetical writings show how this rather pessimistic belief in the continuous temporal deferral of scriptural meaning was frequently counterbalanced by the hopeful expectation that, with the end-time approaching, more and more glimpses of divine truth could be caught through the disintegration of material signifiers. In the "Biblia" – and especially in his commentary on Hebrews and Revelation – Mather thus sketches a hermeneutics that seeks to look beyond the progressively disintegrating referents of the biblical texts and their *sensus literalis* in order to grasp their true significance. Mather's eschatological semiotics, Clark finally points out, differ markedly from the more neo-platonic theory of signs embraced by Jonathan Edwards, who, generally speaking, showed more confidence in the legibility of the scriptures even before the end of days.

The essay by DAVID KOMLINE seeks to elucidate the development of Mather's late eschatology. Since the appearance of Smolinski's edition of the *Triparadisus*, we have known that late in his life, Mather adopted a preterite interpretation of several biblical prophecies (most importantly, those believed to pertain to the national conversion of the Jews and to a great reformation of the church rooted in ecumenical union) that most of his contemporary millenarians, including his own father, believed were yet to be fulfilled prior to Christ's second coming. However, the reasons underlying this shift, says Komline, have not been fully understood. His study, which considers Mather's published works as well as his relevant commentaries in the "Biblia," contends that an essential factor that contributed to Mather's change of position was his response to a conflict in England among the Dissenting churches over Arianism, which erupted in the second decade of the eighteenth century. The so-called Arian controversy severely undermined Mather's conviction that the hoped-for ecumenical regeneration of the Church was imminent. With this hope overturned, Mather slowly changed his mind not merely about the awaited reformation, but also about all the other signs – including the conversion of the Jews – that he had expected to occur before the coming of his Lord. According to Komline, a key-player both in the Arian controversy and in the intellectual drama of Mather's final years was the Newtonian scientist and well-known millennialist William Whiston. Earlier in Mather's life, Whiston had played a prominent role in reinforcing Mather's expectations that the above-mentioned eschatological events would occur in the early eighteenth century and usher in the millennium. As evidenced by multiple revisions in the "Biblia," Whiston's "Arian coming out" deeply disturbed Mather and led him to reconsider his previous acceptance of his theories.

Recent scholarship in early modern intellectual history has given new consideration to the highly complex ways in which the period's changing concepts of gender and race were being constructed and contested through interpretations of the Bible. The essays in **Section 6 (Gender, Race, and Slavery in the "Biblia Americana")** use the untapped resource of the "Biblia" to reassess Mather's positions on the religious or social meaning of human difference in sex and skin color. At the same time, both Gelinas and Stievermann inquire into the practical consequences which Mather's biblical exegesis had on his social activities related to women and African slaves.

HELEN K. GELINAS begins by arguing that, as in so many other respects, when it came to the role of women, Cotton Mather was simultaneously a guardian of orthodoxy and an innovator. On the one hand, Mather upheld a traditionalist understanding of women's subordinate position in the social and ecclesiastical order, largely excluding them from political and economic realms and confining them to a domestic sphere under male authority. On the other hand, with regard to the question as to whether females could or should be offered more than a basic education and what part intellectually gifted women who were pious ought to play in the reformation of church and society, he differed sharply from the majority of earlier Puritan ministers. Not only did he emphasize the spiritual and intellectual equality of women, but he also called for wider access of women to higher learning and hailed their great potential as writers from whose pious labours of the pen church and society might greatly profit. Gelinas's essay helps us to understand that this ambiguous stance grew directly from the scriptural exegesis Mather was pursuing in the "Biblia." Of central importance in this regard are Mather's literalist readings of the Pauline teachings on women that contend with his sympathetic interpretation of Eve before, in, and after the fall. Moreover, the ecclesiology Mather developed in the commentary on Canticles had a significant bearing on his understanding of gender roles. Finally, Gelinas demonstrates that Mather's millennialist eschatology held out an egalitarian promise which seeped increasingly into his reformist agendas as he saw the final days drawing closer.

ROBERT E. BROWN opens up an unusual but very revealing perspective on the negotiation of gender identity in the "Biblia Americana." The essay scrutinizes Mather's commentaries on the Pauline expositions on the gendered significance of long hair in 1 Cor. 11 (natural for women, unnatural for men), expositions which drew considerable attention throughout the early modern period and served as a reference point in the seventeenth-century battles over male hair-fashion. Underlying these battles on both sides of the Atlantic, Brown explains, was an anxiety over the relative instability and mutability of sex that stemmed from the Galenic paradigm of human physiology. Nature and culture, sex and gender thus shared a significant degree of interchangeability. How the body was fashioned, what came into contact with it, and what the wearer imagined or desired his or her appearance to provoke could direct the transformation of the body. Such a prospect was destabilizing to the entire social fabric, premised as it was on the hierarchy of men. In the absence of notions of an anatomically permanent sexual distinctiveness, gender-coded norms such as hair and clothing were vital for stabilizing sexual identity, both physically and socially. Mather's foray into his exposition of 1 Cor. 11, therefore, was heavily freighted with ideological controversy. It is all the more surprising, then, to find Mather take an approach to the text that strongly historicizes Paul's propositions. In so doing, says Brown, Mather relativizes the social and religious meaning of hair. Mather marshals evidence suggesting that men's (and women's) hair styles differed between cultures, differed within cultures over time, and was altered by contextual considerations such as class, occupation, emotional states, and ritual settings. From these insights, Mather constructs an argument that Paul's concerns and instructions for the Corinthians were cultural, particular, and temporally restricted, rather than doctrinal, universal, and indifferent to time or place. If in this specific gloss Mather emphasizes the conventional nature of gender identity, this stress reflects a more general tendency of his commentary to contextualize the Bible and reveals his penchant for anthropological explanation.

JAN STIEVERMANN takes issue with the deeply ingrained habit of American cultural historians of reading modern concepts of race back into the writings of Puritan authors such as Mather. Racism, Stievermann asserts, is not an interpretative framework that allows us to understand why Mather ultimately fell short of calling for an end to the institution of slavery or for a fundamental reorientation of New England's Indian policy, even though he was highly concerned about the breakdown of Anglo-Indian relations and also condemned the evil of the slave trade together with the inhumane treatment of black bondsmen. In fact, Mather's extensive commentaries on Genesis show that he was a guardian of the orthodox belief in mankind's common origin, universal consanguinity, and spiritual unity in Christ, a belief which rendered phenotypical diversity largely insignificant. He defends this position against both the older theories of polygenesis and a new kind of racial thinking which had begun to arise under the impact of developments in early Enlightenment natural philosophy. Moreover, he refutes any theological theories or popular myths, such as the curse of Noah, in which biblical stories were taken as proof that Africans or Native Americans had been expelled from the community of God's children or relegated to perpetual social subordination. With regard to Mather's concrete social agendas, the "Biblia" provides valuable new insights into the scriptural motivation of Mather's stubborn support for the flagging Indian mission in New England, and sheds more light on his increasingly complicated and critical engagement with American slavery. While Mather maintains that the institution of slavery was in principal agreement with Old Testament precepts and had been condoned by Christianity (especially in its Pauline interpretation), he simultaneously argues that the enslaving of innocent Africans on grounds of skin color was by no means scripturally justified and amounted to "manstealing," which the Bible condemned as a deadly sin. As Stievermann proposes, Mather's simultaneous condemnation of the slave trade and defense of the institution of slavery were both a direct outgrowth of Mather's conservative theology and his biblical literalism. The manifest tensions between his growing awareness that, by his understanding of biblical precepts, most slaves were unlawfully brought to the colonies, and his refusal to challenge the legal status of bondsmen already in the colony cannot be adequately explained in terms of Mather's supposed racist attitudes. Instead, these tensions primarily reflect an impasse into which he was led by his radical scripturalism, as well as his closely related social conservatism, and his millennialist expectations.

August 2010   Jan Stievermann (Tübingen) and Reiner Smolinski (Atlanta)

Works Cited

Primary Sources

Bancroft, George. *History of the United States: From the Discovery of the American Continent*. Vol. 1. Boston, 1834.

Calef, Robert. *More Wonders of the Invisible World*. London, 1700.

Calmet, Augustin. *Dictionnaire Historique, Critique, Chronologigue, Géographique, et Littéral de la Bible*. 2 vols. Paris, 1722.

Chandler, Edward. *A Defense of Christianity from the Prophecies of the Old Testament Wherein are Considered All the Objections against this Kind of Proof, Advanced in a Late Discourse of the Grounds and Reasons of the Christian Religion*. London, 1725.

Cotton, John. *A Brief Exposition With Practical Observations Upon the Whole Book of Canticles, or, Song of Solomon*. London, 1642.

Francke, August Hermann. *Manuductio ad lectionem scripturae Sacrae historicam, grammaticam et practicam ...* Halle, 1693.

Henry, Matthew. *An Exposition of All the Books of the Old and New Testaments: Wherein the Chapters are summ'd up in Contents; the Sacred Text inserted at large, in Paragraphs, or Verses; and each Paragraph, or Verse, reduc'd to its proper Heads: the Sense given, and largely illustrated, with Practical Remarks and Observations*. 6 vols. London, 1708–10.

Jenkin, Robert. *The Reasonablenss and Certainty of the Christian Religion*. 1696–97. 6th ed. London, 1735.

Kidder, Richard. *A Demonstration of the Messias. In which the Truth of the Christian Religion is Defended, Especially against the Jews*. London, 1700.

Lowth, William. *A Commentary upon the Prophet Isaiah*. London, 1714.

Mather, Cotton. *The Angel of Bethesda: An Essay Upon the Common Maladies of Mankind*. Ed. Gordon W. Jones. Barre: American Antiquarian Society and Barre Publishers, 1972.

–. *Biblia Americana*. Ed. Reiner Smolinski. Vol. 1. Tübingen: Mohr Siebeck, 2010; Grand Rapids: Baker Academic, 2010.

–. *Bonifacius. An Essay Upon the Good*. 1710. Ed. David Levin. Cambridge: Harvard UP, 1966.

–. *The Christian Philosopher*. 1720/21. Ed. Winton U. Solberg. Urbana: U of Illinois P, 1994.

–. *Diary of Cotton Mather*. Ed. Worthington C. Ford. Collections of the Massachusetts Historical Society. 7th series. Vols. 7–8. Boston: MHS, 1911–12.

–. *Magnalia Christi Americana: Or, The Ecclesiastical History of New England*. 1702. New York: Arno Press, 1972.

–. *Manuductio ad Ministerium*. Boston, 1726.

–. *A New Offer to the Lovers of Religion and Learning*. Boston, 1714.

–. "Cotton Mather's 'Problema Theologicum': An Authoritative Edition." Ed. Jeffrey Scott Mares. *Proceedings of the American Antiquarian Society* 104 (1995): 333–440.

–. *Selected Letters of Cotton Mather*. Ed. Kenneth Silvermann. Baton Rouge: Louisiana State UP, 1971.

–.   *The Threefold Paradise of Cotton Mather: An Edition of the "Triparadisus."* Ed. Reiner Smolinski. Athens and London: U of Georgia P, 1995.

–.   *The Triumphs of the Reformed Religion in America: The Life of the Renowned JohnEliot.* London, 1691.

–.   *The Wonders of the Invisible World.* Boston, 1693.

Mather, Samuel. *Figures and Types of the Old Testament, by Which Christ and the Heavenly Things of the Gospel Were Preached and Shadowed to the People of God of Old. Explain'd and Improv'd in Sundry Sermons.* Dublin, 1683.

Patrick, Simon. *A Commentary upon the Historical Books of the Old Testament.* 2 vols. 3rd ed. London, 1727.

Poole, Matthew. *Annotations upon the Holy Bible. Wherein the Sacred Text is Inserted, and various Readings Annex'd together with Parallel Scriptures, the moredifficult Terms in each Verse are Explained, seeming Contradictions Reconciled, Questions and Doubts Resolved, and the whole text opened. By the Late Reverend and Learned Divine Mr. Matthew Poole.* 2 vols. London, 1683–85.

–.   *Synopsis Criticorum Aliorumque S. Scripturæ Interpretum.* 5 vols. London, 1669–76.

Prideaux, Humphrey. *The Old and New Testament Connected in the History of the Jews and Neighbouring Nations, from the Declension of the Kingdoms of Israel and Judah to the Time of Christ.* 4th ed. London, 1716–18. 3 vols.

Tudor, William. "Books Relating to America: Notice of Mather's *Magnalia.*" *North AmericanReview* 6/17 (1818): 255–72.

Upham, Charles W. *Lectures on Witchcraft.* Boston, 1832; 2nd ed. 1833.

–.   *Salem Witchcraft.* Boston, 1867.

Whitby, Daniel. *A Paraphrase and Commentary on the New Testament.* London, 1706.

Secondary Sources

Adams, Gretchen A. *The Specter of Salem: Remembering the Witch Trials in Nineteenth-Century America.* Chicago: U of Chicago P, 2009.

Aland, Kurt, ed. *Pietismus und Bibel.* Witten: Luther-Verlag, 1970.

Arch, Stephen Carl. *Authorizing the Past: The Rhetoric of History in Seventeenth-Century New England.* DeKalb: Northern Illinois UP, 1994.

Amory, Hugh. "Appendix 1. A Note on Statistics." *A History of the Book in America: The Colonial Book in the Atlantic World.* Ed. Hugh Amory and David D. Hall. New York: Cambridge UP, 2000. 504–19.

Baker, Dorothy Z. *America's Gothic Fiction: The Legacy of Magnalia Christi Americana. Columbus: Ohio UP, 2007.*

Beall, Jr., Otho T., and Richard H. Shyrock. *Cotton Mather: The First Significant Figure in American Medicine.* Baltimore: Johns Hopkins UP, 1954.

Benz, Ernst. "Pietist and Puritan Sources of Early Protestant World Missions (Cotton Mather and A.H. Francke)." *Church History* 20.2 (1951): 28–55.

–.   "Ecumenical Relations between Boston Puritanism and German Pietism (Cotton Mather and August Hermann Francke)." *Harvard Theological Review* 54.3 (1961): 159–93.

Bercovitch, Sacvan. "Cotton Mather." *Major Writers of Early American Literature.* Ed. Everett Emerson. Madison: U of Wisconsin P, 1970. 93–149.

–,   ed. *Typology and Early American Literature*. Amherst: U of Massachusetts P, 1972.

–.   *The Puritan Origins of the American Self.* New Haven: Yale UP, 1975.

–.   *The American Jeremiad*. Madison: The U of Wisconsin P, 1978.

Breitwieser, Mitchell R. *Cotton Mather and Benjamin Franklin: The Price of Representative Personality*. Cambridge: Cambridge UP, 1984.

Bremer, Francis J. *The Puritan Experiment: New England Society from Bradford to Edwards*. Rev. ed. Hanover: UP of New England, 1995.

Brown, Jerry Wayne. *The Rise of Biblical Criticism in America, 1800–1870*. Middletown: Wesleyan UP, 1969.

Brown, Robert E. *Jonathan Edwards and the Bible*. Bloomington: Indiana UP, 2002.

Brumm, Ursula. *Die religiöse Typologie im amerikanischen Denken: Ihre Bedeutung für die amerikanische Literatur- und Geistesgeschichte*. Leiden: Brill, 1963.

Buell, Lawrence. "Introduction: American Literary Globalism?" *ESQ: A Journal of the American Renaissance* 50 (2004): 1–23. Special Issue: American Literary Globalims. Ed. Wai Chee Dimock and Lawrence Buell.

Butler, Jon. *Awash in a Sea of Faith: Christianizing the American People*. Cambridge: Harvard UP, 1990.

Crocco, Stephen D. "Edwards Intellectual Legacy." *The Cambridge Companion to JonathanEdwards*. Ed. Stephen J. Stein: New York: Cambridge UP, 2007. 300–25.

Delbanco, Andrew. *The Puritan Ordeal*. Cambridge: Harvard UP, 1989.

Demos, John. *Entertaining Satan: Witchcraft and the Culture of Early New England*. Rev. ed. Oxford: Oxford UP, 2004.

Dimock, Wai Chee. *Through Other Continents: American Literature Across Deep Time*. New Haven: Yale UP, 2006.

–.   "Introduction: Planet and America, Set and Subset." *Shades of the Planet: American Literature As World Literature*. Ed. Wai Chee Dimock and Lawrence Buell. Princeton: Princeton UP, 2007. 1–17.

Elliott, Emory. "New England Puritan Literature." *The Cambridge History of American Literature*. Gen. Ed. Sacvan Bercovitch. Vol. 1: 1590–1820. Cambridge: Cambridge UP, 1994. 169–307.

Erwin, John. *The Millennialism of Cotton Mather: An Historical and Theological Analysis*. Studies in American Religion. Vol. 45. Lewiston: Edwin Mellon P, 1990.

Feldman, Louis H. "The Influence of Josephus on Cotton Mather's *Biblia Americana*: A Study in Ambiguity." *God's Sacred Tongue: Hebrew & the American Imagination*. Ed. Shalom Goldman. Chapel Hill: U of North Carolina P, 2004. 122–55.

Felker, Christopher D. *Reinventing Cotton Mather in the American Renaissance: Magnalia Christi Ameriana in Hawthorne, Stowe, and Stoddard*. Boston: Northeastern UP, 1993.

Frampton, Travis. *Spinoza and the Rise of Historical Criticism of the Bible*. New York: Clark, 2006.

Frei, Hans W. *The Eclipse of Biblical Narrative: A Study in Eighteenth and Nineteenth-Century Hermeneutics*. New Haven and London: Yale UP, 1974.

Gay, Peter. *A Loss of Mastery: Puritan Historians in Colonial America*. Berkeley: U of California P, 1966.

Giltner, John H. *Moses Stuart: The Father of Biblical Science in America*. Atlanta: Scholars Press, 1988.

Gura, Philip F. "The Study of Colonial American Literature, 1966–1987: A *Vade Mecum*." *William and Mary Quarterly.* Third Series 45.2. (1988): 305–41.

Gutjahr, Paul C. *An American Bible: A History of the Good Book in the United States, 1777–1880.* Stanford: Stanford UP, 1999.

Hall, David D. "Puritanism." *A Companion to American Thought.* Ed. Richard Wightman Fox and James T. Kloppenberg. Oxford: Blackwell, 1995. 559–61.

–.   "Readers and Writers in Early New England." *A History of the Book in America: The Colonial Book in the Atlantic World.* Ed. Hugh Armory and David D. Hall. New York: Cambridge UP, 2000. 117–52.

–.   *World of Wonder, Days of Judgment: Popular Religious Belief in Early New England.* New York: Knopf, 1989.

–   and Russell L. Martin. "Appendix 2. A Note on Popular and Durable Authors and Titles." *A History of the Book in America: The Colonial Book in the Atlantic World.* Ed. Hugh Armory and David D. Hall. New York: Cambridge UP, 2000. 519–22.

Harlan, David. "A People Blinded from Birth: American History According to Sacvan Bercovitch." *Journal of American History* 78.3 (1992): 949–71.

Hatch, Nathan O. and Mark A. Noll, eds. *The Bible in America: Essays in Cultural History.* New York: Oxford UP, 1982.

Holifield, E. Brooks. *Theology in America: Christian Thought from the Age of the Puritans to the Civil War.* New Haven: Yale UP, 2003.

Holmes, Thomas James. *Cotton Mather: A Bibliography of His Work.* 3 vols. Cambridge: Harvard UP, 1940.

Hornberger, Theodore. "Cotton Mather's Annotations on the First Chapter of Genesis." *Texas Studies in English* 18 (1938): 112–22.

Jeffrey, David Lyle. *A Dictionary of Biblical Tradition in English Literature.* Grand Rapids: Eerdmans, 1992.

Jeske, Jeffrey. "Cotton Mather: Physico-Theologian." *Journal of the History of Ideas* 47.4 (1986): 583–94.

Kaufmann, Michael. "Cotton Mather." *A Companion to American Thought.* Ed. Richard Wightman Fox and James T. Kloppenberg. Oxford: Blackwell, 1995. 436–38.

Kammen, Michael. *Mystic Chords of Memory: The Transformation of Tradition in American Culture.* New York: Vintage, 1993.

Kraus, Hans-Joachim. *Geschichte der historisch-kritischen Erforschung des Alten Testaments.* 2nd. ed. Neukirchen-Vluyn: Neukirchner Verlag, 1969.

Levin, David. *Cotton Mather: The Young Life of the Lord's Remembrancer 1663–1703.* Cambridge: Harvard UP, 1978.

–.   "Edwards, Franklin, and Cotton Mather: A Meditation on Character and Reputation." *Jonathan Edwards and the American Experience.* Ed. Nathan O. Hatch and Harry S. Stout. New York: Oxford UP, 1988. 34–50.

–.   "The Hazing of Cotton Mather." *New England Quarterly* 36 (1963): 147–71.

–.   Introduction. *Bonifacius. An Essay Upon the Good.* By Cotton Mather. 1710. Ed. David Levin. Cambridge: Harvard UP, 1966. vii–xxviii

–.   "Trying to Make a Monster Human." *Forms of Uncertainty: Essays in Historical-Criticism.* Charlottesville: U of Virginia P, 1992. 157–76.

Lesser, M.X. "Edwards in 'American Culture.'" *The Cambridge Companion to Jonathan Edwards.* Ed. Stephen J. Stein: New York: Cambridge UP, 2007. 280–300.

Lovelace, Richard. *The American Pietism of Cotton Mather: Origins of American Evangelicalism.* Grand Rapids: Christian UP, 1979.

Lowance, Mason I., Jr. *The Language of Canaan: Metaphor and Symbol in New England from the Puritans to the Transcendentalists*. Cambridge: Harvard UP, 1980.

Manierre II, William R. "Cotton Mather and the Biographical Parallel." *American Quarterly* 13 (1961): 153–60.

Maddux, Harry Clark. "God's Responsibility: Narrative Choice and Providential History in Mather's *Biblia Americana* Commentary on Ezra." *Early American Literature* 42.2 (2007): 305–21.

Marsden, George M. *Jonathan Edwards: A Life*. New Haven: Yale UP, 2003.

Middlekauff, Robert. *The Mathers: Three Generations of Puritan Intellectuals, 1596–1728*. 1971. Oxford: Oxford UP, 1976.

Miller, Perry. *The New England Mind: From Colony to Province*. Cambridge: The Belknap Press of Harvard UP, 1953.

Miller, Peter N. "The 'Antiquarianization' of Biblical Scholarship and the London Polyglot Bible (1653–57)." *Journal of the History of Ideas* 62.3 (2001): 463–82.

Muller, Richard A. "Biblical Interpretation in the 16th & 17th Centuries." *Historical Handbook of Major Biblical Interpreters*. Ed. Donald K. McKim. Downers Grove: InterVarsity Press, 1998. 123–52.

Noll, Mark. *America's God: From Jonathan Edwards to Abraham Lincoln*. New York: Oxford UP, 2002.

–. *The Rise of Evangelicalism: The Age of Edwards, Whitefield and the Wesleys*. Downers Grove: InterVarsity Press, 2003.

–. "Science, Theology, and Society: From Cotton Mather to William Jennings Bryan." *Evangelicals and Science in Historical Perspective*. Ed. David N. Livingstone, D. G. Hart, Mark A. Noll. New York: Oxford UP, 1999. 99–120.

Norton, Mary Beth. *In the Devil's Snare: The Salem Witchcraft Crisis of 1692*. New York: Knopf, 2002.

Oxford English Dictionary Online. Oxford UP. Web. 9 Jan. 2010.

Parrington, Vernon L. *Main Currents in American Thought*. New York, 1927. New York: Harcourt, Brace and Co., 1930.

Poole, William Frederick. "Cotton Mather and Witchcraft." *North American Review* 108 (Apr. 1869): 337–97.

Preston, Thomas R. "Biblical Criticism, Literature, and the Eighteenth-Century Reader." *Books and Their Readers in Eighteenth-Century England*. Ed. Isabel Rivers. Leicester: Leicester UP, 1982 and New York: St. Martin's Press, 1982. 97–127.

Preus, J. Samuel. *Spinoza and the Irrelevance of Biblical Authority*. Cambridge: Cambridge UP, 2001.

Reising, Russell. *The Unusable Past: Theory and the Study of American Literature*. New York: Methuen, 1986.

Reventlow, Henning Graf von. *The Authority of the Bible and the Rise of the Modern World*. Trans. John Bowden. Philadelphia: Fortress Press, 1985.

–. *Epochen der Bibelauslegung. Band IV: Von der Aufklärung bis zum 20. Jahrhundert*. München: Beck, 2001.

Rivers, Cheryl. "Cotton Mather's *Biblia Americana* Psalms and the Nature of Puritan Scholarship." Diss. Columbia U, 1977.

Rogers, Jack B. and Donald K. McKim. *The Authority and Interpretation of the Bible*. San Francisco: Harper & Row, 1979.

Rosenthal. Bernard. *Salem Story: Reading the Witch Trials of 1692*. Cambridge: Cambridge UP, 1995.

Scholder, Klaus. *The Birth of Modern Critical Theology.* Trans. John Bowden London/ Philadelphia: SCM Press Ltd./Trinity Press International, 1990.

Sheehan, Jonathan. *The Enlightenment Bible: Translation, Scholarship, Culture.* Princeton: Princeton UP, 2005.

Sheppard, Gerald T. "Biblical Interpretation in the 18th & 19th Centuries." *Historical-Handbook of Major Biblical Interpreters.* Ed. Donald K. McKim. Downers Grove: InterVarsity Press, 1998. 257–80.

Silverman, Kenneth. *The Life and Times of Cotton Mather.* New York: Harper & Row, 1984.

Smolinski, Reiner. "Apocalypticism in Colonial North America." *The Encyclopedia of Apocalypticism.* Vol. 3: *Apocalypticism in the Modern Period and the Contemporary Age.* Ed. Stephen J. Stein. New York: Continuum, 1998. 36–72.

–. "Authority and Interpretation: Cotton Mather's Response to the European Spinozists." *Shaping the Stuart World, 1603–1714: The Atlantic Connection.* Eds. Alan I. Macinnes and Arthur Williamson. Leyden: Brill, 2006. 175–203.

–. "How to Go to Heaven, or How Heaven Goes? Natural Science and Interpretation in Cotton Mather's 'Biblia Americana' (1693–1728)." *New England Quarterly* 81.2 (2008): 278–329.

–. Introduction. *The Threefold Paradise of Cotton Mather: An Edition of "Triparadisus."* Athens and London: U of Georgia P, 1995. 3–78.

–. "'Israel Redivivus': The Eschatological Limits of Puritan Typology in New England." *New England Quarterly* 63.3 (1990): 357–95.

Solberg, Winton U. Introduction. *The Christian Philosopher.* By Cotton Mather. Ed. Winton U. Solberg. Urbana: U of Illinois P, 1994. xic-cxxxiv.

Stearns, Raymond Phineas. *Science in the British Colonies of America.* Urbana: U of Illinois P, 1970.

Stein, Stephen J. "The Spirit and the Word: Jonathan Edwards and Scriptural Exegesis." *Jonathan Edwards and the American Experience.* Ed. Nathan O. Hatch and Harry S. Stout. New York: Oxford UP, 1988. 118–31.

–. "Edwards as Biblical Exegete." *The Cambridge Companion to Jonathan Edwards.* Ed. Stephen J. Stein: New York: Cambridge UP, 2007. 181–95.

Stievermann, Jan. "Writing 'To Conquer All Things': Cotton Mather's *Magnalia Christi Americana* and the Quandary of *Copia.*" *Early American Literature* 39. 2 (2004): 263–97.

Sweeney, Douglas A. "Evangelical Tradition in America." *The Cambridge Companion to Jonathan Edwards.* Ed. Stephen J. Stein: New York: Cambridge UP, 2007. 217–39.

–. "Jonathan Edwards." *Historical Handbook of Major Biblical Interpreters.* Ed. Donald K. McKim. Downers Grove: InterVarsity Press, 1998. 309–12.

Van Arragon, William. "Cotton Mather in American Cultural Memory, 1728–1892." Diss. Indiana U, 2005.

Van Cromphout, Gustaaf. "Cotton Mather as Plutarchan Biographer." *American Literature* 47 (1975): 465–81.

–. "Cotton Mather: The Puritan Historian as Renaissance Humanist." *American Literature* 49 (1977): 327–37.

Ward, W. R. *Early Evangelicalism: A Global Intellectual History, 1670–1789.* Cambridge: Cambridge UP, 2006.

–. *The Protestant Evangelical Awakening.* Cambridge: Cambridge UP, 1992.

Winship, Michael P. *Seers of God: Puritan Providentialism in the Restoration and Early Enlightenment*. Baltimore: The Johns Hopkins UP, 1996.

Wood, Gordon S. *The Americanization of Benjamin Franklin*. New York: Penguin, 2004.

[II]

BIBLIA AMERICANA.

The SACRED SCRIPTURES of the OLD and NEW Teftament; Exhibited, in the *Order of Time*, wherein the feveral and fucceflive Occurrences, may direct the Placing and Reading of them: Which Exhibition alone, will do the Service of a *Valuable Commentary*. With,

I. A proper Notice taken of thofe Inftances, wherein the moft Polite and Pious Mafters in *Philology*, have expreffed their Wifhes to fee the *Common Tranflation* Amended and Refined.

II. A Rich Collection of ANTIQUITIES, which the ftudious Refearches of Inquifitive and Judicious Men in the later Ages, have recovered; for a fweet Reflection of *Light* from thence upon the Heavenly *Oracles*: Efpecially thofe wherein the *Idolatry*, the *Oeconomicks*, the *Politicks*, the *Agriculture*, the *Architecture*, the *Art of War*, the *Mufic*, the *Habits*, and the *Diets* in the former Ages, may be referr'd unto.

III. The LAWS of the *Ifraelitifh Nation* in thefe *Pandects of Heaven*, interpreted; and the *Original* and *Intention* thereof, refcued from the Mif-interpretations, that fome famous Writers have put upon them. With a particular Hiftory of the City JERUSALEM, under its wondrous Viciffitudes, from the Days of *Melchizedeck*, down to Ours; and a Relation of
the

(12)

the prefent & wretched Condition, in which
it waits, the *Time to favour the fet Time to come on.*

IV. The TYPES of the Bible, accommodated
with their *Antitypes*: And this Glorious Book
of God, now appearing a Field, that yields
a marvellous Mixture of Holy *Profit* and *Plea-
fure*, in thofe Paragraphs of it, which have
fometimes appeared the leaft Fruitful with
Inftruction.

V. *Golden Treafures*, and *more to be defired than
fuch*, fetch'd out of thofe very *unpromifing Heaps*,
the TALMUDS, and other *Jewifh Writings*;
not only to Illuftrate the *Oracles* once *committed* unto the *diftinguifhed Nation*; but alfo to
demonftrate the Truths of *Chriftianity.*.

VI. NATURAL PHILOSOPHY call'd in to
ferve *Scriptural Religion*. The faireft *Hypothefes*
of thofe *Grand Revolutions*, the *Making*, the
Drowning, and the *Burning* of the WORLD,
offered. The *Aftronomical* Affairs, the *Meteors*,
the *Minerals*, the *Vegetables*, the *Animals*, the
Difeafes, the *Anatomical* Curiofities, and what
relates to the *Invifible World* of Good or Evil
Spirits, mention'd in thefe immortal Pages,
reprefented with the *Beft Thoughts of our Times*
upon them. To all which there is added, *The
Chriftian Virtuofo*, with a Commentary of the
more Modern and Certain Philofophy on,
His Work which Men behold; Embellifhed with
the Difcoveries which *our Days at Length* have
made of Things wherein the Glorious GOD
of Nature calls for our *Wonders* & our *Praifes*

(13)

VII. The CHRONOLOGY of this admirable Book, every where cleared, from all its Difficulties; and the *Clock of Time* set right, in its whole Motion, from the Beginning which *He that Inhabits Eternity* gave unto it. Besides the most Accurate *Harmony of the Gospel*, that has yet been offered among them that *know the Joyful Sound.*

VIII. The GEOGRAPHY of it *Survey'd;* The Scituation, especially of *Paradise,* & of *Palestine* laid out: With an Account how the *whole Earth* has been Peopled: And many Notable and Enlightning Things contributed unto this Work, by *Travellers* of unspotted Veracity, by whose *Running to and fro Knowledge has been increased.*

IX. A sort of *Twenty-ninth Chapter of the ACTS;* Or, An elaborate and entertaining History, of what has befallen the *Israelitish Nation,* in every Place, from the Birth of our great REDEEMER to *this very Day*: And the present Condition of that Nation, the Reliques of the *Ten,* as well as of the *Two Tribes,* (and of their Ancient *Sects,*) yet existing in the several parts of the World, where they are now dispersed, at *this Time,* when their approaching Recovery from their sad and long Dispersion is hoped for.

X. The HISTORIES of all Ages, brought in, to show how the *Prophecies* of this Invaluable Book, have had their most punctual Accomplishment,

(14)

plifhment, and ftrongly eftablifhed *Conjectures*, (yet made with all due Modefty,) on fuch as yet *remain to be Accomplifhed:* In the profecution whereof, the Reader finds an entire *Body of Church-Hiftory*, brought into his Poffeffion.

XI. The true Doctrine of the CHILIAD, which more opens & breaks in upon the more confiderate Enquirers, *as the Day approaches,* brought in as a *Key* to very much of the Wealth, which the Church of God enjoys in this *Book of the Kingdom.* Whereto are added, the moft *unexceptionable Thoughts* of the ableft Writers on the *Apocalypfe*; defecated from the more Arbitrary and lefs Defenfible Conceits, of *overdoing Students* in the Prophecies.

XII. Some *Effays* to Illuftrate the *Scriptures* from EXPERIMENTAL PIETY, or the Obfervations of *Chriftian Experience.* With many of the *Excellent Things,* obferved in and extracted from the *Holy Scriptures that make Wife unto Salvation,* efpecially by the *North-Britifh Expofitors,* who with a penetrating and peculiar Search after Hints *for Chriftian Practice,* have been found worthy to *Open* many *Books* of the Bible.

And many Thoufands of curious Notes, found fcattered and fhining, in the Writings both of the *Ancients* and the *Moderns,* laid here together, in a grateful Amaffment of them.

All done with a moft Reiigious & Inviolate and Perpetual Regard unto the *Principles of Religion,* which are the Life of the *Reformed Churches,*

Section I: The Vicissitudes of Mather's Reputation

WILLIAM VAN ARRAGON

The Glorious Translation of an American Elijah: Mourning Cotton Mather in 1728

In 1859, Alonzo Quint, a leading Congregationalist pastor in New England, wrote an article-length biography of Cotton Mather in the denominational journal *Congregational Quarterly*. His purpose, beyond an appraisal of Mather's life and times, was to repudiate Mather's critics, who had maligned him as the archetypal Puritan witch-hunter, the insufferable do-gooder, the self-righteous intolerant bigot.[1] The stigma Quint was trying to erase has been long-lived and influential. In his article "Trying to Make the Monster Human," David Levin talked about the "effigy" into which Mather's detractors had successfully transformed him by the middle of the nineteenth century, a transformation that has influenced Mather scholarship for generations (213). Twentieth-century scholars from Perry Miller to Kenneth Silverman were hardly more sympathetic to Cotton Mather, and Silverman, author of a Pulitzer Prize-winning biography of Mather, bestowed on his subject the dubious title of America's "national gargoyle" (425). As an early combatant against these aspersions on Mather's reputation, Quint cited the immense public outpouring of grief at Mather's death to repudiate the caricature of New England's most famous minister. "The mere existence," he wrote,

> of four sermons upon [Mather's] death; the public sorrow which crowded the streets with spectators of his funeral; the procession of scholars, merchants, clergymen, and officers of government, who, for once, met on common ground, and especially the presence of the Legislature of the Province, with Lieutenant Governor Dummer ... following to the grave a man who held no higher station and performed no other official service, than those of a mere Congregational minister, prove, beyond doubt, the respect and affection which Cotton Mather received from those who knew him. (234)

The decline in Mather's reputation in the nineteenth century to which Quint was referring can be attributed to many factors. In the years after the American Revolution, many early republican historians looked to the colonial past for

1 For advice and guidance on the many versions of this essay I wish to thank: Rebecca Warren, Richard Vaudry, Peggy Bendroth, Roark Atkinson, Doug Winiarski, Ken Minkema, Erik Seeman, Tony Tendero, Mike Grossberg, John Bodnar, Wendy Gamber, and especially Steve Stein. Many thanks also to Reiner Smolinski and Jan Stievermann for their careful and helpful readings of the final draft.

antecedents and icons for the new nation and found useful progenitors in the Pilgrims and Puritans, whose complex history was reduced to the famous national myth of the band of proto-democrats seeking a land of religious liberty. But the Puritan past had to be selectively purged of elements deemed incompatible with the new republican ideals. Thus Cotton Mather was found guilty by many antiquarians and scholars of fomenting the Salem witch trials and, by association, came to represent all in the Puritan past that was un-American: religious fanaticism, priestcraft, political aristocracy. Quint's defense of Mather, meanwhile, was a salvo in the vociferous disputes between nineteenth-century Congregationalists and Unitarians in New England. These denominational squabbles and schisms also included a contest over the meanings of the Puritan past, a legacy to which both parties laid claim, and many Unitarians condemned Mather as the chief exemplar of the brand of harsh, intolerant Calvinism that they accused their orthodox Congregationalist antagonists of trying to preserve. The "systematic depreciation" of Mather by Unitarians (and others), Quint retorted, was the result of their "utter inability" to "understand those deeper spiritual experiences of which their own hearts are ignorant" (237). In sum, Cotton Mather, a "mere Congregational minister," (Quint 234) was a beloved citizen of Boston and a hero of Christianity in his own day, and the denigration of his reputation in the decades after Mather's death was a gross injustice.[2]

Quint's observation about Mather's funeral is my point of departure simply because it suggests the disparity between Mather's reputation in the mid-1800s and how he was regarded in the 1700s, a complex story which I will not recount here. Following Quint – but arriving at different conclusions – I will offer a reading of some of the rituals and texts that originated in response to Mather's death in 1728. How was Mather's reputation constructed when he died, how was so vast and perplexing a figure to be remembered, and what needs did the rituals of commemoration in his honor serve in the immediate aftermath of his death?

This essay will approach Mather's death and funeral commemorations as a series of coherent, scripted cultural performances and rituals which, even as they guided people in mourning Mather as an exemplary saint, were intended to serve important religious and political functions in provincial Boston. Mather's death was not simply the occasion for ritual but an integral part of it. As Mather, the embodiment of the self-fashioned Puritan saint and prophet, succumbed to death, he also gave himself up to the ritualized translation that offered his last private moments and his life as a whole to his ministerial colleagues and admirers for public reflection. As he performed his "final scene," Mather embodied

---

2 Except in passing I will not refer in detail to the issue of Mather's reputation in the 1800s. For more on this topic see E. Brooks Holifield's essay in this collection and my dissertation, listed in the bibliography.

certain typical imperatives and instructions in practical divinity and modeled an exemplary life of personal and public piety. His death was then used by those who celebrated him for integrative social, political, and religious functions. Mather's passing was his "glorious translation," a typical Puritan trope invoking the passage of an earthly saint into the presence of God through death, and this popular figure of speech resonated in the many eulogies and other commemorative acts that sought to translate the meaning of Mather's demise for friends and foes alike. Mather's death was framed liturgically in the very method of his dying, which followed and even exceeded the expectations for the ideal Puritan way of death and which his colleagues and admirers found to be so exceptional that he was hailed as an "American Elijah" (S. Mather, *Elijah* 13). In response, his life and death was celebrated and reified in impressive funeral obsequies by colleagues, friends, and admirers through sermons, procession, and biography. Though Mather was a controversial figure in his day the scale of the outpouring of grief should not necessarily surprise us, since he was the acknowledged leader of New England's Puritan[3] religious order and the most important clergyman in the land. Reflecting his often tumultuous life, what also emerges on the margins of these rituals in honor of Mather are certain ambivalences about his personality and the meanings of his loss together with hints of anxiety about declining ministerial hegemony in New England. But the dominant mood was consolatory, as Mather's memory was harnessed by many in Boston to knit together the grieving community he had left behind.

Scholars of early American religion such as Charles Hambrick-Stowe, David D. Hall, and Erik Seeman have begun to draw our attention to the rituals, practices of piety, and performative dimensions of Puritanism, to what Hall has called "lived religion." They have done so in part by gleaning insights from folklorists and anthropologists such as Victor Turner, who have greatly expanded our vocabulary of performance and ritual. Deborah Kapchan describes performances as aesthetic practices that include "patterns of behavior, ways of speaking, manners of bodily comportment ... whose repetitions situate actors in time and space, structuring individual and group identities." They call attention to themselves as structures and events lifted out of the everyday practices of life that "carry something into effect – whether it be a story, an identity, an artistic artifact, a historical memory, or an ethnography" (479). Crucial to understanding the meaning and creative function of the performance is to observe the dialogic engagement between the performer, the audience, and the shared context. Ceremonies associated with rites of passage (including funerals), for

---

3   This paper avoids the question of whether the label "Puritan" is appropriate to describe New England's religious culture at the turn of the eighteenth century; for comment on this issue see Winship.

example, contain within themselves the elements of a kind of public reflexivity, the built-in space to make social sense of and offer formalized commentary on events of change and transition. Moreover, any performance or ritual is tied to those that precede and succeed them. Over time, the cultural power of ritual and performance comes from its capacity to create or repair a sense of community, which Victor Turner calls "communitus," in the face of imminent or potential social rupture, schism, or ambiguity (123).

Cotton Mather's death and funeral rituals described here followed a familiar and flexible template that had emerged in Puritan New England over three generations.[4] Mather was a particularly assiduous inheritor and shaper of these practices, and throughout his life – which he often described as but a preparation for death[5] – he wrote and preached prolifically on these traditions, as did his ministerial colleagues. Death was the great leveler in early New England, and the language and rituals the Puritans designed to face it had a degree of universality that cut across denominational and cultural lines. What emerges in my analysis is an understanding of the *integrative* functions of Puritan funeral rituals as performances that were fluid and responsive to changing political, religious, and cultural realities. Puritan death and funeral rituals such as those performed by and for Cotton Mather held in harmony what appear to be a number of paradoxical and even oppositional elements. They both leveled and perpetuated the rigid social and cultural hierarchy; in this case, Mather, an exceptional saint and most important cultural leader of the day, also met the fate that would befall all people, regardless of social standing. While they promoted a strong sense of "tribal" identity, this identity was, in the final analysis, not exclusionary but was projected outward, becoming in effect a kind of invitation to those who were uninitiated. While they mourned the loss of a saint as a sign of God's displeasure for New England's moral decline, the classic complaint of the jeremiad, they also promoted the antidote and the means to repair what was often called the hedge of God's protection for all of New England (see Bercovitch). Finally, the unity in consolation that these rituals created was not intended merely for the elect. Funerals were performed as much for the broader public as they were for Puritans themselves.[6]

---

4 On the evolution of Puritan death rituals, see Stannard, Hambrick-Stowe, and Seeman. See also the literature specifically on Puritan funeral elegies and sermons, which is not vast but very suggestive, especially Henson, Ulrich, Bosco, Elliott, and Hammond.

5 "Indeed," he wrote, "what should all our life be but a preparation for death?" (*Bethesda* 318).

6 My analysis in many ways contradicts David Stannard's still-influential *The Puritan Way of Death* (1977). Stannard argues that the elaborate funeral processions and associated rituals of eighteenth-century American Puritanism – Cotton Mather's funeral being a particularly conspicuous example – reflected the underlying pessimism of an increasingly surrounded, tribal Puritan minority. Stannard's analysis follows the classic narrative of Puritan declension, arguing that eighteenth-century Puritan culture was but the depleted and disaffected

By all accounts, Cotton Mather died a splendid death and, as Quint observed: the rituals of mourning it occasioned were massive in scale. When he died, Mather was lauded in Boston's newspapers as "perhaps the *principal Ornament* of this Countrey, & the *greatest Scholar* that was ever bred in it" (*Boston News-Letter* 8–15; February 1728). His ministerial colleagues seconded this praise in their public eulogies delivered from their Boston pulpits. Four of these funeral sermons, by Benjamin Colman, Thomas Prince, Joshua Gee, and Mather's son, Samuel, were subsequently published. His body was escorted through the streets of Boston to the Mather family tomb on Copp's Hill in an expansive procession, and Mather's death was recorded by a number of New England diarists, some of whom remarked the event with more than ordinary feeling, sobriety, and grief. A mass-produced mezzotint print of Mather's portrait, the first of its kind in the colonies, and an appropriately reverent biography penned by his son, Samuel, were sold by subscription in the weeks and months that followed. And news of his passing was noted across the Atlantic by such luminaries as Thomas Hollis and Isaac Watts.[7]

At the center of these rituals was Mather's death itself. His passing was noted in a letter written 13 February 1728, the day Mather died, in which Boston printer Samuel Kneeland wrote of "the Death of Dr. Mather, who went from this World to a better this Morning." He also declared expectantly to his correspondent that Mather's "more than ordinary Joy and Spiritual Triumph in his Sickness and Death you will quickly be informed of" (Kneeland). Benjamin Colman said of Mather's death that "(it may be) one of the brightest Accounts

---

remnant of New England's impressive founding generation. The death of a saint was mourned with such spectacular obsequies because it marked another irreplaceable loss to the dwindling circle of those who remained faithful to the vision of New England's founders. In Stannard's argument, the formality and ostentation of the Puritan funeral rituals increased in direct proportion to the Puritan's growing sense of being a dwindling righteous remnant. Funeral rituals on the size and scale of Mather's had two purposes, Stannard proposes. They gave expression to the profound loss and grief experienced by the concerned Puritan survivors and represented a collective projection of group identity onto a society that was now largely inimical to its historical holy mission to be a redeemer people. "It was the pessimism with which they now viewed the state of their holy mission that drove them to respond to death in ways their spiritual and actual ancestors would have deemed extraordinarily inappropriate," Stannard concludes, "while at the same time it was the continued, if diluted, potency of their cultural presence within New England society that permitted the relatively grandiose acting out of that response" (133).

7 The four published funeral sermons on Mather's death are Benjamin Colman's *The Holy Walk and Glorious Translation of Blessed Enoch* (1728), Thomas Prince's *The Departure of Elijah Lamented* (1728), Joshua Gee's *Israel's Mourning for Aaron's Death* (1728), and Samuel Mather's *The Departure and Character of Elijah Considered and Improved* (1728). Cotton Mather's death is also described in detail in Samuel Mather's biography of his father, *The Life of the Very Reverend and Learned Cotton Mather* (1729). Mather's death and funeral were also announced and described in Boston's newspapers, the *New-England Weekly Journal*, and the *Boston News-Letter*. Diarists who mention Mather's death prominently include Samuel Sewall, Ebenezer Parkman, Israel Loring, and Josiah Cotton.

we yett ever had of *Grace and Peace*, and living Comforts in dying Moments"
(Colman 27).

It should not surprise us, perhaps, that Mather died so well. After all, he
had written countless sermons and books on the necessity of preparing for
death, and he was meticulous, even obsessive, on the particularities of his practice of piety.[8] Mather was nothing if not prudent in expecting and preparing for
his own *"great Leap in the Dark"*: a prudent man, he wrote, "will *dy daily*" (C.
Mather, *Dying Man* 14, 38). He knew and believed, as did many New Englanders, that the peace and tranquility with which a person passed was evidence of
his or her sanctification, that he or she was indeed one of the elect. Like many,
Mather was suspicious of the deathbed confessions of individuals noted in life
for their debauchery or casual indifference to the life of the spirit. He also knew
first hand the inner turmoil of an existence lived by the rhythms of Puritan
psychology, which swung between one's assurance of salvation and the despair
over one's wretchedness before God. While for Mather and his fellow Puritans
certainty could only be found on the other side of the great divide, the manner
in which one crossed over was perceived as an important indication. A good
death, then, was notable in the way that other providential signs were suggestive
of divine realities: as a sign that pointed beyond itself to make legible to the
careful observer the patterns of God's governance of nature and humankind. A
peaceful, tranquil, and holy death (especially by ministers) was more than a
matter for gossip; it was a powerful witness for the truths of Protestant Christianity.[9] As a pastor who was a tireless defender and promoter of these truths,
Mather knew that the way of his dying would speak to the integrity and coherence of his lifelong message.

But there was a method of dying that Mather was keen to emulate. For the
saint, what happened during the process of dying was the beginning of the pu-
rification of the soul, the shedding of the sinful and corrupted body, oftentimes
accompanied by visions of the celestial reward to come. Whether death came
suddenly or gradually, it ideally also brought a definable, sublime moment of
release and surrender, a point at which the dying man or woman saw the approach of death and submitted to it willingly. From this ritualized moment of
surrender, however, also came a heightened and intensified power, as the dying
saint, literally and metaphorically suspended between earth and heaven, modeled the submission shown by Christ himself. The final words of the dying saint

---

8   An ironic lapse on Mather's part, however, was that he died without preparing a will, this
in spite of his repeated published instructions that others should do so. For a description of
the condition of Mather's estate, see Silverman (427–28).

9   Mather was fond of the story of the death of William Ames, who, when "he lay on his
death-bed, ... had such tastes of the 'first-fruits of glory,' as that a learned physitian (who was
a Papist) wondring, said, ... is the latter end of Protestants like this man's?" (*Magnalia*, vol. 1,
bk. 3, pp. 245–46).

had a particular importance, coming as they did from one whose vantage point was drawing nearer to heaven. Mather encouraged those who were dying to "Look up to Heaven for Direction and Assistance; and if thou find thyself able to Speak, Lett fall Some Solemn Words, useful Counsils, awful Charges, which it may for the advantage of the Survivers, to remember all their Dayes" (*Angel of Bethesda* 322).

The language of performance surrounds Mather's death. After Mather died, his kinsman Josiah Cotton wrote from Plymouth to his cousin Samuel Mather to offer his condolences. "Your Father acted his Part well + wonderfully in his Day," he wrote to Samuel. And, anticipating the publication of the funeral sermons and Samuel Mather's biography of his father, he added, "I should be glad to hear what his Concluding moments produced" (Cotton). That Mather acted his final part well was the unanimous evaluation of Mather's "Concluding moments," couched in accounts from funeral sermons, diaries, and newspapers. Mather took to his deathbed in January; he had become ill, and his parishioners feared for his life. The leaders of the North Church (also known as the Second Church, or Old North[10]) called for a day of prayer, to be led by three of Mather's Boston colleagues, Benjamin Colman, Peter Thacher, and Joseph Sewall. The notice in the records of the Second Church, written in the hand of Joshua Gee, on 28 January 1728, Mather's junior pastor, portentously declared, "Whereas in the Holy Providence of our Lord His aged Servant our Rev. & Dear Pastor [Dr. Cotton Mather] is afflicted & brot low by sickness ... who by God has greatly endeared him to us, & threatens his Removal from us by Death, which we would depricate as a most awful Frown of Heaven ..." (*Second Church*). Six week later, however, Mather died peacefully at home.

On the very day of Mather's death, Rev. Ebenezer Parkman of Westborough noted that "The Great Dr. Cotton Mather dy'd this morning 4 A.M. after suffering of an asthma" (Parkman 30). It was not Mather's bodily ailments that were notable to his admirers, however, but the peace and charity with which he bore them. As he lay dying, Samuel Mather and Joshua Gee both reported, Mather professed assurance of his own salvation and intimations of the heavenly world. When Samuel asked him, after praying and receiving his father's blessing, whether he "had a *positive comfortable Assurance* of eternal Glory," his father answered that he "could not *dishonour his great SAVIOUR so much as to doubt of it*," and that he had a "*strong Consolation*." The strength of this conviction was heightened by "*bright and clear views of GOD & CHRIST & Heaven*" (Gee 25).[11] When asked by an "agreeable Friend" what "*Views he had*

---

10   Mather's Old North burned down in 1777. The present Old North, famous for the story of Paul Revere and the lanterns, is an Anglican church that is frequently mistaken for Mather's.

11   Gee noted of these heavenly visions, however, that they were not "so many or lasting as were granted him in [Mather's] former sicknesses" (25).

of the invisible World," Mather replied in the affirmative: *"All glorious"* (S. Mather, *Elijah* 14). The peace and consolation that Mather felt was conveyed to the many guests who visited him on his deathbed. When a member of his church came to pay his respects, he was surprised to find Mather reading. *"Sir,"* the visitor asked, *"what are you reading your Name written in the Lamb's Book of Life?"* Mather replied, *"Yes I have found it,"* and marked down the leaf (S. Mather, *Elijah* 16). To a fellow pastor's query on his state, Mather answered "with a cheerful air and voice ... *'As merry as one bound for heaven'"* (Gee 22). Here the intertextual nature of Mather's performance is demonstrated by the fact that he quoted the English poet Anne Askew (1521–46), who was martyred under Henry VIII and whose tale was found in John Foxe's popular *Acts and Monuments* (1563).[12] His young co-pastor Joshua Gee recounted that "when it was observed to him, that God had heard his prayers for an *easy death*, I think his answer was in this one word, *Grace!* the last word, as I remember, that he was heard to speak" (Gee 30).

Thus runs the very abbreviated narrative of Mather's death, repeated at much greater length in various versions in diaries and the funeral sermons. What individuals like Samuel Kneeland and Benjamin Colman found so remarkable provides the context for understanding the performative aspects of Mather's deathbed scene. It is tempting to see Mather's death as the imaginative construction of his own creation, since the prescription for a good death laid out in many of Mather's own publications and sermons is mirrored exactly in the way Mather's friends and family claimed he died. The staging of Mather's dying seems particularly scripted in Samuel Mather's biography of his father, published in 1729, a lengthy account in which the son interpolated the narrative of his father's death with extended passages from Cotton Mather's own writings on how to die a good death, thus interweaving, as it were, Samuel's play-by-play with color commentary by Cotton himself. Further, the tone of the accounts seems to anticipate the romanticization and sentimentalization of death which, according to David Stannard (167 ff.) and Ann Douglas (200–26), would come to characterize nineteenth-century American culture.

Even if the constructed nature of Mather's glorious death is taken into account, it still seems that there was something genuinely outstanding about it. This outstanding quality comes into view when we compare reports about his passing with formal and informal accounts of other Puritans' deaths. A striking case in point is Increase Mather. In 1723 Samuel Sewall visited Increase Mather three weeks before his death at the age of eighty-four, and found him in intense agony both of spirit and body. "I call'd at the old Doctor's, who was agonizing

---

12 She signed her confession in the words that Mather quotes: "Wrytten by me Anne Askew that neither wishe death, nor yet fear his might: and as meary, as one that is bound towardes heauen" (Foxe 679). Thanks to Reiner Smolinski for this reference.

and Crying out, Pity me! Pity me!" Sewall recorded in his *Diary* on 30 July, 1723. "I told him God pity'd him, to which he assented and seem'd pacified. He pray'd God to be with me" (2: 1007). Cotton Mather's published account of his father's death, meanwhile, did not sugar-coat the details of Increase Mather's dying and essentially corroborates Sewall's version. In his last illness, Increase Mather's health deteriorated over a period of months, during which "he grew at sometimes very forgetful, and even Delirious," and in such moments fell even in doubt about "his Hope of the Future Blessedness." How much were all to be warned about and prepared for the forthcoming terrors of death, Cotton Mather wrote, if someone like his father was "concerned with so much Fear and Trembling, lest he should be deceived at the last?" But Increase Mather often saw these "Accidental Clouds" of doubt dissipate quickly, and resigned himself to death in a manner befitting the "deep Abyss of Humility" of the true saint. About three weeks before he died, however, the agonies that Sewall observed became "Intolerable"; he was tormented by "stones," an autopsy later showed, "some of them above an Inch Diameter, the least of which was big enough to have made a Giant roar." There is an almost apologetic tone in Cotton Mather's description of his father's loss of composure in the last three weeks of his life. He noted the doctor's astonishment at the size of the stones with the reflection that it was a wonder that Increase Mather's "Complaints of the last Three Weeks before he died" had not come earlier. Yet even in his final days, Increase Mather confirmed the belief in his own regeneration; his last words, to Cotton Mather's question of whether he had assurance of salvation, allegedly were, "*I do! I do! I do!*" (*Parentator* 195–197). The point of this illustration is that the Puritan view of death, even in retrospective accounts, was not a sentimental one. Death was often cruel and harsh, and during its rigors even the strongest of saints could be assailed by the temptations and doubts of Satan. For the regenerate individual, however, death was the means to glory, an enemy and a friend, as Cotton Mather said of it as his own death drew near.[13]

Therefore, while there is no doubt a certain ritualized shaping of the narratives about Mather's death, within these texts the physical demise itself is treated in a rather matter-of-fact fashion. Combined with Mather's acknowledged social and religious importance, his peaceful and gracious death inspired superlatives in the biographical parallels used in the sermons preached in his honor. Mather stood in comparison with the biblical examples of Enoch, Elijah, Aaron, each a holy prophet, noted in scripture for their intimate walk with God and for their prophetic leadership. At first glance Mather's death seems in harmony with the well-worn Puritan ritual scripts that Mather himself helped to create. Yet Mather was no ordinary New Englander, and the accounts of his death and

---

13   In his last days Mather wrote to his physician, "my *last enemy* is come; I would say my best friend" (S. Mather, *Elijah* 14).

funeral as mediated by his admirers suggests in places an expansion or stretching of the typical Puritan model. Put another way, Mather's death was even better than the prescriptive literature on dying well warranted. Thus Mather's way of dying as narrated in the funeral sermons could serve as a manual of practical piety even as the superlatives used to describe him placed Mather in a higher spiritual echelon than ordinary believers. His death was the result of lifelong preparation, after all, and even ministers could be intimidated by the holiness of such a death. When Israel Loring, minister in Sudbury, reflected on Mather's death, he challenged himself, "But yet may I not Say, Let me go that I may Die With Dr. Mather." He concluded, "Alas! ... I Come far behind him in fitness for Death" (Loring; 13 February 1728). This insight, of course, is exactly the kind of response that Mather would have hoped his death would provoke in those he left behind.

Mather had accomplished a heroic feat in his death, and the theme of submission, of self-annihilation, is prominent both in Mather's own instructions on preparing to die as well as in the commentary on Mather's death. This appears consistent with what Amanda Porterfield has identified as a strain of female piety in American Puritanism, a gendered typology of self-expression through which both men and women were to exhibit deference to divine authority. Here Mather's cheerful deathbed reference to Anne Askew is pertinent, invoking a female martyr who submitted willingly to her persecutors and to death. Mather, who often felt persecuted in life by opponents and circumstance, no doubt easily identified with Askew's fate as a martyr for the faith. The result of this submission, however, was also a kind of empowerment through grace. "How great was his *Patience* under the Hand of GOD," said Samuel Mather of his father's death; "how did he *annihilate* himself in the Presence of his LORD, and how, like his CHRIST's, was his *Resignation* to the *Will of the Father?*" (S. Mather, *Elijah* 15). This acquisition of Christlike greatness through patience and self-annihilation represents the apex of the well-ordered Christian life. Furthermore, from the gendered imagery of submission that Mather embodied in death emerges its obverse, the very masculine image of the Saint as martial hero and conqueror. As Joshua Gee declared, "To behold a Saint with all the tokens of a divine calm in his breast, not only daring to encounter the king of terrors, but rising above all fears into joyful views of immortality" was a glorious "spectacle" (Gee 15). It was, moreover, a spectacle "inconceivably greater and more glorious than a bold and venturesome hero in a *campaign*, who fearless and unshaken exactly directs the battle, when invironed with fire and death" (Gee 15). In the minds of his observers, Mather was truly the conquering hero and the quiescent saint in the spectacle and performance of his own death. As those left behind to continue his work and assume Mather's place in New England's religious leadership, Mather's admirers celebrated his victory in death, and it is in this sense that Benjamin Colman could say of Mather's death, "Verily *holy dying* is a great and blessed thing" (Colman 29).

In dying well, therefore, Cotton Mather referenced a complex web of historical memory and practical theological instruction that was the collective, if contested, cultural property of citizens of 1720s Boston and New England. Scholars such as David Stannard and Erik Seeman who have written on New Englanders' fascination with deathbed scenes have noted how the clergy tried to order and modulate the paths of death and mourning for laypeople. It was important for the clergy to inculcate the proper dogmatic attitudes toward death in their parishioners.[14] Whatever the relation between the death of laypeople and the death of a religious virtuouso like Cotton Mather, it is interesting to observe that the accounts of Mather's death essentially do declare his justification and sanctification; that Cotton Mather was in heaven was as close to fact as could be ascertained. Perhaps this kind of assurance stretches the generic model of the Puritan deathbed account. After all, it conflicts with the tenor of Reformed dogma, which held in theory that one's eternal fate was ultimately unknowable on this side of the grave. The very imagery describing Mather's "glorious translation" emphasizes his marvelous achievement. Enoch and Elijah were biblical figures who didn't die; they were taken up into heaven, were literally "translated." In all of the literature printed in America from 1630 to 1728, there is only one printed sermon title comparing an individual to Enoch (that of Benjamin Colman's on Mather), and only three which make a comparison with Elijah, two of which, by Thomas Prince and Samuel Mather, were on Cotton Mather. And Mather himself did not compare any of the historical personages he sketches in the *Magnalia* to Enoch or Elijah.[15] These are rarely used, unusual analogues, which suggest the exceptional nature of Mather's death.

According to the sermons preached by Colman, Prince, Gee, and Samuel Mather, the use of these biographical parallels was certainly justified by the saintliness of Mather's life and death, and the terms seem also to be expressive of genuine, widely-held respect and admiration from many friends and admirers. Again, for example, Enoch, the image used by Colman, was a man whose "walk with God was in such a singular manner" that "God distinguished him from the rest of Mortals, and the *Angels* of God took him up in the body" without dying (Colman 25). This was a thinly veiled reference to the peace and tranquility with which Mather died and his exemplary holiness. Aaron, the scriptural analogue used by Joshua Gee, "was the Lord's high-priest; and his

---

14 The clergy were not necessarily as successful as they wished in promoting obedience to their prescriptions on how to die a Christian death. For example, Erik Seeman has argued for the liminality of the deathbed with respect to how laypeople stretched the pastoral model of a godly death. See Seeman, especially ch. 2.

15 I am indebted to Ken Minkema for these ideas from comments on an earlier version of part of this paper.

family was betimes advanced to be at the head of the ecclesiastical order" (Gee 3), obviously a reference to the historical Mather lineage – Richard, Increase, Cotton, and Samuel.

But we can also read anxiety and ambivalence about Mather in the use of these analogues, hints at Mather's proclivity for controversy. Elijah, the subject of Samuel Mather and Thomas Prince's sermons, was "a very zealous and fiery spirited Prophet," yet "at other times ... seem'd to be much discontented that he had no better success and acceptance, and at the Persecution and Hatred of Enemies" (Prince 27). This was a rather plain assessment of the mercurial nature of Mather's temperament in spite of his obvious spiritual greatness, and also an oblique assessment of how Mather's prophetic voice failed to procure the desired moral and spiritual reformation of New England society. More generally, each of these biblical figures was a prophet or a priest of exceptional quality who ministered to God's people in times of increasing corruption and whose godliness was thus all the more remarkable. As a result, the theme common to these funeral sermons is that "The loss of such as these must be very great and dismal, especially in Times of growing Declensions, when we have most need of them" (Prince 12). How could the loss of such an Elijah be compensated?

If the biographical parallels by which Mather was described were rarely employed, suggesting his exceptional holiness and saintliness, another of the prominent themes that characterizes this body of sermons preached in honor of Mather was one typically used on the deaths of ministers, prominent or otherwise, in New England. This theme was the loss of a spiritual father. Samuel Mather, Gee, and Prince in particular elaborated on the death of Cotton Mather as akin to the loss of a "spiritual" and "public" father. "Father" was a multivalent term in eighteenth-century New England, certainly, connoting more than just the head of the family but also evoking the foundational dimension to all social relationships. Samuel Mather summarized these meanings very concisely. "There are several Respects, in which the Denomination and Character of *Father* may be given to Persons," he wrote. It was used in its *"natural Sense,"* for those who were the "Instruments and *Authors* ... of our *Being* and *Life"*; it was used also as a mark of respect for those of age and seniority. When used for civil rulers, the term "father" was used to represent a mode of governing that treats "their Subject Vassals with *Love* and *Goodness*; as *Children*, and not as *Slaves.*" Finally, it was an appropriate epithet for "those who are *Ministers of the Gospel*," who "direct and *warn* their *People as Children.*" As ministers tended their congregations, they were more potently generative than mere biological fathers: "They *beget* them *thro' the Gospel*" (S. Mather, *Elijah* 5).

Obviously these connotations had more personal implications for Samuel Mather, who had just lost his literal father. Charles Hambrick-Stowe has observed how sons in Puritan New England often felt very keenly the spiritual impact of the loss of a father (228). Samuel Mather's choice of biblical text, Elisha's cry after Elijah – "My Father, my Father" (1 Kings 2:12) – captures the sense of profound personal grief and evokes the implications of the public loss for all of New England. Joshua Gee's ruminations on the loss of Cotton Mather as father also straddled these personal and political themes. For Gee, Mather was something of a surrogate father, a parent in faith as well as a nurturing senior colleague. Opening his sermon with a burst of emotional theatricality, Gee professed himself nearly too struck down with grief to speak, yet felt compelled to do so even in his weakness from near filial duty and necessity. Mather was a man for whom Gee had served "as a son in the Gospel." "O my friends," he said, "the hand of the Lord hath touched me, more heavily than you can be supposed to feel it in this providence." He went on to describe how Mather had taken him as a spiritual son, had incited his interest in pursuing the vocation of minister, had directed his "youthful studies," and then accepted him as junior pastor. "He instructed me, admonished, and exhorted me as a father," Gee summarized, "while by his condescending goodness he raised me to the level of a friend and a brother" (Gee 24).

In designating Cotton Mather a public father, a communal *pater familias*, these sermons give voice to the public philosophy advocated by New England's religious leaders – a vision of an organic, orderly, patriarchal society buttressed by the clergy. "Eminent Ministers have the style of *Fathers* very properly given to them," declared Thomas Prince, describing Mather and moving from the private to the public connotations of the term. "They are in a great measure the Glory, Strength, Defense & Safety of a People" (Prince 4). Prince offered the litany of attributes typical of such public figures: eminent ministers are "the Spiritual Fathers of many Spiritual Children"; they instruct, nurture, and reprove their sheep, they defend them from spiritual dangers, and they "set such Examples as to draw their People's Affection, as well as raise their high Esteem & Reverence" (Prince 6). By doing their utmost to "preserve and advance the Religion of CHRIST," on which the health and happiness of society depended, ministers such as Mather performed a crucial public function. In the practice of their vocation they created the space in which public affairs are safely to be conducted. The analysis in these sermons gives a spatial dimension to the minister's role in the social order. Ministers stand apart from culture, as mediators between humankind and God on the one hand, and humankind and Satanic enemies on the other. Thus "Eminent ministers are to be considered as public persons," Joshua Gee argued, and consequently their loss was greatly to be mourned in part because it placed society in great peril from spiritual adversaries and from the force of God's judgment. "What breaches doth [God] make in the wall of safety round about us," Gee asked in a question repeated in each of these sermons, and one typically raised in all sermons on the deaths of ministers and godly magistrates, "by taking away men of great worth and service, not only of a civil but sacred character?" (12, 16).

There were two responses required of New Englanders to the loss of such an Elijah and spiritual father, according to these sermons: ministers must (and would) take up Elijah's mantle and close the breech; and the rest of the people must repent and come to Christ. But if the call for repentance is one message of the loss of such a father, a mitigating tone also emerges by the end of these sermons, particularly in Benjamin Colman's, in which indictment and condemnation (the message of the jeremiad) is ameliorated by words of consolation and hope. Mather's departure was an affliction to those left behind and a potential sign of God's displeasure with his people, but the "proof of the Doctrine" was "That if we do walk with God here in this life," as did Enoch (and Cotton Mather), *"he will take us to himself forever"* (Colman 10). For the saint there was no need to fear death. "Why was *Enoch* taken up, and why is *Christ* risen and ascended, but to *rebuke* such fears?" Colman asked his listeners (19). "It should yield us the highest *Consolations in the death of our Godly friends*, that they have walked with God, and are not, for God has taken them" (21). These words of encouragement to individual repentance were matched by benedictions to the corporate body of God in New England. "May all the bereaved hear an alsufficient God saying to them, *I will never leave you, nor forsake you*," Joshua Gee concluded (33).

While acknowledging Mather's death as a grievous loss, therefore, each pastor also offered assurances to their listeners of the promise of forgiveness and of the continuity of ministerial succession. With the commemoration of Mather as a religious virtuoso and as New England's spiritual father came an affirmation of the social and religious order that ministers and magistrates coveted. Nowhere was that vision more publicly demonstrated than in his funeral procession, which wound its way through Boston's North End a few days after Mather died. Funeral marches were common in Boston's streets, but Mather's was exceptional in size and seemingly brought daily activities to a halt. It was a cloudy and cold morning for the "very large funeral" which circled its way around Old North and up Hull Street and ending eventually at the Copp's Hill burial ground.[16]

In a very visible way, these eighteenth-century funeral processions served to dramatize the unanimity of the ruling classes of provincial Boston, whether or not such harmony existed. By co-opting time and space in Boston's streets, the ruling classes – ministers, merchants, and magistrates – united in an impressive projection of political and cultural power. The procession, observed pastor Ebenezer Parkman, "look'd very sad – almost as if it were the funerall of the Country. Vast Concourse Exceeding long Procession and numberless Spectators," he wrote; "Every heart sad ..." (Parkman 30; 19 February 1728). Here

---

16   Information about the weather and the description of the funeral procession comes from the manuscript diary of Boston merchant Benjamin Walker, entry for February 19, 1728.

Parkman presumed to interpret the mood of the crowd in a manner consistent with ministerial assumptions or expectations about the ideal prescriptive responses to the glorious death of a New England clergyman and cultural leader. Though its primary purpose was liturgical, the procession manifested many things. It made visible in the streets themselves the ideal order of social relations, where pride of place was given to the church, first the bereaved congregation and then the collective church of God in Boston and New England, represented by the ministers of the city. First came Joshua Gee and the council of the Second Church, a mark of particular respect to Cotton Mather and the congregation he served. Next came Mather's coffin, carried first by the rest of Boston's clergy together with a number of the principal members of the Old North Church. The bereaved family followed, with the widowed Lydia Mather, Samuel Mather, and other relatives walking behind the coffin. Next came the officials of secular authority, including the highest figures in the colonial government. Following them came the other pillars of a well-ordered society, visiting ministers, the merchants, and other "principle inhabitants" of Boston. On the periphery, crowding the streets and looking out of windows, stood the rest of Boston, anonymous and silently respectful.[17]

The funeral procession thus mirrored in its arrangement the model of a godly society advocated in the sermons preached on Cotton Mather's behalf. At the center of the procession was Mather's body, which in this performed theology of death was not an inert object but a vivified, active agent. Mather himself wrote of the funeral processions of ministers, "When you see the coffin of this man of God anon carried along the streets, imagine it a mournful pulpit, from whence, 'being dead, he yet speaks'[18] thus unto you: 'Whatever you do, commit your perishing souls into the hands of the Lord Jesus Christ, as you have been advised'" (*Magnalia*, vol. 1, bk. 3, p. 616). This motif of speaking from the coffin reflects a continuation of the performance aesthetic inherent to the process of dying well. And it embodied the integrative function of the ideal Puritan way of death, assuring mourners of the continuity of earthly ministerial presence and social cohesion as the dead Mather became the symbolic agent speaking across the gulf between heaven and earth.

What emerges from these sermons and descriptions of the procession is a selective portrait of Mather, an interpretative projection and collective didactic meditation on the meanings of Mather's glorious life and death. My reading of the ritual of Mather's funeral suggests the construction of ministerial and political amity in response to affliction and loss, though there are hints of anxiety,

---

17 This description is drawn from accounts in Samuel Sewall's *Diary* (2: 1059; 19 February 1728) and the *Boston News-Letter* (15–22; February 1728).

18 Here Mather deliberately echoes John Norton's biography of John Cotton, *Abel being dead yet speaketh, or, The life & death of that deservedly famous man of God, Mr. John Cotton, late teacher of the church of Christ, at Boston in New-England* (1658).

too. The culture of late Puritanism was not united, nor, of course, was Mather universally loved during his lifetime and after. Mather's life story is marked by conflict and personal disputes as he participated in the cultural politics of provincial Boston. And the 1720s in particular were a volatile time for Mather, including such ruptures as the Inoculation Crisis of 1721, the personal attacks of the Franklins and others in the New England *Courant*, his continuing disappointments over the presidency of Harvard, and the earthquake of 1727. And Mather himself was certainly more than ordinarily sensitive to slights against his reputation. How was this contentious Mather reconciled with the "American Elijah"?

These tensions are generally hidden in the sermons and procession but are hinted at in Samuel Mather's biography of his father, published by subscription in 1729, a year after Mather had been buried. The subscription list, appearing in the opening pages of the book, is extensive and includes luminaries, ministers, and intellectuals in New England and Britain. In and of itself, the subscription list gives credence to Thomas Prince's observation about Mather in the preface to the biography. "When about Fourteen Years ago I traveled abroad," Prince recounted, "I could not but admire to what Extent [Cotton Mather's] Fame had reached, and how inquisitive were Gentlemen of Letters to hear and know of the most particular and lively Manner both of his private Conversation and publick Performances among us" (in S. Mather, *Life* 2). The book was awaited expectantly by Cotton Mather's admirers. "If young Mr. Mather publishes his father's Life I should be glad to see his memory honoured with an Elogium wherein his Merits are touched with delicacy, so as to make them shine but not glare," wrote Isaac Watts in a letter to Mather Byles, Cotton Mather's nephew. "That great Man was worthy of the utmost labors of the Muse ..." (qtd. in Silverman 1).

Many of these subscribers no doubt also purchased a new portrait of Mather. Shortly after Mather was laid to rest on Copp's Hill, Peter Pelham, an English artist newly arrived in Boston, introduced an innovation to Boston's cultural scene by offering for sale a portrait of the deceased. Pelham first advertised his proposed mezzotint portrait of the late Cotton Mather a week after his death. Sold by subscription at "The particular desire of some of the late Doctor's Friends," the mezzotint engraving, about 10 by 14 inches, was to be copied from Pelham's original painting of Mather, finished in 1727.[19] Pelham hoped for large numbers of subscribers to keep the price low, and even offered a bargain: "For the Encouragement of Subscribers, those who take Twelve shall have a Thirteenth *gratis*." Pelham promised to complete the work, assuming that "a handsome Number of Subscriptions is procur'd," and to deliver the portraits in

---

19 Pelham's original painting of Cotton Mather is now in the American Antiquarian Society.

two months (*Boston News-Letter*; 22–29 February 1728). Sales must have been abundant, because two months later Pelham was able to inform prospective customers that he would no longer accept credit (*Boston Gazette*; 20–27 May 1728). A month after that Pelham announced that the mezzotints were finished (*Boston Gazette*; 10–17 June 1728). This was the first such mezzotint printing of its type in the colonies, but unfortunately there are no records of the numbers produced or sold. Since the breadth of distribution of Pelham's mezzotint is difficult to trace, any assessments of its iconic impact or cultural use must also be speculative. Certainly the pictures were sent as tokens or given as gifts by Mather's admirers. Thomas Hollis, a London merchant and philanthropist, received a copy of the print from Samuel Mather which, he wrote, "I have put in a frame & hanged in my parlor" (Hollis). Clearly the evidence suggests that Mather's portrait was one many people wished to have in their homes.

It is worth observing that both the portrait and Samuel Mather's biography were thus directed at a smaller public, namely to the religious and cultural elite in which Cotton Mather had been embedded. By contrast, the sermons (in their oral form) and the funeral procession were mass events, aimed at the general public, and are therefore more prescriptive and didactic in character. With Samuel Mather's biography came a greater contraction of the community of memory, a deliberate limitation of the intended audience involved in memorializing Cotton Mather. Though there are dominant, essential continuities between Samuel's rendering of his father's life and the earlier rituals for Cotton Mather, there is thus a distinct shift in tone and message in Samuel's biographical portrait. Here, his son tried to reconcile his father's sometimes contentious life with the image of an American Elijah to those readers – friends and foes – who often knew the subject first-hand. Cotton Mather was an exceptional Christian worthy of wide emulation, Samuel argued, and he also sought to enumerate his father's many spiritual, pastoral, and intellectual achievements. But this also entailed a rather awkward challenge, since Samuel felt himself caught between construing an atemporal, liturgical representation of Cotton Mather's death through a conventional biography and a spirited defense of his father's historical reputation. Much of the book expanded on the themes typically used on the death of Puritan ministers, but rather than encompassing his father's identity through the device of the biographical parallel, as he had in his funeral sermon, Samuel allowed the phases of his father's life – birth, conversion, marriage, his ministerial vocation – to describe and define Cotton Mather's virtues as a pastoral shepherd. When wronged, for example, Cotton Mather thought the best way to respond was "to forgive the *wrong* and bury it in *Silence*" (S. Mather, *Life* 23). He also quoted passages from his father's diary "relating to the *Cure of Pride*, a Sin, which *all* are subject unto, and more especially *Ministers*, and which ought with all Care and all Diligence to be avoided" (28), a subject with which Cotton Mather struggled all his life. Above all, the "Ambition and Character of my Father's life was *Serviceableness*" (49), evident in the many publications he wrote and in years of faithful service as pastor of the Second Church. Samuel Mather also gave a detailed portrait of his father's private devotional and prayer life, the many fasts and night-long vigils, as well as the works of charity and "doing good," in which Cotton Mather was so prolific. The concluding chapter, finally, recounted at length the story of Cotton Mather's last days in a manner congruent with the versions found in the funeral sermons preached at his father's death.

Samuel Mather's assessment of his father's pastoral career was rather conventional and uncontroversial, but he found it more difficult to provide a full and honest appraisal of Cotton Mather's activities in the public arena. "I am here to mention his being concern'd in *State Affairs* (a difficult Section!)," he wrote, "and I must assure my Reader that I am more at a loss what to do about it *than any one* in the whole Book." Samuel Mather faced a two-fold dilemma in composing this section of the biography. If he edited his father's involvement in politics too scrupulously, he would "be a faulty Historian, to leave out what is so considerable." But to expound at length on the public events of Cotton Mather's day was to incur a different risk, since to "write the *ill Managements* of others and the Warmth with which the *Doctor* ever appeared for Truth and Honour as well as for his People & Countrey ... might provoke the Anger of a few Gentlemen and others." Thus Samuel Mather touched very lightly on such potentially uncomfortable topics as Cotton Mather's dispute in the early 1700s with the young Benjamin Colman and the Brattle Street Church,[20] for example, and resolved to "treat of one or two Things only," professing that it was his desire "that this History may be very unexceptionable ... [and] give no one any Offence" (41).

The "one or two" things of which Samuel Mather chose to speak at length were Cotton Mather's involvement in the Glorious Revolution and the Salem witchcraft crisis, the latter especially being the event with which his father would be most closely associated in the centuries to come. Of the first, the Glorious Revolution of 1689 in which the royal governor of the colony, Edmund Andros, was overthrown by Puritan leaders, Samuel Mather argued that his father's role was a moderating and pacifying one. In fact, Samuel Mather claimed, it was only by Cotton Mather's intervention and wisdom that the revolt had not devolved into an anarchic insurrection. At a crucial moment, when "the whole Countrey were now in a most prodigious ferment and Thousands of exasperated People in Arms were come into *Boston*," Samuel Mather described, "'Twas then Mr. Mather appeared – He was the Instrument of preventing the Excesses into which *the Wrath of Man* is too ready to run." Through eloquent and pacifying oratory, Samuel Mather concluded, his father "reasoned down the

---

20   For an account of this controversy see Silverman (146–56).

Passions of the Populace," thus preserving the social order and hierarchy of the colony (42–43).

This heroic version of Cotton Mather in the breech was deliberately culti- vated to counter lingering negative impressions of his father's involvement in the Salem witch trials, wherein some of Cotton Mather's enemies (especially Robert Calef) had accused him of having an incendiary influence. Samuel Mather moved directly to this episode and, in effect, followed the same line of argument that appears in his analysis of the Glorious Revolution. Cotton Math- er, he maintained, had acted as a wise, moderating influence during the witch crisis. Referring to his father's opinions on the use of spectral evidence, the point on which Cotton Mather was later to be much accused, Samuel Mather stated, "Mr. Mather, for his Part, was always afraid of proceeding to convict and condemn any Person as *Confederate* with afflicting *Dæmons* upon so feeble an Evidence as *Spectral Representation*." In saying this, Samuel Mather tried to refute the contention that his father had argued the opposite, that he had in written advice encouraged the judges in the trials to pursue witches ruthlessly.[21] He acknowledged that his father had been "reviled" as "if he had bin the Doer of the hard Things that were done in the Prosecution of the *Witchcraft*" (45). However, the reality of his father's involvement was the same in tone and effect as during the Glorious Revolution. That this event and others brought disrepute and insults was of no ultimate consequence, Samuel Mather concluded, since in life and death Cotton Mather "was high above [the] reach" of his detractors (63). It is a spirited argument, but one that moved Samuel Mather's book from a panegyric on an American Elijah to a self-conscious reflection of the more hu- man Cotton Mather.

There are certainly hints here in Samuel Mather's defensiveness both of the ani- mus that awaited Cotton Mather's cultural reputation and the perplexity his actions in life at times engendered. It is perhaps ironic that in all of the public performances occasioned by Mather's death the product in which the notes of anxiety and ambivalence about him sound most strongly (no doubt uninten- tionally) came from his own son. Obviously, Samuel would not have addressed the events at Salem if his father had not still been in some ways stigmatized by them. We might therefore ask ourselves whether the hagiographic treatments of Cotton Mather after his death accurately depict what those who constructed his image or the wider public really thought of him. None of the rituals and per- formances on Mather's death comes from sources outside the expansive circle of his admirers. Perhaps the superlatives used to describe Mather suggest a level of

---

21   See Mather's "Letter to John Richards" (May 31, 1692), three days before the Salem court convicted Bridge Bishop (June 2) and executed her (June 10). See also *The Return of Several Ministers Consulted* (June 15, 1692) – both reprinted in Levin's *What Happened* (106–11).

ambivalence, insecurity, and anxiety about Mather's political and cultural legacy, or about declining ministerial hegemony in an increasingly pluralistic Boston. Perhaps Mather was too gargantuan a figure to damn with faint praise.[22]
On the other hand, the scale and unanimity of these rituals speak to their impressive consolatory power, and the warm expressions of love, friendship, and
veneration from many quarters are genuine and deeply felt, reflecting how
Mather's memory was cherished by a wide circle of admirers on both sides of
the Atlantic. Cotton Mather's "more than ordinary Joy and Spiritual Triumph"
(Kneeland) could also be New England's if, like him, they submitted themselves to Christ's enfolding love. We are a long way here from the modern re-
constitutions of his image decried by Alonzo Quint in the 1800s, the effigy on
which nineteenth-century scholars, novelists, and theologians hung their own
religious and cultural anxieties. In 1728 the "monster" was still human, and the
American "national gargoyle" had yet to be carved in stone.

Works Cited

Primary Sources

"Baptisms and Admission, 1717–1741," 28^d 11^m 1727. 28 January 1728. *Second Church
(Boston, Mass.) Records*. Vol. 5. Massachusetts Historical Society.
Boston Gazette 20–27 May 1728; 10–17 June 1728.
Boston News-Letter 8–15 February 1728; 15–22 February 1728; 22–29 February 1729.
Colman, Benjamin. *The Holy Walk and Glorious Translation of Blessed Enoch*. Boston,
1728.
Cotton, Josiah. "Letter to Samuel Mather, 19 February 1728." In "Account of the Cotton
Family (1727–1756)." MS Am 1165. Houghton Lib., Harvard College Lib.
Foxe, John. *Acts and Monuments*. 1576. *hriOnline, Sheffield*. Web 13 Aug. 2009.
Gee, Joshua. *Israel's Mourning for Aaron's Death*. Boston, 1728.
Hollis, Thomas. "Letter to Benjamin Colman, 12 February 1729." *Benjamin Colman
Papers, 1641–1763*. Microform. Boston, MHS, 1978. Reel 1.
Kneeland, Samuel. Letter (undated) to "Rev. Sir." MS 363. Boston Public Lib., Depart-
ment of Rare Books and Manuscripts.
Loring, Israel. "Journal of Rev. Israel Loring." TS by Louise Parkman Thomas. *Sudbury
Archives Online*. Web 12 Nov. 2008.
Mather, Cotton. *The Angel of Bethesda: An Essay upon the Common Maladies of Man-
kind*. Ed. Gordon W. Jones. Barre: American Antiquarian Society and Barre Pub-
lishers, 1972.
–. *Magnalia Christi Americana: Or, The Ecclesiastical History of New England*. 1702.
New York: Arno Press, 1972.
–. *Two Mather Biographies:* Life and Death *and* Parentator. Ed. William Scheick.
Bethlehem: Lehigh University Press, 1989.

---

22 Silverman (422–26) sees perplexity, anxiety, and ambivalence about Mather in these funeral rituals.

–.   *The Thoughts of a Dying Man.* Boston, 1697.
Mather, Samuel. *The Departure and Character of Elijah Considered and Improved.* Boston, 1728.
–.   *The Life of the Very Reverend and Learned Cotton Mather, D.D., F.R.S., Late Pastor of the North Church in Boston.* Boston, 1729.
Parkman, Ebenezer. *The Diary of Ebenezer Parkman, 1703–1782.* Ed. Francis G. Walett. Worcester: American Antiquarian Society, 1974.
Prince, Thomas. *The Departure of Elijah Lamented.* Boston, 1728.
Quint, Alonzo. "Cotton Mather." *Congregational Quarterly* 1.3 (July 1859): 233–64.
Sewall, Samuel. *Diary of Samuel Sewall, 1674–1729.* Ed. M. Halsey Thomas. 2 vols. New York: Farrar, Strauss, & Giroux, 1973.
Walker, Benjamin. "Diary, 19 February 1728." *Pre-Revolutionary Diaries at the Massachusetts Historical Society, 1635–1774.* Microform. Boston: MHS, 1983. Reel 10.

Secondary Sources

Bercovitch, Sacvan. *The American Jeremiad.* Madison: The U of Wisconsin P, 1978.
Bosco, Ronald A. Introduction. *The Puritan Sermon in America, 1630–1750.* Ed. Ronald A. Bosco. Vol. 4. *New England Funeral Sermons.* Delmar: Scholars' Facsimiles & Reprints, 1978.
Douglas, Ann. *The Feminization of American Culture.* New York: Harper & Row, 1977.
Elliott, Emory. "The Development of the Puritan Funeral Sermon and Elegy: 1660–1750." *Early American Literature* 15 (1980): 151–164.
Hall, David D., ed. *Lived Religion in America: Toward a History of Practice.* Princeton: Princeton UP, 1997.
Hambrick-Stowe, Charles. *The Practice of Piety: Puritan Devotional Disciplines in Seventeenth-Century New England.* Chapel Hill: U of North Carolina P, 1982.
Hammond, Jeffrey A. *The Puritan Funeral Elegy: A Literary and Cultural Study.* New York: Cambridge UP, 2000.
Henson, Robert. "Form and Content of the Puritan Funeral Elegy." *American Literature* 32.1 (1960): 11–27.
Kapchan, Deborah A. "Performance." *The Journal of American Folklore* 108. 430 (1995): 479–508.
Levin, David. *What Happened in Salem?* 2nd ed. New York: Harcourt, Brace & World, 1960.
–.   "Trying to Make the Monster Human: Judgment in the Biography of Cotton Mather." *The Yale Review* 73. 2 (1984): 210–29.
Miller, Perry. *The New England Mind: From Colony to Province.* Cambridge: Harvard UP, 1953.
Porterfield, Amanda. *Female Piety in Puritan New England: The Emergence of Religious Humanism.* New York: Oxford UP, 1992.
Seeman, Erik R. *Pious Persuasions: Laity and Clergy in Eighteenth-Century New England.* Baltimore: The Johns Hopkins UP, 1999.
Silverman, Kenneth. *The Life and Times of Cotton Mather.* New York: Harper & Row, 1984.
Stannard, David. *The Puritan Way of Death: A Study in Religion, Culture, and Social Change.* New York: Oxford UP, 1977.

Turner, Victor. *The Ritual Process: Structure and Anti-Structure.* Chicago: Aldine, 1969.

Ulrich, Laurel Thatcher. "Vertuous Women Found: New England Ministerial Literature, 1668–1735." *American Quarterly* 28.1 (1976): 20–40.

Van Arragon, William. "Cotton Mather in American Cultural Memory, 1728–1892." PhD Dissertation, Indiana University, 2005.

Winship, Michael P. "Were There Any Puritans in New England?" *New England Quarterly* 74.1 (2001): 118–38.

E. Brooks Holifield

The Abridging of Cotton Mather

The admirers of Cotton Mather in colonial America marveled that a small colony on the outer margins of British civilization could produce "so rising and great a Figure in the literary world" (Prince 2). A preacher who addressed more than a thousand people a week from his pulpit at Boston's North Church, an author with close to four hundred titles to his credit, a scholar honored by membership in the English Royal Society for the Improvement of Natural Knowledge, he was, in their eyes, a model of piety and enlightenment and a defender of the Calvinist faith. Cotton Mather, they thought, could write with authority on almost anything. And indeed he produced books, short and long, on Calvinist theology, natural philosophy, Christian morality, eschatology, supernatural wonders, introspective piety, colonial history, church government, child-rearing practices, sacramental devotion, divine providence, pastoral practice, biography, social and political criticism, ecumenical harmony, evidences of revelation, homiletics, and biblical criticism. For some of his most devoted followers, every word he wrote was worth reading.

Shortly after the publication in 1702 of his *Magnalia Christi Americana*, his long and ambitious history of the New England enterprise, a colleague at the ministerial association in Boston proposed an abridged version of the book. The proposal elicited, from another admirer of his prose and learning, an indignant outcry: "'Tis impossible to abridge it! Abridging it will injure it. ... No man that has a relish for Piety or for Variety can ever be weary of it" (S. Mather 70). The book remained, until the twentieth century, unabridged. But Cotton Mather was not so fortunate. Both his admirers and his critics in the century and a half after his death in 1728 fashioned a stunning abridgment of Mather's intellectual legacy. Cotton Mather shrank. His successors mined the data from his history, praised his admonitions to do good, argued about his views on church government, and bemoaned his credulity about witches, but almost everything else faded into the horizon. In the nineteenth century, he was, for the most part, valued – or deplored – as an authority on church administration. By the end of the century, he was a frequent object of mean-spirited ridicule.

The eclipse of Cotton Mather calls for assessment. In this essay, I draw my conclusions partly from a reading of Mather and his predecessors but primarily from an analysis of 328 books, sermons, journal articles, library listings, and booksellers' catalogues printed between the year of his death and 1870, when

Delano Alexander Goddard in his *The Mathers Weighed in the Balances and Found Not Wanting* described Mather as an example of "the old, old story of heroes lifted a great deal too high in one century, only to be dragged down a great deal too low in another" (5). My sampling is far from exhaustive, but these 108 journal articles and 220 books, sermons, and pamphlets show how Mather's legacy contracted. The reasons for the waning included changes in theological preoccupations, new attitudes toward seemingly supernatural forces, reassessments of what constituted a pleasing literary style, and Mather's failure to find a publisher for his most ambitious project. But among the most important reasons was a deliberate campaign among New England's religious liberals to subvert Mather's reputation as an authority on church government. Mather's legacy was, to some considerable measure, a victim of the political intrigues that threw the Massachusetts religious establishment into turmoil a century after his death.

Mather and New England Theology

Cotton Mather was, above all, a Calvinist preacher and theologian who strove to promote piety, encourage Christian living, and preserve the essentials of Reformed theology. He was no crypto-Arminian, no will-empowering "preparationist," and no disguised rationalist. He urged sinners to do all in their "natural power" to obey God's commands, but he told them that they were utterly unable to "turn" themselves to obedience. He conceded that the doctrine of predestination had its "mysteries" and "abstruse Difficulties," but he also thought it had a "wondrous tendency to the Edification of the Faithful." He warned the unregenerate that they needed to be "prepared" for conversion, but he believed, like earlier New England Puritans, that a sovereign God did the preparing. He urged that the "voice of Reason" was the "voice of God," but he insisted, like his predecessors, that only a revelation above the power of reason could give saving knowledge.[1]

In his *Seasonable Testimony to the Glorious Doctrines of Grace* (1702), he and his ministerial colleagues in the Boston area excoriated English Arminians and reaffirmed the doctrines of original sin, total depravity, the bondage of the will, unconditional election, irresistible grace, and justification by faith through the imputation of Christ's righteousness (2–15). He saw himself as standing in the tradition of such theologians as the "incomparable" John Calvin of Geneva and the "great" Gisbert Voetius of Utrecht, two of the many architects of the

---

1 For this, see Mather's *A Conquest* (28–29) and *The Converted Sinner* (14). On predestination, see his *Free Grace* (2); on preparation *Unum Necessarium* (22, 41), *A Man of Reason* (7), and *Icono-clastes* (18).

Reformed tradition. When he drew on such non-Calvinist theologians as the "incomparable" August Herrmann Francke of Halle, he stayed within Calvinist boundaries (qtd. in Lovelace 57–58). Not until the twentieth century did anyone suggest that Mather departed, even implicitly, from the Calvinist doctrines of grace. To his ministerial partner Joshua Gee he was always "a vigorous defender of the reformed doctrines of grace, and of the mysteries of revealed religion" (19) and insofar as any theologian during the century after his death discussed his views on the "doctrines of grace," they praised – or criticized – him as a conventional Calvinist (Miller 634).[2]

By no means, however, was Mather merely a conventional Calvinist. His successors could have justifiably honored him, with good reason, as a mentor in the apologetic strategies of the Christian enlightenment. They could have seen him as the theologian who expanded the range of New England theology by recognizing the force of the appeal to reason in the intellectual culture of his era. Because he wrestled, more than any other theologian before Jonathan Edwards, with the serious challenge of the Deists, he surpassed his predecessors in the extent of his preoccupation with the reasonableness of Christianity. When he wrote *Reasonable Religion* (1700), *Reason Satisfied: and Faith Established* (1712), *A Man of Reason* (1718), and *The Christian Philosopher* (1721), he invested heavily in the endeavor of the enlightened physico-theologians to use natural science as a source of proofs for God's existence. His natural theology and his employment of the traditional "evidences" for the authenticity of biblical revelation did not distinguish him in principle from the first generation of New England preachers, but the energy he poured into the quest for "proof" and "evidence" could have earned him recognition from a later generation of theologians who shared the same intellectual ambitions.

For the most part, they yawned. Sixteen years after he died, Gamaliel Rogers and John Foule in Boston reprinted his chapter on comets from *The Christian Philosopher*, and in 1815 William Collins revised and published the whole book to make it, as the title page promised, "easy and familiar" (title page) for customers who could find copies in the Middlesex Bookstore in Charlestown, but the publication attracted no attention in the religious press. John Wesley read it in England and reprinted heavily revised excerpts from it; Christian Wolff read it in Germany and praised the "laudable example" of a theologian open to new knowledge; but American theologians looked elsewhere for help in reconciling religion and science. A handful of American physicians and preach-

---

2   On Mather's reputation as a Calvinist see, for instance, the anonymous articles "Dr. Cotton Mather," from *The Christian History* (1743), and "On the Prevalence of Socinianism," from *Hopkinsian Magazine* (1824). See also, the 1745 *Testimony of a Number of Ministers* (12), Wigglesworth's and Chipman's 1746 *Remarks on Some Points of Doctrine* (9), Dunbar's 1751 *Righteousness By the Law* (28), Church's 1810 *The First Settlement* (11), and Willson's 1817 *A Historical Sketch* (129–30).

ers expressed pride that Mather had promoted vaccination against smallpox, but most appeared to lack interest in Mather the natural philosopher (qtd. in Solberg c–ciii).

In addition, "Biblia Americana" – his most ambitious intellectual project – attracted no publisher, so his successors knew little about this effort to interpret scripture in the light of "all the learning in the world" (qtd. in Silverman 166). Readers of the biography of Mather written by his son knew that the manuscript could be described as "by far the greatest amassment of Learning that has ever been brought together to illustrate the oracles of God" (S. Mather 73), and from time to time someone made passing reference to the manuscript's existence. George Edward Ellis told readers in 1857 where to find it in the cabinet of the Historical Society. But his only comment was that Mather held superstitious views of the Bible, and apparently no one read the manuscript, at least for purposes of commenting on it in print. In any case, few would have welcomed his concessions to British and European critics who questioned the Mosaic authorship of the Pentateuch and who contended that later authors emended the biblical texts. Some of his interpretive tactics – reading the Genesis stories, for example, in the light of natural philosophy – became commonplace by the early nineteenth century, but Mather's employment of them remained hidden.[3]

Nor did theologians show much interest in the intense supernaturalism that counterbalanced his commendations of reason. New England theologians had always believed in the existence of angels, for example, but Mather "saw" them – in a series of appearances that began when he was twenty-one and continued the rest of his life – and he had something to say about them in no fewer than 230 of his published works (Lovelace 13). His successors ignored his many comments about angelic beings. New England theologians had always believed in "wonders" – events beyond the power of natural causation – though most had been wary of designating them as "miracles," a term laden with resonances of Catholic apologetics. Mather found the world filled with miracles, collected miracle stories, and announced that they foreshadowed the "age of miracles" that was "now dawning upon the world." He discovered traces of the miraculous in his own prayers when he received what he called "particular faiths," or "special impressions," assuring him that he would receive the "special mercy" for which he prayed. But nineteenth-century Calvinist theologians were wary of talk about miracles – most believed that the "age of miracles" had ceased with the ending of the apostolic era.[4]

---

3   For a reference to the manuscript see, for instance, Willson (129). Mather's negotiations of biblical hermeneutics and natural philosophy are discussed in Smolinski ("Natural Science and Interpretation").

4   For Mather's commentaries on angels, see the 1791 *Catalogue of Books in the Library of Yale College* (107) and his sermons *Coelestinus* (64–67), *Things for a Distress'd People* (36, 69, 73, 80, 84), *Eleutheria* (109), and his autobiography *Paterna* (102–04).

On occasion, a New England outsider commended Mather's accounts of miracles and visions. In 1858 the Methodist Abel Stevens pointed out that John Wesley had also seen ghosts (63), and every now and then a nineteenth-century spiritualist, eager for any proof of communication with the dead, dredged up Mather's references to "spirit touch" (see, for instance, Sargent 37). Liberals and conservatives skirmished for a few weeks in 1825 over his particular faiths. But by the nineteenth century, Mather's supernaturalist imagination made him seem odd. Even the evangelical revivalist Asa Mahan observed in 1855 that the true causes of Mather's "strange phenomena" were "mundane and physical" (98). "His popular reputation," wrote an anonymous reviewer of William B. O. Peabody's biography of Mather in 1840, "is that of a superstitious and credulous man who believed in witchcraft and collected a good many nonsensical stories" (2).[5]

New England theologians had always shared an eschatological sensibility, looking forward to the end-times when Jesus would return, but Mather wrote about the millennial era with an amplitude of detail that surpassed anything written earlier in New England, with the possible exception of his father's musings. After 1691, he published more than forty sermons and essays on eschatology, and he treated the topic extensively in his "Problema Theologicum" (1703), his *Triparadisus* (1726/27), and his "Biblia Americana" (1693–1728). He depicted a heavenly Jerusalem and a transformed world populated by "Raised Saints" and "Changed Saints" relishing the joy of a millennial paradise. During the revivals of the 1740s an occasional theologian remembered his prediction that the day was "at hand," and half a century later Hannah Adams's 1791 *A View of Religions in Two Parts* (pt. 1, p. 151) included Mather's scenario in a descriptive outline of various millennial schemes, but eighteenth and nineteenth century theologians looked elsewhere for help with the final days.[6]

The New England liberals finally reduced Mather to a caricature, but Jonathan Edwards and his New Divinity disciples began, quite unintentionally, the abridging of Mather. They carried theology in new directions. As a theologian, of course, Edwards held much in common with Mather. They both ap-

---

5 For criticism of Mather's supernaturalism see, for instance, the anonymous 1815 *Explanation of Certain Phenomena* (1, 15); for the 1825 debate, see the articles "Prayer of Faith," from *Recorder and Telegraph*, and "Cotton Mather on The Prayer of Faith," from *Western Recorder*.

6 For striking examples of Mather's millennialist visions, see Mares's edition "Cotton Mather's 'Problema Theologicum,'" *Theopolis Americana* (50), and Smolinski's edition of *Triparadisus* (33, 245, 247, 262, 274–75). Reference to Mather's predictions is made, for example, in the preface of Dickinson's 1741 *The True Scripture Doctrine*. Adam's scheme is discussed in the 1796 article "From Miss Adams's View of Religions," in *The Theological Magazine*. Significantly, a nineteenth-century millennialist like Seiss has only one sentence on Mather's eschatology (58). For a scholarly examination of Mather's millennialism, see Smolinski, *"Israel Redivivus."*

propriated ideas from the Enlightenment but struggled against heterodox Enlightenment innovations. Both opposed Arminianism and Deism. They both promoted moral theology while opposing the moral temper of the British philosophers. They shared an apocalyptic sensibility. They had similar ideas about church membership and the signs of a gracious heart. They shared a theological interest in history. Both of them exploited the new distinctions between natural ability and moral inability, and they had similar views about reason and revelation (Holifield 64–78, 102–26).

Yet the differences were as pronounced as the similarities. Edwards worked out a subtle idealist philosophy to accompany and support his Calvinist theology; Mather had different metaphysical assumptions. Edwards organized much of his theology with the help of an ontological understanding of "excellence" or "beauty"; Mather made no similar speculative moves. Edwards was more reluctant than Mather to specify a limited number of essential doctrines that could serve as grounding for ecumenical harmony. They differed in their descriptions of original sin: Mather took the conventional Reformed position that God imputed Adam's guilt to his descendants; Edwards formulated an ontology designed to show that God imputed guilt only because the human race was antecedently guilty of Adam's sin. Mather preached that God normally prepared the heart for grace by engendering a sense of conviction and humiliation; Edwards also spoke of preparatory stages, but he decided by 1738 that repentance, humility, faith, and love were so clearly "united and linked together" that rigid patternings of them missed the point. Mather thought that the return of Christ to inaugurate the millennium was imminent; Edwards expected at least 250 years of "commotions, tumults, and conflicts" before the millennium began, and he thought that the millennial era would precede the final return of Christ.[7]

The Edwardseans who followed in Edwards's footsteps still read Cotton Mather – Nathaniel Emmons, for example, was said to have entered long quotations and abstracts from Mather into his notebooks – but they were clear about their deviations from Mather's theology (see *Memoir of Nathanael Emmons* 69). They were delineated in an 1824 essay entitled "On the Prevalence of Socinianism," which appeared in the *Hopkinsian Magazine*. Mather taught that sinful people had a sinful nature underlying their sinful actions. The Edwardseans said that sin consisted in sinning. Mather said that human beings were guilty because God imputed Adam's guilt to them. The Edwardseans said that sinners became guilty of Adam's sin only by consenting to it. Mather said that Christ was the legal representative of the elect and that by his death he paid their

---

7   For the above-cited differences, see Edwards, *Treatise* (154, 161–62), *Faithful Narrative* (166), "Divine and Supernatural Light," (413), *Original Sin* (390), and "Charity" (332); Mather, *Theopolis Americana* (50) and *Triparadisus* (60–78, 339, 341). See also, Edwards, *Humble Attempt* (107, 129), "Notes on the Apocalypse" (129, 141, 177, 183–84), and *History of Redemption* (462, 478).

debt so that God could impute righteousness to them. He added that Christ died only for the elect. The Ewardseans denied that Christ paid a legal debt and denied that he died only for the elect. They also differed with Mather about the standards for church membership; they disliked the "halfway covenant" that permitted the baptized unregenerate offspring of true visible saints to claim the privileges of baptism for their own children. The Edwardsean Joseph Bellamy said that Mather's support for half-way membership merely exposed his inconsistency.[8]

The Old Calvinist opponents of the Edwardseans agreed with many of Mather's doctrinal views – Ezra Stiles, the president of Yale, affirmed "the Doctrines of Grace as held by the good Old Puritans and by our Ancestors" (qtd. in Morgan 175) – but some of the Old Calvinists wanted to expand full church membership in ways that diverged from Mather's policies. For one thing, they normally disregarded any requirement for a narration of conversion as a prelude to membership. And since ecclesiology was at the heart of the debate between Edwardseans and Old Calvinists, it would not have been wise for them to elevate Mather's authority as a theologian. They found him too strict while the Edwardseans found him not strict enough. On the practical issue that stood behind the complex theological disputes between the Edwardseans and Old Calvinists, neither side found reason to recruit Mather as a fully trustworthy ally. And this meant that Mather the theologian began to lose a voice in the New England conversation (Holifield 149–56).

Legacy

Mather's work in natural philosophy, eschatology, angelology, Calvinist doctrine, the miraculous, natural theology, and Christian evidences failed to retain the interest of his successors. But Americans did not forget Cotton Mather. Between 1728 and 1866, printers in America and England issued seventy-one reprints of one or another of Mather's books. The reprints included twenty-seven titles, which covered topics of piety, history, ethics, witchcraft, and the governance of churches. The printing was a barometer of changing interests in the Protestant churches. In the eighteenth century, devotional guides, with emphasis on children and families, constituted seventy percent of the twenty-four reprinted books. In the early nineteenth century, the pattern shifted. Between 1807 and 1845, Mather's 1710 *Bonifacius: Essay Upon the Good* enjoyed nine-

---

8   For the positions of the Edwardseans on these theological issues, see Jonathan Edwards, Jr., "The Necessity of the Atonement" (337, 358, 368). A good scholarly discussion of these issues in the younger Edwards is provided by Ferm (92, 152, 172). See also Bellamy, "Divinity of Jesus Christ" (38–41) and "The Millennium" (65, 68); Hopkins, *The Importance* (15, 23), *An Inquiry* (137, 142), and *Treatise on the Millennium* (52, 116, 145).

teen printings under the title *Essays To Do Good*, reflecting the activism and moralism that penetrated Protestant churches in the northeast. No other book by Mather received this much attention, and it represented almost sixty percent of the thirty-three imprints that publishers made available during these years. By the late nineteenth century, the printers – and presumably the public – lost interest in his books on piety and ethics, but antiquarian preoccupations and ideological predilections shifted curiosity toward his writings on witchcraft, which were reprinted eight times between 1861 and 1866, the only books reprinted during these five years.[9]

The entrepreneurs who opened bookstores liked the *Essays To Do Good*. A sampling of bookstore catalogues and advertisements between 1768 and 1852 reveals that ten of the fifteen vendors who advertised a Mather publication sold the *Essays to Do Good* while two offered copies of the *Magnalia Christi Americana*. Three had no Mather books to sell, though three of them carried his son's biography of him. The multiple re-printings of Mather's works indicate that book buyers must have had access to new printings of at least twenty-seven titles. Only the essays on doing good and the history of New England appeared in the catalogues. Judging from these advertisements, the only steady seller was the *Essays To Do Good*.[10]

The librarians who assembled America's first public and academic collections preferred the *Magnalia Christi Americana*. Of thirty libraries that publicized their holdings between 1766 and 1864, twenty-four had at least one of Mather's books. Most had no more than two or three titles, though Harvard College had sixty-seven in 1790, Yale College had thirteen in 1808, and the Massachusetts Historical Society had forty-one by 1811. In 1851, Hannah Mather Crocker, a granddaughter of Cotton Mather, sold and donated to the American Antiquarian Society between 900 and 1,000 books from Mather's library, which meant that it probably had the largest Mather collection. Twenty of the libraries had copies – sometimes multiple copies – of the *Magnalia Christi Americana*. No other Mather imprint came close. Only four carried the *Essays To Do Good* and five had *The Christian Philosopher*.

Private clerical libraries tended to emulate the public collections. A sampling of six ministerial libraries in the northeast between 1812 and 1818 finds seventeen books by Mather. Three of the ministers had the *Magnalia Christi Americana*, two had assorted sermons. John Eliot in Massachusetts had 855 books in his library; Mather wrote four of them. Three of the ministers had his son's biography. John Willson claimed in 1817 that "the common people" and "the best clergy of the northern states" read Mather's "smaller works" with "great interest," but he adduced no evidence for the statement (129). In all likeli-

---

9   I here rely on the counts taken from Holmes's bibliography of Mather's works.
10 The bookstore catalogues and advertisements I examined are listed in Appendix A.

hood, the most popular books were sermons, devotional guides, and the *Essays to Do Good.*[11]

Mather's thoughts on morality in the *Essays To Do Good* brought him continuing praise in the religious journals. It helped that Benjamin Franklin had paid tribute to Mather in his autobiography: "If I have been a useful citizen," Franklin wrote, "the public owes the advantage of it to that book" (167). Reviewers praised the book's discussions of prayer and piety, its advice to parents, and its promotion of public benevolence. In an 1828 article entitled "Cotton Mather a Distributor of Tracts," *The Spirit of the Pilgrims* – the journal in which Lyman Beecher impressed his opinions on the conscience of New England – speculated that Mather's promotion of "doing good" might have been "instrumental" in bringing forth "what we, too fondly perhaps, affect to call 'the age of benevolence'" (611). A piece with the telling title "Good Devised" run by the editors of the *Boston Recorder* in 1819 recommended the formation of "Mather Committees" in every community to seek "means to do good." Mather's "active beneficence," they wrote, would have found more "kindred spirits" in the present age than in his own (32).[12]

The *Magnalia Christi Americana* had a more mixed reception. Americans reprinted it twice in the nineteenth century, and libraries sought to own it. Authors cited it more than any other of Mather's books. It provided data for amateur historians, justification for colonial treatment of the Indians, illustrations for sermons, resources for biographical sketches, interpretations of colonial theology, material for political propaganda, and ammunition in church disputes. John Willson described it as "a treasure of historical fact, upon which all the succeeding historians of New England made large draughts" (129). In his *American Institutions and their Influence* Alexis de Tocqueville, no lightweight in the interpretation of American culture, called the *Magnalia* the single most important authority on the history of New England, more valuable to the historian than any other work (450).[13]

The *Magnalia* elicited, however, more than its share of negative reactions. Even Tocqueville described it as "intolerant" and "credulous" (450). Willson, who admired the book, thought that it was "evidently written with great haste," with its facts "neither selected with judgment nor well arranged" (129). *The*

---

11   The library holdings I examined are listed in Appendix B. For the donation to the American Antiquarian Society, see Jewett, *Notices of Public Libraries* (44).

12   Similar praise of Mather's devotional works was expressed in many antebellum religious tracts, journals, and anthologies. For further examples I found, see Appendix C, which also contains full bibliographic references to the texts cited above.

13   Examples for works that use the *Magnalia* in these ways are Emerson's 1766 *A Thanksgiving Sermon* (22), Adams's 1799 *A Summary History* (59), Stiles's 1799 *A Discourse on the Christian Union* (68), DeWitt Clinton's 1811 *A Discourse Delivered Before the New York Historical Society* (58), Samuel Kendal's 1813 *A Sermon* (20, 22), and Beecher's 1815 *On the Importance of Assisting* (6).

New England Theocracy (1858) by the historian Hermann Ferdinand Uhden praised the "great learning" evinced in the book, but he conceded that Mather's prodigious array of "citations from writers ancient and modern" often meant that he barely made it to his subject matter (287). Mather's nineteenth-century readers could not see in the *Magnalia* the rich Baroque sensibility that some contemporary critics have discerned, the amassing of a textual *copia* that shows America as "the culmination of Old World culture." Rather than viewing the history as a rich but ultimately unsuccessful effort to blend example and allusion into a unity expressing a divinely inspired "single truth" (Stievermann 271, 284), they were more prone to criticize Mather for "oddities of opinion" and "fabulous representations" that displayed his "prejudice and false zeal."[14]

Mather's devotional writings enjoyed sporadic bursts of attention. The revivals of the 1740s brought a flurry of interest. In an 1809 retrospective for *The Witness* an anonymous evangelical writer, quoting the clergyman Thomas Prince, claimed that the Awakening created a renewed taste for "pious and spiritual writers," including Mather, and indeed in 1740–41 printers had issued three of Mather's earlier devotional guides – *Family Religion Excited and Assisted* (1740), *Ornaments for the Daughters of Zion* (1741), and *Vital Christianity* (1741). For the next hundred years, the authors of devotional guides occasionally referred to one or another of Mather's pious works, especially his words on family piety and the religiousness of children. Printers continued to issue his books on pious children and religious education. Mather's example of praying with his own children – and his success in seeing that most of them "died in the Lord" – gave authority to his books on family religion.[15]

The Mather who attracted the most attention among the theologians, however, was not the moralist, the devotional writer, or the historian. The Mather about whom theologians continued to argue was, to put it bluntly, the authority on church administration, and his assessments of church polity in his *Ratio Disciplinae Fratrum Nov-Anglorum: A Faithful Account of the Discipline Pro-*

---

14   These characterizations come from the article "Collections of the Massachusetts Historical Society for the Year 1800" (304–16) and from Davis's 1813 *A Discourse Before the Massachusetts Historical Society* (30). For full bibliographic references and a list with more examples for the hundreds of antebellum works containing critical references to the *Magnalia Christi Americana*, see Appendix D.

15   Mather's essential work on the religious education of children is his *Token for the Children of New England* (1700). It was incorporated into the *Magnalia* (1702) and reprinted several times thereafter. The tract was also reprinted in James Janeway's 1771 *A Token for Children*, which went through multiple editions (Philadelphia: B. Franklin, 1749; Boston: T. and J. Fleet, 1771; Boston: Z. Fowle, 1771; Boston: T. and J. Fleet, 1781; Worcester: James Hutchins, 1795). Mather's other important work in this area is his *Corderius Americanus* (1708), which was also twice reprinted (1774; Dutton and Wentworth, 1828; Old South Leaflets, n.d.).

For a sampling of antebellum religious tracts, journals, and anthologies praising Mather's writings on family religion, see Appendix C.

fessed and Practiced in the Churches of New England helped shape the debate over theology and church politics in New England Congregationalism for more than a century. The book was printed in 1726 and never reprinted, though Professor Thomas Upham at Amherst published a book with a similar title in 1829 that occasionally quoted Mather. But from the Great Awakening in the 1740s through the Unitarian controversies in the 1820s, Mather's admirers and critics generated debate over his claims about church government. The battles over the *Ratio Disciplinae* in the eighteenth and nineteenth centuries served for some New England theologians as sufficient grounds for wishing to see Mather's stature diminished.

Contestants in the debates over the Great Awakening viewed Mather still as an authority on both theology and church practice. Partisans of the revivalist George Whitefield praised Mather's defense of "the doctrines of grace." Proponents of itinerancy noted that Mather had celebrated the itinerant preachers in England at the time of the Reformation. Moderate revivalists drew on the *Magnalia* and Mather's *Case of a Troubled Mind*, reprinted in Boston in 1741, to counter an alleged re-emergence of antinomianism among their more extreme brethren. Critics of the revivals drew from the *Magnalia* to decry revival methods as inherently antinomian, and they used his *Warning to the Flocks* (1700) and his *Manuductio ad Ministerium* (1726) to register their opposition to uneducated preachers. When Whitefield in his *The Testimony of a Number of Ministers Convened at Taunton* (1745) disparaged anti-revivalist preachers (12), Mather's praise of the New England clergy served to deflect his censure.[16]

The disputants in the revival era also appealed to his *Ratio Disciplinae*. When the Hampshire Association of the clergy attempted to prevent the ordination of Robert Breck to the pulpit in the First Precinct in Springfield, Massachusetts, on the grounds of his doctrinal errors, Breck's allies charged that the association lacked the authority to tell local congregations what they could and could not do. Writing on behalf of the association, Jonathan Edwards used Mather's book as a warrant for its intervention. Writing on behalf of Breck, William Cooper used the same book as a warrant for congregational precedence. Mather had become a player, posthumously, in colonial church politics (see Edwards 12: 111, 122, 138, 152).

By the late eighteenth century, the New England debate expanded to include liberal theologians who were beginning to move outside older Calvinist

---

16 For references to Mather in the debate with Whitefield, see Wigglesworth and Chipman (9), "Dr. Cotton Mather" (36), and Dunbar (28). For the discussion of itinerancy, see Chauncy's 1743 *Seasonable Thoughts* (58). For the antinomianism issue, see Dickinson's 1743 *A Defence of the Dialogue* (40) and Eells's 1745 *Religion is the Life of God's People* (38). On the question of preachers, see Niles's 1745 *Tristitae Ecclesiarum* (4, 12), Chauncy's 1742 *Gifts of the Spirit to Ministers* (29, 39), and Hancock's 1743 *Dangers of an Unqualified Ministry* (16). On praise for the clergy, see Chauncy, *Seasonable Thoughts* (142).

boundaries. The debates between liberals and conservatives raised again the question of the power of the associations. Traditionalist clergy wanted to use these organizations to stop liberal innovation. In 1815, a committee of the General Association of Churches in Massachusetts appealed to a manuscript that Mather had written to support his effort in 1705 to strengthen the power of associations of ministers to exercise "watch and care" over each other.[17] The manuscript was an early draft of a circular letter of a ministerial convention to the Congregational churches containing the substance of what came to be called the "Massachusetts Proposals." Mather apparently wrote the draft for a convention of ministers in 1704, for it was his granddaughter Hannah Mather Crockett who gave a copy of the original to William Jenks, a Congregational minister, who was also a member of the publications committee of the Massachusetts Historical Society. Jenks copied the manuscript and had it published in *The Panoplist* in July 1814 (320–21). Everyone assumed that Mather was the author. The conservatives on the Association committee cited the published manuscript in support of their desire to erect institutional safeguards against liberal innovations.[18]

Liberal critics attacked both the proposal and Mather's authority. The committee had no warrant, wrote John Lowell in an 1816 pamphlet, for bringing forth a manuscript of Cotton Mather "with as much parade as if he had been an apostle." Mather represented a "credulous age, and he partook, as largely as any man, of the imperfections of the times. ... What authority ought such a man to enjoy, in a state of society, in which his works can scarcely be read without a smile at his weakness and prejudices?" (40, 44, 59). Lowell charged that the conservatives were using the misreading of scripture in Mather's *Ratio Disciplinae* to further their own interests. As if in response, conservatives began to tout the virtues of Cotton Mather. By 1822 New Haven's *The Christian Spectator* in a "Review of New Publications" lamented that Mather – that "good man" – would have been deeply "wounded" if he could have foreseen liberal "reproaches" of the orthodox Puritan fathers (313).

In August, 1816, Jedediah Morse's *Panoplist*, the main journal of the conservatives in Massachusetts, began publishing excerpts from Mather's diary to acquaint readers with his piety (362, 495). In November, the journal set forth the "Reasons in Favor of a Consociation of Churches," elevating the authority of Mather as "one of the best ministers in Massachusetts." For the next twenty years, the liberals and the orthodox battled about the power of consociations. The publication of an 1820 edition of Mather's *Magnalia Christi Americana*,

---

17 The appeal appeared as "Report of the General Association," in the *The Panoplist* (1815).
18 The document also appears in Walker's *Creeds and Platforms of Congregationalism* (483–84).

which contained a discussion of associations,[19] was a reminder of Mather's position, and after Thomas Upham published his own *Ratio Disciplinae* in 1829, with frequent reference to Mather,[20] an article in the May 1831 issue of Lyman Beecher's journal *Spirit of the Pilgrims* suggested that every Congregationalist minister should have a copy ("Communion of Churches" 254). Many continued to recognize Mather's book as a guide to Congregational church government. They used it to defend Congregational polity, promote small group devotions, clarify the rights of members, regulate local church discipline, and support clerical education. But liberal clergy, wary of the conservative use of Mather, were no longer willing to look to him for much help on anything.[21]

By the 1820s, the Congregational churches in Massachusetts were veering toward liberalism, aided by an 1820 Massachusetts court decision that gave the liberal parish of Dedham the right to elect a liberal pastor despite the objections of the visible saints in the church. The Dedham quarrel returned Cotton Mather to the field of battle. Opponents of the court decision insisted – as defenders of the prerogatives of church members in Dedham had stated the matter in 1818 – that Cotton Mather rightly held "high authority in the church" ("Statement of the Proceedings in the First Church" 28), and that his *Ratio Disciplinae* gave churches, not civil bodies, the right to elect pastors. Friends of the court decision, however, found evidence in Mather's book that some New Englanders had always considered the church's claim to precedence as "odious and offensive." But the liberals had less and less use for the authority of Cotton Mather. They were especially adamant on the point that an antiquated book written in the eighteenth century should enjoy no overweening place in nineteenth-century church governance.[22]

Once begun, the campaign against Mather gained a life of its own. Even apart from the issue of the power of associations, the liberals saw Mather as a symbol of the religious dogmatism they were trying to escape. In a review of the "Lectures on Witchcraft," by Charles Upham, Jr., the Boston-based *Christian*

---

19 Mather discussed synods in the 1702 edition of *Magnalia Christi Americana* (bk 5, pp. 37–38, 45–46). When the Congregationalist minister Thomas Robbins republished the volume in 1820 as a gesture to both political and religious conservatism, the discussion of synods came once again to public view just as the Unitarian-Orthodox conflict was heating up. See Felker (87, 91, 93).

20 For Upham's references to Mather see, for example, *Ratio Disciplinae* (43, 103, 106, 142, 156, 170, 183, 186).

21 See the 1822 article by Laicus in the *Christian Watchman*. In the same year appeared Snell's "Result of Council" in the *Boston Recorder* and the anonymous article "Ecclesiastical," in the *Christian Register*; see also Chauncy, *Seasonable Thoughts* (416), Ross's 1773 *A Sermon* (49), and the 1816 pamphlet *The Controversy Between the Inquirer and Philo* (36).

22 The liberal responses are quoted from the 1821 "Article I," in *Christian Register*, and from the 1827 "Review: The Rights of the Congregational Churches of Massachusetts," in the *Christian Examiner*. For the court decision, see *A Statement of the Proceedings in the First Church* (28).

Examiner, the leading Unitarian journal, argued in 1831 that Mather had been "intensely disliked" even in his own day because of his "miserable vanity, coupled with jealousy" (241, 251). One caustic Unitarian speaker at Harvard named William P. Lunt assured his audience in 1851 that "no one of us would like to have Cotton Mather for a neighbor or for a spiritual guide." "Cotton Mather's brain," he said, "was all alive with maggots" (346). The lay theologian Orestes Brownson, having found a home in the Catholic Church after years of spiritual wandering, suggested in his satiric novel *The Spirit-Rapper* that Harvard "may have ceased to cherish his memory" and that the Second Church in Boston now "blushes" with embarrassment at the mention of his name (122). A reviewer for the *Christian Examiner* (using the abbreviation G. E. E.) pointed out in an 1856 article entitled "Review of A Half Century of the Unitarian Controversy," that Mather had tried to deny Congregationalists the use of the label "Independent." But our churches, the reviewer insisted, *were* indeed independent and our ministers are *now* independent (76). By implication, they were especially independent of the authority of Cotton Mather. By the 1850s the once radical opinion to which the Deist Philip Freneau had given poetic expression in the late eighteenth century had become the liberal consensus: "All pity the wretches that liv'd in those days/(ye modern admirers of novels and plays)/when nothing was suffered but musty dull rules/and nonsense from Mather, and stuff from the schools" (288).

The chief weapon in the Unitarian subversion of Mather's authority was the unceasing accusation that he had been the dark figure in the background of the 1692 witchcraft trials. The flogging of Cotton Mather for mismanaging the witchcraft episode had begun during his own lifetime when the Boston merchant Robert Calef published *More Wonders of the Invisible World* (1700) to ridicule him as the man whose recklessness and folly resulted in a fatal debacle. By the late eighteenth century, New England liberals had latched on to the witchcraft episode. A new printing of Calef's book appeared in 1797 with a Salem publisher. Two years later, the liberal minister William Bentley in Salem published a history of the town in which he argued that Mather and the other elders had been "too timid to speak, or perhaps too weak to think, until the destruction was sure" (267).

After the outbreak of the Unitarian controversy, liberal authors and journals found renewed reason to link Mather to witchcraft. How could a book written by "the most superstitious among the vulgar" in the witchcraft trials be allowed to determine how nineteenth-century rational Christians govern their churches? In 1816, the same year that Morse's *Panoplist* began to publish winsome excerpts from Mather's diary, the *North American Review*, controlled by the liberals, asserted in an anonymous review that Mather's "folly and his credulity were unlimited." No one, wrote the journal, had done more than Mather to "excite and renew the persecutions." Robert Calef had been as superior to

Mather "in reasoning as he was in good sense and courage" ("More Wonders of the Invisible World" 317).

Even after the battle about associations faded away, Mather remained the Unitarian example of orthodoxy's latent dangers and the chief exhibit for the prosecution was Salem. "In his writings," argued the anonymous writer of the 1825 article "The First Settlement of Our Country," which was published in the *Boston Monthly Magazine*, "we have specimens of the greatest fanaticism, the most shameless credulity, that ever escaped the lips or pens of mortals" (227). In 1831, a young Unitarian minister in Salem, Charles W. Upham, published his *Lectures on Witchcraft*, in which he charged that Mather had been "instrumental in causing the delusion" in 1692 as a way to promote religious revival. He had viewed the events "with secret pleasure" (107, 113–14). Significantly, the laudatory review of the lectures published in 1831 by the *Christian Examiner* put a special emphasis on "what relates immediately to Cotton Mather." It turned out that Upham's only shortcoming was that he had been "too generous" to Mather (245, 248). Three years later, George Bancroft, who had tried his hand at the Unitarian ministry before turning to Democratic Party politics and the writing of history, published the first volume of his *History of the United States*, in which he promoted Upham's view that Mather's yearning for "religious excitement," supplemented by his "boundless vanity," had prompted him to exploit the accusations against innocent people (1: 83–84, 95, 38). Critics of Bancroft derided the charge as "indecent," but by then, as one of Mather's defenders complained, Cotton Mather was firmly cast as a fanatic. ("The Salem Witchcraft" 64). Upham would later repeat the charges in his 1867 *Salem Witchraft* (2: 366–71) and defend them in his *Salem Witchcraft and Cotton Mather* (1869).[23]

Not everyone accepted the accusation that Mather was particularly to blame for Salem. An anonymous reviewer of Peabody's biography of Mather in *The North American Review* argued in 1840 that Mather simply shared the assumptions of his time (2), and when Samuel G. Drake reprinted in 1866 the documents of "the witchcraft delusion," he urged that his readers get beyond "vituperative denunciations" (lxx).[24] A few Americans tried to move back from the theological wars, and they reminded each other that Cotton Mather offered other possibilities. Mather had, after all, tried to escape theological wrangling by urging the combatants of his own era to unite around a few "essential maxims." In an article with the speaking title "Testimony of the Forefathers of New England, in Favour of Christian Charity and Against Illiberality and Bigotry," the *Christian Register* reminded its readers in 1821 that Mather had been the

---

23 For full bibliographic references and a sampling of other antebellum writings expressing similar opinions about Mather's role in the witch trials and his religious intolerance, see Appendix E.

24 A rather exceptional defense of Mather is Poole's 1869 "Cotton Mather and Salem Witchcraft."

author of *Blessed Unions* (1692), a book marked by "liberality" and the hope that all Christians could be "united in one profession" (78). The following year it quoted one of his ecumenical sentiments in an "Extract from Cotton Mather": "Now, if good men are so united in the maxims, which are the End, for the serving wherefore they declare that they pursue their controversies; why should not this uniting piety put an end unto their controversies?" (1). From the more conservative side, the Baptist James Winchell recalled that Mather had eventually accepted New England Baptists as "worthy Christians" and preached at the ordination of a Baptist minister in Boston (6–9). But Baptists and Quakers had long been critical of Mather, and some Baptist writers continued to depict him – in the words of a 1823 article on "Roger Williams" that appeared in the *Salem Gazette* – as a "bigoted" example of "intolerance" (20).[25]

By the 1850s, Mather was fair game for religious liberals. "Dr. Mather was a man of narrow views, a conceited heart, and unsound judgment" (Lossing 27). Dr. Mather's credulity was a "sore evil" (Knap 24). Dr. Mather was an example of "wretched fanaticism" (Berg 9). *The Southern Quarterly Review* was already using him in 1848 as an example of northern foolishness. He had, as an anonymous reviewer of the "Writings of Washington Irving" noted, published 382 books despite his "arduous duties of examining and burning witches, in which recondite science he was supposed to be more expert than any learned man of his day." Writers of this character, the article added, were "hardly calculated to inspire a respect for native [literary] productions" (73).

The popular mass magazines were even less restrained. Cotton Mather, wrote the editor of *Harper's New Monthly Magazine* in 1861, was "one of the dreadfulest" of a "grim, gloomy, severe race" ("Editor's Easy Chair" 556). The problem with going to heaven was being compelled to "endure the presence of Cotton Mather." Who could tolerate "the idiotisms of Cotton Mather"? ("Editor's Drawer" 422). By the 1850s Mather became a stock figure in popular fiction – a blue-nosed, persecuting, credulous, superstitious fanatic who cowered before ghosts and relentlessly pursued anyone accused of being a witch. Cotton Mather was a "good man," the reader's of *Harper's* "Editor's Easy Chair" were told in 1855, "and to that extent, an ass" (846).

Not only the hack writers of popular stories but also the classic figures of the New England literary renaissance used Mather to symbolize dogmatism, intolerance, and superstition. Nathaniel Hawthorne depicted him as the agent of the disaster in Salem, Washington Irving took pains to undercut his reputation, and Harriet Beecher Stowe dropped subtle hints that her respect for fig-

---

25   Mather's ecumenism is also foregrounded in Webster's 1772 *Ministers Labourers Together With God* (20) and in the 1834 article "Roger Williams," in *Princeton Review* (see Appendix C). For earlier critiques, see Arscott's 1734 *Some Considerations* (13), Bolles's 1756 *To Worship God* (72), Backus's 1764 *A Letter* (13–14), and *A History of New England* (253, 328, 355).

ures like Jonathan Edwards and Samuel Hopkins did not extend so far as to embrace Mather. Some of the serious New England authors used Mather's *Magnalia* as a source for wondrous tales and historical trivia, but they had more affection for the book than for the man.[26]

Drake's introduction to Mather's *Wonders of the Invisible World* assured readers that Mather was on the mend: "So far from the Reputation of Dr. Mather being in a Decline, his writings have never been so much sought after as at the present time. So much so that even reprints ... are at once taken up, and at high prices" (lxxi). Drake might have been right, but the books in demand by 1860 were not the theological texts that Mather would have liked to see in the bookstores. The most frequently reprinted books now were the documents from the witchcraft crisis. Throughout the earlier nineteenth century, these books had reappeared during periods of disillusionment with religious conservatism. Mather's *Another Brand Pluckt Out of the Burning*, a narrative of his pastoral care of the bewitched Margaret Rule, was reprinted in 1798, when religious liberalism was on the rise in New England, and in 1823 and 1828, during the Unitarian controversy. But by the 1850s and 1860s, when four more editions appeared, the documents of the Salem trials now served mainly purposes of historical curiosity. Mather was becoming a lens through which to peer at a benighted past. Between 1862 and 1866, publishers also issued four editions of Mather's *Wonders of the Invisible World*. By then he was known not primarily for his historical work, his natural philosophy, his eschatology, his angelology, his Calvinist doctrine, his biblical criticism, his ethics, his natural theology, or his treatment of the Christian evidences. He was not even remembered, in the popular imagination, for his devotional guides, his treatment of children's piety, or his ecumenical instincts. Cotton Mather was trapped in Salem. He suffered the ultimate abridgment.

APPENDIX A:

A Sampling of Booksellers' Catalogues and Advertisements with References to Works by Mather (Listed in Chronological Order; Page Numbers Indicate References to Mather)

Imported in the Last Vessels from England, and to be Sold by David Hall, at the New Printing Office, in Market Street, Philadelphia, the Following Books. Philadelphia: David Hall and William Sellers, 1768.

Beers, Isaac. *A Catalogue of Books, Sold by Isaac Beers, at his Bookstore in New Haven.* New Haven: Thomas and Samuel Green, 1791. 8.

---

26 Two particularly striking examples for negative fictionalizations of Mather are Herman Melville's "The Apple Tree Table, or, Original Spiritual Manifestations" (1856) and the anonymous "Alice–A Story of Cotton Mather's Times" (1849). For the literary constructions of Mather, see Buell (218–24, 233), Baker (8, 66), and Felker (106, 130, 276). Buell recognizes that the "hazing" of Mather was a "legacy of the Unitarian Controversy" (218).

Pelham, William. *A Catalogue of Books for Sale by W. Pelham*. Boston: E. Lincoln, 1802.
9.

Beecher, Lyman. *The Remedy for Dueling*. New York: J. Seymor, 1806. Advertisement,
53. "Works in the Press." *The Monthly Anthology and Boston Review* 5.14 (Apr. 1,
1808): 228.

Cooke, Oliver Dudley. *Hartford, Connecticut, Respectfully Offers to the Public the Following Select Catalogue*. Hartford: n.p., 1809. 2.

Comstock, Cyrus. *Essays on the Duties of Parents and Children*. Hartford: Oliver D.
Cooke, 1810. Advertisement, 344.

Fuller, Andrew. *The Great Question Answered*. New Haven: Increase Cook, 1810. Advertisement, 2.

Jameson, John. *The Use of Sacred History*. Hartford: Oliver Book, 1810. Advertisement,
490.

Hopkins, Samuel. *The System of Doctrines Contained in Divine Revelation*. Boston:
Lincoln and Edmands, 1811. Advertisement, 1056.

Catalogue of Books the Sale of Which Will Commune at Public Auction. Feb. 11, 1812.
New York: n.p., 1812. n.pag.

Amory, Francis. *Catalogue of a Large and Valuable Assortment of Books to be Sold,
Without Limitation, at the Store of Francis Amory*. Boston: Wells and Zilley, 1814.
13.

A Catalogue of Books, Offered to the Public by Oliver D. Cooke and Horatio G. Hale.
Hartford: Cooke and Hale, 1818. 10.

A Catalogue of Books, For Sale by Howe and Spalding, Booksellers ... New Haven, 1st
November 1818. New Haven: Flagg and Gray, 1818. 20.

"Excellent Assortment of Religious Books." *The Portsmouth Weekly Magazine* 1.43
(Apr. 13, 1825): 4.

The Book Buyer's Manual. New York: G. P. Putnam, 1852. 89.

APPENDIX B:

*A Sampling of Public and Private Library Holdings from the Antebellum Period with
References to Works by Mather* (Listed in Chronological Order; Page Numbers Indicate
References to Mather)

The Charter, Laws, and Catalogue of Books of the Library Company of Philadelphia.
Philadelphia: Franklin and Hall, 1765. n.pag.

Catalogue of Books in the Library of Yale College, New Haven. New Haven: T. & S.
Green, 1791. 22, 31, 37.

A Catalogue of Books, Belonging to the Library Company of Burlington [New Jersey].
Burlington: Isaac Neale, 1792. 34.

Catalogue of Books in the Massachusetts Historical Library. Boston: S. Hall, 1796. 10,
25–26.

Catalogue of Books in the Library of the American Academy of Arts and Sciences. Boston: n.p., 1802. 31, 35.

"For the Library." *The Boston Weekly Magazine* 1.29 (May 14, 1803): 117–18.

*By-Laws of the Proprietors of the Portland Library with the Names of the Proprietors,
and Catalogue of the Books*. Portland: Thomas B. Wait, 1806. 12.

Catalogue of Books Belonging to the Library Company of Philadelphia. Philadelphia: Bartram and Reynolds, 1807. 272, 592.

Catalogue of Books in the Theological Library, in the Town of Boston, March 1, 1808. Boston: Snelling and Simons, 1808. 22.

Catalogue of Books in the Library of Yale College, New Haven, January 1808. New Haven: Oliver Steele, 1808. 16, 41, 62, 65, 74, 76.

Catalogue of Books in the Boston Athenaeum. Boston: n.p., 1810. 106.

Catalogue of Books At The Washington Circulating Library. New York: Olmsted, Levy, 1810. n.pag.

Catalogue of the Books Belonging to the Salem Athenaeum. Salem: Thomas Cushing, 1811. 44.

Catalogue of the Books, Pamphlets ... in the Library of the Massachusetts Historical Society. Boston: J. Eliot, 1811. 29, 45–46, 54, 58, 85.

Catalogue of the Library of the Late Rev. J. S. Buckminster. Boston: John Eliot, Jr., 1812. 47.

Catalogue of the Books belonging to the Library of the Three Monthly Meetings of Friends of Philadelphia. Philadelphia: For the Society, 1813. 61.

Catalogue of the Library of the Late Rev. John Eliot. Boston: n.p., 1813. 10, 18.

The Constitution and By-Laws of the New Haven Library Company. New Haven: n.p., 1815. 15, 25, 26.

Catalogue of the Library of the United States. Washington, D.C.: Jonathan Eliot, 1815. 24.

Catalogue of Rare, Curious, and Valuable Books ... to be Sold at Auction at Francis Amory's Auction Room ... February 22, 1816, Being the Library of the late Reverend John Lathrop. Boston: n.p., 1816. 6, 7, 9, 10.

Catalogue of the Washington Circulating Library. Boston: T. Bangs, 1817. 9.

Torrey, Jesse. *The Intellectual Torch.* Ballston Spa, NY: Jesse Torrey, 1817. 29.

Catalogue of Books Belonging to the Hartford Library Company, April 1, 1818. Hartford: Hamlen and Newton, 1818. 25.

Catalogue of Valuable Books being the Library of the Late Rev. Samuel Cary of Boston. Boston: Munroe and Francis, 1818. 12, 15.

Catalogue of the Select Library of the late Rev. Joseph McKean. Boston: John Eliot, 1818. 28–37.

Catalogue of the Entire and Select Library of the Late Rev. Samuel Cooper Thacher. Boston: Wells and Lilly, 1818. 19–20.

Catalogue of the Library Belonging to the Theological Institution in Andover. Andover: Flagg and Gould, 1819. 92.

Jewett, Charles C. *Notices of Public Libraries in the United States of America.* Washington, D.C.: House of Representatives, 1851. 44.

A Classed Catalogue of the Cambridge High School. Cambridge: J. Bartlett, 1853. 225.

Catalogue of the Library of the City of Boston. Boston: J. Wilson and Son, 1854. 99.

Catalogue of the Mercantile Company of Boston. Boston: J. Wilson and Son, 1854. 163.

The Catalogue of the New York State Library. Albany: C. Van Benthuysen, 1856. 489.

A Catalogue of the Library of Bowdoin College. Brunswick: Bowdoin, 1863. 417.

The Alphabetical Library of the Library of Congress. Washington, D.D.: Government Printing Office, 1864. 742.

APPENDIX C:

A Sampling of Religious Tracts, Anthologies and Journal Articles Praising Mather's Works on Practical Charity, Devotion, and Family Religion (Listed in Chronological Order; Page Numbers Indicate References to Mather)

Chandler, Thomas Bradbury. *The Appeal Defended, Or the Proposed American Episcopate Vindicated.* New York: Hugh Gaine, 1769. 167.

Worcester, Francis. *A Bridle for Sinners and a Spur for Saints.* Boston: E. Russell, 1782. 13.

"Anecdotes." *Panoplist, or Monthly Missionary Magazine* 2.1 (June 1806): 31.

"Theology." *The American Register* 2 (Jan. 2, 1807): 166.

Collier, William. *Evangelicana, or Gospel Treasury.* Boston: Etheridge and Bliss, 1809. 307.

The Friendly Instructor. Boston: Lincoln and Edmonds, 1809. 81.

Griffin, John. *A Child's Memorial, or New Token for Children.* Charleston: S.T. Armstrong, 1809. 41.

Prince, Thomas. "Revival of Religion in Boston in 1740." *The Witness* 1.6 (June 1, 1809): 61.

Hutton, Joseph. *The New American Reader.* Philadelphia: David Hogan, 1813. 90.

Codman, John. *A Sermon on Prayer.* Boston: S.T. Armstrong, 1814. 11.

Twelve Witnesses to the Happy Effects of Experimental Religion on Life and Death. Boston: N. Willis, 1814. 187

Buck, Charles. *The Practical Expositor, or Scripture Illuminated by Facts.* Philadelphia: W.W. Woodward, 1815. 38.

"To the Editor of the Christian Minister." *The Christian Minister* 2.1 (Jan. 1, 1815): 8–11.

"Essays to Do Good." *Christian Monitor* 2.3 (Oct. 1816): 1.

Sampson, Ezra. *The Brief Remarker on the Ways of Man.* Hudson: Stone and Corss, 1818. 358.

"Good Devised." *Boston Recorder* 4.8 (Feb. 20, 1819): 32.

Mather, Cotton. "'Ministers of the Gospel.'" *The Religious Intelligencer* 7.18 (Sept. 28, 1822): 285.

"Cotton Mather a Distributor of Tracts." *The Spirit of the Pilgrims* 1.11 (Nov. 1828): 611.

"Hints Concerning Prayer Meetings." *The Princeton Review* 3.1 (Jan. 1831): 42.

"Roger Williams." *Princeton Review* 6.4 (Oct. 1834): 451–87.

APPENDIX D:

A Sampling of Writings Containing Criticism of the Magnalia Christi Americana (Listed in Chronological Order; Page Numbers Indicate References to Mather)

Hutchinson, Thomas. *The History of the Colony of Massachusetts Bay.* Thomas and John Fleet, 1764. 1.

Emerson, Joseph. *A Thanksgiving Sermon Preached at Pepperell, July 24, 1766.* Boston: Edes and Gill, 1766. 22.

Belknap, Jeremy. *American Biography*. Boston: Isaiah Thomas and Ebenezer Andrews, 1794. 155, 362.

Collections of the Massachusetts Historical Society for the Year 1795. Boston: Samuel Hall, 1795. 107.

Stiles, Ezra. *A Discourse on the Christian Union*. Brookfield: E. Merriam, 1799. 53, 68.

Adams, Hannah. *A Summary History of New England, From the First Settlement at Plymouth, to the Acceptance of the Federal Constitution*. Dedham: H. Mann and J.H. Adams, 1799. 31, 59.

"Collections of the Massachusetts Historical Society for the Year 1800." *The American Review and Literary Journal* 1.1 (Jan. 1, 1801): 314–15.

Holmes, Abiel. *The History of Cambridge*. Boston; Samuel Hall, 1801. 16, 41, 47, 49, 52, 54.

Morse, Jedediah and Elijah Parish. *A Compendious History of New England*. Charlestown: Samuel Etheridge, 1804. 14, 100, 102, 180.

Holmes, Abiel. *American Annals, or, A Chronological History of America*. Cambridge: W. Hilliard, 1805. 183.

Popkin, John Snelling. *Two Sermons on Quitting the Old and Entering the New Meetinghouse in the first Parish of Newbury*. Newburyport, MA: W. and J. Gilman, 1806. 62.

Allen, Timothy. *A Collection of American Epitaphs and Inscriptions*. New York: Whiting and Watson, 1812–14. 121.

Davis, John. *A Discourse Before the Massachusetts Historical Society, Boston, December 22, 1813*. Boston: John Eliot, 1814. 26, 30.

Smith, William. *History of New York*. Albany: Roger Schermerharn, 1814. 20.

Clinton, DeWitt. *A Discourse Delivered Before the New York Historical Society ... 6th December 1811*. New York: Van Winkle and Wiley, 1814. 58

Field, David O. *Centennial Address*. Middletown: W.B. Casey, 1853. 55.

Thompson, Pishey. *The History and Antiquities of Boston*. Boston: J. Noble, 1856. 412.

Goodrich, S.S. *Peter Parley's Pictorial History of North and South America*. Hartford, CT: Peter Parley Publishing, 1858. 422.

Spencer, J.A. *History of the United States*. New York: Johnson Fry, 1858. 60.

APPENDIX E:

A Sampling of Writings Blaming Mather for Salem and Religious Intolerance (Listed in Chronological Order; Page Numbers Indicate References to Mather)

Freneau, Philip Morin. *Poems Written Between the Years 1768 and 1794*. Mt. Pleasant: Freneau Press, 1795. 288.

Calef, Robert. *More Wonders of the Invisible World*. 1700. Salem: William Carlton, 1797.

Collections of the Massachusetts Historical Society for the Year 1798. Boston: Samuel Hill, 1798. 68.

Adams, Hannah. *A Summary History of New England, From the First Settlement at Plymouth, to the Acceptance of the Federal Constitution*. Dedham: H. Mann and J.H. Adams, 1799. 164

Bentley, William. "A Description and History of Salem." *Collections of the Massachusetts Historical Society for the Year 1799*. Boston: Samuel Hall, 1800. 266–67.

"Richard [sic. Robert] Calef." *The Port-Folio* 3.2 (Feb. 1810): 122.

"'Witchcraft of New England' from 'Knickerbocker's History of New York.'" *The Huntingdon Library Museum* 1.6 (June 1, 1810): 265.

"More Wonders of the Invisible World." *The North American Review and Miscellaneous Journal* 3.9 (Sept. 1816): 317.

"The First Settlement of Our Country." *Boston Monthly Magazine* 1.5 (Oct. 1825): 227.

"Review: The Rights of the Congregational Churches of Massachusetts." *Christian Examiner and Theological Review.* (Mar.-Apr. 1827): 128.

Knap, S.L. "The Mathers of New England." *Christian Watchman* 9.6 (Febr. 8, 1828): 24.

"Lectures on Witchcraft, Comprising a History of the Delusion in Salem in 1692, by Charles Upham, Jr." *Christian Examiner and General Review* 11.2 (Nov. 1831): 241, 245, 248, 251.

Bancroft, George. *History of the United States: From the Discovery of the American Continent.* Vol. 1. Boston: Little, Brown, 1834. 38, 83, 84, 95.

"Writings of Washington Irving." *The Southern Quarterly Review* 8.15 (June 1848): 73.

"Alice–A Story of Cotton Mather's Times." *The United States Democratic Review* 25.135 (Sept. 1849): 249–57; and 25.136 (Oct. 1849): 341–42.

Lunt, William P. "The Faculty of Imagination in its Relations to Religion." *Christian Examiner and Religious Miscellany* 53.5 (Nov. 1852): 346.

Berg, Joseph Friedrich. *Spirit Rappings: A Fraud.* Philadelphia: W.S. Young, 1853. 9

Brownson, Orestes A. *The Spirit-Rapper: An Autobiography.* Boston: Little, Brown, 1854. 122.

"Editor's Drawer." *Harper's New Monthly Magazine* 9.51 (Aug. 1854): 422.

"Editor's Easy Chair." *Harper's New Monthly Magazine* 11.66 (Nov. 1855): 846.

Lossing, Benson John. *Our Countrymen: Or, Brief Memoirs of Eminent Americans.* Philadelphia: Lippincott, Gambo, 1855. 27

G.E.E. "Review of A Half Century of the Unitarian Controversy." *Christian Examiner and Religious Miscellany* 60.1 (Jan. 1856): 76.

Melville, Herman. "The Apple Tree Table, or, Original Spiritual Manifestations." *Putnam's Monthly Magazine* 7.41 (May 1856): 456–76.

"Editor's Easy Chair." *Harper's New Monthly Magazine* 22.130 (Mar. 1861): 556.

Upham, Charles W. *Salem Witchcraft.* Vol. 2. New York: Frederick Ungar, 1867. 366–71.

Works Cited

Primary Sources

Adams, Hannah. *A Summary History of New England, From the First Settlement at Plymouth, to the Acceptance of the Federal Constitution.* Dedham: H. Mann and J.H. Adams, 1799.

–. *A View of Religions in Two Parts.* Boston: John West Folsom, 1791.

Arscott, Alexander. *Some Considerations Relating to the Present State of the Christian Religion.* Philadelphia: n.p., 1734.

"Article I." *Christian Register* 1.4 (Sept. 7, 1821): 15.

Backus, Isaac. *A History of New England*. Boston: Edward Draper, 1777–97.

–. *A Letter to the Reverend Mr. Benjamin Lord*. Providence: William Goddard, 1764.

Beecher, Lyman. *On the Importance of Assisting Young Men of Piety and Talent in Obtaining an Education for the Gospel Ministry*. Andover: Flagg and Gould, 1815.

Bellamy, Joseph. "Divinity of Jesus Christ." *Sermons Upon the Following Subjects, viz, The Divinity of Jesus Christ, The Millennium, The Wisdom of God in the Permission of Sin*. Boston: Edes and Gill, 1798.

–. "The Millennium." *Sermons Upon the Following Subjects, viz, The Divinity of Jesus Christ, The Millennium, The Wisdom of God in the Permission of Sin*. Boston: Edes and Gill, 1798.

Bolles, John. *To Worship God in Spirit and Truth*. New London: Timothy Greene, 1756.

Catalogue of Books in the Library of Yale College, New Haven. New Haven: T & S Green, 1791.

Chauncy, Charles. *The Gifts of the Spirit to Ministers*. Boston: Rogers and Fowle, 1742.

–. *Seasonable Thoughts on the State of Religion in New England*. Boston: Rogers and Fowle, 1743.

Church, John Hubbard. *The First Settlement of New England: A Sermon Delivered in the South Parish in Andover April 5, 1810*. Sutton: Sewall and Goodridge, 1810.

Clinton, DeWitt. *A Discourse Delivered Before the New York Historical Society ... 6th December 1811*. New York: Van Winkle and Wiley, 1814.

"Communion of Churches." *Spirit of the Pilgrims* 4.5 (May 1831): 245–56.

The Controversy Between the Inquirer and Philo on Christmas. Newburyport: William B. Allen, 1816.

Calef, Robert. *More Wonders of the Invisible World*. London, 1700.

"Cotton Mather on The Prayer of Faith." *Western Recorder* 2.43 (Apr. 26, 1825): 1.

Dickinson, Jonathan. *A Defence of the Dialogue Intitled, A Display of God's Special Grace*. Boston: J. Draper, 1743.

–. *The True Scripture Doctrine Concerning some Important Points of Christian Faith*. Boston: G. Rogers, 1741.

"Dr. Cotton Mather." *The Christian History* (Nov. 5, 1743): 36.

Drake, Samuel G., ed. *The Witchcraft Delusion in New England*. Roxbury: W. W. Woodword, 1866.

Dunbar, Samuel. *Righteousness By the Law Subversive of Christianity*. Boston: S. Kneeland, 1751.

"Ecclesiastical." *Christian Register* 1.45 (June 21, 1822): 1.

Edwards, Jonathan. "Charity and its Fruits." *The Works of Jonathan Edwards. Ethical Writings*. Ed. Paul Ramsey. Vol. 8. New Haven: Yale UP, 1989. 123–397.

–. "A Divine and Supernatural Light." *Sermons and Discourses, 1730–1733*. Ed. Mark Valeri. *The Works of Jonathan Edwards*. Vol. 17. New Haven: Yale UP, 1999. 405–27.

–. *A Faithful Narrative of the Surprising Work of God. The Works of Jonathan Edwards. The Great Awakening*. Ed. Clarence C. Goen. Vol. 4. New Haven: Yale UP, 1972. 97–211.

–.   *An Humble Attempt to Promote Explicit Agreement and Visible Union of God's People in Extraordinary Prayer. The Works of Jonathan Edwards. Apocalyptic Writings.* Ed. Stephen J. Stein. Vol. 5. New Haven: Yale UP, 1977. 307–436.

–.   "Notes on the Apocalypse." *The Works of Jonathan Edwards. Apocalyptic Writings.* Ed. Stephen J. Stein. Vol. 5. New Haven: Yale UP, 1977. 95–297.

–.   *A Treatise Concerning Religious Affections. The Works of Jonathan Edwards. Religious Affections.* Ed. John Smith. Vol. 2. New Haven: Yale UP, 1959. 84–461.

–.   *The Works of Jonathan Edwards. Original Sin.* Ed. Clyde H. Holbrook. Vol. 3. New Haven: Yale UP, 1970.

–.   *The Works of Jonathan Edwards. A History of the Works of Redemption.* Ed. John F. Wilson. Vol. 9. New Haven: Yale UP, 1989.

–.   *The Works of Jonathan Edwards. Ecclesiastical Writings.* Ed. David D. Hall. Vol. 12. New Haven: Yale UP, 1994.

Edwards, Jonathan Jr. "The Necessity of the Atonement and the Consistency Between that and Free Grace and Forgiveness." *Theological Tracts.* Ed. John Brown. 3 vols. London: Fullarton, 1853.

Eells, Nathaniel. *Religion is the Life of God's People.* Boston: S. Kneeland and T. Green, 1743.

Emerson, Joseph. *A Thanksgiving Sermon Preached at Pepperell, July 24, 1766.* Boston: Edes and Gill, 1766.

Explanation of Certain Phenomena Supposed to Be Supernatural. Boston: SPCK, Munroe, and Francis, 1815.

"Extract from Cotton Mather." *Christian Register* 2.1 (Aug. 16 1822): 1.

Franklin, Benjamin. *Essays, Works of the Late Doctor Benjamin Franklin.* Easton, MD: Henry Gibbs, 1810.

"From Miss Adams's View of Religions: Millenarians, or Chiliasts." *The Theological Magazine* 1.5 (Mar.-Apr. 1796): 377–82.

Gee, Joshua. *Israel's Mourning for Aaron's Death* Boston: S. Gerrish, 1728.

Goddard, Delano Alexander. *The Mathers Weighed in the Balances and Found Not Wanting.* Boston: Daily Advertiser, 1870.

Hancock, John. *The Dangers of an Unqualified Ministry.* Boston: Rogers and Fowle, 1743.

Hopkins, Samuel. *The Importance and Necessity of a Christians considering Jesus Christ in the Extent of his High and Glorious Character.* Boston: Kneeland and Adams, 1768.

–.   *An Inquiry into the Future State of Those Who Die in their Sins.* Newport: Solomon Southwick, 1783.

–.   *Treatise on the Millennium.* Edinburgh: G. Caw, 1806.

Janeway, James. *A Token for Children.* Boston: Z. Fowle, 1771.

Kendal, Samuel. *A Sermon Delivered at Weston on the Termination of a Century Since the Incorporation of the Town.* Cambridge: Hilliard and Metcalf, 1813.

Laicus. "Religious Association." *Christian Watchman* 3.51 (Nov. 30, 1822): 202.

Lowell, John. *An Inquiry into the Right to Change the Ecclesiastical Constitution of the Churches of Massachusetts.* Boston: Wells and Lilly, 1816.

Mahan, Asa. *Modern Mysteries Explained and Exposed.* Boston: J.P. Jewett, 1855.

"Massachusetts Proposal." *The Panoplist and Missionary Magazine* 10.7 (July 1814): 320–21.

"*Mather's Diary.*" *The Panoplist, or Monthly Missionary Magazine* 12.8 (Aug. 1816): 362.

Mather, Cotton. *Another Brand Pluckt Out of the Burning.* In Robert Calef.

–. *Bonifacius: Essay Upon the Good, That is to Be Devised and Designed.* 1710. Ed. David Levin. Cambridge: Harvard UP, 1966.

–. *The Case of a Troubled Mind.* Boston: B. Green for S. Gerrish, 1717.

–. *The Christian Philosopher.* 1721. Ed. Winton U. Solberg. Urbana: U of Illinois P, 1994.

–. *The Christian Philosopher.* Rev. ed. William Collins. Charlestown, MA: Thomas M'Kown, 1815.

–. *Coelestinus: A Conversation in Heaven.* Boston: S. Kneeland, 1723.

–. *A Conquest Over the Grand Excuse of Sinfulness.* Boston: Timothy Green, 1706.

–. *The Converted Sinner.* Boston: Nathaniel Belknap, 1724.

–. *Corderius Americanus: An Essay Upon the Good Education of Children.* Boston: John Allen, 1708.

–. *Eleutheria: Or, An Idea of the Reformation in England.* London: n.p., 1698.

–. *Family Religion, excited and assisted.* Boston: n.p., 1707.

–. *Free Grace Maintained and Improved.* Boston: B. Green, 1706.

–. *Icono-clastes: An Essay Upon the Idolatry Too Often Committed.* Boston: John Allen, 1717.

–. *Magnalia Christi Americana: Or, The Ecclesiastical History of New England.* 1702. New York: Arno Press, 1972.

–. *A Man of Reason: a brief essay to demonstrate that all men should hearken to reason.* Boston: John Edwards, 1718.

–. *Manuductio ad Ministerium.* Boston, Thomas Hancock, 1726.

–. *Ornaments for the Daughters of Zion.* Boston: S. G. B. for Samuel Phillips, 1691.

–. *Paterna: The Autobiography of Cotton Mather.* 1699–1702, 1717–1727. Ed. Ronald A. Bosco. Delmar, NJ: Scholars Facsimiles and Reprints, 1976.

–. *Ratio Disciplinae Fratrum Nov-Anglorum: A Faithful Account of the Discipline Professed and Practiced in the Churches of New England.* Boston: S. Gerrish, 1726.

–. *Reason Satisfied: and Faith Established.* Boston: John Allen for S. Boare, 1712.

–. *Reasonable Religion: Or The Truth of the Christian Religion Demonstrated.* Boston: T. Green for Benjamin Eliot, 1700.

–. *A Seasonable Testimony to the Glorious Doctrines of Grace.* Boston: n.p., 1702.

–. *Theopolis Americana.* Boston: B. Green, 1710.

–. *Things for a Distress'd People to Think Upon.* Boston: B. Green and J. Allen, 1696.

–. *The Threefold Paradise of Cotton Mather: An Edition of the "Triparadisus".* Ed. Reiner Smolinski. Athens: U of Georgia P, 1995.

–. *Token for the Children of New England.* Boston: Timothy Green, 1700.

–. *Unum Necessarium: Awakenings for the Unregenerate.* Boston: B. H., 1693.

–. *Vital Christianity: A Brief Essay on the Life of God.* Charles-Town: Samuel Kilmer, 1725.

–. *A Warning to the Flocks Against Wolves in Sheeps Cloathing.* Boston: n.p., 1700.

–. *The Wonders of the Invisible World.* Boston: Benjamin Harris for Sam Phillips, 1693.

Mather, Samuel. *The Life of the Very Reverend and Learned Cotton Mather, D. D., F. R. S., Late Pastor of the North Church in Boston.* Boston: Samuel Gerrish, 1729.

Memoir of Nathanael Emmons. Boston: Congregational Board of Publication, 1861.

Niles, Samuel. *Tristitae Ecclesiarum: Or, A Brief and Sorrowful Account of the Present State of the Churches in New England*. Boston: J. Draper, 1745.

"On the Prevalence of Socinianism." *Hopkinsian Magazine* 1. 12 (Dec. 1824): 270–76.

Peabody, William B.O. *Life of Cotton Mather*. Boston, 1844.

"Prayer of Faith." *Recorder and Telegraph* 10.17 (Apr. 22, 1825): 65.

Prince, Thomas. Preface. *The Life of the Very Reverend and Learned Cotton Mather*. By Samuel Mather. Boston: Samuel Gerrish, 1729.

Poole, William. "Cotton Mather and Salem Witchcraft." *North American Review* 108 (Apr. 1869): 337–96.

"Report of the General Association." *The Panoplist, or Monthly Missionary Magazine* 11.8 (Aug. 1815): 236–45.

"Review Article IX." *The Christian Disciple and Theological Review* 2.10 (July 1, 1820): 257–87.

"Review of New Publications." *Christian Spectator* 4.4 (June 1, 1822): 299–318.

"Review: The Rights of the Congregational Churches of Massachusetts." *Christian Examiner and Theological Review* (Mar.-Apr. 1827): 124–53.

"Review of Life of Cotton Mather By William B.O. Peabody." *North American Review* 108 (July 1840): 1–23.

"Roger Williams." *The Salem Gazette* 2.5 (Feb. 1, 1823): 20.

Ross, Robert. *A Sermon Preached at Newtown, December 8th, 1773, on Church Government and Church Discipline*. New Haven: Thomas and Samuel Green, 1773.

"The Salem Witchcraft," *The American Whig Review* 311 (January 1846): 60–68.

Sargent, Epes. *Peculiar: A Tale of the Great Transition*. New York: Carleton, 1864.

Seiss, Joseph Augustus. *The Last Times and the Great Consummation*. Philadelphia: Blakeman and Mason, 1863.

Snell, Thomas, et al. "Result of Council." *Boston Recorder* 7.4 (Jan. 26, 1822): 16.

A Statement of the Proceedings in the First Church and Parish Respecting the Settlement of a Minister. Dedham: n.p., 1818.

Stevens, Abel. *The History of the Religious Movement in the Eighteenth Century, Called Methodism*. New York: Carlton and Porter, 1858.

Stiles, Ezra. *A Discourse on the Christian Union*. Brookfield: E. Merriam, 1799.

–. *The Testimony of a Number of Ministers Convened at Taunton, in the County of Bristol, March 5, 1744–45*. Boston: S. Kneeland and T. Green, 1745.

"Testimony of the Forefathers of New England, in Favour of Christian Charity and Against Illiberality and Bigotry." *Christian Register* 1.20 (Dec. 28, 1821): 78; 1.21 (Jan. 4, 1822): 82.

Tocqueville, Alexis de. *American Institutions and their Influence*. New York: A.S. Barnes, 1851.

Uhden, Hermann Ferdinand. *The New England Theocracy*. Boston: Gould and Lincoln, 1858.

Upham, Thomas C. *Ratio Disciplinae or the Constitution of the Congregational Churches*. Portland, ME: Shirley and Hyde, 1829.

Walker, Williston. *The Creeds and Platforms of Congregationalism*. New York: Charles Scribner's Sons, 1893.

Webster, Samuel. *Ministers Labourers Together With God*. Salem, MA: S. & E. Hall, 1772.

Winchell, James M. *Jubilee Sermon*. Boston: Truer Weston, 1819.

Whitefield, George. *The Testimony of a Number of Ministers Convened at Taunton.* Boston: S. Kneeland and T. Green, 1745.

Wigglesworth, Samuel and John Chipman. *Remarks on Some Points of Doctrine.* Boston: S. Kneeland and T. Green, 1746.

Willson, James R. *A Historical Sketch of Opinions on the Atonement.* Philadelphia: Edward Earle, 1817.

Secondary Sources

Baker, Dorothy Z. *America's Gothic Fiction: The Legacy of Magnalia Christi Americana.* Columbus: Ohio UP, 2007.

Buell, Lawrence. *New England Literary Culture: From Revolution through Renaissance.* Cambridge: Cambridge UP, 1986.

Felker, Christopher D. *Reinventing Cotton Mather in the American Renaissance: Magnalia Christi Ameriana in Hawthorne, Stowe, and Stoddard.* Boston: Northeastern UP, 1993.

Ferm, Robert L. "Jonathan Edwards the Younger and the American Reformed Tradition." Diss. Yale U, 1958.

Holifield, E. Brooks. *Theology in America: Christian Thought from the Age of the Puritans to the Civil War.* New Haven: Yale UP, 2003.

Holmes, Thomas James. *Cotton Mather: A Bibliography of His Work.* 3 vols. Cambridge: Harvard UP, 1940.

Levin, David. "The Hazing of Cotton Mather." *New England Quarterly* 36 (1963): 147–71.

–. "Trying to Make a Monster Human." *Forms of Uncertainty: Essays in Historical Criticism.* Charlottesville: U of Virginia P, 1992. 157–76.

Lovelace, Richard. *The American Pietism of Cotton Mather: Origins of American Evangelicalism.* Grand Rapids: Christian UP, 1979.

Mares, Jeffrey ed. "Cotton Mather's 'Problema Theologicum': An Authoritative Edition." *Proceedings of the American Antiquarian Society* 104.2 (1994): 334–430.

Miller, Perry. "A Note on the *Manuductio ad Ministerium.*" *Cotton Mather: A Bibliography of His Works.* Ed. Thomas James Holmes. Vol. 2. Cambridge: Harvard UP, 1950). 634.

Morgan, Edmund S. *The Gentle Puritan: A Life of Ezra Stiles, 1727–1795.* New Haven: Yale UP, 1962.

Silverman, Kenneth. *The Life and Times of Cotton Mather.* New York: Harper & Row, 1984.

Smolinski, Reiner. "How to Go to Heaven, or How Heaven Goes? Natural Science and Interpretation in Cotton Mather's 'Biblia Americana' (1693–1728)." *New England Quarterly* 81.2 (2008): 278–329.

–. "*Israel Redivivus*": The Eschatological Limits of Puritan Typology in New England." *New England Quarterly* 63.3 (1990): 357–95.

Solberg, Winton U. Introduction. *The Christian Philosopher.* By Cotton Mather. Ed. Winton U. Solberg. Urbana: U of Illinois P, 1994. xic-cxxxiv.

Stievermann, Jan. "Writing 'To Conquer All Things': Cotton Mather's *Magnalia Christi Americana* and the Quandary of Copia." *Early American Literature* 39.2 (2004): 263–99.

Section 2: Mather in the Context of
International Protestantism

Francis J. Bremer

New England Puritanism and the Ecumenical Background of Cotton Mather's "Biblia Americana"

In 1979 Richard Lovelace effectively argued for a strong connection between the American Pietism of Cotton Mather and German Pietism. In doing so he made a major contribution to our understanding of Cotton Mather and also to the Atlantic dimension of colonial American religious history in general. Since then numerous scholars have emphasized Mather's engagement with the best learning of his age and particularly the pietist movement. Winton Solberg's edition of Mather's *The Christian Philosopher* (1994) and Reiner Smolinski's edition of *Triparadisus* (1995) are notable in this regard. Many of the others who gathered in Tübingen in 2008 to discuss Mather's "Biblia Americana" have also made significant contributions to our understanding of the transatlantic scholarly and religious communities in which Mather operated. All too often, however, the focus on Mather and Pietism has been presented as something new and unprecedented. Ernst Benz, in his classic studies of the "Ecumenical Relations between Boston Puritanism and German Pietism," asserted that until the eighteenth century "the established churches of the continent and the Puritan churches of New England had viewed each other with suspicion" and that productive contact between Continental divines and colonial clergy was only possible in the first two decades of the eighteenth century (162).[1] Some scholars have noted that there were strains in puritanism that anticipated these connections,[2] but by focusing on Mather they have often over-emphasized the Boston clergyman's agency as opposed to examining the roots of such an engagement. This essay makes the case that Mather's ecumenical interests were actually the product of a long history of puritan contacts with Continental reform.

---

1 Benz's other important study is his article "Pietist and Puritan Sources of Early Protestant World Missions," which equally emphasizes Cotton Mather's trailblazing role in bringing New England into the ecumenical network of international Protestantism. A similar interpretation can be found in Lovelace's recent essay, "Cotton Mather." Though both scholars underestimate the roots of such ecumenism, they make significant contributions to our understanding of Mather's links to Continental reformers.

2 The terms "puritanism," "puritans," and "puritan" will be lower-cased throughout this essay to emphasize that there was no institutional identity or official body of beliefs among the manifold and very heterogeneous groups of church reformers in England during the sixteenth and seventeenth centuries.

The failure to recognize the historical roots of Mather's interests and activities in this regard are largely attributable to the failure of American historians to appreciate the transatlantic dimension of the history of early New England. While some specialists such as David Hall and Michael Winship have empha- sized the international aspects of puritan thought, too many have portrayed the seventeenth-century New England colonies as alienated from European reli- gious movements. Even Perry Miller argued that early in their history the colo- nists turned their backs on English puritanism when their one time allies moved towards accepting toleration.[3] But the fact is that from its earliest roots through the seventeenth century and on into the Great Awakening, puritan clergy main- tained important contacts with Continental colleagues and pursued with them the goals of a united Christendom and the creation of a "holy and happy socie- ty." Two points are critical here: it is important to examine actual contacts, and not simply the familiarity of one individual with the works of another; more- over, we should recognize that contact did not necessarily mean agreement, but the existence of creative dialogue.

The wellspring of puritan international ecumenism is to be found in the early history of the Church of England. This is a point that was made over sixty years ago by Franklin L. Baumer in his studies of English views of the body of Christendom and over forty years ago by John T. McNeil in his study of *Unitive Protestantism*. Though we rightly think of the Church of England as a national church governed by the reigning monarch, Archbishop Thomas Cranmer and other leaders of the church were committed to the search for Christian unity. Those links were further strengthened when Cranmer invited Martin Bucer to be Regius Professor of Divinity at Cambridge and the Italian Protestant Peter Martyr to hold the Regius chair of Divinity at Oxford. Both became actively involved in trying to shape the English church in ways that drew it towards the Continental Reformation. Rudolf Gwalther, the Zurich theologian, recorded his contacts he made on a visit to England in his unpublished "Ephimerides Peregri- nationes." He became a key figure in communicating between Cranmer and the Swiss reformers (see Gordon). Another key figure in keeping the English church engaged with Continental Protestant thought was John a Lasco (Jan Łaski), who was named superintendent of the Strangers' Church in London in 1550, oversee- ing congregations of a Dutch church and a congregation of French Walloons. Lasco returned to Poland at the accession of Queen Mary, but his *Forma ac Ratio* (1555), which set out the forms of worship of the Stranger Churches, in- fluenced English puritans in Elizabeth's reign, as well as Scottish, Palatinate,

---

3   For examples of studies that clearly include a transatlantic dimension, see D. Hall's *The Faithful Shepherd*, Bremer's *Congregational Communion*, Winship, and Bozeman. Based in part on an erroneous dating of a key source, Miller argued in *Errand into the Wilderness* that the colonists turned their backs on English puritans in the 1640s, a mistake that has been made by others, including, most recently, by Carla Pestana.

and Dutch Protestants. In 1552, Cranmer tried to persuade Heinrich Bullinger, John Calvin, and Philipp Melanchthon to come to England to join him in an international church council comparable to the Catholic Council of Trent.[4]

During the reign of Queen Mary, many English Protestants found refuge on the Continent, where they engaged in discussion with divines such as Calvin, Bullinger, and Melanchthon as well as observed local religious practices at work. Relationships formed at this time continued after the exiles returned home with the accession of Queen Elizabeth. During the vestinarian controversy of 1566, English authors on both sides of the quarrel appealed to the works of Continental divines (Milton 109–11). At the same time, the license given to communities of foreign Protestants to establish their own congregations in England provided opportunities to further dialogue between English Protestants and Continental faiths. London reformers were particularly engaged with the reestablished "stranger churches."

During the course of Elizabeth's reign it was the proponents of further reform, increasingly called puritans, who were most engaged with Continental leaders. Their concern for practical piety, their fierce anti-Catholicism, and their interest in millennial speculation – all provided common ground with Continental reformers, as did the interest that some puritans displayed in educational reform, alchemical speculation, and scientific advances. Forced to leave England because of his criticisms of the inadequacy of church reforms in 1574, Thomas Cartwright matriculated as a student at the University of Heidelberg, where he met and exchanged views with divines such as Caspar Olevian, Immanuel Tremellius, Jerome Zanchius, Zacharias Ursinus, and Franciscus Junius. When the Calvinist Elector of the Palatinate died and was succeeded by the Lutheran Ludwig VI, Cartwright left the Palatinate, resettling first in Basel, and then in Antwerp before he was able to return to England. In all he spent twenty years on the Continent, and his engagement with international Calvinism was reflected in his correspondence and his published works.[5]

William Ames was another English puritan who spent much of his career abroad. Suspended from his positions at Cambridge because of his puritanism, Ames first settled in The Hague as chaplain to Sir Horace Vere, the commander of English forces in the Netherlands. He became engaged in the debates within Dutch Calvinism as an opponent of the teaching of Arminius and served as an adviser to Johannes Bogerman, the presiding clergyman at the Synod of Dort. This led to his appointment as professor of theology at the University of Franeker, where he taught from 1622–1633. English students matriculated at Franeker to study under Ames, as did young men from the Continent. Dozens of Hun-

---

4 The best source of information for these connections during the reigns of Henry VIII and Edward VI is McCullough.
5 For the standard biography of Cartwright, see Pearson.

garian students travelled to Franeker to study under Ames, and through them English practical divinity was introduced into the schools in their homeland (Murdock 59–60). Ames achieved an international reputation among Reformed theologians, yet continued his engagement with the English puritan movement. William Perkins, yet another Englishman commonly identified as a puritan, had an impact on Continental Protestantism through his 1597 *A Reformed Catholicke*, in which he set forth the doctrines that distinguished true Protestantism from the teaching of Rome (see Jinkins).

One of the ways in which the ties that bound English puritans to international Protestantism were forged and sustained in the early seventeenth century was through students studying abroad. English students were most likely to journey to the Netherlands, and over nine hundred enrolled at the University of Leiden alone between 1575 and 1675 (Milton 112). Among them was Francis Rous, who became a prominent lay puritan in the events leading to and following upon the English Civil Wars (Van Den Berg 26). And students came from the Continent to study in England especially after 1618, as refugees from the Thirty Years War sought a haven in England. One such was John Nicolaus Rulice, who left Heidelberg in the early 1620s, staying briefly at Cambridge, and then taking up residence with John Cotton in Boston, Lincolnshire. He eventually returned to the Continent and settled in Holland. Maximillian Teelinck also prepared for the ministry in Cotton's household. Teelinck returned to the Continent and became minister at Vlissingen. He introduced another Dutch minister, Timothy Van Vleteren, to Cotton. Peter Griebius was a German student described by Cotton as "a good young man," who studied with Ames at Franeker and then with Cotton in Boston, England. He later settled in Middelburg and translated the Dutch liturgy into English. Though most of Cotton's correspondence from this period has not survived, what remains contains references to other young men from the Continent who stayed with him and became correspondents with whom he would continue to discuss the concerns of international reform.[6] Cotton was not the only English puritan who took Continental Protestant youth into his domestic academy, though his engagements with Continental scholars may have been of particular importance for his grandson, Cotton Mather. Jonas Proost studied with Thomas Gataker, and Wilhelm Thilenius attended Richard Blackerby's academy. Before he became a preacher in Heidelberg, John Rulice was an assistant to John White in Dorchester, England. White also sheltered refugees from the Palatinate in the early 1630s. John Davenport supported the studies in England of Bernhard Decker, the son of a deceased professor of theology at the University of Heidelberg (Grell 70, 181, 195).

Some of those who studied with Cotton may have been directed there by a group of London reformers who were actively engaged in the affairs of Conti-

---

6   The surviving correspondence has been well collected and edited by Bush.

nental Protestantism. In 1626 four London puritan clergymen – Thomas Taylor, Richard Sibbes, William Gouge, and John Davenport – issued a circular letter calling for assistance to relieve the

> lamentable distress of two hundred and forty godly preachers with their wives and families of about four score desolate widows and sundry thousands of godly private persons with them cast out of their houses and home, out of their callings and countries, by the fury of the merciless papists in the upper Palatinate, whose heavy condition is such as they are forced to steal up their exercises of religion in woods and solitary places, not without continual fear and danger of their lives, and whose grievous want is such as they would be very thankful for coarse bread and drink if they could get it. (Davenport 26–27)

The concerns of these English puritans may have been heightened by the reports of Samuel Hartlib, who would become a key figure in furthering the connection of English puritans with Continental clergy. Hartlib had been born and raised in Elbing (Poland), but by 1625 was in England, studying at Cambridge under the tutelage of John Preston, one of the leaders of the puritan movement. Shortly thereafter he moved to London and began to weave a network of international correspondents dedicated as he was to the advancement of knowledge in general as well as the cause of international Protestantism. By the 1630s he had organized a newsletter service, the *Ephemerides*, which provided information about books, scientific discoveries, educational proposals, and the state of religion to correspondents throughout Europe. Hartlib knew Davenport and the other authors of the clerical circular letter seeking support for Protestant refugees. He may have provided them with some of their information, and he himself took in some of the refugees.

On a visit to Elbing, in 1627, Hartlib met the clergyman John Dury, who became a friend and key member in the Hartlib circle. Dury was the son of a Scottish minister who had been banished from Scotland and took up residence in the Netherlands. Educated in Leiden and at the Huguenot academy in Sedan, France, Dury was for a time the preacher at the Walloon Reformed church in Cologne before settling in Elbing. His exposure to various Reformed traditions fueled a lifelong dedication to trying to bring about a union of all Protestants and, potentially, a united and reformed Christendom, a campaign that would be supported by many English puritan clergy and laymen (Grell 183).[7] The principal strategies espoused by Hartlib and Dury were the promotion of practical divinity as opposed to a doctrinal approach and the establishment of a set of fundamental doctrines on which all Christians could agree. In these efforts they anticipated similar projects among puritans of Cotton Mather's generation, who sought to unify Christianity under an *Evangelium Aeternum* that he eventually reduced to as few as three maxims (see Benz "Ecumenical Rela-

---

7   Lady Barnardiston left a legacy to Dury to support his work.

tions"). Pointing to the words uttered to Daniel that at the onset of the millennium, "Many shall run to and fro, and knowledge shall increase" (Dan. 12:4), the "Great Instauration," which Hartlib and his associates promoted, was a rapid growth in all forms of learning that they believed would precede the second coming of Christ. Joining Hartlib and Dury in seeking to advance these irenic goals was the Moravian Calvinist Jan Amos Comenius, whom Hartlib had first heard about from Moravian missionaries.

Comenius sought to effect "world reformation through a collaborative and systematic effort to identify the fundamental principles underlying all knowledge" (Woodward 53–54).[8] His "Pansophism" was influenced by the writings of reformers such as Tomasso Campanella, J.V. Andrae, Francis Bacon, and Comenius's professor at the academy of Herborn in Nassau, Johann Heinrich Alsted. Hartlib became deeply engaged in the early 1630s in trying to advance the educational reform ideas of Comenius, who believed that learning and spiritual growth were linked and sought to reform education as a means of promoting religious truth. His goal, as he expressed it, was "nothing in fact less than the improvement of all human affairs, in all persons and everywhere." One of the radical elements of this program was the belief that education was for all men and women, not, as he put it, "that all men should become learned but that all men may be made wise unto salvation." With basic education ordinary men and women would be able to read the scriptures, sift truth from error, and strive for moral and religious perfection, "embracing of that Golden Age of light and knowledge, which hath been so long foretold." That light and knowledge would include greater insight into the natural world, which Comenius referred to as "the first and greatest book of God" (qtd. in Woodward 59).[9] This fit in smoothly with Hartlib's interest in promoting and publicizing scientific discoveries and technological innovations. As they later would be by Cotton Mather, millennialism, the advancement of science, and universal religious reform were perceived as shared objectives by the members of the Hartlib circle. The Hartlib Papers are filled with comments on Continental and English clergy and their works as well as numerous examples of efforts to unite Christendom. They informed their subscribers of projects to work towards a common Protestant catechism, Gustavus Adolphus's interest in a harmony of doctrinal confessions, news from the Swiss churches, comments on useful works of practical divinity, the preparation of concordances that would contribute to a common interpretation of scriptures, and much more. Because of our interest in tracing a path to Cotton Mather, I want to focus on information gleaned from those collections

---

8   Dr. Woodward's important work was just published by the University of North Carolina Press. The page references here are still to the dissertation.

9   For more on these interactions, see Hotson, *Johann Heinrich Alsted* and *Paradise Postponed*.

that involve puritans who played a part in the colonization and development of New England.

The extent to which efforts to promote Protestant union influenced the course of English religious debates sheds much light on the character of puritanism at this time. Even as many puritans were increasingly concerned about the direction in which Charles I and his bishops were taking England and her church, their commitment to unity led them to accept a greater measure of conformity than they were comfortable with. Around 1624 John Davenport wrote a letter to Alexander Leighton, a member of the semi-separatist Jacobs Church in London, in which he argued that "when we consider the distresses of the reformed churches in these days, we shall soon conclude with him that said these are not times for disputing but for praying." Rather than disputing among themselves, he proposed it were better "to unite our forces against those who oppose us in fundamentals rather than to be divided among ourselves about ceremonials." "Who can," he asked, "without sorrow and fear, observe how atheism, libertinism, papism, and Arminianism, both at home and abroad, have stolen in and taken possession of the house whilst we are at strife about the hangings and paintings of it?" (Davenport 23–26).

As they sought to mute their differences with the national church, especially in areas of the country where they had sufficient autonomy to ignore disliked ceremonies, puritans had for some time been devoting their attentions to issues of practical divinity. These efforts had a considerable impact on the Continent. According to Anthony Milton they "provided a vital stimulus to the Dutch 'further reformation' (*andere reformatie*) – the movement to reform personal and public piety manifested in the works and actions of divines such as Voetius, Willem Teellinck," and others (118). Voetius was noted for close bonds with puritans (van den Berg 25). Teellinck, of course, had sent his son Maximillian to study with John Cotton and was a friend of Thomas Gataker. English puritan practical divinity also had an impact on what contemporaries referred to as "puritanism" in Hungary as well. Many leading Hungarian students came to England to study, some of them joining together in London in 1638 to form a "League of Piety" (see Milton 119). In Hungary itself, puritan influence was reflected in calls for tighter moral discipline, educational reforms, and a drive to reform liturgical practices (see Murdock 44).

Of course most Continental Protestants could not read works in English. Spurred by John Dury, members of the Hartlib circle organized an effort "to translate into Latin or compose such seasonable treatises" as needed by refugee clergy on the Continent who had lost their own libraries in the devastation of war and who were thus "destitute of the crumbs of those powerful helps" enjoyed by Englishmen. Among the subscribers recorded by Hartlib were a variety of puritan laymen and clergy, including John Stoughton, Richard Saltonstall, Peter Bulkeley, John Davenport, and Brampton Gurdon. The hope was that the tracts would be works of "spiritual divinity" rather than explorations of controversies, and would thus advance "love and peace," heal "divisions and great distractions," and "solder and unite their spirits" (Hartlib 23/2/17A–18B).[10]

Among the men who later crafted the New England puritan experiment, John Davenport was particularly engaged with the Hartlib circle. In 1630, in a letter to Dury in which he expressed the view that "moral wisdom is far to be preferred before anything which this world can afford," Hartlib rejoiced "greatly that you found Mr. Davenport so forward, earnest, and judicious in the work." Others who were recruited for the work included John Cotton, Philip Nye, Richard Sibbes, and John White (Hartlib 46/6/33A–b). In 1631 Davenport was one of the many signers of Dury's "Instrumentum Theologorum Anglorum," a subscribed letter advocating church unity. Indeed, until the rising Laudian tide made his position untenable, Davenport was noted for taking the position that Protestants must unite against the common Catholic foe rather than squabble among themselves.

Davenport's admiration for Dury led him to invite the reformer to join the Great Migration to Massachusetts. His exposure to the views of Comenius influenced his ideas about colonial education. Through these men Davenport also was exposed to the writings of Johann Valentin Andreae, Johann Arndt, Valentin Weigle, and Jakob Boehme (Archer 145). Members of the network shared their manuscript works with each other – for example, Dury lent Davenport his notes on Colossians (Hartlib 33/3/9A–10B) – and recommended works to one another. Hartlib and others in the network were noted for their philo-semitism.[11] Davenport likely explored this interest during his time in Amsterdam, and it has been suggested that the town plan of New Haven was derived from the current understanding of the layout of the Old Testament Jerusalem and the Temple (see Archer; Popkin 120–22).[12]

Davenport and others who sought to advance universal reform were also connected with the stranger churches in London. Dury and Hartlib were closely associated with the Dutch church at Austin Friars in London, and Hartlib

---

10 This and other references to the Hartlib Papers are drawn from the electronic edition prepared by Greengrass and Hannon for the University of Sheffield Humanities Research Institute in 2002. In 1638 one of the subscribers to Hartlib's newsletter service, the clergyman John Stoughton, wrote a millenarian tract about the church in Transylvania (Murdock 66). At the same time, puritan viewpoints were spread through the translation of various works into European languages. For instance, Istvan Telkibanyi translated William Bradshaw's *English Puritanism* and had it published in Utrecht in 1654 (Murdock 191). For puritan efforts to publish works of practical divinity for the benefit of Continental Protestants, see Peacey.

11 Referencing Katz, Walsham points to "the philo-semitism of intellectuals such as Samuel Hartlib and John Dury" (245). On this, see also Popkin.

12 For a discussion of Christian interest in discovering the design of the original Temple in Jerusalem, see Popkin.

may have been a member (Grell 135). Along with other puritans such as Hugh Peter, Stephen Marshall, and James Ussher, Davenport was in correspondence with Cesar Calandrini, the pastor of the Italian church in London (Grell 63–64).

From the mid-1620s on, the initiatives of the king and his bishops made conformity more and more difficult, and puritans such as John Cotton, Thomas Hooker, Hugh Peter, and John Davenport were forced from or abandoned their livings. The initial movement of many of these – including Peter, Hooker, and Davenport – was to relocate for a time to the Netherlands, where there were over twenty-five English Reformed churches recognized by the Dutch authorities, not to mention congregations centered on puritan chaplains serving with English regiments there. By the early 1630s, however, the pressure exerted by the English government on Dutch authorities made the situation of these exiles more difficult, leading to the decision to settle in New England. At the same time, indicative of his identification of his puritan enemies with Continental reform and his efforts to separate the Church of England from the Reformed tradition, Archbishop Laud sought to restrict the rights of the foreign "stranger churches" in England, referring to them as "nurseries of ill-minded persons to the Church of England" (qtd. in Murdock 65).[13]

Following their emigration to America, colonists sustained their ties with European allies and friends. Sometimes this had practical consequences – around 1634 Richard Saltonstall arranged with Dutch friends for a shipment of horses and cattle from Friesland to Massachusetts (Grell 183n45). For our purposes, we want to trace some of the intellectual exchanges. Following the outbreak of the English Civil Wars, the Parliament convened the Westminster Assembly in an effort to chart the reformation of the national church. Though not one of the original members of the Assembly, John Dury was soon added. These efforts were supported by New Englanders and also by the puritans' friends on the Continent.[14] In the Netherlands, regional synods observed days of fast and prayer on behalf of English reform, raised funds for the relief of distressed Englishmen, and petitioned the States General to support the English Parliament's efforts (Milton 115). New Englanders and Continental divines became engaged in the debates over Presbyterian and Congregational reforms being considered by the Westminster Assembly. For example, when the Dutch pastor William Apollonius wrote a sharp attack on Congregational principles, he was answered by the Massachusetts clergyman John Norton, whose defense of Congregationalism was published in London with an introduction by Thomas Goodwin, Philip Nye, and Sidrach Simpson (see Norton). Following the puritan triumph

---

13   Sprunger offers the best general treatment of the subject. Thomas Hooker's story can be found in Williams, et al. See also Bush and Shuffleton. I am currently working on a biography of John Davenport which will pay attention to his career in the Netherlands.

14   For New England's support, see Bremer, *Congregational Communion*.

in the Civil Wars, there were attempts to pursue strategies for uniting Protestantism during the Cromwellian Protectorate, including discussion between Cromwell and Transylvanian authorities about a proposed alliance of Protestant countries (Murdock 280).

During this period, John Davenport continued his contacts with his friends in the Hartlib circle. At one point he wrote to John Winthrop, Jr., that he had "received letters and books, and written papers from my ancient and honored friends Mr. Hartlib and Mr. Dury, wherein I find sundry rarities of inventions and projects for common good" which were "too many to be transmitted ... by passengers" (19 August 1659; Davenport 141–42). As late as 1660 Davenport was writing in support of Dury's ecumenical efforts. In a letter to Dury from that year, the New Haven clergyman expressed his concern about "those broils and strifes, and animosities, and schisms and scandals, which offend the weak and afflict the good, and are no little satisfaction to the enemies of Gospel-Truth" and his hope that the reformed churches throughout Europe and America would be "held together in the strictest bonds of Love and unity" (Davenport 175).

The millennial expectations of the Hartlib group led to particular interests in the American colonies. One of the early explanations proposed for the background of the Native Americans was the suggestion that they were the descendants of the lost tribes of Israel, which was significant in that one of the signs of the approaching millennium would be the conversion of the Jews. In a preface he wrote for Thomas Thorowgood's *Iewes in America* (1650), John Dury "waxed eloquent about the way God's direction of history was emerging in America and how this would lead to the reappearance of the lost tribes ... [,] the conversion of the Jews, the restoration of Jerusalem, and the millennium" (Popkin 125; see also Cogley 35–36). He inquired of Menasseh ben Israel about the Jewish view on the location of the lost tribes, and their correspondence led Menasseh to write *The Hope of Israel* (1650), in which he accepted that the evidence indeed indicated that at least one lost tribe had settled in America.

This belief spurred efforts to convert the Natives in New England. Many of the members of the Hartlib Circle were supporters of the Corporation for the Promoting and Propagating of the Gospel of Jesus Christ in New England, which was founded in 1649 to finance the efforts of John Eliot and others colonial missionaries.[15] Its successor, the Company for the Propagation of the Gospel, would include among its governors the scientist Robert Boyle. Both organizations played a key role in fostering transatlantic communications.

Through correspondence, Davenport introduced Hartlib to the younger Winthrop, who was particularly interested in the former's scientific connec-

---

15 See also Clark's new edition of Eliot's Indian tracts and Eliot's correspondence with English supporters.

tions. Hartlib helped Winthrop to expand his own contacts in England, which led to Winthrop's admission to the Royal Society and to him becoming a chief conduit through which the latest European thought was introduced into New England in the decades following the Restoration. Whereas Davenport was focused primarily on the religious thoughts of the age, Winthrop's interests included attention to the scientific discoveries of the age that would also characterize the lives of Increase and Cotton Mather. As a young man in England, Winthrop had, according to a recent student of his thought, been attracted to the Rosicrucian Movement, and its incorporation of "alchemy, geometry, mathematics, cabala and natural magic, and above all, religious and spiritual illumination, all in the service of millenarian reform" (Woodward 27). On one of his trips to England in the early 1640s, he met with intellectuals engaged in the pansophic movement in Amsterdam, The Hague, and Hamburg. Winthrop sought to draw upon the scientific insights of the age, including alchemy, to assist him in his efforts to develop the resources of New England and to further his medical practices. In Hamburg he became friends with Johannes Tanckmarus; in Wedel he met Johann Rist, a noted Hebrew scholar and mathematician; it was perhaps in Amsterdam that he was introduced to the Dutch Reformed minister and Comenius supporter Johann Moriaen. And it is likely that he met Comenius himself when he was in London (Woodward 62–71). These men and others he encountered became members of his friendship network.

One of the missed opportunities for New England involved the effort to establish in the region a university modeled on the ideas of Comenius. John Davenport, who had been impressed with the Moravian's educational program when he first encountered the ideas in England, had hoped to establish a college in New Haven from the early days of that colony. In 1643 he wrote to Hartlib seeking an update on Comenius's plans. In response Hartlib informed the New Haven clergyman of his own efforts to raise funds for a Comenian educational effort in the colonies.[16] Walt Woodward has suggested that if, as Cotton Mather recorded in the *Magnalia* (bk. 4, p. 14), Winthrop, Jr., had indeed invited Comenius to head a college in New England it was likely to have been a new venture in New Haven (where Winthrop had ties) rather than, as Mather indicated, Harvard (Woodward 170–72). While Comenius, if he was indeed offered such a post, turned it down, plans did go ahead for a New Haven College in the early 1650s, with Hartlib and Dury both being consulted. Two events brought the effort to an end: the decision of William Leveritch to decline an offer to assume the college presidency, and legal tangles that prevented the use of a legacy that Edward Hopkins had left for the purpose. But the character and purposes

---

16   Hartlib to Davenport, Hartlib Papers 7/35/1A–2B. Woodward correctly points out that it was Davenport, not Winthrop, Jr., who was the recipient of this letter (Woodward 192–236).

of the intended college were clearly shaped by the transatlantic exchanges between the colonists and European reformers.

While, as noted previously, Davenport expressed support for Dury's
schemes in 1660, and in 1658 had been in communication with John Beale (a
future member of the Royal Society) who wished him to compile a natural history of New England, there is little surviving evidence of his ongoing interaction with members of the Hartlib Circle in the post-Restoration era. Davenport
was committed to the losing battle to prevent New Haven from being absorbed
by its neighbor colony, Connecticut. He also fought against the Half-Way Covenant, and then engaged in the controversy that resulted from his acceptance of
the post of pastor of the First Church in Boston in 1668. Of course Hartlib had
died in 1662, and that disrupted the normal channels of communication among
the members of the circle. Dury had to leave England following the Restoration
because of his previous connections with the leaders of the puritan revolution.
His influence subsequently waned – or at least it appears to have done so, a conclusion that might be revised by a thorough examination of the neglected collections of his papers in Zurich.

But if Davenport's role in the international community of thinkers waned,
that of his friend John Winthrop, Jr., increased. During his 1661 visit to England
to secure a royal charter for Connecticut, Winthrop renewed friendships and
built further on those connections. He became the first colonist to be elected a
member of the new Royal Society, in part on the recommendation of Hartlib.
The extent of his communications with Robert Boyle and other members of the
Royal Society as well as other scientists and thinkers of the time has been obscured by the fact that the published volumes of the twentieth-century edition
of the *Winthrop Papers* only extends to 1653. And the attention given to the
contributions of the Royal Society to the burgeoning scientific revolution has
obscured the fact that, as a few scholars have noted, for many of its members,
their "vision of science, trade, empire and reformation" was wedded to a millenarian mood similar to that which had spurred Hartlib, Comenius, and others
earlier in the century. As suggested above, the conversion of the American Indians was a goal that attracted many of the members of the Royal Society and
was the subject of correspondence between Boyle and Winthrop (Woodward
337, 353).

Another figure emerged at this time as a key broker in the transatlantic
exchange of ideas, Increase Mather. Increase had journeyed to England in 1657,
following his graduation from Harvard. Availing himself of introductions to
the leading English thinkers of the time, he soon developed a network of friends
and correspondents that he retained after returning to Massachusetts in 1661. I
have previously written about Mather's network of friends and how it facilitated the exchange of religious, political, and scientific news and books between
New Englanders and England. My focus there was on Anglo-American rela-

tions, and I did not explore the Continental dimension of the network. But there was such a dimension. Mather's circle also included Continental thinkers such as Abraham Kick in Amsterdam and John Leusden in Utrecht. Some of his closest English friends, including Matthew Mead and John Howe, and his brother Nathaniel, spent some of the post-Restoration years in exile in the Netherlands. They immersed themselves in the Protestant community on the Continent and communicated their news to Mather (see Bremer, "Increase Mather's Friends").[17]

Mather had returned from England as the controversy over the Half-Way Covenant was commanding the attention of New Englanders. He had identified with John Davenport in opposition to the proposed change in baptismal practices. Though Davenport was not invited to the 1662 Massachusetts synod that debated the issue, he travelled to Boston and used Mather to present his views to the delegates. It was at this time that the two became close friends (M. Hall, *Increase Mather* 58). They had common correspondents in England such as Philip Nye and they shared manuscripts and news from abroad. Davenport included Mather in the close circle that had contact with the hidden English regicides Whalley and Goffe. When Davenport died many of his papers passed to Mather, and consequently some are to be found in the Mather Papers of the American Antiquarian Society. Included in these were copies of his correspondence with Dury and members of the Hartlib circle.[18] Mather also had access to Davenport's library of over 1,000 books.

In some respects Increase Mather combined the religious interests of John Davenport with the scientific interests of John Winthrop, Jr., a broad outlook that would also be characteristic of his son, Cotton Mather. Thus, in 1683 he and Cotton organized the Boston Philosophical Society, modeled after England's Royal Society. The effort pointed to the continuing interest of some New Englanders to remain engaged with the latest thinking of the age; its collapse after less than a year points to the fact that the number of New Englanders who shared such a commitment had dwindled over the course of the century (Solberg xxxiv).

It has generally been considered that Harvard was more open to some of the new sciences and ideas than Oxford and Cambridge. At Harvard, students like the young Cotton Mather were exposed to works such as the "Philosophical Exercises" of Adrian Heerebord of Leiden, who was a disciple of Descartes. The younger Mather became deeply interested in the latest scientific discoveries and what they implied for religion. His *Christian Philosopher* has been called

---

17 John Leusden dedicated his *Psalterium Hebraeo Latinum* to Increase Mather and made reference to the conversion of the natives.

18 Davenport's 1660 letter to Dury survives as copied by Cotton Mather in the *Magnalia Christi Americana* (bk. 3, pt. 1, pp. 54–55). The original was in the hands of Cotton's son Samuel in 1738 (Davenport 175 n1).

"the first comprehensive account of the physical and natural sciences written by an American" (Solberg xxi). Keeping abreast of the latest scientific and religious writings through his contacts in England and the Continent, he accumulated a library that exceeded three thousand volumes by 1700 (see Solberg xxvii). He was an avid reader of the *Transactions* of England's Royal Society and the works of its members such as John Winthrop's friend Robert Boyle. As was the case with the members of the Hartlib circle earlier, he saw scientific progress not as an end in itself but rather a means to bringing about general society reform and – as he tried to do with the "Biblia Americana" – achieve a better understanding of the scriptures. In an effort to promote his "Biblia Americana," he described it as "an American offer to serve the great interests of learning and religion in Europe" (qtd. in Solberg xxxix). Starting in 1712 he sent over eighty-two letters to the English Royal Society in which he described American scientific curiosities, and in 1713 he was chosen a Fellow of the Society (see M. Hall, "Cotton Mather"). Interestingly, he modeled his contributions after the scientific publications of the German philosophical society, which he referred to as the "German Ephemerides," a term that evokes the *Ephemerides* of Hartlib (Solberg xl).

At the start of the seventeenth century, many puritans who lacked the political power to impose their views on the nation sought to build the kingdom of God one convert at a time, through persuasion. They pursued a unitive Protestantism and emphasized practical divinity in preference to focusing on ceremonial and doctrinal issues that divided them from their fellow Englishmen and from reformers on the Continent. That practical divinity fed reform movements on the Continent, as close to England as the Netherlands and as far away as Transylvania. When they came into power in New England in the 1630s and in England during the Interregnum, the puritan focus shifted to efforts to set perimeter fences to distinguish acceptable belief and behavior from what was unacceptable. It is debatable if these efforts contributed to puritan progress or not, but the ability to impose their views came to an end with the Restoration of 1660 in England and the loss of the Massachusetts Charter in 1684. Once again puritanism became a movement that relied on persuasion to spread itself. As their predecessors had done earlier in the century, English clergy such as Richard Baxter emphasized the importance of unity over uniformity.

During his charter mission to England at the time of the Glorious Revolution, Increase Mather worked to unite the divided elements of the former puritan movement through the Heads of Agreement, producing the (briefly) Happy Union of Congregationalists and Presbyterians. During the latter seventeenth century puritans such as John Bunyan had rediscovered the value of practical divinity and appeals to personal piety, and this orientation persisted into the eighteenth century. In the case of Cotton Mather his turn towards practical piety was stimulated by his contacts with Richard Baxter and other English divines as well as Continental thinkers. It was clearly reflected in 1700 when he gave two weekday lectures on the imitation of Christ (Winship 81). But this commitment was strengthened through his contacts with Halle Pietism. In Mather's correspondence with August Hermann Francke he welcomed news of the "warmth from the fire of God, which ... flames in the heart of Germany" (qtd. in Lovelace, "Cotton Mather" 116).[19] He sent Francke a copy of his *Magnalia Christi Americana* and focused on the links between Halle Pietism and American Pietism. He embraced the leavening effects of Pietism in approaches that anticipated the Great Awakening.

As the essays in this collection demonstrate, Mather was anything but a provincial scholar with a narrow outlook. His range of knowledge and engagement with the writings of past authorities as well as his contemporaries place him firmly in the tradition of Dury and Hartlib, Davenport and Cotton.[20] But he was more than a scholar. In a stance that reminds us of the outlook of the puritan reformers of the previous century, he viewed all of his writings, including "Biblia Americana," as attempts to enlighten the mind as a prelude to warming the heart. In doing so, he was part of a long tradition of an Atlantic community of ecumenical Protestants who sought to deploy knowledge and piety to unite Protestants everywhere and ultimate move all men towards bringing about the kingdom of God on earth.[21]

Works Cited

Primary Sources

Bradshaw, William. *English Puritanism*. London, 1605.
Cotton, John. *The Correspondence of John Cotton*. Ed. Sargent Bush, Jr. Chapel Hill: U of North Carolina P, 2000.
Davenport, John. *The Letters of John Davenport*. Ed. Isabel M. Calder. New Haven: Yale UP, 1937.
Eliot, John. *The Eliot Tracts: With Letters from Eliot to Thomas Thorowgood and Richard Baxter*. Ed. Michael P. Clark. Westport: Praeger, 2003.
Hartlib, Samuel. *The Hartlib Papers*. Ed. Mark Greengrass and Michael Hannon. 2nd ed. Sheffield: Humanities Research Institute, 2002. CD ROM.

---

19 The original quotes comes from Mather's 1715 *Nuncia Bona e Terra Longuinque* (9), in which he advertised his correspondence with Francke. See also the essays by Benz.
20 See, in addition to the essays in this collection Smolinski, "Natural Science and Interpretation."
21 Other points that he had in common with the Atlantic community ecumenists of the early period are his attempt to develop a unifying definition of twenty-four principles of Christian faith in Spanish (see his 1699 *La Fe Del Christiano*), and his interest in efforts to bring about the conversion of the Jews.

Hooker, Thomas. *Thomas Hooker: Writings in England and Holland.* Ed. G.H. Williams et al. Cambridge: Harvard UP, 1975.

Lasco, John a. *Forma ac ratio tota ecclesiastici Ministerii, in peregrinorum, potissimum uero Germanorum Ecclesia. ...* London, 1555.

Leusden, John. *Psalterium Hebraeo Latinum.* Utrecht, 1688.

Mather, Cotton. *The Christian Philosopher.* Ed. Winton Solberg. Urbana: U of Illinois P, 1994.

–. *La Fe Del Christiano.* Boston, 1699.

–. *Magnalia Christi Americana: Or, The Ecclesiastical History of New England.* 1702. New York: Arno Press, 1972.

–. *Nuncia Bona e Terra Longuinque.* Boston, 1715.

–. *The Threefold Paradise of Cotton Mather: An Edition of "Triparadisus."* Ed. Reiner Smolinski. Athens: The U of Georgia P, 1995.

Menasseh Ben Israel. *The Hope of Israel.* London, 1650.

Norton, John. *Responsio ad Totam Questionum.* London. 1648.

Perkins, William. *A Reformed Catholicke.* Cambridge, 1597.

Thomas Thorowgood. *Iewes in America; or, Probabilities that the Americans are of that race.* London, 1650.

Secondary Sources

Archer, John. "Puritan Town Planning in New Haven." *Journal of the Society of Architectural Historians* 34 (1975): 140–49.

Baumer, Franklin Le Van. "The Church of England and the Common Corps of Christendom." *Journal of Modern History* 16 (1944): 1–21.

Benz, Ernst. "Ecumenical Relations between Boston Puritanism and German Pietism: Cotton Mather and August Hermann Franke." *Harvard Theological Review* 54.3 (1961): 159–93.

–. "Pietist and Puritan Sources of Early Protestant World Missions (Cotton Mather and A.H. Francke)." *Church History* 20.2 (1951): 28–55.

Bozeman, Theodore Dwight. *The Precisianist Strain: Disciplinary Religion and Antinomian Backlash in Puritanism to 1638.* Chapel Hill: U of North Carolina P, 2004.

Bremer, Francis J. *Congregational Communion: Clerical Friendship in the Anglo-American Puritan Community, 1610–1692.* Boston: Northeastern UP, 1994.

–. "Increase Mather's Friends: The Trans-Atlantic Congregational Network of the Seventeenth Century." *Proceedings of the American Antiquarian Society* 94 (1984): 59–96.

Bush, Sargent, Jr. *The Writings of Thomas Hooker: Spiritual Adventures in Two Worlds.* Madison: U of Wisconsin P, 1980.

Cogley, Richard W. "Some Other Kind of Being and Condition: The Controversy in Mid-Seventeenth Century England over the Peopling of Ancient America." *Journal of the History of Ideas* 68.1 (2007): 35–56.

Gordon, Bruce. "Gwalther, Rudolf (1519–1586)." *Oxford Dictionary of National Biography.* Ed. H.C.G. Matthew and Brian Harrison. Vol. 24. Oxford: Oxford UP, 2004. 336–37.

Greengrass, Mark, Michael Leslie, and Timothy Taylor, eds. *Samuel Hartlib and Universal Reformation.* Cambridge: Cambridge UP, 1994.

Grell, Ole Peter. *Dutch Calvinists in Early Stuart London: The Dutch Church in Austin Friars 1603–1642.* Leiden: Brill, 1989.

Hall, David D. *The Faithful Shepherd: A History of the New England Ministry in the Seventeenth Century.* Chapel Hill: U of North Carolina P, 1972.

Hall, Michael G. *The Last American Puritan: The Life of Increase Mather, 1639–1723.* Middletown: Weleyan UP, 1988.

–. "Mather, Cotton (1663–1728)." *Oxford Dictionary of National Biography: From the Earliest Times to the Year 2000.* Ed. H.C.G. Matthew and Brian Harrison. Vol. 37. Oxford: Oxford UP, 2004. 265–68.

Hotson, Howard. *Johann Heinrich Alsted, 1588–1638: Between Renaissance, Reformation and Universal Reform.* Oxford: Oxford UP, 2000.

–. *Paradise Postponed: Johann Heinrich Alsted and the Birth of Calvinist Millenarianism.* Dordrecht: Klewer Academic Publishers, 2001.

Jinkins, Michael. "Perkins, William (1558–1602)." *Oxford Dictionary of National Biography Oxford Dictionary of National Biography: From the Earliest Times to the Year 2000.* Ed. H.C.G. Matthew and Brian Harrison. Vol. 43. Oxford: Oxford UP, 2004. 781–84.

Katz, David S. *Philo-Semitism and the Readmission of the Jews to England.* New York: Oxford UP, 1982.

Lovelace, Richard. *The American Pietism of Cotton Mather.* Grand Rapids: Christian UP, 1979.

–. "Cotton Mather." *The Pietist Theologians: An Introduction to Theology in the Seventeenth and Eighteenth Centuries.* Ed. Carter Lindberg. London: Blackwell, 2005. 115–28.

McCullough, Diarmaid. *Thomas Cranmer.* New Haven: Yale UP, 1996.

McDermott, Gerald. *One Holy and Happy Society: The Public Theology of Jonathan Edwards.* University Park: Penn State UP, 1992.

McNeil, John T. *Unitive Protestantism: The Ecumenical Experience and its Persistent Expression.* Richmond: John Knox, 1964.

Miller, Perry. *Errand into the Wilderness.* 1956. Cambridge: Harvard UP, 2004.

Milton, Anthony. "Puritanism and the Continental Reformed Churches." *The Cambridge Companion to Puritanism.* Ed. John Coffey and Paul C.H. Lim. Cambridge: Cambridge UP, 2008. 109–27.

Murdock, Graeme. *Calvinism on the Frontier, 1600–1660: International Calvinism and the Reformed Church in Hungary and Transylvania.* Oxford: Oxford UP, 2000.

Peacey, Jason. "Seasonable Treatises: A Godly Project of the 1630s." *English Historical Review* 113 (1998): 667–79.

Pearson, A.F. Scott. *Thomas Cartwright and Elizabethan Puritanism, 1553–1603.* Cambridge: Cambridge UP, 1925.

Pestana, Carla. *The English Atlantic in an Age of Revolution, 1640–1661.* Cambridge: Harvard UP, 2004.

Popkin, Richard. "Hartlib, Dury and the Jews." *Samuel Hartlib and Universal Reformation.* Ed. Mark Greengrass, Michael Leslie, and Timothy Taylor. Cambridge: Cambridge UP, 1994.

Shuffleton, Frank. *Thomas Hooker, 1586–1647.* Princeton: Princeton UP, 1977.

Smolinski, Reiner. "How to Go to Heaven, or How Heaven Goes? Natural Science and Interpretation in Cotton Mather's 'Biblia Americana' (1693–1728)." *New England Quarterly* 81.2 (2008): 278–329.

Solberg, Winton. Introduction. *The Christian Philosopher.* By Cotton Mather. Ed. Winton Solberg. Urbana, IL: University of Illinois, 1994. xic-cxxxiv.

Sprunger, Keith. *Dutch Puritanism: A History of English and Scottish Churches of the Netherlands in the Sixteenth and Seventeenth Centuries.* Leiden: Brill, 1982.

van den Berg, Johannes. *Religious Currents and Cross-Currents: Essays on Early Modern Protestantism and the Protestant Enlightenment.* Leiden: Brill, 1999.

Walsham, Alexandra, *Charitable Hatred: Tolerance and Intolerance in England, 1500–1700.* Manchester: Manchester UP, 2006.

Winship, Michael P. *Seers of God: Puritan Providentialism in the Restoration and Early Enlightenment.* Baltimore: John Hopkins UP, 1996.

Woodward, Walter W. "Prospero's America: John Winthrop, Jr., Alchemy, and the Creation of New England Culture (1606–1676)." Diss. U of Connecticut, 2001.

–. *Prospero's America: John Winthrop, Jr., Alchemy, and the Creation of New England Culture, 1606–1676.* Chapel Hill: U of North Carolina P, 2010.

OLIVER SCHEIDING

The World as Parish: Cotton Mather, August Hermann Francke, and Transatlantic Religious Networks

The World begins to feel a Warmth from the *Fire of God*, which thus flames in the Heart of *Germany*, beginning to extend into many Regions; the whole world will e're long be sensible of it!
Cotton Mather, *Nuncia Bona e Terra Longinqua* (1715)

In the Frederician Academy, which flourisheth amongst the People of Halle, and which ought to outshine all the Academies in the World, as a Pattern and Rule for the rest; this was the Lord's Doing, was done for the Lord also, and it is marvellous in our Eyes, to whom the Fame of the Fact has arrived, though so far remote as America.
Cotton Mather, *Cotton Mather's Student and Preacher; or, Directions for a Candidate of the Ministry* (1789)

For quite some time now, the religious and literary history of the Atlantic world has been studied from a comparative perspective. However, most works done within this transatlantic paradigm still focus on the Anglo-American Puritan community in the seventeenth century.[1] Other areas in which religious networks have been established, for instance, between New England Puritanism and German Pietism, require further investigation.[2] Only a small number

---

1 See, for instance, the groundbreaking studies by Bremer (*Puritanism* and *Congregational*) and Cressy on the Anglo-American Puritan community in the seventeenth century. Searle focuses on the "Transatlantic Puritan Republic of Letters," examining the correspondence of two American ministers (John Eliot and John Woodbrigde) with the English Nonconformist Richard Baxter. In their collection of essays programmatically entitled *Transatlantische Religionsgeschichte* (2006), Lehmann and Wellenreuther make a strong plea to study more closely the multiple communicative relationships and networks of the colonial ministry and their European counterparts (see also Wellenreuther, "Pietismus"; "Mission"). In contrast to an earlier focus on particular regions and local communities, either in colonial North America or in Europe, current studies emphasize the importance of transregional pastoral and professional relations in the early modern Atlantic world. Scholars such as Lindberg, Noll, and Ward focus on the ways in which religious networks maintained a sense of community that worked beyond notions of exceptionalism, nationalism, and insularity. As David Hall and others have shown, the exchange of spiritual and textual practices is central for studying the intense flow of ideas and thoughts that crisscrossed the Atlantic.
2 The close connection between Puritanism and Pietism has been recognized in scholarship since the seminal work of church historian F. Ernest Stoeffler (*Rise of Evangelical Pietism*). While Perry Miller had primarily emphasized the orthodox Calvinist orientation of the Pu-

of studies have so far explored the conversation between Cotton Mather (1663–1728) and August Hermann Francke (1663–1727) that occurred in the opening decades of the eighteenth century. Much of what has been said about it is based on the early archival studies of Kuno Francke and the church historian Ernst Benz. Their work led to important findings that still form the basis for the few more recent discussions of the subject. Both scholars gave emphasis to the cosmopolitan ethos of Mather's theology, called attention to his interest in German Pietism and his practical view of religion, and showed the closeness of Mather's and Francke's attempts to unite Christianity under the "MAXIMS of PIETY."[3] However, the actual extent and importance of this exchange between Boston and Halle, Saxony, has never been fully examined. One reason for this neglect has certainly been the cumbersome access to archival material housed in the Franckesche Stiftungen in the city of Halle over the last fifty years and the paucity of original documents to be found. Many of the original documents (all written in Latin) have been lost and there are only scattered hints of the exchange in diaries and letters of third persons. Critical assessments of the correspondence range from reading it as proof of the "strong relationship between

---

ritan congregations in England and North America, Stoeffler opened up Puritan studies by shifting the focus from Calvinist theology to the shared practical and pastoral traditions in both English Puritanism and continental Pietism (see Stoeffler, *Continental Pietism*). While the term "Pietism" remains difficult to define, recent scholarship stresses the lasting social and political influence of Pietism in North America (see Roeber; Strom 1–10). Although this shift in Puritan studies has resulted in many important revisionist works, which try to reassess Puritanism as a "devotional movement, rooted in religious experience" (Hambrick-Stowe i), major deficiencies in scholarship remain evident. On the one hand, Puritan studies, dominated by Anglo-American approaches, focus on the first phase of the European colonization of North America, from 1607 to 1660, and concentrate almost exclusively on New England Puritans (see Foster; Peterson). Transregional studies are rare, and topics like the Reformed churches of the New Netherlands, for example, in New York and New Jersey, have been insufficiently explored. Nor has enough attention been given to the period from 1660 to 1776. Given the increasing number of people emigrating from Continental Europe to North America, ethnic and religious pluralism characterizes this period of the British Atlantic world. In the wake of the Act of Toleration of 1689, the variety of Protestant denominations in the New World expanded significantly, mainly in the mid-Atlantic and southern colonies of British North America (see Durnbaugh, Fogleman, Grabbe).

3   These "MAXIMS of PIETY" were first published in Cotton Mather's *Things to be more thought Upon* (1713), then in *The Stone Cut out of the Mountain* (1716), *Malachi: Or, the Everlasting Gospel, Preached unto the Nations* (1717) and elsewhere. They served as a basis upon which all Christians, of whatever denomination, might unite. In his sermon, Mather proposes "[t]hat there should be formed SOCIETIES of Good Men, who can own some such Instrument of PIETY, and make it their most inviolate Law, to bear with *Differences* in one another upon the *Lower* and *Lesser* points of Religion, and still at their Meetings have their *Prayers* for the growth of the People, who being Established on the Grand MAXIMS of Christianity are to become a *Great Mountain and fill the whole Earth*, accompanied with Projections of the most *unexceptionable Methods* to accomplish it" (*Malachi* 92–93). Similar thoughts on church union and piety can be found in Mather's *Three Letters from New-England, Relating to the Controversy of the Present Time* (9), and in his late *Manuductio ad Ministerium* (119). On this, see Middlekauff (305–19).

New England Puritanism and continental pietism" (Benz, "Ecumenical Relations" 192–93) to simply calling it a minor footnote in the history of Puritanism that ultimately demonstrates Mather's Calvinist tenacity (Holifield 68–69). The truth probably lies somewhere in between.

On the one hand, one must not blow out of proportion the importance and exceptionality of this particular transatlantic conversation. According to Silverman's estimates, Mather wrote and "sent literally around the world" "more than five thousand letters," and his surviving letters alone (about 600) make for "the largest extant correspondence of an American Puritan" (Silverman 199). Francke, supported by a large office of clerks, had about 5,000 correspondents and was in constant contact with at least three to four hundred. Even if some of Francke's letters to New England were lost over the course of history, Mather was definitely not amongst Francke's main correspondents. On the other hand, the Boston-Halle connection is of real significance that is easily overlooked by those who focus too much on the volume and frequency of their epistolary correspondence. Its chief value lies in the insights which the exchange, despite its limited scale, gives into the genuine affinities and, most importantly, mutual exchange of ideas that existed between Franckean Pietism and third-generation American Puritanism – something which most scholars of the period have been slow to recognize.[4] This essay will present fresh evidence that the transatlantic conversation between Mather and Francke enjoyed much greater reciprocity in terms of mutual interest and influence than is commonly understood or acknowledged. After reviewing the extant archival record together with the current state of the scholarly debate, I will examine the *Narratio Epistolica Ad Cott. Matherum* (1735), a historical narrative written in part by August Hermann Francke, but completed, edited, and published by his close associate Johann Heinrich Callenberg (1694–1760), a Lutheran church historian and important second-generation promoter of the Pietist movement. As I will demonstrate, this hitherto ignored document (composed in Latin but never translated into German or English) reveals substantial new information about Halle's relationship with Mather. To quote from the preface to the *Narratio*, both Francke and Callenberg regarded their bond with their Boston colleague as "a highly pleasant friendship ... because of their similarity of intentions and undertakings" ("Preface" i; see appendix).

---

4 The most recent assessment of the correspondence between Boston and Halle by Wolfgang Splitter comes to the conclusion that it was very short-lived and ultimately rather insignificant. Although Splitter meticulously reconstructs the chronology of the extant letters (102–22), he does not take into account the *Narratio Epistolica* and fails to recognize the role Callenberg played for the exchange between Boston and Halle after 1720. In light of the *Narratio*'s preface it can certainly be no longer maintained that "[a]fter 1719, Francke never corresponded with Mather again" (112).

In the late nineteenth century, Kuno Francke, professor of German literature at Harvard, rediscovered some letters written by Cotton Mather to August Hermann Francke and immediately set out to reconstruct the epistolary record. What he actually found was a highly fragmented body of writings which hardly deserves to be called a "correspondence," if by that term we understand a continuous and mutual exchange of letters over a longer period of time. Kuno Francke edited one short letter of Mather, written in 1711 ("Correspondence" 194–95), and reprinted August Hermann Francke's long Latin reply composed in 1714, in which Mather's correspondent chronicles the history of Pietitist undertakings at Halle up to that very year ("Further Documents" 32–53). Kuno Francke also added to his transcription of August Hermann Francke's handwritten letter Mather's revised and much altered English version of it which Mather had published in his 1715 as *Nuncia Bona e Terra Longinqua: A Brief Account of Some Good and Great Things A Doing for the Kingdom of God, In the Midst of Europe. Communicated in a Letter to* (1–13; K. Francke, "Further Documents" 54–66). Mather's immediate appropriation of the information provided in Francke's letter reveals his intention to appear before his home audience as an eminent minister who corresponds with "Persons of a Superiour Character on the other side of the wide *Atlantick*" (*Nuncia* 1).[5] Kuno Francke not only brought to light the immediate usefulness of the account for Mather's self-fashioning as one of New England's leading ministers, but Francke's research also drew attention to important mediators in establishing the network between Boston and Halle, namely the London-based Society for Promoting Christian Knowledge (SPCK). In particular, he pointed to the central role of Anton Wilhelm Böhme (1673–1722), the German chaplain at the English court and translator of Francke's works in England. Böhme had published August Hermann Francke's *Segensvolle Fußstapfen des noch lebenden und waltenden liebreichen und getreuen Gottes* (1701), an institutional history of the charity school in Halle, under the English title *Pietas Hallensis: or a Publick Demonstration of the Foot-steps of a Divine Being yet in the World: In an Historical Narration of the Orphan-house, and other Charitable Institutions at Glaucha near Hall in Saxony* (1705).[6] The translation documented the accomplishments of the educational and social reforms at Halle. Through this and other activities Böhme was actively building an international audience for Francke, and by informing Cotton Mather of the various activities of the German Pietist reform

5   A number of scholars have pointed out that Mather's international correspondence with Lutheran Pietists must be seen as part of his attempts to overcome the stigma of provincialism and to highlight his own importance. Citing Silverman's judgment, W.R. Ward argued in his *The Protestant Evangelical Awakening* (1992) that if "'Mather obsessively wanted to put America on the cultural map,'" he had to "get a foothold in the most energetic spiritual movement of his middle years, that of Halle Pietism" (274).
6   In 1710, Böhme published the second part, which documented the events in Halle up to the year 1708, and the third part with a long preface in 1716.

movement he helped promote the ecumenical and missionary endeavors of both men in the English-speaking world of the British Atlantic empire (Wallmann 131–32).[7] After World War II, the German church historian Ernst Benz continued where Kuno Francke had left off. Influenced by the newly established "Pax Americana," Benz read the relation between New England Calvinism and continental Pietism in terms of an "Early Protestant World Missions" ("Pietist"). He promised to prepare a publication of the "complete extant correspondence between Cotton Mather and August Hermann Francke" (51). The result of his research was, however, mainly related to Mather's missionary endeavors and based on some of his printed documents, which Benz interpreted in the context of another letter Mather had sent to Francke in 1717.

In the third part of his *Pietas Hallensis* (1716), Böhme had revealed to a wider Christian audience the existence of a transatlantic religious network of fellow Protestants in North America and Europe, and had specifically mentioned the connection between Halle and Boston.

> ... [E]ven some Rivulets of Christian Benevolence have been derived from *New-England* in *America*; where the History of *Pietas Hallensis* falling into the Hands of some Publick-Spirited Persons, hath not only excited them to a kind Contribution, to refresh the Bowels of the Poor at *Hall*, but engaged them also to a useful *Correspondence* for mutually advancing the Good of the Church universal. This agreeable Mingle of Gifts and Benefactions, of Persons and Nations, of near and far, of great and low, and of divers Denominations of *Lutherans* too, sets off the better the whole Undertaking, and evinceth the sweet and concurring Harmony of those that have the same *End* in View, though personally distanced by Sea and Land from one another. (Francke, *Pietas* xiii)

Given Böhme's reference to a "useful *Correspondence*," it seems likely that prior to 1716 more than the two extant letters may have crossed the Atlantic. What we do know for certain is that Mather felt stimulated by Böhme's public account to continue in his endeavors to strengthen ties with Halle. After 1717, Mather wrote at least one more letter to Francke of which, unfortunately, only a tran-

---

7 For a discussion of the close relationship between Mather and the SPCK's secretary Benjamin Coleman, see Brunner. He characterizes the different ecumenical views of the Anglican Society for the Propagation of the Gospel in Foreign Parts (SPG) and those of the SPCK as follows: "Much of the SPCK's uniqueness resulted from the fact that it was *not* an officially-chartered Society. While the SPG drew the attention and involvement of the episcopate, the SPCK proceeded quietly and unassumingly, controlled for the most part by dedicated, pious, and reform-minded laymen. It allowed foreign Protestants to become subscribing members and to exercise a considerable influence in setting a course for the Society. ... The SPCK was much more pragmatic and less theological than its sister Society, accepting for over one hundred years the validity of the ordinations of German Lutheran missionaries in India, something which the SPG repeatedly refused to do in America" (222). For Mather's criticism of the SPG's missionary objectives, see *Selected Letters* (124, 186) and *Diary* (2: 412); for the relationship between Halle and the SPCK, see Schmidt (39–41) and Wellenreuther ("Mission" 198–203).

script (dated 1724) has survived.[8] Yet, the epistolary record reconstructed by Kuno Francke and Benz seems to suggest that for some reason these endeavors remained unreciprocated from this point onward. In his *Diary* as well as in his letters to Böhme and to his correspondents in London, Mather also complained about flagging responses from Halle. Still, through his SPCK friends, he kept sending books and money to his Pietist friends in Germany, but apparently to no avail.

Unable to find further archival documents, Benz was at a loss how to explain this breakdown of communication in the final decade of Mather's and Francke's careers other than by the latter's loss of interest in a further exchange. Nor could Richard F. Lovelace's *The American Pietism of Cotton Mather* – the only American study that has considered in any detail Mather's connection with German Pietism – offer new hints as to why this hiatus occurred. Building on Benz, Lovelace's conclusion was that Mather's project to promulgate an "American Pietism" might have been temporarily fueled by his enthusiasm for the Halle Pietists, which was reflected in his desire "to communicate to them his own theological reflections on the ecumenical significance of the Pietist awakening" (34).[9] This enthusiasm, however, remained largely unrequited and ultimately did not play a decisive role for his reformulation of Puritanism. "[T]he influence of German Pietism on Mather," Lovelace writes, "was a matter of indirect stimulation, the resonance of two sympathetic traditions, rather than a direct transfer of content between the two Pietisms" (*American Pietism* 307).

---

8   While some have survived in the original, most of the letters written either by Mather or Francke between 1711 and 1724 are only available in transcripts whose dates of composition are at variance with those assigned by the copyists. The following letters are available in the archives at Halle, Franckesche Stiftung (AFSt): Boston, May 28, 1711, original letter (D 42, S 743–744; cf. D 57 136–139; reprinted in K. Francke's "Beginning"); Boston, January 10, 1712, original letter (C 229, S 32a); Boston, n. d., original letter, probably written in 1717 (D 121: 6a; for chronology, see Benz, "Ecumenical"). In "Wirtschaftsarchiv" (business archives), there is a copy of a letter dated January 10, 1712, and another archival record in the green card catalogue ("Grüne Kartei") dates the very same letter as Nov. 23, 1724 (cf. AFSt, W Tit. II Sect. 23 Schr. Ia Fach F: 3); Boston, June 23, 1724, copy (see files of Danish-Halle Mission, signature 9/19, 32; a note says: "Ad Franck. Dec. 1724, with two other Packets"). In addition to Mather's letters that were sent together with some of his books in 1711 and 1713 (see Mather's *Diary* and Francke's "Narratio de Orphanotropheo"), there is Francke's 1714 response, a long letter that was published and translated in English in 1716 by Böhme, as "Letter to a Friend" (A. H. Francke, *Pietas* 1–60); this first long letter by Francke dated December 12, 1714. Gustav Kramer reprinted Francke's Latin "Narratio de Orphanotropheo Glauchensi" (1–26). Furthermore, there is a brief exchange of letters with German missionaries in India; see Mather, "Notitia Indiarum," in *India Christiana* (1721) 49–87. See also AFSt, DHM 9/19, 31, 33 and M 1 C 16, 25.

9   In his preface to *The Heavenly Conversation* (1710), Mather writes that his essay may be "Entituled, American Pietism" (n. p.). The essay shows Mather's early enthusiasm about German Pietism shortly before he wrote his first letter to Francke in 1711: "Go on, my dear *Franckius*, and thy co-adjutors. *The Lord is with you, ye mighty men of* Piety!" (Preface, n. p.). On this issue, see Lovelace, "Cotton Mather."

The majority of scholars who have considered this issue followed Benz and Lovelace by interpreting the Halle-Boston connection as one that did not involve much of a reciprocal exchange. Its significance, limited as it was, is largely seen in having contributed to a growing network of Protestant world missions. Relying on Benz, Mather's letters to the Lutheran missionaries in India, his promotion of the Indian mission in New England, and his observations on the Greek Church are often cited as "impressive document[s] of the ecumenical consciousness of Boston Puritanism" ("Ecumenical" 182).[10]

In judging the nature of his relationship with Halle, most historians have clearly focused on Mather's side, while Francke's interest in entering the conversation with his Boston colleague has received little if any attention. Moreover, no one has considered that Francke's response to the books, letters, and money Mather mailed to Halle may not have been transacted as continuous exchange of personal letters, but instead took the form of what Böhme called a "Historical Narrative" (in Francke's *Pietas Hallensis* v), that is, of quasi-official reports (or circulars) about activities in Halle which Böhme sent to Mather to promote the ongoing reform work of continental Pietism in New England. As indicated above, a first seventy-page report in Latin, summarizing events and accomplishments in the years since 1709, reached Mather in 1714. While scholars have known about this report for a long time, it has largely been disregarded. What is more, the sequel to this first historical narrative, which covers Francke's ongoing interest, has been virtually ignored. This negligence may well have been caused by the document's late publication date (1735) and its obscure Latin title *Narratio Epistolica Ad Cott. Matherum Theologum Anglicanum Ecclesiae Et Academiae Bostoniensis In America Directa Qua Continetur Historia Ecclesiastica Halensis Annorum Huius Saeculi Septem XV. Usque Ad XXI Nec Non Genuina Relatio De Principis Saxonici Ad Ecclesiam Evangelicam Reditu Beati Cuisdam Viri Hortatu Et Nomine Scripti Io. Henr. Callenberg Phil. Prof. Publ.*[11] What may have further contributed to this document's obscurity is that it was published under the signature of Francke's close associate Johann Heinrich Callenberg several years after both Mather and Francke had passed away. However, archival records reveal that the original narrative was supervised by

---

10   This view has recently been challenged by Hermann Wellenreuther in one of his articles on Protestant mission in the eighteenth-century Atlantic world ("Pietismus" 167, 185), in which he argues that given the modest success of New England's missionary activities among Native Americans, the German Pietists found the Puritan mission less stimulating and inspiring than many other evangelical activities around the globe.

11   The translated title reads, *Epistolary Narration for Cotton Mather, English theologian and director of the Boston church and academy in America, containing the Halle church history of the years 1715 to 1721 and an accurate report on the return of the Saxon prince to the Lutheran church. Johann Heinrich Callenberg, public professor of philosophy wrote this at the behest of a blessed man.*

Francke and completed in 1722, more than 13 years before it was published.[12] It is a direct continuation of his first report to Mather and begins where the old one had left off, documenting the ecclesiastical history of Halle, as the subtitle says, up to the year 1721.[13] Both of Francke's narratives continue his previous conceptualizations of the Hallensean church history and the universal reform, as is evident in Francke's report on Lutheran improvement "Der Große Aufsatz" (1704–16) and in his *Pietas Hallensis*.[14]

The original manuscript of the *Narratio Epistolica*, comprising some fifty handwritten pages in Latin by Francke, Callenberg, and some of their assistants, was a joint piece of writing composed under the strict supervision of Francke. A note by Callenberg refers to his editorship and explains that he forwarded the account to Mather in late March of 1722. It also mentions a third document which, however, has not been found. The *Narratio Epistolica* was forwarded to Anton Wilhelm Böhme, who was supposed to dispatch it to Mather. Among the papers of the SPCK exists a copy of a letter written by Henry Newman, the society's secretary, which informs Mather in early August of 1722 of the death of Böhme. It also notes that Böhme's executors had given him a long letter from Francke to be shipped to Mather. Newman transmitted this report to Mather together with a long account of the death of Böhme, whom he called the "life & soul of our Correspondence in religious affairs with Germany" (Allen and McClure 232; see also my appendix). Possibly this package to Mather got lost, as there is no evidence in Mather's papers that he ever received it.[15] This loss may explain much of Mather's frustration over Halle's apparent lack of response, which, however, would then have been caused, at least partly, by mischance rather than by Francke's dwindling interest in his American correspondent.

---

12   See AFSt, W Tit. II Sect. 23 Schr. Ia Fach F: 3. This extended account is dated March 6, 1722. It was sent to "Reverendo Mathero" on March 27, 1722, as notes in the manuscript indicate.

13   In the first republication of the 1714 report to Mather ("Narratio de Orphanotropheo"), which was edited by Gustav Kramer in 1863 on the occasion of the bicentennial celebrations of the Francke Foundations, there is a reference to its continuation in Callenberg's *Narratio Epistolica*. Apparently, Kuno Francke when he translated and published that same report again in 1897 did not know about Kramer's edition, and until very recently, no one has followed up on Kramer's hint. There are brief references to the *Narratio Epistolica* in Wellenreuther's "Die atlantische Welt" (15) and in Grabbe (8–9), but neither offers a detailed interpretation.

14   Another motivation for the Halle Pietists to chronicle their achievements lies in the anti-Pietist attitude of the orthodox Lutheran clergy. Spener's *Wahrhafftige Erzehlung dessen, was wegen des so genannten Pietismi in Teutschland vor einiger Zeit vorgegangen* (1697) is one of the first historical narratives that has influenced later Pietist church histories (see Peters).

15   However, in his "Preface" to the *Narratio* Callenberg suggests that the 1722 letter, with its account of Duke Moritz's re-conversion, greatly pleased Mather and was incorporated by him into a sermon. Since no evidence of this sermon can be found, and Mather never mentions the 1722 letter, the case is inconclusive.

In discussing the *Narratio Epistolica*, I would like to re-assess the received opinion that, in the words of Lovelace, the influence of German Pietism on Mather was a matter of "indirect stimulation," which did not result in a "direct transfer of content between the two Pietisms" (*American Pietism* 307). While this statement may be true to some extent for the initial stage of the conversation between Halle and Boston,[16] the long manuscript account of 1722 and Callenberg's 1735 published version of it show the increasing closeness of both patriarchs, who in their later careers considered religion more as a matter of "practical conduct and of tangible results than abstract contemplation of a transcendent divinity" (Miller 632). Francke's narrative can be read as a response to Mather's goal to establish a church in which "the PIETY of the Grand *Evangelical Maxims*, is most Animated and Exhibited" (Mather, *Manuductio* 128). In his role as the official church historian of Halle Pietism, Callenberg, who was obviously deeply impressed by Mather's *Magnalia Christi Americana* (see Callenberg's *Narratio*, "Preface"), offers in his edition of Francke's reply a history of Pietism that emphasizes Halle's understanding of theology as a "habitus practicus" (Spener, *Pia Desideria* 69). The focus on Duke Moritz Wilhelm's reconversion to Lutheranism (ch. 18; see appendix for my translation) serves as a showcase of Francke's "Erziehungstheologie," his belief in a growth of faith, and his pride in the pious men and women it had created. This emphasis suggests that Francke and Callenberg regarded practical piety, informed by a belief in a continual improvement of life through religious education, as the most important common ground with Mather that formed the starting point as well as the center of their transatlantic conversation. Overall, Callenberg's *Narratio Epistolica* suggests that he and Francke considered Mather a serious dialogue partner in matters of church reform rather than just a kindred spirit coming from "sympathetic traditions" within Pietism (Lovelace, *American Pietism* 307).

As I will argue, the *Narratio Epistolica* was strongly motivated by questions of institutional politics and Francke's project of universal improvement of the Protestant Church, which he had begun to promote in 1716 on a large scale. Francke shared Mather's idea of the Reformation being in decay, an idea both had borrowed from Philipp Jakob Spener's works (see *Pia Desideria*, pt. 1). It is fair to say that in their chiliastic hopes, they conceived of themselves as coworkers in attaining a more perfect Reformation. The *Narratio Epistolica* di-

---

16 Mather notes in his *Diary* on March 15, 1713: "I take notice of admirable Piety, shining among the Professors of the modern Pietism (tho they are not without their Errors:) and I look on the Strains of Piety conspicuous in them, as notable Dawns of the Kingdome of God among the Children of Men. I would endeavour as in Reading their Books, I find the Passages of a raised and noble Piety occurring, to pant and strive after a lively Impression thereof, on my own Mind. And in this Way I would seek a particular præparation for Services which I may do, in the coming on of the Kingdome of God" (*Diary* 2: 193).

rectly addresses the usefulness of their exchange for the churches in New England, and the narrative serves as a promotional tract for continental Pietism in North America. What makes Callenberg's re-publication even more interesting is an inserted catalogue of Halle's book production, one of the first attempts to draw attention to its printing press that could supply North America with the appropriate literature of continental Pietism.[17] Moreover, Callenberg's edition of the conversation marks its entrance into a new international network of personal and informal contacts in the 1730s that is closely connected to his own efforts to establish the *Institutum Judaicum* at Halle, which he had founded in 1728 as one of the centers to reform Christian society at large. Callenberg used the correspondence between Mather and Francke as a means to attract a broader Christian public sympathetic to the Pietist movement and, in doing so, hoped to enlist the help of pious Englishmen and Americans.

Before I examine the *Narratio Epistolica* within the framework of the international relationships that sustained the Francke Foundations, a few words on Callenberg seem in order. In his 1955 article on the "Annales Hallenses ecclesiastici," Kurt Aland drew attention to Callenberg's role as an important church historian of Halle Pietism (590; see also Peters 120–8). However, today, Callenberg is mostly remembered as the founder of the *Institutum Judaicum* and its printing office, whose goal was to aid missionary work and promote the conversion of the Jews. Although Callenberg maintained an international network of Christian correspondents and continued to inform the Christian public about the achievements of Francke's institutions, his function as a mediator between Francke and Mather has gone unnoticed. Callenberg was the progeny of the Pietists' "second generation" and studied at the Frederician University of Halle, where he attended the lectures and seminars of August Hermann Francke. On Francke's recommendation, he became professor of philology in 1727. Callenberg, as one critic observed, "was among those poor students who earned their keep by recording the master's words in writing" (Clark 48). In his preface to the *Narratio Epistolica*, he tells his readers,

---

17 While working on the narrative, Callenberg assembled a long list of Mather's books, essays, and sermons. Many of the titles on Callenberg's list correspond with Mather's diary entries in which he mentions book packets shipped to Halle. Francke and Callenberg knew much of the printed material, as the narrative and Francke's letters show (see *Pietas Hallensis* 1–2; see also the "Introduction" to the *Narratio Epistolica* in my appendix); see also "Scriptiones de Cottonius Matheri," AFSt/H D 121:5. The list contains entries for the following years: 1699 (2); 1701 (3); 1702 (3); 1703 (3); 1704 (none); 1705 (none); 1706 (4); 1707 (5); 1709 (5); 1710 (4); 1711 (2); 1712 (9); 1713 (12); 1714 (8); 1715 (2); 1716 (4); 1717 (9); 1718 (3); 1719 (none); 1720 (3); 1721 (2). Callenberg's booklist also mentions two entries without year ("sive mentione anni"), among them Mather's *New Offer to the Lovers of Religion and Learning*, his announcement and prospectus of the "Biblia Americana." The prospectus appeared without printer's name, place, or any date. As Mather's *Diary* indicates, he indeed had sent copies of it to Europe (2: 283; see Holmes 2: 729–35).

That blessed man, whose encouragement and fame gave me reason to compose this narration, is August Hermann Francke, pride and joy of the Lutheran church. His writings, above all his description of the institutions in Glaucha, had come into the possession of the theologian Mather, acclaimed in America, and they had induced him to start a correspondence with Francke. … [T]he theologian from Halle could write about nothing more pleasurable to the American than what was pursued in Halle and what happened there. When I made acquaintance with Francke in the year 1721, Mather had been informed of events up to the year 1714. So, Francke encouraged me to write the sacred history of the remaining years in his name. After it was written, proof-read – by him as well as by certain assistants of his – , and approved of, Francke sent it to Mather in the year 1722. ("Preface" ii)

Although the preface is written in a characteristically Pietist fashion that minimizes Callenberg's own role in comparison to Francke's achievements, the printing of the exchange more than seven years after his master's and Cotton Mather's deaths shows how Callenberg sought to reassess the correspondence within the framework of his own promotional network. "The Ecclesiastical History of Halle from the Years 1715 to 1721 Which Contains the True Report of the Reconversion of the Prince of Saxony to the Evangelical Church," as the whole subtitle reads, was published under the name of the *Institutum Judaicum*. Callenberg purchased his own printing press in 1730 and obtained the royal privilege to publish books two years later. At the same time, he corresponded with the SPCK in London and exchanged and translated books and reports, in the hope that the *Institutum* would garner the support of pious English diplomats and merchants in Asia, Africa, and America to distribute theological texts printed in Halle. Like Francke's charitable institutions, the *Institutum* largely depended on donations from the Christian community. Mather, for instance, had sent money several times to support Francke's reform work in Halle.

One of the reasons for publishing and translating Francke's *Segensvolle Fußstapfen* (*Pietatis Hallensis*) was not only to propagate universal reform, but also to maintain a policy of financial transparency that informed the Christian public about all donations and expenditures. It has been argued, therefore, that one of the most modern achievements of the Pietist movement was its successful tapping of the "financial resources of an anonymous Christian public" (Clark 53). For this reason, special historical narratives were published. These were not merely account books or annals, but carefully edited publications that contained excerpts from correspondences, letters, missionary diaries, accounts of the daily affairs at Halle, and passages from the works of Christian authorities relating to the church's reformation. Letters were frequently complemented by reports of missionary activities or institutional accounts to create an atmosphere of dialogue. Copies of the reports were sent to Christian correspondents across Europe and beyond. Callenberg's printed version of the correspondence between Mather and Francke follows the editorial policies of these narrative church histories and is part of a long line of similar texts he had published since 1727.[18]

In 1733, Samuel Mather had published his Latin biography of August Hermann Francke in Boston. Cotton Mather's son praised the German Pietist preacher and pastor as an "incomparable theologian" (*Vita* 1). Friedrich Michael Ziegenhagen (1694–1776), who took Böhme's place in the SPCK, informed his Hallensean friends about this publication in a letter to Francke's son (Schmidt 40). Samuel Mather's biography, which addresses both the students of Harvard and the New England ministry, listed the Latin publications of Francke (*Vita* 31). In the "Catalogus Librorum," Samuel Mather regrets not being able to give a complete list of Francke's Latin and German publications. To the book catalogue is appended a narration ("Narratio") about the "Most Memorable Things of the Evangelical Churches throughout Germany and Other Regions and Provinces that Occurred in the Year 1730," as the chapter's title states (*Vita* 1–11). It explicitly mentions Callenberg's missionary activities. Given this second-generation effort in continuing to promote the bonds between the two branches of Pietism, Callenberg, probably encouraged by Francke's son Gotthilf August and Halle's growing interest in Pennsylvania and Georgia (Beyreuther, *Geschichte* 164–65), printed the earlier epistolary account for two immediate purposes: to expand the distribution of Pietist texts in North America, and, in doing so, to encourage a Christian public in England and the colonies to support the Hallensean activities financially.[19]

Like the *Institutum's* reports, Callenberg's book publication is carefully edited and seeks to capture the conversational tone of the exchange. While the original document is only loosely structured, the printed version uses a frame narrative (chs. 1, 21) that embraces nineteen closely knit chapters. The introduction (see appendix for my translation of ch. 1) and the concluding chapter were written by August Hermann Francke himself. In tone and style, the opening chapter follows the introduction of Francke's first long account that informed Mather about institutional affairs up to the year 1714 (see the *Pietas Hallensis*). Both texts contain the same argumentative structure and consist of three parts: the first refers to letters and books that Mather sent to Francke; the second part discusses briefly the current state of the Reformed Churches and the attempts of both men to instigate universal reform; in the concluding lines Francke apologizes for the intermittent flow of information, which he explains by his inces-

---

18   For a survey of this textual genre, see Peters, who also discusses Callenberg's unpublished manuscript, "Neueste Kirchenhistorie," a 23-volume handwritten church history, which encompasses the years from 1689 to 1724.
19   There are two undated letters in the Halle Archive by Samuel Mather and Gotthilf Francke which attest to their mutual interest in prolonging the exchange (cf. AFSt, M 2 H 3:1, 2 H 3:2).

sant overload of work, and then proposes to publish longer summaries that would keep Mather informed about the state of affairs in Germany.

The following chapters of Callenberg's *Narratio*, however, deviate from the earlier account in various aspects. One of the most striking features is the mixed character of Callenberg's printed version. Similar to Böhme's earlier attempts to promulgate Halle Pietism throughout the English-speaking world by translating Francke's journal, Callenberg's reproduction of the exchange is a "historical narrative" in which he publicizes Francke's achievements. At the same time, however, it is a "sacred history," as Callenberg characterizes the narrative in his preface. He compares the narration to Mather's own church history, *Magnalia Christi Americana* (1702), which both Callenberg and Francke had studied. In his 1717 letter, Mather had suggested to Francke a German publication of his church history and his *Bonifacius* (1710), as he had become aware of the expanding business of translated books distributed by Francke's book shop since 1716 (ch. 1, pp. 1–4; see also Wilson, "Übersetzungen"). The ensuing chapters differ from Francke's earlier account by embedding numerous conversion stories and exemplary tales (chs. 7–9), whose dramatic style of narration contrasts with the more account-like chapters which give long lists of expenditures, donations, books, and Bible translations (chs. 1–6, pp. 13–16). Furthermore, Callenberg highlights the beginnings of Hebrew Studies at the University of Halle (ch. 12). The narration culminates in Francke's missionary journey through Germany (ch. 17) and his widely acclaimed success in re-converting Duke Moritz Wilhelm of Saxony-Zeitz to Lutheranism in 1718 (ch. 18). It also contains excerpts of Francke's 1717 university address celebrating the jubilee of the Reformation (*Oratio Jubilea de Reformatione*, publ. in 1721), in which he complains about the halfway-state of reforming Christianity (ch. 14, pp. 78–83). Callenberg ultimately portrays Francke as the patriarch of Halle Pietism.

To set up a dialogic atmosphere, Francke's introductory letter explicitly refers to Mather's long letter of 1717, in which the Boston pastor appears as the self-appointed spokesman of "American Pietism." In his introductory letter, Francke alludes to key themes that he finds relevant for re-opening the conversation with Mather. The letter does not discuss theological principles that Mather had addressed in his earlier letter.[20] Instead, Francke writes in accordance with Mather's call for establishing a "*Universal Religion* of PIETY ... wherein all *Good Men* are *United*, whatever *Different Persuasions* in other Matters may alienate them from one another" (*Menachem* 38–39). Unlike earlier Protestant conversations that frequently offered a confession of faith for public

---

20 In the first part of his 1717 letter, Mather had given the fourteen maxims of Pietism; one year later, in a letter to the Halle-trained missionary in Tranquebar Bartholomäus Ziegenbalg, reprinted in his *India Christiana* (62–74), Mather reduced them to three maxims: belief in the Trinity, complete reliance on Christ for salvation, and the love of one's neighbor for the sake of Christ (see Benz, "Ecumenical Relations"; Holifield 69).

discussion, Mather and the German Pietists were interested in accumulating practical experiences which would support their understanding of history and strengthen their movement of renewal and reform of Christianity. As Ward points out, they "sought their legitimation in the hand of God in history" (2). Francke stresses Mather's immense book production ("more than 250 booklets in different languages") and discusses his "biblical opus, which you want to call *Biblia Americana.*" He calls his "hermeneutic approach" an "active piety" of a mind "which has been purified by the Holy Spirit." At the same time, he underscores the importance of Mather's reading of Johann Arndt, Philipp Jakob Spener, and some of his own "little works" (ch. 1, p. 2). In fact, Francke also seems to be very much motivated by his own growing interest in the North American book market. He retells the enormous success of their earlier encounter that became known to a large Christian public in New England by Mather's and Böhme's intervention. Francke declares,

> However, with how much joy my rather fruitful letter has imbued you and all of your people from New England and how much praise the churches of New England sang to God and to our Christ, after the letter had been read, cannot be expressed in words. I confess, this message has very much moved me and it has prompted me to work on the continuation of so fruitful a history. (ch. 1, p. 4)

The manuscript lists 150 out of the 300 book titles of Francke's press and names another 84 books published between 1714 and 1721. Callenberg's *Narratio Epistolica* version contains a more condensed list which is divided into three parts: Theology, the "other sciences," and Francke's own publications. The book catalogue contains Latin editions published by Francke's printing office as well as vernacular translations, either from English or Latin into German. It strongly promotes the achievements of the University of Halle in the field of medicine and law, and in the burgeoning discipline of biology. The output further covers theology, natural sciences, philology, mathematics, physics, and history. The theological section advertises, among other titles, the writings of Philipp Jakob Spener, together with German translations of the "pious works" of the Evangelical Puritan Thomas Goodwin and the medieval mystic Johannes Tauler. Callenberg's list also reveals the beginning of the translation of English revival texts that were collected at Halle from 1722 to 1755. Mather's *The Minister: A Sermon, Offer'd unto the Anniversary Convention of Ministers, From Several Parts of New-England* (1722), in which he discusses the "Spirit of Piety" (31), was one of the first books in this collection (Wilson, "Übersetzungen" 93). The science section names numerous books by the chemist and medical practitioner Georg Ernst Stahl, who was the originator of the phlogiston theory, which dominated chemistry until the end of the eighteenth century. Francke's press printed his *Opusculum Chymico-Physico-Medicum* in 1715, as well as some of his animistic medical pieces and tracts of his disciple Michael Alberti. The press also promoted Bartholomäus Ziegenbalg's linguistic achievements by publishing his Tamil grammar, as Callenberg's book catalogue shows. The first two sections of this catalogue thus read like an annotated bibliography, whereas the last part consists mainly of titles and long excerpts from Francke's texts and sermons, focusing on his Christocentric and practical reform writings.

Callenberg's printed narrative is a well-balanced piece of writing that moves back and forth between describing particular successes achieved at Francke's model institutions and the universal progress of Christianity at large. The large-scale output of the print shop and the worldwide distribution of religious literature demonstrate the power of the printed word. The narrative also advances Francke's "praxis pietatis" in reading the Holy Scripture. The 45 theological books, together with the 34 scientific titles listed by Callenberg, signal a biblical hermeneutics that did not oppose the sciences but saw them as part of what Francke had called the "lectio practica," a reading to distinguish the "kernel" from the "husk," terms he used to uncover the deeper meaning and religious center of the Bible (Peschke, "Einleitung" xvi). This, of course, is an approach strikingly similar to Mather's own. With a view to Mather's project of publishing the "Biblia Americana," Callenberg's introduction states: "You certainly have not neglected any subject to support its elegant style. You have carefully consulted mathematics, philosophy, and whatever researchers of our age have found out about the classics, philology, and natural science." Indeed, science was seen by Mather as a welcome support of Christian religion, and he considered studying the "two great Books of God, Nature and Scripture" (Holmes 1: 135) as complementary endeavors.

Another chapter of Callenberg's narration (ch. 15) describes the difficult publication history of the *Biblia Hebraica* that was finally published in 1720 after eighteen years of strenuous editing. This episode could be indirectly read as an attempt to encourage Mather not to give up on his ambitious literary undertaking, whose publication Mather by that time already considered ill-fated (see *Diary* 2: 511).[21]

---

21 Mather's repeated requests to get his own books translated into German as well as the advertisement of the "Biblia Americana" which Mather sent to Halle seem to have been ignored by his Pietist friends on the other side of the Atlantic. One of the reasons for this might have been a growing sense of competitiveness at Halle. In 1721, when Francke resumed the correspondence with Mather, Halle Pietism had reached an importance hitherto unknown in Protestant history. Renate Wilson ("Übersetzungen") has shown that, around this time, Halle Pietists began to carefully guard their position in the religious literary market of Germany and beyond. They translated popular medical texts into English, but increasingly refrained from translating religious literature. For all their interest in establishing ecumenical relations across the Atlantic, the Halle Pietists thus also wanted to secure a leading role for their own prints throughout the fast-growing and competitive markets for religious literature overseas. Halle used its middlemen in London and the support provided by the SPCK to distribute its own books, but was generally reluctant to help with the distribution of publications by others in order not to weaken its standing in the transatlantic book trade.

Francke's concluding letter refers to a catalogue of 83 essays and sermons written by Mather between 1693 and 1721, which Callenberg had collected. Francke briefly informs Mather about these documents, so that the latter may see how many of his writings are known by Francke. In his final remarks, Francke encourages Mather to send more of his books and pamphlets. Callenberg's handwritten "Scriptiones de Cottonis Matheri" reads like one of the first attempts to generate a bibliography of Mather's "American Pietism." It also demonstrates how closely Halle observed Mather's output of his "little Engines of Piety" (*Diary* 2: 333), as Mather himself termed the devotional and practical tracts, lectures, and essays that he published in his middle years. Callenberg's catalogue gives in chronological order running title and captions and even lists some anonymous publications that were only later identified as Mather's work by his son. Halle's interest in surveying Mather's writings obviously shifted over the years. While earlier the focus rested entirely on missionary publications and Mather's accounts of the state of Christianity, from 1706 onwards a strong emphasis is given to Mather's "Instruments of Piety" (*Diary* 2: 23) and how the "Consideration of CHRIST [may] be brought into all the Life of a Christian" (*The Heavenly Conversation*, n. p.). Callenberg records, for instance, Mather's "An ESSAY, On the CARE taken in the Divine PROVIDENCE For CHILDREN when their PARENTS *forsake* them" – otherwise known as *Orphanotrophium. Or, Orphans Well-Provided For* (1711) – a reform piece which is greatly inspired by the orphanage Francke had founded in Halle. Other titles recall Mather's efforts for universal union of the Church, as he delineates it in his *Malachi. Or, the Everlasting Gospel, Preached unto the Nations* (1717). Finally, there are texts which were signed by Mather as a "FELLOW of the Royal Society," such as his philosophical approach to the nature of the soul discussed in *Coheleth* (1720) and his more poetic and inspirational piece, *The Salvation of the Soul Considered* (1720).

The "transatlantic turn" in religious history has given rise to a closer study of the letters, diaries, and journals of pastors, theologians, and laymen as important documents to better understand the "shared network of theological convictions, reading, and family connections" that can be found over geographical distance and generations (Searle 305). Moreover, recent studies in the field of the history of the book call our attention to the "extraordinary diversity of the trans-European Reformation" (Anderson 19). Replacing religious parochialism with Protestant internationalism, transatlantic religious history foregrounds a "cosmopolitan mind" (20) that characterized the Protestant Atlantic world. Moreover, given the lack of strict denominational conformity in British America (except perhaps for early New England congregationalism), it was vital for colonial ministers to contact their mother churches on the Continent in spiritual and pastoral matters in order to maintain their status, power, and knowledge within their local religious communities. Also, the quantity of

books, treatises, and essays published by New England congregational ministers both in England and on the Continent demonstrate their strong conviction
of belonging to a transatlantic Christian brotherhood to which they contributed. Both with regard to their printed output as well as through pastoral practice,
the colonial ministry is certainly one of the most important social groups in the
eighteenth-century transatlantic world.

The transatlantic exchange between Mather and Francke demonstrates the
multiple motivations that informed the connection between German Pietism
and New England Calvinism. It also shows how far Mather was willing to go in
spite of his concern for orthodoxy. Critics see Mather as a transitional figure
who drew his inspiration from Puritanism, Pietism, and from nascent Enlightenment ideas. Robert Middlekauff notes however that "Pietism was not something [Mather] picked up to repair the sagging authority of the ministry in New
England. It expressed the intensity of his own spirit" (306). New England Puritans undoubtedly shared ideas of practical Christianity with their Continental brethren and felt solidarity with them in terms of what Francke called "Universalverbesserung," or universal improvement. Networks of correspondents,
helpers, and donors in Europe and beyond also created the impression of a religious experience that united all Protestants in their common endeavor to reinte-
grate the Reformation into a broader Christian tradition. Erhard Peschke sees a
"gläubigen Realismus," a spiritual realism (*Studien* 2: 221), at work within Pietism that intends to reconcile inwardness with the primacy of the outward
world. According to Peschke, what is real to Francke are the footsteps of God,
as he describes his own reform activities, as well as the daily experience of God's
grace, and doing good to others. In this respect, too, the continental model of
Francke's Pietism may very well have served as a catalyst for Mather's thinking.

And yet, one should not forget that among all affinities there are fundamental theological differences between Pietism and Puritanism. The Puritan
way to set the "*Truths* on *Fire*," as Mather has it in his *Manuductio ad Ministerium* (105), differs greatly from German Pietism's more institutional approach
towards benevolence and reform. There is one group of critics who see Mather,
regardless of his affinity for ecumenical Pietism, as someone who, in the final
instance, insisted on orthodox Calvinism as the sole truth. Others who approached the two Pietisms from a theological point of view claim that "Puritanism and Pietism simply do not share common expectations about the way
Christian faith is experienced" (Tipson 706). Spener's and Francke's optimistic
belief in a progress in grace does not agree with Calvinism's preparational theology and stages of conversion. As valid as these objections may be, they keep
Mather caught in a "continuing oscillation ... between the progressive and conservative poles" (Lovelace, *American Pietism* 41). However, Mather's career as
pastor and evangelist shows that New England Puritanism did not develop

along the lines of a fixed set of orthodox creeds. Mather's Puritanism rather resembles a "distillation system" that subsumes "legalistic elements, leaving a predominant stress on inner piety by the end of the seventeenth century" (Lovelace 38–39). Even though Perry Miller falsely interpreted the innovations of third-generation Puritans as signs of decadence and a decline in piety, he was therefore right in regarding Mather not simply as "guardian of orthodoxy" (631), but as someone who moved with his time. He read Mather's late pastoral manual *Manuductio ad Ministerium* (1726) as a "fascinating melange of seventeenth- and eighteenth-century attitudes," a book that airs the "contradictory winds of doctrine" that are blowing through the dawning Age of Reason. This view emphasizes Mather's growing investigation into science and natural philosophy so that the *Manuductio ad Ministerium* appears not as a "variant on the traditional treatise of the pastorate," but has to be read "in connection with others of his own works such as *Reasonable Religion, Reason Satisfied: and Faith Established, A Man of Reason,* and *The Christian Philosopher*" (631).

However, Mather did not only incorporate science and natural philosophy, but also an experiential practice-oriented approach to religion that can be found in the Pietist works of Spener and Francke.[22] I therefore agree with Silverman who has suggested that "Mather's program for Doing Good," which found its most famous expression in his *Bonifacius: An Essay Upon the Good* (1710) "gained confidence and direction from his reading of the German Pietists, one of the most pervasive spiritual and intellectual forces on his adult life" (230).[23] As pastors, educators, and theologians Mather, like the Halle Pietists, did not pursue abstract doctrines, but developed a practice of devotion and good works that answered to the religious and social needs of their time. They believed in

---

22 For all his enthusiasm about ecumenism, Mather was fairly realistic about a possible union of Lutherans and Calvinists. In one of the concluding chapters of the *Manuductio ad Ministerium,* entitled "The *Genuine* and *Catholic* Spirit of *Christianity,* described, and commended" (115–30), Mather experiments with what he calls a "*Syncretism* of PIETY" (122). As the ensuing dialogue between "Master *Lutheran*" and "Master *Calvinist*" illustrates, there can never be a union in terms of religious principles. Therefore, Mather departs from "the Churches that will keep up *Instruments of Separation*" (127) and promotes a "*Christian Fellowship,*" a "*Coalition*" (127) of those of "Visible PIETY" (125). Mather admonishes his New England students that they should "let the *Table* of the Lord have no *Rails* about it, that shall hinder a Godly *Independent,* and *Presbyterian,* and *Episcopalian,* and *Antipedobaptist,* and *Lutheran,* from sitting down together there" (127). Miller puts it aptly: "Grandfathers Cotton and Mather must have turned uncomfortably in their graves when he who bore both their names thus renounced what had been the single purpose of their lives" (634). Already at the very beginning of his correspondence with Francke, Mather maintains that as there is "a *Fanatick,* so there is an *Orthodox,* a *Reformed,* an Heavenly Pietism" (*Heavenly Conversation* n. p.). This heavenly Pietism unites them and demonstrates that Pietism has to be seen as a whole way of life, and as such, for both of them, Pietism matters.
23 We also know from Mather's *Diary* (2: 413, 481) that he carefully studied Francke's theology and biblical hermeneutics, reading the *Manuductio ad Lectionem Scripturae Sacrae* (1693) and Francke's preface to the Greek New Testament (*Praefatio Nova,* 1702).

reason to distinguish the Holy Spirit from the other spirits of *"Fanatick … Pietism"* (Mather, *Heavenly Conversation* n. p.). What united them was indeed their shared commitment to the core tenets of Protestantism, which they regarded as being in accordance with reason, and their strong belief in an applied theology directed against the *"Indifferency in Religion"* and the "Corruptions of the *Market-place"* (*Diary* 2: 16, 19).

Francke's report of 1722 demonstrates that the two Pietisms were building a network that bridged the North Atlantic in both directions. As Bremer has shown, networks tie together people in "a variety of ways and perform different services for each other" (*Congregational Union* 10). Despite all denominational differences, this early transatlantic Pietist network was fueled by the ardent desire to bring about religious renewal. Callenberg's printed version of the 1722 report, and also Mather's letters to the Francke's missionaries in India, illustrate that it became a multifarious network in which transactions were based on attitudinal congruence, affections, and shared religious dispositions. Mather's assumption that *"American Puritanism* [is] so much of a Peece with the *Frederician Pietism"* (*Diary* 2: 411) sounds in many ways highly idealistic. At least with regard to the notion of universal religious improvement, however, Mather's statement is a realistic assessment of an essential similarity between the two strands of Pietism which enabled and motivated their co-operation in an international Protestant setting.

Appendix

English Translation from: Johann Heinrich Callenberg. *Narratio Epistolica Ad Cott. Matherum Theologum Anglicanum Ecclesiae Et Academiae Bostoniensis In America Directa Qua Continetur Historia Ecclesiastica Halensis Annorum Huius Saeculi Septem XV. Usque Ad XXI. Nec Non Genuina Relatio De Principis Saxonici Ad Ecclesiam Evangelicam Reditu Beati Cuiusdam Viri Hortatu Et Nomine Scripsit Io. Henr. Callenberg Phil Prof. Publ.* Halle: Verlagsbibliothek der Buchhandlung des Waisenhauses, 1735. i–ii; 1–4, 115–133.

Preface

That blessed man, whose encouragement and fame gave me reason to compose this narrative, is August Hermann Francke, pride and joy of the Lutheran church. His writings, above all his description of the accomplishments in Glaucha,[24] had come

---

24 Glaucha, which is situated near Halle in Saxony, became the center of Pietist social welfare projects. In 1698, August Hermann Francke founded an orphanage there, which was connected with a modern system of secondary schools. Francke's orphanage became a model that was frequently imitated in England and in North America.

into the possession of the theologian Mather, who is acclaimed in America, and they induced him to start a correspondence with Francke. Mather's pious mind is burning with the desire to win his people's support for active devotion to heavenly truth and to propagate this very truth among the Indian tribes. I have seen several pamphlets of his written for this purpose. However, I was above all pleased when I read the great book, which has been composed by him, with the title *Magnalia Dei*.[25] In this, an ecclesiastical history of New England can be found. Therefore, it is not astonishing that a highly pleasant friendship has been formed between such men, because of their similarity of intentions and undertakings. Until Francke's death, this friendship flourished for many years, as far as spatial distance allowed it, and was cultivated by mutual letters. However, the theologian from Halle could write about nothing more pleasurable [ii] to the American than what was pursued in Halle and what happened there. When I made acquaintance with Francke in the year 1721, Mather had been informed of events up to the year 1714.[26] So, Francke encouraged me to write the sacred history of the remaining years in his name. After it was written, proof-read – by him as well as by certain assistants of his –, and approved of, Francke sent it to Mather in the year 1722.[27] The fact that this narration was thoroughly agreeable to him was made clear by the fact that he incorporated the episode about the Saxon ruler who was brought back to the Lutheran church into an English sermon which he published in Boston.[28] I hope that our edition of the whole narration will also be appreciated by many readers, if not by all, and that it will bring sacred joy to their minds while they read it, so that it will be linked to acts of grace and to the imitation of good examples.

I have written this in Halle on May 8, 1735.

Chapter I: Introduction

Repeatedly, our honourable *Boehmius* has sent your small gifts to me, namely, booklets written by you, which are witnesses of your holy eagerness and constancy in developing and continuing the proclamation of the gospel among your Ameri-

---

25 Callenberg refers to Mather's *Magnalia Christi Americana*, which was published in London in 1702. Together with his letter, Mather had sent his church history and his *Bonifacius* (1710) to Halle. He wished them to be translated into German ("Narratio Orphanotropheo" 1). There are some single page translations from Mather's *Magnalia* concerning the Indian mission in New England, but no copies of the books can be found in the archive.

26 See Francke's "Viro maxime reverendo atque amplissimo D. Cottono Mathero" ([1714]; "Narratio Orphanotropheo") and Böhme's English translation of it in the third edition of *Pietas Hallensis* (1–60).

27 In the SPCK's archive there is one letter written by the society's secretary Henry Newman in which he informs Mather about Böhme's death. The letter comes with a superscription ("To the Reverend Dr. Cotton Mather at Boston, New England, by Captain Beale, dated 3. Aug. 1722) which states, "Reverend Sir, – I just now received the Letter herewith sent from good Mr. Martini, one of our late Dear Mr. Boehm's Executors and with it send a long Letter from your Excellent Mr. Professor Franck to you, which Mr. Boehm when living told me was coming to him by piece meals as opportunity presented of conveying it, and I believe the last part of it must have been receiv'd but just before his Death" (qtd. in Allen and McClure 231).

28 I was unable to find a sermon matching this description in Holmes bibliography.

cans. While I was contemplating the mind of the people, which is so avid for the glory and salvation of Christ, and while I was thinking about the remaining effort and assiduity, and about the fruits and successes which normally follow this, it cannot be expressed how much joy and inducement I derived from it to thank the Lord, who elicits such sweet and efficacious words in the furthest and most secluded region.

Your preceding letters consist among other things of this: In your New England there are almost 200 churches of the English and 30 of Indians who have been converted to the Christian faith. In all of these the effort towards the Protestant doctrine and true piety [2] are eminent. You strenuously continue in the Protestant ministry, which you took over when you were seventeen, until today when you are fifty two.[29] You not only promulgate the Gospel by word of mouth, but also through your deeds and the scripture. You have written more than 250 booklets in different languages, all of them for the cause of Christ, and you have brought them to the public. Taken together they comprise an ample history of the churches, which Christ has founded in America. Until today you have worked on a biblical opus, which you want to call Biblia Americana.[30] You have certainly not neglected any subject to support its elegant style. You have carefully consulted mathematics, philosophy, and whatever researchers of our age have found out about the classics, philology, and natural science. Nevertheless, you did not find anything more important in your entire hermeneutic approach than active piety, a mind which has been purified by the Holy Spirit, and the writings of experts who transmitted the knowledge of the Holy Scripture. Amazingly, the writings of Arndt, Spener, and my little works of various content, namely, instruction about the reading of the Holy Scripture and the book of programs, have pleased you.[31] There are seven preachers of the Holy Word in your city of *Boston*, who are joined with you in special love, which I hold in high regard, and hand in hand with you nourish the people, whose care has been entrusted to you.[32]

---

29   Francke repeats the content of an earlier letter by Mather (1717) in which he mentions his age. Mather was, however, sixty years old in 1722, when Francke's reply was composed.

30   See the copy of Mather's letter to Anton Wilhelm Böhme (6 August 1716): "When I readd [sic] the preface of our excellent *Frankius* to his Greek New Testament, it revived in me some Hopes; that our glorious Lord, may in His Time inspire and incline some capable Persons to bring our, *Biblia Americana*, into the World. ... I can without Vanity assure you, that the Church of God, has never yett [sic] had so rich an Amassment of the most valuable Things together tendered unto it. But after all, the most valuable Things, are those which such men as your *Arndt*, and *Franck*, and others of the like truest Erudition, have led into. ... If this work ever see the Light, I expect, it will be from the Countenance and Contribution, of men of our *Universal Religion*; who will every way appear more and more in the several Forms of Christianity" (*Diary* 2: 413).

31   Johann Arndt (1556–1621); as Mather's *Diary* and numerous other references to "my *Arndt*" (*Diary* 2: 348) show, he was well acquainted with Arndt's *De Vero Christianismo*, a devotional book which is central for seventeenth-century Lutheran Pietism. Mather had studied Spener's *De Natura et Gratia* (1715), which he had received in 1717 (*Diary* 2: 490), an experience he considered vital "to render me a finished Christian" (2: 497). Francke had sent his own *Manuductio ad Lectionem Scripturae Sacrae* (1693) and, among the short programmatic treatises, was Francke's preface to the Greek New Testament (see Brecht 462).

32   For church establishments in Boston in the opening decades of the eighteenth century, see M. Hall (293–301, 343–50).

[3] May God protect this fellowship of the holy work, may He command that the proclamation of heavenly truth among immature people, which He has instigated, be eternal and may He favor the proclamation by bestowing on us new successes day by day!

In doing so we share your happiness about the divine gifts, which have been granted to your part of the world.[33] I want you to share our joy, which is caused by the abundance and the permanence of goods, which flow into our mouths from above; I want to show which pieces of evidence of propitious providence God has put forth to the accomplishments of *Glaucha* recently. As their perception gave us reason to rejoice, in spite of various unfavourable events, their exposition is hopefully delightful to you.

This you have confirmed yourself beforehand and you have therefore asked me to continue writing letters to you, which should be as long as possible. I will satisfy your wish and narrate, in a number of words, in what state our affairs have been since the year 1714, when I composed my last narrative to you.

Yet I hope that this letter achieves the same effect that – as you write – the mentioned letter and booklet had,[34] in which the achievements of Halle are depicted. Evidently, you have shared that booklet, which contains the amazing yet true history, with your faithful people, who, after they had contemplated God's miraculous footsteps with incredible and unutterable pleasure of the mind [4], praised these divine providences most profusely. Why? Because through the generous communication of this letter, as many attempts at piety as possible have been instigated in the eastern regions of India, just like glowing charcoal which has been picked up from the altar. However, with how much joy my rather fruitful letter has imbued you and all of your people from New England and how much praise the churches of New England sang to God and to our Christ, after the letter had been read, cannot be expressed in words. I confess, this message has very much moved me and it has prompted me to work on the continuation of so fruitful a history.

I had been considerably moved by your letters and I was ashamed for having deferred the response I owe you for so long. Yet, I could not fulfil my obligation instantly, though the delay was not my fault but was due to necessity. The number of people from my immediate environment who accosted me was so great that I was forced to somewhat neglect my supporters from far away. This happened against my will and among complaints about the missed chance and the offence to people who do not know about my situation. I therefore urgently ask you, dear Sir, not to blame me for the delay, which was not my fault. However, as a compensation for the delay you will now kind-heartedly receive a longer letter. If anything occurs in this

---

33 Here Francke refers to the first part of Mather's 1717 letter to him, in which he defends the churches in New England against the prevalent view in Europe that the New World had only a marginal role in the history of salvation. In light of Mather's claim of "balancing globes" in matters of church union (Engler, Fichte, Scheiding 19), Francke's letter shows that "[b]oth sides become conscious of their congruity, and the new light of American Puritanism flows together with the light of continental pietism, strengthening their common endeavor" (Benz, "Ecumencial" 167).

34 Reference to *Pietas Hallensis* (1716), which Mather had read and in which Böhme had published Francke's first long letter to Mather (see Francke, "Narratio de Orphanotropheo").

letter which seems to be in favour of my reputation, I strongly ask you to think that I have mentioned it for no other reason than the praise of divine goodness.

Chapter 18:

On the Saxon Sovereign Who Was Brought Back to the Lutheran Church

Returning from this journey,[35] I succeeded in something that I will set forth in a little more detail, as it is a plentiful cause of joy and a reason to thank the *Lord. Mauritius Guilielmus,*[36] a prince of Saxony, who was descended from an excellent family, came from the town of *Zeitz.* He had once been ruler of the diocese and was now ruler of the territory (of Zeitz). Easily the best educated of the sovereigns of our century, he had openly renounced the evangelical religion and now approved of the papal religion; the Jesuit Schmeltzerus from the town of Vienna,[37] who was partly the originator of this error and partly reinforced it, surrounded him for a long time.

Never had I seen this sovereign before, nor had I ever talked to him, [116] as there had never been an opportunity to make an attempt to. But when I was sojourning on this way, some friends told me, more than once, that several people – above all Her Most Serene Highness, aunt of our king – believed it would not be futile if I would leave my journey, go to the sovereign, and converse with him about religion; something which this sovereign, due to his exceptional education, would certainly not be reluctant to do. However, I responded that I could not come without any explicit invitation, and in order to be useful to him in such an important matter, I would not dare to offend him. Back home, I refused with the same words the demand of many; especially because I did not know until then if they really wanted me to come to this place.

But after some time had passed, a letter from this region, written on July 13, 1718, was brought to me, in which some Lutheran minister asked me for arguments to bring the sovereign back to the path of truth. I recommended to him a small book by *Spenerus,* edited in the year 1684, entitled *Instructions about the Blessed Return to the Evangelic Truth of those Who Suffered from Being Led Away from it to Errors, Especially Papal Ones, and Who Are Now Driven to Repentance by the Holy Spirit.*[38] Furthermore, I told him to lay open in his theological meetings what

---

35   The previous chapter dealt with Francke's journey to South Germany which he undertook from August 1717 to April 1718.

36   Duke Moritz Wilhelm of Sachsen-Zeitz (1664–1718) was from early on interested in theology and profoundly inspired by Philipp Jacob Spener's Pietist thought; both men had met in Frankfurt am Main where Spener had propagated many of his ideas. In 1715, under the influence of his brother Christian August, who had converted to Catholicism in 1697 and was widely known as the "Cardinal of Saxony," the prince himself adopted the Catholic faith. His conversion was made public in 1717.

37   Franz Heinrich Schmelzer (1678–1738), a Jesuit priest whose name Protestant pamphleteers ridiculed, referring to him as "Schelm" (rogue), an anagram of his German last name Schmelzer; see Böttiger (287).

38   Reference to Philipp Jakob Spener, *Christlicher Unterricht von seliger Wiederkehr zu der Evangelischen Wahrheit der jenigen, welche sich von derselben zur irriger Lehr sonderlich dem Papstthum verführen lassen und nun von Gottes Geist wiederumb zur buß gerühret werden; samt einem Gebet in solchem zustand* (1684). Spener had disproved the Tridentine doc-

he wrote about this matter everywhere in an illustrious manner; and I also recommended a small book by the Christian *Aletophilus*[39] (which is a pseudonym), in which this Aletophilus demonstrates vis-à-vis someone who calls himself a *conscientious* Christian[40] [117] that a man could completely achieve eternal salvation in the Lutheran religion. I added: If he told me more about the sovereign's soul and told me what one would have to aim at, then I would give advice more appropriate to the goal that was to be reached. Other business then kept me from writing a longer letter. But this friend wrote back that Her Most Serene Highness, wife of the sovereign,[41] wished that I come myself, and that she strongly asserted that this would not be unpleasant to the sovereign. I saw that if I persisted in refusing thus brusquely, those people would judge that I either lacked the love to attempt to bring the erring man back to the right path, or that my conviction to defend the evangelical truth before the papal scholar was weak. So I answered that I would comply with Her Most Serene Highness, wife of the sovereign, as a sign of God's will, and, once my business was done, I would go there.

So I departed from here on August 10 and went to *Zeitz*, at first to Her Most Serene Highness. Happy about my coming, she ordered the news of my arrival to be taken to His Most Serene Highness, her husband, who, at this time, sojourned in *Weida*; and she commanded to let him know that I would see him on my return from *Köstritz* where I was hurrying because of other business. There, in Köstritz, a letter was given to me, in which it was made clear that my coming would be welcome to the sovereign. Having received this message, I departed, and when, on August 13, I had come to the place where the sovereign was residing, [118] I was instantly invited by him to lunch.

Before we sat down to eat, he inquired in a most educated manner about the state of my academy and of our plans. During lunch, we had a varied, but valuable conversation. Then, when the sovereign felt that I had nothing more to say, he posed the following question: Which religion is the best? Among the guests, the Jesuit *Schmeltzerus* was present; and with these words, the sovereign intended to give me the opportunity to enter into a conversation with Schmeltzerus. When I had grasped the intention of the sovereign and understood his words, I said that he

---

trine of justification and its simple relationship between God and man. Instead, he put a strong emphasis on man's "new birth" and preferred regeneration ("Wiedergeburt") to conversion ("Bekehrung"). Regeneration leads to the "inflaming" ("Entzündung") of faith and the forgiveness of sins (justification and adoption), as well as the reception of a new nature. Spener's order of salvation was based on resignation and the "understanding that God will work in us what is pleasing to him without opposition" (Spener 84; see *Theologische Realenzyclopädie* 28: 331–35).

39 Johann Fischer (pseudonym: Christianus Aletophilus, 1636–1705), *Wahrer Christen vernünfftiger Gottesdienst, in Prüfung der Glaubens-Lehre nach der Schrifft, gegen den unvernünfftigen blinden Gehorsam in Glaubens-Sachen, / aus Gottes Wort verthätiget von Christiano Alethophilo* (1685). This polemic treatise refuted the position of the Catholic priest Johannes Breving, which was presented in his *Des Glaubens- und Religions-Scrupel durch der Herren Protestierenden Antwort vermehret und nicht gebessert. Das ist: Kurtze Voraugenstellung der vergeblichen Antwort, so der Christian Conscientiosus ... von einem zu Riga ungegründeter Weiss erhalten hat* (1683); see Deppermann (317).

40 Johannes Breving (d. 1686); ironic allusion to his Roman Catholicism.

41 Maria Amalia von Brandenburg-Schwedt (1670–1730), daughter of the Great Elector Friedrich Wilhelm.

could easily conjecture which side I would support and defend; obviously the pure and apostolic belief was found in the Protestant religion; the papal religion, on the other hand, suffered from great and abominable mistakes, of which I would now only mention two. Firstly, I mentioned that the papists did not regard the word of God, revealed in the Holy Scripture, as the only basis and measure of faith and life, but added to it the tradition.[42] Secondly, I pointed out that the papists added to the only and invisible head of the church, Jesus Christ, something else which is visible, although the Holy Scripture did not know it and rejected it. This way, a dispute started, which centered on the rule of believing. Some guests, old and young noblemen alike, joined the discussion with other servants, who all listened with the greatest attention to what was said, [119] while neither the sovereign nor anyone else interrupted. But after this opportunity to speak had been given to me, I gave a confession – free and affirmed by reason – about the truth of the doctrine which was bequeathed in the *confessio Augustana*[43] which the Lutheran church professes.

I showed openly what is to be thought of the papacy's false convictions by explaining: men, as long as they are not content with the rule of God's word, are led to an uncertain and unsteady destination, and they are driven to a most dangerous aberration. As a consequence, they can attain no certain knowledge, but are forced to depend on the pope's arbitrariness, or – since not all can see the pope every day – of any clergyman, and to approve, in some sort of faith, of blind doctrines. The evangelical doctrine, on the contrary, consistent with the apostolic instructions, I explained, orders men to follow the Holy Scripture as the one norm of faith, incapable of deception. For evidence, I cited the most famous sentences: 2. Timoth. 3. 15. 16. 17. and John 2. 10. 31. 32.[44] In reply to this, nothing came back from *Schmeltzerus*, who could only have replied with dubious argumentation. However, he took refuge in what the papists usually reply to people in these situations, but which has for long and abundantly been proven wrong.

Later, I understood what I had not then known: That the discussion of this matter must not be undertaken without godly advice; as with regard to the state of his soul, no other question seemed more urgent to the sovereign. [120] For this had been the beginning of his apostasy from the evangelical religion: That he had not firmly held the Holy Scripture as the one and only basis upon which faith was to be built. I also found that this rather free and passionate speech of mine, concerning

---

42 Francke refers to differences between Protestant and Catholic doctrine in the area of tradition. The Lutheran church claims that the Bible alone is intended by God to be the source of doctrinal truth. Catholicism differs from Protestantism since it maintains that many doctrines have been revealed to the Church over the centuries. For instance, there is the veneration of Mary, her immaculate conception and her bodily assumption into heaven. There is also the apocrypha, transubstantiation, praying to saints, the confessional, penance, and purgatory.

43 The confession of Augsburg, drawn up by Luther and Melanchthon in 1530, contains the principles of Protestants, and their reasons for separating from the Roman Catholic Church.

44 2 Tim. 3:15–17: "And that from a child thou hast known the holy scriptures, which are able to make thee wise unto salvation through faith which is in Christ Jesus"; "All scripture is given by inspiration of God, and is profitable for doctrine, for reproof, for correction, for instruction in righteousness"; "That the man of God may be perfect, thoroughly furnished unto all good works." John 8:31–32, "Then said Jesus to those Jews which believed on him, If ye continue in my word, then are ye my disciples indeed"; "And ye shall know the truth, and the truth shall make you free."

the papacy and the evangelical doctrine, had not insulted the listeners, but had been of great use to them. One of the noble ministers, who had been present at lunch, confirmed that if I had not given this speech, it would have brought about various concerns with many of the people; through my speech, however, all had been affirmed.

Together with one of the sovereign's counselors and *Schmelzerus*, I stayed with the sovereign after we had eaten. I revealed to him in a friendly manner that from his words I had understood that he, in his soul, had not yet returned to God. I could not tell and advise him anything better than to turn with all of his soul to God. I told him if he had not yet been in a true school, he could not know the importance of the soul going back to God. The sovereign seemed to have taken this with contempt and did not respond much. But I said everything not with hatred, but out of true love. I hoped it would be efficacious at the right time so that, when the light of the Holy Spirit has helped, he might have a brighter insight into the evangelical doctrine and, under its proper use, attain eternal salvation!

[121] Then, in private and far into the night, the sovereign talked to me about what he reprehended in the evangelical religion and what had urged him to leave it. Holding the Holy Bible in his hand, he carefully examined passages from it and analyzed them most accurately. After he had expressed his doubts, he attentively listened to their solution. What aggrieved him most was this: [that] it could not be that all that we were told by the Christian religion to believe and all that was accepted by the Christian church without any discussion was infallibly shown by the Holy Scripture; therefore the help of the traditions was necessary and above all the help of the synods, in particular of the ecumenical ones; in the judgment of which he finally acquiesced, believing that he would enter with his soul a carefree and secure path under their authority. He brought forward some dogmas which, he believed, could not have been unobjectionably approved of by the Holy Scripture, regarding the eternal godliness of Christ and of the Holy Spirit, regarding the mystery of the Trinity, the baptizing of infants, the Sunday – with what right was this day celebrated by the Christians instead of the seventh day, etc. I clarified, with God's help, that these things were in fact based on a statement of the Holy Scripture, so that the sovereign thereupon said: On this or that matter, more light was shed to him than he had had before. However, as long as something was not yet verified clearly, he did not hesitate to challenge it; he was exempt from that fault of zealots who often leap from one matter to the next although the first has not yet been thoroughly thought through.

[122] On the next day, August 14, I was again invited to lunch. Here I again discussed much of what I thought germane to the topic and useful in order to drive the wrong ideas out of the sovereign's mind. Even though the Jesuit *Schmeltzerus* was present and heard all this, he still said nothing against it. After lunch, the sovereign told me to come with him into his private room, where he continued the discussion he had started the day before. Over and over again he had seriously thought about the things I had said, and he had written down what still seemed opposed to the truth of what I said. After I had responded to this with numerous words, he again declared: A greater knowledge of many things had been bestowed on him. During this talk, he also thought of what he had once heard from *Olear-*

ius,[45] a professor from Leipzig, about the synods that were not supposed to be added to the Holy Scripture. These words now seemed to utterly unleash their force. The talk lasted until dinner in which the sovereign wanted me to take part.

It was again the sovereign's disposition that determined the talk during dinner. He then confirmed openly that much light had been shed on many things, but [that] he still was not entirely sure. Before this was the case, he would not admit to anything inconsiderately. If he were indeed convicted of an error, he would not feel it disreputable to return to the truth. Still, he revealed very openly that it appeared hard to him to profess this.

[123] But I slipped in a word of Christ for him: "For what is a man profited, if he shall gain the whole world, and lose his own soul?"[46] [I said that] none of the wiser men would accuse him of a sin if he said that in the beginning, when he had poorly perceived the matter, he had acted according to this feeling; now, however, after he had succeeded in understanding these things better, he thought it a sign of sincerity to follow the discovered truth. The days to come bore witness several times that I did not believe this man would die in the papal religion.

At one point, the sovereign remembered that Luther had said that he had adopted his opinion about the *mass* from an evil spirit.[47] The sovereign sent for the Jesuit and told him to search Luther's writings for the passage. With a few words I rejected this old defamation which had been made up by malevolent people from words of this blessed man, which were perverted into an alien direction; a defamation which many – and among them, *Seckendorffius,*[48] in his history of Lutheranism, book I, section 45 – had with numerous words refuted: In a letter, I later showed this passage to the sovereign. After a disputation about the *mass* had thus begun, I explained: The greatest part of this cult had been introduced into the church by human arbitrariness, which the Holy Scripture not only does not ask for,

---

45 Gottfried Olearius (1672–1713), theologian in Leipzig and writer of religious tracts and treatises, among others *Commentatio theologica de redem[p]tione ex inferno et liberatione a morte* (1707) and *De certitudine salutis* (1711). Olearius was also influenced by Spener's works.

46 Francke refers to Matt. 16:26.

47 For the history of Luther's alleged conference with the devil, see *The Religious Magazine* (1829/30): 462–64. The doctrine of justification was at the heart of Luther's conflict with the papacy, and eventually the mass became central to this conflict. His objection was to the concept of mass as sacrifice. The Roman teaching that in the mass the priest offers a sacrifice and thus appeases God's anger denies the efficacy of Christ's atoning work. Luther argued that it distorts the nature of Christianity, changing it from a religion of grace to one of works. In his *Admonition Concerning the Sacrament* (1530), Luther contended, "They made the sacrament which they should accept from God, namely, the body and blood of Christ, into a sacrifice and have offered it to the selfsame God. ... Furthermore, they do not regard Christ's body and blood as a sacrifice of thanksgiving, but as a sacrifice of works in which they do not thank God for His grace, but obtain merits for themselves and others and first and foremost, secure grace. Thus Christ has not won grace for us, but we want to win grace ourselves through our works by offering to God His Son's body and blood. This is the true and chief abomination and the basis of all blasphemy in the papacy" (Luther 38: 117–18).

48 Veit Ludwig of Seckendorff (1629–93), one of the teachers of August Hermann Francke and vehement proponent of Lutherism in his *Commentarius historicus et apologeticus de Lutheranismo, sive de reformatione religionis ductu D. Martini Lutheri* (1688/89) published in a translation as *Ausführliche Historie des Luthertums und der heilsamen Reformation* (1714).

but even condemns. Without the precept of the Holy Scripture we must not ponder anything with regard to the way we worship God.

The next day, August 15, I went to a count nearby, in the region of Glaucha; but I was back before the evening service. [124] On August 16, I was again invited to lunch and went there: And, as no one touched upon the controversy, I intended to get rid of the false assumption about true Christianity and about the right perception of the divine truth; and I showed what it is to really know God and Christ, and [what it is] to live as a Christian and by the guidance and the evidence of the godly scriptures. To this end, I also mentioned a few stories, for the telling of which the occasion arose and which seemed to have some importance for setting their minds into motion.

Again, after leaving the table, we spent the rest of the day in a private talk about the purity of the evangelical doctrine. *Schmeltzerus* referred to *Irenaeus* and *Cyrillus*[49] and said that these men highly favored the *mass* and, because of *Grabius's* words,[50] *Schmeltzerus* spoke for the old usage. The sovereign gave me writings of both Church Fathers in order to read them thoroughly at home; after I had done this, I could easily invalidate their reproaches. I also showed the sovereign a directory, attached to the Anglican edition of the writings of Cyrillus, in which papal errors are listed with Cyrillus's refutation of them. From *Halle*, I later sent him an essay by a theologian from Jena called *Buddeus*,[51] in which he, having rejected Grabius's view, made clear that neither the Roman *Clemens*[52] nor *Irenaeus*, so often called upon by the Jesuit to support his opinion, defended the *mass*.

On August 17, however, I did not join them for lunch because of bad health: [125] Still, at noon, I went into the courtyard on behalf of the sovereign. Here, I explained to him the difference between the evangelical and the papal doctrine in a more detailed way, and with him I pursued those passages of the Holy Scripture in which the Roman church was depicted through an image of Babylon and the reign of Antichrist. I also gave him some booklets that he should read after my departure: That is to say, the above-mentioned writing of *Spenerus* on the beneficial return to the truth and another writing[53] by the same man on persistence in the truth: And I promised that I would send him a letter of a certain *Langius*.[54] Because of this letter a famous man in the year 1699 was kept from leaving the evangelical truth. The sovereign knew *Langius*.

---

49   Saint Irenaeus (c. 135–202), early Church Father. His writings were formative in the early development of Christian theology; he stressed traditional elements in the church. Cyril of Alexandria (c. 375–444), defender of the orthodox faith and writer of dogmatic works.

50   Johannes Ernst Grabe (1666–1711), initially a Lutheran theologian, who under the influence of the Jesuit Robert Bellarmin questioned Protestantism. He migrated to England from Königsberg and became chaplain of Christ Church in Oxford.

51   Johann Franz Buddeus (1667–1729), professor of philosophy in Halle, later taught theology at the University of Jena.

52   Pope Clement I (called Clemens Romanus) was the first of the successors of St. Peter, and he is the first of the Apostolic Fathers.

53   See Spener's *Sieg der Wahrheit und der Unschuld* (1692).

54   Joachim Lange (1670–1744), pedagogue, theologian, and later professor of theology. He was one of Francke's students and became a stout defender of Halle Pietism against orthodox offenses; see Peters (114–19). Lange's works were known to Cotton Mather (see *Diary* 2: 348).

In the letter, [Langius] expertly calls back to mind that this mystery of sin, implanted from birth, which has a prominent place in the papacy, is hidden in all of us: [that] opposed to it, the kingdom of God, which is based on justice, peace and the joy of the Holy Spirit, and which is offered by the evangelical doctrine, is not acquired from the outside, but it should be built up within ourselves and we should sincerely approach it. Nobody must boast that he is freed from the papacy from the outside, but everyone should take care that he is purified of it within himself and that he admits to himself the kingdom of God instead of the papacy.

On August 18, I finally bid farewell to the sovereign and went back to *Halle.* Later, I went on to continue in written form what I had begun orally. [126] I was not only concerned about the scruples that might still be there and that needed to be removed, but also about showing the divine order – God promised to grant knowledge of the truth to those who make use of it. This order demands that we devote our soul to God and our mind to praying, ready to do what God wants. I wrote that Christ had said: If any man will do his will, he shall know of the doctrine, whether it be of God, or whether I speak of myself.[55] And in the same way I said that the bare knowledge of the evangelical truth would neither be of any use to us in this life nor in the next. For in Christ, nothing is worth anything except the new creature. I concluded that we must make our steps according to this principle and way if we wish to take part in peace and mercy.[56]

But as this man was still doubtful and as the danger was increasing with difficulties coming up from the outside, I wrote him a letter again, on September 27, with the following content: [that] I had heard of the effort of people who tried to cut off his path back to the evangelical truth. Alarmed by this message, I tried to write him something in order to admonish him in the most submissive way, in the light of my care for his eternal salvation. His doubts, I wrote were of the sort that, with God's help, he could easily be freed from. [127] And, just as I had already responded to all his objections, I was utterly ready to explain with even more words what he, until then, thought of as uncertain. I wrote that on the last day, no guilt should be on me for having neglected his soul. But he should beforehand consider this fact which no one can deny is reasonable: the soul is strengthened by God alone.[57] Our mind was for a long time stirred and torn here and there, until, with God's advice and pacification, it could come to rest. The Pharisees served as an example: Their genius, their knowledge of the scriptures and Christ's instruction, had been of no use in understanding the truth, but they had remained in error. That is why Christ announced: If someone did not obey the will that was given him, then this man could by no means reach the knowledge of the truth. In this manner, no better way of gaining a thorough insight into the truth could be shown to him than the one inculcated by Christ on the Pharisees. In the future, it would not be enough to explore the evangelical doctrine in the Holy Scripture – he had given an outright promise to be, in the future, bound to these only – but it was also neces-

---

55 John 7:17. [original footnote].
56 Gal. 6:15–16 [original footnote]. Francke paraphrases the original text: "For in Christ Jesus neither circumcision availeth any thing, nor uncircumcision, but a new creature" (6:15); "And as many as walk according to this rule, peace be on them, and mercy, and upon the Israel of God" (6:16).
57 Prov. 16:2 [original footnote]. "All the ways of a man are clean in his eyes; but the Lord weigheth the spirits."

sary to bring back to the reality of life the knowledge of the truth and to shun attentively whatever he felt resisted the revealed will of God. For this reason, God, on his own behalf, and to be called upon continually [128] so that He would grant the Holy Spirit; and, as Peter told us to, one had to remain watchful, praying in moderation and sobriety. He should make use of his courage and begin this certain course of life – not only one of perceiving the truth, but also one of attaining eternal salvation. On this road, he would have God as a helper, a defender, and an aid: Through his virtue, he would not only subordinate his reason to obedience to Christ, but he would also overcome all deceit and the power of Satan and of those who held him back in error; and he would certainly come to know that God is the compensator of those who seek Him. He knew that the papists were little concerned with his eternal salvation, but that they were content if only he followed their party outwardly, and if he, for proving that his soul was devoted to them, took part in the *mass*: In all other respects, they let him be a slave to sin and hurry right to his downfall. Therefore, as he had come to know this and as he had already obtained so much light from God that he saw a better way now, I implored him to confidently elude the darkness and its power, to turn his soul to the living God, and to arm himself with God's word that is distinguished from all else as a solid foundation. He should begin with more intense prayers and after he had gathered his faith in God, he should no longer hesitate to profess this truth anew – a truth that the wise *Fridericus*[58] and others of his ancestors, all of them most outstanding men, had been ready to approve after their blood was shed. I wrote to him that if he went on delaying the realization of his plan, [129] I was afraid that the other side would cause so many troubles that there would be no way left to set him free. And, if he could not take part in evangelical comfort, how much would this strike him with fear in the hour of his death? What, eventually, would he answer Jesus Christ at the time when his greatness and glory became apparent and when Jesus Christ would bring this as a reproach: That Jesus Christ had supported him so readily after his desertion and that he had shown him a way to overcome the doubt and to attain the eternal life; from which, for profane reasons, he had shrunk back. He should consider that he was advanced in years and not as healthy as he used to be. And even if I prayed for him, namely for a long life and a full recovery of his physical strength, still it was evident from the Holy Scripture that only a hand's breadth lay between us and entrance into eternity. What would all the glory of his life be good for then? Or how were these things to be judged with regard to the eternal agony by which his soul was to be tormented? Now, if there were indeed any scruples, I implored him in God's name to speak to me about them, so that I would not leave anything untried and so that he could be sure to have tried everything for a calm conscience. In the meantime I would persist in my pleas with God and I would pray that the duke would finish the incomplete work on his eternal salvation.

[130] On October 3 he answered to these things: That he still remained in a state of self-examination and consideration. So, after I had designed a letter, I reminded him again on October 6, among other things, of the following: That what he wrote, i.e., that he had still been examining himself and contemplating was a consolation for me. I wished, however, that he imagined himself as if he were in that eternal life, and from there he should see what had to be done just before death in order to devote his soul to God all the more easily and to make use of God's bright

58   Frederic III (1463–1525), elector of Saxony.

word – just like a torch – so that, by force of His word, he would dare to profess in the presence of all people the truth he had experienced, wholeheartedly and with faith in God, following the example of Josiah.[59]

Let us praise the Lord who, after many preceding temptations and plots, has finally overcome the sovereign's soul! Thus, on October 16 after discussing the matter with only very few people and against the hope and expectation of all the others, he went to the church of the Lord in *Pegau*, openly renounced the papal denomination and went to the holy supper, following the evangelical ceremony, accompanied by the singing of songs which indicated supplication for a most serious misconduct. The sovereign was dressed in clothes of mourning, and his countenance expressed that his soul was in an utterly pious and submissive state. Sending me a messenger, he instantly let me know about it by means of a letter and with the following words: With the support of God's favor, he had conquered himself [131], and according to the precept of our savior, Jesus Christ, he had taken part in the holy supper in the church meeting of *Pegau*. With speedy letters, he indicated his return to the Lutheran church also to the King of *Prussia* and to the other sovereigns.

So I congratulated the sovereign and, at the same time, I reassured him concerning the value of the godly word – a value he had now realized – and I showed him its legitimate implementation; I implored him to live a life worthy of the evangelical creed and to follow Christ, the light of the world. I prayed that he would attain assurance of faith and strengthening of spirit to protect him from falling away from God's love in Jesus Christ, for the Lord loved us so much that neither death, nor life, nor angel, nor principality, nor worldly power, nor anything past, present, or yet to come, nor anything high or low, might ever make us stumble and fall away.[60] With regard to the hostile pursuit of men, I recommended David's Psalm XXVII for his perusal.[61] As some colleagues of mine were together with me just at that moment when the messenger had come to me and as they became partakers in the same joy, they, too, decided to collectively write a letter to the sovereign. In this letter, after giving the most serious reasons why the community of the papal worship was to be left, [132] they called on him with the words of the Apostle Judas: But you, dear friends, although you are putting yourselves over your most holy belief, pray to the Holy Spirit and save yourselves in God's love, expecting mercy of our Lord Jesus Christ for eternal life.[62] In a friendly manner, they also remarked that it was not enough to have returned outwardly to the true church; an inner improvement of the soul, according to the most holy belief, was required – this they said, was achieved and continued by means of modest prayers. Otherwise, he would, in the future, not be apt to overcome wicked agitation. He should strug-

---

59 Josiah was king of Judah from 641 to 609 BCE. His example refers to righteousness in time of wickedness. Josiah's faithfulness was seen in numerous ways throughout his life. He sought after God, broke down the altars of Baal, and punished the idolatrous priests.

60 Rom. 8:38–39 [original footnote], "For I am persuaded, that neither death, nor life, nor angels, nor principalities, nor powers, nor things present, nor things to come, nor strength, (8.39) nor height, nor depth, nor any other creature, shall be able to separate us from the love of God, which is in Christ Jesus our Lord."

61 Cf. Ps. 17:4, "Concerning the works of men, by the word of thy lips I have kept me from the paths of the destroyer."

62 Ps. 20–21. [original footnote].

gle over the belief that was promised to the saints, using the forces that God would give him, in view of the power of God's glory, to begin this good struggle; so that, having finished all this and having kept his belief to the very end, he would one day obtain this crown that was reserved in heaven, etc.

In a most gentle manner, he replied to this on November 5. In this letter, one reads words so very clear and worthy of a Christian man that we realized that God was completing the work He had initiated in him. However, a message was delivered soon after that the sovereign had, due to a disease of few days, similar to the small-pox, departed from life most devoutly and in constant belief on November 14: On hearing this, I was very depressed because there had been hope that he would, after this change of mind, have taken better care of his matters and those of his subjects in the future. Nevertheless I praised the Lord, who, during all this business, did not appear before our eyes with any obscure omens and who was now revealed openly to those who observed the effort and fight of the soul in the accomplishment of this return to the truth. This way one could understand how precious the salvation of men is to God and how He wishes to relieve them of all errors and how readily He frees them of an error if, once they have abandoned their persistence in resisting and refusing the Holy Spirit, they lend their ears to God's word, and if it is near to their heart to learn about the truth. For God wants all people to be saved and to reach knowledge of the truth. Let us therefore praise Him together for all His favor, even if it cannot be described!

Works Cited

Primary Sources

Callenberg, Johann Heinrich. *Narratio Epistolica Ad Cott. Matherum Theolgum Anglicanum Ecclesiae Et Academiae Bostoniensis In America Directa Qua Continetur Historia Ecclesiastica Halensis Annorum Huius Saeculi Septem XV. Usque Ad XXI. Nec Non Genuina Relatio De Principis Saxonici Ad Ecclesiam Evangelicam Reditu Beati Cuiusdam Viri Hortatu et Nomine Scripsit Io. Henr. Callenberg. Phil. Prof. Publ*. Halle, 1735.

Francke, August Hermann. "Narratio de Orphanotropheo Glauchensi. Viro maxime reverendo atque amplissimo D. Cottono Mathero, ecclesiae Christi Bostonensis in America ministro fidissimo, Augustus Hermannus Franckius uberrimam in Christo salutem dicit." *Natalicia Secularia Augusti Hermanni Franckii Die XIII. Mensis Martii Anni MDDCCLXIII. in Aula Magna Orphanotrophei Hora IX. Publice Celebranda Directorii Aedium Franckianarum Nomine ex Officio Indicit Fridericus Augustus Eckstein*. Halle, 1863. 1–26.

–. *Pietas Hallensis: or, an Abstract of the Marvellous Foot-Steps of Divine Providence, Attending the Management and Improvement of the Orphan-House at Glaucha near Hall; and of Other Charitable Foundations Relating to It*. London, 1716.

Luther, Martin. "Admonition Concerning the Sacrament of the Body and the Blood of Our Lord." 1530. *Luther's Works*. Ed. Martin E. Lehmann. Vol. 38: *Word and Sacrament* IV. Philadelphia: Fortress Press, 1971. 93–137.

"Luther's Alleged Conference with the Devil." *Religious Magazine, or Spirit of the Foreign Theological Journals and Reviews* 4 (1829/1830): 462–64.

Mather, Cotton. *Cotton Mather's Student and Preacher; or, Directions for a Candidate of the Ministry.* London, 1789.

–. *Diary of Cotton Mather.* Ed. Worthington C. Ford. Collections of the Massachusetts Historical Society, 7th series. Vols. 7–8. Boston: MHS, 1911–12.

–. *The Heavenly Conversation. An Essay Upon the Methods of Conversing with a Glorious Christ, in Every Step of Our Life. With Directions Upon That Case, How May the Consideration of Christ, Be Brought into All the Life of a Christian?* Boston, 1710.

–. *India Christiana. A Discourse, Delivered unto the Commissioners, for the Propagation of the Gospel among the American Indians. ...* Boston, 1721.

–. *Malachi. Or, the Everlasting Gospel, Preached unto the Nations. And those Maxims of Piety, which Are to Be the Glorious Rules of Behaviour, the Only Terms of Communion, and the Happy Stops to Controversy. ...* Boston, 1717.

–. *Manuductio ad Ministerium. Directions for a Candidate of the Ministry. ...* Boston, 1726.

–. *The Minister: A Sermon, Offer'd unto the Anniversary Convention of Ministers, From Several Parts of New-England, Met at Boston, 31 d. II m. 1722.* Boston, 1722.

–. *Nuncia Bona e Terra Longinqua: A Brief Account of Some Good and Great Things a Doing for the Kingdom of God, In the Midst of Europe. Communicated in a Letter to – .* Boston, 1715.

–. *Selected Letters of Cotton Mather.* Ed. Kenneth Silvermann. Baton Rouge: Louisiana State UP, 1971.

–. *The Stone Cut Out of the Mountain.* Boston, 1716.

–. *Things to Be More Thought Upon.* Boston, 1713.

–. *Three Letters from New-England, Relating to the Controversy of the Present Time.* London, 1721.

Mather, Samuel. *Vita B. Augusti Hermanni Franckii.* Boston, 1733.

Spener, Philipp Jakob. *Pia Desideria. Umkehr in die Zukunft. Reformprogramm des Pietismus.* 1675. 5th ed. Ed. Erich Beyreuther. Giessen: Brunnen Verlag, 1995.

–. "Resignation." *Pietists: Selected Writings.* Ed. Peter C. Erb. New York: Paulist P, 1983. 83–87.

Secondary Sources

Aland, Kurt. "Die Annales Hallenses ecclesiastici: Das älteste Denkmal der Geschichtsschreibung des Halleschen Pietismus." *Kirchengeschichtliche Entwürfe: Alte Kirche, Reformation und Luthertum, Pietismus und Erweckungsbewegung.* Gütersloh: Gerd Mohn, 1960. 580–650.

Allen, W. O. B., and Edmund McClure. *Two Hundred Years: The History of the Society for Promoting Christian Knowledge, 1698–1898.* London: Society for Promoting Christian Knowledge, 1898.

Anderson, Douglas. *William Bradford's Books: Of Plimmoth Plantation and the Printed Word.* Baltimore and London: Johns Hopkins UP, 2003.

Benz, Ernst. "Ecumenical Relations between Boston Puritanism and German Pietism (Cotton Mather and August Hermann Francke)." *The Harvard Theological Review* 54.3 (1961): 159–93.

–.   "Pietist and Puritan Sources of Early Protestant World Missions (Cotton Mather and A. H. Francke)." *Church History* 20.2 (1951): 28–55.

Beyreuther, Erich. *August Hermann Francke und die Anfänge der Ökumenischen Bewegung*. Hamburg-Bergstedt: Herbert Reich Evang. Verlag, 1957.

–.   *Geschichte des Pietismus*. Stuttgart: Steinkopf, 1978.

Böttiger, Karl Wilhelm. *Geschichte des Kurstaates und Königreich Sachsens*. Vol. 2: *Von der Mitte des sechzehnten Jahrhunderts bis auf die neuste Zeit, 1553–1831*. Hamburg: Perthes, 1831.

Brecht, Martin. "August Hermann Francke und der Hallische Pietismus." *Geschichte des Pietismus*. Ed. Martin Brecht Vol. 1: *Der Pietismus vom siebzehnten bis zum frühen achtzehnten Jahrhundert*. Göttingen: Vandenhoeck & Ruprecht, 1993. 439–539.

Bremer, Francis J. *Congregational Communion: Clerical Friendship in the Anglo-American Puritan Community, 1610–1692*. Boston: Northeastern UP, 1994.

–, ed. *Puritanism: Transatlantic Perspectives on a Seventeenth-Century Anglo-American Faith*. Boston: Massachusetts Historical Society, 1993.

Brown, Matthew Pentland. *The Pilgrim and the Bee: Reading Rituals and Book Culture in Early New England*. Philadelphia: U of Pennsylvania P, 2007.

Brunner, Daniel L. *Halle Pietists in England: Anthony William Boehm and the Society for Promoting Christian Knowledge*. Göttingen: Vandenhoeck & Ruprecht, 1993.

Clark, Christopher M. *The Politics of Conversion: Missionary Protestantism and the Jews in Prussia, 1728–1941*. Oxford: Clarendon P, 1995.

Cressy, David. *Coming Over: Migration and Communication between England and New England in the Seventeenth Century*. Cambridge: Cambridge UP, 1987.

Deppermann, Andreas. *Johann Jakob Schütz und die Anfänge des Pietismus*. Tübingen: Mohr Siebeck, 2002.

Durnbaugh, Donald F. "The Flowering of Pietism in the Garden of America." *Christian History* 10 (1986): 23–27.

Engler, Bernd, Jörg Fichte, and Oliver Scheiding, eds. *Millennial Thought in America: Historical and Intellectual Contexts, 1630–1860*. Trier: WVT, 2002.

Fogleman, Aaron. *Jesus is Female: Moravians and Radical Religion in Early America*. Pennsylvania: U of Pennsylvania P, 2007.

Forster, Stephen. *The Long Argument: English Puritanism and the Shaping Argument of New England Culture, 1500–1700*. Chapel Hill: U of North Carolina P, 1991.

Francke, Kuno. "The Beginning of Cotton Mather's Correspondence with August Hermann Francke." *Philological Quarterly* 5 (1926): 193–95.

–.   "Cotton Mather and August Hermann Francke." *Studies and Notes in Philology and Literature* 5 (1896): 57–67.

–.   "Further Documents Concerning Cotton Mather and August Hermann Francke." *Americana Germanica* 1 (1897): 31–66.

Garret, Clarke. *Spirit Possession and Popular Religion: From the Camisards to the Shakers*. Baltimore: Johns Hopkins UP, 1987.

Grabbe, Hans-Jürgen. Introduction. *Halle Pietism, Colonial North America, and the Young United States*. Ed. Hans-Jürgen Grabbe. Stuttgart: Steiner, 2008.

Hall, David D. *Ways of Writing: The Practice and Politics of Text-Making in Seventeenth-Century New England*. Philadelphia: U of Philadelphia P, 2008.

Hall, Michael G. *The Last American Puritan: The Life of Increase Mather*. Middletown: Wesleyan UP, 1988.

Hambrick-Stowe, Charles E. *The Practice of Piety: Puritan Devotional Disciplines in Seventeenth-Century New England*. Chapel Hill: U of North Carolina P, 1982.

Holifield, E. Brooks. *Theology in America: Christian Thought from the Age of the Puritans to the Civil War*. New Haven: Yale UP, 2003.

Holmes, Thomas James. *Cotton Mather: A Bibliography of his Works*. 3 vols. Cambridge: Harvard UP, 1940.

Hoskins, J. P. "German Influence on Religious Life and Thought in America during the Colonial Period." *Princeton Theological Review* 5 (1907): 225–27.

Lehmann, Hartmut. "Transatlantic Migration, Transatlantic Networks, Transatlantic Transfer." *In Search of Peace and Prosperity: New German Settlements in Eighteenth-Century Europe and America*. Ed. Hartmut Lehmann, et al. University Park, Pennsylvania: Pennsylvania State UP, 2000. 307–30.

–, and Hermann Wellenreuther, eds. *Transatlantische Religionsgeschichte: 18. bis 20. Jahrhundert*. Göttingen: Wallstein, 2006.

Lovelace, Richard F. *The American Pietism of Cotton Mather: Origins of American Evangelicalism*. Grand Rapids: Christian UP, 1979.

–. "Cotton Mather." *The Pietist Theologians: An Introduction to Theology in the Seventeenth and Eighteenth Centuries*. Ed. Carter Lindberg. Oxford: Blackwell, 2005. 115–27.

Middlekauff, Robert. *The Mathers: Three Generations of Puritan Intellectuals, 1596–1728*. New York: Oxford UP, 1971.

Miller, Perry. "A Note on the Manuductio ad Ministerium." *Cotton Mather: A Bibliography of his Works*. Ed. Thomas James Holmes. Vol. 2. Cambridge: Harvard UP, 1940. 630–36.

Noll, Mark A., et al., ed. *Evangelicalism: Comparative Studies of Popular Protestantism in North America, the British Isles, and Beyond, 1700–1990*. New York: Oxford UP, 1994.

Peschke, Erhard. Einleitung. *August Hermann Francke: Schriften zur Biblischen Hermeneutik I*. Ed. Erhard Peschke. Vol.1. Berlin: De Gruyter 2003. xiii–xxi.

–. *Studien zur Theologie August Hermann Franckes*. 2 vols. Berlin: Evangelische Verlagsanstalt, 1966.

Peters, Christian. "'Daraus der Lärm der Pietismi entstanden': Die Leipziger Unruhen von 1698/90 und ihre Deutung durch Spener und die hallischen Pietisten." *Pietismus und Neuzeit* 23 (1997): 103–30.

Peterson, Mark. *The Price of Redemption: The Spiritual Economy of Puritan New England*. Stanford: Stanford UP, 1997.

Roeber, Gregg A. "Der Pietismus in Nordamerika im 18. Jahrhundert." *Geschichte des Pietismus*. Ed. Martin Brecht and Klaus Deppermann. Vol.2: *Der Pietismus im achtzehnten Jahrhundert*. Göttingen: Vandenhoeck & Ruprecht, 1995. 666–99.

Schmidt, Martin. "Das hallische Waisenhaus und England im 18. Jahrhundert. Ein Beitrag zum Thema: Pietismus und Oikumene." *Theologische Zeitschrift* 7 (1951): 38–55.

Searle, Alison. "'Though I Am a Stranger to You by Face, yet in Neere Bonds of Faith': A Transatlantic Puritan Republic of Letters." *Early American Literature* 43 (2008): 277–308.

Silverman, Kenning. *the Life and Times of Cotton Mather*. New York: Harper & Row, 1984.

Splitter, Wolfgang. "The Fact and Fiction of Cotton Mather's Correspondence with German Pietist August Hermann Francke." *New England Quarterly* 83.1 (2010): 102–22.

Spurr, John. "From Puritanism to Dissent, 1600–1700." *The Culture of English Puritanism, 1560–1700.* Ed. Christopher Durston and Jaqueline Eales. Houndsmill, Basingstoke: MacMillan, 1996. 234–65.

Stoeffler, F. Ernest, ed. *Continental Pietism and Early American Christianity.* Grand Rapids: Eerdmanns, 1976.

–. *The Rise of Evangelical Pietism.* Leiden: Brill, 1965.

Strom, Jonathan, Hartmut Lehmann, and James Van Horn Melton, eds. *Pietism in Germany and North America 1680–1820.* Farnham, Burlington: Ashgate, 2009.

Theologische Realenzyclopädie. Ed. Gerhard Krause, Gerhard Müller, et al. 42 vols. Berlin: De Gruyter, 1997–2007.

Tipson, Baird. "How Can the Religious Experience of the Past Be Recovered? The Examples of Puritanism and Pietism." *Journal of the American Academy of Religion* 43 (1975): 695–707.

Wallmann, Johannes. *Der Pietismus.* Göttingen: Vandenhoeck & Ruprecht, 2005.

Ward, W. R. *The Protestant Evangelical Awakening.* Cambridge: Cambridge UP, 1992.

Wellenreuther, Hermann. "Die atlantische Welt des 18. Jahrhunderts: Überlegungen zur Bedeutung des Atlantiks für die Welt der Frommen im Britischen Weltreich." *Transatlantische Religionsgeschichte: 18 bis 19. Jahrhundert.* Ed. Hartmut Lehmann. Göttingen: Wallstein, 2006. 9–30.

–. "Mission, Obrigkeit und Netzwerke: Staatliches Interesse und Missionarisches Wollen vom 15. bis ins 19. Jahrhundert." *Pietismus und Neuzeit* 33 (2007): 193–213.

–. "Pietismus und Mission: Vom 17. Jahrhundert bis zum Beginn des 20. Jahrhunderts." Ed. Hartmut Lehmann. *Geschichte des Pietismus.* Vol. 4: *Glaubenswelt und Lebenswelt.* Göttingen: Vandenhoeck & Ruprecht, 2004.

Wilson, Renate. "Continental Protestant Refugees and their Protectors in Germany and London: Commercial and Charitable Networks." *Pietismus und Neuzeit* 20 (1994): 107–24.

–. "Übersetzungen englischer und deutscher Erweckungsliteratur im Spiegel der Bestände der Hauptbibliothek der Franckeschen Stiftungen zu Halle 1700–1750." *Pietismus und Neuzeit* 26 (2000): 81–93.

Adriaan Neele

Peter van Mastricht's *Theoretico-practica Theologia* as an Interpretative Framework for Cotton Mather's Work

> But after all there is nothing that I can with so much Plerophorie Recommend unto you, as a *Mastricht*, his *Theologia Theoretico-practica*. That a Minister of the Gospel may be *Thoroughly furnished unto every Good Work*, and in one or two *Quarto* Volumns enjoy a *well furnished Library*, I know not that the Sun has ever shone upon an Humane Composure that is equal to it.
> Cotton Mather, *Manuductio ad Ministerium* (1726)

Cotton Mather's generous praise of Peter van Mastricht's *Theoretico-practica Theologia* (hereafter *TPT*) in *Manuductio ad Ministerium* (85), Mather's handbook for students studying for the ministry, echoed throughout eighteenth-century New England.[1] In fact, Mastricht's work was highly valued by such well-known New England theologians as Benjamin Colman (27–28), Joseph Seccombe (title page), Mastricht's editor and translator of "On Regeneration" (*Treatise*), Samuel Hopkins (769), and Joseph Bellamy (xiv).[2] If the words of Edwards Amasa Park (9) can be relied upon, Jonathan Edwards, Jr., read Mastricht's *TPT* seven times. Above all of these, however, Jonathan Edwards bestowed the highest praise on his Dutch colleague's work: "But take Mastricht for divinity in general, doctrine, practice and controversy; or as a universal system of divinity; and it is much better than Turretin or any other book in the world, excepting the Bible, in my opinion ..." (*Works* 16: 216–17, 223, 266).

Mastricht's reputation amongst New England theologians, first established by Cotton Mather, lasted over a hundred and fifty years. It therefore comes as a surprise that his *TPT* has received little attention by scholars today.[3] Perhaps this neglect is a direct result of Perry Miller's dismissive claim that the theology of Cotton Mather's generation was intellectually muted and drifting to practi-

---

1 The author would like to thank Reiner Smolinski and Jan Stievermann for their constructive comments on this essay and Kenneth P. Minkema for his valuable suggestions.

2 Tyron Edwards (1809–94) notes that Jonathan Edwards lent a copy of Mastricht's work to Bellamy. See Haykin (85n 2).

3 For studies that mention Mastricht, see Miller (96, 105, 226), Bogue, Harinck (88, 91–94), Guelzo (3–4), Morimoto (18–20), Vlastuin (92), and Plantinga (12).

cal piety.[4] Richard Lovelace, however, offers an important corrective. He argues that New England's theology is better associated with English Puritanism *and* German Pietism. Unfortunately, these movements are still largely viewed independently from one another. More recent scholarship recognizes the Pietist movement as a working out of the theology of seventeenth-century Reformed orthodoxy, as found in English Puritanism, German Pietism, and the Dutch *Nadere Reformatie*, which includes methodological aspects of scholasticism and Renaissance humanism. In fact such critics as Hof, van Asselt, and Muller have come to view Mastricht's *TPT* as an integral part and outgrowth of post-Reformation theology. In turn, the concern for both the theory and the practice of theology can be traced to the medieval cathedral schools and monasteries, and their preoccupation with both speculative and practical theology. Nearer to home, however, this close joining of speculative and practical theology was also mirrored soon after the Reformation and perhaps even rooted in the dispute among Reformed and Lutheran theologians regarding the so-called third use of the law (*tertius usus legis*), wherein the divine law is understood to retain a use or role in not only the first sense (*usus paedagogicus* or *elenchtichus*) of reminding the sinner of his sin and by consequence, salvation, or the second (*usus politicus*), the preservation of social order, but also in a third sense, in the sanctification of the believer. That is, by extension of the first use (*usus paedagogicus*), a third use is articulated in the renewing of the Christian (*usus in renatis*); the foundational theology in the *tertius usus* which joined the speculative beliefs, teachings, principles or laws with the practical life and responsibility of the Christian in his dealings and acts as a Christian was critical preparation for not only the post-Reformation theology found in Mastricht's *TPT*, but also the flourishing of humanist anthropology and most all forms of moral theology in Pietism on the Continent, British Isles and colonies. Viewed from this perspective, Mather's thorough knowledge of post-Reformation sources (Woody 4; Lovelace 25–57) invites questions about the structure of his theology and, ultimately, Mastricht's potential influence on New England's theologians in the eighteenth century.

In his *Manuductio*, Mather praises Mastricht's *TPT* more than any other "system of divinity." Indeed, addressing divinity students, Mather writes, "you will next to the *Sacred Scripture*, make *Mastricht* the *Store-house* to which you may resort continually" (85). Furthermore, he states emphatically, "And, I wish, all that study *Divinity* might hear" the dying words of Mastricht, "*Se nulla Loco et Numero habere Veritatis Defensionem, quam sincera Pietas et Vitæ Sanctitas, individuo nexu non comitetur*" (85).[5]

---

4 Miller's views of Mather (most strongly expressed in *The New England Mind: From Colony to Province*) have been convincingly challenged by Middlekauff, Levin, and Silverman.

5 This citation, which translates as "that he has no place and value for truth that is not de-

Thus Mather's admiration for *TPT* as a *"Store-house"* of systematic theology and for *"Pietas et Vitae Sanctitas"* (85), a piety and holy living, are well worth remembering. My discussion will begin with an introduction of Mastricht's life and work, with particular attention to the *theoretico-practica* motif or paradigm, followed by some observations on Mather's theology as found in his *Bonifacius, The Christian Philosopher*, the "Biblia Americana," and *Manuductio*. Finally, I shall offer some concluding remarks.

Peter van Mastricht (1630–1706)

Biographical studies of Mastricht's life and work commonly foreground three aspects: his importance as a Hebraist and exegete, as a philosopher and opponent of Cartesianism, and as a Reformed theologian.[6] Mastricht studied Hebrew and Old Testament at the University of Utrecht (1647–52) with his former catechetical teacher Johannes Hoornbeeck and with Gisbertus Voetius, who taught him a thorough knowledge of Hebrew as the necessary prerequisite for the study of theology and of the rabbinic commentaries and Talmud (Long 51). An assessment of Mastricht's exposition of the doctrine of God in the *TPT* demonstrates that he heeded his teachers' advice, for his linguistic skills are as pronounced as his knowledge of the rabbinic commentaries by such well-known medieval, Renaissance, and early modern rabbis as Elijah Levita, Hakkadosch, Salomon Jarchi, David Kimchi, Maimonides, Nachmanides, Abraham Ibn Ezra, Isaac ben Abraham, and Spinoza's teacher in Amsterdam, Manasseh ben Israel.[7] Moreover, Mastricht refers to his "Jewish masters" and the Targum and Mishnah throughout *TPT* (2.16.2, 251; 3.7.1, 339; 5.1.3, 392; 5.3.34, 432; 5.8.11, 479; 5.17.4, 605; 8.1.32, 884). He also cites from the Hebrew grammars and lexica of such Christian Hebraists as Paul Fagius, Henricus Alting, and John Lightfoot (*TPT* 2.12.2, 134; 8.2.24, 906; 8.2.32, 911) and recommends Matthew Poole's mainstay *Synopsis Criticorum* (1669–76), with its detailed references to rabbinic sources.[8]

---

fended with sincere piety and holy living," is found in the *Laudatio Funebris* by H. Pontanus that was added to the 1724 edition of Mastricht's *TPT*.

6 For eighteenth and nineteenth-century accounts of Mastricht's life, see the entries in Jöcher's *Allgemeines Gelehrten-Lexicon*, in Aa's *Biographisch woorderboek* and the biographies by Paquot and Pontanus. For contemporary scholarly biographies, see my article in Bautz, *Biographisch-Bibliographisches Kirchenlexikon* and Tellingen.

7 See Mastricht's *TPT* (2.4; 2.6; 2.17). My citations from Mastricht refer to the books, chapters, and, where necessary, to the paragraph and page numbers of the *TPT*.

8 Mastricht, *TPT*, De Optima Concionandi Methodo Paralipomena (1228): *"Exegeseos adminicula repetantur ... A Commentatoribus praestantissimis, cum criticis & verbalibus; tum analyticis ac realibus, Calvino, Piscatore, Polo &c."* Mastricht rarely makes use of Calvin's *Commentary*, refers sometimes to Piscator, but is in regular dialogue with Poole. For example, compare *TPT* (1.1.2, 2) and *Synopsis* (5: 1087); *TPT* (1.3.2, 47) and *Synopsis* (5: 1106); *TPT*

His academic appointments include a professorship of Hebrew at the Viadrina at Frankfurt an der Oder (1667–70), which at that time was the European center of studies of the Talmud and Judaica, and subsequently at the University of Duisburg (1670–77). These appointments underscore Mastricht's significance as a post-Reformation humanist, whose in-depth acquaintance with Hebrew and rabbinic scholarship provided him with a solid linguistic foundation, exegetical aids, and expertise in support of his theological and philosophical endeavor.

Moreover, Mastricht had a life-long interest in contemporary philosophy. His work on scripture and philosophy *Vindicae veritatis* (1655),[9] his philosophical work *Gangraena* (1677) – a work also positively used and highly recommended by seventeenth-century Lutheran and Roman Catholic theologians – and his anti-Cartesian polemic *Contra Beckerum* (1692) demonstrate Mastricht's warning against reducing theology to an axiom of philosophy or against making philosophy an "infallible interpreter of Scripture" (*Contra Beckerum* 25). Most of all, Mastricht was concerned with strengthening matters of salvation through the *praxis pietatis*.

With respect to theology, Mastricht's theological itinerary began at the Reformed church at Cologne, continued with his studies at Duisburg, Heidelberg, and Oxford, and concluded with his comprehensive training in Reformed orthodoxy and Protestant scholasticism joined with piety at the University of Utrecht. In this manner, theoretical and practical concerns in theology became a central theme in Mastricht's intellectual preparation for his office as pastor and teacher.

Mastricht's *TPT*, a work written for the students of divinity (*De Optima Concionandi*), represents the culmination of his theoretical and practical experience that includes his early theological works such as the *Prodomus*, the *Methodus Concionandi*, and on *Faith*, as well as his later disputations on the nature of theology (*De natura theologiae* 1–4) and on the covenant. The prominence of the *theoretico-practica* and *theologia practica* is advanced and codified by Mastricht in his masterpiece that today is synonymous with its author's name: *Theoretico-practica Theologia*, a text which constitutes a pivotal achievement of Post-reformation Reformed and scholastic theology with emphasis on exegetical, doctrinal, elenctical, and practical methods. It should be emphasized that for Mastricht the practical application of his theology arises from the biblical text; it is the improvement and use for the Christian life – the application of pi-

---

(2.6.2, 98) and *Synopsis* (4: 1147); *TPT* (2.11.2, 128) and *Synopsis* (4: 114); *TPT* (2.12.2, 134) and *Synopsis* (4: 1212); *TPT* (2.14.2, 152) and *Synopsis* (5: 57); and, lastly, *TPT* (2.21.2, 219) and *Synopsis* (1: 166).

9 Mastricht's work was one of the early Reformed responses to Christopher Wittichius, whose *Dissertationes Duae* (1653) argued in favor of Descartes's Copernican beliefs and made an attempt to reconcile theology and philosophy.

ety (*TPT* 1.2.2, 18). The *practica* is a living unto God – a result of the *theoretica* or contemplation. Mastricht, as I have proposed elsewhere (Neele, *Reformed Orthodoxy*), unites his long-standing interest in speculative and practical theology that ran counter to the bifurcation of Reformed doctrine and piety mentioned earlier.[10] The combination of speculative and practical theology into one force had a far-reaching impact on Protestant theology in Europe as well as in English North America. In New England, Cotton Mather was the first to recognize Mastricht's importance.

Cotton Mather, Mastricht, and Theoretico-Practica

The full title of Mather's *Bonifacius*[11] reminds one of the opening question of the Westminster Catechism (1647),[12] which in turn resembles Calvin's first inquiry in the *Geneva Catechism* (1545).[13] The great end of life, for Calvin, the authors of the English Catechism as for Mather, was to glorify God and therefore desire "to do good, while they live" (*Bonifacius* title page). For Mather, moreover, this endeavor was rooted in the Christian scriptures (vi). To do good works, he argues, one needs to have "A Glorious work of GRACE on the Soul," which is a divine work of regeneration (33–34), with the "Dispositions" (39) to glorify God through good works (38). Mather shared this understanding with Mastricht and other Reformed thinkers such as William Perkins and William Ames, who formulated Christian theology in terms of its ultimate goal (*finis*), the glory and enjoyment of God (*fruitio Dei*). Here theology is practical insofar as it aims for a *dispositio* or *habitus* of love and glorification of God, which is the knowledge and the *praxis* of salvation (*TPT* 1.1.2, 1).

Contrary to any suggestion's of crypto-Arminianism in Mather's work, his understanding of doing good therefore rests, first, upon the regenerating work of the Holy Spirit which disposes one by faith to the "*Good Works* of the *Christian Life*" (*Bonifacius* 36) and, second, on post-Reformation orthodoxy.

---

10   On this, see Goeters, Graafland (340), Heppe, Knappert (234), Krull, Osterhaven (183), Proost, Reitsma (338), and Stoeffler.

11   *An Essay Upon the Good, that is to be Devised and Designed, by those Who Desire to Answer the Great End of Life, and to Do Good While they Live* (1710).

12   "Question 1: What is the chief and highest end of man? Answer: Man's chief and highest end is to glorify God and fully enjoy him forever" (*The Larger Catechism. First agreed upon By the Assembly of Divines at Westminster* 73).

13   *Le Catéchisme de l'Eglise de Genève* (1541): "1. Le Ministre: Quelle est la principale fin de la vie humaine? L'Enfant: C'est de connaître Dieu. 2. M : Pourquoi dis-tu cela? E : Parce qu'il nous a créés et mis au monde pour être glorifié en nous. Et c'est bien raison que nous rapportions notre vie à sa gloire puisqu'il en est le commencement." *Le Catéchisme de l'Eglise de Genève* was written by Calvin as the result of a doctrinal confession (1536) and primarily intended for children. It was first published in French in 1541, and then slightly modified in Latin in 1545.

Both of these considerations together are the foundation of Mather's *Bonifacius*. For instance, in ch. 3, he discusses the relationship between an individual's home and his neighbors; here he adds the introductory commendation that when we do good, "we Adorn the Doctrine of God our Saviour" (50–51). His avowed intention echoes the broad concept of Mastricht's formulation of doctrine and piety: "*doctrina, quae est secundum pietatum*" (*TPT* 1.1.9, 4). We should therefore not be surprised that in his address to ministers (*Bonifacius* ch. 4), teachers (ch. 5), and civil magistrates (ch. 7), Mather advocates piety, the essence of doing good, as an expression of the individual's faith in God. In his conclusion to *Bonifacius*, Mather reminds his reader that God rewards his humble servants in spite of outward and inward afflictions. Calvin put it as follows: "[B]ecause I have served him who never failed to pay his servants what he had once promised" (qtd. in *Bonifacius* 193). In essence, the *summum bonum* in Mather's understanding is to practice the Christian life for the glory of God. With Mather, the believers' expression of orthodoxy is the *ortho-praxis* of living unto God: "bring them [students] to Express *Resolutions of Serious Piety*. Sirs, you may do a thousand Things, to render you *Pupils Orthodox* in their Principles, *Regular* in their Practices …" (109).

Closely related to his Pietist goal in *Bonifacius* is Mather's interest in making natural philosophy (science) subservient to the adoration of God. His best-known work on this topic is *The Christian Philosopher: A Collection of the Best Discoveries in Nature with Religious Improvements* (1721). This work, as Beall, Stearns, Silverman, Solberg and others suggests, aims at harmonizing natural science and theology by "surveying science from a religious perspective" (Solberg xxxv). Although primarily a work of physic-theology, *The Christian Philosopher* can also be fruitfully viewed through the lens of Mastricht's *TPT*. As Thomas Bradbury puts it in his dedicatory address to Mather's work, "every Observation improv'd to the End of Devotion and Practice" (*The Christian Philosopher* iv). Mather echoes this observation, for example, in his essay "Of the Light." Although he closely attends to the scientific theory of light, he also urges readers to allow such contemplations with "devout Thoughts" or "Lessons of Piety" (13). *Theoria* and *praxis* do not "indicate a tendency toward metaphysical rationalization on the one hand and pragmatic enterprise on the other" (Muller 1: 340). Quite the opposite seems to be true: Theory should lead to practice. This connection is especially apparent in his essay "Of the Stars," where Mather exhorts his soul to praise God: "*O my soul*, why art thou *slow* in thy Contemplations of GOD, and CHRIST, and HEAVEN; fly thou thither, with a Swiftness beyond that of the *Light*" (*The Christian Philosopher* 16). His purpose was to glory in the greatness of God, as he attests in numerous essays such as "Of the Rainbow," "Of the Snow," "Of Insects," and "Of Man."[14] In the

---

14   See also the following passages in *The Christian Philosopher* where Mather finds similar

latter essay, though Mather is impressed with mankind's greatness as exemplified by such learned post-Reformation divines as Voetius, Witsius, and Alsted, he never loses track of his didactic aim: to "enkindle the *Dispositions* and the *Resolutions* of PIETY ... is the intention of all my ESSAYS" (284, 294). For Mather, this means to adore God in Christ (295, 297). Mather's conclusion resonates well with Mastricht's definition of theology, which both theologians define as a living unto God in Christ. These selections from the *The Christian Philosopher*, in which he synopsizes the "Best Discoveries in Nature," (title page) clearly indicate that his goal of "religious improvements" (title page) was identical with that of Mastricht: the *theoria* was a beholding or contemplation, and the *praxis*, a didactic application in everyday life.

With these preliminary findings in *Bonifacius* and *The Christian Philosopher*, which suggest that the motif of *theoretico-practica* played a role in Mather's theological thought, let us turn to the "Biblia Americana." Here, we will briefly focus on some of the historical books of the Old Testament and on a selection of commentaries on the Pentateuch. Comparing Mather's "Biblia" and Mastricht's *TPT*, we notice a principal difference between the two theologians. Whereas Mather is interested in a causal analysis of issues, Mastricht aims at exegetical results that contribute to the formulation of doctrine and *praxis*. Their differing goals appear, for instance, in their discussion of Josh. 24. Mather focuses his attention on v. 33 and provides "some remarks upon the Sepulchre of the Ancients" [*BA*, Josh. 24:33]. In this verse, Mather is principally concerned with describing the form and architectural design of ancient tombs. Mastricht, however, is more interested in v. 19 with its focus on divine sanctity and its practical application to a holy life before God. Comparing Mather's choice of biblical text exposition with that of Mastricht, one often notices a different focus and exegesis. This difference, however, does not signify Mather's lack of interest in the principles of *theoretico-practica*. Interestingly, a closer examination of Mather's and Mastricht's exegetical work on the same biblical text reveals an even greater dissimilarity. For instance, in his exposition on Judg. 10:6, Mather wonders, "How come the people easily, to forsake the Lord?" Mather identifies as the cause the Israelites' idolatry and neglect of the law. Mastricht, by contrast, places this text in a broader exegetical context (*TPT* 8.2.24, 906) and urges the reader to remember the Lord. Unlike Mastricht, Mather does not present a practical application. This is not true, however, for his gloss on 1

---

cause to praise God: "May we *look upon the Rainbow, and praise Him that made it!*" (58); "When we see *the Snow* ... *Lord*, let a Work of real *Sanctification*, at the same time upon me, render me *purer than the Snow*" (60); "For what ENDS are all these little Creatures made? Most certainly for great ENDS, and for such as worthy of a GOD" (163); "I will transfer this *Meditation* to the Exercises which are to fill a *Life of Piety*" (164); "This is not all that we have to think upon; we see an incomparable *Wisdom* of God in His *Creatures*. ... *How glorious, how wondrous, how lovely art thou* ..." (301).

Chron. 29:29. Here, Mather examines the distinction between a seer, prophet, and discerner – a topic that Mastricht also addresses in his chapter *On the Holy Scriptures* (*TPT* 1.2.1–84, 18–47). Mather acknowledges in his exposition his reliance on the commentaries of his Dutch colleagues Hermann Witsius (*Miscellanea Sacra*) and Johannes Cocceius – both contemporaries of Mastricht. Furthermore, like Mastricht, Mather cites John Lightfoot, Johannes Buxtorf, and the Babylonian Talmud to explain the difference between these types of prophets and their function in the Old Testament [*BA*, 1 Chron. 29:29].[15] Although Mather invests more than 5 pages (folio) on this issue, his conclusion is succinct: "But the Church of God, now being *furnished* with so compleat a *Rule* of *Beleef* and *Practice*, as the Holy Scriptures, we must not wonder if those Gifts are not now granted, as they were in the former Ages" [*BA*, 1 Chron. 29:29].

Mastricht reaches a similar conclusion in the elenctical section of the chapter *On the Holy Scriptures*, but ends on a practical note: Scripture is a perfect rule or norm for living to God, in as far as such is described and contained in scripture.[16] Although both Mather and Mastricht draw a practical application that shares an understanding of scripture as a norm for faith and obedience, Mastricht is here more elaborate on the *practica* than Mather allows for.[17] The question then arises, to what extent, if any, do the exegetical results on a biblical text differ for both theologians? The exegetical commentary on Genesis and Proverbs may provide a preliminary answer to this question.

First, for Mastricht the doctrine arises from the biblical text and belongs to the *theoria* of theology. Significantly, both ministers arrive at similar conclusions in their reflections on Gen. 3:15 and 17:11. The former biblical text refers both exegetes to the promise of restoration of a violated covenant (*TPT* 5.1.2, 392; Mather (*BA* 1: 485–89)). The latter is foundational in their discussion on the initiating seal of the covenant of grace, i.e. circumcision or sacrament in which God promises "to be a God unto thee" (*TPT* 7.3.2, 808; Mather (*BA* 1: 923–24)).

Second, one notices that Mather, like Mastricht, refers to rabbinic commentaries by Kimchi [*BA*, Josh. 14, 23, 24; Judg. 2, 5, 14, 16; 1 Sam. 1, and 6], Ibn Ezra, and others.[18] Mather's commentary on Proverbs draws on R. Levi Gershom [*BA*, Prov. 2:3; 2:16; 3:2], R. Solomon [*BA*, Prov. 2:16; 5:9; 5:14; 6:11], and

---

15 The transcription of this commentary is 54 pages long.

16 *TPT* (1.1.36, 12; 1.2.3, 19): "Patet itaque, *sacram Scripturam, perfectam esse Deo vivendi regulam*" and "sacrâ autem Scriptura, nil aliud intelligimus, quam *doctrinam vivendi Deo, quatenus illa literis continetur descripta.*"

17 *TPT* (1.3.1, 47): "Artifi cium istud vivendi Deo, cujus *norma* est Scriptura; certis *partibus* repraesentare … verbis præfixis (2 Tim. 1:13)." See also *TPT* (2.1.1, 50): "*Vita* illa *Dei*, cujus *normam* praestat Scriptura, perinde ut *naturalis*, duos actus concludit: *primum*, quo *possumus* operari spiritualiter, quem præstat fi *des* … *secundos*, quos fi des producit, actus scil. *Observantiae.* …"

18 Mastricht was most likely directly acquainted with these commentaries, while Mather

Ibn Ezra [5:16; 6:10; 6:11], though primarily through the consultation of Sebastian Münster's *Hebraica Biblia* and Michael Jermin's *Paraphrasticall Meditations*. Mastricht, on the other hand, consults Proverbs primarily in support of his practical formulation of exegesis and doctrine (*TPT* 5.8.25, 486; 5.4.14, 575, 6.1.32, 644; 6.8.35, 752). The difference in emphasis, therefore, is not the result of one being more practical than the other, but of the principal distinction between the different genres of their respective works. Mather's primary concern in his "Biblia" appears to be the *contemplatio* of the biblical text, while Mastricht's aim in the *TPT* is to move from the biblical text analysis (*theoretica*) to the practical implications (*practica*).

The degree to which Mather appreciated Mastricht's *TPT* can be seen in his letter to Jacob Wendel (May 10, 1720), a Dutch merchant living in Albany, New York: "The world has never yet seen so valuable a system of divinity. ... Tis orthodox, 'tis concise, 'tis complete. In one word it is everything." Mather then requests more copies of the *TPT* from Holland, for "the sake of our young ministers and of the churches that expect services from them" (*Selected Letters* 306, 307, 432). His great admiration for Mastricht's work raises the question of how much Mastricht may actually have influenced Mather's theology.

Both Mather's *Manuductio* and Mastricht's *TPT* were intended for the students of divinity. The two manuals, however, differ in that Mather supplies his readers with a catalogue for a well-furnished Library (148–49) whereas Mastricht's reiterates the exegetical mainstay of the four-fold approach to *theoretico-practica* theology: exegesis, doctrine, elenctic, and practical. These differences aside, Mather demonstrates in the *Manuductio* a sense of continuity in post-Reformation Reformed thought. Moreover, when compared with August Hermann Francke's *Methodus studii theologici* (Woody 10) and Gysbertus Voetius's *Exercitia et bibliotheca studiosi theologæ* (Long), Mather's *Manuductio* shares the same overall vision: theology must be known and practiced. As Mather put it in *Manuductio*, we must practice "the Method of living unto GOD" (8), that is, "with a *single Eye*, to keep up a Regular and Perpetual *Aim* at the RIGHT END, of all that I *do* ... the *Life of* GOD and of His CHRIST, be thus *manifested in me!*"(9).

Mastricht's argument resonates in Mather's opening of the *Manuductio* that the "art of living to God" (*TPT* 1102; Ames 2) consists of two aspects: how to awaken the individuals spiritually and to lead them to a life unto God (*Deo vivere*). Furthermore, Mather's attention to the study of the original languages as laid out in the *Manuductio* (30–32) is shared by post-Reformation scholastics such as Mastricht (*TPT* 1.2.7–12, 20–21; Ames 172). Finally, Mather's suggested reading in divinity, beginning with the "SACRED SCRIPTURES," followed

---

may have cited these commentaries indirectly via Matthew Poole and Bomberg's famous edition of the Hebrew Bible.

by "SYSTEMS OF DIVINITY," and "POLEMIC DIVINITY" resembles Mastricht's approach to theology: exegesis, doctrine, polemic and practice – whereby both share this aim in their studies: the preparation of a sermon and edification of the congregation (*TPT* 1225; *Manuductio* 80–86). Both emphasize that the study of theology is to thrust the individual into a *theoretico-practical* science, whereby the *praxis* is understood as *doctrina* (teaching) (Muller 1: 351). This distinction should not be overlooked, when one reads Mather's earlier works such as the *Bonifacius* and *The Christian Philosopher*.

In conclusion, the *theoretico-practica* paradigm offers a possible framework for the study of Mather's theology. More specifically, his appreciation of Mastricht's *TPT* could provide a key to understanding Mather's fascination with German Pietism and its emphasis on practical application to a life unto God. This emphasis may have compelled both Mather and Mastricht to view reason "not as an enemy" but as a servant in the study of scripture (*The Christian Philosopher* 1). The occasionally suggested dichotomy of Mather as theologian *and* natural philosopher might be less pronounced if he is understood within the *theoretica-practica* framework. In this conception, philosophy is merely an instrument aiding in the apparent perception of the object by confirming and clarifying truths by the light of nature, a tool to prepare the heart and intellect to receive the essence of theology, which is the glory of God. Theory and practice are not separate dimensions but converge in the service of piety. Method establishes the doctrine, enables the minister to support his argument, and allows him to drive home the practical applications. The pietism of Peter Mastricht, of Cotton Mather, as well as of their German colleague August Hermann Francke share one overarching concern: theory is never an end unto itself but must lead to *praxis*. Given this common perspective, Mather's admiration for Mastricht's *TPT* was therefore almost natural.

A word of caution is here in order: My short and limited survey of Mather's "Biblia Americana" should not be understood as a proposal to interpret his theological endeavor solely on the basis of Mastricht's *theoretico-practica*. Their difference may very well be grounded in the different genres in which each of them works. Nevertheless, it is my preliminary contention that the incorporation of the proposed *theoretico-practica*-paradigm helps to avoid a suggested bifurcation in Mather's works: His theology and philosophy, as well as his doctrine and piety, do not pursue separate ends. What is called for, then, is the study of post-Reformation sources and their transatlantic impact on the colonies of English North America. Cotton Mather's "Biblia Americana" serves as an excellent resource to begin such a study, for Mather is much more of a post-Reformation exegete, theologian, and philosopher than is commonly understood.

Works Cited

Primary Sources

Aa, Abraham Jacob van der. *Biographisch woordenboek: bevattend levensbeschrijvingen van zoodanige personen, die zich op eenigerlei wijze in ons vaderland hebben vermaard gemaakt.* Amsterdam, 1852–78.

Allgemeines Gelehrten-Lexicon: Darinne die Gelehrte aller Stände. Ed. Christian Gottlieb Jöcher. Leipzig, 1750–51.

Ames, William. *Marrow of Sacred Divinity, drawne out of the holy Scriptures, and the Interpreters thereof, and brought into Method.* London, 1642.

Bellamy, Joseph. *The Works of Joseph Bellamy, D. D.* Boston, 1853.

Le Catéchisme de l'Eglise de Genève, c'est à dire le Formulaire d'instruire les enfans la Chretienté fait en manière de dialogue ou le ministre interrogue et l'enfant respond. Geneve, 1545.

Colman, Benjamin. *A Dissertation on the Image of God wherein Man was created.* Boston, 1736.

Edwards, Jonathan. *The Works of Jonathan Edwards. Letters and Personal Writings.* Ed. George S. Claghorn. Vol. 16. New Haven: Yale UP, 1998.

Euangelisch Magazijn, of Gemengde Bijdragen ter Bevordering van Kennis en Beöefening der Goddelijke Waarheden. Rotterdam, 1775.

Hopkins, Samuel. *The system of doctrines: contained in divine revelation, explained and defended: showing their consistence and connection with each other: to which is added, A treatise on the millennium.* Boston, 1793.

Jermin, Michael. *Paraphrasticall meditations, by way of commentarie, upon the whole book of the proverbs of Solomon.* London, 1638.

Long, Isaac le. "Gysbertus Voetius, Reedenvoeringe." *Hondert-Jaarige Jubel-Gedachtenisse de Academie van Utrecht.* Utrecht, 1736.

Mastricht, Petrus van. *Ad virum clariss. Bathasarem Bekkerum epanorthosis gratulatoria occasione articulorum, quos venerandae Classi Amstelodamensi exhibuit, die 22 Janu. 1692.* Utrecht, 1692.

–. *De fide salvifica syntagma theoretico-practicum: in quo fidei salvificae tum natura, tum praxis universa, luculenter exponitur; cum praef. de membris Ecclesiae visibilis seu admittendis, seu rejiciendis, oborienti scismati moderno applicanda.* Duisburgi ad Rhenum, 1671.

–. *De Foedere Gratiae, pars prima Ex theologiae theoretico-practicae libro quinto caput primum.* Utrecht, 1682.

–. *De mediatore foederis gratiae, pars tertia, Ex theologiae theoretico-practicae libro quinto, caput secundum.* Utrecht, 1682.

–. *De optima concionandi methodo Paralipomena: in usum theologiae theoretico practicae.* Utrecht, 1681.

–. *Methodus Concionandi.* Francofurti ad Viadrum, n.d.

–. *Novitatum Cartesianarum Gangraena, Nobiliores plerasque Corporis Theologici Partes arrodens et exedens, Seu Theologia Cartesiana detecta.* Amsterdam, 1677.

–. *Theologiae didactico-elenchtico practicae prodromus tribus speciminibus.* Amsterdam, 1666.

–. *Theologiae theoretico-practicae, sub relo sudantis, specimen de natura theologiae primum.* Utrecht, 1680.

—. *Theoretico-practica theologia: qua, per singula capita theologica, pars exegetica, dogmatica, elenchtica et practica, perpetua successione conjugantur; accedunt historia ecclesiastica, plena quidem, sed compendiosa, idea theologiae moralis, hypotyposis theologiae asceticae etc proin opus quasi novum. Ed. nova, priori multo emendatior et plus quam tertia parte auctior.* Utrecht, 1699.

—. *A Treatise on Regeneration. Extracted from his System of Divinity, called Theologia theoretico-practica; and faithfully translated into English; With an Appendix containing Extracts from many celebrated Divines of the reformed Church, upon the same Subject.* New Haven, [n.d].

—. *Vindicae veritatis et autoritatis sacrae scripturae in rebus Philosophicis adversus dissertationes D. Christophori Wittichii.* Utrecht, 1655.

Mather, Cotton. *Biblia Americana.* Ed. Reiner Smolinski. Vol. 1. Tübingen and Grand Rapids: Mohr Siebeck, Baker Academic, 2010.

—. *Bonifacius. An Essay Upon the Good, that is to be Devised and Designed, by those Who Desire to Answer the Great End of Life, and to Do Good While they Live.* Boston, 1710.

—. *The Christian Philosopher: A Collection of the Best Discoveries in Nature with Religious Improvements.* London, 1721.

—. *Manuductio ad Ministerium. Directions for a candidate of the ministry: Wherein, first, a right foundation is laid for his future improvement; and, then, rules are offered for such a management of his academical & preparatory studies; and thereupon, for such a conduct after his appearance in the world; as may render him a skilful and useful minister of the Gospel.* Boston, 1726.

—. *Selected Letters of Cotton Mather.* Ed. Kenneth Silverman. Baton Rouge: Louisiana State UP, 1971.

Paquot, Jean Noël. *Mémoires pour servir à l'histoire littéraire des dix-sept provinces des Pays-Bas, de la principauté de Liége, et de quelques contrées voisines.* Louvain, 1765.

Pontanus, Hendricus *Laudatio Funebris In excessum Doctissimi Et Sanctissimi Senis, Petri van Mastrigt, S. S. Theol. Doctoris & Professoris: Quam jussu amplissimi Senatus Academici D. XXIV. Februarii / postridie sepulturae dixit Henricus Pontanus.* Rotterdam, 1706.

Seccombe, Joseph. *Some Occasional Thoughts on the Influence of the Spirit with Seasonable Cautions against Mistakes and Abuses.* Boston, 1742.

Westminster Larger Catechism. The Larger Catechism. First agreed upon By the Assembly of Divines at Westminster. Edinburgh, 1649.

Secondary Sources

Asselt, W.J. van, and L. Rouwendal, eds. *Inleiding in de Gereformeerde Scholastiek.* Zoetermeer: Boekencentrum, 1998.

Beall, Otho T. and Richard Shyrock. *Cotton Mather: First Significant Figure in American Medicine.* 1954. New York: Arno Press, 1979.

Bogue, Carl W. *Jonathan Edwards and the Covenant of Grace.* Cherry Hill: Mack, 1975.

Goeters, W. *Die Vorbereitung des Pietismus in der Reformierten Kirche der Niederlande bis zur Labadistischen Krisis 1670.* Leipzig: J.C. Hinrichs'sche Buchhandlung, 1911.

Graafland, C. "Gereformeerde Scholastiek VI: De Invloed van de Scholastiek op de Nadere Reformatie (2)." *Theologia Reformata* 30 (1987): 109–131, 313–340.

Guelzo, Allen C. *Edwards on the Will.* Middletown: Wesleyan UP, 1989.

Harinck, C. *De Schotse Verbondsleer, van Robert Rollock tot Thomas Boston.* Utrecht: De Banier, 1986.

Haykin, Michael A.G., ed. *A Sweet Flame. Piety in the Letters of Jonathan Edwards.* Grand Rapids: Reformation Heritage Books, 2007.

Heppe, H. *Geschichte des Pietismus und der Mystik in der Reformierten Kirche, namentlich der Niederlande.* Leiden: Brill, 1879.

Hof, W.J. op 't. *Engelse piëtistische geschriften in het Nederlands, 1598–1622.* Rotterdam: Lindenberg, 1987.

Knappert, L. *Geschiedenis der Nederlandsche Hervormde Kerk gedurende de 16e en 17e Eeuw.* Amsterdam: Meulenhoff & Co., 1911.

Krull, A.J. *Jacobus Koelman: Eene Kerkehistorische Studie.* Sneek: J. Campen, 1901.

Levin, David. *Cotton Mather. The Young Life of the Lord's Remembrancer 1663–1703.* Cambridge: Harvard UP, 1978.

Lovelace, Richard F. *The American Pietism of Cotton Mather. Origins of American Evangelicalism.* Grand Rapids: Christian UP, 1979.

Miller, Perry *The New England Mind: the Seventeenth Century.* Cambridge: Harvard UP, 1939.

–. *The New England Mind: From Colony to Province.* Cambridge: Harvard UP, 1953.

Middlekauff, Robert. *The Mathers. Three Generations of Puritan Intellecuals 1596–1728.* New York: Oxford UP, 1971.

Morimoto, Anri. *Jonathan Edwards and the Catholic Vision of Salvation.* University Park: Pennsylvania State UP, 1995.

Muller, Richard A. *Post-Reformation Reformed Dogmatics: The Rise and Development of Reformed Orthodoxy, ca. 1520 to ca. 1725.* 4 vols. Grand Rapids: Baker Academic, 2003.

Neele, Adriaan C. "Mastricht, Petrus van." *Bautz Biographisch-Bibliographisches Kirchenlexikon.* Vol. 26. Nordhausen: Verlag Traugott Bautz, 2006.

–. *Petrus van Mastricht (1630–1706) Reformed Orthodoxy: Method and Piety.* Leiden: Brill, 2009.

Osterhaven, M. Eugene. "The Experiential Theology of Early Dutch Calvinism." *Reformed Review* 27 (1974): 3–15.

Park, Edwards Amasa. "New England Theology." *Bibliotheca Sacra* 9.1 (1852): 2–32.

Plantinga Pauw, Amy. *The Supreme Harmony of All. The Trinitarian Theology of Jonathan Edwards.* Grand Rapids: Eerdmans, 2002.

Proost, P. *Jodocus van Lodenstein.* Amsterdam: J. Brandt en Zoon, 1880.

Reitsma, J. *Geschiedenis van de Hervorming en de Hervormde Kerk der Nederlanden.* 5th ed. Gravenhage: Martinus Nijhoff, 1949.

Silverman, Kenneth. *The Life and Times of Cotton Mather.* New York: Harper & Row, 1984.

Solberg, Winton U. Introduction. *The Christian Philosopher.* By Cotton Mather. Ed. Winton U. Solberg. Chicago: U of Illinois P, 1994. xic-cxxxiv.

Smolinski, Reiner. "How to Go to Heaven, or How Heaven Goes? Natural Science and Interpretation in Cotton Mather's 'Biblia Americana' (1693–1728)." *New England Quarterly* 81.2 (2008): 278–329.

Stoeffler, F. Ernest. *The Rise of Evangelical Pietism*. Leiden, 1965.

Sweeney, Douglas A. *The New England Theology. From Jonathan Edwards to Edwards Amasa Park*. Grand Rapids: Baker Academic, 2006.

Tellingen, A. E. van. *Het leven en enige aspecten uit de theologie van Petrus van Mastricht (1630–1706)*. Master Thesis: Faculty of Theology of University of Utrecht, 2003.

Vlastuin, W. van. *De Geest van Opwekking, Een onderzoek naar de leer van de Heilige Geest in de opwekkingstheologie van Jonathan Edwards (1703–1758)*. Heerenveen: Groen, 2001.

Woody, Kennerly M. "Cotton Mather's *Manuductio ad Ministerium*. The 'More Quiet and Hopeful Way.'" *Early American Literature* 4.2 (1969): 3–48.

Section 3: Enlightenment Rationalism, Biblical Literalism, and the Supernatural

Winton U. Solberg

Cotton Mather, the "Biblia Americana," and the Enlightenment

Cotton Mather was highly regarded in his own day. Although often disparaged in our time, the Puritan priest remains an iconic figure in American culture. A learned man of deep religious conviction, Mather lived during the early Enlightenment. His literary output was truly impressive. The two most important books he published during his lifetime were the *Magnalia Christi Americana* (1702), a two-volume ecclesiastical history of New England, and *The Christian Philosopher* (1721), a treatise on the harmony between science and religion. Mather also left behind a massive manuscript commentary, the "Biblia Americana" (1693–1728). *The Christian Philosopher* demonstrates that Mather was an apostle of the Enlightenment. What does the "Biblia Americana" reveal about Mather and the Enlightenment?

Mather was highly qualified to write both the book and the manuscript mentioned. Born in 1663, he spent his entire life in Boston, Massachusetts. His ancestry and talents were such as to convince him that he was a chosen vessel of God, destined for greatness. Mather entered Harvard in 1675, graduated B.A in 1678, and received an M.A in 1681. He began preaching when he was eighteen. In 1685 he became his father's colleague as minister of the North Church in Boston, where he remained as a minister until his death in 1728.[1]

A New England Puritan, Mather believed in the supremacy of scripture. He viewed the Bible as the guide to personal salvation and the pattern for ecclesiastical and civil polity. He was keenly interested in the new sciences, to which he had been exposed at Harvard. To know the physical creation, he thought, was a way of knowing its creator. In 1723 the British Royal Society, a prestigious scientific body, confirmed his 1713 election as a Fellow for his "Curiosa Americana" – letters sent to London describing aspects of nature that he came upon in America. In *The Christian Philosopher* Mather reported the best discoveries in the sciences from Copernicus to Newton. A treatise on physico-theology, this was the first book by an American to describe all of the physical and natural sciences known at the time.

---

1 For the most recent comprehensive biography, see Silverman.

When Mather began the "Biblia Americana" in late summer of 1693, he intended to assemble a mass of illustrations of Scripture in the scattered books of
learned men. At the rate of one illustration a day he would be able to gather in
seven years "a Number of *golden Keyes* ... and curious *Notes* on His Word, far
beyond any that had yet seen the Light" (*Diary* 1: 170). Mather, then thirty, was
well equipped for this ambitious enterprise. A man of considerable learning, he
knew ancient history and ecclesiastical history. He was intimately familiar with
the Bible, fluent in Hebrew, Greek, and Latin, and had a retentive memory.
Moreover, he was skillful in assembling sources and summarizing them simply
and clearly. His personal library of more than three thousand volumes was perhaps the largest private library in the American colonies, and he had access to
the Harvard College Library. Both collections were strong in standard theological treatises and ecclesiastical histories, including older tomes written within a framework of the new science and the argument from design.[2] Mather's
avowed aim to heap up a mass of commentaries on the Bible suggests that he
hoped to impress readers by the magnitude of his effort. When he wrote, Latin,
which had long been the language of learned discourse, was in the process of
being replaced by vernacular languages. However, Mather's "Biblia Americana," largely an English-language composition, includes considerable Latin, a
good bit of Greek, and some Hebrew. Apparently, the author assumed an audience of educated gentlemen, of which there were more in England than in New
England.

Mather was supremely confident of his capacity to advance the proposed
project. "I am able with little study to write in seven languages," he boasted. "I
feast myself with the sweets of all sciences, which the more polite part of mankind ordinarily pretend to. I am entertained with all kinds of histories ancient
and modern. I am no stranger to the curiosities which by all sorts of learning,
are brought to the curious" (qtd. in Tuttle 294). Worthington C. Ford, the editor of the *Diary of Cotton Mather*, sharply criticized the "Biblia" manuscript as
"a great indigested mass of material, drawn from many sources, and with no
evidence of design or settled plan" (*Diary* 1: 170n.). This critique deserves consideration, but one might well wonder if it is borne out by study of the manuscript itself.

In some years Mather amassed more than a thousand commentaries dispersed in hundreds of volumes. On 28 May 1706, after a labor of thirteen years,
Mather declared that he had finished his undertaking. He continued to gather
illustrations, but henceforth his main concern was to get his manuscript published. It was too big for an American press, so in September 1706 he sent to
England "AN AMERICAN OFFER *to serve the Great Interests of Learning*

---

2   For Mather's library see Tuttle; for the Harvard library, see the 1723 *Catalogus Librorum*.

and Religion in Europe" (Diary 1: 570; also 563–64, 567). He tried again in 1711, 1714, and 1715 to enlist dissenting clergymen and other correspondents in London to raise subscriptions to underwrite publication of the "Biblia," which he described as "the richest collection of the most valuable Treasures, in so little a Room, that ever the Ch: of God was entertained withal" (*Diary* 2: 331; also 283, 309–19).

Meeting discouragement, Mather felt sorry for himself. Dissenters did not over-value literature, he lamented, and some Englishmen seemed to believe that "a poor *American*" must not be thought capable of doing anything worth regarding. Yet "it may be," he declared, "God our Saviour will in His Time, dispose the Minds of some eminent and opulent persons, to cast a benign Aspect upon a work which may hand down their Names with lasting Acknowledgements unto posterity" (*Diary* 2: 331–32).

It will be instructive to evaluate Mather's scholarly enterprise from two perspectives. One is from his vantage point. Surely Mather was influenced by impressive contemporary models. During his lifetime many authors compiled biblical commentaries, guides to interpretation, and studies of ancient Hebrew history and antiquities. These works went through many editions. As a group they comprise a kind of "received interpretation" of the Old and New Testaments (Preston 98–99).

Short volumes introduced readers to the contents of the Bible and the basic methods of interpretation. Among these were books by John Wilson (1663–1755), John Owen (1616–83), and William Lowth (1661–1732). According to these authors, all things necessary for salvation are plainly stated in the scriptures, and no biblical text should be interpreted so as to contradict fundamental Christian doctrine (Preston 99–100). Biblical commentaries that aimed at different types of readers were also available. Matthew Poole (1624?-79) published a four-volume synopsis of his own critical labors and those of others entitled *Synopsis Criticorum Aliorumque Sacrae Scripturae Interpretum* (see Keene). These tomes, originally written in Latin and published between 1669 and 1674 were for a scholarly audience. In the 1680s Poole's *Annotations upon the Holy Bible* appeared in English for the common people, and Matthew Henry (1662–1714), a Presbyterian minister, published a four-volume exposition of the Old Testament from 1707 to 1712 (see Wykes).

In addition, Henry Ainsworth (1569–1622), Simon Patrick (1626–79), and William Lowth compiled commentaries on the Old Testament, while Henry Hammond (1605–60), William Burkitt (1650–1703), Samuel Clarke (1675–1729), and Daniel Whitby (1637/8–1726) wrote on the New Testament. These works were models for a self-styled "poor American." Mather would show that a provincial could compete with the best English expositors.

It will also be instructive to evaluate the "Biblia Americana" in the context of the Enlightenment. As a historical movement the Enlightenment began with an early, radical stage that lasted from the late seventeenth century to the early eighteenth century. This upheaval led to a conservative or counter-Enlightenment beginning about 1750, and the Radical Enlightenment then underlay the French Revolution in the late eighteenth century. The early Enlightenment broke the cake of custom. In the mid-seventeenth century, about the time Mather was born, the established structures of political, social, and intellectual authority that had long dominated Europe were still in place. Monarchs and the pope ruled their respective domains, society was hierarchical in structure, the Aristotelian-scholastic synthesis ruled in the universities, Trinitarian Christianity commanded wide assent, and the conflicts were largely along confessional lines. About 1660, however, a ferment of new ideas began to disrupt the traditional order (see M.C. Jacob; Israel). It was no coincidence that this intellectual awakening began in the Netherlands, a country characterized by socio-political and cultural conditions which were unique in Europe at the time. The Dutch Republic was a Protestant country with religious tolerance and thriving commercial activity. Relative freedom from censorship, a general atmosphere of free inquiry, a free press, universities with able professors, and the presence of many printers and booksellers combined to make Holland the center of learned communication in the republic of letters. After the revocation of the Edict of Nantes in 1685, many Huguenots sought refuge in the Netherlands, which was more hospitable than any other European country to Jews and dissidents who fled oppressive regimes in their native lands (Golden 13–25).

Benedict Spinoza, who was born in late 1632 in Amsterdam of Sephardic Jewish parents, grew up in an orthodox Jewish community in his native city. He became the foremost spokesman of the ideas unleashed during the Radical Enlightenment. As a youth he questioned the accepted Jewish beliefs that he was taught, and he was not satisfied with what he read in biblical texts and Jewish theological authors. Spinoza associated with freethinking Protestants and a group of radical Cartesians. Prominent among the latter was Franciscus Van den Enden (1602–74), an ex-Jesuit, who taught Spinoza Latin and a little Greek and helped develop his interest in the science of nature, called *philosophia* or mathematics. In July 1656 the Amsterdam synagogue expelled Spinoza on account of his heresies and his behavior (see Klever). A man of science, Spinoza specialized in optical theory. He made observations with the microscope and the telescope, and he corresponded with the English scientists Robert Boyle (1627–91) and Henry Oldenburg (c. 1619–77), secretary of the Royal Society, and with the Dutch astronomer and mathematician Christiaan Huygens (1629–95). In 1656 Spinoza wrote an unfinished treatise explaining his intellectual development, and in 1661–62 he composed a short work on God, man, and his well-being that prefigures his *Ethics*. Spinoza was committed to a life of reason and a search for the causal explanation of things. Ministers of the Reformed Church discovered that he identified God with nature in unpublished manuscripts, so they accused him of atheism and warned their flocks against his pernicious doctrines. Feeling insecure, in October 1665 Spinoza began composing his *Tractatus Theologico-Politico*. This book, described by one scholar as "the most important seventeenth-century work to advance the study of the Bible and religion generally" (Preus x), was published anonymously and with a false imprint in 1670. Spinoza, whose personal life was above reproach, died in 1677. His principal work, the *Ethics*, appeared posthumously in that year. Because our concern here is primarily with Mather, biblical scholarship, and the Enlightenment, this paper will focus on Spinoza's *Theological-Political Treatise*.

Spinoza devotes the preface and first fifteen chapters of his book to countering the false interpretations and political misuse of Scripture by theologians and to defending himself as a scientist. Fear and dread give rise to superstition, he writes, and the worst kind of people use religion to win over those who are superstitious. Such people see church offices as lucrative positions. Prophecy is certain knowledge revealed to men by God, but prophecy depends on imagination alone, and it is inferior to natural knowledge *(Treatise*, chs. 1–2*)*. The natural divine law, which is to love God, is common to all men because it is deduced from the universal law of human reason (*Treatise*, ch. 4).

Scripture proclaims that there is a God who is to be adored and who cares for all people, but it is impossible to infer from the Bible what God is. Christ was a moral teacher and philosopher whose thought had little or nothing to do with what ecclesiastics and theologians made of it. But Christ was in no way divine, and in Spinoza's eyes, as he admitted in a letter to Henry Oldenburg, secretary of the Royal Society in London, the resurrection never took place (Israel, xviii). The order of nature is fixed and immutable. Since nothing happens contrary to nature, Spinoza rejects the possibility of miracles (ch. 6). The true method of interpreting Scripture is for Spinoza the same as that of interpreting nature, a method that reduces all reality to the empirical. The rule is to claim nothing as a biblical doctrine that is not derived from the Bible's history, and to explain a given passage as a product of natural forces (chs. 7–14).

Biblical exegetes had long maintained that Moses was the author of the Pentateuch. The belief that God spoke to Moses supposedly guaranteed the truth of the text. Spinoza was among those who disputed this view. Aben Ezra (1092–1167), a medieval Spanish rabbi who was recognized by Christian and Jewish scholars as an important Bible commentator, was the first to describe the established view as a misconception. Moses could not have written the passage in Deut. 33 about his own death, Aben Ezra observed. In the late seventeenth century the authenticity of the text became a problem. Thomas Hobbes (1588–1679), Isaac La Peyrère (1594 or 1596–1676), and Samuel Fisher (bap. 1604, d. 1665) all demonstrated that Moses could not have been the author of the Pentateuch, and Spinoza devoted several chapters of his *Theological-Political Treatise* to illustrating that Moses did not write the Pentateuch and that other books of the Old Testament were not written by the persons after whom they were named (see *Treatise* chs. 8–9; see also Popkin).

Spinoza devotes the last six chapters of his book to his political theory. Here his major concern is to balance the power of the state with the liberty of the individual. The state has the authority to rule, but the state should guarantee religious toleration and individual freedom. Spinoza granted that religion has a positive dimension. Religious teaching based on the Bible provides the rudiments of true morality and is indispensable in underpinning society. But Spinoza differentiates between the high-minded visions of the founders of the great religions and the corruption of their ideals by self-seeking priests motivated chiefly by ambition and greed. He attacks ecclesiastical authority and priestcraft. For the state to prescribe doctrine could only lead to sectarianism and dissension among the people (*Treatise*, chs. 15–20; see also De Deugd).

Spinoza wrote with a view to reconstructing society. His *Theological-Political Treatise* challenged traditional views on biblical interpretation, religion, and politics. He and his fellow Spinozists wanted to weaken ecclesiastical authority, lower the status of theology, promote toleration, widen individual freedom, and expand equality and democracy. Wherever Spinoza's radical agenda spread it provoked controversy. Theologians and civil officials denounced Spinoza as an atheist who wrote a vile book. Realizing the book's dangerous implications, authorities in the Netherlands, Germany, France, Italy, and elsewhere on the Continent banned Spinoza's treatise, and in 1674 the Roman Catholic Church placed it on its Index of Prohibited Books (see Totaro).

Despite efforts to refute and suppress Spinoza's radical views, new editions of his *Theological-Political Treatise*, published with false imprints, circulated clandestinely. Pierre Bayle (1647–1706), a refugee Huguenot editor and publisher, fixed on Spinoza a label which became a reference point for later interpretation of Spinoza's thought. Bayle's *Dictionaire* [sic] *Historique et Critique*, published in Rotterdam in 1697 (expanded in 1702 and published in an English translation in London in 1710) described Spinoza as "a *Jew* by birth, who forsook Judaism, and at last became an Atheist. ... He was a Systematical Atheist, and brought his Atheism into a new method, tho' the substance of his Doctrine was the same with that of many Ancient and Modern Philosophers, both in Europe and the Eastern Countries." Bayle labeled the *Treatise* "a Pernicious and Execrable Book" (*Dictionnaire Historique et Critique* 2: 1083–84; *Historical and Critical Dictionary* 4: 2785; see also Simonutti 195).

Nevertheless, Spinoza attracted a small but passionate following. The diffusion of his thought is central to the history of the Enlightenment. Paul Vernière has examined Spinoza and French thought before the Revolution, while Pierre-Françoise Moreau has traced Spinoza's reception and influence in Europe from the seventeenth century to the years after 1945 (see Vernière; Moreau). What about the reception of Spinoza in America?

French authors were not among Mather's most important sources, but he does draw on several of them in his "Biblia Americana." Police censorship prevented allegedly radical books from entering France. A French translation of the *Theological-Political Treatise* appeared in the Netherlands in 1678. This clandestine work had no close connection with Spinoza himself, and it cannot have reached a wide audience in France (Spink 238). "Spinozism," or a misconception of Spinoza's teaching, was known in France as early as 1673, when a Swiss adventurer named Stouppe published in Paris a book titled *La Religion des Hollandois*. Stouppe, who had met and conversed with Spinoza in Utrecht, summarized the *Treatise* by means of the familiar theory that all religions have been invented as a means of governing (Bayle, *Dictionary* 4: 2785; Wade 1–29, 124–40; Israel 302–03).

French authors often decried Spinoza without having read him, but Pierre-Daniel Huet (1630–1721), the bishop of Avranches and a man celebrated for profound and extensive erudition, knew Spinoza and openly fought him. The bishop described the *Theological-Political Treatise* as "that horrible and sacrilegious book full of impiety, ignorance, and madness." Huet, in his *Demonstratio Evangelica* (1679), held that proof based on the evidence of history and scripture was no less solid and certain than proof derived from mathematical reasoning. He tried to establish religious truth inductively out of the materials of comparative religion that were being explored at the time (Huet, *Memoirs* 1: 30; Spink 242; Sullivan 30; Israel 487–88). These views appealed to Mather, who often quotes Huet in the "Biblia Americana."

Mather's closest intellectual and cultural ties were with Britain. During the late seventeenth century and the early eighteenth century many English authors feared that their country was drifting toward Deism and even atheism (Redwood, *Reason* 9–15; see also the Appendix II in O'Higgins). Leading English authors engaged Spinoza either positively or negatively. Many viewed Hobbes as a more powerful subverter of orthodoxy than Spinoza, but Hobbes could not serve as the philosophical basis of a broad-based philosophical radicalism because of his absolutism in politics, High Church sympathies, and pessimism about human nature. Thus Spinoza was the stronger formative influence on radical thought in Britain (Israel 602).

The negative response to Spinoza was swift and sharp. Edward Stillingfleet (1635–99), the bishop of Worcester, had Spinoza in mind when, in "A Letter to a Deist" (written in 1675, published in 1677), he admitted that he was deeply troubled by a "late author mightily in vogue among many, who cry up any thing on the Atheistical side, tho' never so weak and trifling." It was not difficult, declared Stillingfleet, to mark the "false Reasonings, and inconsistent Hypotheses" of the *Treatise*. If the book was translated into English and reached the common people to advance irreligion, Stillingfleet hoped that someone would defend "Religion and Morality" (*Works* 2: 118; see also Popkin, "The Philosophy of Bishop Stillingfleet").

Neoplatonists at Cambridge University joined in denouncing Spinoza. In December 1676 Henry More (1614–87) informed Robert Boyle that he had learned out of Holland that a number of men there were "scoffers at religion, and atheistical," and that "*Spinosa*, a Jew first, after a Cartesian, and now an atheist, is supposed the author of the Theologico-Politicus." The *Treatise* was "such an impious work" that More had to confute it, which he did in his *Epistola altera* (1677) and the weighty *Confutatio* (1678).[3] Ralph Cudworth (1617–88), another Cambridge Neoplatonist, attacked the views of materialists in his *True Intellectual System of the Universe, Wherein all the Reason and Philosophy of Atheism is Confuted and Its Impossibility Demonstrated* (1678). Here Cudworth's primary targets were Hobbes and Spinoza. He dismissed the *Theological-Political Treatise* as being in "every way so Weak, Groundless and Inconsiderable" that it was not worth confuting" (Pallin 565).

The Boyle lecturers from 1692 to the middle of the eighteenth century wrestled with the problem of God posed by changing relations between religion and science. They defended Anglican orthodoxy, Newtonian science, reason, and the argument from design. Richard Bentley (1662–1742), the inaugural lecturer, used his lecture to refute Spinoza's doctrine that God is extended substance. Samuel Clarke (1675–1729), whose 1704 lecture was published as *A Demonstration of the Being and Attributes of God* (1705), criticized Spinoza's "absurd definition of substance." Clarke characterized Spinoza as "the most celebrated patron of Atheism in our time" (Clarke 20; see also Redwood, *Reason* 103–08; Israel 600, 603; Gascoigne).

Despite these denunciations, a number of English worthies espoused ideas advanced by Spinoza. Charles Blount (1654–93) published a number of tracts that promoted natural religion, anti-clericalism, toleration, and freedom of the press. In these early works Blount was sparing in the acknowledgement of influences, but in *Miracles, No Violations of the Laws of Nature*, published anonymously in 1683, Blount associated himself with the philosophy of Spinoza. He included in this work a translation of Spinoza's chapter on miracles in the *Treatise*. This was the first English translation of any of Spinoza's writings (Redwood, "Charles Blount" 492–95; Pfanner 294–95).

Thomas Browne replied to Blount in *Miracles, work's above and contrary to nature, or, An answer to a late translation out of Spinoza's Tractatus Theologico-Politicus, Mr. Hobbs's Leviathan, &c. published to undermine the truth and authority of miracles, Scripture, and religion* (1683). The author charged

---

3   On this, see also Colie 66–93; Alexander Jacob's *Henry More's Refutation of Spinoza* includes, in addition to a biographical introduction, the Latin text and an English translation of the *Confutation*.

that Blount's tract was based on Spinoza's heresy of equating God with nature, thus denying God's existence above and beyond nature. Browne viewed Blount's undeclared smuggling of Spinoza into England as a subversion of both religion and civil authority. Blount's books were burned by the common hangman, but his championing of natural religion, toleration, and freedom of the press spread, and judging by the number of his critics he was widely read (Redwood, "Charles Blount" 495; Israel 605).

In 1689 an anonymous translator, probably Blount, published in London the first complete English translation of Spinoza's *Theological-Political Treatise* (Israel 601–02, 604–05). In the introduction to the book, the translator admitted that those who upheld the established religion and government would severely criticize the treatise, but he defied the "Crape Gown and the Long Robe" to prove that there were any tenets in the whole treatise "half so dangerous or destructive to the Peace and Welfare of human Society, as those Doctrins [sic] and Maxims are, which have of late Years been broached by "time-serving Churchmen and Mercenary Lawyers."[4]

Matthias Earbery (1658–1735), a vicar and schoolmaster, published *Deism examin'd and confuted* (1697) in answer to the *Theological-Political Treatise*. Earbery emphasized the centrality of Spinoza in the forming of British Deism. The perfect Deist, Earbery wrote, was inordinately fond of Spinoza, who took away all divine authority from prophecy, miracles, and inspiration. Earbery described the *Treatise* as rapidly producing in England a "general corruption of manners, contempt of the clergy, and advancement of irreligious ideas."[5]

Nehemiah Grew (bap. 1641, d. 1712), a distinguished botanist and physician, shared the widespread English fear that Spinoza's ideas would spread to the common people. In 1701 Grew published *Cosmologia Sacra, Or, A Discourse of the Universe As It Is the Creature and Kingdom of God*. "The many Leud Opinions, especially those of Anti-scripturists, which have been published of late Years; by Spinoza and some others, in *Latin, Dutch*, and *English*," Grew wrote in his preface, were the occasion of writing his book. "Not only Men of Erudition, but the Citizens themselves," Grew observed, "are very dangerously infected. In so much, that every Apprentice … formeth all his Thoughts, Words, and Actions, by This, as his Bible." In his *Cosmologia Sacra*, Grew offered proof of God's existence on philosophical and natural philosophical

---

4 The text appeared under the title *A Treatise Partly Theological, and Partly Political, Containing some few Discourses, To prove that the Liberty of Philosophizing (that is Making Use of Natural Reason) may be allow'd without any prejudice to Piety, or to the Peace of any Commonwealth; And that the Loss of Public Peace and Religion it self must necessarily follow, where such a Liberty of Reasoning is taken away*. The quotations are taken from the introduction entitled "The Translator to the Reader" (A3 verso).
5 Finder's article on Matthias Earbery, the younger, also provides information on Matthias Earbery, the elder. See also Israel (608).

grounds and defended the miracles described in the Old and New Testaments (Preface; bk. 4, ch. 5; bk. 5, ch. 3).

The three most prominent early English Deists, John Toland (1670–1722), Matthew Tindal (c. 1657–1733), and Anthony Collins (1676–1729), all had a strong ideological tie to Continental radicalism. Toland, supposedly the son of an Irish priest and his concubine and a man of quick intelligence and boisterous mannerisms, was a key link between early English Deism and Continental Deism. His *Christianity Not Mysterious* (1696) was both a Deist manifesto and an assault on priestcraft. It emphasized reason over revealed religion. In the early eighteenth century Toland spent considerable time on the Continent. While in Holland he came under the influence of Spinoza's ideas, and he devoted a considerable part of his *Letters to Serena* (1704) to a discussion of Spinoza's philosophy. Toland's approach to biblical exegesis was much like that of Spinoza. In 1709, while at The Hague, Toland published anonymously two radical tracts under the title *Dissertationes Duae*. One of these, *Adeisidaemon*, dedicated to Anthony Collins, virtually equated all organized religion with superstition and portrayed religion as a conspiracy between priests and rulers. The other, *Origines Judaicae*, was a sustained piece of biblical criticism that attacked a work by the French bishop Huet and denied that the Old Testament was the word of God or the work of His Spirit. According to Toland, Moses had not written the Pentateuch but had invoked the supernatural in order to legitimate his rule over the Jewish people. Moses set a pattern for the imposture that marked the subsequent history of Judaism.[6]

Tindal, a Fellow of All Soul's, Oxford, published *The Rights of the Christian Church Asserted* (1706), an onslaught against ecclesiastical authority. Critics charged that his argument was borrowed from Spinoza and grounded on atheism (Israel 619–22). Collins was a member of the gentry with a large and excellent library. While remaining a member of the Church of England, he was both anti-clerical and anti-Christian. A self-proclaimed apostle of freethinking, Collins emphasized reason over revelation. He owed much to Spinoza among others and was influenced by Toland. Collins published several works during Mather's lifetime, including *Essay concerning the Use of Reason in Propositions* (1707), *Priestcraft in Perfection* (1709), *A Discourse of Free-Thinking* (1713), and *A Philosophical Inquiry Concerning Human Liberty* (1717). Collins believed that wresting from priests their power over people and allowing freedom to philosophize would greatly benefit society.[7]

---

6 On this, see also Sullivan (1–50, 134, 182, 183); Daniel (4, 5, 7, 10, 11, 40, 106–07, 120–21, 125, 128, 187, 194–96, 211, 115); Champion, *The Pillars of Priestcraft Shaken* (130–31, 157–58) and *Republican Learning* (1–21, 69–90); Israel (613).

7 See O'Higgins (11–12, 13, 17, 36–37, 40, 51–56, 76, 201, 204, 234); Israel (614–18); see also Drury (1–45); Stephens.

In sum, Spinozism spread from Holland to continental Europe and England. The erudite in Amsterdam, Berlin, Venice, Naples, Paris, London, Cambridge, and Oxford were aware of the radical challenge to traditional views about church, state, the Bible, and religious belief. Mather flourished during the time that Spinoza's influence was making its way into the North Atlantic countries. Admittedly, Mather lived on the periphery of the republic of letters, but he kept in close touch with religious developments in England. His *The Christian Philosopher*, published in 1721, endorses a moderate Enlightenment. This Enlightenment was based on Newtonian science, empiricism, and belief in the compatibility of faith and reason. Mather had ample opportunity to be aware of Spinoza and his ideas about God, the Bible, and interpretation. The question arises, what did he know, and how did he respond to the radical challenge of his day?

Mather's practice in composing the "Biblia Americana" was to amass a multitude of sources on the biblical passage under review. He quotes and paraphrases not only from sources he identifies but also from the sources of his sources. He is erudite but prolix. His method of presentation is a question-and-answer format. He proceeds within a tradition of typology, which was a well-established interpretive practice during his day. Mather is in the mainstream of late seventeenth-century Protestant hermeneutics. He accepts the principle of the analogy of faith: no biblical text should be interpreted so as to contradict fundamental Christian doctrine (*Diary* 1: 231; see also Preston). While favoring a literal interpretation of the text, he is not enslaved to it. The law of Moses was not merely a literal command to the Jews, he affirms, it also contained the figure and image of good things to come (*BA* 1: 940–41).[8] Mather finds it impossible to give a literal sense to the last words of the dying Jacob, because only by giving them a spiritual and mystical significance can we discover in them a worthy meaning (*BA* 1: 1013).[9] He notes approvingly that Augustine was full of allegories (*BA* 1: 1016–17, 1: 938–39), and he endorses the mystical sense of an argument about Esau and Jacob (*BA* 1: 932–33). The Christian doctrine of miracles had been elaborated in the exegesis and defense of the biblical narratives well before Mather's time (Pelikan 1: 137). Mather follows this line in writing about the miracles recounted in the Bible.

Among Mather's sources are some who denounced Spinoza, although Mather may not have known as much. One is Johann Heinrich Heidegger (1633–98), a Swiss Reformed theologian and professor in Zurich. "Our Heidegger," as Mather lovingly calls him, published on the history of the patriarchs from 1667 to 1671. In Heidegger's obituary of Johann Ludwig Fabricius (1632–96), a Protestant theologian and professor of systematic theology at Hei-

---

8   Here and in the following I rely on Smolinski's transcriptions and annotations of Mather's commentary on Genesis.
9   Mather borrows this point from Jacques Saurin, one of his sources.

delberg, Heidegger wrote that after reading that "horrible book" (the *Theological-Political Treatise*) Fabricius hoped that this blasphemous material would never be allowed to be promulgated inside the German borders (see Klever 43; Killy and Vierhaus 3: 246 and 4: 507). Another source Mather invokes is Pierre-Daniel Huet. The learned French bishop denounced Spinoza, and in *Origines Judaicae* Toland denounced Huet (*Origines Judaicae* 101–99).

Mather came across the name of Spinoza in at least two of his sources. Nehemiah Grew denounced Spinoza in his *Cosmologia Sacra*. Mather draws on that book in both *The Christian Philosopher* and the "Biblia Americana." Mather also came across the name of Spinoza from works by Jean LeClerc (1657–1736). LeClerc was born in Geneva, and after a brief sojourn in London he settled in Amsterdam in 1683. A year later he became a professor at the Remonstrant or Arminian university in that city. LeClerc was an editor, author, critic, and intermediary of the main intellectual currents of the day. Having read the work of the French Oratorian priest Richard Simon (1638–1712), *Histoire Critique du Vieux Testament* (1678), which was published in an English translation in 1682, LeClerc thought he could improve on it. So in 1685, with feigned indifference, he wrote a treatise of twelve letters, *Sentimens de Quelques Théologiens de Hollande sur L'Histoire Critique du Vieux Testament*, in rebuttal of Simon's book. An English excerpt of *Sentiments* was published in 1690 under the title *Five Letters Concerning the Inspiration of the Holy Scriptures*.

LeClerc's stated purpose in this composition was to engage "Learned Men" to write on the subject of inspiration. The letters probe the possibility that ecclesiastical history would be true only when reexamined in the clear light of reason. Letter I attacked the use of inspiration in writing history and argued that truth derived from factual sources and from right reason should be the bases for all kinds of histories. Letter II doubted the inspirational qualities generally attributed to the Apostles. Letter III satirized Simon and commented on the irresponsibility of modern critics. Letter IV answered objections that Simon had raised, while Letter V rebutted the allegation that LeClerc was a Deist (see *Five Letters*).

The *Five Letters* was widely read in England, France, Germany, and Holland. Some British theologians vehemently opposed LeClerc's views on the inspiration of sacred writers. For example, William Wotton (1666–1727), a linguist and theologian, wrote *A Discourse Concerning the Confusion of Languages at Babel. Proving It to Have Been Miraculous, Contrary to the Opinion of LeClerc and Others*. The *Discourse* was not published until 1730, after Mather's death, but in 1715 John Chamberlayne published a Latin translation. Mather may have learned about LeClerc from Chamberlayne, but, as Reiner Smolinski demonstrates, he could also have learned about LeClerc from other sources (Smolinski, "Authority and Interpretation," 183–84, 189–90; "Natural Science and Interpretation" 320–21).

In commenting on Gen.11 and the confusion of languages at Babel, Mather writes, "There is Reason to take the History which *Moses* gives us of that great Occurrence ... in the most literal Sense," and to believe that God struck the minds of the builders of Babel so as "to produce *miraculously* a Difference of Languages among them." He adds, "the opinion of LeClerc and others, that there was now produced no more than a bare Difference of *Opinions*; among them, does not come up to the Truth, & the glorious *Miracle* of the Matter" (*BA* 1: 810–11).

In the "Biblia Americana," Mather demonstrates awareness of the challenge to the old view that Moses was the author of the Pentateuch. Gen. 12:6, in the Authorized Version used by Mather, reads, "Abram passed through the Land unto the Place of Sichem, unto the Plain of Moreh. And the Canaanite was then in the Land." According to the biblical narrative, Abram (later, Abraham), migrated from Haran (in Mesopotamia) to Canaan, the pre-Israelite name for Palestine, and coming to Shechem, a fortified city in the northern part of the Hill Country of Israel, he built an altar there to the Lord who had appeared to him. Spinoza wrote that this passage must have been written after Moses's death, at a time when the Canaanites had been expelled and no longer possessed that territory" (*Treatise*, ch. 8). Richard Simon, in his *Critical History of the Old Testament* (1678), lists Gen.12:6 as one of many places in the Pentateuch that rendered Moses' authorship unlikely because the Canaanites were not then in the land (bk. 1, ch. 1, 2–6; ch. 2, 19; ch. 5, 36–46). Mather, however, is determined to uphold the traditional view that Moses was the author of the Pentateuch. So he writes in his gloss on Gen. 12:6, "Spinosa, and after him, the Author of the Five Letters, [One for Immoralities, a Monster of Mankind,] urge, That Moses could not bee the author of the Book of Genesis, or, as F. Simon saies, of any more than Part of it. For the Canaanite was not in the Land when it was written. The Canaanite was then in the Land; And that Moreh was a Man, and not a Place" (*BA* 1: 706–11). The reference to Spinoza by name is probably unique in the "Biblia Americana." As Reiner Smolinski writes, Mather's commentary on this passage, and on other controversial passages in the "Biblia Americana" reveals that Mather wrestled with each of the underlying issues "to rescue the scriptures out of the hands of their historical detractors" (Smolinski, "Authority and Interpretation" 181).

Prominent English authors shared Mather's hostility to Spinoza and LeClerc. William Lowth, for example, a theologian and Anglican priest, published *A Vindication of the Divine Authority and Inspiration of the Writings of the Old and New Testament* (1692), in which he charged that the atheistic party led by Spinoza kept alive the dispute over the integrity and authority of the scriptures and that LeClerc was not only a Spinozist but worse, an improver on Spinoza (see preface). C. G. De La Mothe (1547–1713), a Reformed minister, charged that Spinoza had led the way in attacking the inspiration of the sacred books but LeClerc had digested Spinoza's notions into a system (see La Mothe).

Most of the books that Mather draws on in the "Biblia Americana" date from before the late seventeenth century. He was probably less aware of the literature of the conflict caused by Spinoza during his own lifetime than he was of earlier, traditional tomes. But he does cite books that were published as late as the 1720s in both *The Christian Philosopher* and the "Biblia Americana."

Cotton Mather was not the very first colonial American to name Spinoza as an antagonist in a published work. His father, Increase Mather, viewed the extolling of natural reason above revelation as the cause of Pelagianism and Socinianism in the past and of Deism in his own day. To counter it he penned *A Discourse Proving that the Christian Religion, Is the Only True Religion* (1702). In this treatise Increase Mather wrote, "*I have not taken notice of the Objections and Sophismes produced by Atheists or Deists, (such as that Prodigy of a Jew Spinosa, from which the late Execrable Blunt has borrowed some of his Oracles)*" (Holmes, *Increase Mather* 1: 183–84). Cotton Mather shared his father's hostility to Spinoza and his fear that Spinozism undermined revelation and led to Deism. The younger Mather also inveighed against the writings of the Deists and exalted reasonable religion in treatises published in 1712, 1713, and 1718 (Holmes, *Cotton Mather*, 2: 879, 885). In these works, as in the "Biblia Americana," Mather wished to establish the Christian religion on the basis of reason, which he largely identified with the voice of God. Mather's conception of reason was not that of the reason advanced by Spinoza and his disciples.

Jonathan I. Israel persuasively writes that Spinoza dominated the debates over science, philosophy, and politics in the late seventeenth and early eighteenth centuries, and that the Radical Enlightenment, which was transnational rather than merely national, paved the way for modernity and the emancipation of man. Democratic, egalitarian, tolerant, and secularist, this Enlightenment changed the world by demolishing structures of intellectual, political, and social authority that had remained basically unshaken since the Renaissance and the Reformation. Israel's *Radical Enlightenment: Philosophy and the Making of Modernity 1650–1750* makes a notable contribution to understanding the complexity of early modern thought (see Israel; also Ricuperati and Grafton).[10]

Mather lived when the Radical Enlightenment was shaking the pillars of the past. A religious conservative, he valued tradition and was an exponent of the moderate strand of the Enlightenment. This Enlightenment was based on British empirical natural philosophy, especially Newtonian science and Lockeian epistemology, and the conviction that faith and reason are compatible. Mather's

10   In his *The Enlightenment and Religion: The Myths of Modernity* Barnett questions the influence of an educated elite in the rise of "modernity."

commitment to these ideas is evident in his *The Christian Philosopher* and in his immensely learned "Biblia Americana," wherein he defended the scriptures, the Christian faith, and human reason. Mather was one of the first Americans to oppose Spinoza and the thrust of his radicalism, but he was not alone. Many professors and theologians in North Atlantic countries hoped that Spinozism would never be allowed inside their borders, but in the western world "modernity" has triumphed to an appreciable degree. Nevertheless, to many Americans the religious convictions affirmed by Mather in *The Christian Philosopher* and the "Biblia Americana" remain attractive and convincing.

Works Cited

Primary Sources

Bayle, Pierre. *Historical and Critical Dictionary.* Vol. 4. London, 1710.
–. "Spinoza, Benoît de." *Dictionaire Historique et Critique.* Vol. 2. Rotterdam, 1697. 1083–1100.
[Blount, Charles]. *Miracles, No Violations of the Laws of Nature.* London, 1683.
Browne, Thomas. *Miracles, work's above and contrary to nature, or, An answer to a late translation out of Spinoza's Tractatus Theologico-Politicus, Mr. Hobbs's Leviathan, &c. published to undermine the truth and authority of miracles, Scripture, and religion, in a treatise entituled, Miracles no violation of the laws of nature.* London, 1683.
Catalogus Librorum Bibliotheca Collegij Harvardini Quod est Cantabrigiae in Nova Anglia. 1723. In *The Printed Catalogues of the Harvard College Library: 1723–1790.* Eds. Bond, W. H. and Hugh Amory. Boston: Colonial Society of Massachusetts, 1996. 1–130.
Clarke, Samuel. *A Demonstration of the Being and Attributes of God and Other Writings.* 1705. Ed. Ezio Vailati. Cambridge: Cambridge UP, 1998.
Collins, Anthony. *A Discourse of Free-Thinking.* London, 1713.
–. *Essay concerning the Use of Reason in Propositions, the Evidence whereof depends on Human Testimony.* London, 1707.
–. *A Philosophical Inquiry Concerning Human Liberty.* London, 1717.
–. *Priestcraft in Perfection: or, A detection of the fraud of inserting and continuing this clause (The church hath power to decree rites and ceremonys, and authority in controversys of faith) in the twentieth article of the articles of the Church of England.* London, 1709.
Cudworth, Ralph. *The True Intellectual System of the Universe: The First Part; Wherein, All the Reason and Philosophy of Atheism is Confuted; and its Impossibility Demonstrated.* London, 1678.
Earbery, Matthias. *Deism examin'd and confuted. In an answer to a book intitled, Tractatus theologico politicus.* London, 1697.
Grew, Nehemiah. *Cosmologia Sacra: Or A Discourse of the Universe As It Is the Creature and Kingdom of God. Chiefly Written, to Demonstrate the Truth and Excel-*

lency of the Bible; Which Contains the Laws of His Kingdom in this Lower World. London, 1701.

Henry, Matthew. *An Exposition of All the Books of the Old and New Testaments: Wherein the Chapters are summ'd up in Contents; the Sacred Text inserted at large, in Paragraphs, or Verses; and each Paragraph, or Verse, reduc'd to its proper Heads: the Sense given, and largely illustrated, with Practical Remarks and Observations.* 6 vols. London, 1708–10.

Huet, Pierre-Daniel. *Demonstratio evangelica ad serenissimum Delphinum.* Parisiis, 1679.

–. *Memoirs of the Life of Peter Daniel Huet.* Trans. John Aikin, 2 vols. London, 1810.

La Mothe, C.G. *The Inspiration of the New Testament Asserted and Explained in Answer to Some Modern Writers.* London, 1694.

LeClerc, Jean. *Sentimens de quelques Théologiens de Hollande.* 1685. A translated segment appeared as *Five Letters Concerning the Inspiration of the Holy Scriptures.* London, 1690.

–. *Twelve Dissertations Out of Monsieur Le Clerk's Genesis Genesis. ... Done out of Latin by Mr. Brown.* London, 1696.

Lowth, William. *Directions for the Profitable Reading of the Holy Scriptures.* London, 1708.

–. *A Vindication of the Divine Authority and Inspiration of the Writings of the Old and New Testament in answer to a treatise lately translated out of French, entitled, Five letters concerning the inspiration of the Holy Scriptures.* Oxford, 1692.

Mather, Cotton. *Biblia Americana.* Ed. Reiner Smolinski. Vol. 1. Tübingen and Grand Rapids: Mohr Siebeck and Baker Academic, 2010.

–. *The Christian Philosopher.* 1720. Ed. Winton U. Solberg. Urbana: U of Illinois P, 1994.

–. *Diary of Cotton Mather.* Ed. Worthington C. Ford. Collections of the Massachusetts Historical Society 7th series. Vols. 7–8. Boston: MHS, 1911–12.

–. *Magnalia Christi Americana: Or, The Ecclesiastical History of New England.* 1702. New York: Arno Press, 1972.

More, Henry. *Ad V.C. Epistola altera, Quae brevem Tractatus Theologico-Politici confutationem complectitur.* 1679. In *Opera Omnia.* Vol. 2. London, 1675–79. 3 vols. 563–614.

–. *A Brief and firm Confutation of the ... two Propositions in Spinoza which are the chief Columns of Atheism.* 1678.

–. *Henry More's Refutation of Spinoza.* Ed. Alexander Jacob. Hildesheim: Olms, 1991. 55–119.

Owen, John, Συεσις Πνευματίη, *or, the causes, waies & means of understanding the mind of God, as revealed in his word. ...* London, 1678.

Poole, Matthew. *Annotations upon the Holy Bible. Wherein the Sacred Text is Inserted, and various Readings Annex'd, together with, Parallel Scriptures, the more difficult Terms in each Verse are Explained, seeming Contradictions Reconciled, Questions and Doubts Resolved, and the whole Text opened. By the Late Reverend and Learned Divine Mr. Matthew Poole.* 2 vols. London, 1683–85.

–. *Synopsis Criticorum Aliorumque Sacrae Scripturae Interpretum.* 5 vols. London: 1669–76.

Simon, Richard, *A Critical History of the Old Testament*. Trans. H. Dodwell. London, 1682.

Spinoza, Benedict de. *Ethics with the Treatise on the Emendation of the Intellect and Selected Letters*. 1677. Ed. S. Feldman. Trans. S. Shirley. Indianapolis: Hacket, 1992.

–. *Tractatus Theologico-Politico*. 1670. Ed. Jonathan Israel. Cambridge: Cambridge UP, 2007.

–. *A Treatise Partly Theological, and Partly Political, Containing some few Discourses, To prove that the Liberty of Philosophizing (that is Making Use of Natural Reason) may be allow'd without any prejudice to Piety, or to the Peace of any Commonwealth; And that the Loss of Public Peace and Religion it self must necessarily follow, where such a Liberty of Reasoning is taken away*. [Trans. Charles Blount?] London, 1689.

Stephens, William. *An Account of the Growth of Deism in England*. 1696. Ed. James E. Force. The Augustan Reprint Society, Publication Number 261. Los Angeles: William Andrews Clark Memorial Library, 1990.

Stillingfleet, Edward. "A Letter to a Deist." In *Origines Sacrae: Or, a Rational Account of the Grounds of Natural and Reveal'd Religion*. In *The Works*. Vol. 2. London: 1710. 118.

Stouppe, Jean Baptiste. *La Religion des Hollandois*. Cologne, 1673.

Tindal, Matthew. *The Rights of the Christian Church Asserted*. London, 1706.

Toland, John. *Christianity Not Mysterious*. London, 1696.

–. *Dissertationes Duae: Adeisidaemon et Origines Judaicae*. The Hague, 1709.

–. *Letters to Serena*. London, 1704.

Wilson, John. *The Scripture's genuine Interpreter asserted: or, a Discourse concerning the right Interpretation of Scripture*. London, 1678.

Wotton, William. D.D. *A Discourse Concerning the Confusion of Languages at Babel; Proving it to have been miraculous, from the Essential Difference between them, contrary to the Opinion of Mons. Le Clerc, and others*. 2nd ed. London, 1730.

Secondary Sources

Barnett, S.J. *The Enlightenment and Religion: The Myths of Modernity*. Manchester: Manchester UP, 2003.

Champion, Justin A.I. *The Pillars of Priestcraft Shaken: The Church of England and Its Enemies, 1660–1730*. Cambridge: Cambridge UP, 1992.

–. *Republican Learning: John Toland and the Crisis of Christian Culture, 1696–1722*. Manchester: Manchester UP, 2003.

Colie, Rosalie L. *Light and Enlightenment: A Study of the Cambridge Platonists and the Dutch Arminians*. Cambridge: Cambridge UP 1957. 66–93.

Daniel, Stephen H. *John Toland: His Methods, Manners, and Mind*. Kingston: McGill-Queen's UP, 1984.

De Deugd, Cornelis, ed. *Spinoza's Political and Theological Thought: International Symposium under the Auspices of the Royal Netherlands Academy of Arts and Sciences*. Amsterdam: North-Holland Publishing, 1984.

Drury, John, ed. *Critics of the Bible, 1724–1873*. Cambridge: Cambridge UP, 1989.

Finder, John. "Earbery, Matthias (1690–1740)." *Oxford Dictionary of National Biography*. Ed. H.C.G. Matthew and Brian Harrison. Vol. 17. Oxford: Oxford UP, 2004. 558–59.

Gascoigne, John. "Clarke, Samuel." *Oxford Dictionary of National Biography*. Ed. H.C.G. Matthew and Brian Harrison. Vol. 11. Oxford: Oxford UP, 2004. 912–17.

Golden, Samuel A. *Jean LeClerc*. New York: Twayne, 1972.

Grafton, Anthony. "Where It All Began: Spinoza and the Dutch Roots of the Enlightenment." *Times Literary Supplement* 9.11 (2001): 3–4.

Holmes, Thomas J. *Cotton Mather: A Bibliography of His Works*. 3 vols. Cambridge: Harvard UP, 1940.

–. *Increase Mather: A Bibliography of His Works*. 2 vols. Cleveland, 1931.

Israel, Jonathan I. *Radical Enlightenment: Philosophy and the Making of Modernity, 1650- 1750*. Oxford: Oxford UP, 2001.

Jacob, Margaret C. *The Radical Enlightenment: Pantheists, Freemasons, and Republicans*. London: George Allen & Unwin, 1981.

Keene, Nicholas. "Poole [Pole], Matthew." *Oxford Dictionary of National Biography*. Ed. H.C.G. Matthew and Brian Harrison. Vol.44. Oxford: Oxford UP, 2004. 841–43.

Killy, Walther and Rudolf Vierhaus, eds. *Dictionary of German Biography*. Vols. 3–4. München: Saur, 2002.

Klever, W.N.A. "Spinoza's Life and Works." *The Cambridge Companion to Spinoza*. Ed. Don Garrett. Cambridge: Cambridge UP, 1996. 13–60.

Moreau, Pierre-François. "Spinoza's Reception and Influence." *The Cambridge Companion to Spinoza*. Ed. Don Garrett. Cambridge: Cambridge UP, 1996. 408–33.

O'Higgins, James. *Anthony Collins: The Man and His Works*. The Hague: Martinus Nijhoff, 1970.

Pallin, David A. "Cudworth, Ralph (1617–1688)." *Oxford Dictionary of National Biography*. Ed. H.C.G. Matthew and Brian Harrison. Vol. 14. Oxford: Oxford UP, 2004. 565.

Pelikan, Jaroslav. *The Christian Tradition: A History of the Development of Doctrine*. Vol.1. Chicago: U of Chicago P, 1971.

Pfanner, Dario. "Charles Blount (1654–1693)." *Oxford Dictionary of National Biography*. Ed. H.C.G. Matthew and Brian Harrison. Vol.6. Oxford: Oxford UP, 2004. 294–95.

Popkin, Richard H. "The Philosophy of Bishop Stillingfleet." *Journal of the History of Philosophy* 9.7 (1971): 303–19.

–. "Spinoza and Bible Scholarship." *The Cambridge Companion to Spinoza*. Ed. Don Garrett. Cambridge: Cambridge UP, 1996. 385–99.

Preston, Thomas R. "Biblical Criticism, Literature, and the Eighteenth-Century Reader." *Books and Their Readers in Eighteenth-Century England*. Ed. Isabel Rivers. Leicester: Leicester UP, 1982. 97–126.

Preus, J. Samuel. *Spinoza and the Irrelevance of Biblical Authority*. Cambridge: Cambridge UP, 2001.

Redwood, John. "Charles Blount (1654–93), Deism, and English Free Thought." *Journal of the History of Ideas* 35.7–9 (1974): 490–98.

–. *Reason, Ridicule and Religion: The Age of Enlightenment in England, 1660–1750*. Cambridge: Harvard UP, 1976.

Ricuperati, Giuseppe. "In Margine al Radical Enlightenment di Jonathan I. Israel." *Rivista storica Italiana* 115.4 (2003): 285–329.

Silverman, Kenneth. *The Life and Times of Cotton Mather.* New York: Harper & Row, 1984.

Simonutti, Luisa. "Spinoza and the English Thinkers. Criticism on Prophecies and Miracles: Blount, Gildon, Earberry." *Disguised and Overt Spinozism around 1700: Papers Presented at the International Colloquium held at Rotterdam, 5–8 October 1994.* Ed. Bunge, Wiep Van and Wim Klever. Leiden: Brill, 1996. 191–211.

Smolinski, Reiner. "Authority and Interpretation: Cotton Mather's Response to the European Spinozists." *Shaping the Stuart World, 1603–1714: The Atlantic Connection.* Eds. Alan I. Macinnes and Arthur Williamson. Leyden: Brill, 2006. 175–203.

–.   "How to Go to Heaven, or How Heaven Goes? Natural Science and Interpretation in Cotton Mather's 'Biblia Americana' (1693–1728)." *New England Quarterly* 81.2 (2008): 278–329.

Spink, J.S. *French Free-Thought from Gassendi to Voltaire.* London: Athlone Press, 1960.

Sullivan, Robert E. *John Toland and the Deist Controversy: A Study in Adaptations.* Cambridge: Harvard UP, 1982.

Totaro, Pina. "La Congrégation De L'Index Et La Censure Des Oeuvres de Spinoza." *Disguised and Overt Spinozism around 1700: Papers Presented at the International Colloquium held at Rotterdam, 5–8 October 1994.* Ed. Bunge, Wiep Van and Wim Klever. Leiden: E.J. Brill, 1996. 353–76.

Tuttle, Julius H. "The Libraries of the Mathers." *Proceedings of the American Antiquarian Society.* New Series 20 (1910): 269–356.

Vernière, Paul. *Spinoza et La Pensée Française Avant la Révolution.* Paris: Presses Universitaires de France, 1954.

Wade, Ira O. *The Clandestine Organization and Diffusion of Philosophic Ideas in France from 1700 to 1750.* Princeton: Princeton UP, 1938.

Wykes, David L. "Henry, Matthew." *Oxford Dictionary of National Biography.* Ed. H.C.G. Matthew and Brian Harrison. Vol. 26. Oxford: Oxford UP, 2004. 582–84.

Michael Dopffel

Between Biblical Literalism and Scientific Inquiry: Cotton Mather's Commentary on Jeremiah 8:7

In 1712 Cotton Mather sent a package of thirteen letters to Dr. John Woodward and Richard Waller of the Royal Society in London which contained his first offering of "Curiosa Americana." The first letter, in which the Boston clergymen sought to establish the basis for an ongoing dialogue with the Society's learned fellows, gives us some insights into the intellectual impetus behind the "Curiosa," of which he would compose about seventy more over the course of the next twelve years. While Mather's simultaneously subservient and pompous strategy of communication certainly betrays a colonial anxiety for acknowledgment by the metropolitan center of scientific learning, the introductory writing leaves no doubt about the main impetus behind the "Curiosa": First and foremost, they were composed out of a genuine hope for the ongoing progress which the modern age would make both in the fields of natural philosophy and scriptural exegesis. Significantly, the statements most expressive in this regard were woven into a rhetorically disguised advertisement of Mather's "Biblia Americana," which he presented as the project of an unnamed acquaintance:

> There is an *American* Friend of yours, who tho' he never travelled out of *America*, has had the Honour to be Related unto one of your *European* Universities; and has been desirous to oblige a Number of the best people in *Europe*, with a composure, which now arises to Two considerable Volumes in *Folio*, wearing the Title of, *BIBLIA AMERICANA*. He had long since been of your Excellent *Boyl's* opinion, That *you should no more measure the Wisdome of God couched in the Bible, by the Glosses and Systems of Common Expositors, than Estimate the Wisdome He has expressed in the Contrivance of the World, by* Maginus's, *or* Eustachius's *Physicks*; and agreed with him in hopes, that Learned Men would go on to make more admirable Explications and Discoveries, in that *wonderful Book*, than what usually occurr'd in the *Vulgar* (tho' very *useful*) *Annotations*. (qtd. in Levin 759; Mather, *Selected Letters* 111)

The "Biblia," he promised his addressees, examined the main events of sacred history through the lens of cutting-edge natural philosophy, and provided the "fairest *Hypotheses* ... of those grand Revolutions, the *Making*, and the *Drowning*, and the *Burning*, of the World. ..." Moreover, "[t]he *Meteors*, the *Minerals*, the *Plants*, the *Animals*, the *Diseases*, the *Astronomical* affaires, & the Powers of the *Invisible World*, mentioned in the Book of God, are here considered with the *Best Thought of the Our Times* upon them" (qtd. in Levin 760–61; Mather, *Selected Letters* 112).

Mather's unpublished Bible commentary and his letters to the Royal Society, which encompassed descriptions of and speculations on extraordinary natural phenomena from North America relating to "virtually all the sciences of his time, including astronomy, botany, zoology, geology, and meteorology" (Silverman 247), were thus conceived as part of one larger endeavor. In the spirit of Boyle, Mather wished to contribute from his corner of the earth to the rapid advancements in interpreting both the book of nature as well as the book of scriptures. And he hoped to do so by undertaking more fruitful cross-pollinations between biblical scholarship and the empirical findings of the new sciences that would further man's knowledge of God's truth.

In fact, a good number of the "Curiosa" which Mather dispatched to London (for reasons not the least of which was a way to generate interest in his larger work) were originally written for the "Biblia" and copied out of the manuscript. Strange as this may seem to us today, some of the most extraordinary scientific theories he put forth over the years in the letters to the Royal Society directly grew from his illustrations on certain scriptural verses. In contrast to those "Curiosa" that are mainly concerned with the description of American flora and fauna, these bible-based "Curiosa" mostly concern occult phenomena; that is, phenomena of nature which he either had observed himself or which had otherwise been credibly recorded or reported to him, and whose causes and full significance were still hidden from human understanding. Although Mather was never one to rule out the supernatural, he usually presented these occult phenomena as something that in all probability lay within the realm of nature, but could not yet be explained by man's still very limited knowledge (Levin 757). The speculative explanations which Mather gives for these phenomena in the manner of a scientific hypothesis are developed on the basis of specific biblical passages that are read in strictly literalist fashion as reliable, quasi-empirical sources of knowledge. Of this kind is not only the best known of the "Curiosa Americana," which claims that the bones of an antediluvian giant (mentioned in Gen. 6:4; *BA* 1: 582–99; see Levin) had been unearthed near Albany in 1705, but also numerous other discourses such as Mather's discussion of extraordinary cases of childbearing and longevity that was spun out from a scriptural illustration on the population development before the flood (see his entry on Gen. 4:25, *BA* 1: 528).

Largely ignored by existing studies, the "Curiosa" derived from the "Biblia Americana" are of special interest because they shed much light on the relationship in Mather's thinking between orthodox scripturalism and a scientific approach to the world, a relationship which, despite his own rhetoric of harmonious progress, was in fact riddled by tensions and increasing problems.[1] More

---

1 Discussions of the "Curiosa" can be found in Kittredge, Beall, Beall and Shyrock (42–50), Stearns (405–25), Silverman (244–49), Levin, and Solberg (xl-xliii).

specifically, these texts throw into relief the complicated interplay between a literalist hermeneutics and an empiricist epistemology that especially marks his later writings. Of course, Mather has long been recognized as a herald of a Christian or moderate Enlightenment in British North America. But until very recently, scholars interested in this aspect of Mather have focused almost exclusively on his physico-theological works, in particular *The Christian Philosopher* (1721). Even though these works undoubtedly show Mather's overall *wish* to harmonize an orthodox faith based on a belief in the literal truth of the Bible and the new sciences, they tell us very little about his growing difficulties in actually giving convincing proof of this reconcilability.[2] After all, by arguing from the design of nature for the general goodness of God or the world's providential order, he could avoid the very pitfalls that inevitably open up as soon as one attempts to bring specific doctrines of revealed religion such as God's creation of the world in six days into agreement with new scientific knowledge. It is therefore only when we additionally examine Mather's detailed reading of the scriptures, as Smolinski has done ("Natural Science and Interpretation") that we begin to understand how difficult Mather and other Christian advocates of the Enlightenment found it to come to terms with science.

If in many entries of the "Biblia" Mather felt either forced to abandon a traditional literalist hermeneutics or to embrace openly anti-scientific supernaturalism, the "Curiosa" developed from scriptural illustration offer, as I will show in my analysis of one particularly striking example, a quite different picture. In those "Curiosa" concerned with as yet occult phenomena of nature, Mather was free, as it were, to engage in wishful thinking rather than having to squeeze biblical revelations into a Procrustean bed of natural laws irrefutably established by science; and in so doing he left us significant testimony of what he had hoped for from the marriage between science and religion. Since he was dealing with phenomena for which the sciences had as yet no convincing answer, or which were outside the reach of its methods of observation, literalism and empiricism could still be rendered as complementary, mutually reinforcing methods of interpretation. Here, Mather could offer a speculative hypothesis that was empiricist in its basic approach or rationale and, at the same time, based on a strictly literalist reading of a specific verse of the Bible. As long as natural sciences or natural history knew nothing of extinct species like the Mastodon, he was free to claim, for instance, that a literal reading of Genesis provided a sound explanation for the findings at Claverack, near Albany. At the same time, he was able to represent the giant bones as physical proof for the historical exist-

---

2 For good discussions of Mather's physico-theology, see Jeske and especially Solberg's introduction to his 1994 edition of *The Christian Philosopher*. The growing difficulties amongst Puritan clergymen of Mather's generation to reconcile theology and science are emphasized by Middlekauff (esp. 284) and Winship (esp. 195) without, however, examining in any detail his biblical scholarship.

ence of the biblical Nephilim (Gen. 6:1–4) and hence disprove allegorical interpretations arguing, "That the *Antediluvian Giants* were but *Metaphorical* ones"
(qtd. in Levin 763; *BA* 1: 585).

In the following, I will undertake a close reading of the scriptural commentary that Mather turned into the second part of his third "Curiosa Americana," which was transmitted to London in the first package of letters.[3] In it
Mather constructs the hypothesis that the migratory birds, whose whereabouts
during the absences from their normal habitats was then still a mystery to science, were flying to planetoids circling between the earth and the moon. Bizarre
and ridiculous as Mather's hypothesis may appear from our perspective, it was
actually not fundamentally different from many other discourses published at
the time under the rubric of *curiosa* in perfectly respectable venues of scientific
learning (Silverman 249). Indeed, his theory responded to an ongoing scientific
debate in Europe and North America about whether the moon could be the
place whereto the birds disappear during their seasons of migration. In large
parts, Mather's speculations were based on a posthumous publication by Charles
Morton (1627–98), the former vice-president of Harvard and author of the famous "Compendium Physicae" (1680), who, in his college days had been a peer
of Boyle and other leading empiricist scholars who would form the core of the
Royal Society. It is therefore not altogether surprising that, as Silverman has
shown, the Royal Society responded very well to Mather's first package, including the third letter.[4] A summarized account of Mather's "particular fancy"
about the migratory birds was consequently published as part of an eight-page
digest of his first series of "Curiosa" in the 1714 *Philosophical Transactions*, a
publication which followed upon the nomination (belatedly confirmed in 1723)
for the highly prestigious membership in October 1713.[5]

---

3   The third letter of the first series of "Curiosa" (addressed to John Woodward of the Royal
Society of London) was edited in slightly shortened form by Silverman (Mather, *Selected Letters* 113–15). Generally speaking, the second part of the letter, which contains the theory
about bird migration, follows the entry in the "Biblia" (Jer. 8:7) very closely. The few but
significant differences that do exist will be discussed in the conclusion of this essay. The first
part of the letter offers "an addition to the treasure of your ornithology" by providing detailed description of the American hummingbird and passenger pigeons (Mather, *Selected
Letters* 113).
4   On this, see Silverman's convincing assessment: "Secretary Waller reported to him in July
1713 that his first series of Curiosa 'very well pleased and Entertained' the members, and that
his future communications would be 'extremely acceptable.' Waller and Dr. Woodward also
prepared some more detailed notes on their or the members' reactions ... withal indicating
that the "Curiosa" received respectful and thoughtful attention" (Mather, *Selected Letters*
253). Therefore, I do not share Stearn's assessment that the Royal Society was unappreciative
of Mather's contributions (Stearns 414).
5   Printed in the Apr.-June issue, the part of the digest derived from the third letter reads, "...
he takes notice of vast Hights of [*illeg.], coming and departing at certain Seasons: And as to
this, he has a particular fancy of their repairing to some undiscovered Satellite, accompanying
the Earth at a near distance" (64).

What makes Mather's theory about migratory birds an especially intriguing and forceful example for the specific interplay between literalism and empiricism in the "Biblia" is, for one thing, the fact that he developed it from Jer. 8:7, a passage which was usually read in a figurative sense and was very likely intended by the biblical author to be read in this way. By making this passage the textual basis for his scientific speculations about undiscovered planetoids, Mather not only generally insisted on the literal truthfulness of even a rather obscure part of the Bible that, at first glance, simply looked like a figure of speech. He in fact implied that folded into the literal meaning of Jer. 8:7 was a hitherto secret truth about nature which had not just escaped commentators, but also exceeded the prophet's own horizon of knowledge. In this way, he apparently intended to make his hypothesis about bird migration (which he hoped improvements in telescopes would soon prove to be valid) evince the divine inspiration of the Bible and its absolute authority as the book of books comprising, even if partly in hidden ways, the whole truth about this world and the one to come.

Before entering into a detailed discussion of these issues together with the eschatological conjectures to which they give rise, I will very briefly survey the parallel evolution and eventual collision of scientific empiricism and hermeneutic literalism in the early modern period, a development which needs to be taken into account to help us appreciate the complexities of Mather's interpretative maneuvers.

From the vantage point of today, a scientific approach to the world and an insistence on the literal truth of the Bible almost inevitably appear as opposing principles. Most people of faith have made their peace with the separation of science and religion as two separate fields of human inquiry concerned with fundamentally different kinds of truths. But before the early nineteenth century such a view was a minority opinion. Indeed, historically speaking, the two principles of scientific empiricism and scriptural literalism sprung up together at the beginning of the early modern period and evolved alongside each other for more than two centuries before they ultimately came into irreconcilable conflict. The Renaissance revolution in natural philosophy and the Reformation's call for *sola scriptura* were part of one larger paradigm shift in Western culture which centered intellectual interest on the factual, be it the physical facts of nature or the facts of (biblical) history, and which increasingly made empirical evidence the decisive criterion for the authority of any kind of knowledge. To be sure, this shift from its very beginnings brought forth challenges to the absolute truth-claims of the scriptural revelations as the scientific and geographic discoveries raised troublesome questions about the reliability of the biblical world picture (Scholder 9–26). But for a long time these challenges did not carry enough weight to unsettle the status of the Bible as the ultimate frame of reference for human learning. Rather, the focus on the factual led to a new understanding of the scriptures which, at least in the discursive mainstream of Western culture, did not entail a diminution, but a reinterpretation of the Bible's authority as a quasi-scientific source text containing a kind of knowledge that could be held to the new standards of evidentiality. The Protestant concern with the *sensus literalis sive historicus*, together with humanist biblical scholarship invested in producing an unadulterated scripture text and in understanding the historical circumstances that gave rise to it, simultaneously responded to and, at the same time, reinforced a view of the Bible as an ancient but fully reliable document. When interpreted in a literal fashion the scriptures were thought to yield factual truths about nature, man, and history in their relationship to God.

With the turn to empiricism and literalism, then, the Bible was brought into the realm of scientific discourse in which it was simultaneously treated as an authoritative source and as an object of the increasingly far-reaching empirical investigations into the natural cosmos, an endeavor which was undertaken during the period of the early Enlightenment. "Far from the scientific revolution of the seventeenth century contributing to the demise of scripture," writes Colin Kidd following Peter Harrison's groundbreaking study *The Bible, Protestantism, and the Rise of Natural Science* (1998),

> the emergence of early modern science went hand in hand with a positive reappraisal of the scientific value of the Bible. Indeed, Protestant scientists read the Bible and the natural world – God's book of nature – in tandem as complementary 'texts.' In addition ... early modern Protestant exegesis witnessed a marked retreat from the symbolic and allegorical readings of scripture toward a more literal treatment of the Bible. To be sure, Protestant exegesis did consider typological readings of scripture in which some events or characters in the Old Testament were seen to prefigure developments in the New Testament; but ... these approaches were quite distinct from allegorical readings and were not out of step with a literal interpretation of the Bible as a reliable guide in the fields of science and history. The Old Testament set out, in plain terms and unmediated by allegory – so early modern Protestant scholars believed – the creation of the world, the origin of humankind and the ancient history of the world from earliest times. In parallel, the realm of nature too was denuded of symbolic significance. Nature and scripture consisted of facts, not of signs and symbols. (Kidd 56–57)

The literalist approach to the scriptural texts and hence the attempt to ground their contents in the factual and historical was also extended to prophecies and kerygmatic proclamations of the Bible. Many Protestant and especially Reformed exegetes insisted on non-allegorical readings of the final stages of redemptive history, including the millennial reign of Christ. As is evident in Mather's own writings, this insistence went hand in hand with a tendency to locate eschatological sites, such as the New Jerusalem or heaven itself, in empirical space (P. Harrison, *The Bible* 148).

While it did not break apart until the early nineteenth century, the inherent problems of this coalition between an empiricist epistemology and a literal hermeneutics began to push to the surface with increasing vehemence since the late seventeenth century. For one thing, it became more and more clear in some areas of theological discussion that literalism, more than anything, had been a theoretical promise to reach an unambiguous truth through rationalized methods of interpretation. In practice, however, these methods usually did not yield any indisputable factual knowledge that could be translated, after the manner of the natural sciences, into unequivocal propositional forms. On the contrary, the push for literal interpretations only highlighted the invincibly metaphorical, highly ambiguous, and frequently completely obscure nature of many parts of the Bible. Rather than simply yielding the one inherent meaning of the scriptures through an unmediated approach to the text itself, the Protestant penchant for a literalist hermeneutics created the need for ever more excessive historical contextualization and philological investigations. But instead of providing certainties, these methods forced exegetes to recognize how inextricably rooted the meanings of scriptural writings were in a historically distant and culturally alien world view, as well as how insurmountably difficult it was to create a single catholic text.

Literalism thus not only engendered what Peter Miller calls "the antiquarianization of biblical scholarship," but also gave rise to historical-critical exegesis, which eventually "led to a completely secular reading of the Bible" (Popkin 11). Moreover, in the late seventeenth century the fundamental problems involved in reconciling many parts of biblical revelation with the Newtonian view of a universe governed by uniform natural laws became increasingly evident. In Mather's day the first advocates of a secular reading of the Bible such as Hugo Grotius, Thomas Hobbes, and Benedict Spinoza, had thus already called for a separation of theology and science. Yet at the time these were radical and hence relatively marginal voices easily drowned out by the large chorus of scholars who continued to proclaim the happy marriage of Enlightenment empiricism and traditional scripturalism. In the long run, however, it turned out that the attempt to redefine scriptural truths in terms of the factual inevitably worked to undermine the authority of the Bible, and "that once the sacred was made fully and finally historical, it ceased to be sacred" (Miller 465). While Mather certainly never reached that conclusion, his biblical scholarship (in contrast to his physico-theological writings) shows the mounting tensions he perceived between a scientific outlook on the world and the tenets of Reformed orthodoxy.

The "Biblia" was produced at a critical turning point in intellectual history and is in many ways a transitional work that stands between the optimism of the early Enlightenment with its high-flying expectation of reinforcing the authority of the Scriptures through empirical methods and the advent of "Higher

Criticism" in the late eighteenth century. On the one hand, Mather's scriptural commentary, as his above-cited advertisement to the Royal Society suggests, was still secure in its basic confidence that the revealed truths of the Bible could be demonstrated to agree with the "fairest *Hypotheses*" offered by new sciences concerning the laws of nature. On the other hand, as Smolinski has convincingly demonstrated (see "Natural Science and Interpretation"), the "Biblia" in some entries betrays Mather's anxious awareness that holding on to a strictly literalist understanding of a particular passage such as the Mosaic *hexameron*, the description of Noah's flood, or miraculous events like Joshua's arrest of the sun, would eventually undermine the Bible's truth-claim because the *sensus literalis* contradicted the evidence produced by the great scientific discoveries from Copernicus to Newton. Unwilling to separate natural philosophy from theology, Mather in these cases sacrificed the literalist principle and with it the conservative claim for full verbal inspiration of all scriptural texts in order to rescue the general authority of the Bible. Arguing that it was "[t]he doctrine, not the letter of the text, [which] is vouchsafed by the Holy Spirit," he here moved towards a form of accommodationist hermeneutics (Smolinski, "Authority and Interpretation" 198). Whereas the truths informing the scriptural revelations were inspired and thus could not conflict with scientific knowledge, according to Mather's reasoning, he conceded that the language in which these truths had been expressed was time-bound and reflected the authors' limited, even faulty knowledge of the workings of nature as well as the primitive mind-set of the audience to which they had to accommodate their teachings. In those parts of the "Biblia" that he decided to send to London as "Curiosa," however, Mather felt no pressure to give up the orthodox understanding of the inerrancy of the letter, and to take the escape route of accommodationism because the respective biblical passage did not conflict with contemporary scientific knowledge. Instead, he could uninhibitedly engage in hypothetical speculations that tightly locked together an empiricist form of inquiry with a hyper-literalist interpretation of scripture. In so doing, he created a circular structure of reasoning in which a quasi-scientific form of reasoning relying on physical evidence is represented as supporting the factual truth of a scriptural text and vice versa.

This is certainly true for Mather's commentary on Jer. 8:7. As already suggested above, the formulation "Yea, the stork in the heaven knoweth her appointed times; and the turtle and the crane and the swallow observe the time of their coming" was intended by the biblical author to serve as a metaphorical vehicle for his moral indictment of the Jewish nation: "but my people know not the judgment of the LORD." Accordingly, most Protestant exegetes and popular commentators of the time read the passage with an eye to the historical context of Jeremiah's prophetic mission to reproach a wayward people, while foregrounding the general significance of his exhortations to modern Christians.

This was, for instance, the way Matthew Henry's *Exposition of all the Books of the Old and New Testament* (1708–10) glossed on the verse:

> They *know not* how to improve the *Seasons of Grace* that God affords them, when he sends them his Prophets; not how to make use of the Rebukes they are under, when *his Voice cries in the City*. They *discern not the Signs of the Times*, Matth. 16. 3. nor are aware how God is dealing with them. They know not that *way of Duty*, which God hath prescrib'd them, though it be written both in their Hearts and in their Books. (4: 243)

Mather, of course, was aware of how the passage was usually read and was by no means suggesting that the figurative interpretation should be rejected altogether. In his tract *Reasonable Religion Or The Truths of the Christian Religion Demonstrated* (1713), he in fact expounded the same passage in just such a figurative and didactic fashion. In this primarily pastoral text Mather appeals to his audience's faculty of reason to abstain from "the vile things, which the very *Brutes*, by the meer *Instincts of Nature* avoid" and to live a good Christian life in accordance with reason. "God," he argues, "has implanted a *Natural Instinct*, into the *Unreasonable Creatures*, partly that so the *Reasonable* ones, may by them be *Hieroglyphically* Cautioned and Instructed. ..." Accordingly, he employs Jer. 8:7 as an admonishment to "let not slip the Seasons of Grace, but Seasonably apply your selves, to Do the Service, and Get the Blessing of God. If you do it not, the Stork, & the Turtle, the Crane, and the Swallow, will reproach your Sleepiness" (41–42). By way of contrast, the entry in the "Biblia" that was then included in the "Curiosa" has no interest in the verse's potential for "hieroglyphical" or allegorical instruction. Instead it serves as a kind of launching pad for a scientific speculation on a scientific mystery of the times: where do birds go when they migrate?

The absence of entire bird populations during certain seasons had been debated since antiquity. In Mather's days the mystery was still unsolved, and different answers continued to be proposed. It was not until the second half of the eighteenth century that a theory was developed from enough empirical evidence ultimately to establish what we now recognize as the truth. George Edwards (1694–1773), the "father of British ornithology," had collected sufficient data over the years on the basis of which he could with absolute certainty prove the seasonal flight of birds to warmer climates.[6] In a 1795 publication of his *A Discourse on the Emigration of British Birds*, he also gives an introductory summary of older theories, which is useful for our purposes here because it helps us appreciate the context in which Mather had formulated his earlier speculations.

---

6   To corroborate his theory, Edwards notes, that he had "filled volumes with remarks; have strictly observed ... the exact time each species appear and disappear ... compared them with the observations of others, examined the journals of seamen, collected the relations of travellers, and made every other information that was in our power, in order to arrive at a *perfect* knowledge of this subject" (xii-xiii).

After expressing his belief in the ongoing progress of knowledge,[7] Edwards chides the absurdity of "the many chimerical notions, the many groundless conjectures, the many foolish, unreasonable, impertinent, and incongruous hypotheses" that were put forth about migratory birds in the past. These are then grouped into "four opinions how these birds encounter the winter" (1–2). The first opinion that had, for instance, been expressed by Aristotle and Pliny maintained that birds hide in caves and nooks during the winter in a state of hibernation. As Edwards argues, several factors contradict this assumption, including the inadequate anatomy of the birds. For similar reasons, Edwards also dismisses the second opinion, which held that the birds slept under the ice of lakes. As the most ludicrous of them all, however, he chides the third hypothesis, according to which birds migrate to the moon or some other distant globe circling the earth. Finally, he offers and endorses the fourth opinion that the birds migrate to warmer climates (2–19). While modern readers will unanimously agree with Edwards, a few decades prior to his treatise, all of these theories still had reputable proponents and were discussed as serious possibilities.

In the English-speaking world of Mather's time, the third opinion mentioned by Edwards, the "moon theory," was most forcefully represented by an anonymous tract that was first published in 1694 and later attributed to the close friend of the Mather family, Charles Morton.[8] Under the title *An Enquiry into the Physical and Literal Sense of that Scripture, Jeremiah viii.7. The Stork in the Heaven knoweth her appointed times; and the Turtle, and the Crane, and the Swallow observe the time of their coming*, the tract listed several logical conjectures, empirical observations, as well as readings of biblical passages as evidence for its argument.[9] Morton's hypothesis apparently remained popular at least until the second half of the eighteenth century as it was reprinted in different versions for several decades.[10] Since Morton's tract was Mather's main source, a rough outline will be provided here.

---

7 "New observations and new discoveries may be made in one age, that are not in another, by the hints that one generation transmits to another. Human reason is still aiming for perfection" (viii).

8 Morton had been an English Puritan preacher as well as an esteemed scholar before he left for New England in 1686, where Increase Mather apparently intended him to become president of Harvard; the revocation of the Massachusetts charter forced Morton to take up a parish in Charlestown. Morton and Cotton Mather were both suspected by the governor's council of conspiracy, and they both shared common views on the use of spectral evidence during the Salem witch trials. Morton was later named vice president of Harvard, where he lectured on scientific subjects; his "Compendium Physicae" was one of the most popular textbooks in that institution. He died in 1698. For a concise biography, see the entry in the *American National Biography* (945–46).

9 T. Harrison (323), following an entry in Halkett's and Laing's *Dictionary of Anonymous and Pseudonymous English Literature* (173), suspects that this version is the earliest. It is included in the *Harleian Miscellany* (5: 498–511), published in 1808.

10 Later reprints include *An Essay toward the Probable Solution of this Question: Whence come the Stork and the Turtledove, the Crane, and the Swallow, when they Know and Ob-*

While the title identifies the Bible as the main starting point of the theory, the largest portion of the arguments are of an empirical rather than an exegetical nature. Morton's first statement in his prolegomena is that "the Creator made the universe for the manifestation of his own glory" (501), after which he notes that the "rational creature (man)" (501) has the capacity to observe and comprehend this creation.[11] Through the accumulation of knowledge over the ages and the improvements in the sciences, man's understanding of nature, according to Morton, will be increasingly perfected until he fully understands the "end and use" (502) of even the smallest thing in creation. After reciting Copernicus, Morton finally comes to the empirical evidence he has collected for his specific hypothesis: "I do suppose ... 'that the moon's body ... is of a composition like our earth, and may have in it dry land and water, mountains and vallies, fountains, streams, seas, &c.'" (502). This assumption allows him to argue for the moon as a conceivable location to which the birds travel. Furthermore, he describes the arrival and departure of the seasonal birds as so sudden, that they probably come straight down from the atmosphere, where gravitation is supposedly weaker, making it easier to hover and fly with hardly any resistance. Another observation he provides is the difference in the texture of their flesh, from which he conjectures "that they have another kind of nourishment before they come here, than what this earth doth afford" (505). That the earth cannot be the place to which the animals retreat seems certain to Morton, since a witness to the birds' resting somewhere on the planet surely would have written it down at some point in history (503). Morton continues by giving evidence of the birds' behavior. Because some of them refuse to fly off to sea, he conjectures that they never come from or fly to "any part of the earth, that lies beyond our seas" (505). Likewise, he finds support for his argument in the behavior of storks, which gather and then, after a silence in their chattering, "rise together, and fly in one great flock, or cloud, fetch many great rounds, first near the earth, but after higher, like the spiral Ascent of a goss-hawk when she lowers ... till it utterly disappears" (506). In this manner, he writes, the stork surely must ascend to the moon since "directly upright is not the way to any part of this globe" (506).

At this point Morton turns to his other source of support, Jer. 8:7: "And lastly, Consider some remarkable words in the text; one is their *tempus iteneris*, the time of their journey; so, instead of coming, do the learned render it" (506).

---

serve the Appointed Time of their Coming (1703); *A Solution to the Question, Where the Swallow, Nightingale, Woodcock, Fieldfare, Cuckow, and other Birds of Passage Go, and Reside, when Absent from us* (1733); *Essay towards the probable solution to this question, whence comes the stork, the turtle, the crane, and the swallow. ... By a person of learning and piety* (1739). On this, see T. Harrison (323).

11   The pagination here refers to the version published in the *Harleian Miscellany* in 1808, as it is most likely a reprint of the earliest tract (see footnote 9).

For this reason, the distance which the birds travel, must be "such a distance as may deserve the name of journey" (506). Another hint that Morton finds in the Bible is the distinction between the phrase "in the Heaven," which is used to describe the stork and turtledove in Jer. 8:7, and the "Fowls of the Heaven," mentioned throughout the Old Testament. According to Morton, "in the heaven" is only employed by the scriptures to refer "to those things, that have the heaven for their proper place, and as contra-distinct from the earth" (507) such as, for example, the moon. Thus, the usage of this phrase in Jeremiah can only mean that the migratory birds mentioned there actually live "in the Heaven" for a longer period of time, rather than just occasionally residing there, while flying by:

> [I]t remains therefore, that the stork ... does go unto, and remain in some one of the cælestial bodies, and that must be the moon, which is most likely, because nearest, and bearing most relation to this our earth, as appears in the Copernican scheme, yet is the distance great enough to denominate the passage thither an itineration or journey. (508)

Morton concludes his tract by addressing several possible objections which might be offered to his theory such as the question as to whether the birds could really gain the speed necessary to fly to the moon in the time of their absence. He computes that if the distance of the earth to the moon is 179,712 miles, the birds would have two months for each of their flights, traveling at a speed of 125 miles an hour, which would still be slower than a racehorse. He adds that the lack of gravity and resistance from the air in the outer atmosphere would allow for at least such swiftness.[12] Yet in his postscript, he again addresses the problem of distance and velocity and offers another possible solution to those that cannot believe the moon theory: "'[w]hether there may not be some concrete bodies, at a much less distance than the moon, which may be the recess of these creatures, and may serve for little else but their entertainment'" (511). Serving as "ætherial islands" (511) to the migratory birds, these globes would have to be so small or at such a distance as to be invisible from the earth.

Morton's theory thus rests on three pillars: the Copernican Scheme and its conjectures on the composure of the moon, further developed by John Wilkins; Morton's own collection of empirical observations on the behavior of seasonal birds; and the biblical texts, in particular Jer. 8:7. The literalistic exegesis of the verse thus provides the impetus and serves as the intellectual framework of the discourse, while the bulk of Morton's arguments rely on logic and observation.

---

12 Morton based his computations of the distance on John Wilkins' treatise, *The Discovery of a New World in the Moon* (1638). Wilkins, a founder of the Royal Society, in a later reprint of the tract also discussed the possibility of humans travelling to the moon, including some ideas on the effects of gravitation (T. Harrison 325).

Mather apparently read this treatise at some point and must have known that it had been written by Morton, who had quite likely passed away before the publication of the paper. Fascinated by the field of ornithology, Mather then evidently decided to engage in the debate by proffering his own opinions. The general arguments proposed by Morton appear to have convinced him, so that he copied an abstract of them into his commentary on Jer. 8:7 in the "Biblia Americana," from which he then later derived the third letter of the "Curiosa." Therefore, both texts present arguments that are, for the most part, very similar to Morton's. The few differences, however, are highly interesting. While Morton conjectured that the birds' journey was to the moon, Mather, in both the "Biblia" and the "Curiosa" argued for the possibility which Morton added as an alternative possibility in his postscript, namely that the birds flew to hitherto undiscovered planets circling earth closer than the moon. Moreover, Mather's own versions also differ significantly from each other. In his Bible commentary he proposes both a different foundation for his argument and offers an extraordinary conclusion that is missing from the letter sent to London.

The third "Curiosa"-letter, as noted earlier, was completely dedicated to ornithology, offering some description of American birds such as the passenger pigeon and the humming-bird before launching into his theory on bird migration (*Selected Letters* 113–15). Mather here accurately identifies Morton as the originator of the theory that had been presented in an anonymous pamphlet after the author's death, and then repeats his arguments, in fact copying the above-cited empirical evidence almost word for word: the lack of information concerning the possible resting-place of the birds anywhere on earth, the manner of the birds' coming and going, the texture of their flesh, their reluctance to fly over water and so on. Even several examples and similes such as of the storks' circling like a goshawk are included verbatim. It is only on the question of the actual destination of the birds' migration that Mather proposes another answer: "it seems no unreasonable presumption to imagine," he writes to Woodward, "that there are nigh unto our terraqueous globe, sundry minute planetary bodies" (114) to which the birds relocate during the time of their absence.[13] Thus Mather rejects as "faulty" the theory presented in the main body of Morton's tract and seeks to prove the necessary existence of the planetoids mentioned in the afterword. He adds a witty analogy to the inhabitants of the "Coast of Barbary" and their lack of familiarity with the island of Ascension out at sea, from which seafowl travel to their lands. Similar to their ignorance is science's lack of knowledge concerning the existence of these planets (115). In this fashion Mather closes his letter to Woodward.

---

13   Unfortunately, the computations Mather employed to refute the "moon theory" are not included in the *Selected Letters*; however, it is likely that the arguments are similar to those in the "Biblia" version and will be fully discussed in that context later.

What is perhaps most striking in the "Curiosa"-letter is the total lack of biblical evidence which stands in marked contrast to Morton's treatise. Jer. 8:7 is used merely as a rhetorical introduction to the letter but not presented as a source of knowledge about nature: "They are not only Birds (Of) the Heaven but also Birds (In) Heaven (Jer VIII 7)" (114), Mather writes without any further reference to the scriptural text. He presents his theory as directly derived from Morton, as strictly empirical and with no connection whatsoever to literalist exegesis. This is surprising, since Mather seldom missed a chance to emphasize the harmony between the books of nature and scripture, as in his *Christian Philosopher*, or in the first letter of the "Curiosa," in which he allowed the "anonymous" author of the "Biblia" to claim the bones found at Albany were the remnants of a Nephilim, as described in the Bible. It appears as if Mather in this case chose exclusively to focus on reason and empirical evidence and to omit any proof from the Bible, thereby effectively separating the realms of scientific and scriptural knowledge. His letter recapitulates the essentials of Morton's hypothesis for the Royal Society and then offers some suggestions for corrections. In so doing, Mather presents his own version of the theory as a purely scientific investigation into an occult phenomenon of nature.

In his commentary on Jer. 8:7 in the "Biblia" from which the "Curiosa" was derived, Mather, by contrast, not only repeats Morton's scriptural interpretations, but actually exceeds him in his literalist approach. Like Morton, he stresses the importance of the correct translation of "Time of their Coming" as "Time of their Journey" and the fact that the migratory birds are called "Fowls in the Heaven" rather than "Fowls of the Heaven." And like Morton, he presents these philological niceties as evidence that is as valid as empirical investigations to corroborate a scientific hypothesis. But Mather goes even farther than Morton in his concern for the literal meaning of the original Hebrew text. The commentary on Jer. 8:7, preceding his entry that includes the speculation on bird migration, illustrates this painstaking exactness very well:

> Q. Among the *Season-Birds*, we read of, the *Crane*, and the *Swallow*; Are the Names truly translated? v. 7.
> A. *Bochart* saies, *No*; but reads, The *Swallow*, and the *Crane*.
> The Hebrew / סוס / *sus*; or rather / סיס / *sis*, is to be translated, not, a *Crane*, but a *Swallow*. To confirm This, we have the Consent of the LXX and of *Theodotion*, and of *Jerom*, and *Symmachus*, and the *Arabic*. By the Sound of the Name, *Sis*, which is ὀνοματοποιητικὸν,[14] the Hebrewes express the ψιθυρισμος, of the *Swallow*; and the *Italians* therefore, near *Venice* call that little Bird, *Zisilla*.
> The Hebrew עגר *Agor*, is to be translated, not a *Swallow*, but a *Crane*.

With Samuel Bochart's *Hierozoicon* at his elbow, Mather here insists that the King James Bible erroneously changed the order of the birds. While this mis-

---

14   Mather here cites Samuel Bochart's *Hierozoicon* (vol. 2, col. 62).

take is completely insignificant for a figurative reading of the passage, from a literalist perspective it amounts to a distortion of the truth about the (natural) world contained in this and every other scriptural verse. The "Biblia" is filled with such small corrections, all of which demonstrate Mather's strong investment in reconstructing a catholic translation of the biblical texts that alone would guarantee their reliability as a source of factual knowledge. Even a seemingly trivial philological improvement of the text might lead to the deciphering of a hitherto unnoticed meaning.

Rather than merely offering a slightly theologically tinged introduction as in the "Curiosa," the commentary on Jer. 8:7 thus presents the theory on bird migration as derived from the text of the Bible:

> [W]hat will you say, if I do from this Text, offer you a singular & curious *Hypothesis* concerning them? I will then suppose that the Annual Recesses of these little *Birds* are in some remote Regions of *Heaven*; they are not only *Birds [Of] the Heaven*, but also *Birds [In] the Heaven*, from whence, at their *Appointed Times*, they take their *Journey* hither. They find something either in the Temper of their own *Bodies* or in the *Alterations* of their Lodgings at home or in the *Effluvia* of the Earth upon the new Reflections of the Sun there upon, which invites them to change their Quarters; and so, *they know their Season.*

While Mather's arguments again echo Morton's, they are quite different from the discussion in the "Curiosa." The structure of the argument is clearly arranged to present the literal sense of the Bible as the inspiration and main factual foundation for the theory. Charles Morton is not even mentioned as the originator of these speculations. As a way to reference the "moon theory" Mather instead offers an allusion to the fictional story of Domingo Gonsales, who flew to the moon with the aid of geese (*ganzas*).[15] This rhetorical gesture, which effectively belittles the "moon theory" as a piece of fiction, is certainly meant as a sideswipe at Morton, even though Mather's own conjectures about the planetary bodies were so much indebted to him.

The actual arguments which he offers for his theory in the "Biblia" are then again exclusively based on the conjectures and observations proposed by Morton. While the structure of the argument is slightly more ordered than in the "Curiosa," the content of the evidence is again entirely the same: The arguments against the birds migrating to some location on the surface of the earth, a description of their behavior before take-off, and of the texture of their flesh. Mather then presents his own calculations concerning the distance between the

---

15 Mather refers to a story written by Francis Godwin (1562–1633), bishop of Hereford, which was published in 1638. T. Harrison, recounting the story, assumes that Morton might ultimately have fetched the idea of birds flying to the moon from this romance, via Wilkins (325–28).

moon and the earth, and the approximate velocity of the birds.[16] According to Mather, the originator of the "moon theory" (kept anonymous in the "Biblia") employed the wrong measurements and computations, namely those expressed by Ptolemy and used by the Arabians. Under these circumstances, "wee cannot consent unto so great a Swiftness [of the birds]; especially, since the true Distance of the *Moon* from the *Earth* is much greater than what was conceived by *Ptolomy*." Mather therefore arrives at his own conclusion that the birds must rest somewhere nearer than the moon. Apparently, "the greatest Philosopher in this age, has already affirm'd that some *Christalline*, or *Semipellucid* Bodies, between the *Earth* & the *Moon* have already been discovered," and therefore, with a little advancement in the range of telescopes these globes might soon be discovered.[17]

Up to this point, both versions of Mather's theory are nearly identical, the "Biblia" version being slightly extended and actually more in accord with Morton's theory, insofar as it rests on a literalistic exegesis. Indeed, while the "Curiosa" is almost devoid of scriptural references, Mather's main interest in the "Biblia" entry seems to be to offer a striking example of how in the case of Jer. 8:7 literalism and empiricism work as complementary approaches.

Mather clearly states that his intention is to go beyond both the physico-theological issues and the strictly empirical version later published in the "Curiosa." He does not only wish to "magnify the Power, & Wisdome, & Goodness of our God, in some Circumstances of the Creation hitherto unheeded" but rather to "serve the *Illustrations* of the Scripture, by exciting the further Enquiries of ingenious Men." This statement echoes his advertisement for the "Biblia" in his first "Curiosa"-letter that promises to utilize science in order to "make more admirable Explications and Discoveries, in that *wonderful Book*" (qtd. in Levin 759). Indeed, demonstrating the mutual compatibility of science and orthodox theology can be regarded as one of the key elements and ambitions of his *magnum opus*. He therefore represents his bird theory as equally based on a strictly literalistic reading of the Bible on the one hand, and on empirical evidence, mathematics, and logic on the other. Together he hoped they would lead to new explanations for an occult phenomena in nature and to a more complete comprehension of other "Texts in the Bible, which have hitherto wanted a tolerable *Commentary*; especially about, the *Windowes of Heaven opened for the Flood*; about, *the Treasures of the Snow & Rain, reserved against the Time of Trouble*; and some things, referring to the *New Jerusalem*, at the Second Coming of our Lord." Methodologically, Mather therefore moves in a kind of hermeneutical cycle, which starts with an example of literalist exegesis,

16   This part was not included in Silverman's edition of the letters (see above); however, it is likely that the arguments are similar or the same to those in the "Biblia".
17   The philosopher here mentioned is quite likely Galilei Galileo, as Mather mentions in the "Curiosa" that he had died in the former century.

from which he then develops a scientific hypothesis. This hypothesis is supported with empirical observations and mathematical computations. Ultimately, however, all of these efforts again aim at gaining new insights into the hidden *sensus literalis* of other biblical passages which previously had only been interpreted in a figurative manner. This approach shows Mather's conviction that through the improvements in theology and science one would eventually be able to unlock the literal truth of all scriptural texts, even in cases such as Jer. 8:7, in which the author had obviously not been fully aware of this truth that the Holy Spirit embedded in his words.

Mather's cross-references to the other biblical verses in the passage quoted above deserve more attention than can be given in this context; I can merely offer a short side-glance here. The references are to Gen 7:11, a verse which addresses the origin of the water of the deluge, as well as to Job 38:23, in which God admonishes Job for challenging him and his judgment.[18] Yet Mather's "Biblia" commentary on these verses does not engage in any literalist interpretation, but rather affirms traditional figurative readings. Nor do Mather's glosses make a connection to Jer. 8:7.[19] It seems, therefore, that while writing his commentary on Jeremiah, he came up with new ideas on how to revise earlier entries into a more literalist fashion, but then never actually got around to doing it. I will therefore focus on the other cross-reference to Rev. 21, which foretells that the New Jerusalem will come down from heaven. In this case, Mather seemed to have indeed used his ideas from Jer. 8:7 as the basis for further scriptural interpretations.

In his *Triparadisus*, written between 1726/27, Mather put forth his belief that the New Jerusalem, the city of the resurrected saints in the New Heaven,

---

18   Here, God condescends to remind his erstwhile questioner about all the wonders of creation: "Hast thou entered into the treasures of the snow? Or hast thou seen the treasures of the hail, which I have reserved against the time of trouble, against the day of battle and war?"

19   I here quote Mather's commentary on Gen 8:19, as it deals more directly with the "Windowes of Heaven": "About the Descent of any *Supra-Cœlestial Waters*, on this Occasion, we shall find a Difficulty to conceive any thing. The *Windowes of Heaven*, are a very apt Metaphor for the *Clouds*. The *Opening* and *Shutting* of *Heaven*, are Expressions, by which the *Coming* or the *Failing* of *Rain* from the *Clouds*, is described. A great *Plenty* afforded from *Heaven*, is called, *An Opening of the Windowes of Heaven*" (*BA* 1: 648). Mather's commentary on Job 38:23 runs as follows:

Q.   What may bee intended by, *The Day of Battel*, against which the *Treasures of Hail* are said here to bee Reserved? v. 23.

A.   The Story of the *Egyptians*, in Exod. 9.23. But why may it not also refer unto the *Day of the Battel* that *Joshua* had with the *Amorites*? If we suppose this Passage written before that Battel, why may it not be a Prophecy of it? Thus *Hannah* prophecied of the Thunder, wherewith Heaven afterwards fought against the *Philistines*.

Indeed, this Book being probably written before any of those Events, I shall be rather satisfied with *Patricks* Paraphrase. "I need no other Weapons than those, if I please to use them, for the Destruction of Mine Enemies."

would be *"coming down from GOD out of Heaven"* (244). Smolinski has demonstrated that in Mather's view the New Jerusalem of the raised saints would
neither be located in New England, nor anywhere on the face of the earth. It
would be hovering above the surface of the Earth: "The Situation of it, will be
in a Part of the *Atmosphaere*, which will be nearer to the *Earth*, where the *Nations* are to Walk in *the Light of it*, than as yett it is, and it will be conspicuous
to the Nations" (245). The New Jerusalem, gigantic in its proportions, would
descend from the regions of the sky where it was hitherto stationed, "a *Material
City*" (244). It may be that Mather had just such a flying planetoid in mind when
he wrote in his commentary on Jer. 8:7 about a celestial body small enough to
escape the naked eye, perhaps even transparent, and as yet invisible, but soon to
be "experimentally demonstrated" by the technological innovations of the
modern age.

Mather had adapted the concept of the corporeal city from Tertullian's
Against Marcion, who in turn had been ridiculed for building "Castles in the
Air," just the phrase Mather had used when he proposed his "planetoid theory"
earlier in his "Biblia" commentary on Jer. 8:7: "wee might soon discern some
very significant *Globules* in our Supern Regions, without coming under the
Scoffs of those, that *Build Castles in the Air*." There appears to be a direct connection here to the gloss on Jeremiah. This supports the assumption that Mather used the "Biblia" as a source for his *Triparadisus* (244–67).

Another element to consider is Mather's third argument concerning the
migration of birds: the texture of their flesh, which he believes comes from a
different source of nourishment than that to be found on earth. He remarks that
the taste is finer and the flesh more tender. It might seem a rather trivial argument until one considers that the nourishment of heaven could account for this
increased culinary worth. As men and birds alike are of matter, they need matter to survive. Again, the *Triparadisus* states that "The *Place* for the Communication of GOD unto us [the New Jerusalem], must be where the most Noble
and Sublime Creatures find the Noblest & Purest *Matter*. This Place is in the
Heavens, and no doubt in that Part of the *Heavens*, where the best Part of that
rare *Matter* is to be met withal" (244–45). Mather does not define what this
matter is, but he strongly suggests that it is vastly superior to any matter on
earth, and so the term there might include some sort of heavenly nourishment,
even if it were to be found on a different planetoid than that of the celestial New
Jerusalem. Hence, Mather obviously felt that his theory about bird migration
might simultaneously shed more light on the literal truth of some of the "dark
passages" in St. John's prophecies on the latter days.

The fact that Mather had developed (if not fully fleshed out) all of these
ideas in the context of the "Biblia" raises one final question that deserves consideration here: Why would he later expunge these materials from his "Curiosa"-letter? Obviously, a number of explanations are conceivable. However, given

Mather's growing recognition of the difficulty of proving empirically the unproblematic harmony of natural and scriptural truth (see Smolinski, "Natural Science and Interpretation"), I believe that it was simple caution that led him to exclude his scriptural interpretations. Because they constituted examples for a much more complex and daring hermeneutical interplay between literalist exegesis and natural philosophy than the run-of-the-mill arguments from design, the risk of error was considerably greater than in a regular physico-theological discussion. The failure to actually discover the planetoids of the birds would have undermined the larger contention that a hyper-literalist exegesis of the Bible could lead to discoveries of hitherto occult truths in the realm of nature that might simultaneously improve man's understanding of the scriptural prophecies. The refutation of his theory on bird migration might have unintentionally served as a welcomed case in point for the advocates of a stricter separation of science and theology, a danger Mather apparently hoped to evade in the "Curiosa"-letter.

While the letter thus displays Mather's insecurities when addressing the Royal Society and potentially a larger audience of scientifically-minded gentlemen, the "Biblia" entry offers a contrasting view. Here, Mather could "successfully" demonstrate the unity of the books of nature and scripture. Although not provable at the time, his hypothesis was also not outside the bounds of contemporary scientific discussion. Nor were his exegetical speculations unusually farfetched, as the comparison with Morton's tract has shown. Indeed, it appeared not wholly unlikely that empirical observations through new telescopes would eventually support Mather's theory of the planetoids, which he, however, developed from literalistic exegesis on a seemingly straightforward passage of scripture. In this case, both science (solving the mystery of bird migration) and theology (gaining insight into the events of the last days) would have been enriched and the compatibility of empiricism and literalism made manifest.

In the materials sent to the Royal Society, however, he found it safer to separate his literalist interpretation of the scriptural text from, as he puts it in the letter to Woodward, "the conjecture (I had almost said, hypothesis) which I am now laying before you, for your judgment upon it, how far it may pass the ordeal of reason and experiment" (*Selected Letters* 113–14). The irony is, of course, that in pursuing this cautious strategy Mather effectively made his "Curiosa"-letter an example for the increasing tendency to divorce the truth-claims of theology from those of the empirical sciences.

Appendix: Transcription of Mather's commentary on Jeremiah 8:7

Q. Wee read concerning, *The Stork in Heaven, knowing her Appointed Times, & and the Turtle, and the Crane, & the Swallow, which observe the Time of their*

Coming, or as I read it, *The Time of their Journey*. Have you any Curiosity to offer about these little *Season-Birds*? v. 7.

A.   There are certain little Birds, which wee may call *Season-Birds*, for their Visiting of us at certain *Seasons*, either of *Summer* or *Winter*; and that I may now give you a *Break-fast* of those little *Birds*, what will you say, if I do from this Text, offer you a singular & curious *Hypothesis* concerning them?

I will then suppose, That the Annual Recesses of these little *Birds*, are in some Remote Regions of *Heaven*; they are not only *Birds [Of] the Heaven*, but also *Birds [In] the Heaven*, from whence, at their *Appointed Times*, they take their *Journey* hither. They find something either in the Temper of their own *Bodies* or in the *Alterations* of their Lodgings at home, or in the *Effluvia* of the Earth upon the new Reflections of the Sun, thereupon, which invites them to change their Quarters; and so, *they know their Seasons*.

To Illustrate this Matter, Lett mee mind you; First, If these Birds, during their Absence from us, did Reside in any Part of this Earth, wee should after so many Ages at last, have heard, *where* it is; but no Man hath yett seen any Numbers of them, out of their *Seasons*: nor have wee had any but *old Wives Fables* concerning the finding of any, except a poor Bird or so, that by some *Lameness* ha's been left behind his Fellowes.

Secondly, The Birds come in a Manner so sudden, so surprising, so unobserv'd, as if *dropping down from above* upon us. In a Nights Time, the whole Countrey is full of them; & that not in *Flocks*, but extremely *separated*. Probably they keep Hovering towards the upper Part of our *Atmosphære*, which, being there freed from the Inconveniences of *Gravitation*, they may do with Ease, till by the Blowing of certain *Winds*, they perceive agreeable *Steams* calling for them; and then down they fall, tho' by some Accidents disadvantaged somewhat as to their Designed Pitching-Places. Hence, by the Way, sometimes one of these Birds ha's made his Descent upon a Vessel, farther off at *Sea*, than ever any such *Land-birds* were known to Fly.

Thirdly, At the first Coming of these Birds, they are generally of a *Texture* very different, from what they have, after they have been here a while. Their *Tast* is finer; they eat Short; their *Flesh* is Tender; they have little or no *Blood* in them. Which argues, that they have had another Sort of Nourishment, than what this *Earth* affords.

Fourthly, The *Flight* of these Birds, while they abide among us, for the most Part, is but *Short*; and those, which on such an Island as *Great Britain*, are found near the *Sea-Shore*, yett being disturbed, never will offer *towards* the Sea. Wherefore, tis probable, they *never* came thither from *beyond* the Sea.

Fifthly, There are very odd *Phænomena* among these Birds, at or near the Time of their *Departure*. They don't grow Duller, their *flights* are higher, their *notes* are brisker, & they *gather together* as having a noble Design for another World. Particularly to mention, the first Bird in out Text; The *Storks*, in the *Low-Countreyes*, when the *Time of their Departure is at hand*, they all, to a Bird, Assemble together; there they continue chattering for diverse Dayes, till the last are come in to this *general Rendezvous*; then in the Midst of all the Din, there is a sudden *Silence*, for a little while: after which, upon some *Signal*, they all Rise together, and fly in one great Flock or Cloud, fetching many great Rounds, higher & higher still, much like the *Spiral Ascent* of a *Goshawk*, when shee Towers, till at last, their

Distance makes them appear less & less, & so they utterly disappear. They seek a comfortable Repose, by flying *Directly Upward*, which is not the Way to any other Land on our Earth.

I expect, that you will now demand, what & where bee the *Heavenly Receptacles*, whither wee may imagine, these little *Season-Birds* Retiring?

Truly, I will not say with the Author of *Gonsales* his *Ganzas*, *The Moon*. For if wee do but allow unto the *Moon*, such a small Distance from the *Earth* as the *Arabians*, after *Ptolomy*, have assigned; namely *Forty-nine* Semidiameters of the Earth, which is in English Miles, counting according to *Cluverius* fifty-five Miles to a Degree on the great Circle of the Earth, 154350 Miles; and if wee suppose the Birds to Travel at least one Third of the Year, according to which, they can have but sixty-one Dayes for their Journey, they must then fly every Day, at least 1530 miles, which is omitting Fractions about 63 miles *per Hour*, which is nigh as fast again, as the swiftest Race-horse, who moving at the rate of four Miles in seven Minutes, & an half, dispatches in an Hour but *Thirty two Miles*. Now, tho' much might bee said about the Possibility of an unsuspected Velocity in a Bird, sett at some Liberty from the grosser & heavier Parts of the *Atmosphære*, yett wee cannot consent unto so great a Swiftness; especially, since the True Distance of the *Moon* from the *Earth*, is much greater than what was conceived by *Ptolomy*.

Know then, That it is no unreasonable Præsumption, to imagine, That there are nigh unto our *Terraqueous Globe* several *Planetary Bodies*, which partly from the Smallness of their Bulk, and partly from some other Qualities, may not bee visible unto *Us*, without the Help of Instruments. Until wee were assisted with *Telescopes*, who ever dreamt of the *Satellites* which move about *Jupiter*, and some other of the Planets? or, who ever thought of catching *Saturn* by his *Ears*? I say, if *Glasses* were a little more Improved, & Mens Attention to the Discovering of their *Glasses* a little further awakened, it is possible wee might soon discern some very significant *Globules* in our Supern Regions, without coming under the Scoffs of those, that *Build Castles in the Air*. Yea, the greatest Philosopher in this Age, ha's already affirm'd That some *Christalline*, or *Semipellucid* Bodies, between the *Earth* & the *Moon* have already been Discovered. Certainly, the *Negroes* on the Coast of *Barbary* that know not of such a Rock, as the Isle of *Ascention*, which tho' it bee thirty Miles in Compass, ha's not a Drop of any Fresh-Water on it, will ignorantly think the prodigious Multitudes of *Sea-fowl* which visit them from that *Rock*, to be bred on their own Shoar, because they know not of such a notable Place. Thus it may bee in the Case before us.

I would not have so much as mentioned these *Curiosities*, much less would I have been so large & long upon them, if I had not been willing to serve the *Illustrations* of the Scripture, by exciting the further Enquiries of Ingenious Men, about this Matter. For if it shall bee experimentally Demonstrated, that there is any thing in what I have written, there will bee a glorious Opportunity, not only to magnify the Power, & Wisdome, & Goodness of our God, in some Circumstances of the Creation, hitherto unheeded, but also to Illustrate many Texts in the Bible, which have hitherto wanted a Tolerable *Commentary*; especially, about, *The Windowes of Heaven opened for the Flood*; about, *The Treasures of the Snow & Rain, reserved against the Time of Trouble*; and some things, referring to the *New Jerusalem*, at the Second Coming of our Lord; About all of which, you shall have in your ordinary Annotators, far more exorbitant things, than any that I have this Morning tendred you.

Works Cited

Primary Sources

Bochart, Samuel. *Hierozoicon Sive bipertitum opus De Animalibus Sacrae Scripturae. Pars Prior. De Animalibus in genere. Et de Quadrupedibus viviparis et oviparis. Pars Posterior. De Avibus, Serpentibus, Insectis, Aquaticis, et Fabulosis Animalibus.* 2 vols. 1646. London, 1663.

Edwards, George. *A Discourse on the Emigration of British Birds.* London, 1795.

Godwin, Francis. *The Man in the Moone: Or A Discourse of a Voyage thither By Domingo Gonsales The speedy Messenger.* London, 1638.

The Harleian Miscellany. Ed. William Oldys and John Malham. London, 1808.

Henry, Matthew. *An Exposition of all the Books of the Old and New Testament: wherein the Chapters are Summ'd up in Contents. ... In Six Volumes. By Matthew Henry.* 3rd ed. Vol. 4. London, 1721–25.

Mather, Cotton. *The Christian Philosopher.* Ed Winton U. Solberg. Urbana: U of Illinois P, 1994.

–. and Daniel Williams. *Reasonable Religion Or The Truths of The Christian Religion Demonstrated.* London, 1713.

–. *Selected Letters.* Ed. Kenneth Silverman. Baton Rouge: Louisiana State UP, 1971.

–. *The Threefold Paradise of Cotton Mather: An Edition of "Triparadisus."* Ed. Reiner Smolinski. Athens and London: U of Georgia P, 1995.

Morton, Charles. "An Enquiry into the Physical and Literal Sense of that Scripture, Jeremiah viii.7. The Stork in the Heaven knoweth her appointed times; and the Turtle, and the Crane, and the Swallow observe the time of their coming, &c. Written by an eminent Professor for the use of scholars, and now published at the earnest desire of some of them." *The Harleian Miscellany* 5: 498–511.

–. *An Essay toward the Probable Solution of this Question: Whence come the Stork and the Turtledove, the Crane, and the Swallow, when they Know and Observe the Appointed Time of their Coming.* London, 1703.

Philosophical Transactions of the Royal Society 29 (Apr.-June 1714): 64.

Secondary Sources

Bates, George E. "Seventeenth- and Eighteenth-Century American Science: A Different Perspective." *Eighteenth-Century Studies* 9.2 (1975–76): 178–92.

Beall, Otho T. "Cotton Mather's Early 'Curiosa Americana' and the Boston Philosophical Society of 1683." *William and Mary Quarterly.* Third Series. 18.3 (1961): 367–68.

–. and Richard Shryock. *Cotton Mather: First Significant Figure in American Medicine.* 1954. New York: Arno Press, 1979.

Halkett, Samuel and John Laing. *Dictionary of Anonymous and Pseudonymous English Literature.* Ed. James Kennedy. Vol. 2. Edinburgh: Oliver and Boyd, 1926.

Harrison, Peter. *The Bible, Protestantism, and the Rise of Natural Science.* Cambridge: Cambridge UP, 1998.

–. *The Fall of Man and the Foundations of Science.* Cambridge: Cambridge UP, 2007.

–. "Original Sin and the Problem of Knowledge in Early Modern Europe." *Journal of the History of Ideas* 63. 2 (2002): 239–59.

Harrison, Thomas P. "Birds in the Moon." *Isis* 45.4 (1954): 323–30.

Hornberger, Theodore. "The Date, the Source, and the Significance of Cotton Mather's Interest in Science." *American Literature* 6 (1935): 413–20.

Jeske, Jeffrey. "Cotton Mather: Physico-Theologian." *Journal of the History of Ideas* 47.4 (1986): 583–94.

Kennedy, Rick. "The Alliance between Puritanism and Cartesian Logic at Harvard, 1687–1735." *Journal of the History of Ideas* 51.4 (1990): 549–72.

Kidd, Colin. *The Forging of Races: Race and Scripture in the Protestant Atlantic World, 1600–2000.* Cambridge: Cambridge UP, 2006.

Kittredge, George Lyman. "Cotton Mather's Scientific Communications to the Royal Society." *Proceedings of the American Antiquarian Society.* New Series. 26 (1916): 18–57.

Levin, David. "Giants in the Earth: Science and the Occult in Cotton Mather's Letters to the Royal Society." *William and Mary Quarterly.* Third Series. 45.4 (1988): 751–70.

McManus, Edgar J. "Charles Morton." *American National Biography.* Vol. 15. Eds. Carnes, Mark C. and John A. Garraty. New York: Oxford UP, 1999.

Middlekauff, Robert. *The Mathers: Three Generations of Puritan Intellectuals 1596–1728.* New York: Oxford UP, 1971.

Miller, Peter N. "The 'Antiquarianization' of Biblical Scholarship and the London Polyglot Bible (1653–57)." *The Journal of the History of Ideas* 62.3 (2001): 463–82.

Popkin, Richard H. "Spinoza and Bible Scholarship." *The Books of Nature and Scripture: Recent Essays on Natural Philosophy, Theology, and Biblical Criticism in the Netherlands of Spinoza's Time and the British Isles of Newton's Time.* Ed. James E. Force and Richard H. Popkin. Dordrecht: Kluwer, 1994. 1–20.

Scholder, Klaus. *The Birth of Modern Critical Theology.* Transl. John Bowden London/ Philadelphia: SCM Press Ltd./Trinity Press International, 1990.

Silverman, Kenneth. *The Life and Times of Cotton Mather.* New York: Harper & Row, 1984.

Smolinski, Reiner. "Authority and Interpretation: Cotton Mather's Response to the European Spinozists." *Shaping the Stuart World, 1603–1714: The Atlantic Connection.* Ed. Alan I. Macinnes and Arthur Williamson. Leyden: Brill, 2006. 175–203.

–. "How to Go to Heaven, or How Heaven Goes? Natural Science and Interpretation in Cotton Mather's 'Biblia Americana' (1693–1728)." *New England Quarterly* 81.2 (2008): 278–329.

Solberg, Winton. Introduction. *The Christian Philosopher.* By Cotton Mather. Ed. Winton Solberg. Urbana, IL: University of Illinois, 1994. xic-cxxxiv

Stearns, Raymond P. *Science in the British Colonies of America.* Urbana: U of Illinois P, 1970.

Winship, Michael P. *Seers of God: Puritan Providentialism in the Restoration and Early Enlightenment.* Baltimore: The Johns Hopkins UP, 1996.

Paul Wise

Cotton Mather and the Invisible World

This man [Robert Calef], out of Enmity to mee, for my public Asserting of such Truths, as the Scripture has taught us, about the Existence and Influence of the *Invisible World*, hath often abused mee, with venomous *Reproaches*, and most palpable *Injuries*. ... I understand, that hee apprehends the shortest way to deliver People, from the *Beleef* of the Doctrines which not I only, but all the Ministers of Christ in the World, have hitherto mentained, will bee, to show the World, what an *ill Man* I am.
Cotton Mather, *Diary* (1: 264)

I often find, that when I preach of the Angels, or on a Subject (such as the Glory of the Lord Jesus Christ,) very singularly agreeable to the Angels, I have a more than ordinary Assistance in my public Ministrations. My mind, and Voice and Strength, is evidently under some special Energy from the invisible World; and a notable Fervency and Majesty and Powerful pungency setts off my Discourses.
Cotton Mather, *Diary* (1: 396)

Anyone who is even vaguely familiar with Cotton Mather today almost immediately associates his name with the Salem witch trials (1692–93). It is fair to argue that this brief episode in early American history has received an inordinate amount of attention in the popular and academic press and Mather an undue amount of blame.[1] Over the last three decades, historians have thoroughly revised traditional narratives of what happened in Salem and, in so doing, they also painted a more nuanced picture of Cotton Mather. Where once he simply figured as the monstrous villain of the witchcraft drama, his role is now perceived to have been ambiguous and conflicted, but ultimately rather moderate.[2] Sadly, all of this has done little to alter Mather's popular image, and it is questionable whether future scholarship will be able to effect such change. But this paper is not about improving Mather's reputation or about offering any apologies for his actions in the context of Salem. It is primarily concerned with

---

1 On the impact of Salem on Mather's reputation see, for instance, Adams, van Arragon, and the essay by E. Brooks Holifield, "The Abridging of Cotton Mather," in the present collection. D. Levin ("Monster" 157–76) aptly survey's Mather's stereotypical image in the popular press.

2 The literature on Salem is vast, and virtually every study has something to say on Mather. For important and fair-minded interpretations of Mather's role in the trials, see Levin (*Cotton Mather* 195–222), Silverman (83–138), Rosenthal (esp. 135–48, 202), and Norton (esp. 203–07, 212–15, 246–52, 268–69, 284–85).

properly understanding Mather's beliefs in supernatural forces, including witchcraft, with carefully contextualizing these beliefs, and with offering historical explanations for why these beliefs were so important to him and so many others at the time. Neither singling him out for his gullibility, nor simply assuming that "everybody believed it then," I will examine his opinions on the invisible world – as he expressed them both in the "Biblia Americana" and in some of his other writings – against the background of the increasingly controversial discussions of the seventeenth and early eighteenth centuries.

I will start out by looking at the two main sources of Mather's great investment in the reality of the invisible world: the specific religious tradition he grew up in and which he defended so vehemently, and his Enlightenment interests. That Mather championed the new sciences at the same time that he unequivocally affirmed the existence of ghosts and witchcraft may seem contradictory to many people today, but would have been normal to most contemporary theologians and other intellectuals in both old and New England. In the broad mainstream of the so-called moderate Enlightenment, in which Solberg has located Mather, there was an almost unanimous consensus that demons and witches existed as reported in the scriptures, a consensus that was carried by a strong alliance of biblical literalism and empiricism. Before the second third of the eighteenth century, only a small group of philosophical thinkers such as Thomas Hobbes and Baruch Spinoza, who are now usually associated with the term of the Radial Enlightenment, would have questioned this consensus. But for the majority of learned men, as for Mather, the reality of spirits and devils could not be separated from the reality of God's spirit or the immortality of the soul. Hence, in their view to "assert the reality of supernatural phenomena" against the skeptical philosophers was equivalent to "defending Christianity itself" (Silverman 92).

The essay will then proceed to show how, in the "Biblia" and elsewhere, Mather's approach to many of the scriptural passages that speak about the supernatural, whether demonic or angelic, is decidedly empiricist in orientation. On the one hand, he frequently argues from empirical evidence, including his personal experiences with the supernatural, which he had (often after long sessions of praying and fasting) throughout his life. In fact, it may have been Mather's capacity for "particular faiths" and dream visions, his ability to witness visitors from the invisible world, that gave his biblical interpretations such a decidedly literal cast. On the other hand, Mather's deliberations on such experiences always aim at demonstrating, in quasi-scientific manner, the literal truth of the biblical revelations about the invisible world, and at establishing the laws of the supernatural realm in order to link these into the known laws of the natural realm. In this context, I will pay particular attention to how exactly Mather understood the nature of witchcraft and discuss in some detail his speculations about a connecting medium or agency he termed the *Nishmath-Chajim* ("breath of life") through which he hoped to explain how the supernatural interacted with the natural world. Finally, the essay will look at how the debate over witchcraft and other supernatural phenomena developed over the course of Mather's life and in the decades after it. By surveying a sampling of relevant publications from roughly 1650 to 1750, I will demonstrate that public expression of skepticism of, or of outright disbelief in, the reality of the world of spirits was a rare exception before the second half of the eighteenth century; even then the tide was turning only very slowly.

Experiencing the Invisible World

Growing up in a family of Puritan divines steeped in a religious culture that put a premium on first-hand encounters with the invisible world, a strong belief in the supernatural came naturally to young Mather.[3] He was raised amidst supernaturally inflected household conversations, sermons, family devotions, and tales of prodigies, wonders, and witchcraft. Like John Cotton and Richard Mather before him, Increase Mather left records of his own experience with the invisible world and became the American spokesperson for a "Design" put forward by the English divine Matthew Poole (1624–79) "for the Recording of illustrious Providences." Increase answered Poole's suggestion with a book entitled *An Essay for the Recording of Illustrious Providences* (1684), describing various kinds of discernable effects from the invisible world, including apparitions and activities of witches.[4] Thus, Cotton Mather was from the beginning predisposed to paranormal experiences of his own. In fact, as he grew older he seems to have gained more familiarity with the invisible world than any of his immediate predecessors (Middlekauff 305–19). What appears to have made him especially susceptible to such experiences was his great zeal in performing the practices of meditation, strenuous praying and fasting that were so important to the Puritan culture of piety.[5] As so many religious traditions before them, both Christian and non-Christian, English Puritans and Continental Pietists regarded fasting as an effective means of bringing about altered states in which one might "be absent from the body, and ... present with the Lord" [*BA*, 2 Cor. 5:8]. Cotton learned the spiritual benefits of fasting and extended periods of prayer both from the Bible and by the example of Increase. While praying in his study,

---

3   The wide-spread supernatural beliefs in all segments of early modern New England society and the magical elements of both orthodox and folk religion are treated in Butler, Hall (*World of Wonder*), and Demos.

4   See K. B. Murdock (167–75) and M. G. Hall (167–74).

5   For Cotton Mather's holistic approach in applying the methods of natural science to prayer see G. Faithful (175–87). For a related discussion that examines how Calvinist psychology shapes Mather's response to the Salem phenomenon, see D. Harley (307–30).

Increase Mather was frequently visited by *"Praesagious Impressions"* and once wrote, "me thought I saw God before my eyes" (qtd. in Silverman 8–9). Following the lead of his father, Cotton, like the prophet Daniel, would thus often "set [his] face unto the Lord God to seek by prayer and supplications, with fasting" angelic guidance in all ordinary and extraordinary occurrences (Dan. 9:3; 10:5–19). Samuel Mather relates that his father was engaged in a combination of fasting and strenuous prayer for at least 450 days of his life (*Life* 110). Through these exercises, which he begun at age fourteen, Cotton Mather, like his father, found the "substance of things hoped for and evidence of things not seen" (Middlekauff 192; Heb. 11:1). He often retired to his study in the "Dead of the Night" and, while prostrate on the floor in the dust, was "rewarded with unutterable Communications from Heaven" (S. Mather, *Life* 123).[6]

During at least one of the many sessions of fasting and prayer in his youth, Cotton Mather ecstatically experienced the presence of an angel, an event which left a lasting impact on the young clergyman. This event probably occurred in 1685 when he was twenty-two years old: He recorded the experience on the verso of the cover of his journal for 1685:[7]

> A strange and memorable thing. After outpourings of prayer, with the utmost fervor and fasting, there appeared an Angel, whose face shone like the noonday sun. His features were those of a man, and beardless; his head was encircled by a splendid tiara; on his shoulders were wings; his garments were white and shining; his robe reached to his ankles; and about his loins was a belt not unlike the girdles of the peoples of the East. And this Angel said which it is not fit to set down here. But among other things not to be forgotten he declared that the fate of this youth should be to find full expression for what in him was best: and this he said in the words of the prophet Ezekiel [Mather quotes Ezek. 31: 3, 5, 7, and 9]. (*Diary* 1: 86–87)

Significantly, Mather's description of the event closely resembles the famous vision of the Prophet Ezekiel. The wheels within a wheel filled with winged bovines and angelic creatures described by Ezekiel in chapters 1 and 10 are a representation of God's *merkabah*, or "holy throne-chariot," symbolic of the visionary or ecstatic state in which mental pictures "are beheld as realities." The ancient Hebrews considered it "perilous to penetrate into these mysteries." Only older or more experienced men dared to undergo initiation into such "mysteries" (see Kohler). Ezekiel relates that the sky above the creatures' heads was of a "terrible" radiance like "chrystall," and the beating of their wings sounded "like the noise of great waters, as the voice of the Almightie, the voice of speech, as the noise of an hoste." There was a "voice from the firmament"

---

6   In his commentary on Heb. 11.1 in the "Biblia Americana," Mather defines the word *substance* as *"confident expectation"* [*BA*, Heb. 11:1], what the NRSV translates as *"assurance."* Thus, through prayer and fasting, Mather found assurance of the invisible world by repeated experience with evidence of things not ordinarily seen.

7   See Levin, "When" (271–75) and *Cotton Mather* (106–08).

above their heads (Ezek. 1: 22, 24, 25).[8] Although Mather keeps silent about the things he deems "not fit to set down here [diary]," his references to Ezekiel's vision reveal more than they conceal. What this episode shows is that for Mather, both biblical teachings and visionary experiences were inextricably linked. While scriptural precedents obviously shaped his extraordinary experiences, they experimentally verified for him at the same time the inspiration of the prophets and the reality of their revelations. Mather may well have taken his own encounters to mean that the Lord might indeed be raising up a new prophet in him, for as Mather comments in his "Biblia Americana," God *made Himself known to the Prophets in a Vision* ... when they were Awake, as if they had perceived ... [things] by their Senses, which yett at the same Time were locked up, and all was transacted by a Divine Operation upon their Mind & Imagination" [*BA*, Numb. 12:6].

Such manifestations of the divine very much assured Mather that any Hobbist or Cartesian nullibist, who denied the existence of angels and spirits, was in the wrong. Indeed, besides the ecstatic joys Mather felt when his religious exercises yielded such extraordinary visions, the main reason for his great interest in these experiences of the supernatural, whether first- or second-hand, was that they offered extra-biblical proof for the literal truth of the scriptures. The Bible in many places spoke of angels, demons, and witches, and proving their factual reality simultaneously corroborated the literal truth of the more fundamental biblical revelations. And here we see the link between Mather's scripturalism and his well-known engagement with the natural sciences and their empiricist epistemology. While Mather recognized that man could not know God "face to face," he, like so many learned man in his age, eagerly sought and found empirical evidence of, as it were, the lower regions of the invisible world. "[E]ven my *Senses* have been convinced of such a World," he wrote in *The Christian Philosopher*, "by as clear, plain, full *Proofs* as ever any Man's have had of what is most obvious in the *sensible World*" (306).

More specifically, Mather searched for evidence of the realm between heaven and earth, which, in his *Triparadisus*, he called the "Second Paradise." He was convinced that this spiritual dwelling place or abode was reserved for the souls of the departed who must linger before the resurrection of the body and before being ushered into the highest heaven or "Third Paradise" at judgment day to dwell with God. Types of preternatural evidence of the "Second Paradise" and workings of God's Providence occurred in cases of witchcrafts and demon possession which, like other Christian scientists of his day, Mather carefully documented. For instance, he insists in the "Epistle Dedicatory" to *Mem-*

---

8   Interestingly enough this youthful vision also closely resembles Mather's Christian interpretation of the Jewish concept of Theophany, the Shechinah. On this, see Paul Peterson's essay in this volume.

orable Providences (Boston, 1689; London, 1691) that it was "partly my own *Ocular Observation* and partly my *undoubted Information*, [that] hath enabled me to offer unto the publick Notice of my Neighbours" the record of such cases. Collected with a scientific concern for *"Truth in Matter of Fact,"* Mather's *"undoubted"* information was based not only upon physical eye and ear witness but also upon the overwhelming evidence of his own perceptions of the "Second Paradise" (*Triparadisus* 112–52). His criteria for judging the reality of this "other" world were therefore in keeping with the requisites of contemporary "natural philosophy."

Several instances illustrate how Mather sought to gather tangible proof of the numinous world around him. He found the story of Joseph Beacon so compelling that Mather employed it in at least three separate publications: *Wonders of the Invisible World* (79–81), *Magnalia* (bk. 6, pp. 77–78), and *Triparadisus* (115–16). A young man from Boston, Beacon witnessed at his bedside the apparition of his brother who had been murdered in faraway London. The ghost revealed exact details about the day, time, and manner of the murder as well as the villain's identity. Later, through "common ways of communication," it was confirmed that Beacon's brother was murdered in London on the same day and hour (May 2nd at 5 a.m.) at which the apparition appeared to Joseph Beacon in Mather's Boston (*Triparadisus* 115–16). As Mather summarized the empirical data, he saw "no Cause to think" that these *"Humane Souls"* were indeed any other than those whom they represented. For God "who enables our *Will*, while we are yett in our *Bodies*, under certain Limitations to Command and Perform such Motions as we *Will*, may so extend the Sphaere of Activity to the *Souls* taken out of their *Bodies*, that they shall be able, when they *Will*, to form such an Human *Voice*, or *Shape*, as they have been us'd unto, and render it *sensible* to the Survivers" (117).

Besides such stories of apparitions, deathbed narratives were particularly suitable for presenting empirical evidence of the beyond. As a minister, Mather witnessed the last moments of many a dying parishioner at whose bedside he took note of reports from the invisible world. In fact, his *Diary*, *Magnalia Christi Americana*, *Coelestinus* (157–161), and *Triparadisus* (138–47) contain collections of deathbed narratives including the dying ecstasies of both his daughter Katharine and his sister, Mrs. Jerusha Oliver. Mather collected and published these narratives to substantiate the existence of the world beyond. He understood these narratives as confirmation that once converted Christians had gained a taste of heaven by dropping in and out of consciousness, they lost all fear of death. "On her Last *Satureday*," he relates of his daughter Katharin, who lay dying of the consumptive aftereffects of a measles epidemic, "she long'd, that she might have her *Sabbath* in the *Paradise* of GOD." But when she was told that "it was thought she might live another Day, she replied; *No, I have received other Advice; It has been said unto me,* THIS DAY THOU SHALT BE

WITH ME IN PARADISE. A little after Midnight, she said, *My Soul is in perfect Ease; –* And with those Words expired" (*Triparadisus* 143). Although Mather records just a glimpse of Katharin's dying agony, his diary reveals the anguish of a doting father who witnessed thirteen of his fifteen children die a premature death. "I have been for many Months a dying in my feeling the dying Circumstances of my lovely *Katy*," he jotted down his own anguish on December 16, 1716. "And now, this last Night, she is actually dead; but how triumphantly did she go away!" (*Diary* 2: 388, 389).[9]

Mather also read other accounts, both historical and contemporary, about the ecstatic experiences of the dying. In particular he admired James Janeway's *Token for Children* (1676).[10] In 1700, Mather collected and published similar materials about the lives of dying children of New England, which was appended to Janeway's book and entitled *A Token for the Children of New England* (1700). This work included hagiographies, conversion experiences, and deathbed narratives of children showing remarkable signs of grace. Characteristic features of these texts include triumph over fear of death, reluctance of the dying to return to earth from the heavenly state they had witnessed, the hearing of celestial music, ineffable visions of radiant forms of relatives and angels, and feelings of happiness and joy beyond expression. Although Mather was conscious that deathbed experiences might well be the results of delusion, he remained convinced that at least some of them were real enough:

> I do most readily grant, that some Relations, which we have had *of Dying Extasies,* may impose upon us, no other than the Delirious and Extravagant *Fancies,* of Whimsical *Visionaries.* They must be read with *Discretion.* But yett some of these *Dying Extasies* have been attended with such Circumstances, that it would be a Rash & a Weak & a very *Indiscreet* thing to make meer *Fancies* of them, and nothing but the *Vapours* of Imagination. ... The *Views* and the *Joys* to which these *Holy Souls* have been raised, before they have quite left their *Bodies,* have been such as to make them utterly Insensible of their *Bodily Ails,* & strangely take away the *Sting of Death,* and give them a Surprizing Triumph over the *King of Terrors.* (*Triparadisus* 138)

Mather's empiricist investigation into such phenomena and his interpretation is hardly unique. Founding members of the Royal Society of London such as Henry Moore and Joseph Glanvill also compiled records of deathbed experiences, ghosts, apparitions, and witchcraft and created a model for documenting such cases. In fact, the best of Mather's own accounts closely resemble those collected in Henry More's *The Immortality of the Soul* (1662) or in Joseph Glanvill's ever popular *Saducismus Triumphatus* (1681), which went through at least four editions and as many reprints with different titles during Mather's

---

9   D.E. Stannard's analysis of Katherin Mather's dying moments is highly useful here (82–83). See also William Van Arragon's essay in this collection.
10   I wish to thank Professor Andrew DiNicolla of South Georgia College for drawing my attention to this book.

lifetime. He studied their works assiduously and compared their scientific observations with those he witnessed in his own Boston vicinity, years before the devil would come down in Salem and frighten New England with preternatural manifestations of his power. In his own writings on the supernatural, Mather thus made an effort to satisfy the standards for verification set up by his peers. A case in point is the story of a dying woman from Salem who on her deathbed received information from "Several Shining Persons, who told her, *That they were not now come for her, but on that Day Six Weeks hence, they would come for her, & fetch her away with a Glorious Equipage.*" The woman immediately asked her pastor what the word "*EQUIPAGE*" meant (*Triparadisus* 142). Mather rejoiced that the woman's ignorance of the term was proof in and of itself that her close encounter of the spiritual world was tangibly real. What strengthened her case all the more, Mather felt, was that she died exactly six weeks to the day, just as the "Shining Persons" had foretold (142). With such palpable proof of the spiritual realm, Mather felt assured that the Bible's relation of angels and spirits (both good and evil) was anything but superstition.

Mather's Views on Witchcraft

When Mather came of age, belief in witchcraft was still the norm all over the Christian world, although the skeptical voices grew louder. Since the Bible explicitly affirms the reality of black magic or sorcery, the stakes in these debates were high. While the "Biblia Americana" clearly documents that Mather never changed his convictions after Salem, it also shows he did not simply dismiss off-hand those who claimed that witchcraft did not exist or did not actually involve demonic forces. That he carefully examined both the empirical and exegetical issues raised by skeptics can be seen in two, unfortunately undated, commentaries he wrote on the famous episode of Saul's encounter with the witch of Endor [*BA* 1 Sam. 28:14; 28:25].

In the first gloss Mather unequivocally affirms the existence of witches and their familiarity with demonic spirits. Following the arguments laid out by Gisbert Voetius, Henry More, Increase Mather, as well as many other apologists, he argues that a denial of the reality of witches and of the true source of their powers could only be justified by either refuting the literal truth of the Bible in this and other places, or by deceitfully twisting its true meaning:

> My Parent, in his *Remarkable Providences*; and, [John] *Edwards*, in his *Exercitations*; have handled this problem as well as [Gisbert] *Voetius, De Spectris*. And this is the Summ of what they say upon it. The Men, who, like [John] *Webster*, go to make this whole Transaction, a Cheat, a Trick, an Artifice; I know not which is greater, their *Stupidity* or their *Profanity*; but both are very great. The *Witch-Advocates* find the History, to be such a Proof of *Witches*, That they [skeptics] try very

odd Shifts to evade their Proof. Dr. [Henry] *More* saies, *They play more Hocus-Pocus tricks in the Explication of that Passage, than the Witch herself did in the Raising of Samuel*. When they have done all, we must conclude with Dr. *Edwards, we are to look upon this famous Relation of the Witch of Endor, as an undeniable Proof of Witches transacting with Evil Spirits*. [*BA*, 1 Sam. 28:14][11]

This is essentially what Mather had also argued in his *Wonders of the Invisible World*. The second entry [1 Sam. 28:25], which was written sometime after 1706 and focuses on the exact nature of the apparition of Samuel and how it had been conjured up, offers more intriguing insights into Mather's thinking on witchcraft in the context of ongoing exegetical debates. His principal source here is Pierre Jurieu's *Critical History of the Opinions and Worships* (1705–06), which Mather puts to good use throughout "Biblia Americana."

What actually happened between Saul, the witch, and the spirit of Samuel in this biblical passage had been long disputed by biblical exegetes and demonologists. Matthew Poole's invaluable *Synopsis Criticorum* (1: 426, 2: 242–46) is the most accessible summation of the various positions that Mather draws on. For instance, the Jesuit scholar Martin Antoine Del Rio (1551–1608) and the Anglican Joseph Glanvill argued that the spirit raised by the witch of Endor was truly that of Samuel, whose soul was "fetch'd by the *Witch* herself." A similar position had also been advocated by Josephus, Justin Martyr, Origen, and Sulpicius Severus. "The Souls of the Godly" are "lodged somewhere near unto us," they argued, "from whence they might be with ease recalled." Another group of the fathers – including Tertullian, Cyril of Alexandria, Gregory Nazianzen, Nyssen, Basil, Jerome, Eustathius of Antioch, and perhaps Augustine (who "disputes the Matter on both sides"), Bede, Anselm, Rabanus, and Aquinas – insisted that the spirit which appeared in Samuel's likeness was not the real Samuel but a demon impersonating the holy man. This position was held by "the Generality of our Protestant Divines," as Mather writes with Jurieu at his elbow. "They believe that the Apparition they saw were probably "Cacodaemons, which feigned themselves to be the *Spirits* of Men departed." Neither these demons nor the juggleries of magicians had power over "the souls of Holy Men departed." This was also how Mather chose to interpret the matter. The remaining question, then, was how exactly did the witch of Endor create the false image of Saul?

Building on Jurieu, Mather distinguishes between different types of necromancy depending on the "Instruments used by the Magicians, for the Evocation

---

11 Mather here refers to John Edwards' *Exercitations Critical, Historical, Philosophical, Theological on Several Important Places of the Writings in the Old and New Testament* (London, 1702) 80, to Gisbert Voetius' summary of the debate in *Selectarum disputationum ex priori parte theologiae nona, de spectris* (Utrecht, 1637), to John Webster's *The Displaying of Supposed Witchcraft* (London, 1677), and to Henry More's *Antidote Against Atheisme, Or An Appeal to the Natural Faculties of the Minde of Man, whether there be not a God* (London, 1653).

of the Dead." If a "Looking-glass" is employed, "it was called, *Catoptromancy*." However, if a "deep *Vessel*" was used, "it was called, *Gastromancy*." If the vessel was filled with water, "*Hydromancy*," because "the Soul of the Deceased appeared with an Humane Shape in the Water" and generally accompanied by "confused Noise," and "a Voice" arising "from under Ground, at a considerable Distance, answering the Quaestion that had been proposed." Those who used "a *Bottel*, a *Barrel*, a *Cask*, or a very deep Vessel" practiced "*Lecanomancy*," a term derived from the Greek word for "*A Basin*." Those who inquired of the dead, cast "a Peece of Gold into a *Basin*, upon which they poured the Water; and then offering certain Sacrifices, with Invocation to the Daemons, there was heard a kind of Groaning or Grumbling in the Bottom of the Vessel, whereupon the Daemon appearing in a visible Shape; did with a low Voice utter his Words." Again demonstrating the empiricist bend of his supernaturalism, Mather added that he personally had heard reports of cases of both *Catoptromancy* (employing a mirror) and *Lecanomancy* coupled with *Hydromancy* (a deep vessel filled with water). "I can myself add Surprizing Exemples of both Sorts of *Sorceries*, which have been known to have been practiced in my Neighbourhoods." Which practice, or combination of practices, the witch of Endor had employed could not be known with certainty. But surely the image of Samuel could have been conjured up only with the help of a demon.[12]

---

12   In his *Seers of God* (132–34), Michel P. Winship compares these two entries of the "Biblia" and comes to the conclusion that the second, later commentary suggests a change in Mather's position on witchcraft to the extent that, while still affirming a general belief in witches, he now backed away from the idea so important in the Salem trials that witches derive their powers from familiar spirits bound through a covenant. Winship bases his claim on the fact that Mather approves of Jurieu's suggestion for an alternative translation of the Hebrew word "ob." While in the first entry he still supports the traditional translation "familiar spirit," the second entry concedes that it also might be rendered as "bowl," a translation that supported the idea that practices of either *Lecanomancy* or *Hydromancy* were used for conjuring Samuel. While Winship's observations in themselves are correct, I cannot follow the larger claims he derives from these, claims which support his overall argument that Mather in his later years toned down his earlier language of an unabashed supernaturalism in order to make his writings more acceptable to the higher circles of learned gentlemen in England who increasingly distanced themselves from the religious culture of prodigies and wonders. To my mind, this thesis is not borne out by the entries in the "Biblia Americana," nor by any other of Mather's later writings for that matter. After all, Mather still contended that the witch of Endor had made a demon to impersonate Samuel. In my opinion, to argue that these entries demonstrate that Mather "quietly tore down the strongest biblical sanction for the traditional religious conception of the covenanting witch" and "dismantled the scaffolding of witchcraft as the inverse parallel of organized religion" (133) is an overstatement. Moreover, since Mather was in the habit of incorporating in the "Biblia" opposing, even conflicting, interpretations, Winship's assumption that Mather's excerpt from Jurieu replaced or negated his earlier statement on the issue is misleading. In virtually all cases where Mather firmly changed his mind, he either removed the outdated passages or explained why he revised his point of view.

   I'm similarly skeptical of Winship's contention that by the time of Mather's death beliefs in witchcraft, prodigies and divination were already thoroughly discredited amongst the edu-

Mather's view that a demon had impersonated the holy prophet Samuel signals his continuing reservations about the use of spectral evidence in the convictions of witches. For, as one of the accused at Salem, Susannah Martin, deftly complained before Judge Hathorne, "He that appear'd in the shape of a *Samuel*, a Glorify'd Saint, may appear in anyone's shape" (Mather, *Wonders* 116). In *Wonders* Mather had cautioned amongst similar lines that it was a "Great and Just Suspicion, that the *Dæmons* might Impose the *Shapes* of Innocent Persons in their *Spectral Exhibitions* upon the Sufferers, (which may perhaps prove no small part of the *Witch-Plot* in the issue)" (xiii). As if to back up his public position, his commentary on Samuel [*BA*, 1 Sam. 28] examines conflicting interpretations of the passage to show links between witches and demons from ancient authors to authors in his own time. Because of its implications about the use of spectral evidence in the Salem trials, what these writers had to say about the apparition of Samuel was particularly relevant to Mather. If the shape of Samuel conjured by the witch of Endor had not been Samuel but a lying demon, as Mather argues, then the devil might assume the shape of anyone, including that of an innocent person, a saint, or even Mather himself [*BA*, 1 Sam, 28:14]. This point is crucial to understanding why Mather and his clerical colleagues warned the Salem court against relying on "spectral evidence" to convict the accused.[13] By showing the passage's historical context and its likeness to that of modern incidents of witchcraft, Mather addresses both philological and empirical aspects of the question. His commentary in the "Biblia" thus casts into sharp relief his theoretical viewpoint on magic, witches, demons, and spectral evidence

cated elite. Even "The Account" of the Rev. Ebenezer Tur(r)ell (1702–78) of Medford, which Winship cites as clear evidence that by 1728 "the whole genre of authentic accounts of encounters with the supernatural" was passé, is in fact highly equivocal. Turell's account of the brief witchcraft episode in Littleton, Massachusetts (1720), is based on the confessions of a repentant woman who, decades after she and her young siblings accused an ill woman in the neighborhood of witchcraft, revealed that their accusations were groundless and the mere sports of children. Turell freely admits that "I knew but little of the dark story I have now told the world, and was entirely ignorant of her being an actor in it. It was therefore to my great surprise, that ... the day before she was to be received into the church, she came to visit me under the deepest concern and trouble of mind imaginable" and confessed to her malicious actions (18). If Turell's incredulity seems exemplary for the generation born sixty years after Mather's and ten after the Salem debacle, Turell still feels the need to ward off potential charges of Sadducism by stating that he, too, "firmly believe[s] the existence of spirits, an invisible world, and particularly the agency of Satan, and the instruments, in afflicting and tormenting children of men, (when permitted by God;) yet I fear," he adds in hindsight, "the world has been wretchedly imposed upon by relations of such matters. ... Many things have been dubb'd witchcraft, and called the works of the devil, which were nothing more than the contrivance of the children of men, who are wise to do evil, and which by strict examination might have been detected" (6).

13   In his "Letter to Judge John Richards" (May 31, 1692), Mather explicitly warned the court against reliance on spectral evidence more than ten days before the first victim was executed. The same caution appears in *The Return of Several Ministers* (June 15, 1692), in D. Levin, *What Happened in Salem?* (106–10, 110–11).

found in all of his earlier writings on witchcraft. A close reading of *Wonders*, of *Triparadisus*, and of his commentaries in "Biblia Americana" reveals that Mather's views on the devil's ability to assume the shape of innocent individuals remained the same throughout his lifetime.

Closely related to the question whether or not witches were able to raise the souls of the dead and whether demons could impersonate the likeness of innocent people was the debate in Mather's time about the true meaning of the Hebrew word *kashaph* (Exod. 22:18). As is well known, the translators of the King James Version (1611) fatefully rendered this term *witch* in rendering the Mosaic decree "Thou shall not suffer a witch to live." Significantly, the relevant commentaries in the "Biblia" omit any etymological consideration of *kashaph*. Although Mather refers to Josephus Flavius' *Antiquities* in many places, including that of the Jewish historian's comments on both the witch of Endor and the apostasy of the Jews living among the Gerasenes, he disregards Josephus' comments on *kashaph*, the key word in the passage. Significantly, to Josephus the scriptural application of the term signifies *poisoner, fortune-teller, sorcerer, or magician (Antiquities* 6.14.23).[14] The word was translated in the Vulgate as *veneficos*, a poisoner, or enchanter, and in the Septuagint as *pharmakos*, from which derives the modern English word *pharmacy* (see Walton's *Biblia Sacra Polyglotta* 1: 322–23). While skipping over the issue in the "Biblia," Mather did address it in his tract "A Brand Pluck'd Out of the Burning." In describing the symptoms of Mercy Short, which somewhat resembled that of poisoning, near the time of the Salem witch trials, Mather comments: "Behold a Proper Venefic Witchcraft!" (265). The incident called to his mind the ideas of others who also commented on the relationship between witches and poisons:

> Because the Name for Sorcerers in the Bible may signify Poisoners, tis a foolish Thing thence to infer that by witches, the Scripture means no more than such as commit Murders by Poisons. One great Skill, and way of Afflicting People in Witchcraft, is by another sort of Poisoning than what may bee seen by common Eyes. Yea I suppose, all the Bewitched have undergone such Spiritous Infection that wee may count them in a manner poisoned. ("A Brand" 265)

---

14 In Mather's lifetime, several translations of Josephus's Greek original existed – a Latin translation done by Edward Bernard (which covers *Antiquities*, bks. 1–5), an English translation by Thomas Lodge (which went through several editions and reprints), and a revised English translation based on the French version by Arnauld d'Andilly (*The Works of Josephus*, London, 1683). They all render the word in question as "Enchantress" (D'Andilly) or "enchantress" or "sorceress" (Lodge). The most popular English translation, done by William Whiston in 1733, renders *kashaph* as "fortune-teller." But in the footnote to his translation of *kashaph* (*Antiquities* 4.8.34), Whiston explains, "What we render a witch, according to our modern notions of witchcraft, Exodus 22:15, Philo and Josephus understood of a poisoner, or one who attempted by secret and unlawful drugs or philtra, to take away the senses or the lives of men."

By the early 1700s the greater part of the scholarly community would still have agreed with Mather and rejected the view that the biblical texts did not in fact speak of supernatural practices and powers.

Eminent biblical commentators upon whom Mather drew were also great believers in the supernatural character and demonic origin of witchcraft. As mentioned earlier, the famous scholar and biblical exegete Matthew Poole was the originator of the "Designe for registering of illustrious providences," a project to collect accounts to be used as evidence of the works of the hand of God, and this idea was later put into form in North America by Increase Mather in *An Essay for the Recording of Illustrious Providences* (1684). Poole, in his *Annotations upon the Holy Bible* (1683) intended for generalist readers, comments upon Exod. 22:18 ("Thou shalt not suffer a witch to live") by defining a witch as "Any person that is in league with the Devil and by his help either doth any mischief, or discovers and practices things above the reach of other men and women." Poole does not touch upon the meaning of the key Hebrew word, *kashaph*, but he points out that the word for *witch* is of the feminine gender. The association of witchcraft with the female sex occurs partly, he says, because women are most "prone to these Devilish acts, and most frequently guilty of them." However, in his huge *Synopsis Criticorum* (1: 426), Poole identifies all the authors – ancient and modern – who render the Hebrew *kashaph* [Strong # 3784] not only as *pharmacon* (*wizard*), but also as *mixers of poison* and *enchanters* and *sorcerers*. Matthew Henry (1662–1714), the English nonconformist still revered for his pious *Exposition of the Old and New Testaments* (1708–10) and his mild manners, stands fully behind Moses' law that "justly" made witchcraft a capital crime (Exod. 22:18). Alluding, perhaps, to the favor of the English in God's sight, Henry maintains the justice of the death penalty for witchcraft as being especially true "among a people that were blessed with a divine revelation, and cared for by divine Providence above any people under the sun." Henry also supports current English law against "consulting, covenanting with, invocating or employing, and evil spirit to any intent whatsoever, and exercising any enchantment, charm, or sorcery whereby hurt shall be done to any person whatsoever." Such acts as "pretending to identify the location of lost and stolen goods, or the like," he adds, should be punished by death upon conviction for the second offence. He concludes that the "justice of our law herein is supported by the law of God recorded here" (*Exposition*, Exod. 22:18).

A glance at the biblical commentary by Simon Patrick (1626–1707), bishop of Ely, on the same verse yields much the same viewpoint on the matter. Simon Patrick's *Commentary upon Exodus* (1697) is one of Mather's main sources [*BA*, Exod. 22:18], but Mather follows Patrick only up to the point when Patrick's discussion turns to Maimonides' observations on astrology in *Moreh Nebuchim*, or *Guide to the Perplexed*. Significantly, Maimonides associates the "worship of the stars" with witchcraft and other activities, including the planting of herbs at certain positions of the zodiac, purportedly to affect their growth and potency. Thus, like Maimonides, Mather relates witchcraft to astrology, which he also blames for inciting the Salem episode, but steers clear of associating witches with the cultivation of plants, a factor that Maimonides plainly intended.[15]

Mather's Interpretation of the *Nishmath-Chajim*

Mather's insistence on the reality of supernatural forces interacting with the natural world must also be seen as part of his attempt to refute the Cartesian position that all matter was subject to physical laws only and that the universe always ran in orderly and unchanging fashion by itself. Instead, Mather promoted the Newtonian worldview that allowed for God's willful intervention as well as for other kinds of supernatural interruptions of the natural order. But in a scientific age when many were disposed to discover empirical causes for all previously unexplained phenomena, Mather, like others, sought for the modus operandi through which supernatural forces interacted with the natural world. How did God, Satan, or a witch act upon material bodies to influence human affairs? In *The Christian Philosopher* (1720/21) and in *Coheleth* (1720), Mather wrote about the difficulties of identifying the interactive link between the different realms of being, between soul and body: "Some of the most Sublime Philosophers, who make the *Union* of the SOUL with the *Body*, to consist in the *Conformity of our Thoughts to what is done in the Body*, do well confess, That it is *Inexplicable*; and that we *must have Recourse to a Superiour Power for the Explication of it*. Yea, and so you must, Syrs, for the *Operation* of it" (*Coheleth* 11–12). Wrestling with this question, Mather found frequent reference in the Bible (also described in other ancient Hebrew writings) to the *Nishmath-Chajim*, or "breath of life" (נשמת חיים, see, for instance, Gen. 2:7). This ancient concept he re-interpreted to be the mysterious medium that constituted the *"Vital Ty"* between the *"Rational Soul* and the *Corporeal Mass"* (*Triparadisus* 122), through which, indetectable to the human senses or existing scientific instruments, the invisible world could interact with the material. Mather lays out his understanding of the *Nishmath-Chajim* in *Triparadisus* (122–26), in *The Angel of Bethesda* (28–38), in *Coheleth* (see esp. 11–17), and in "An Appendix Containing Some General Stores" at the end of the manuscript of "Biblia Americana."[16]

---

15 Significantly, Mather makes positive mention of several herbalist practices in his medical handbook *The Angel of Bethesda* (not to be mistaken for a sermon with the same title), which was not edited and published until 1972.
16 For useful discussions of this issue, see Beall and Shryock (66–80), Warner, and Silverman (408–10). An important source for Mather's re-interpretation of the *Nishmath-Chajim*

In all of these texts, Mather, amongst other things, attempted to reconcile biblical teachings of the invisible world of the soul with the new view of the natural world as a uniform space governed by universal physical laws. He was convinced that the communication between the visible world of matter, or the body and the invisible world of the spirit or the soul took place in the *Nishmath-Chajim*. In the *Triparadisus* Mather describes it as the *"Medium of Communication"* by which the *"Rational Soul* and the *Corporeal Mass* ... work upon one another"* (122). Citing 2 Cor. 12:3, Mather asserts that the *"Soul,"* when out of the body, may be able to "See and Hear Things that are Unspeakable" and that a disembodied soul "yett has an Ear to hear, and an Eye to see, what no Body in This World has a Tongue to utter" (120). To Mather, the *Nishmath-Chajim* was also key to understanding how impalpable sins directly impacted the physical body and, conversely, how the diseases of mind and body could be redressed through spiritual exercises. It is the *Nishmath-Chajim*, according to Mather, that "is more eminently the Seat of our Diseases, or the Source of them" (*Triparadisus* 122). What is more, Mather identified the *Nishmath-Chajim* as a vehicle for the imputation of the original sin and, "in conjunction with the concept of indestructible animalcules, the *Nishmath-Chajim* could help explain the ultimate Resurrection of the Dead" (Silverman 410).

It was also this intermediate realm linking soul with body, spirit with matter, that allowed ghosts, witches, demons, and angels to operate in the natural world. In *Triparadisus* Mather writes, "In the Indisputable and Indubitable Occurrences of *Witchcrafts* and *Possessions*, there are many things, which because they are *Hard* to be understood, the *Epicurean Sadducees* content themselves in their Bekkerian Manner [Balthazar Bekker], only to laugh at. But the *Nishmath-Chajim* well understood would give to more Sober Men a Key to lett us very far into the Meaning of them" (126). Moreover, Mather speculated that it was through the *Nishmath- Chajim* that apparitions occurred and a witch's specter could be formed. Mather writes,

> It is probable, That when we *Dy* the *Nishmath-Chajim* goes away as a Vehicle to the *Rational Soul*; and continues unto it an Instrument of many Operations. Here we have some Solution for the Difficulties, about the *Place*, and the *Change* of it, for such an *Immaterial Spirit* as the *Rational Soul*; And some Account for the *Apparition of the Dead*, which are called both, *Spirits*, and *Phantasms* in our Gospel. (*Triparadisus* 126)

---

was Spinoza's teacher Rabbi Menasseh ben Israel (1604–57), whose treatise on the immortality of the soul, *Sefer Nishmat Hayyim*, published in Hebrew in Amsterdam in 1651, much resembled Joseph Glanvill's *Saducismus Triumphatus* in purpose and content (Chajes 136). Like Glanvill's work, it is filled with detailed accounts of wonders, demons, and witches. Another important source was the Swiss physician Jean Baptiste van Helmont, who developed a similar theory in *Oriatrike or, Physick Refined* (1662), a work that would be of importance to the development of Mesmerism.

In Mather's mind, the *Nishmath-Chajim* was an all-encompassing psychosomatic link that even involved in the digestion of the stomach. "'Tis," as Mather puts it, "the *Nishmath-Chajim* after all, that is the Main Digester" (*Triparadisus* 125). It is "of a *Middle Nature*, between the "*Rational Soul* and the *Corporeal Mass*" and "wonderfully receives Impressions from Each of them ... by which they work on one another" (122).

As Kenneth Silverman so well observed, the *Nishmath-Chajim*, which in many ways anticipates the concept of animal magnetism later propagated by Franz Anton Mesmer and many others, was Mather's daring "attempt to harmonize his scientific and religious ideas, his understanding of matter and of spirit, his natural philosophy and pneumatology, his vitalistic and mechanistic views of the universe – Mather's own unified field theory" (Silverman 408–9). Deeply convinced of the viability of his theory and confirmed in his supernatural beliefs by the empirical evidences he collected over a lifetime, he thus felt justified until the end to defend the literal truth of what he understood the Bible to teach about the forces of the invisible world, including witchcraft.

Contrary to the linear narratives of secularization that earlier generation of scholars liked to tell, the alliance of supernatural religiosity and science that Mather embodies did not disappear from American culture with his generation. In fact, recent studies show that it continued to prosper with great intensity through the age of the founding fathers, producing a plethora of new movements in the late eighteenth and early nineteenth centuries, such as Mesmerism and Spiritualism. Like Mather, the followers of all of these movements hoped to bridge the gap between matter and spirit that the Enlightenment had opened up and sought to prove their theories of a unified cosmos by empirically observable phenomena of spiritual healings, ghostly encounters, and clairvoyance. Even by the early twentieth century, when William James conducted a search after hard evidence for life after death with the American Society for Psychical Research, most of these phenomena were not universally deemed to be beyond the realm of science.[17] Only witchcraft had decidedly gone out of fashion. So the question remains, when did this happen (why it happened is another question which cannot be addressed here) and how unique were Mather's beliefs at the end of his lifetime?

---

17 For a magisterial recent survey of religious movements in American history that put a premium on the supernatural, see Albanese. For the colonial period and the nineteenth century, see Butler. William James obsession with Spiritualism is examined by Blum.

The Belief in Witchcraft and its Decline in the Context of the Early Enlightenment

I already suggested above that England's most eminent biblical scholars in Mather's day, including Matthew Poole, Matthew Henry, and Simon Patrick, all shared Mather's convictions. The following survey discusses a wider sampling of English and other European writings on witchcraft from Cotton Mather's time in order to place his views in perspective. (My appendix provides a list of publications representing both sides of the issue, published in England and America between 1688 to 1750). Here treated chronologically, the examined works demonstrate that throughout his life Mather's belief in the reality of witchcraft chimed with the great majority of interpreters while outright skepticism was still an embattled minority opinion. Only around the time of his death did the balance slowly begin to shift amongst the learned. It was not until the second half of the eighteenth century, however, that the majority of academic theologians followed the trend.

Cotton Mather's first published attempt at documenting witchcraft cases and explaining his views on the matter is *Memorable Providences Touching Witchcraft and Possessions* (1689, 1691, 1697). As is well known, the book in many ways build upon the model of his father's *An Essay for the Recording of Illustrious Providences* (1684), which in turn was inspired by Matthew Poole. The 1691 London edition of *Memorable Providences* carried an imprimatur in the form of a preface by the eminent English Puritan minister Richard Baxter (1615–91), a person with close ties to both Mathers. In his preface to the 1691 London edition of Cotton Mather's *Memorable Providences*, Baxter outlines the theory behind the recording of empirical evidence of witches, demons, and apparitions. His preface to Mather's book argues that knowledge of the soul's immortality is made "more than probable by natural evidence" and "fully ascertained by Scripture" – the same type of argument that Henry More, Joseph Glanvill, Richard Baxter, and Cotton Mather used as rationale while documenting empirical evidence of the supernatural. Hard proof of the true existence of spiritual forms substantiated biblical interpretations that witches had acquired supernatural powers through a pact with Satan. Baxter writes, "*I have ... taken it for a great mercy of God, to cause Devils themselves by* Witches, Apparitions, Possessions, *and* Temptations, *to be made even to* Sense, Convincers *of the* Sadducees. ..." He adds, "*Indeed were not our* Sadducees *mad with incredulity, the Histories of* [Jean] Bodin *and* Remigius [Nicholas Remy] *alone (both Judges) besides the* mallei maleficarum *and all others might have fully convinced them*" (*Memorable Providences* [1691], "Preface").[18] Both sides of the debate, therefore, invoked science to either prove or disprove witchcraft. Mather verified

---

18   Baxter alludes to Jean Bodin's *De la démonomanie des sorciers* (1580), to Nicholas Re-

second-hand evidence with what he had himself heard, felt, and seen. In *Certainty of the Worlds of Spirits* (1691), written near the end of his life, Richard Baxter fills over 250 octavo pages with empirical accounts of apparitions, demons, witchcrafts, prodigious acts, and sightings of angels. Baxter's book alludes several times to recent occurrences of witchcraft in New England. He writes, "They that will read Mr. *Increase Mathers* Book, and especially his Sons, Mr. Cotton Mathers Book of the Witchcrafts in *New-England*, may see enough to Silence any Incredulity that pretendeth to be Rational (80).[19]

How the "modern Sadduccees" (who disbelieved the immortality of the soul, the efficacy of witchcraft, and the existence of the invisible world in general) were treated can be seen in the case of Dr. Balthasar Bekker (1634–98), astronomer, philosopher, theologian, and Calvinist minister of Amsterdam, whose *De Betooverde Wereld* (1691), or *The World Bewitched* appeared in an English translation in 1695. Applying Cartesian reasoning to scriptural interpretation, Bekker rejected the idea that immaterial spirits could act on material bodies. He denied such notions as the witches' flight, the witches' pact, copulation with the devil, and other phenomena commonly associated with witchcraft (Maxwell-Stuart 27; Bostridge 98; Fix 3–12, 125–48). Bekker's preface to *De Betooverde Wereld* addressed the ongoing argument over the translation of the English word *witchcraft*: "I searched deeper into this matter, expounding the Greek word Φαρμακός [*pharmakos*], which the French and Dutch interpreters have translated *Poisoning*, and the *English, Witchcraft*." Bekker refuted, both from the pulpit and in print, what he terms the "common Opinion" and "vulgar error" expressed by the English translation of certain Hebrew and Greek words as *witchcraft*. Upon publishing his denunciation of witchcraft in 1691, over 200 ministers in Friesland (a province in northern Holland) condemned his book, which, as Bekker put it, "ought to have taught me how dangerous it is to write upon such matters; there being neither favour nor profit to be expected for such Authors as rid themselves of all prejudices ..." (Preface). Tellingly enough, as a result of his controversial views of scripture, Bekker lost his position as rector in 1692 (Robbins 46).

In Germany in 1631, the Jesuit Frederick Spee (1591–1635) published *Cautio Criminalis* (1631), claiming that those then being prosecuted as witches were not in fact guilty of scriptural witchcraft. Though the work was published anonymously, Spee was immediately identified as the author and accused of promoting heretical opinions. The book shocked some of Spee's Jesuit brothers, and Peter Roestius, professor of theology in Cologne, wanted to have the book added to the "papal Index of Forbidden Books" (Hellyer xiv). Christian Tho-

---

my's *Daemonolatrioe libri tres* (1595), and Heinrich Kramer and Jacob Sprenger's *Malleus Maleficarum* (1486).

19 Baxter (*Certainty* 80) refers to Increase Mather's *Essay for the Recording of Illustrious Providences* (1684) and to Cotton Mather's *Memorable Providences* (1689, 1691).

masius (1655–1728), influenced by Spee's *Cautio Criminalis*, published *De Crimine Magiae*, in Latin in 1701. It was translated into German in 1703, appearing under the title, *Kurze Lehr-Sätze*. Thomasius did not believe in the witches' pact and thought that all prosecutions for witchcraft should immediately cease (Levack 36). He believed that even if the devil could be proven to have caused illness or harm, in no case could the accused be proven guilty of the deed by means of a pact with the devil. Disagreement was so sharp with Thomasius that the University at Halle, which he helped to found, was known disparagingly as the "University of Hell [Hölle]" (Robbins "Christian Thomasius" 496).

In 1706 the Rev. Francis Hutchinson (1660–1739), an Anglican clergyman and perpetual curate of St. James's at Bury St Edmonds, site of the "notorious" witch trials in 1662 and of the 1645 mass trials of "Witch Finder General," Matthew Hopkins, interviewed many of the survivors and sent several chapters he had written condemning the trials to Archbishop Tenison, who discouraged Hutchinson from publishing them because of potential consequences. Thus at nearly the same time that the writings of Bekker and Thomasius questioning witch beliefs caused trouble in Holland and in Germany, Hutchinson's criticism of witch trials was being suppressed by the Archbishop of Canterbury, in England, this thirteen years after the Salem witch trials ended.

Back in England in 1715, medical writer Richard Boulton published a treatise, *A Compleat History of Magic, Sorcery, and Witchcraft*, which strongly upheld belief in Satan's minions by attempting to show empirical evidence for ghosts, demons, and witches. Three years later, in 1718, after more than ten years delay, Francis Hutchinson finally *did* publish the material he earlier sent to the archbishop in *An Historical Essay Concerning Witchcraft*, partly as a response to Richard Boulton's *Compleat History*. Hutchinson's *Historical Essay* is acknowledged by many scholars to be the *coup de grace* that marked the end of the witchcraft debate in England. In 1722, Boulton attempted to refute Hutchinson with *A Vindication of A Complete History*, but Boulton's rejoinder was considered by most a weak response to Hutchinson's reasoned arguments and did nothing to assuage growing skepticism toward witchcraft, or to lessen condemnation of procedures used during the witch trials.

Francis Hutchinson devoted chapter 5 of his *Historical Essay* to criticizing the Salem witch trials. He singles out three works: Increase Mather's *Illustrious Providences* (1684), Cotton Mather's *Memorable Providences* (1690), and Richard Baxter's *Certainty of the World of Spirits* (1691) for helping to incite the witch epidemic in Salem. Basing some of his criticism on that of Boston merchant Robert Calef's *More Wonders of the Invisible World* (1700), which accused Mather of getting up the witchcraft hysteria to control his parishioners, Hutchinson singled out Cotton Mather, whom he most often refers to simply as "Mr. Mather." Hutchinson also dedicates a chapter to criticizing the trials

Mather abstracted in *Wonders* and to those that the Lord Chief Justice of England Matthew Hale (1609–76) had conducted at Bury St Edmonds in 1664. Mather presented Hale's Bury St Edmonds trials as having been an example to the Salem judges. In addition, Hutchinson specifically criticizes the three English authorities – William Perkins, Richard Bernard, and John Gaule – whom Mather had summarized in *Wonders* on signs used to detect and identify witches. Hutchinson credited the Royal Society with the decline in witch beliefs since its inception in 1660. He pointed out that the Royal Society based its discourse on facts, not on immeasurable quantities like God or the Soul. Perhaps he had the Salem trials in mind when he wrote,

> for if any wicked Person affirms, or any crack'd brain Girl imagines, or any lying Spirit makes her believe, that she sees any old Woman, or other Person pursuing her in her Visions, the Defenders of the vulgar Witchcraft tack an imaginary, unprov'd Compact to the Deposition, and hang the accus'd Parties. ... How many miserable Creatures have been hang'd or burnt as Witches and Wizzards in other Countries, and former Ages? In our own Nation, even since the Reformation, above a hundred forty have been executed, if my Book hath any Truth in it, very much upon the Account of one ill translated Text of Scripture (*Historical Essay* 4–5).

Hutchison believed, as did many of his peers, that the Hebrew word for *witch* (Exod. 22:18) signified something quite different from that in the popular conception of a witch who allegedly had acquired powers through a covenant with the devil. Greatly to his credit, the 1718 Bolton-Hutchinson witchcraft debate appears to have decided the outcome in favor of the skeptics – twenty-six years after Mather published his *Wonders*.

The last witch trial in England was that of Jane Wenham, which took place in 1712. Wenham was sentenced by a jury, but pardoned by the judge. In 1736, eight years after Cotton Mather's death, the English witchcraft statute was repealed. Yet even after prosecution for witchcraft became illegal, widespread belief in witches, demons, and apparitions persisted, as evidenced by statements such as that of the Rev. John Wesley in 1768 that "[t]he giving up of witchcraft is, in effect, giving up the Bible" (qtd. in Robbins 170). Writing to his brother Charles in 1774, Wesley confessed he had no doubt about the validity of the accounts of witchcraft in either Joseph Glanvill or Cotton Mather (Sharpe 253). Treatises proclaiming the reality of witchcraft continued to be published and re-published throughout the eighteen century. Richard Boulton's book *A Vindication of a Complete History* was published in 1722. The last eighteenth-century edition of Joseph Glanvill's *Saducismus Triumphatus* was published in 1726. As James Sharpe points out in the conclusion to his book *Instruments of Darkness: Witchcraft in Early Modern England*, it is certain that belief in witchcraft was virtually ubiquitous among the general population in England, if no longer amongst the learned, far into the second half of the nineteenth century. The same is certainly true for North America.

By this time, of course, academic theologians, together with the rest of the learned world, had clearly abandoned the belief in witches. While beliefs in other spiritual or charismatic phenomena persisted in all segments of American culture, including the educated elite, and are still widespread today, witchcraft (at least in its demonic interpretation) lost much of its popularity.[20] But for Mather these different manifestations of the supernatural were inseparable. Indeed, he thought that giving up on witchcraft ultimately meant to surrender wholesale the biblical revelation, and thus he saw the turn of the intellectual tide towards the end of his life as a sign of declining piety that portended God's apocalyptical judgment. "The foolish, and flouting, & bruitish, & short-winded Way of passing a Sentence upon *Extraordinary Descents from the Invisible World*, which we have seen in our Days," Mather commented ruefully thirty years after the Salem debacle, "is a sufficient Indication, how much the most Shocking *Signs of the Times* are lost upon us" (*Triparadisus* 342).

Note to the Appendix

As we can see, until the mid-eighteenth century the treatises in general accepting the actuality of witchcraft and the necessity for punishment clearly far outnumber those treatises in general skeptical of witchcraft and of the evidence presented at trials. And even though in 1736 was published "An Act to Repeal the Statute made in the First Year of the Reign of King James the First, intitled, *An act against conjuration, witchcraft, and dealing with evil and wicked sprits,*" works continued to be published on the subject and popular belief in witchcraft in America, England, and elsewhere remained widespread for the entire eighteenth century and beyond.

Witchcraft Treatises, Pamphlets, and Works on Demonic Possessions (1688–1750)[21]

Works Generally Credulous of Witchcraft, Attributing Its Effects Primarily to Supernatural Causes. Generally Accepting of Evidence Presented at Witch Trials.	**Works Generally Skeptical of Witchcraft, Attributing Its Effects Primarily to Natural Causes. Generally Skeptical of Evidence Presented at Witch Trials.**

---

20 For the current popularity of beliefs in angels and other supernatural phenomena, see Wuthnow (114–42). Of course, witchcraft has also made a rather spectacular comeback in American culture with the rise of neo-paganism and other new religious movements which, however, mostly understand the powers of witches as non-demonic in origin.

21 Unless otherwise noted, all texts are printed in London.

Year
1688

1. Crouch, Nathaniel (1632?-1725?) (pseudonym of Richard Burton). *The Kingdom of Darkness* (1688).
2. Glanvill, Joseph (1636–1680). *Saducismus Triumphatus.* (1688).
3. *Saducismus Triumphatus.* (1689). 4th ed.
4. Blagrave, Joseph (1610–82). *Astrological Practice of Physick* (1689).
5. Mather, Cotton (1663–1728). *Memorable Providences* (Boston, 1689).

1690

6. *The full tryals, examination, and condemnation of four notorious witches. At the assizes held at Worcester, on Tuesday the 4th of March* (1690).
7. Baxter, Richard (1615–91). *The Certainty of the Worlds of Spirits* (1691) 3rd ed. (1691).
8. *The distressed gentlewoman; or, Satan's implacable malice* (1691).
9. Mather, Cotton. *Late Memorable Providences Relating to Witchcrafts and Possessions* (1691).
10. *A true and faithful relation of the sad and dreadful accident, which hath lately happen'd by Lincoln-Inn-Fields, in the person of a maiden Gentlewoman, whose body is possess'd by an evil spirit* (1691).
11. Lawson, Deodat. *A brief and true narrative of some remarkable passages relating to sundry persons afflicted by witchcraft, at Salem village* (Boston, 1692).
12. *A Further Account of the Tryals of the New-England Witches* (1693).
13. Hale, Matthew. *A Collection of Modern Relations of Matter of Fact, Concerning Witches & Witchcraft* Part 1. (1693).
14. M.D. *A most strange and wonderful, tho' true relation of one Sarah*

Bowre ... who is at present [be]s-
sett with an evil spirit. (1693?)

15. Mather, Cotton. *The Wonders of the Invisible World* (Boston, 1693).

19. Lawson, Deodat. *Christ's Fidelity the Only Shield Against Satans Malignity* (Boston, 1693).

20. Mather, Cotton (1663–1728). *Wonders of the Invisible World.* 1st London ed. (1693).

21. *The Wonders of the Invisible World.* 2nd London ed. (1693).

22. *The Wonders of the Invisible World.* 3rd London ed. (1693).

22. Mather, Increase (1639–1723). *Cases of Conscience Concerning Witchcraft and Possessions* (Boston, 1693).

23. Petto, Samuel (1624?-1711). *A faithful narrative of the wonderful and extraordinary fits which Mr. Tho. Spatchet (late of Dunwich and Cookly), was under by witchcraft* (1693).

1695

24. Maule, Thomas (1645–1724). *Truth Held Forth and Maintained* (New York, 1695).

25. *Truth Held Forth and Maintained According to the Testimony of the Holy Prophets, Christ and His Apostles Recorded in the Holy Scriptures. Some Account of the Judgments of the Lord Lately Inflicted Upon New-England By Witch Craft* (New York, 1695).

26. *Observations Concerning the Original and Various Forms of Government.* 2nd ed. (1696).

27. *Observations Concerning the Original and Various Forms of Government, As Described.* 3rd ed. (1696).

28. Mather, Cotton. *Memorable Providences.* 2nd ed. (Boston, 1697).

29. Cullen, Francis Grant, Lord (1658–1726). [*True narrative of*

1. Keith, George (1639?-1716). *A Refutation of Three Opposers of Truth, By Plain Evidence of the Holy Scripture* (Philadelphia, 1690).

2. C.M. *A true account of the tryals, examinations, confessions, condemnations, and executions of divers witches, at Salem* (1692).

3. Willard, Samuel (1640–1707). *Some miscellany observations on our present debates respecting witchcrafts* (Philadelphia [i.e., Boston], 1692).

4. Filmer, Robert, Sir (d. 1653). *An Advertisement to Jury-Men of England Touching Witches* (1696): 309–346.

5. Bell, John (1676–1707). *Witchcraft proven, arreign'd, and condemn'd in its professors, professions and marks* (Glasgow, 1697).

6. Howson, Robert. *The second part of the boy of Bilson: or, A true and particular relation of the impostor, Susanna Fowles ... who pretended her self to be posses'd with the devil* (1698).

the sufferings and relief of a young girle; strangely molested, by evil spirits and their instruments, in the west]. Sadducismus debellatus: or, A true narrative of the sorceries and witchcrafts exercis'd by the Devil and his instruments upon Mrs. Christian Shaw, daughter of Mr. John Shaw, of Bargarran in the County of Renfrew in the West of Scotland, from Aug. 1696 to Apr. 1697 (1698).

30. Jollie, Thomas (1629–1703). *A vindication of the Surey demoniack as no impostor* (1698).

31. R.C. (Richard Chamberlayne). *Lithobolia: or, The stone-throwing devil.* (1698).

32. T.P. *A relation of the diabolical practices of above twenty wizards and witches of the sheriffdom of Renfrew in the kingdom of Scotland, contain'd, in their tryalls, examinations, and confessions; and for which several of them have been executed this present year, 1697* (1698).

33. Higgs, Daniel. *The wonderfull and true relation of the bewitching a young girle in Ireland, what way she was tormented, and a receipt of the ointment that she was cured with* (1699).

1700

34. Bell, John. *The tryal of witchcraft: or, Witchcraft arraign'd and condemn'd: In some answers to a few questions anent witches and witchcraft. Wherein is shewed, how to know if one be a witch, as also when one is bewitched: with some observations upon the witches mark, their compac with the Devil, the white witches* (Glasgow, 1700?).

35. Blight, Francis. *A true and impartial account of the dark and hellish power of witchcraft, lately*

7. Calef, Robert (1648–1719). *More Wonders of the Invisible World* (1700).

8. Hale, John (1636–1700). *A Modest Enquiry into the Nature of Witchcraft* (Boston, 1702).

9. Aubin, Nicolas (b. ca. 1655). [*Histoire des diables de Loudun.* English]. *The cheats and illusions of Romish priests and exorcists. Discover'd in the history of the devils of Loudun* (1703).

10. Aubin, Nicolas. [*Histoire des diables de Loudun.* English [*The*

exercised on the body of the
Reverend Mr. Wood, Minister of
Bodmyn (Exeter, 1700).

36. Glanvill, Joseph. *Saducismus
Triumphatus* (1700).

37. *A full and true account of the
apprehending and taking of Mrs.
Sarah Moordike, who is accused
for a witch* (1701).

38. *Some Few Remarks Upon A
Scandalous Book, Against The
Government And Ministry Of
New-England, Written, By One
Robert Calef* (Boston, 1701).

39. Hathaway, Richard. *The tryal
of Richard Hathaway, upon an
information for being a cheat and
impostor, for endeavouring to
take away the life of Sarah Mor-
duck, for being a witch* (1702).

40. Greenwel, Thomas. *A full and
true account of the discovering,
apprehending and taking of a
notorious witch, who was carried
before Justice Bateman in Well-
Close* (1704).

41. Lawson, Deodat. *Christ's Fidelity
the Only Shield Against Satan's
Malignity.* 2nd London ed. (1704).

1705

42. Davis, Ralph. *The Northamp-
tonshire witches. Being a true
and faithful account of the births,
educations, lives, and conversations, of Elinor Shaw, and Mary
Phillips, (the two notorious
witches) that were executed at
Northampton in 1705.* 2nd London
(1705).

43. R.B., [Nathaniel Crouch] *The
Kingdom of Darkness.* 3rd London
ed. (1705).

44. *A full and true account of the tryals, examination, and condemnation of Lewin Brown, a Jesuite,
and one Father Lewis, pretended
Bishop of Landaff, at the last
assizes at Lancaster, March 16th*
(London, 1706).

history of the devils of Loudon]
In three books (1705).

45. Johnson, Mary (d. 1706). *A full and true account of the tryal, examination, and condemnation of Mary Johnson a witch* (1706).
46. *The black art detected and expos'd: or, a demonstration of the Hellish Impiety, of Being, or desiring to Be a Wizzard, Conjurer, or Witch* (1707).
47. *The dreadful effects of going to conjurers* (1708?)

1710

48. Bragge, Francis (1664–1728). *A defense of the proceedings against Jane Wenham, wherein the possibility and reality of witchcraft are demonstrated from scripture, and the concurrent Testimonies of all Ages* (1712).
49. *A full and true account: of one Mrs. Elisabeth Bates, the only daughter of an eminent merchant living at Hackney, who sold herself to the Devil* (1712?).
50. G.R., A.M. *The belief of witchcraft vindicated: proving, from scripture, there have been witches; and from reason, that there may be such still. In answer to a late pamphlet, intituled, The impossibility of witchcraft* (1712).

11. *The Case of the Hertfordshire Witchcraft Consider'd* (1712).
12. *The Impossibility Of Witchcraft, Plainly Proving, From Scripture And Reason, That There Never Was A Witch; And That It Is Both Irrational And Impious To Believe There Ever Was* (1712) 2nd ed. (1712).
13. Physician in Hertfordshire. *A full confutation of witchcraft. … In which The Modern Notions of Witches are overthrown, and the Ill Consequences of such Doctrines are exposed by Arguments; proving that, Witchcraft is Priestcraft* (1712).
14. Massachusetts. [Laws, 1711–10–17] Province of the Massachusetts-Bay. *An act, made and passed by the Great and General Court or Assembly of Her Majesty's province of the Massachusetts-Bay in New-England, held at Boston the 17th day of October, 1711* Boston, 1713.

1715

51. Boulton, Richard (b. 1676). *A Compleat History of Magick, Sorcery, and Witchcraft* (1715).
52. Anonymous. *A Tryal of Witches, at the Assizes* (1716).
53. Hale, Matthew Sir (1609–76). *Pleas of the Crown* (1716).
54. *A Tryal of Witches, at the Assizes Held at Bury St. Edmonds For the*

15. Hutchinson, Francis (1661–1739). *An Historical Essay Concerning Witchcraft* (1718).

County of Suffolk; On the Tenth Day of March, 1664. Before Sir Matthew Hale ... Taken by a person then attending the court (1716), 2nd ed. (1716).

1720

55. Boulton, Richard. *The Possibility and Reality of Magick, Sorcery, and Witchcraft, Demonstrated. Or, a Vindication of a Compleat History of Magick, Sorcery, and Witchcraft. In Answer to Dr. Hutchinson's Historical Essay ... in Two Parts. By Richard Boulton* (1722).

56. Beaumont, John (d. 1731). *Gleanings of Antiquities.Containing ... III. Some Notes Concerning Familiar Spirits* (1724).

1725

57. Glanvill, Joseph. *Saducismus Triumphatus* (1726).

58. *Saducismus Triumphatus ... in Two* Parts (1726).

59. Defoe, Daniel (1661?-1731). *The History of the Devil, As Well Ancient As Modern* (1727) 2nd ed. (1727).

60. R.B. (1632?-1725?). *The Kingdom of Darkness. By Robert Burton* 4th ed. (1728).

1735

61. Oates, Titus (1649–1705). *The Witch of Endor: Or, a Plea For the Divine Administration By the Agency of Good and Evil Spirits* (1736).

62. Church, Thomas (1707–56). *An essay towards vindicating the literal sense of the Demoniacks, in the New Testament; in answer to a late enquiry into the meaning of them* (1737).

63. Twells, Leonard (1683–1742). *An answer to the enquiry into the meaning of Demoniacks in the New Testament* (1737).

64. Whiston, William (1667–1752).

16. *An historical essay concerning witchcraft. With observations upon matters of fact; Tending to clear the Texts of the Sacred Scriptures, and confute the vulgar Errors about that Point.* 2nd ed. (1720)

17. An Act to repeal the Statute made in the first Year of the Reign of King James the First, intitled, *An Act against Conjurations, Witchcraft and dealing with evil and witched Spririts*, except so much thereof as repeals an Act of the fifth Year of the Reign of Queen Elizabeth, *Against Conjuration, Inchantments and Witchcraft*, and to repeal an Act passed in the Par-

An account of the *Dæmoniacks,
and of the power of casting
out Dæmons, both in the New
Testament, and in the four first
centuries* (1737).

65. Church, Thomas. *A reply to the
Farther enquiry into the meaning
of the Demoniacks in the New
Testament* (1738).

66. Twells, Leonard. *An answer to the
Further enquiry into the meaning
of Demoniacks in the New Testament: In a second letter to the
author* (1738).

1750

67. Church, Thomas. *A vindication of the miraculous powers,
which subsisted in the three first
centuries of the Christian church*
(1750).

liament of *Scotland* in the ninth
Parliament of Queen MARY,
intitled, *Anoetis Witchcrafts*, and
for punishing such Persons as
presented to exercise or use and
Kind of Witchcraft, Sorcery, In-
chantment or Conjuration (1736).

18. *A discourse on witchcraft. Occasioned by a bill now depending in
Parliament, to repeal the statute
made in the first year of the reign
of King James I, intituled, An act
against conjuration, witchcraft,
and dealing with evil and wicked
spirits* (1736).

19. Juxon, Joseph, d. 1757. *A sermon
upon witchcraft. Occasion'd by
a late illegal attempt to discover
witches by swimming* (1736).

20. *The Famous history of the
Lancashire witches: Containing,
the manner of becoming such;
their enchantments, spells, revels,
merry pranks* (c. 1750–1775?).

21. *The History of the Lancashire
witches: Containing, the manner of their becoming such* (c.
1750–1790).

Works Cited

Primary Works

Ben Israel, Menasseh. *Sefer Nishmat Hayyim*. Amsterdam, 1651.
Bekker, Balthazar. *De Betoverde Weerled*, or *The World Bewitched*. 1691. London, 1695.
Bible. King James Version.1st ed.
–. New Revised Standard Version (NRSV).
Bodin, Jean. *De la démonomanie des sorciers*. Paris, 1580.
Boulton, Richard. *Compleat History of Magic, Sorcery, and Witchcraft*. London, 1715.
–. *A Vindication of a Compleat History of Magic, Sorcery, and Witchcraft*. London, 1722.
Baxter, Richard. *The Certainty of the Worlds of Spirits*. London, 1691.
–. Preface. *Memorable Providences Relating to Witchcrafts and Possessions*. By Cotton Mather. London, 1691.

Calef, Robert. *More Wonders of the Invisible World*. London, 1700.

Edwards, John. *Exercitations Critical, Historical, Philosophical, Theological on Several Important Places of the Writings in the Old and New Testament*. London, 1702.

Flavius, Josephus. *The Complete Works of Josephus*. Ed. and trans. William Whiston. 1737. Grand Rapids: Kregel Publ., 1960.

Glanvill, Joseph. *Saducismus Triumphatus: Or, Full and Plain Evidence Concerning Witches and Apparitions. In Two Parts*. 1681. London, 1689.

Henry, Matthew. *An Exposition of All the Books of the Old and New Testaments: Wherein the Chapters are summ'd up in Contents; the Sacred Text inserted at large, in Paragraphs, or Verses; and each Paragraph, or Verse, reduc'd to its proper Heads: the Sense given, and largely illustrated, with Practical Remarks and Observations*. 6 vols. London, 1708–10.

Hobbes, Thomas. *Leviathan*. London, 1651.

Hutchinson, Francis. *An Historical Essay Concerning Witchcraft*. London, 1718.

Janeway, Jane. *A Token for Children: Being the Account of the Conversion, Holy and Exemplary Lives, and Joyful Deaths, of several young Children*. London, 1676.

Jurieu, Pierre. *Critical History of the Opinions and Worships (Good and Evil) of the Church*. 2 vols. London, 1705–06.

Kramer, Heinrich and Jacob Sprenger. *Malleus Maleficarum*. 1486. Trans. Christopher S. Mackay. 2 vols. Cambridge: Cambridge UP, 2006.

Maimonides, Moses. *Guide for the Perplexed*. Ed. and trans. M. Friedländer. New York: Dover, 1956.

Mather, Cotton. *The Angel of Bethesda*. Ed. Gordon W. Jones. Barre: American Antiquarian Society, 1972.

–. *Biblia Americana*. Ed. Reiner Smolinski. Vol. 1. Tübingen and Grand Rapids: Mohr Siebeck and Baker Academic, 2010.

–. "A Brand Pluck'd Out of the Burning." 1914. *Narratives of the New England Witchcraft Cases*. Ed. George Lincoln Burr. Mineola: Dover, 2002. 259–87.

–. *The Christian Philosopher*. London, 1720/21. Ed. Winton U. Solberg. Urbana: U of Illinois P, 1994.

–. *Coheleth*. Boston, 1720.

–. *Coelestinus*. Boston, 1723.

–. *Diary of Cotton Mather*. Ed. Worthington C. Ford. Collections of the Massachusetts Historical Society 7th series. Vols. 7–8. Boston: MHS, 1911–12.

–. "A Discourse on Witchcraft." In *Wonders of the Invisible World*. Boston, 1693.

–. "An Extract of Several Letters from Cotton Mather, D.D to John Woodward, M.D. and Richard Waller, Esq." *Philosophical Transactions of the Royal Society*. 29 (1712): 62–71.

–. *Magnalia Christi Americana: Or, The Ecclesiastical History of New England*. 1702. New York: Arno Press, 1972.

–. *Memorable Providences*. 1689. In *Narratives of New England Witchcraft Cases*. Ed. George Lincoln Burr. 1914. Mineola: Dover, 2002. 89–143.

–. *The Threefold Paradise of Cotton Mather: An Edition of* "Triparadisus." Ed. Reiner Smolinski. Athens: U of Georgia P, 1995.

–. *A Token for the Children of New England*. Boston, 1700.

–. *The Wonders of the Invisible World*. Boston, 1693.

Mather, Increase. *An Essay for the Recording of Illustrious Providences*. 1684. In *Narratives of New England Witchcraft Cases*. Ed. George Lincoln Burr. 1914. Mineola: Dover, 2002. 1–38.

256   *Paul Wise*

Mather, Samuel. *The Life of the Very Reverend and Learned Cotton Mather, D.D. &
    F.R.S.* Boston, 1729.
More, Henry. *The Immortality of the Soul.* London, 1662.
Poole, Matthew. *Annotations upon the Holy Bible. Wherein the Sacred Text is Inserted,
    and various Readings Annex'd together with Parallel Scriptures, the more difficult
    Terms in each Verse are Explained, seeming Contradictions Reconciled, Questions
    and Doubts Resolved, and the whole Text opened. By the Late Reverend and
    Learned Divine Mr. Matthew Poole.* 2 vols. London, 1683–85.
–. *Synopsis Criticorum Aliorumque S. Scripturæ Interpretum.* 5 vols. Londini, 1669–
    76.
Remy, Nicholas. *Daemonolatrioe libri tres.* Lyons, 1595.
Spee, Friedrich von Langenfeld. *Cautio Criminalis, or a Book on Witch Trials.* Trans.
    Marcus Hellyer. Charlottesville: U of Virginia P, 2003.
Thomasius, Christian. *De Crimine Magiae.* Halle, 1701.
Tur(r)ell, Ebenezer. "Brief Abstract." *Collections of the Massachusetts Historical Society.*
    2nd Series. Vol. 10 (1823). Rpt. Boston: MHS, 1843: 6–22.
Walton, Brian. Editor. *Biblia Sacra Polyglotta.* 6 vols. Londini, 1653–57.

Secondary Works

Adams, Gretchen A. *The Specter of Salem: Remembering the Witch Trials in Nine-
    teenth-Century America.* Chicago: U of Chicago P, 2009.
Albanese, Catherine L. *A Republic of Mind and Spirit: A Cultural History of American
    Metaphysical Religion.* New Haven: Yale UP, 2007.
Beall, Jr. Otho T. and Richard H. Shryock. *Cotton Mather: First Significant Figure in
    American Medicine.* Baltimore: Johns Hopkins UP, 1954.
Blum, Deborah. *Ghost Hunters: William James and the Search for Scientific Proof of Life
    After Death.* New York: Penguin, 2006.
Bostridge, Ian. *Witchcraft and Its Transformations: 1650–1750.* Oxford: Oxford UP,
    1997.
Butler, Jon. *Awash in a Sea of Faith: Christianizing the American People.* Cambridge:
    Harvard UP, 1990.
Chajes, Jeffrey Howard. *Between Worlds: Dybbuks, Exorcists, and Early Modern Juda-
    ism.* Philadelphia: U of Pennsylvania P, 2003.
Demos, John. *Entertaining Satan: Witchcraft and the Culture of Early New England.*
    Rev. ed. Oxford: Oxford UP, 2004.
Faithful, George. "Cotton Mather's Scientific Method for Prayer." *Theology and Science*
    7.2 (2009): 175–87.
Fix, A. *Fallen Angels: Balthasar Bekker, Spirit Belief, and Confessionalism in the Seven-
    teenth-Century Dutch Republic International Archives of the History of Ideas.*
    Dordrecht: Kluwer, 1999.
Hall, David D. *World of Wonder, Days of Judgment: Popular Religious Belief in Early
    New England.* New York: Knopf, 1989.
Hall, Michael G. *The Last American Puritan: The Life of Increase Mather.* Middletown:
    Wesleyan UP, 1988.
Harley, David. "Explaining Salem: Calvinist Psychology and the Diagnosis of Posses-
    sion." *American Historical Review* 101.2 (1996): 307–30.

Hellyer, Marcus. "Translator's Introduction." *Cautio Criminalis, or a Book on Witch Trials*. Trans. Marcus Hellyer. Charlottesville: U of Virginia P, 2003. vii–xxxvi.

Kohler, Kaufmann. "Merkabah." *The Jewish Encyclopedia*. Web. 11 Dec. 2009.

Kramer, Heinrich and Jacob Sprenger. *The Hammer of Witches: A Complete Translation of the Malleus Maleficarum*. Trans. Christopher S. Mackay. Cambridge: Cambridge UP, 2009.

Levack, Brian. "General Reasons for the Decline in Prosecutions." *Witchcraft and Magic in Europe: The Eighteenth and Nineteenth Centuries*. Ed. Bengt Ankarloo and Stuart Clark. U of Pennsylvania P, 2003. 7–47.

Levin, David. *Cotton Mather: The Young Life of the Lord's Remembrancer, 1663–1703*. Cambridge: Harvard UP, 1978.

–. "Trying to Make a Monster Human: *Judgment in the Biography of Cotton Mather*." *Forms of Uncertainty: Essays in Historical Criticism*. Charlottesville: UP of Virginia, 1992. 157–76.

–. "When Did Mather See the Angel?" *Early American Literature* 15 (1980/81): 271–75.

Mackay, Christopher. "Introduction." *The Hammer of Witches: A Complete Translation of the Malleus Maleficarum*. Cambridge: Cambridge UP, 2009. 1–58.

Maxwell-Stuart, P.G. *Witchcraft in Europe and the New World: 1400–1800*. Houndmills, Basinstroke: Palgrave, 2001.

Middlekauff, Robert. *The Mathers: Three Generations of Puritan Intellectuals, 1596–1728*. 1971. Oxford: Oxford UP, 1976.

Murdock, Kenneth Ballard. *Increase Mather: The Foremost American Puritan*. Cambridge: Harvard UP, 1926.

Norton, Mary Beth. *In the Devil's Snare: The Salem Witchcraft Crisis of 1692*. New York: Knopf, 2002.

Robbins, Rossell Hope. "Christian Thomasius." *The Encyclopedia of Witchcraft and Demonology*. New York: Crown, 1959.

–. "James I." *The Encyclopedia of Witchcraft and Demonology*. New York: Crown, 1959.

Rosenthal. Bernard. *Salem Story: Reading the Witch Trials of 1692*. Cambridge: Cambridge UP, 1995.

Sharpe, James. Instruments *of Darkness: Witchcraft in Early Modern England*. Philadelphia: U of Pennsylvania P, 1996.

Silverman, Kenneth. *The Life and Times of Cotton Mather*. New York: Harper & Row, 1984.

Stannard, David E. *The Puritan Way of Death: A Study in Religion, Culture, and Social Change*. New York: Oxford UP, 1977.

Van Arragon, William. "Cotton Mather in American Cultural Memory, 1728–1892." Diss. Indiana U, 2005.

Warner, Margret Humphreys. "Vindicating the Minister's Medical Role: Cotton Mather's Concept of the *Nishmath-Chajim* and the Spiritualization of Medicine." *Journal of the History of Medicine and Allied Sciences* 36.3 (1981): 278–95.

Wuthnow, Robert. *After Heaven: Spirituality in America Since the 1950s*. Berkeley: U of California P, 1998.

Section 4: Mather's Historical Method and His Approach
to the History of Religions

Rick Kennedy

Historians as Flower Pickers and Honey Bees: Cotton Mather and the Commonplace-Book Tradition of History

When describing in his *Diary* the purpose for compiling the "Biblia Americana," Mather wrote that he desired to fetch "all together by laborious Ingenuitie" the "Treasures of *Illustrations* for the Bible, dispersed in the Volumes of this Age" (1: 170). In a promotional pamphlet for his *magnum opus* he presented himself as a dinner host offering delicacies "together set upon the Table ... a Feast of *Fat Things full of Marrow, of Wines in the Lees well refined*" (*A New Offer* 5–6). He advertised the "Biblia" as "a sort of *Library*" and referred to it as "this *Common Hive*" (*A New Offer* 4). So, too, in the *Magnalia Christi Americana* he had noted that good historical work should be a *polyanthea*, a flower arrangement of "choice *Flowers*" directly from the fields of "Ancient or Modern Writings" (100–01). There is nothing incidental about these rather humble and social images (particularly those of flowers and hives) that Mather chose to characterize his writings, and especially the "Biblia." Through these metaphors and images he linked his method of composition to a commonplace-book tradition of history that was rooted in Aristotelian rhetoric and had long been promoted through a Stoic-Christian alliance. His claim to "laborious Ingenuitie" was therefore not a claim to originality; rather, it was the claim of one who, in line with this tradition, perceives the historian's or exegete's role to consist primarily in gathering and organizing in communication with the living and dead. It is the purpose of this paper to shed new light both on the underlying structure of the "Biblia" and Mather's self-understanding as a historian or historical exegete by reconsidering his work against the background of the Aristotelian commonplace-book tradition. I will do this by tracing the flower-and-hive imagery as code words signifying a methodological approach of gathering that is predicated on a metaphysical assumption about time-tested consensus.

Throughout this article I will use the genre designation "commonplace-book tradition" interchangeably with "Aristotelian historiography." There are other conceptual frameworks to analyze Mather's method of composition that are useful; however, they tend to emphasize the elephantine rather than the apian. For instance, Jan Stievermann, in his excellent article, "Writing 'To Conquer All Things': Cotton Mather's *Magnalia Christi Americana* and the Quandary of *Copia*," analyzes Mather's striving for "verbal opulence," and his goal of an "universal historiographic intertext ... a monological discourse that represents one divine truth ... a textual utopia of limitless but at the same time well-or-dered abundance" (263, 270, 276). Stievermann puts Mather's *Magnalia* in the context of the rhetorical ideal of *copia* that is intimately tied to the classical no-tion of the *consensus gentium*. This notion, which was still widely accepted in early modern Europe, Gustaaf Van Cromphout puts at the heart of Mather's self-definition as a historian (Lovejoy 83; Van Cromphout 333). The universal ideals of *consensus gentium* and its counterpart, *consensus omnium*, are linked to what C.S. Lewis calls the medieval "love of the labyrinthine" (Lewis 193–94). Peter Gay writes dismissively, but correctly, that the meaning in Mather's *Magnalia* "lies concealed in the maze of its organization and the tangled wilder-ness of its prose" (Gay 59). It is certainly appropriate to associate Mather with all-encompassing and labyrinthine grandiosity. Here, however, I want readers to appreciate that, in the "Biblia" more than anywhere else in his writings, Mather accepted the purposefully humble role of a commonplace-book histo-rian of the flower-picker and honey-bee type.

Ann Moss, in her very insightful book *Printed Commonplace-Books and the Structuring of Renaissance Thought* (1996), introduces readers to the breadth and diversity of pre-modern concern given to assembling bits of information into varied schemes of commonplaces. In the sixteenth century commonplace-books were published in various forms. Erasmus's *Adages* was a very popular aphoristic collection. Melanchthon's *Loci Communes* helped students organize and use theology. By the seventeenth-century there was a great diversity of ways commonplace-books were being organized and promoted (Moss 24). Moss notes that, beginning in the twelfth century, collections of classical quotes (called flowers) also began to proliferate. In the Renaissance these collections were often called *anthologies* or *florilegia*. In Greek, *anthos* means flower; an *anthology* is a flower arrangement. *Florilegium* is the Latin version of the same image. Moss follows the trail of sixteenth-century *anthologies* and *florilegia* back into the Aristotelian system of *topics* and further into the widespread role of commonplace-books in humanist pedagogy. She advises us to be alert for references to flowers, a term that "acquired an almost technical sense" (246). Moss illuminates how a simple floral image could link an author to a long Aris-totelian tradition which, in turn, could be "a valuable clue to distinctive features of early modern culture in general and to the working practice of individual writers in particular" (vii).

Cotton Mather referred to flowers, bees, hives, and *polyanthea* (literary flower arrangements) when defining commonplace-books and history in both the *Magnalia* and his *Manuductio ad Ministerium*, which also contains reading guidelines for the candidates of the ministry (*Magnalia* 94–106; *Manuductio* 44, 45, 72, 120). In the context of such passages Mather wrote that he would "make

unto the Church of God an humble Tender of our BIBLIA AMERICANA"
(*Magnalia* 105–06). The humility here invoked was not self-delusional. The art
of being a historian, for Cotton Mather, was an art best depicted as flower-pick-
ing and the work of a honey bee. He also liked the image of a library. In the
Manuductio he praised the massive *Great Historical Dictionary* and the *Critical
History* of Pierre Bayle as "*A Library*," an "*Immense Treasure* of *History*" (70).
Four paragraphs later he advised young scholars to start a commonplace-book.
"In a few Years, you will have a *Treasure*" and "prepared an *Hive*" (72).

In his *Diary* Mather characterized himself as a gatherer of quotes "scattered" among the books of learned men (1: 230). "Seldome any *new book* of
Consequence finds the way from beyond-Sea, to these Parts of *America*," he
claimed, "but I bestow the Perusal upon it. And, still, as I read, I note Curiosities in my blank Books, which I entitle, *Quotidiana*" (*Diary* 1: 548). Mather
lived the life of the bee, and proudly noted in 1711 that in year alone he added
more than a thousand passages to the "Biblia" (*Diary* 2: 162).

Hugo Grotius, well remembered for his handbook for missionaries *De
Veritate Religionis Christianae* (1639), wrote of the first gatherings of commonplace-books in a "Prolegomena" to an edition of Johann Stobaeus' *Antholo-
gion/Florilegium*. Grotius described how the Greeks would mark an χ next to a
useful quote to signify "χρηστον [chreston], *id est*, utile *esse*" (xxvii). These useful bits would be gathered into a χρηστομάθειαν, a chrestomathy. A chreston
eventually came to be associated with a flower, and a chrestomathy came to be
called an *anthologion* or *florilegia*. In this tradition, citation of sources was encouraged. The gatherer was distinct from the author of the useful bit.

In the "Biblia," Mather, more than anywhere else in his writings, freely
cited his sources. In his question-and-answer format he even allowed himself,
lightheartedly, to banter about his sources. For example, commenting on Acts
17:28 where Paul tells the Greeks of the Areopagus that their poets have written
of the Christian God, Mather wrote

> Q.   On that Quotation which our Apostle marks, *As certain also of your own Po-
> ets have said*; We may make some Remarks, not unworthy of a Room among our
> *Illustrations*.
> A.   Some were made by an Ingenious Man, one Mr. *John Sherman*, more than fifty
> Years ago, in some *Common-places*, which he published under the Title of, *A Greek
> in the Temple*. And from the Hints then & there given by him, I have my Thoughts
> awakened, to take notice of several things. [*BA*, Acts 17:28]

Mather reported his heavy reliance on certain authors with intimacies such as
"one *Sherman*" and "my excellent *Witsius*" [*BA*, Acts 17:27; 9:6]. He often
would announce something about his source such as "Dr. *Whitby* has collected
the Expositions of the Ancients upon it" [*BA*, John 6:71]. The announcement
might carry some information, as when writing on the roots of the term "East-

er," Mather praised "a Sermon preached by Dr. *Hill*, the Master of Trinity College in *Cambridge*," in which "I find a passage of this Importance which I think it not amiss to recite and leave it to the Credit of the Author" [*BA*, Acts 6:5]. He explained the circumstances of the long "Historia Apostolica or PROLEGOMENA to the *Acts* of The APOSTLES." The section is from "The Happy Pen of a Learned but Nameless Person ... wherein he has cultivated that Subject with an uncommon Penetration and *written Excellent Things*" [*BA*, Prolegomena to Acts]. Mather noted that he had the work in front of him and proposed "to make an *Extract* from it, and an *Abstract* of it, but in doing so, still use the Liberty of Style that may best suit my Main Intention" [*BA*, Prolegomena to Acts]. Mather believed in reading history *"with Discretion,"* so it is not surprising that, in the catholicity of the "Biblia," he at times offered warnings.[1]

When illustrating John 1:14, for example, Mather wrote that he would be assisted by Dr. John Scott "in the Thoughts I am now going to give you. ... [I am] beholden unto this Author, for the chief Materials, of the *Illustration* I am now going to give you"; however, Scott did not "write alwayes with so good a Spirit, as I could have wish'd for, nor show so good an Insight" [*BA*, John 1:14].[2] Overall, as much a gatherer as a commentator, Mather allowed a wide diversity of authors to speak freely in the "Biblia." At one point he matter-of-factly dropped an issue in the reader's lap. After gathering many long quotations about worship related to Acts 15:20, Mather declared, "Having done with Dr. *Spencer*, I will now take the Scales in hand, and throw into them, two brief Discourses, on this controverted Theme ... and leave it unto your Consideration, which præponderates" [*BA*, Acts 15:20]. Through this method of composing the "Biblia Americana," Mather thus fashioned himself as a provincial American commonplace-book gatherer. Of the trilogy of Mather's most important books – one natural history, one regional-ecclesiastical history, and one synoptic commentary – the "Biblia Americana" is the most honest and humble. The *Christian Philosopher* tends to hide Mather's reliance on authorities. The *Magnalia* was constructed largely upon unnamed hearsay testimony. The "Biblia," however, is overflowing with references within references to sources both ancient and modern. By calling the "Biblia" a "hive," Mather embraced the historiographical tradition that emphasized simple gathering of flowers into a commonplace-book style of history.

Though there is simplicity and humility in the structure, the commonplace-book tradition was embedded with metaphysical assumptions about the emergent power of truth over error. The image of a hive is never only about gathering and organizing. It is also about the mysterious production of honey.

---

1   For Mather's advice on reading with discretion, see *Manuductio* (60–64).
2   The reference is to Scott's 1728 *An Appeal to the Understanding of the Meanest Capacities for the Truth of the Christian Religion.*

John Wallis, in the preface to another of Mather's oft-cited sources, Samuel Clarke's *Marrow of Ecclesiastical History*, wrote of this emergent power implicit in the imagery of flowers, bees, and hives:

> And now (Christian Reader) craving pardon for our tediousness, whereby thou hast been long detained out of this pleasant Garden, we desire that God's direction and blessing may accompany thy passage through it: that whilst thou seest thy self surrounded with sweet and fragrant flowers, thou mayest adore the inexhaustible fulness of Jesus Christ, from whom all graces and consolations do continually flow. And because an inward and supernatural principle is necessary to the right improvement of such helps, (as the Bee by an innate quality, which other creatures want, maketh Honey out of Flowers) we commend thee to the God of all Grace, that by the abilities of his Spirit, thou mayst be abundantly benefited in spiritual respects, by the Serious surveying of this useful book. ("To the Reader" n.pag.)

Although Wallis here has the bee making the honey, the "inward and supernatural principle" at work in the commonplace-book tradition was usually more vaguely associated with the long storage and repeated affirmation of wise and informative passages. Hugo Grotius, in the conclusion to his "Prolegomena" to Stobaeus' *Anthologion/Florilegium* (lv) affirmed the authority of gathered quotations that grow stronger over time. Long endurance proved vitality and strength. In the long tradition of Aristotelian historiography, this is the power of time-testing, the power of consensus through time. Mather, in the *Magnalia*, quoted Cicero's time-honored definition of history: "History is Time's witness, the messenger of Antiquity, the lamp of Truth and embodied soul of Memory, the guide of human life" (94).

In one of Mather's shorter hives called *The Good Old Way or Christianity described appearing in lives of primitive Christians and Ancient Church History*, he declared that "the *Idea of Primitive Christianity* ... shall be fetched from the *Lives* of the more *genuine Christians*" (11). He would fetch them "by Raising the *Primitive Christians* out of their *Graves* and Setting them in the midst of our Congregation" (5). This is one of Mather's most striking depictions of his role as historian. He helps dead people speak to the living. As in the pamphlet, his massive and complex "Biblia" allowed ancient and foreign writers to emerge with authority. Mather, the commonplace-book historian, often cited quotations at second hand from other commonplace-book historians. Often there are multi-layers of citations that have carried an ancient or foreign author through history and across space before Mather gathers that citation into his collection. Authority emerges in the consensus of many citations. Bee-like, the historian participates in the mysterious production of honey. Every generation and every place needed its own commonplace-book history in order to both participate in the long tradition and fetch what was to be had at that particular time and place. Maybe this is one of the reasons Mather titled his "Biblia" so particularly as *American*. Whatever the full extent of his purpose and meanings, Mather meant for the "Biblia Americana" to be a personal help to himself and his readers. When advising young men to fetch together their own commonplace-books, Mather told them: "if you live to *Old Age*, you will find, that, like Old *Photius*, you have prepared an *Hive* then to live upon" (*Manuductio* 72).

Photius was a ninth-century collector of quotes who modeled his work on St. Basil the Great who had, in the fourth century, offered the metaphor of the flower-picker and bee in support of "plucking the blooms" from classical literature. Mather, by linking himself and his readers through the hive image to Photius, brings into view the ancient models for the "Biblia."[3] Systematic thinking about historical flower-picking was rooted in the ancients, most influentially in Aristotle's *Topics* and *Rhetoric*, two works known to every schoolboy in the early modern era. The garden images were promoted by a Stoic-Christian alliance that was also well known to schoolboys. Mather had only to mention a "hive," and his readers knew the tradition to which he referred.

The "Biblia Americana" manifests a type of pre-modern or rhetoric-based Aristotelian historiographical tradition. *Anthologies* and *florilegia* were rooted in Aristotle's belief that there was a large category of knowledge that was social, not individual. An individual philosopher or mathematician might know much by intuition or self-evident truths. An individual naturalist or physicist might figure out lots of things by using his senses. However, if one wanted information about past events, distant lands, foreign customs, or ancient wisdom, an investigator could not do it alone. The investigator had to gather ready-made, already fully-formed information from people, living or dead, in oral or written form. Knowledge that could be worked-up by oneself was called *invented*. Knowledge already worked up and gained from a human source was called *exploited*. The former was *internal* and the latter was *external*. The former, which could be produced by one's own skill or art, was *artificial*. The latter was *inartificial*. The former Aristotle labeled *technical* (*entechnoi* / εντεχνοι) and the latter *non-technical* (*atechnoi* / ατεχνοι). At Harvard college when Increase and Cotton Mather were intimately involved with the curriculum, the distinction was taught in all three types of humanist logic textbooks: Aristotelian, Ramist, and Cartesian.[4]

Aristotle most clearly described this distinction in his *Rhetoric* where he further declared that the gathering of *non-technical* information from external sources was the method most suitable for investigation of the past, what Aristotle called forensics (dikanikon / δικανικόν). Aristotle went further to distin-

---

3   St. Photius I (c. 810–93) collected 279 extracts from classical authors in his *Bibliotheca or Myriobiblon*. See St. Basil the Great (c.330–79) ("To Young Men" 4.391).
4   For an overview of the whole history of this textbook tradition, see Kennedy, *History of Reasonableness*. For these distinctions taught at Harvard between 1675 and 1735, see Kennedy and Knoles (199–201) and Kennedy, *Aristotelian and Cartesian Logic at Harvard* (169, 227–30, 313–14).

guish two types external sources or witnesses: "some ancient, some modern." Ancient witnesses he vaguely described as "poets and all those other famous men whose judgment are well known" (*Rhetoric* 1375b; 1.15.13). Modern witnesses were good for establishing modern facts while ancient testimony carried more authority and wisdom. Either way, the work of the forensic investigator was to gather testimony from witnesses, dead or alive. When Mather called the "Biblia" a "hive" he used a code word with a visual reference. Mather taking notes at the harbor bookshop, the bee flitting among flowers, the flower-picker wandering in literary fields are visual representation for what can also be schematically visualized by diagramming passages in Aristotle's *Rhetoric* (Figure 1). The "Biblia Americana," in light of this diagram, is a huge Aristotelian project of historical-social investigation.

Figure 1.
Commonplace-book History in Aristotle's *Rhetoric*
1358 (1.1.3) & 1368–77 (1.10–15)

Three Types of Oratory
Based on three types of hearers

Spectator in Present	Judging the Future	**Judging the Past**
Display	Deliberative	**Forensic**
ἐπιδεικτικόν	συμβουλευτικόν	**δικανικόν**
About the present	About the future	**About the past**

All three need to use 2 types of information, 1356 (I.ii.2)

Invented	**Exploited**
εντεχνοί	ατεχνοί
Technical	**Non-Technical**
Artificial	**Inartificial**

"Non-technical proofs are a peculiarity of forensic"

Ancient witnesses   Modern witnesses

This sterile scheme was easily translated into garden imagery with *non-technical* information represented by flowers and pollen, and *non-technical proofs* represented as something to be gathered from fields of testifiers. This was done most flippantly by Aulus Gellius (c. 125-after 180) in *The Attic Nights*, a sort-of extended commonplace book that became a popular collection of short essays. Gellius wrote that he "made notes from books known as *Chronicles*" and planned "to strew" his *Attic Nights* ... lightly here and there with a few of these flowers of history (*historiae flosculis*)" (17.21.1). Tore Janson, in *Latin Prose Prefaces: Studies in Literary Conventions*, cites Gellius as a source for later Latin flower-picking imagery (81–83).[5] Greek imagery reaches back at least to Isocrates, a contemporary of Aristotle. He was the first we know of who associated bees and flowers with dialectic and rhetoric. Isocrates had "the bee settling on all the flowers, and sipping the best from each" as an example of gathering useful knowledge from all sources (1.52). A natural-history book associated with Aristotle, *Parts of Animals*, declared that bees "are more intelligent than many animals" (2.2). One of the great passages in Aristotle's *Politics* compares the intellectual powers of humans to bees: "And why man is a political animal in a greater measure than any bee or any gregarious animal is clear. For nature, as we declare, does nothing without purpose; and man alone of the animals possesses speech" (1253a.5–10; 1.1.10). Lucretius, in the first century before Christ, had a bee on flowery glades sipping the words of eternal life from Epicurus (3.11).

The Stoic-Christian alliance with dialectic and rhetoric enhanced the metaphysical depth in these images by linking them to the tradition that storage and retrieval systems had a mysterious power to confirm, encourage, and advance truth. Flower pickers and honey bees were not uncommon in early Christian historical writing. Aristotle had earlier infused all his thought with belief in purposefulness, an infusion that greatly facilitated its subsequent Christianization. He believed gregariousness, consensus over time, to have emergent power. Aristotle had a teleological optimism that truth was more persuasive than error, that truth outs itself when it stands the test of time, and is best seen in agreements between authorities (Guthrie 106–12). His writings also, as W.K.C. Guthrie notes, show "constant anxiety to give due consideration to the opinions of others" and "defiant championship of the *consensus omnium*" (91).[6] The later Latin term *consensus omnium* invokes the optimum situation in which there is greater likelihood of truth in consensus. In Christian tradition the Holy Spirit was considered to be evident in consensus, whether evident in an unanimous vote in favor of a creed or bishop or by the development of agreement around

5   Gellius' *Attic Nights* was one among many handbooks written "to help readers shine at cultured tables."
6   See also Oehler (234–71, esp. 237–41).

the canon of scriptures or rights of the church. In the vague stoicism of Roman government, the unanimity of the *vox populi* or the consensus of SPQR (Senate and the People of Rome) had within it a transcendent power. Mather's beloved Congregational system has roots in this Aristotelian assumption.

Aristotle, however, was more subtle than the term *consensus omnium* indicates. In *Topics* Aristotle valued "general opinions" (100a.25–100b.25). In *Nicomachean Ethics*, he wrote that authority should be accorded to "all, the majority, or the most notable and illustrious" of the philosophers, and to "the undemonstrated remarks and beliefs of experienced and older people" (1143b.5–15). In *Politics*, Aristotle plucked fact after fact from old histories expecting that such gathered-up facts would manifest a truth. "History shows," Jowett has him declare in his translation of "φανερόν δ' ἐκ τῶν συμβεβηκότων." Rackham in the Loeb edition has "this is manifest from the facts of history" (Jowett 216; Rackham 439). The word, συμβαινω / *sumbaino*, implies the act of agreement and consensus as an aspect of knowledge about past events. Discussing the history of education, Aristotle cited the authority of the "witness of ancients" (ἀρχαίων ... μαρτυρίαν) using essentially the same terms that he used in *Rhetoric* when he declared that "ancient witnesses (παλαιοί ... μαρτυριῶν) are the most trustworthy of all, for they cannot be corrupted" (*Politics* 8.3.1; *Rhetoric* 1.15.17). Quintilian, following Aristotle, found wisdom in majorities. "The safest and most rational course," Quintilian advised on one debatable issue, is "to follow the authority of the majority" (3.4.12). Cassiodorus, when recommending old respected books, wrote, in the preface to the first book of his *Institutions*, "It will always be better for you not to be drinking in striking novelty; but to satisfy yourself at the spring of the ancients" (4). Following Aristotle, Cassiodorus taught that "credence is sought in the words and actions of our ancestors by recalling the words and deeds of the ancients" (2.2.16). Quintilian wrote, "As for antiquity, it is commended to us by the possession of a certain majesty, I might almost say sanctity." Famed orators and historians should be accorded special authority. "Even error brings no disgrace, if it results from treading in the footsteps of such distinguished guides" (1.6.1–3).[7] Ancient traditions have the mystical authority of growing consensus through time. One ancient tradition was to envision this ancient tradition in the life of bees.

For early modern historians, Lucius Annaeus Seneca in his *Epistulae* (84) offered the classic bee and honeycomb image to encourage scholarly bookishness. "Reading," he declared, "is indispensible." It

> nourishes the mind and refreshes it when it is wearied with study; nevertheless, this refreshment is not obtained without study. ... We should follow, men say, the exam-

---

7 "*Vetera maiestas quaedam et, ut sic dixerim, religio commendat.*" The following quote refers directly only to orators, but in context refers to historians too: "*... et velut error honestus est magnos duces sequentibus. ... Omnia tamen haec exigent acre iudicum.*"

ple of the bees, who flit about and cull the flowers that are suitable for producing honey, and then arrange and assort in their cells all that they have brought in. ... It is not certain whether the juice which [the bees] obtain from the flowers forms at once into honey, or whether [the bees] change that which they have gathered into this delicious object by blending something therewith and by a certain property of their breath. ... We also, I say, ought to copy these bees, and sift whatever we have gathered from a varied course of reading, for such things are better preserved if they are kept separate; then, by applying the supervising care with which our nature has endowed us, – in other words, our natural gifts, – we should also blend those several flavours into one delicious compound that, even though it betrays its origin, yet it nevertheless is clearly a different thing from that whence it came. (2: 277–79)

The writings of Seneca were well known by Mather. A common tradition held that Seneca and St. Paul knew each other in Rome. St. Jerome included Seneca in "the list of the Saints" because letters between Paul and Seneca that had been read by many gave him "just cause" to include him.[8] Similarities between Seneca and Paul were key to a sense of a Christian commonality with Stoicism. Mather was critical of Stoics in the "Biblia" discussion in Acts 17 because of their "spiritual pride." In general, however, he appreciated the ideas that were compatible with Christianity – especially those in Seneca's letters and moral essays [BA, Acts 17:27].

Important for understanding Mather's description of the "Biblia" as a "Common Hive" is to note that he did not place as much emphasis as Seneca did on the powers of the honey bee. In The Christian Philosopher, Mather offered his readers a short compendium on "these industrious and marvelous Creatures!" He compared a bee to "an exquisite Chymist, or at least a diligent Purveyor and Collector of the Honey-dews, provided by Heaven for him on the Leaves of the Plants in the Field, which he lays up in convenient Cells." The bee, for Mather, participates in the making of honey, but his emphasis was on the gathering and storing. Mather quoted Aristotle that bees should be reckoned "among the ζωα πολιτικά, or Civil People" (162).

In his Miscellanies (Stromateis), as a collection of essays on the relationship of human and divine learning, Clement of Alexandria used agrarian images throughout. He compares the philosopher to "the wild olive" needing to be "engrafted in the truly fair and merciful Word" (6.15). He encouraged scholars to think of his Miscellanies as "promiscuously variegated like a meadow." He further encouraged readers to gather from his work that which the researcher "will turn out to his benefit and advantage" (6.1). After writing on the importance of training in the arts then the relationship of theology and philosophy, Clement wrote how the student can become productive and able to see the truth.

---

8   See Sevenster (6–25, esp. 11–12).

"Go to the bee," he declared, "and learn how laborious she is; for she, feeding on the whole meadow, produces one honeycomb" (1.6).[9]

Eusebius of Caesarea was Mather's most influential model of historiography. Eusebius's *History of the Church* is one of the most innovative books in the development of ancient history-writing. Arnaldo Momigliano writes that "a new chapter of historiography begins with Eusebius not only because he invented ecclesiastical history, but because he wrote it with a documentation which is utterly different from that of the pagan historians" (92).[10] Momigliano sees in Eusebius the roots of our modern usage of quotes and footnotes. Momigliano is right to see these roots, but we here need to note that these roots were in the commonplace-book tradition of clunky accumulations of long quotations. Eusebius, Jerome noted, wrote a book on *topics* that is now lost, and we can see the careful use of Aristotle's principles of *non-technical proofs* being applied to subjects throughout the book. Eusebius had extensive concern for various types of witnesses as evidence, the traditions connecting generations of witnesses, and the growing tradition of a canon of scriptures used by a consensus of churches.[11] In the introduction to his *The History of the Church*, he wrote the most famous flower-picker line in history: "Thus from the scattered hints dropped by my predecessors I have picked out whatever seems relevant to the task I have undertaken, plucking like flowers in literary pastures the contributions of earlier writers, to be embodied in the continuous narrative I have in mind" (12).

St. Jerome, who fetched together a collection of *Lives of Illustrious Men*, a grab bag of information about 135 Christian authors, linked the principles and method of his historical work to Eusebius. Like Eusebius he has no bees, only flowers. Jerome complained that his collection of *lives* was harder to create than earlier models by Suetonius, Varro, and Cicero because "They, opening the old histories and chronicles could, as if gathering from some great meadow, weave some small crown at least for their work" (359). They had easier access to sources.

When Jerome wrote that his pagan predecessors wove crowns out of easily picked flowers, he was tapping into an old image used by Plutarch in an essay to young boys called "On Listening to Lectures":

> One ought, therefore, to strip off the superfluity and inanity from the style, and to seek after the fruit itself, imitating not women that make garlands, but the bees. For

---

9   Grant (28–29) comments on Eusebius's connection to Clement's bee. It is not a stretch to see the meadow image as a Roman agrarian analogy for Aristotle's *topics*. Clark (3–14) writes that though Clement rarely gave much credit to Aristotle, he used Aristotelian *topics* when writing on the definition of faith. She also notes that Clement's dialectic links him directly to Aristotelian pedagogical literature if not Aristotle himself.

10   See also Grafton and Williams.

11   See especially Eusebius (III).

those women, culling flower-clusters and sweet-scented leaves, intertwine and plait them, and produce something which is pleasant enough but short-lived and fruitless; whereas the bees in their flight frequently pass through meadows of violets, roses, and hyacinths, and come to rest upon the exceeding rough and pungent thyme, and on this they settle close, and when they have got something of use, they fly away home to their own special work. (41.8)

For Plutarch, the flower imagery was more feminine and less substantial than the work of bees. On the other hand, Eusebius did not claim to be a bee. He claimed to be a flower-picker, and his *Church History* became a standard model for history chock full of many voices in long quotations. Cassiodorus, the historiographical founder of "national history," used the flower-picking analogy twice, maybe three times. The first two come in the *Variae*, describing his authorship of the *History of the Goths*.[12] "From Gothic origins," Cassiodorus claims to have "made a Roman history, gathering, as it were, into one garland, flower-buds that had previously been scattered throughout fields of literature" (*Variae* 9.4–5). Cassiodorus's second use of the image is in the preface to his *Variae* where he again describes his *History of the Goths*. In Barnish's translation, Cassiodorus reports that he composed "the history of the Goths in twelve books, anthologizing their successes" (11). The third use of the flower-picking and weaving image comes at the conclusion of Jordanes's *Gothic History*: "I have followed the writings of my ancestors, and have culled a few flowers from their broad meadows to weave a chaplet for him who cares to know these things" (316). Jordanes is the named author, but Jordanes wrote that he was remembering Cassiodorus' text.

Cotton Mather's description of the "Biblia Americana" as "this *Common Hive*" carries a lot of freight. The programmatic image roots him in the structure of Aristotelian rhetoric and connects him with the historiographical commonplace-book tradition promoted by authors that Mather honored such as Seneca, Clement, Eusebius, Jerome, and Cassiodorus. Gentle garden imagery supplied code words within the tradition. Subtle distinctions such as whether flower-weaving was feminine compared to the bee or the amount of influence the bee had in the production of honey would have been known to readers of Plutarch and Seneca; however, the usefulness of the garden imagery was the picture it gave to Aristotelian historiographical methods and assumptions. The historian in this tradition is primarily a gatherer who trusts the power of truth to make itself known better by such gatherings.

Mather wrote that he "make unto the Church of God an humble Tender of our BIBLIA AMERICANA" (*Magnalia* 105–06). Typical of Mather, he made

---

12   For Cassiodorus as the creator of national history see Kelley (106), Goffart (105), and Markus (5). Momigliano explores deeper roots in "Fabius Pictor and the Origins of National History" (80–108).

a show of being humble. However, when describing the "Biblia," he accurately presented it as something he gathered more than he wrote. More than any other work of his, he took care to point his readers to his sources. It is a massively humble work. Mather understood himself to be a historian of the flower-picking, honey-bee type, more a gatherer and organizer than writer. In the "Biblia," more carefully than anywhere else in his publications, he directed his readers to his sources and humbly limited his own comments. He trusted truth to out itself.

Of the thousands of long historical digressions in the "Biblia," his long discussion of "The *Wisdome of the Egyptians*" is an example of Mather at his best within the flower-picking, pollen-gathering tradition. Given a reference to this wisdom in Acts 7:22, Mather wrote that Dr. Thomas Burnet "has bestowed a chapter on it" in his *Archeologiae*.[13] Mather culls from Burnet, maybe while standing in a bookstall, four distinct, tightly-packed pages that he later inserted into the already bulging manuscript of the "Biblia." Mather gathered from Burnet information about Egyptian mathematics, astronomy, agriculture, medicine, music, philosophy, theology, and mythology. He included a section on how we know what we know about ancient Egyptians and how the Egyptians influenced the Greeks and Hebrews. He bemoans Egyptian idolatry and intellectual decline. "'Tis pitty," he ends, "that we have Lost the Writings of *Severus*, a Roman Sophist mentioned by *Suidas* who travelled over *Egypt*, & compiled what he found in all its Monuments" [*BA*, Acts 7:22]. The long section is informative and fair and gathered out of a named source.

The *Suidas* mentioned at the end as an information gatherer adds to our understanding of Mather's necessary humility. *Suidas* is a book, not a person, an error that lived long in commonplace-book tradition. The *Souda* was a tenth-century Byzantine philological commonplace-book, a massive encyclopedia and dictionary. Today it is online.[14] In early eighteenth-century Boston, Cotton Mather had no access to such a work. He learned of it through Burnet, who heard of it from some other commonplace-book history promulgating in the erroneous tradition of it being a person rather than a book.

David Levin described Mather as "essentially a faithful historian" who gathered from sources and was "a consistently intelligent editor and reporter whose paraphrases and summaries are remarkably free of distortion" (255). The "Biblia Americana" in its entirety is overwhelming and extends Stievermann's interpretation of Cotton Mather as a historian desirous "To Conquer All Things." But in page after page in the "Biblia" we can see the truth of Mather's characterization of himself as humble gatherer trusting layers of other gatherers for information. The book has no single authorial voice. Its authority emerges

---

13   See Burnet's *Archeologiae Philosophicae*.
14   http://www.stoa.org/sol/

in the fact that it is a hive. Cotton Mather understood the historiographical tradition within which he worked. Like a flower-picker and a honey-bee, he gathered and believed that something good would come of it.

Works Cited

Primary Sources

Aristotle. *Nichomachean Ethics*. Trans. Terence Irwin. Indianapolis: Hackett Publishing, 1985.
–. *Parts of Animals*. Trans. A.L. Peck. Cambridge: Harvard UP, 1955.
–. *Politics*. Trans. H. Rackham. Cambridge: Harvard UP, 1932.
–. *Politics*. Trans. Benjamin Jowett. Mineola: Dover Publications, 2000.
–. *Rhetoric*. Trans. H.C. Lawson-Tancred. New York: Penguin, 1991.
–. *Topica*. Trans. E.S. Forster. Cambridge: Harvard UP, 1960.
Basil the Great, St. "To Young Men, On How They Might Derive Profit From Pagan Literature." *The Letters*. Trans. Roy J. Deferrari and Martin R.P. McGuire. Cambridge: Loeb Classical Library, 1970.
Burnet, Thomas. *Archeologiae Philosophicae*. London, 1692.
Cassiodorus. *Institutions of Divine and Secular Learning and On the Soul*. Trans. James W. Halporn. Liverpool: Liverpool UP, 2004.
–. *The* Variae *of Magnus Aurelius Cassiodorus Senator*. Trans. S.J.B. Barnish. Liverpool: Liverpool UP, 1992.
Clement of Alexandria. "The Stromata." Trans. Roberts-Donaldson. *Early Christian Writings*. Web. 10 Sept. 2009.
Eusebius. *The History of the Church*. Trans. G.A. Williamson. Rev. Trans. Andrew Louth. New York: Penguin Classics, 1989.
Gellius, Aulus. *The Attic Nights of Aulus Gellius*. Trans. John C. Rolfe. Cambridge: Loeb Classical Library, 1927.
Grotius, Hugo. "Prolegomena." In Johann Strobaeus. *Anthology*. Ed. Thomas Gaisford. Oxford: Clarendon, 1822.
Isocrates. "To Demonicus." *Isocrates*. Trans. George Norlin. 3 vols. Cambridge: Loeb Classical Library, 1980.
Jerome. "Lives of Illustrious Men." *Nicene and Post-Nicene Fathers of the Christian Church*. Trans. Ernest Cushing Richardson. Vol. 3. 2nd ed. Grand Rapids: Eerdmans, 1979. 359–84.
Jordanes. *The Gothic History of Jordanes*. Trans. Charles Christopher Mierow. Princeton: Princeton UP, 1915.
Lucretius. *De Rerum Natura*. Trans W.H.D. Rouse and M.F. Smith. Cambridge: Loeb Classical Library, 1935.
Mather, Cotton. *The Christian Philosopher*. 1721. Ed. Winton U. Solberg. Urbana: U of Illinois P, 1994.
–. *Diary of Cotton Mather*. Ed. Worthington Chaucey Ford. 2 vols. Massachusetts Historical Society Collections (Seventh Series, Vol. VII–VIII). Boston: MHS, 1911–12.

–. *The Good Old Way or Christianity described … appearing in lives of the primitive Christians. …* Boston, 1706.

–. *Magnalia Christi Americana* (Books I and II). Ed. Kenneth B. Murdock. Cambridge: Harvard UP, 1977.

–. *Manuductio ad Adminsterium: Directions for a Candidate of the Ministry.* Ed. Thomas J. Holmes and Kenneth B. Murdock. New York: Columbia UP, 1938.

–. *A New Offer to the Lovers of Religion and Learning.* Boston, 1714.

Plutarch. "On Listening to Lectures." *Moralia.* Trans. Frank Cole Babbitt. Cambridge: Loeb Classical Library, 1927.

Quintilian, *Institutio Oratoria.* Trans. H. E. Butler. Cambridge: Harvard UP, 1920.

Scott, John. *An Appeal to the Understanding of the Meanest Capacities for the Truth of the Christian Religion.* London, 1728.

Seneca. *Ad Lucilium Epistulae Morales.* Trans. Richard M. Gummere. 3 vols. Cambridge: Harvard UP, 1920.

Wallis, John and Simeon Ash. "To the Reader." In Samuel Clarke. *The Marrow of Ecclesiastical History.* London, 1654.

Secondary Sources

Clark, Elizabeth. *Clement's Use of Aristotle: The Aristotelian Contribution to Clement of Alexandria's Refutation of Gnosticism.* New York: Edwin Mellen Press, 1977.

Gay, Peter. *A Loss of Mastery: Puritan Historians in Colonial America.* New York: Vintage Books, 1968.

Goffart, Walter. *The Narrators of Barbarian History A. S. 550–800: Jordanes, Gregory of Tours, Bede, and Paul the Deacon.* Princeton: Princeton UP, 1988.

Grafton, Anthony and Megan Williams. *Christianity and the Transformation of the Book: Origen, Eusebius, and the Library of Caesarea.* Cambridge: Harvard UP, 2006.

Grant, Robert M. *Eusebius as Church Historian.* Eugene: Wipf & Stock, 2006.

Guthrie, W. K. C. "Aristotle: An Encounter." *A History of Greek Philosophy.* Vol. 6. Cambridge: Cambridge UP, 1981.

Janson, Tore. *Latin Prose Prefaces: Studies in Literary Conventions.* Stockholm: Alquist & Wiksell, 1961.

Kelley, Donald R. *Faces of History: Historical Inquiry from Herodotus to Herder.* New Haven: Yale UP, 1999.

Kennedy, Rick. *Aristotelian and Cartesian Logic at Harvard: Charles Morton's* A Logick System *and William Brattle's* Compendium of Logic. Boston: Colonial Society of Massachusetts, 1995.

–. "Faith, the Conference on Faith and History, and Aristotelian Historiography." *Fides et Historia* 41 (2009): 1–21.

–. *A History of Reasonableness: Testimony and Authority in the Art of Thinking.* Rochester: U of Rochester P, 2004.

– and Thomas Knoles. "Increase Mather's 'Catechismus Logicus': An Analysis of the Role of a Ramist Catechism." *Proceedings of the American Antiquarian Society* 109 (1999): 145–223.

Levin, David. *Cotton Mather: The Young Life of the Lord's Remembrance, 1663–1703.* Cambridge.: Harvard UP, 1978.

Lewis, C. S. *The Discarded Image: An Introduction to Medieval and Renaissance Literature*. Cambridge: Cambridge UP, 1964.

Lovejoy, Arthur O. "The Parallel of Deism and Classicism." *Essays in the History of Ideas*. Baltimore: Johns Hopkins UP, 1948. 78–98.

Markus, R. A. "Bede and the Tradition of Ecclesiastical History." *The Jarrow Lecture 1975*. Jarrow: U of Durham P, 1976.

Momigliano, Arnaldo. *The Conflict between Paganism and Christianity in the Fourth Century*. Oxford: Clarendon, 1963.

–. "Fabius Pictor and the Origins of National History." *The Classical Foundations of Modern Historiography*. Berkeley: U of California P, 1990.

Moss, Ann. *Printed Commonplace-Books and the Structuring of Renaissance Thought*. Oxford: Clarendon, 1996.

Oehler, Klaus. "*De Consensus Omnium* als Kriterium der Wahrheit in der Antiken Philosophie und der Patristik." *Antike Philosophie und Byzantinisches Mittelalter: Aufsätze zur Geschichte des Griechischen Denkens*. Munich: Beck, 1969. 234–71.

Suda On Line: Byzantine Lexicography. Web. 10 Sept. 2009.

Sevenster, J. N. *Paul and Seneca*. Leiden: Brill, 1961.

Stievermann, Jan. "Writing 'To Conquer All Things': Cotton Mather's *Magnalia Christi Americana* and the Quandary of *Copia*." *Early American Literature* 39.2 (2004): 263–97.

Van Cromphout, Gustaaf. "Cotton Mather: The Puritan Historian as Renaissance Humanist." *American Literature* 49 (1977): 327–37.

KENNETH P. MINKEMA

"Flee From Idols": Cotton Mather and the Historical Books

The happy lot that has fallen to me as a member of the editorial team of Cotton Mather's "Biblia Americana" is the Historical Books – actually, the Historical Books "Lite," because my assignment begins with Joshua and ends, not with Esther, but with Chronicles. The following brings together a preliminary reading of the entries for these books, giving a taste of Mather's range and erudition in just this one section, but also, more importantly, of the potential that his reflections on the Historical Books hold for more extensive study. To these ends, this essay provides a brief overview of some of the methods and themes Mather explored in his commentary on these books, and then focuses in on a frequent topic – namely, idols and idolatry – that reached into several areas of inquiry for Mather and for biblical commentators and critics of his day.

Mather on Joshua-Chronicles

First, to quantify just a little, in this part of the second of the six manuscript volumes of the "Biblia," Mather amassed some 1250 entries on Joshua through Chronicles over some 500 manuscript leaves, which translates into a transcript, preserving original line lengths, that amounts to nearly 1600 pages. Entries vary from a single sentence to as long as ten leaves containing ten thousand words (for instance, essays on the apparent inconsistencies in the Historical Books or on the distinctions between prophets, seers, and discerners).[1] Within this run, Kings accounts for nearly one third of the total entries. Samuel and Chronicles each warrant about three-quarters of the entries devoted to Kings (that is, about 300 entries each on Samuel and Chronicles, compared to 400 for Kings) – this, despite the fact that Kings is the shortest of these three "twinned" books.[2] On the other side of the spectrum, not surprisingly, is the book of Ruth, on which there are only six entries, though the last one, on the

---

1 On Mather's understanding of prophets, see Smolinski ("Authority and Interpretation"). See also Calvin's reflections on prophets and seers in the preface to *A commentary upon the prophecie of Isaiah.*
2 Of course, biblical scholars before and after Mather tell us that originally Kings and Chronicles, and possibly Samuel, were each one book, but were divided when translated into Greek.

union of Boaz and Ruth, runs to some eight leaves on the nature and strictures of Leviratic matrimony.

Some of the topics Mather covers at length were right in keeping with what synoptic commentators of the late seventeenth century likewise took pains to explicate: Joshua's making the sun stand still; the exploits of Samson; the height of Goliath and the weight of his armor and weapons, and the sacrifice of Jephthah's daughter. Yet Mather's manner of treating these topics could be distinctive. If we look at only one of these incidents in the biblical narrative – Joshua's making the sun stand still (Josh. 10:13–14) – as representative, we see what Reiner Smolinski ("Natural Science and Interpretation" 324–27) describes as Mather's "ambidextrous approach," in which he neither denied nor insisted on the miraculous nature of the event but rather attributed the description of it to "poetical hyperbole." Compare this with the more conservative Matthew Henry (39, col. 1), who in his gloss on the text referred simply to the "miraculous Arrest of the Sun" and treated the event as an instance of the efficacy of prayer and of the Spirit's inspiration. Or, compare it to Jonathan Edwards (129–31), who in his treatment of the passage was most expansive in identifying the typological elements of the incident, specifically, the sun as Christ and the moon as the church.

Other exegetical strategies likewise reflected Mather's addressing of controversial passages in a manner that built on tradition but also contained some inimitable twist or feature of his own. As part of the effort to defend the veracity and accuracy of the biblical texts against the rising tide of rationalist criticism led by Thomas Hobbes, Baruch Spinoza, Richard Simon, and others, Mather was concerned with reconciling the seeming discrepancies in the historical accounts and explaining the dizzying genealogies of the various kings and the lengths of their reigns (see Frampton; Scholder). Also, he offered what he called "evangelical illustrations" on occasion, the most dramatic instance being the entry on 2 Kings 6:38, which provided no less than seventy topics for pious meditation from the House of God in Jerusalem, "digested" from John Bunyan's *Solomon's Temple Spiritualized*. Even so, Mather sought for the most part to let the Hebrew texts speak for themselves, at least in his commentary on these particular books. An exception, not a surprising one, was his interest in maintaining the link between the testaments through typology, clearly evident in entries treating Joshua, Gideon, Samson, Ruth, David, Elijah, Elisha, Solomon, and other figures and events as types of Christ, the church, or other aspects of the gospel dispensation; these two dozen or so entries constitute the great majority in which the name of Jesus is even mentioned.[3]

---

3   Mather drew materials for these entries on personal types from Samuel Mather's *The Figures or Types of the Old Testament*. For parallels on Joshua, as an example, see pp. 100–103 and the entry on Josh. 24:33 in the "Biblia."

Mather also exhibited the contemporary interest in ancient Hebrew life-style and society, which included everything from their articles of clothing to the architecture of their houses and tombs to the order and method of their worship. In this sense, he was part of the movement that Jonathan Sheehan calls "antiquarian biblical scholarship," which focused on customs, practices, and languages of biblical times in response to radical and liberal challenges (*Enlightenment Bible* 20, 23; see also his "Sacred and Profane"). This scholarship included entire treatises on the most minute topics – Mather himself (in the entry on Judg. 3:23) whimsically remarked entire books describing the shoes, shoe-buckles, rings, earrings, and gloves of God's chosen people – because even such mundane objects lent themselves to spiritualization. Here, as with Mather's spiritualization of Solomon's Temple, we can speculate that he had a dual purpose: asserting the verity of the received biblical text against the rising tide of critics, as well as providing sources of spiritual contemplation for pious readers.

Other entries reflected the various disciplines Mather adopted. Though the seventeenth century saw a temporary downturn in Middle Eastern travel journals written by Europeans, Mather nonetheless had an eye to geography, explaining the locations of cities and features mentioned in Scripture that were lost (see Krieger). At the end of Joshua, where Mather gave a lengthy "choreography," as he described it, of the conquered Promised Land, he even included a printed fold-out map of the Holy Land (taken from Nicholaes Visscher the Elder's *Terra Sancta*). Drawing on mathematics professor George Reynold's publications, Mather presented estimates of David's wealth, of Solomon's annual revenue (142 million pounds sterling, which translates to nearly 24 billion in 2007 Euros, or $33 billion), and of the cost of the Temple (1.3 billion pounds sterling, or over 218 billion Euros, or $300 billion).

Still other topics are perhaps more stereotypically, though of course not exclusively, Mather. Fine examples of these, for those interested in Mather primarily because of his relation to witchhunts – and you know who you are – are entries on Saul and the witch of Endor, or on the wizard Apollonius Tyaneaus. The angelic realm makes its appearance as well, as in the entry on Judg. 6:22, in which Mather identified the "stars in their courses" as "the ministry of angels." Likewise, the "ambushments" described in 2 Chron. 20:22 that Jehovah set against Judah's enemies were, for Mather, angels in disguise.

Fallen angels were among the cast of characters as well. The "ambushments" entry, written a few months after the Salem witchcraft episode had subsided, led Mather to relate an incident that occurred "when the Troubles from the *Invisible World* were upon us": in the sky above the town of Gloucester appeared spectral French soldiers who fired many "Smart guns" on the townspeople, who, Mather claimed, still had in their possession some of the balls fired at them. Mather's explanation was that these specters were demons (though, it must be said, conventional British wisdom barely distinguished between devils and the French).[4]

Idolatry in the Historical Books

As the reader can see, there is no lack of topics to pursue. But let us zero in on one that seems to be key not only by virtue of the number of times Mather returns to it but by its relevance to contemporary scholarly, polemical, and apologetic concerns, namely, the theme of idols and idolatry. Certainly, the frequency with which false gods, idolatrous worship, and related occult and magical practices appear in the Historical Books made the topic virtually unavoidable, and the single most prominent theme could be said to be the respective fates of those who follow Yahweh or other gods. Even so, Mather explored the topic with marked frequency and depth. In this regard, he was riding the wave of seventeenth-century scholarship. Frank Manuel, for example, has noted the

> vast literature, primarily English and Dutch, on the idolatrous practices mentioned in the Bible. With the aid of rabbinic sources a valiant effort was made to identify, describe, and catalogue the abominable rituals which were merely mentioned in the Hebrew text. The same passion for collecting which lay behind the gathering of botanical specimens and culminated in Linnaeus possessed the scholars who grouped the rituals and "superstitious" practices of universal paganism (8).[5]

If this evidence plays into the popular image of Mather as consumed with dark forces, it also locates him squarely within the early Enlightenment as well as Pietistic efforts to identify practical meanings for Christians individually and collectively.

Even a quick reading of the Historical Books reveals the ease with which the Hebrews and Israelites could dilute or abandon the worship of the true God, often adopting the deities and practices of surrounding peoples.[6] In other words, the Historical Books, as so many other histories, were written by the "winners" (see Assmann). Mather discussed the origin and nature of false gods, the wor-

---

4 Mather included a first-hand version of this episode (by Rev. John Emerson of Gloucester) entitled "A Faithful Account of many Wonderful and Surprising Things, which happened in the Town of Glocester, in the Year, 1692" in *Decennium Luctuosum*. In his afterword to the "Faithful Account," he referred to 2 Chron. 20:22 and the likelihood of angelic ministry (see content parallels in the first paragraph of this entry and in *Decennium Luctuosum* 112). See also "Niles's History of the Indian and French Wars" (231–32); Swan (160–65); Norton (231–32).

5 Some of the figures Manuel refers to include John Selden, John Spencer, Gerhard Vossius, Pierre Jurieu, Hermann Witsius and Pierre-Daniel Huet.

6 More recent scholarship has posited that many of the deities and magical practices utilized by the Hebrews and Israelites were actually cultural continuities from Egypt and elsewhere, or the religion of the "strangers" who accompanied the Hebrews out of Egypt, which were challenged and eventually overcome by the Yahwehists. See, for example, LaRocca-Pitts.

ship of them, their priests, and related topics, as part of the cyclical, inverse relationships between the rise, decline, and re-establishment of the worship of the one true God and the many false gods. He wrote no less than fifty entries that dealt with the topic either in whole or in part. Distinct idols considered by Mather included Ashtaroth, Baal, Baal-berith, Chemosh, Dagon, Beelzebub, and Nisroch; related entries treated images set up by Jeroboam, Omri, the Assyrians, Maacha, and Manasseh. In addition, Mather repeatedly noted the propensity of the ancient Hebrews in general to idolatry.

The Historical Books are full of the lesson that false religion, in whatever form, will be punished. The Canaanites were doomed to destruction by Joshua and the Hebrews because they went "a whoring after idols" [*BA*, Josh. 1:18]. Mather objected that Jael was described unjustly by some commentators as "no better than a trapanning sort of an hussy," because her dispatching of the slumbering Sisera by driving a spike through his head was "a peece of Justice on him, as an horrible Idolater" [*BA*, Judg. 4:19]. And the Philistines were cursed of Jehovah for their continued worship of other gods, despite the many correctives they had received at the hands of the Hebrews and Israelites [*BA*, 1 Sam. 6:5].

However, so long as Israel worshipped Jehovah according to the law and covenant, and maintained Jerusalem as the high place, they prospered. The reign of David and most of the reign of Solomon were prime examples of this lesson. David did not allow any "strangers," that is, heathens, to reside in the land, and his closely heeding the word of God (in comparison to Saul) was one reason he was favored of Jehovah [*BA*, 2 Chron. 2:17]. Solomon after him married Pharaoh's daughter, but she was, Mather deduced, a proselyte to the true religion – and as such a type of the gentile church – and so never was a "snare" to him to take up false worship [*BA*, 2 Chron. 1:1]. It was only later, with his huge assortment of wives and concubines, that he became careless. Certain later kings, such as Asa, Hezekiah, and Josiah of Judah, were righteous and therefore blessed. Hezekiah's son Manasseh, for Mather, provided the most explicit example of the effect of reformation from this evil. As a young prince he was easily drawn into idol worship by the "great men" who didn't sympathize with the reforms of his father. Eventually he became a most wicked king, was taken captive to Babylon, repented, and then allowed to return to Jerusalem, where "he abolished the Idolatrous profanations, both of the Temple, and throughout the Land, which he had formerly Established, and Restored all things according to the Reformation of his Father *Hezekiah*; and all *Judah* with him Conformed unto the True Worship of God all the rest of his Days." To clinch his argument, Mather pointed out that Manasseh "continued in prosperity after this, to the End of his Reign; which extended unto full Fifty-five years."

After Solomon, the stories of Israel and Judah were ones of increasing darkness and degradation, penetrated only here and there by some light. When the leaders and people fell into following false gods and superstitious practices, they, like their neighbors, became the objects of divine wrath. Judg. 18:30 relates that Jonathan, the grandson of Moses, first set up public idolatry in the tribe of Dan; for that reason, Mather noted, that tribe was "not named, in the Revelation, among the *Sealed of the Lord.*" The nation divided into the ten tribes of Israel and the two of Judah because of false worship established by Jeroboam – at least according to Mather.[7] According to 1 Kings 16:19, Zimri ruled only seven days in punishment for continuing in Jeroboam's idolatry. Omri, as Mather described in his entry on 1 Kings 16:25, did "worse than all that were before him": "He Introduced the Idolatries, which his Son *Ahab* afterwards established. Or, He compelled the people to worship the *Calves,* and by Severe Lawes restrained them from going up to *Jerusalem,*" the place where Israelites had hitherto been required to go. Ahab, one of the most wicked of the kings, scoffed at Elijah for not being punished for his idolatry, whereupon, for failing to keep his mouth shut, Elijah pronounced the judgment: no rain for three and a half years. Finally, on the plague visited on Jehoram, who multiplied high places and caused Judah to commit ritual fornication, Mather, relying on the sixteenth-century German theologian Victorinus Strigelius, wrote,

> There was no Calamity to be thought of, which did not befal this wicked Prince. His Kingdome was destroyed by the fiercest Nations; His Treasures ransacked; His Wives Carried into Captivity; His Children butchered; And he Himself Labouring under a sore Disease for Two Years together; Finally, Dying without the Honour of a Royal Sepulture. All these Calamities were threatned, in the Writing sent him in the Name of *Elijah.* The *People* suffer in this *Great Plague,* because their Base Fear made them comply with him in his Idolatry. He was also punished in the Loss of them. [*BA,* 2 Chron. 21:14][8]

Ultimately, idolatry, superstition, magical arts, human additions to and corruptions of ordained worship, and the failings attending them – unbelief and disregard for God's law and the temple at Jerusalem – caused the downfall of the kingdoms of Israel and Judah, and resulted in their Babylonian captivity.

The Enlightenment and Paganism

If Mather showed a microscopic interest in the details of Hebrew life and history as a way of illuminating these texts, he also looked outward to other cultures in a comparative manner. Following the lead of a troop of seventeenth-century scholars such as Simon Patrick and John Selden – probably the most

---

7   The real reason, biblical scholars today tell us, seems to have had something to do with oppressive taxation.
8   Mather's source here possibly is *Victorini Strigelii viri clarissimi orationes XXX: de praecipuis patriarchis, prophetis et regibus, quorum historie in libris Moysis, Samuelis, Regu & Paralipomenon recitantur ...* (1583).

cited authors in this run of entries – Mather collected a number of instances in which biblical figures and events were to be found in "pagan antiquitie," that is, in myths and histories of the Greeks, Romans, and other cultures.[9] So, for example, Joshua, in the hands of non-Hebrew storytellers, became Apollo; Samson was transformed into Nisus, the king of the Megarenses; and commemoration of Hezekiah's sundial going back ten degrees found its way into the rites of the Persian priests of Mithras. Mather was not alone in asserting that all such "gentile" or heathen accounts were only derived from, and corrupt variants of, the Hebrew account, which, for him, was "the antientist history." These parallels were the result of dilutions and corruptions of the original revelation of true religion given to Adam at the beginning of time. Theophilus Gale, exemplifying this Euhemeristic approach in his massive *Court of the Gentiles* (1660), confirmed that "the greatest part of *Human Literature* owes its original to the *sacred Scriptures*, and *Jewish Church*" (8).

Alongside increasing interest in etymology and narrative details in the original Hebrew, scholars such as Manuel, Peter Gay, Jan Assman, and others have noted the interest in paganism – classicism, Egyptology, and "world religions," ancient and contemporary – that arose in the seventeenth and blossomed in the eighteenth century. And they have linked the trend in pagan studies to the rise of Romanticism in the late eighteenth and early nineteenth century, making Mather's contribution to later notions of the "noble savage" and primitive versus modern minds possible topics of contemplation. Also, the early Enlightenment saw the development of social sciences such as anthropology as scholarly disciplines. Mather drew on these pursuits for the "Biblia," grouping together false religion, idol and image use and worship, and pagan and occult practices (see Manuel; Gay; Laplanche). He leavened his own exploration of these phenomena with the work of orthodox apologists such as the Cambridge Platonists, who battled materialist thought by latching onto accounts of occult activity as proof of the existence of the supernatural world (Redwood 151–53). Too, Eric Midelfort, in his work on witchcraft and the occult in early modern Germany specifically, and in Europe generally, has pointed out that seventeenth-century writers commonly joined sorcery, witchcraft, and idolatry in all its forms as chief among the challenges to true religion (12–13). This brings us, then, to the polemical and more pietistic implications of the lessons of the Historical Books in Mather's presentation.

---

9 See Patrick's *Commentary upon the historical Books* (1727) and Selden's *De Diis Syris Syntagmata* (1617); Mather's entries on idols and idolatries relied much more on Selden than Patrick. Others in this group used by Mather include Bochart's *Hierozoicon* and *Geographia Sacra*, Kircher and Vossius.

Modern Idolatry and the Threat to True Religion

The latest forms of idolatry, as Mather enumerated them in other writings, were threefold: Catholic brands of idolatry as portrayed by Protestants, the false worship of reason amongst free-thinkers, and idolatry of the heart as practiced by Protestants themselves. Mather does not address all of these categories equally in his commentary on the Historical Books, but they do provide a helpful framework for understanding how he may have wished his commentary to be applied.

The first, Catholic idolatry, can most readily be found in these "Biblia" entries. Anti-Catholic bias was still going strong within the English and Dutch reforming communities two centuries after the Reformation.[10] Protestants castigated Catholics for excising the first and second commandments from the Decalogue, for idolatrous worship of the Pope, the saints, images, and the eucharistic host – all, as Mather put it, with his love of word-play, "a Mass of *Idolatry*." In the "Biblia" entry on Judg. 6:25, he identified Baal-Berith and Baal-Meon as places where Baal was worshipped, and put them on a par with sites dedicated to "The Lady of *Loretto*, and, The Lady of *Walsingham*, among the popish Idolaters, of the *Latter Dayes*." Considering Samson's betrayal by Delilah as a type in Judg. 13, Mather pointedly declared that "The *Harlot* Church of *Rome*, betray'd our Lord Jesus Christ." And in the entry on 1 Kings 12:28, relating to Jeroboam's images of the two calves, Mather noted that false gods were given feminine genders, which led him to "Query, How far this Leads us to think on the worship of a *Mary*, which the *Jeroboam* of *Rome* has introduced."

This form of spirituality, which Mather considered to be idolatry based on delusion and false teaching, was part of the Antichrist's efforts to corrupt true religion. This polemic had a millennial dimension to it, touching the cosmic struggle between the forces of true and false Christianity, in works such as William Perkins's *Warning against the idolatrie of the last times* (1601). Mather himself was a prime practitioner. The threat of a Romish captivity of the "true" church was still very real for writers of the generation of Mather, who, we must remember, composed the great part of the "Biblia" during the War of the Grand Alliance and the War of the Spanish Succession, which pitted England against its Catholic rivals France and Spain. For his part, Mather called "*Rome*" the "*Idolatrous Babylon*" of the Apocalypse. In the *Magnalia* (bk. 7, pp. 9–11) he devoted three pages to the story of "one in *some* Authority" in early Massachusetts who defiantly cut the cross of St. George out of the ensign because it was a "Popish *Idol*," an incident Nathaniel Hawthorne would later make into the short story "Endicott and the Red Cross."

---

10   For the Reformation background, see Crew; Eire; Wandel.

Other seventeenth-century English authors such as Henry Ainsworth and Henry Hammond addressed the need to eschew forms of idolatry and superstition as a means of further church reform in the time of Civil War and the Interregnum. Catholicism was described as containing countless continuities and accommodations of pagan traditions, a syncretism that had to be eliminated, the accretions of centuries peeled back, to reveal the primitive purity of Christianity. One of the more colorful attempts in this vein was Ezekias Woodward's Interregnum diatribe against Christmas observance, a pamphlet that makes anyone trying to revise Puritan stereotypes in the popular imagination nearly abandon hope. Beginning in the very title, Woodward portrayed the holiday as *"the superstitious mans idol day, The multitudes idle day, Whereon, because they cannot do nothing: they do worse then nothing."* The Restoration period saw similar warnings and critiques from Edward Stillingfleet, Daniel Whitby, Charles Blount, and a long line of polemicists. Still others during this period, such as Mather's grandfather Richard and, later, his uncle Samuel in Dublin, turned the charge of "idolatry and superstition" against the Church of England's ceremonies and forms of worship.[11]

Yet another manifestation of this modern form of idolatry was the deification of reason. Reason, Mather allowed, was a noble and admirable faculty, but we must not exalt it too high. In his sermon, *A Man of Reason*, Mather cautioned, "Vain Man, Do not imagine, That thy *Light within*, or the *Light* of *Reason*, is a *Sufficient Guide* without the *Scripture*. ... To make a *Christ*, and a *God* of that *Light*, it is a dangerous *Idolatry*" (16). This was the sin of those who set reason above revelation:

> When Men will Receive nothing that is *Reveal'd* from GOD, Except they can fathom it by *Reason*; When Men must Comprehend the *Mysteries* of *Revealed Religion*, or else they will *Reject the Counsel of GOD*. Such *Free-Thinkers*, are one Tribe of *Idolaters*. The Men that Writes [sic], *Christianity not Misterious*, have set up an *Idol*, that proves a *Stumbling-block of Iniquity* unto Them. (*Icono-clastes* 18)

Mather's allusion to John Toland's *Christianity Not Mysterious* (1696) and to those who thought like him clearly indicated that he placed them among modern idolaters.[12]

Beyond these polemics, Mather identified a practical, experiential application against a more subtle, nefarious brand of idolatry plaguing even the most "refined" churches, that is, the Protestant dissenting churches. Certainly radical groups such as the Baptists and Quakers were tarred by the orthodox with this form of idolatry – idolatry of water-baptism, or idolatry of the inner light

---

11 See Perkins; Ainsworth; Hammond; Stillingfleet; Whitby; Blount; Richard Mather in *Magnalia* (bk. 4, pp. 147–48); S. Mather, *A Testimony from the Scripture Against Idolatry & Superstition*.
12 On the controversy over Toland's book for his appropriation of Locke's epistemology, see Yolten (188–226).

(see Fuce; Miller). But it also applied to more orthodox believers. In the entry on Josh. 1:1, for example, Mather drew a parallel between the Hebrews' descent into false worship in the wilderness and the interior life of his readers. "The Carriage of Israel in the Wilderness," he observed, "is a Glass, wherein we may see the Corruption of our own Hearts."

An incident from Mather's life serves as an illustration of this modern form of idolatry. In March 1716, a Boston artisan was hired by individuals at Cape Francois to carve a statue – in wood, presumably – of St. Michael. "Whether it be only an ornamental Business, or an Idol to be worshipped by the bruitish Papists," Mather wrote in his *Diary*, "I know not." For their part, Bostonians assumed it was the latter. Mather himself had taken it upon himself to speak "a transient and pleasant Word" to the artisan's wife, who had "improved that Word, in their own Favour, and made a formal, a lying, Story out of it," so that Mather's name was being dragged through the mud (but what else was new?), "as if I had encouraged the making and sending of an Idol, for the Papists at Cape *Francois*, to make an Object of their Adoration (2: 441, 445).

The result, the following year, was the sermon *Icono-clastes*, where Mather began: "The *Glorious Gospel of the Blessed GOD*, has rescued us from the *Grosser* sort of *Idolatry*. But then, there is a *Finer* sort of more *Spiritual Idolatry*, which we are all still in danger of: And the *Finer* it is, the Greater is our *Danger* of it." This *"Spiritual*," or "*Heart-Idolatry*," came from setting self above God. One component was "*Will-Worship*," in which "*Inventions* of Men" were brought into the "*parts* and *means* of *Worship*." These human additions become idols in their own right. The solution was to heed the scripture-warrant and to "Keep to the *Primitive Worship*" (*Icono-clastes* 2, 3, 5, 10, 12, 14, 15, 18). Inherent in these warnings was the danger that truly Reformed churches could acquire Catholic-like layers of superstition and human fancy.[13] But Mather's *Diary* makes it clear that in this sermon he moved beyond anti-Catholic animosity and into a pietistic mode. "Under these Dispositions," he wrote, "the best Thing I could think of, was to publish a little Treatise on *Idolatry*, that may serve all the Interests of practical Piety" (2: 446).

False Worship and the Demonic

An aspect of false worship to which Mather devoted much room in the "Biblia" was its perversion, its unnaturalness. He explicitly connected idolatry with child sacrifice, prostitution, orgies, bestiality, incest, and other unclean and licentious behavior. Practitioners of idolatry were brutes, beasts, slaves to

---

13   On "spiritual idolatry," see, for example, Henry More, *An appendix to the late antidote against idolatry* (53–58).

their lusts. In the entry on Judg. 6:25, Mather continued his discussion of Baal-peor, "a monster ... An Idol, that *Shewed all* that *Adam* covered with Fig-leaves. The Ancients, as *Jerom*, and *Isidore*, make him to be the Same, with the Beastly *Priapus*."[14] Mather added that some commentators thought the worship of this particular manifestation of Baal to have included eating the "sacrifices of the dead," or *inferiae*, offering sacrifices to "gastly ghosts." (So too, the groves of idols mentioned in the scriptures were haunted by the "manes," or spirits, of heroes.) His gloss on Judg. 11:24 mentions Chemosh, "The Abomination of Moab," which was "held in *Coparceny* [equal sharing of an inheritance], as here we see betwixt the *Moabites* and the *Ammonites*. Thus as *Moab* and *Ammon*, once parted the Incestuous Extraction, from the same Grandfather, so now they mett again at the Idolatrous Adoration of the same God." The name *Chemosh* denoted "unnatural Cruelty, Like that of *Saturn* in devouring his Children." So when David conquered the Ammonites, he ordered that they be burnt in lime-kilns, "the very place where the Idolaters had Sacrificed their Children unto *Moloch*" [*BA*, 2 Sam. 12:30].

There was a gendered dimension at work here for Mather that bears exploring: the Israelites' associations with foreign women, either through marriage or illicit relations, were a major factor in their various falls into heathenism. In the entry on Judg. 18:7, Mather contended that idolatry was introduced among the Hebrews by an Ephraimite woman. Also, the people were further drawn into worship of Baal-peor through intimacies with Midianite women. Jerome, Selden, and the seventeenth-century French Protestant theologian Pierre Jurieu helped Mather to characterize Chemosh as "That filthy *Idol*, whereto *Fornication* was the *consecration*" [*BA*, 1 Kings 11:33]. Mather lamented, "That *Solomon* should Erect an Altar unto this Idol, on the Mount of *Olives*! *Horrendum*!" However, the Israelites were tame in comparison to how women were employed in the religious rituals of other cultures. Mather, in his comments on 2 Kings 17, devoted five entries in a row to the Assyrian deities. At the temple of

> the Babylonian *Mylitta*, or *Venus Urania* ... the young women satt there apart in several *Tents*, where any Stranger, that had paid his Devotions to Madam *Mylitta*, pulling what String he pleased, was accommodated with a Wench at the End of it, ready to be prostituted unto his Libidinous Inclinations. All women, it seemeth, Once in their Life, exposed themselves unto Conversation with a Stranger, though some waited a pretty while, before they had the Luck of it. Both *Herodotus* and *Strabo*, gives the more ample Story of this Diabolical Business.

The very images of these infernal powers themselves denoted uncleanness, filth, and degradation. The Philistines' gift of images of "emrods" and mice in 1

---

14   Priapus was the Greek god of fertility who was often portrayed as an ugly little man with an enormous phallus.

Sam. 6, to which Mather devoted four entries, was to divert the plagues with which Jehovah afflicted them, when mice ate up their corn, and emrods, or emerods – hemorrhoids, tumors, or boils – afflicted their "bottom parts" (and I leave it to the reader's imagination what these images may have looked like). These objects were properly talismans, and Mather attributed real, though infernal, power to such images, as well as to human agents such as conjurors, wizards, and astrologers, whether biblical or post-biblical. In this entry, for instance, he included a story from Gregory of Tours who told of a bridge in Paris beneath which images of serpents and dormice had been found; when the images were removed, the area was infested with those very vermin. Getting back to unclean deities, Mather portrayed Dagon as "part *Humane*, part *Marine*," that is, half woman, half fish. Assyrian gods included Ashima, a goat; and Nibchaz, a dog or an ass. And then there was Beelzebub, Lord of the Flies. Mather gave several substantial entries to the consideration of this rather disgusting Philistine deity. The name itself, Mather claimed, was actually a satirical Hebraic variation, referring to the flies that swarmed around Beelzebub's temple attracted by the meat sacrifices, in comparison to the temple of Jehovah, which reportedly never had any flies or insects despite the veritable rivers of blood that flowed from sacrificed animals.

These false gods, for Mather, were not cultural constructions or expressions of collective experience; they were nothing less than Satan and his servant demons. If Mather was like Pierre Bayle in condemning paganism, he was more like the Swiss theologian and biblical scholar Jean LeClerc, perhaps, and indeed the early Church Fathers, in attributing demonic origins to virtually all aspects of non-Christian religions.[15] Satan, Mather maintained in the "Biblia," sought to mimic worship of the true God as a way of aggrandizing himself and of luring believers to him. So, for example, the name Baal-berith, or "Lord of the Covenant," was "fetched" from the God of Israel, just as Adonis came from Adonai, and "Federator" was one of the titles of Jupiter. In the entry on 1 Sam. 6:5, Mather declared that the Philistine astrologers saw that Moses had been directed to make the brazen serpent in the wilderness to relieve the Hebrews from "fiery serpents." Because "the Divel will bee Gods *Ape*," Mather added, using Luther's phrase, "that became the Original, as I suppose, of all the *Telesmatical* practices, Afterwards used in the World." Since Mather was convinced that superstitious and occult practices – even seemingly innocent ones such as hanging up a horseshoe or a glass globe to ward off evil spirits – had demonic origins, he, like his father before him, was of the group that W. R. Ward characterizes as "trying to get the magic out of Christianity" (19).[16]

---

15   For Bayle's comments on paganism, see the many references in *An historical and critical dictionary*. On Bayle generally, see Manuel (35). On LeClerc and Mather, see Smolinski ("Authority and Interpretation").

16   Mather's simultaneous acknowledgement and distrust of magical and talismanic powers,

All of the portrayals of worship of the false gods, and the rites accompanying them, including child sacrifice, prostitution, and lewd activity, paralleled pictures of devil worship and satanic rituals as popularly imagined at the time. So for example, Ashtaroth, as Mather wrote in his entry on Judg. 2:13, drawing again largely on Selden, was also known as Minerva, Juno, Venus, and especially Astarte. This deity was represented as both male and female, and, Mather added, "being in reality a *Devil*, 'tis no Wonder the Sacred Scriptures observe not a Difference of Sexes for it." Baal-peor, of Judg. 6:25, was a demon as well. And in one of his entries on Beelzebub, Mather joined a number of these themes, relating that the power of this "prince of Darkness" was imported from Scandinavia, where conjurors used "magical Darts," or "Gans," to revenge themselves on their enemies. These gans were a sort of demon-fly, like those supposedly employed by Native American shamans:

> 'Tis a Little *Divel*, of which the *Finlanders* that excel most in this Art, keep great Numbers in a *Leathern Bag*, and they dispatch daily some of them abroad; and if they destroy no Men, they Rove about until they meet with something, that they find capable of inflicting Destruction upon. It is well known, That in my own Countrey of *New England*, the *Indian Powawes* will form a Peece of Leather, like an *Arrowes* Head, and then to Tye an Hair to it; and over these to employ certain Magical Ceremonies; whereupon a *Dæmon* presently Snatches them away, and conveyes them into the Bodies of Persons to be Afflicted. And as the *Laplanders* do send their *Gans*, or *Flies* to destroy People, so a *Dæmon* will pretend unto our *Powawes*, to bring a Portion of the Spirit of a Person closely Imprisoned in a *Flye*; and as they deal with the *Flye*, so it fares with the *Body* of the Person they Design to Afflict. [*BA*, 2 Kings 1:2b]

Though it is difficult to ascertain, Mather was apparently describing Native American "medicine bundles," which actually were collections of objects carried in a pouch that served as mnemonic devices for preserving tribal and personal memories.[17] For Mather, however, these were less innocent: "Consider, my reader," he concluded, "whether these northern *Gans*, flew as far as *Judaea*" [*BA*, 2 Kings 1:2b]. He could have added, "as far as New England."

Israel Redux

Mather provided two significant entries, each twenty pages in length, one, on 1 Kings 12:33, an overview of the "propensity" of the Israelites to idolatry, the other, on 2 Kings 17:41, tracing the fate of the ten tribes after they were car-

---

along with other mystical pursuits, complicates Ward's identification of the main characteristics of Pietism as anti-confessionalism, mysticism, apocalypticism, theosophy, and cabbalism. On Mather's Pietism, see also Lovelace.

17   On medicine bundles, see Gibson.

ried into captivity. The first entry relied largely on seventeenth-century Dutch theologian Herman Witsius's *Dekaphylon* (1683) and traced the career of Jeroboam, who "flies to wicked Arts" to preserve his rule over Judah. After nineteen kings and 235 years, the kingdom fell, most of the Judeans were carried into captivity, to be re-established in Palestine under Roman rule.

The other entry used Samuel Lee's *Israel Redux* (1677)[18] for its basic points. The ten tribes were carried into captivity to northeastern Mesopotamia and the area of the Caspian Sea, from whence they spread out. As of the late seventeenth century, Lee continued, they resided in Assyria and Media, Ethiopia, and India. Would they ever return from the diaspora? Here, at least, Mather answered yes, after a few historical preconditions: the Messiah had to appear, and they had to be converted to the Messiah and his law, coincident with the destruction of Gog and Magog (i.e. the Turks). They will rule from Jerusalem over Babylon and their ancient enemies, possessing a far larger, more prosperous domain than in the days of Solomon, and all nations will look to them. This, Lee stated, was to be a literal, not a spiritual, relocation (see Smolinski, "*Israel Redivivus*").[19]

In *Icono-clastes*, Mather provided a memorable vignette: "One of our Sufferers in the horrid, bloody, *Marian* Days," he recounted, "wore about his Neck, this Admonition, DEUM TIME, IDOLUM FUGE; *Fear GOD, and Flee from Idols.*" Mather saw himself as the iconoclast of the sermon's title, exploding false objects of worship, whether the errors of the Catholics, or the latest forms of infidelity forwarded by free-thinkers, or the spiritual idolatry of Protestants. If Mather's grand chronicle, the *Magnalia*, showed the decline of New England,[20] the "little Israel," his "Biblia" entries on Israel in the Historical Books offered an even greater, literal precedent for the decline of God's people as found in the tragic rise and fall of the *original* chosen nation. If the *Magnalia* held out the possibility of return by remembering the New England founders and their acts, Mather's observations in "Biblia" (and elsewhere) on Israel offered a more certain, and yet a more expansive, and more mystical, return. For Mather, the model of New England as part of God's new chosen people, grounded in the national covenant, held.[21] That covenant dictated that decline and captivity would

---

18   Actually two works under one title, the first by Giles Fletcher, the second by Samuel Lee, *Israel redux, or, The restauration of Israel, …; the second, a dissertation concerning their ancient and successive state, with some Scripture evidences of their future conversion, and establishment in their own land* (1677).

19   We must note that this was written considerably before the *Triparadisus* (1726/27), where Mather renounced a literalist view of the conversion and restoration of the Jews in favor of a "spiritual" conversion of a "true" Israel not necessarily composed solely of Jews (Smolinski, Introduction 21–37). Hence, we must assume that he would have most likely revised this entry if given the opportunity.

20   For the classic statement on this topic, see Bercovitch.

21   See Mather's use of the 1679 Reforming Synod's affirmation of covenant renewal, *The necessity of reformation with the expedients subservient thereunto*, asserted in the *Magnalia*, (bk. 5, p. 93).

come with apostasy, whatever its form, in the corruption of true religion. For Mather, too, the prevalence of modern forms of idolatry that he saw around him – spiritual, internal, based on faith in the self, in human strength, works, will, righteousness, or reason – testified to the church's danger of sharing the fate of Israel unless repentance and reformation were immediate and continual. The Hebrew history, the "antientist history," taught the inevitable return of the spiritual Israel. Just as captive Israel in its scriptures was promised the reconstitution of its former glorious domain and rule, so too would the New Israel partake in that glory, despite the constant lure of false idols, superstition, unbelief, skepticism, and the Devil himself.

Works Cited

Primary Sources

Ainsworth, Henry. *An arrow against idolatrie.* London, 1640.

Bayle, Pierre. *An historical and critical dictionary. By Monsieur Bayle. Translated into English, with many additions and corrections, made by the author.* 4 vols. London, 1710.

Blount, Charles. *Great is Diana of the Ephesians, or, The original of idolatry.* London, 1680.

Bochart, Samuel. *Geographia Sacra. Cujus Pars Prior: Phaleg De Dispersione gentium & terrarum divisione facta in ædificatione turris Babel; Pars Posterior: Chanaan De Colonijs & sermone Phoenicum.* Caen, 1646.

–. *Hierozoicon Sive bipertitum opus De Animalibus Sacrae Scripturae. Pars Prior. De Animalibus in genere. Et de Quadrupedibus viviparis et oviparis. Pars Posterior. De Avibus, Serpentibus, Insectis, Aquaticis, et Fabulosis Animalibus.* 2 vols. 1646. Londini, 1663.

Bunyan, John. *Solomon's temple spiritualiz'd, or, Gospel-light fetcht out of the temple at Jerusalem, to let us more easily into the glory of New-Testament-truths.* London, 1688.

Calvin, John. *A commentary upon the prophecies of Isaiah.* London, 1609.

Edwards, Jonathan. *The Works of Jonathan Edwards. Notes on Scripture.* Ed. Stephen J. Stein. Vol. 15. New Haven: Yale UP, 1998.

Fletcher, Giles and Samuel Lee. *Israel redux, or, The restauration of Israel, exhibited in two short treatises: the first contains an essay upon some probable grounds, that the present Tartars near the Caspian Sea, are the posterity of the ten tribes of Israel ...; the second, a dissertation concerning their ancient and successive state, with some Scripture evidences of their future conversion, and establishment in their own land.* London, 1677.

Fuce, Joseph. *The fall of a great visible idol.* London, 1659.

Gale, Theophilus. *The court of the gentiles, or, A discourse touching the original of human literature, both philologie and philosophie, from the Scriptures and Jewish church.* Oxford, 1660.

Hammond, Henry. *Of idolatry.* Oxford, 1646.

Henry, Matthew. *Exposition of all the books of the Old Testament; Viz. Joshua, Judges, Ruth, I and II. Samuel. ...* Vol. 2. London, 1725.

Huet, Pierre-Daniel. *Demonstratio evangelica ad serenissimum delphinium.* Parisiis, 1679.

Jurieu, Pierre. *Critical History of the Doctrines and Worships (both good and evil) of the church from Adam to Our Saviour Jesus Christ.* London, 1705.

Kircher, Athanasius. *Œdipus Ægyptiacus. Hoc est universalis hieroglyphicae veterum doctrinae temporum iniuria abolitae instauratio opus ex omni Orientalium doctrina & sapientia conditum, nec non viginti diversarum linguarum, authoritate stabilitum.* Tomi tres. Romae, 1652–54.

Mather, Cotton. *Decennium Luctuosum.* Boston, 1699.

–. *Diary of Cotton Mather.* Ed. Worthington Chaucey Ford. 2 vols. Massachusetts Historical Society Collections 7th Series, Vol. VII–VIII. Boston: MHS, 1911–12.

–. *Icono-clastes. An Essay upon the Idolatry too often committed under the Profession of the most Reformed Christianity; And a Discovery of the Idols which all Christians are Every where in danger of.* Boston, 1717.

–. *Magnalia Christi Americana: Or, The Ecclesiastical History of New England.* 1702. Facsimile rpt. New York: Arno P, 1972.

–. *A Man of Reason. A brief essay to demonstrate, that all men should hearken to reason; and what a world of evil would be prevented in the world, if men would once become so reasonable.* Boston, 1718.

–. *The Threefold Paradise of Cotton Mather: An Edition of "Triparadisus."* Ed. Reiner Smolinski. Athens: UP of Georgia, 1995.

Mather, Samuel. *A Testimony from the Scripture Against Idolatry & Superstition.* Cambridge, 1670.

–. *The Figures or Types of the Old Testament, by which Christ and the Heavenly Things of the Gospel were Preached and Shadowed to the People of God.* 2nd ed. London, 1705.

Miller, Joshua. *Antichrist in Man the Quaker's Idol.* London, 1655.

More, Henry. *An appendix to the late antidote against idolatry Wherein the true and adequate notion or definition of idolatry is proposed. Most instances of idolatry in the Roman Church thereby examined. Sundry uses in the Church of England cleared. With some serious monitions touching spiritual idolatry thereunto annexed.* London, 1673.

"Niles's History of the Indian and French Wars." *Massachusetts Historical Society Collections,* 3rd series, 6 (1837): 231–32.

Patrick, Simon. *Commentary upon the Historical Books of the Old Testament.* 2 vols., 3rd cor. ed. London, 1727.

Perkins, William. *A warning against the idolatrie of the last times.* Cambridge, 1601.

Selden, John. *De Diis Syris Syntagmata.* Londini, 1617.

Spencer, John. *De Legibus Hebraeorum Ritualibus.* Cantabrigiae, 1685.

Stillingfleet, Edward. *A discourse concerning the idolatry practised in the Church of Rome.* London, 1671.

Strigel(ius), Victorin(us). *Victorini Strigelii viri clarissimi orationes XXX: de praecipuis patriarchis, prophetis et regibus, quorum historie in libris Moysis, Samuelis, Regu & Paralipomenon recitantur.* Strassbourg, 1583.

Visscher, Nicolaes. *Terra sancta, sive promissionis, olim Palestina recens delineatio, et in lucem edita per Nicolaum Visscher.* Amstelaedami, 1659.

Vossius, Gerhard. *De theologia gentili, et physiologia Christiana; sive, De Origine ac Progressu Idololatriae.* Amstelaedami, 1641.

Witsius, Hermann. *Ægyptiaca et Dekaphylon, sive, De Ægyptiacorum sacrorum cum Hebraicis collatione libri tres, et De decem tribubus Israelis liber singularis: accessit diatribe de legione fulminatrice Christianorum, sub imperatore Marco Aurelio Antonino.* Amstelaedami, 1683.

Woodward, Ezekias. *Christ-mas day, the old heathens feasting day, in honour to Saturn their idol-god. The Papists massing day. The prophane mans ranting day. The superstitious mans idol day. The multitudes idle day. Whereon, because they cannot do nothing: they do worse then nothing. Satans, that adversaries working-day. The true Christian mans fasting-day. Taking to heart, the heathenish customes, Popish superstitions, ranting fashions, fearful provocations, horrible abhominations committed against the Lord, and His Christ, on that day, and days following.* London, 1656.

Whitby, Daniel. *The absurdity and idolatry of host-worship.* London, 1679.

Secondary Sources

Assmann, Jan. *Moses the Egyptian: The Memory of Egypt in Western Monotheism.* Cambridge: Harvard UP, 1997.

Bercovitch, Sacvan. "New England Epic: Cotton Mather's *Magnalia Christi Americana.*" *English Literary History* 33 (1966): 337–50.

Crew, Phyllis Mack. *Calvinist Preaching and Iconoclasm in the Netherlands, 1544–1569.* Cambridge: Cambridge UP, 1978.

Eire, Carlos. *War Against the Idols: The Reformation of Worship from Erasmus to Calvin.* Cambridge: Cambridge UP, 1986.

Frampton, Travis. *Spinoza and the Rise of Historical Criticism of the Bible.* New York: Clark, 2006.

Gay, Peter. *The Enlightenment, An Interpretation: The Rise of Paganism.* New York: Knopf, 1966.

Gibson, Arrell Morgan. *The American Indian: Prehistory to the Present.* Lexington: Heath & Co, 1980.

Krieger, Barbara. "Seventeenth Century English Travelers to Palestine." *Hebrew and the Bible in America: The First Two Centuries.* Ed. Shalom Goldman. Hanover: UP of New England, 1993. 43–58.

Laplanche, Francois. "Tendances actuelles de la recherche: présentation générale des XVIe–XVIIe siècle." *Les Religions du Paganisme Antique Dans L'Europe Chrétienne XVIe-XVIIIe Siecle.* Paris: Presses de l'Université de Paris-Sorbonne, 1988. 11–35.

LaRocca-Pitts, Elizabeth C. *"Of Wood and Stone": The Significance of Israelite Cultic Items in the Bible and Its Early Interpreters.* Harvard Semitic Monographs No. 61. Winona Lake: Eisenbrauns, 2001.

Lovelace, Richard. *The American Pietism of Cotton Mather: Origins of American Evangelicalism.* Grand Rapids: Christian UP, 1979.

Manuel, Frank. *The Eighteenth Century Confronts the Gods.* Cambridge: Harvard UP, 1959.

Midelfort, Eric. "Social History and Biblical Exegesis: Community, Family, and Witchcraft in Sixteenth-Century Germany." *The Bible in the Sixteenth Century*. Ed. David Steinmetz. Durham: Duke UP, 1990.

Norton, Mary Beth. *In The Devil's Snare: The Salem Witchcraft Crisis of 1692*. New York: Knopf, 2002.

Redwood, John. *Reason, Ridicule, and Religion: The Age of Enlightenment in England, 1660–1750*. Cambridge: Harvard UP, 1976.

Scholder, Klaus. *The Birth of Modern Critical Theology: Origins and Problems of Biblical Criticism in the Seventeenth Century*. Trans. John Bowden. London: SCM Pres, 1990.

Sheehan, Jonathan. *The Enlightenment Bible: Translation, Scholarship, Culture*. Princeton: Princeton UP, 2005.

–.   "Sacred and Profane: Idolatry, Antiquarianism and the Polemics of Distinction in the Seventeenth Century." *Past and Present* 192.8 (2006): 35–66.

Smolinski, Reiner. "Authority and Interpretation: Cotton Mather's Response to the European Spinozists." *Shaping the Stuart World, 1603–1714*. Ed. Macinnes, Alan I. and Arthur H. Williamson. Leiden: Brill, 2006. 175–203.

–.   "How to Go to Heaven, or How Heaven Goes? Natural Science and Interpretation in Cotton Mather's 'Biblia Americana.'" *New England Quarterly* 81.6 (2008): 279–329.

–.   Introduction. *The Threefold Paradise of Cotton Mather: An Edition of "Triparadisus."* Ed. Reiner Smolinski. Athens: UP of Georgia, 1995. 3–78.

–.   "'*Israel Redivivus*'": The Eschatological Limits of Puritan Typology in New England." *New England Quarterly* 63 (1990): 357–95.

Swan, Marshall W.S. "The Bedevilment of Cape Ann." *Essex Institute Historical Collections* 117 (1981): 153–177.

Wandel, Lee Palmer. *Voracious Idols and Violent Hands: Iconoclasm in Reformation Zurich, Strasbourg, and Basel*. Cambridge: Cambridge UP, 1995.

Ward, William R. *Early Evangelicalism: A Global Intellectual History, 1670–1789*. Cambridge: Cambridge UP, 2006.

Yolten, John W. *John Locke and the Way of Ideas*. Oxford: Oxford UP, 1956.

REINER SMOLINSKI

"Eager Imitators of the Egyptian Inventions": Cotton Mather's Engagement with John Spencer and the Debate about the Pagan Origin of the Mosaic Laws, Rites, and Customs

> To deny a people the man whom it praises as the greatest of its sons is not a deed to be undertaken lightheartedly – especially by one belonging to that people. ... It might have been expected that one of the many authors who recognized Moses to be an Egyptian name would have drawn the conclusion, or at least considered the possibility, that the bearer of an Egyptian name was himself an Egyptian. ... What hindered them from doing so can only be guessed at. Perhaps the awe of Biblical tradition was insuperable. Perhaps it seemed monstrous to imagine that the man Moses could have been anything other than a Hebrew.
> Sigmund Freud, "Moses ein Ägypter" (*Imago*, 1937); *Moses and Monotheism* (1939, 1969)

We don't know if the father of psychoanalysis and formulator of the proverbial Oedipus complex appreciated the implicit irony of symbolically "killing" the father of monotheism – in denying Moses his Hebrew parentage. There is no doubt, however, that for Sigmund Freud and his contemporaries more than mere curiosity in the mythic founder of Judaism or fascination with a remote age were involved. For if Freud was afraid that publishing his "Moses ein Ägypter" (1937) might "cause psychoanalysis to be forbidden in a country [Austria] where its practice was still allowed" (132), then his anxiety reveals the subversive potential the argument about the Egyptian origins of Moses and his religion still held at the time.[1] Of course, developments in the field of biblical criticism and the wider acceptance of a historicist-comparative approach to the scriptures have since done much to defuse the explosiveness of the subject. But even today Jews and Christians who are invested in the literal truth of their sacred texts are bound to struggle with the claim about the pagan origin of the Mosaic religion.[2] Indeed, in the words of Freud, it seems monstrous for some

---

1 This subversive potential is illustrated by the controversy started by the German Assyriologist Friedrich Delitzsch (1850–1922) three decades before Freud wrote his "Moses ein Ägypter." In his famous lecture *Babel und Bibel* (1902), Delitzsch posited that most of the cultic rites and creedal points of the Israelites must have been adopted from their Babylonian-Assyrian neighbors, whose civilization was significantly older and much more advanced than that of ancient Israel. The argument caused considerable uproar in its wake (see Lehmann).

2 More recently, the debate about an Egyptian origin of Moses and of the cultic rites of the Israelites has been rekindled by the German Egyptologist Jan Assmann, whose *Moses the Egyptian* (1998) has sparked an international controversy that Assmann tries to redress in his

believers to imagine that the divine lawgiver could have been born and bred an Egyptian. For literalists, it appears blasphemous to allege that many of the Mosaic laws, rites, and customs did not originate in God's divine revelation on Mt. Horeb but were borrowed from the Israelites' Egyptian neighbors. Equally hard to accept is that the God of Israel would have Moses make use of idolatrous rites, turn them upside down, and adapt them to new uses in the service of the true God. After all, from this perspective the truth claims of the Judeo-Christian religions – founded on supernatural revelation – would be critically undermined if they turned out to be mere borrowings of pagan sacraments. If the modern disciples of Johann Salomo Semler (1725–91), Johann Gottfried Eichhorn (1752–1827), Ferdinand Christian Baur (1792–1860), or of Julius Wellhausen (1844–1918), the formulators of Higher Criticism, no longer wince at such rationalist studies of God's law, we can well imagine how Cotton Mather and his peers must have responded when they encountered such iconoclastic assertions in works by serious and well-respected scholars. Perhaps the most notorious example in Mather's time was *De Legibus Hebræorum Ritualibus et Earum Rationibus Libri Tres* (1685), a thousand-page analysis of the grounds and reasons of Hebrew ritual laws, by John Spencer (1630–93), Christian Hebraist extraordinaire and master of Corpus Christi College, Cambridge. Reprinted in The Hague in 1686, in Leipzig in 1705, and in a considerably expanded and revised version in Cambridge in 1727, *De Legibus Hebræorum Ritualibus* appeared in its final imprint in Tübingen, in 1732, from the press of the renowned Tübingen publisher Johann Georg Cotta.[3]

Spencer's *De Legibus* is a massive work of late Renaissance erudition as only scholars of immense learning and leisure (or tenure) could compose. In its revised and expanded edition, it consists of four books (or parts) in polished Latin, complete with full-scale citations from Greek and Roman antiquity, the Church Fathers, and Rabbinic literature. Here, Spencer sets forth what was then a heterodox thesis: that most of the ceremonial and cultic laws of the Levites were not given to Moses by Yahweh, the God of the Israelites, but were indeed translated (in the tradition of *translatio studii*) and adapted from their

---

Die Mosaische Unterscheidung oder der Preis des Monotheismus (2003), the English translation appearing most recently as *The Price of Monotheism* (2010). In the latter work, he responds to charges (reprinted in the German edition) that his argument about the establishment of monotheism having caused untold bloodshed throughout the millennia is a form of disguised anti-Semitism.

3   This Tübingen edition (which constitutes the 5th edition of Spencer's work) is particularly noteworthy for its valuable "*Dissertatio Præliminaris*," a review of Spencer's critical reception among English and Continental theologians. The preface was composed by Christoph Matthäus Pfaff (1686–1760), a moderate Lutheran theologian and chancellor of the University of Tübingen, and bound with the 1732 edition. All citation references are to this Tübingen edition which, incidentally, uses identical pagination for the main text as the Cambridge edition of 1727 does.

Egyptian, Chaldaean, and Canaanite neighbors. Moses "was learned in all the wisdom of the Egyptians, and was mighty in words and in deeds," as we learn from Acts 7:22.[4] But according to Spencer, Moses was also a visionary states-man who fully understood that a new nation was not born in a day, that a nation of slaves and a mixed multitude of gentiles could not easily form a new identity as a separate people, let alone adopt a new system of beliefs and laws contrary to what they had imbibed for centuries. After more than four-hundred years in Egypt, they were fully assimilated; they were slaves not only in the sense of making bricks for their Egyptian overlord but also in worshipping their idols, whose adoration and customs they had completely internalized. To accommo-date the habits of a fractious people and to indulge their penchant for pagan rituals and tangible idols, but redirect their devotions and instead offer them in the service of Yahweh, the invisible desert God of their ancestors, was therefore perfectly logical. Through this divine ruse Moses could make them embrace their unique identity as God's peculiar possession and have them believe in a self-sufficient cult shaped in contradistinction to the idolatry of their pagan neighbors. If this evolutionary process of cultural assimilation and identity for-mation makes good sense to modern historians, then John Spencer's *De Legibus* is all the more noteworthy as an early example of comparative religion. He ex-amined the Mosaic ritual laws from the point of view of religious history to reconstruct the historical zeitgeist and conditions that brought them forth. In-stead of reading the ceremonial laws – as most Christian exegetes at the time were doing – as prophetic or typological foreshadowing of Christ in whom they were abrogated, Spencer insisted on historical literalism. He examined the ori-gin of these laws in the context of the cultural and religious norms of the Egyp-tian and Phoenician neighbors, pagan rules which he deemed to be the true ori-gin of the Mosaic laws. The allegorical and typological use of the law Spencer relegated to a subordinate or secondary purpose, which he covers in less than

---

4 All biblical quotations are from the King James Version. The Jewish philosopher Philo Judaeus (c. 20 BCE – c. CE 50) of Alexandria seems to be the first to argue that Moses was well trained in the wisdom of the Egyptians. Moses was an eager scholar, who had "all kinds of masters, one after another, some coming of their own accord from the neighbouring coun-tries and the different districts of Egypt, and some being even procured from Greece by the temptation of large presents. But in a short time he surpassed all their lessons by the excellent natural endowments of his own genius; so that everything in his case appeared to be a recol-lecting rather than a learning, while he himself also, without any teacher, comprehended by his instinctive genius many difficult subjects; [22] for great abilities cut out for themselves many new roads to knowledge." Moses received lessons "by Egyptian philosophers, who also taught him the philosophy which is contained in symbols, which they exhibit in those sacred characters of hieroglyphics, as they are called, and also that philosophy which is conversant about that respect which they pay to animals which they invest with honours due to God" (*De Vita Mosis* 1.20–22, 23; *Works* 461). Mather, too, spoke of Moses's "Education in the Court of *Egypt*; His Fellowship in the Colledge of *Diospolis* [Thebes] ... His Conversation with the wisest Men of *Arabia*, and *Idumæa*, and, perhaps *Phœnicia*, during his long Exile" (*BA* 1: 380). See also Edward Stillingfleet's *Origines Sacræ* (bk. 2, ch. 2, pp. 119–34).

sixteen pages out of more than 1,200, in a chapter titled, "The Ritual Laws of Moses restricted to a secondary [minor] purpose" (*De Legibus*, bk. 1, ch. 15, pp. 208–23). Zealous interpreters are so eager to discover hidden meanings, Spencer complained, that in their hands the Law becomes as malleable as a wax nose ("nasum cereum"), running this way or that just as it pleases them (208).

Although *De Legibus* was unrivalled in its academic profundity, Spencer was neither the first nor only scholar in his own day to notice the close correspondence between the Levitical laws and the cultic rituals of Israel's gentile neighbors. Nor was he the first to argue that Moses translated the mysteries of the Egyptian religion into his own laws. What rendered Spencer's thesis so subversive, however, is that he appeared to relinquish divine revelation as the sole basis of the Judeo-Christian religion, implicitly arguing for a gradual historical evolution from pagan polytheism. The often vehement reactions to Spencer's thesis are also partly explained by the charged atmosphere in which *De Legibus* was published. Hobbists and Spinozists were shaking the foundation of civil and ecclesiastical governments, even as such highly respected (albeit controversial) theologians as Richard Simon (1632–1712) and Jean LeClerc (1657–1736) were challenging the Mosaic authorship of the Pentateuch and the dogma of the Bible's verbal inspiration.[5]

In Mather's period, Spencer's supporters and detractors approached the controversy from essentially three different positions: First, those who agreed with Spencer argued that the Israelites, an obscure and primitive people, borrowed their ceremonial rites and sacrifices from their more powerful neighbors, especially from the Egyptians, the most advanced civilization of the time. This list of proponents is relatively small and in the early modern era includes such noteworthies as Franciscus Moncaeus, Jacques Gaffarel, Athanasius Kircher, John Marsham, Charles Blount, John Toland, Augustin Calmet, and William Warburton. Second, others who clearly recognized the value of Spencer's research but were unprepared to concede his conclusion argued that neither Israelites nor gentiles borrowed their religion from one another, because the cultic similarities were either accidental or, more likely, sprang from the fountainhead of their common ancestor: the patriarch Noah. Noah's sons, Shem, Ham, and Japheth, they argued, had carried the religion of their patriarch, the *prisca theologia*, into all the corners of the world, before the true religion that God had taught Adam and passed down to Noah became corrupted by the passage of time, the dispersal of the people after Babel, and the admixture of human inventions and errors. It was for these reasons that many similarities can be found between the ancient myths the world over and the stories and heroes in the He-

---

5   See section 3 of my introduction to Cotton Mather's *Biblia Americana* (Genesis) 1: 113–74.

brew Scriptures.[6] Third, predictably, the most vociferous and numerous group of theologians to oppose Spencer's thesis charged him with heterodoxy and flatly denied the validity of his argument. They employed Spencer's own evidence but reversed its thrust: The Egyptians, Chaldeans, Greeks, and Romans stole their rituals and ceremonies from God's chosen people whose sacred religion, magnificent temple, propitious sacrifices, and elaborate ceremonies were the envy of their polytheistic neighbors; the chronology of the Pentateuch and the genealogy of the patriarchs down to Moses clearly demonstrates, so they argued, that the Hebrew God was the source of all wisdom and the Bible his revealed word from which all pagans derived their philosophy.[7] The French Huguenot divine Jacques Basnage de Beauval (1653–1723) at The Hague, whose *History of the Jews* (1708) Mather abstracts in his "Biblia Americana," succinctly sums up the variety of positions more than twenty years after Spencer published his *De Legibus*. Although only partially agreeing with Spencer's position on the origin of the Mosaic laws, Basnage knew only too well that many learned men maintained

> the *Heathens* took their Religion and Mysteries from the *Jews*. Some think the Patriarchs *Abraham* and *Joseph* instructed the *Ægyptians*: Others say, the *Phenicians* were the Channel that convey'd this Knowledge into the Isles of the *Ægean* Sea, *Greece* and *Sicily*, even to *Spain* and *England*, whither this nation had sent Colonies, who brought with them the Religion which their Ancestors had receiv'd but at the second hand. ... *Lastly*, They fancy, that when the Books of *Moses* were publish'd, the *Heathens* seiz'd on them, and attempted to form a Religion like the *Jewish*, by copying the Writings of the Lawgiver. We take the quite opposite Opinion, as believing 1. That the Religion of the *Ægyptians* was much ancienter than that of the *Jews*. 2. That each Nation deified its Heroes, or made its Gods, without begging them from others. 3. That if there be any conformity betwixt the *Heathen*

---

6 Rudiments of this position can be found in Lord Herbert of Cherbury (*De Religione*, ch. 3), Thomas Burnet (*Doctrina Antiqua* 89–136), John Woodward (*Wisdom*, esp. 52–102), John Toland (*Letters to Serena*, esp. 19–128), and Isaac Newton ("Theologiæ Gentilis Origines Philosophicæ") and, later in the eighteenth century, especially in Jacques Basnage (*History of the Jews*, bk. 3, chs. 17–19) and in William Warburton (*Divine Legation*, vol. 2, bk. 4, sec, 6, pp. 281–357). On this issue, see Assmann (*Moses the Egyptian* 91–143). David Hume turned this argument against its original intentions and insisted that superstition and polytheism – not primitive monotheism – were the sources of mankind's religion (Schmidt 21–27). Pierre Jurieu, like many others, frequently occupies a middle position and accepts certain aspects of Spencer's thesis while rejecting others. See also Rossi's excellent discussion on Moses's Egyptian culture (123–32).

7 In his valuable *"Dissertatio Præliminaris,"* Christoph Matthäus Pfaff catalogues most of the well-known and lesser-known theologians of the day who rose up against Spencer's thesis. Pfaff's introductory essay is particularly useful, because he arranges his list of critics according to the particular subject and issue they target in Spencer's *De Legibus*. Pfaff's inventory includes detailed bibliographical information to locate each critic's counterargument. Among the many theologians who argued that the Egyptians and all other pagan neighbors borrowed their religion and ceremonies from the Israelites are Gerhard Vossius, Pierre-Daniel Huet, Theophilus Gale, Hermann Witsius, and John Edwards.

Religion and the *Jewish*, 'tis only in some faint Strokes that are artfully heightned.
4. But especially we are certain that the *Jews* deriv'd their *Cabbala*, and the method
of teaching we are in quest of from the *Ægyptians*, which is what we are going to
prove; but first we will relate the Opinion and Reasons of those that think this Science was brought into *Ægypt* by the Patriarchs. (bk. 3, ch. 17, p. 207; see also chs.
18–19)

Basnage's huge *History* is perhaps the most evenhanded discussion of the topic.
It identifies the principal advocates of each standpoint, states their main arguments, and then allows ample space for opponents to take their stand. Where
more passionate minds might engage in polemics to denounce their opponents,
Basnage allows reason and evidence to settle the points dispassionately. So
Mather. Responding to and frequently moving between all of the three major
positions, Cotton Mather in his "Biblia Americana" rehearses, as it were *in
nuce*, the extensive controversy about the Egyptian origins of the Mosaic laws,
rites, and customs.

My examination will be largely restricted to Mather's critical engagement
with the first and most controversial of the three positions and its rationale.[8] By
focusing on his interpretation of several cultic instruments (Aaron's golden calf,
the polymorphous cherubim, and the ark of the covenant), we can gauge just
how far Mather was prepared to go along with Spencer's argument and why he
disagreed with Spencer and his supporters. As I will demonstrate, Mather generally welcomed Spencer's historical contextualization of the Mosaic laws and
their origin within the dictates of ancient Egyptian culture. He incorporated
Spencer's learned exegesis wherever it appeared relevant and acceptable to his
own purposes and praises Spencer for his vast reading and erudition. However,
Mather was hardly prepared to go along with Spencer's radical conclusions
where they appeared to threaten the divine authority of the scriptures. In order
to understand better Mather's sometimes ambivalent engagement with Spencer,
we must look at the most important of Spencer's predecessors and place his
thesis in its contemporary intellectual context.

---

8   Given the limitations of space in our collection of essays, I am forced to exclude Mather's
response to Spencer's thesis on the Egyptian origin of such ritual sacrifices as the paschal
lamb, the red heifer, and the scapegoat Azazel, as well as Mather's typological readings of
these central issues in Christian exegesis. I shall return to this discussion at a later point.

John Spencer and Maimonides: Adaptation and Accommodation

"Indeed, all the *Mosaic Rites*, did in some remarkable Circumstances, vary from the *Egyptian*," Cotton Mather confessed with amazement as he studied the piacular laws governing the sacrifice of the red heifer [*BA*, Num. 19:2].[9] He was even more surprised that God's incommunicable name I AM THAT I AM seemed to correspond to the mysterious inscription on the statue of Isis at Saïs (Nile Delta). As Plutarch rendered the sacred name, "Εγω ειμι παν το γεγονος, και ην, και εσομενον, *I am all that is, and was, and shall bee*: which," insisted Mather, "is a plain reference to this Name of God in *Exodus*." And if "the Inscription of EI, in the Temple of *Delphos*," can be trusted, then "EI, is the compleat Appellation of God," for when we speak to God, "wee say, *Thou art*; attributing to Him, this True, Certain, & only Appellation, which agrees to Him alone, who is called, *Being*, or, *Existing*" [*BA*, Exod. 3:14].[10] Mather's shock of recognition upon perusing Spencer's *De Legibus Hebræorum* is, perhaps, not all that surprising. After all, Spencer's contextual analysis explores the historical grounds and reasons for the Mosaic rites through the whole corpus of ancient and modern literature that few if any of his peers had mastered or put to the same use.[11] To be sure, Spencer was not the first to assert that God had Moses groomed in the Pharaonic court at Heliopolis, the Egyptian city On in lower Egypt, initiated into the priesthood of the inner adytum of the temple, and trained in the esoteric and exoteric mysteries of Egyptian hieroglyphics.[12] No

---

9   The Lord Bishop of Gloucester William Warburton (1698–1779) – more than ten years after Mather's death – was perhaps less surprised than cautious in endorsing Spencer's thesis, even though the thrust of Warburton's whole argument fully supports Spencer's *De Legibus*. In his *Divine Legation* (1739–41), Warburton conceded, "I mean to charge myself with no more of his [Spencer's] Opinions than what directly tend to the Proof of this Part of my Proposition, *viz.* that there is a great and surprising Relation between the *Jewish* and *Egyptian* Rites, in Circumstances both *opposite* and *similar*" (vol. 2, bk. 4, sec. 6, p. 299).

10   Plutarch, *De Iside et Osiride* (9.354c, line 6).

11   Spencer was not interested in the Egyptian religion per se; he was not a nascent Egyptologist like the German Jesuit Athanasius Kircher (1601–80), whose huge *Oedipus Ægyptiacus* (1652–54) testifies to his heroic, but ultimately unsuccessful endeavor to crack the hieroglyphic code. That honor, of course, belongs to Jean-François Champollion (1790–1832) and his peers who, upon the discovery in 1802 of the Rosetta Stone, laid the foundation for modern Egyptology. Spencer did not have access to the scientific record of modern archeology; the only excavations he could undertake were to dig through tomes of Latin, Greek, Hebrew, and Arabic manuscripts in Cambridge and London. Dannenfeldt illustrates the problems scholars faced during the Renaissance to access information on Egypt given the limited availability of original or translated sources in print. For those faced in the seventeenth and eighteenth centuries, see Iversen (88–145).

12   See Philo Judaeus (note 4 above). In his commentary on Lev. 27:34, Mather relates that "*Moses* was adopted by a Princess of *Egypt*, & educated in the Court of *Egypt*, and all agree, that he was a Man of mighty Interest among the *Egyptians*. They counted him so admirable a Person, that they challenged him for their own; they would needs have him to be an *Heliopolitan*. Doubtless they received many good Instructions from him. And when he opposed

wonder, then, that Moses was able to translate the rites of Egypt into his Levitical laws, and the mysteries reserved for Egypt's priests and pharaohs into the
ceremonies of the Mosaic religion. As Spencer put it in *De Legibus*, "Some ceremonies long practiced [among Idolaters were] reshaped and transferred into
God's own worship. [That] ... when the Law was given, God suffered not a few
ancient ceremonies and rites to be transferred into his worship so as to accommodate unto himself the mores and devotions of the people."[13]

That God saw the need to accommodate his people's addiction to their
idolatrous customs can be inferred from the story of Aaron's molten calf (Exod.
32:4–8), Spencer thought. For while the divine lawgiver received the Decalogue
high up on Mt. Horeb, the Israelites down below (fearing that Moses was dead)
longed for the fleshpots of Egypt, reverted to the abomination (taboo) of their
Egyptian masters, and fell to worshipping their golden idol. Quite obviously,
their forty-year triage in the Sinai desert, as Moses quickly realized, was insuf-
ficient time to break their idolatrous habits. To transfer their former adoration
of the Egyptian god Nemur (the sacred calf Mnevis of On or the Apis bull of
Noph) to Yahweh, their ancestral desert God, whose most conspicuous quality
was his invisibility, his proscription against carved images, and his injunction
against pronouncing his unutterable name – such Draconian measures seemed
too much for a people accustomed to slavery. According to Spencer, the sacrifice
of the paschal lamb (the Egyptian ram god Khnum, Amun-Ra, aka. Jupiter
Hammon) at Passover, the ashes of the red heifer (sacred to the Egyptian Isis
and Typhon) for ritual lustration, the scapegoat Azazel (the embodiment of Typhon) on the Day of Atonement, even the Ark of the Covenant, its cherubic
statues, as well as the high priest's Ephod and its oracular Urim and Thummim
– these and many more seemingly inexplicable institutions of the Mosaic religion had their origin and counterpart in Egypt, Phoenicia, and among the so-
called Zabians.[14] Innumerable parallels between the rites and sacred instruments

---

their Tyranny with such amazing Plagues from Heaven upon them, they could not but conceive a mighty *Fear* of him, *Fear*, which is no small Instrument and Incentive of *Religion* in the
World. *Suidas* tells us, That there had been Prophecies among the *Egyptians*, concerning the
Exploits, which this great Person was to do upon them. And they were as ready to worship
what *Harmed* them, as what *Served* them."

13   The Latin original reads, "Ritus aliquos longo usu receptos reformando, eosque ad Dei
ipsius cultum transferendo. [Ut] ... Deum cum legem daret, cultus antiquitus usitati et institute non pauca tolerasse, et in cultum suum transtulisse, ut seipsum populi moribus et affec-
tibus accommodaret" (*De Legibus*, bk. 1, ch. 13, p. 196).

14   See esp. Spencer's *De Legibus* (bk. 3, diss. 1, chs. 1–2, 639–663) and John Edwards's out-
rage at Spencer's claims ([Polypoikilos Sophia], ch. 8–9, esp. pp. 246–59; 276–84). The designation "Zabians," also spelled "Sabians," is best translated as "pagans." The term is variously
claimed to be an "invention" of Maimonides (*Guide* 3.29–30.514–23), whose study of the
Chaldean book *The Nabatean Agriculture* (allegedly translated by Ibn Wahshiyya in 904)
provided Maimonides with the grounds and reasons why Moses instituted certain ritual laws
to combat pervasive Sabian idolatry. Mather refers to the Sabians throughout his commentary
on the Pentateuch and distinguishes them from the Magians and Zoroastrians of Persia, in his

of the Hebrews and those of the Egyptians and Phoenicians supply Spencer with the means to document his claims (*De Legibus*, bk. 3, diss. 1–8).

Spencer's main thesis was partly adumbrated in Maimonides's *More Nebuchim* (c. 1190; 1551; 1629), in Aquinas's *Summa Theologica* (c. 1265–74), in Franciscus Moncaeus's *Aaron purgatus sive De vitulo aureo* (1606), in John Selden's *De Diis Syris Syntagmata II* (1617), in Jacques Gaffarel's *Curiositez inouyes sur la sculpture talismanique des Persans* (1629), in Gerard Vossius's *De Theologia Gentili, et Physiologia Christina, sive De Origine ac Progressu Idololatriæ* (1641), in Lord Herbert of Cherbury's *De Religione Gentilium* (1663), and in John Marsham's *Chronicus Canon Ægyptiacus Ebraicus Græcus* (1672).[15] All of these ponderous works are put to good use in Spencer's *magnum opus* and, ultimately, in Mather's "Biblia Americana." While Spencer's material evidence is laboriously exhumed from all the classical sources at his disposal, he does acknowledge in his "Prolegomena" his special indebtedness to the Sephardic philosopher Maimonides (1135–1204), whose *More Nebuchim, Doctor Perplexorum* (1551) made a lasting impact on many Christian Hebraists.[16] He praises Maimonides as his great master and his priceless book as his vademecum because its rationalist foundation runs counter to the pervasive mystical and allegorical readings of the Bible alike practiced by Jews and Christians (*De Legibus*, "Prolegomena," chs. 1 and 3, sec. 4, pp. 1, 12–13).

Concerned with the preponderance of Aristotelian philosophy of his day, Maimonides tried to establish a rational foundation for the Mosaic laws, whose dual intent and utility he believed were to purify the morals of the people and to lead them to the true faith by preventing their regression into paganism.[17] Significantly, in *More Nebuchim* (*Guide* 3.31–33.523–34), Maimonides focuses on those ceremonial rites that appear to be without rhyme or reason. He objects to those among the zealots who insist that man should not enquire into the utility of God's laws because God is beyond human comprehension and the incomprehensibleness of his laws is therefore positive proof of their divine origin. If man can penetrate their mystery, so they argue, our laws would only lose their divine

---

fifth essay "V. *Antiqua*. Or, Our Sacred Scriptures illustrated, with some Accounts of the *Sabians* and the *Magians*," as well as in "An Appendix," that follows Mather's commentary on Revelation. For useful discussions of Maimonides and the Sabians, see esp. Elukin's "Maimonides" and Assmann's *Moses the Egyptian* (57–68).

15 For Aquinas, see especially his *Summa* (Pt. 1–2, Q. 98–103; 2:1025–87); for Vossius, see *De Theologia Gentili* (bk. 1, ch. 29, pp. 213–20); and for Lord Herbert, *De Religone* (ch. 3). For the other authors in this list, see my discussion below.

16 In the seventeenth century, Maimonides's brilliant work was available in several Latin translations. The most popular one appears to have been Johann Buxtorf's 1629 translation *Rabbi Mosis Majemonidis Liber* מורה נבוכים *Doctor Perplexorum ... Translatus: ... in Linguam Latinam persicuè & fideliter Conversus*. Hereafter, all citations of Maimonides's work are from the translation of Shlomo Pines, in *Guide of the Perplexed*.

17 See Pines's "Translator's Introduction" (lxi–lxxviii) and M. Friedländer's "Analysis" (xxxix–lix).

status and diminish our reverence because they could then have been devised by man. Maimonides's explanation takes the opposite stance: The rational benefit of the laws is the only possible proof that they are of supernatural origin. Why else would believers take pride in their wisdom?[18]

John Spencer welcomed Maimonides's reasoning in part because Spencer himself attempted to counter what he regarded as "Judaizing tendencies" among radical Calvinists coming out of Cromwell's Interregnum, whose interest in reintroducing the observance of sabbatical labor laws during the Restoration ran counter to Spencer's belief in Christian liberty and the rationalist tendencies of what we now call the early Enlightenment (*De Legibus*, "Prolegomena," ch. 3, sec. 2, pp. 7–11). However, Spencer does not rest there. His larger aims are fundamentally different from those of Maimonides. On the one hand, Maimonides underscores the rational utility of God's laws because he wants to stress their abiding significance. Only in those cases where this explication fails does Maimonides allow that certain ceremonial and cultic laws were borrowed from Israel's pagan neighbors. Spencer on the other hand does his best to demonstrate that *all* ceremonies and sacrifices derived from pagan origin. Their utility originated in the temporal expediency of combating paganism and, therefore, they are now completely abrogated. Such ceremonial institutions as the Sabbath, ritual lustrations, observations of the new moon, the ark of the covenant, the use of the Urim and Thummim in divination, and many others, derived from Egyptian customs and demonstrate the extent to which the Mosaic laws were clearly indebted to pagan institutions. Spencer's historicist approach thus pursues a rather negative if not destructive aim; it borders on completely disavowing revelation as the origin of the Old Testament.

Why conservative exegetes would feel threatened by Spencer's heterodox approach is particularly apparent in the first book of *De Legibus*. As indicated in its subtitle "In quo fuse agitur de generalibus legum & rituum Judaicorum

---

18   Maimonides argues, "They [opponents] think that if those laws were useful in this existence and have been given to us for this or that reason, it would be as if they derived from the reflection and the understanding of some intelligent [human] being. If, however, there is a thing for which the intellect could not find any meaning at all and those do not lead to something useful, it indubitably derives from God; for the reflection of man would not lead to such a thing." The case is quite different, Maimonides insists, because the divine wisdom of the laws is revealed in its usefulness to us (Deut. 6:24; 4:6). "Now if there is a thing for which no reason is known and that does not either procure something useful or ward off something harmful, why should one say of one who believes in it or practices it that he is *wise and understanding* and of great worth? And why should the religious communities think it a wonder? Rather things are indubitably as we have mentioned: every *commandment* from among these ... [613] *commandments* exists either with a view to communicating a correct opinion, or to putting an end to an unhealthy opinion, or to communicating a rule of justice, or to warding off an injustice, or to endowing man with a noble moral quality, or to warning them against an evil moral quality. Thus all [the commandments] are bound up with three things: opinions, moral qualities, and political civic action" (*Guide* 3.31.524).

causis" (bk. 1, p. 19), Spencer is mainly concerned with rationalizing how the Mosaic laws were instituted as a means of abolishing idolatry and of separating the Israelites from their pagan neighbors by casting aspersions on pagan deities. To Spencer, this intent of the law – to segregate God's people to keep them pure – is the principal means to justify the temporality of the Jewish ceremonial laws, whose purpose would become abrogated when the cause for their original establishment had been accomplished. This abrogation would occur either when idolatry among the Israelites was eradicated through their successful separation or in Christ's sacrifice in which all temporal laws become null and void. For these reasons, Spencer argues, the laws governing the Sabbath, circumcision, diet, lustrations, processions, sacrifices, and blood rituals are obsolete because they were tied to specific times, persons, or locations, and borne out of a historical necessity no longer existent. In contrast to Spencer, Maimonides insists on the perpetual validity of these laws which – though they had their origin in a particular historical necessity – remain relevant because of their intrinsic value. These laws could only be abolished by a new revelation whose divine origin is validated by miracles.

Spencer's radicalism is, perhaps, most apparent in book three. In eight dissertations and great historical detail he establishes the translation of pagan customs into the Mosaic laws: "De ritibus e Gentium moribus in Legem translatis," "De ratione & origine sacrificiorum," "De lustrationibus & purificationibus Hebræorum," "De Neomeniarum Festis," "De origine Arcæ & Cherubinorum," "De Ratione & Origine Templi, De Urim & Thummim," and "De Hirco Emissario, & præcipuis Expiationis *Judaicæ* Ceremoniis." It is in these eight dissertations that Spencer's greatest contribution to the historical study of religion and religious customs is to be found. And it is here that the diverging interests of Maimonides and Spencer become evident.

Why did Moses and Aaron, his high priest, sanction such arcane and incomprehensible practices? Man's fallen nature cannot change from one extreme to another on a sudden, Maimonides contends in his *Guide for the Perplexed*. For this reason, God wisely accommodated his laws to the limited capacity of man, because man is powerless to cast off practices to which he had been accustomed for centuries. As Maimonides explains the issue, "the universal service upon which we were brought up consisted in offering various species of living beings in the temples in which images were set up, in worshipping the latter, and in burning incense before them." God used a "gracious ruse" which "did not require that He give us a Law prescribing the rejection, abandonment, and abolition of all these kinds of worship." Knowing that sinful man – like a leopard – cannot change his spots, God wisely allowed these forms of worship to continue, "but transferred them from created or imaginary and unreal things to His own name." He therefore "commanded us to build a temple for Him" (Exod. 25:8), just as we had seen the archetype in Egypt; "to have an altar for

His name" (Exod. 20:21–24), just as we used to have for the idols of Egypt; "to have the sacrifice offered up to Him" (Lev. 1:2), just as we used to do for our idols in Goshen; "to bow down in worship before Him; and to burn incense before Him," just as we used to do before the gods of our Egyptian masters. But in the Holy Land, God outlawed "the performance of any of these actions" for any other god but Himself (Exod. 22:20; 34:14). "Through this divine ruse," Maimonides reasons, "the memory of *idolatry* was effaced" and worship of the one true God established, "while at the same time the souls had no feeling of repugnance and were not repelled because of the abolition of modes of worship to which they were accustomed" (*Guide* 3.32.526, 527). By divine direction, then, many inexplicable and seemingly arbitrary laws of Moses constitute a counterreligion, a "normative inversion" of idolatrous practices turned upside down and recycled in the worship of God.[19] To be sure, this process of re-educating his people was slow and never-ending. Change, therefore, was not effected instantaneously through a miracle, but gradually, through a long process of training and accommodation. If God had been inclined to change man's habits through a miracle, the whole Mosaic pedagogy, all the prophets, and "all giving of the Law would have been useless" (*Guide* 3.32.529).

Ironically, Maimonides's explication of the Mosaic ceremonial laws – though grounded in the need to justify their rationality – turned out to be a double-edged sword. For in explaining, for instance, why a kid must not be boiled in its mother's milk (Exod. 23:19; 34:16; Deut.14:21), or why linens and woolens or the seeds of different plants must not be mixed (Lev. 19:19; Deut. 22:9, 11), why tattoos and cross-dressing are strictly forbidden (Lev. 19:28; Deut. 22:5), why the blood of slaughtered animals must be poured on the ground and covered with soil (Lev. 19:26), or why only predominantly male animal sacrifices (rams, goats, and bulls) – but no females – were acceptable to God (Lev. 1:3, 10; 22:19), or, finally, why God commanded salt to be added to the meat offerings, but objected to honey (Lev. 2:11, 13), Maimonides claims that these rituals originated among the Egyptians and Zabians (gentiles), whose rites were so pervasive that they could only be erased by turning them on their head and by doing the exact opposite.[20] Since the ancient ram-god Khnum

---

19 During the past twenty years, the seventeenth-century controversy surrounding Spencer and Maimonides has been re-examined by scholars from various disciplines. See Funkenstein (202–43) and especially Assmann's recent "The Mosaic Distinction," *Moses the Egyptian* (55–90), "Moses as Go-Between," *Of God and Gods* (127–45), and *Price*; see also Parente, Stroumsa (19–21), and Sutcliffe (70–71, 199–200).

20 For the proscription against seething a kid in its mother's milk, see Maimonides (3.48.599), Spencer (bk. 2, ch. 9, pp. 333–42), Mather [*BA*, Exod. 23:19]; against mixing linens and woolens, and seeds, see Maimonides (3.26.507; 3.37.544, 548–49), Spencer (bk. 2, ch. 33, pp. 544–51), Mather [*BA*, Lev. 19:19]; against tattoos and cross-dressing, Maimonides (3.37.544–45), Spencer (bk. 2, chs. 19–20, pp. 403–17), Mather [*BA*, Lev. 19:28]; against consuming blood, Maimonides (3.46.585–86), Spencer (bk. 2, ch. 15, pp. 376–84), Mather [*BA*,

(Amun-Ra) was widely revered in Egypt, the Israelites demonstrated their defiance by slaughtering their sacred animal. That is why the blood of the paschal lamb (ram) was smeared on lintels and the abomination (taboo) of the Egyptians sacrificed to the one God. "In this way," Maimonides reasons, "an action considered by them [Egyptians] an extreme act of disobedience was the one through which one came near to God and sought forgiveness for one's sins. Thus wrong opinions, which are diseases of the human soul, are cured by their contrary found at the other extreme" (*Guide* 3.46.581–82).[21] Either way, this divine ruse was grounded in the temporal necessity of preventing God's people from backsliding into the abomination of their former overlords.[22]

Maimonides's problem to explain the dual function of the Mosaic ritual laws becomes apparent since neither function is rooted in divine revelation, but in the quite human need to adapt already existing pagan rituals to the divine service of God. The bulwark of revelation upon which monotheistic religions built their claims to divine truth is thus relegated to the status of political expe-

---

Lev. 17:1, 19:26]; sacrificing predominantly male animals, Maimonides (3.46.588–90), Spencer (bk. 2, ch. 4, pp. 293–300; bk. 3, diss. 2, ch. 2, pp. 755–57), Mather [*BA*, Exod. 12, insert; Lev. 1:3, 17]; against sacrificing honey, Maimonides (3.46.582); Spencer (bk. 2, ch. 11, pp. 345–49), Mather [*BA*, Lev. 1:17, 2:11].

21 Maimonides argues that the first intention of maintaining sacrificial laws is to keep God's people from "worshipping someone other than Me. ... It is for the sake of that principle that I transferred these modes of worship to My name, so that the trace of *idolatry* be effaced and the fundamental principle of My unity be established" (*Guide* 3.32.530). For a much earlier example of this form of accommodationism, see *Soncino Midrash Rabbah* (Lev. 22:8). As the parable goes, the king cures his son from eating forbidden things by having him always eat from his table.

22 As a resident of Egypt late in his life, Maimonides was probably familiar with the writings of the Egyptian Manetho (fl. 280 BCE), high priest of Heliopolis. Manetho's *Ægyptiaca*, a history of Egypt from pre-historical times to 342 BCE, relates that in the eighteenth Dynasty, sometime during the reign of Amenophis (Amenhotep III), one of the priests of Hêliopolis called Osarsêph, rose in rebellion against the Egyptian king and commanded his fellow rebels "that they should neither worship the gods nor refrain from any of the animals prescribed as especially sacred in Egypt, but should sacrifice and consume all alike, and that they should have intercourse with none save those of their own confederacy." He framed "a great number of laws like these [that were] completely opposed to Egyptian custom. ..." Osarsêph and his Shepherd allies despoiled the sacred temples, defaced the images of the Egyptian gods, and turned their temples into "kitchens to roast the sacred animals which the people worshipped: and they would compel the priests and prophets to sacrifice and butcher the beasts, afterwards casting the men forth naked." When Osarsêph incited his followers to rise up in rebellion, "he changed his name and was called Moses" (*Ægyptiaca*, fragm. 54, in *Manetho* 127, 131). Likewise, the Roman historian Tacitus (c. 56-c. 120 CE) comments on the Mosaic inversion of Egyptian rites. "To ensure his future hold over the people," Tacitus reports in his *Annals*, "Moses introduced a new cult, which was the opposite of all other religions. All that we hold sacred they held profane, and they allowed practices which we abominate. They dedicated in the innermost part of the Temple an image of the animal whose guidance had put an end to their wandering and thirst, after first killing a ram, apparently as an insult to Ammon. They also sacrifice bulls because the Egyptians worship the bull Apis" (*Histories* 5.4.234–35).

dience to control the common masses. Maimonides tries to solve this conundrum by limiting the inversions of pagan customs to those cases in which they are bound up with the polytheistic cosmology of the Israelites's pagan neighbors. Yet when their function can be separated from their heathen origin, Maimonides does not object to their wholesale adaptation and integration into the Mosaic code.

His vindication of the Mosaic laws satisfied many to whom their divine origin was borne out most of all in their rational utility for man. There were many others, however, who severely censured Maimonides for depriving these laws of their supernatural foundation. Moshe ben Nachman of Gerona, Spain (c. 1290–1375), Bachya ben Asher of Saragossa (c. 1255–1340), and many other Rabbinic commentators reproached the great rabbi for questioning the mystery of divine revelation, the sole claim to the trustworthiness of revealed religion, and for reducing the ceremonial laws to little more than the farsighted policies of mortal man. According to Maimonides's rationale, not God but man seemed to have devised the time-honored ceremonies encoded in the Torah! "The disease of idolatry would surely have been far better cured if we were to eat [these animal-deities] to our full, which would be considered by them forbidden and repugnant, and something they would never do!" Nachmanides fumed. "Far be it that they should have no other purpose and intention except the elimination of idolatrous opinions from the minds of fools" (*Commentary* 3:20, on Lev. 1:9). And Rabbi Bachya ben Asher warned, "The whole subject of animal sacrifice dating back as it does to the first man is a subject replete with mystical significance. It contains hidden elements of the interrelations between different parts of G'd's creation. … All those who do understand these matters are dutybound to conceal their knowledge and not publicise it indiscriminately. This knowledge may only be revealed for the sake of the Creator's honour to selected individuals, exceptionally pious persons" (*Torah Commentary* 5: 1486).[23]

Christian theologians were generally more accepting of Maimonides's rationalism. They welcomed Maimonides because he seemed to confirm their belief that the real purpose of the ceremonial laws of Moses was to serve as shadowy types and figures of Christ in the Old Testament and whose binding force was terminated in his crucifixion in the New. The ceremonies, whose mystical function was to foreshadow the new covenant, had now accomplished their office and were no longer applicable to his Church. Why else did God use the Romans in 69 CE to raze Jerusalem and its temple and thus stopped all sacrifices offered on his alter? To be sure, Maimonides would not have agreed with his Christian counterparts on any of these issues. The law that God gave to Moses would last forever. Neither the moral, ceremonial, or any other part of

---

23 For much the same argument, see Rabbi Yaakov ben Rabbeinu Asher's *Tur on the Torah* (3: 786–88).

the Mosaic pedagogy would ever be abrogated. In fact, once the Jewish messiah arrived, he would lead his people back to their ancestral heritage, cast out all foreign oppressors from the Promised Land, rebuilt Jerusalem and its temple, and once again resume the ancient sacrifices in the only locale where God allowed them to be offered.[24] For the most part, the Christian church did not expect the resumption of animal sacrifices in Jerusalem even if its members shared the belief in the return of the Jews to the holy land. After all, Jesus Christ's ultimate sacrifice had atoned for the sins of true believers once and for all.[25]

I already mentioned that Spencer, by way of contrast, did no more than pay lip-service to such a typological interpretation of the Mosaic laws and rites. His interest in Maimonides was rather different from that of most of his Christian peers. For him Maimonides's rationalizing account of the laws' evolution served as a springboard for much larger claims about the pagan origins of the Jewish religion. Spencer's own position becomes clear in the third book of *De Legibus*,

24 See esp. Goldish, Idel, Katz and Popkin (3–88), Ravitzky, and Scholem (103–98).

25 Although their exoteric function had been abrogated in the death of Christ, theologians in the medieval church argued that animal sacrifices by themselves might yet be a useful tool in bringing pagans into the Christian fold. The medieval church was particularly prone to accommodate the demonology and rituals of pagan converts as long as they could be redirected and given a Christian signification. Perhaps the most prominent example of this sort is preserved in the *Historia Ecclesiastica Gentis Anglorum* (731), composed by the Venerable Bede (c. 673–735), the Father of English History. Writing the history of the English Church, Bede incorporates a missive of Pope Gregory the Great (c. 540–604) to Abbot Mellitus, who was about to go on a missionary journey to Britain. The letter is dated 17 June 601 and deserves to be quoted at length; it illustrates just how far the wisdom of Mosaic accommodationism was operating even in the medieval Church. Pope Gregory I gives the following instructions: "We have been giving careful thought to the affairs of the English, and have come to the conclusion that the temples of the idols among that people should on no account be destroyed. The Idols are to be destroyed, but the temples themselves are to be aspersed with holy water, altars set up in them, and relics deposited there. For if these temples are well-built, they must be purified from the worship of demons and dedicated to the service of the true God. In this way, we hope that the people, seeing that their temples are not destroyed, may abandon their error, and flocking more readily to their accustomed resorts, may come to know and adore the true God. And since they have a custom of sacrificing many oxen to demons, let some other solemnity be substituted in its place, such as a day of Dedication of the Festivals of the holy martyrs whose relics are enshrined there. ... They are no longer to sacrifice beasts to the Devil, but they may kill them for food to the praise of God, and give thanks to the Giver of all gifts for the plenty they enjoy. If the people are allowed some worldly pleasures in this way, they will more readily come to desire the joys of the spirit. For it is certainly impossible to eradicate all errors from obstinate minds at one stroke, and whoever wishes to climb to a mountain top climbs gradually step by step, and not in one leap. It was in this way that the Lord revealed Himself to the Israelite people in Egypt, permitting the sacrifices formerly offered to the Devil to be offered thenceforward to Himself instead. So He bade them sacrifice beasts to Him, so that, once they became enlightened, they might abandon one element of sacrifice and retain another. For, while they were to offer the same beasts as before, they were to offer them to God instead of to idols, so that they would no longer be offering the same sacrifices ..." (*History* 1.30.86–87). Clearly, then, Pope Gregory's directives are of a kind with those that Moses gave Aaron in the wilderness: to allow ritual sacrifices to continue but to consecrate them to the true God.

which consists of eight dissertations that move well beyond Maimonides's concern in *More Nebuchim*. For instance, Spencer's explication of the festivity of the New Moon and its origin ("De Neomeniarum Festis") is particularly interesting, because it is well known that of all the sin offerings only the sacrifice offered up on Yom Kippur, the Day of Atonement, is called "the sin offering unto the Lord" (*De Legibus*, bk. 3, diss. 4, pp. 804–28; diss. 8, pp. 1039–87). Maimonides explains that "only the *he-goat* offered on the *New-Moon as a sin-offering* is called in [Scripture] *a sin-offering unto the Lord*" (Num. 28:15). This piacular designation was devised to ensure that no one would mistake the sacrifice of a he-goat "to be a sacrifice to the moon, such as was offered by the Copts of Egypt at the beginning of the months." The purpose and common origin of this ritual thus becomes apparent. Maimonides, however, tries to rationalize the use and function of the sacrificial goat, the time, and day of the ceremony (first day of the new moon) by insisting that the goat is the most suitable sin offering and that it is to be distinguished from its pagan cousin by the designation "*unto the Lord*" (*Guide* 3.46.590). Spencer agrees but insists that the real reason was that Moses intended to cast aspersions on the goat, whose statue the people revered as a demonic god whom they sought to assuage through a live sacrifice. Nonetheless, the rite of the scapegoat, though originating among the pagans, served with minor variations an almost identical purpose among the Israelites (*De Legibus*, lib. 3, diss. 8, ch. 7, pp. 1059–63). Although his conclusions were certainly the most bold, Spencer, as I suggested above, was neither the first nor the only Christian theologian in his own period to argue that the Israelites borrowed their ceremonial rites from their pagan neighbors, especially from the Egyptians, whose civilization was the most advanced and powerful in the hemisphere.[26] Thus, before I proceed to discuss Mather's position it seems appropriate to offer a short survey of the early modern debate about the origins of the Mosaic laws.

All the Wisdom of Egypt: Mosaic Ceremonies and Pagan Religion

In the early seventeenth century, the learned French antiquarian Franciscus Moncaeus (François de Monçeaux, fl.1550–1600) had much to say on the issue. In *Aaron purgatus, sive de Vitulo aureo libri duo* (1606), he alleged that

---

26   In fact, this argument was frequently maintained by some of the earliest Church Fathers, who interpreted the sacrificial rituals as part of the Mosaic pedagogy to break the Israelites' addiction to their Egyptian customs. See St. Irenaeus (*Against Heresies* 4.14.2–15.2, and esp. 4.17.3; in *ANF* 1: 479–80, 482–84); Eusebius of Caesarea (*Proof of the Gospel* 1.6.16c–17d); Tertullian (*Against Marcion* 2.18; in *ANF* 3: 311–12); Theodoret of Cyrus (*Questions on the Octateuch* 1:309; 2:3–4, 11; on Exod. Quest. 55; on Lev. Quest. 1.1–3, 5); St. Augustine (*Letter to Marcellinus* 136.2; 138.2, 5, 8; in *NPNF* 1: 473, 481–83). Benin's excellent discussion in "Cunning" and *Footprints* provide useful background on these issues.

the winged cherubim on the ark of the covenant, the golden calves of Aaron and Jeroboam, Micah's teraphim, and many other ceremonial implements were all borrowed from their Egyptian or Phoenician neighbors. The statues of the golden calves just like those of the teraphim, Moncaeus claimed, derived from the polymorphous cherubim and were perfectly lawful in ancient Israel. These bovine, winged cherubim originally were effigies of the Egyptian Apis bull set upon the ark of the covenant and served as the mercy seat upon which God is seated (*Aaron purgatus*, bk. 1, ch. 3, pp. 105–06). The cherubim were *not* angels shaped like humans – as is commonly believed – but rather winged calves or bulls (bk. 1, ch. 6, p. 111), because their purpose was to convey God like a ruler riding on steeds. Angels in human shape would not at all be suitable for such a purpose (bk. 1, ch. 4, pp. 107–10). These bovine statues were no idols at all, but legitimate instruments through which the devout – lying prostrate before God's throne – could direct their prayers to Jehovah (bk. 1, ch. 21, pp. 154–56). However, those who erroneously worshipped the winged bulls as their god were idolaters. Although the devotions of the pious and profane were outwardly the same, their true disposition was discovered when they were forced to drink the water of separation (bk. 2, chs. 7–8, pp. 168–72).[27] Furthermore, Moncaeus posited that the golden calves in Jeroboam's temples at Bethel and Dan (1 Kings 12:26–30) were really replicas of Aaron's golden calf (Exod. 32:1–4), of the mercy seat of the Mosaic ark, and of the cherubim decorating the veil of the Mosaic tabernacle and of Solomon's temple (Exod. 36:8, 37:6–7; 1 Kings:7–8). In Ezekiel's merkabah vision (Ezek. 1:6–10, 10:1, 14–22), these cherubim are mixed creatures with four faces – man, lion, ox, and eagle – and thus explain the polymorphous cherubim in Solomon's temple (1 Kings 6:21–35, 7:25) and the presence of the twelve brazen oxen supporting the huge laver ("moulten Sea") of the abattoir. Had Jeroboam's golden calves not been exact copies of those in Jerusalem's temple he tried to supplant, Moncaeus argued, the Israelites in the northern kingdom would not have accepted them but continued their thrice-annual pilgrimages to Jerusalem. Jeroboam was therefore no idolater as is commonly believed, but merely a schismatic. If Moncaeus tried to justify the use of icons, images, and statues in the temple, his novel argument was taken quite seriously because he dared to spell out what many had suspected all along. His *Aaron purgatus* appeared in the wake of sporadic iconoclasms that swept through Protestant countries during the Counter-Reformation. Worse yet, emphasizing the profane origin of certain Mosaic institutions, Moncaeus implicitly questioned the Bible's claim as an inspired book. Perhaps that is why he was cen-

---

27   Abraham Ibn Ezra (Exod. 32:20) says as much that when Moses forced the Israelites to drink the waters that contained the gold dust of the Aaron's calf from the floor of the tabernacle, "the water caused a sign to appear on the face of those who served the calf or their bellies swelled up. For otherwise, how could the Levites know who worshipped the golden Calf?" (*Commentary* 676–77).

sured by Roman Catholics and Protestants alike.[28] Significantly, the English and Dutch editors of *Criticorum Sacrorum* (1660, 1698) deemed his *Aaron Excused, or Concerning the Golden Calf* sufficiently noteworthy to reprint the Latin text – along with its official condemnation – in their nine-volume commentary (1: 86–192).[29]

Never quite willing to let a good controversy die without making the most of it, the French scholar Jacques Gaffarel (1601–81), astrologer extraordinaire and librarian to Cardinal Richelieu, published his *Curiositez inouyes sur la sculpture talismanique des Persans* (1629), for which he was censured by the theologians of the Sorbonne and forced to retract. *Unheard-of Curiosities* (1650), the English title of Gaffarel's book, was a popular work in its time. It went through at least three French editions before Edmund Chilmead, chaplain of Christ-Church, Oxford, translated it into English. "The Cherubim, which *Moses* made to the Arke, were in the figure of Calves" in imitation of Aaron's bovine creature, Gaffarel opined with Moncaeus's work to back his claims. As Moses's high priest, Aaron would have done "nothing, but what he conceived *Moses* himselfe would have done." These cherubim were made "after the patterne that was shewed to *Moses*," Aaron, "and the seventy Elders" in the mount, with the face of a man, a lion, a calf, and an eagle – just as we find them later described in Ezekiel's vision (Ezek. 10:14). "If the People afterwards provoked God to wrath" by venerating these tauromorphous creatures, "it was not for making the Calfe, but for worshipping it" (*Unheard-of* 20, 22). Gaffarel then takes Moncaeus's argument one step further and equates the cherubim with the teraphim. Images such as the cherubim and teraphim, Gaffarel avers, were clearly employed in divinatory rites, even in Solomon's temple (*Unheard-of* 68–75). Like his predecessor, then, Gaffarel does not object to the veneration of images per se but only to their receiving the adoration that is due to God alone. But who can separate the idolaters of Aaron's golden calf from those who directed their prayers towards the bovine effigy as a representation of the God of Moses? Gafferel wondered.

The unusual frankness of such arguments rendered the motives of Moncaeus and Gaffarel sufficiently suspect that most of their peers dismissed their scholarship as heterodox. It was quite a different matter with *Chronicus Canon Ægyptiacus Ebraicus Græcus* (1672), by Sir John Marsham (1602–85), a learned Kentish antiquarian and chronologer. In more than six-hundred pages, he compares the history and chronologies of the Egyptians, Chaldeans, Greeks, and

---

28 Moncaeus's *Aaron purgatus* was placed on the *Index* in 1607; see *Index Librorum prohibitorum* (627). Robert Visorius, professor of theology at the Sorbonne, published his refutation *Aaronis purgati* (1609).

29 Sheehan (40–41) provides a brief but helpful discussion of Moncaeus. A detailed summary of Moncaeus's argument is furnished in Matthew Poole's *Synopsis Criticorum* on Exod. 32:1–35 (1: 480–92) and a translation appears in *Exegetical Labors* (5: 349–87).

Hebrews. In Marsham's reading, the similarities between the cultural, legal, and religious institutions of these peoples make obvious their close contact and mutual influence. The Egyptian civilization and its astronomical periods far surpass those of its neighbors, Marsham argues. The Hebrews, long touted by pious believers as the most ancient civilization, received many of their religious and civil laws from the Egyptians, whose chronology and kings list of thirty dynasties surpassed those of the Old Testament by thousands of years. "Immense are the religious institutions of the Egyptians, whether we examine the most ancient worship or varieties." According to Marsham, then, "the divine and semi-divine dynasties before the flood" had to be properly arranged, "even if they contradicted the Mosaic chronology, which the superstitious people begin with the age of Enosh" (*Chronicus* 54).[30] Marsham tries to reconcile these diverging chronologies by arguing that the thirty Pharaonic dynasties were not successive but simultaneous, for they reigned at the same time in different parts of Egypt. Marsham received high praise from many of his peers in England and on the Continent (*Chronicus canon* was reprinted in Leipzig in 1676 and at Franeker in 1696) for having bestowed order and harmony on Egypt's preposterously long chronology and for making a comparative history with Israel and its neighboring kingdoms possible.[31]

His critics were far less kind. For instance, the French Oratorian Richard Simon (1638–1712) chastised Marsham in the "Avertissement" to the Rotterdam edition of Simon's own *Histoire Critique Du Vieux Testament* (1685) for asserting that Moses borrowed his laws from Egypt: "Je veux dire l'*Histoire chronologique des Égyptiens* de Marsham, qui semble n'avoir point d'autre but que d'insinuer dans l'esprit de son lecteur que toute la religion de Moïse et des Hébreux a été prise sur celle des Égyptiens" ("Avertissement" 796–97).[32] This dismissive criticism is rather ironic since Simon postulated in his *Histoire Critique Du Vieux Testament* that Moses was *not* the author of the Pentateuch, but

---

30   "Immensa res est Ægyptiorum Religio, seu cultus vetustatem spectemus, seu varietatem. Deorum Semideorúmque Dynastias ante Diluvium collocavimus: neque refragatur chronologia Mosaica, quæ superstitionem Gentium refert ad *Enosi* ætatem" (*Chronicus* 54).

31   Marsham (2–12) corrects the ancient Egyptian chronology of 36,525 years by establishing that the kings list of thirty dynasties does not signify the consecutive, but coterminous dynastic rule in several Egyptian regions. This discovery allows Marsham to align the chronologies of Egypt with those of the Hebrews and Greeks. Basnage (bk. 3, ch. 18, secs. 5–6, p. 212) summarizes the discovery of the coterminous rule of regional and local kings. The ultimate collapse of the Bible's traditional chronology and its consequences for biblical interpretation is described by Rossi (145–52 and 158–67) and Grafton. For a discussion of the historical-philological criticism of the Old Testament, see section 3 of my introduction to Cotton Mather's *Biblia Americana* (Genesis) 1: 113–74.

32   "I should like to say that Marsham's *Chronological History of the Egyptians* appears to have no other intent than to insinuate in the mind of his reader that the whole religion of Moses and the Hebrews was taken from that of the Egyptians" ("Avertissement" 796–97). See also Rossi (126).

only of some small parts, and that much of the Old Testament was periodically rewritten by "écrivains publics" who were responsible for keeping the ancient records up to date (107–41).[33]

The contemporary ecclesiastical and political implications of the debate can be seen in the Right Reverend Samuel Parker (1640–88), bishop of Oxford, who seems to have borrowed his thesis from Moncaeus and Gaffarel. In his *Reasons for Abrogating the Test [Act]* (1688), Parker pleaded for toleration, especially for Roman Catholics, because the use of images and statues of saints did *not* constitute idolatry. If modern divines would "soberly enquire into the Nature and Original of *Idolatry*," Parker argued, they would soon discover that they completely misunderstood God's prohibition against graven images (Gen. 20:4–5). It is "not the meer Image it self that is the Idol," Parker opined, "but the Image as representing a false God, tho it be only a Symbol, and not a Picture of him, as most of the Heathen Images were, of the *Sun*, as the *Calf*, and the *Ram*" (79). That Moses did not proscribe effigies per se, but only images that represented false gods, like those worshipped by Israel's pagan neighbors, can be seen in the use of the two polymorphous cherubim, which God instructed Moses to set upon the ark of the covenant to serve as his mercy seat (Exod. 25:20–22). The most learned scholars – Hugo Grotius, John Spencer, Juan Bautista Villalpandus, and Samuel Bochart – likewise concluded they were of a mixed form, "in which that of a Bullock had the biggest share; but compounded of these four shapes, a Man's Face, an Eagles Wings, a Lyons Back, an Oxes or Bullocks Thighs and Feet" (123) (Ezek. 1, 10; Rev. 4:6–7). These sphinx-like cherubim with four faces "were the most solemn and sacred part of the Jewish Religion; and therefore, tho Images, so far from Idolatry; that God made them the *Seat* of his Presence, and from between them delivered his Oracles; so that something more is required to make *Idolatry*, than the *use of Images*" (125–26).

Dr. Edward Stillingfleet's polemic *A Discourse concerning the Idolatry Practiced in the Church of Rome* (1671) therefore does not stand up to scrutiny, Parker insisted. For when the learned doctor asserted that Moses and the Israelites "only directed their Worship *towards* the Images," but did not worship the cherubim, he seems to be equivocating. The Israelites bowed toward these images "as the Symbols of God's Presence, and that is to Worship God by *Images*, or to give the same Signs of Reverence to his *Representations*, as to *Himself*. ... And if so much outward Worship may be given to Images, as Symbols of the Divine presence, it is enough to justifie it" (126).[34] If anyone did not accept

---

33 For a discussion of Richard Simon's *Histoire Critique* and Mather's response, see my introduction to *Biblia Americana* (1: 113–74).

34 In his *Institutes* (2: 62–66), Francis Turretin (1623–87), a Reformed theologian of Geneva, also explores the question of images and their legal use in sacred places. Surprisingly, he presents some of the same arguments as Parker does.

his authority on this matter, Bishop Parker was only too glad to refer his readers to "that admirable Book of Dr. *Spencers*, concerning the Jewish Laws and the Reason of them." For anyone who loves the wisdom of the ancients "may have his glut of Pleasure and Satisfaction" in reading Spencer's *De Legibus* (98). The danger which Spencer's historicist argument posed to Protestant orthodoxy then becomes all too apparent. In the hands of distracters, it might be employed for all sorts of questionable purposes, perhaps even return icons, images, and saints' statues through the backdoors of Protestant churches from which the Reformers had much ado to cast them out almost in living memory. Ultimately, Spencer's research might even have the (unintended) purpose of breaking down the wall of separation between sacred and profane religions. Worse yet, in tracing the origin of the Mosaic ceremonies to their alleged roots in paganism, Spencer's historical parallels might turn the Judeo-Christian religions into something akin to variants of Oriental creeds whose sacred or profane status was relative to the succession of their respective prominence accorded to them by the dominant power structure.[35]

Spencer and Mather on the Idols of Egypt

It is now high time to cross the Atlantic and to sketch Cotton Mather's involvement in the controversy over the Egyptian origin of Hebrew ceremonial laws and cultic instruments. As is well known by now, "Biblia Americana" is a vast storehouse of arcane and modern knowledge, which clearly indicates how far the English colonies in North America participated in the scholarship and intellectual debates of the period. Let me single out some of the most significant examples to illustrate how Mather negotiates the conflict between Reformed and heterodox exegesis: "There ha's been an Opinion, very plausibly maintained and laboriously defended," Mather raises the issue in "Biblia Americana,"

> That the *Egyptians* were they who had the first Rules and Rites of *Religion* among them; and that not only the *Religious Rites* of other Nations, but even [those] of the *Israelites* themselves, were derived from the *Egyptians*: And that in the Reformation whereto the Great God brought the *Israelites*, He wisely considered, how strongly they were tinctured with the *Egyptian* Superstitions; And He therefore Allowed the Continuance of many of them; only He Corrected them, He Improved them, He Applied them unto better Purposes. Tis a prodigious Ostentation of Lit-

---

35 Curiously, William Warburton, Lord Bishop of Gloucester, did not seem to be overly concerned about the matter of what the Mosaic accommodation of pagan ceremonies might mean for Christianity and revelation as such. In his *Divine Legation*, he asks, "And what is it, we lose? Nothing sure very great or excellent. The imaginary Honour of being original in certain Rites, indifferent in themselves; and only good or bad as is the *Authority* that enjoyns them, and the *Object* to which they are directed." Well, there it is (vol. 2, bk. 4, sec. 6, p. 355).

erature, which [John Marsham, Athanasius Kircher, and John Spencer] our *Hero's* have made, in the Asserting of this Opinion. [*BA*, Lev. 27:34]

Having thus identified the bone of contention, Mather engages the theses of Marsham and Spencer in a process of give and take. The works of Samuel Bochart (1599–1667), John Edwards (1637–1716), Herman Witsius (1636–1708), Pierre Jurieu (1637–1713), and Thomas Tenison (1636–1715) among many others provide Mather with much useful ammunition to combat the alleged enemies of the sacred scriptures. Mather is not content, however, with presenting a one-sided interpretation of the matter. He is prepared to give both traditional and heterodox readings a fair hearing.

For instance, John Edwards, conservative English theologian that he was, tried his utmost to defend the sanctity of the Bible by somehow palliating the story of Aaron's golden calf (Exod. 32:1–8), in *A Discourse Concerning the Authority, Stile, and Perfection of the Books of the Old and New Testament* (1693–95). Here, Edwards saw a veiled allusion to the lean and fat cows in Pharaoh's dream vision (Gen. 41:1–7, 25–31), which Joseph providentially explicated to save the people from starvation. The Egyptian Apis or Serapis bull of Memphis (Noph), Edwards opined, was really nothing but "a true Hieroglyphic of *Joseph*," whose memory was sacred to the Egyptians for saving them from catastrophic famine. Similarly, Joseph's association with the Egyptian Serapis bull seemed also evident to the Roman monk and historian Ruffinus, who relates that "a *Bushel* was placed on its Head; signifying, that *Joseph* was the Giver of *Corn*, and measured it with exact Proportions in his giving of it. Yea, tis probable, that *Serapis*, was originally *Sorapis*; a Compound of *Sor*, an Ox; and *Apis*, an Egyptian Word, perhaps of the same Importance" (*BA* 1: 440).[36] Edwards's argument suggests that the Israelites dancing around Aaron's golden calf revered as their savior no one else but the hieroglyphic of Joseph, their famous

---

36   Edwards (*Discourse* 1: 214–15, 216). Edwards's diatriabe against Marsham and Spencer is particularly prominent in *Compleat History* (chs. 6–8). The Greco-Egyptian Osiris-Apis or Serapis is the deified representation of the Apis bull of Memphis (Plutarch's *Moralia* 5: 70–73; *De Iside et Osiride* 29.362c-d). Revered as lord of Hades, Osirapis (Pluto) delivered his oracles and cures through dreams. The association of Joseph as "Zaphnath-paaneah," meaning "the revealer of secrets" (Gen. 41:45); i.e., the interpreter of Pharaoh's dream of the seven fat and lean cows (Gen. 41:1–45), is here taken to be the biblical hero commemorated in the Serapis cult – if Gerard Vossius (*De Theologia Gentili*, bk. 1, ch. 29, pp. 213–20), Theophilus Gale (*Court* [1672], pt 1, bk. 2, ch. 7, pp. 92–95), and their disciples can be relied upon. Pierre Jurieu, however, begs to differ; he traces the debate in his "Treatise of the Golden-Calf," but ultimately rejects as erroneous the figurative representation of the patriarch Joseph as the Apis bull, in his 1705 *A Critical History* (2: 183–89). The Roman monk and historian Rufinus Aquileiensis (c. 345–410) describes a statue of Serapis in his *Historia Ecclesiastica* (2.23; PL 21. 532a-533b) and argues that King Apis fed the starving inhabitants of Alexandria from his own granaries. That is why – in the best tradition of Euhemerus – the Alexandrians deified their king and revered him in the shape of the sacred Apis bull, a bovine being universally useful to mankind.

ancestor, who had saved them once before when starvation threatened Jacob's entire family. Edwards's Euhemeristic reading, it appears, did not satisfy Mather, who revisits the story several times over. This is especially the case in Mather's lengthy synopsis of Herman Witsius's *Ægyptiaca, et Dekaphylon* (1683), one of the earliest polemics against Marsham and Spencer, which Mather incorporates in his commentary on Leviticus (ch. 27).[37] Mather agrees with Spencer (*De Legibus* bk. 3., diss. 5, sec. 4, 857–62) that *"Calf-Worship"* originated in Egypt and that God's people "became eager imitators of the Egyptian inventions." Mather quotes Philo Judaeus affirmatively on this issue (*Vita Mosis* 2.161, p. 505). As if to out-Spencer Spencer, Mather enlists Strabo (17.1.22, 27, 31), Cicero (*De natura deorum* 1.82), Pliny (8.71), and Pomponius Mela (*De chronographia* 1.49) – all confirming that the Egyptian *"Apis,"* a living black bull with white markings, was "worshipped by the *Memphites*, and *Mnevis*, by the *Heliopolites*, under the Figure of *Oxen*" [*BA*, Lev. 27:32]. More to the point, a golden image of a cow or Βοῦν διάχρυσον, representing the image of Osiris's soul, was worshipped by the Egyptians, Mather assures us after consulting Plutarch's *Isis and Osiris* (39.366d-f).[38] To back up his point, Mather consults Samuel Bochart's trusty 1646 *Hierozoicon sive Bipertitum de animalibus sacræ scripturæ* (pt. 1, bk. 2, ch. 34, cols. 329–60), a massive study of biblical bestiaries, which provides him with much useful information on the topic. According to Bochart, Aaron's golden calf must have been "an Imitation of the *Egyptian Apis*," the considerably older cousin of the *Serapis* bull, which was not known in Egypt before the time of Alexander the Great (356–323 BCE). Or, if Philo Judaeus can be trusted, Aaron's bovine idol was really an effigy of the Egyptian *Typhon* (Seth), ancient personification of chaos and jealous brother deity of Osiris and Isis, who was worshipped in the shape of a red bull [*BA*, Exod.

---

37 It is fair to argue that Witsius (*Ægyptiaca* [1696], bk. 3, ch. 14, pp. 280–92) opposes Spencer's *De Legibus* on seven major points: (a) it is dishonorable to God to argue that he resorted to tricks to teach the Israelites (282); (b) God did not set up a new republic that was a patchwork of Egyptian or Canaanitish garbage, but one that was based on the model given to Moses on Mt. Horeb (282–83); (c) God did not permit any pagan rites to be adapted after the giving of the Law or to deviate from it even in the slightest manner (283); (d) God did not permit or command the Israelites to worship him after the fashion of the gentiles (283–84); (e) God did not accommodate the Israelites by indulging their penchant for pagan rituals, but gave them Laws that were to break their stubbornness (285); (f) God's Laws intended to separate the Israelites from their pagan neighbors by creating an aversion in his people to all idolatry (287–88); and finally (g), God's Laws were types and shadows of divine things; his Laws were therefore unlikely to be accommodations of Egyptian rites (289).

38 For the same argument, see John Selden's 1617 *De Diis Syris* (synt.1, ch. 4, pp. 46–64), and Simon Patrick's annotations on Exod. 32:4 (*Commentary* 1: 341). According to Plutarch, the Apis bull at Memphis is "the image of the soul of Osiris, whose bodies also lies there." Apis, whose hide is marked with lunar symbols, "is the animate image of Osiris, and he comes into being when a fructifying light thrusts forth from the moon and falls upon a cow in her breeding-season" (20.359b; 43.368c).

32:9 ff].[39] Whatever the origin and function of Aaron's idolatrous calf, its source, Mather argues, must be sought in Egypt, because the adoration of bovine creatures was much older than the departure of the Israelites from Egypt. These idols were the *"Abominations* of the *Egyptians,"* a sacrosanct taboo whose violation would have been monstrous had the Egyptians witnessed "their *Gods* made a *Sacrifice"* by the enslaved Israelites [*BA*, Lev. 27:32].

All things considered, the Egyptian origin of Aaron's golden calf is perhaps not all that controversial an issue because the worship of bovine deities in Egypt, Phoenicia, Assyria, and Babylonia was well known throughout the ages. It was a different matter, however, with the most sacred instrument in the Mosaic religion: the ark of the covenant and the two winged cherubim between which the Shechinah of the Lord appeared as the visible symbol of his divine presence. Again, Spencer relates the historical evidence "of the ancient usage of the arks in the ceremonies of the gentiles," who carried sacred chests (cistae) and images in their religious services and temples of their gods.[40] Furthermore, he reports that "the shapes of cherubim took their origin from the Egyptian symbols and images"[41] and were joined with the ark. The biblical description of the building material, dimension, and function of the ark was clear enough, because God had given Moses specific instructions (Exod. 25:10–22). But the cherubim seemed to be a totally different matter. Apart from their wings, posture, and position little can be discerned in the Pentateuch. Their form and appearance must have been well known to Moses's contemporaries because he did not go into any detail. What was their size, shape, function? And how come that God punished the renegade Israelites for worshipping Aaron's calf, and then had Moses place images on the sacred ark? Did Almighty God's Decalogue not specifically proscribe "any graven image, or any likeness of any thing that is in heaven above, or that is in the earth beneath, or that is in the water under the earth"? And did he not specifically command "Thou shalt not bow down thyself to them, nor serve them"? (Exod. 20:4–5). If these laws were not explicit enough, how come that God instructed the Hebrew lawgiver to place iconic statues of cherubim at opposite ends of the ark of the covenant and centuries later permitted Solomon to set up in the inner sanctum of the temple two gigantic cherubim "each ten cubits high" and their extended wings of "ten cubits" touching in the middle and both sides of the temple walls? (1 Kings 6:21–35;

---

39 Significantly, Rabbi Abraham Ibn Ezra (1089-c.1164) seemed to exculpate Moses's brother, positing that those who worshipped Aaron's golden calf did not commit idolatry intentionally, because they believed that the invisible God of Moses "was to be identified with the calf" (*Commentary* 678) just as much as the Egyptians believed that the spirit of their gods resided in their images.

40 "a cistarum usu perantiquo in Gentium ceremoniis" (*De Legibus*, diss. 5, ch. 1, sec. 1, p. 831).

41 "Cherubinorum formas a symbolis & simulacris Ægyptiis originem accepisse" (diss. 5, ch. 4, sec. 4, p. 857); see also chs. 8 and 9, pp. 876–89.

[*BA*, 1 Kings 6:28]). And lastly, what is one to make of the statues of twelve oxen carrying the laver, with graven lions, oxen, and cherubim decorating not only its basis, but also the embroidered veil that separates the foyer from the adytum of the inner temple? Would the faithful Israelites not bow toward the veiled enclosure occupied by two enormous cherubim from between which God's oracle spoke to the high priest? (1 Kings 6:21–35; 7:23–36 [*BA*, 1 Kings 6:38]). Given Israel's proclivity to worship false gods, surely such prominent images in Solomon's temple and on the Mosaic ark must somehow be reconciled with God's explicit prohibition against graven images unless something completely different is meant by that proscription![42]

Francis Moncaeus, Jacques Gaffarel, and John Spencer tackled these issues historically by examining the Bible for evidence of similar graven images and linking them with parallel iconic statues and rituals among Israel's pagan neighbors. For instance, they speculated that Moses's winged cherubim were closely related to the talismanic teraphim which Rachel stole from her father and which King Saul's daughter Michal placed in David's bed to deceive her husband's attackers (1 Sam. 19:13). They were used for divination, Mather cites Pierre Jurieu's *Critical History* (1705) on Gen. 31:19 (*BA* 1: 1042–47) affirmatively, but their original was derived from worshipping dead ancestors whose effigies were placed on *kenotaphia* or empty tombs: "Upon these they sett the *Teraphim*, or the Images of their Ancestors, at the Two Extremities of the *Tombs*. And indeed, there was a little Resemblance to the *Cherubim* on the *Ark* of the *Israelites*" (*BA* 1: 1045), because the cherubim were also stationed at opposite ends of the Mosaic ark, and the voice of God was heard issuing from between the two images standing on his mercy seat.[43] In this sense, then, the divinatory function of the teraphim in delivering oracles was alike present in the cherubim of the ark, in Solomon's temple, as well as in the Urim and Thummim in the ephod of Aaron's breastplate.[44] They were all instruments of divine communication with

---

42   See also Mather's discussion of the huge cherubim in Solomon's temple [*BA*, 1 Kings: 6–7].

43   Mather here cites Jurieu (*Critical History* 2: 98). For these "kenotaphia" (empty monuments, tombs, or images), see also Diodorus Siculus (3.40.8) and 1 Kings 19:13 (LXX).

44   This connection is established in Spencer's *De Legibus* (diss. 7, chs. 3–4, pp. 929–94), but Mather rebuffed it vehemently: "Now, in the first Place, I do with much Distaste *Reject* the Opinion of *Spencer*. ... And because I *Reject* it, I will not so much as *Translate* it, but give it unto you in his own Words." Just a few short paragraphs later. Mather again lashes out at Spencer: "This harsh, and hard, (and I may say, *Horrid*) Opinion of *Spencers*, is well confuted, by a Learned Foreigner, one *Philippus Riboudealdus*, in a Book printed in *Geneva*, 1685, unto whom I refer you, if you want further Satisfaction. ... Whereas this unhappy Scholar [Spencer] employes a vast Learning, to make the *Urim* and *Thummim*, (that illustrious Oracle) with which the God of Heaven distinguished His ancient People, to be *Their Ordinances*, or the Diabolical Ordinances of the *Egyptians* and *Canaanites*, Imitated and Continued by the Holy *Angels* of Heaven. *Maimonides* utters more Christianity, than this Gentleman, when he asserts, *That the Jewish Rites, præscribed that People by God, were not an imitation of the Pagan Rites, but were in absolute Opposition to them*" [*BA*, Exod. 28:30].

the invisible world. This liminal blurring of things sacred and profane was too much for Cotton Mather, who knew only too well where such an argument might lead. "The Opinion of *Moncæus*, and *Gaffarel*, and *Spencer*, is by no means to be allow'd, That the *Cherubim* and the *Teraphim*, were the same," Mather responded with Jurieu's *Critical History* (2: 99) to back him up. "The *Cherubim* were a Mixed Figure, of no less than Four Animals; as they are described by *Ezekiel*: whereas the *Teraphim* were purely of an Humane Shape. And yett we may say, That the *Teraphim* were among the *Idolaters*, what the *Cherubim* were unto the *Israelites*. The Number *Two*, is one Instance of the Resemblance; *Two Images* for a Tomb were indeed enough" (*BA* 1: 1045).[45] No doubt, the teraphim were much older than the Mosaic cherubim, Mather agreed, but the former were not employed for divinatory purposes until "the Oracle of the Ark, & of the *Cherubim*" had been set up by Moses. It was then that "the Divel," imitating God's oracle, made the teraphim "serve as Instruments of Magick, & of Necromancy; making the Tombs to be the Seats of them, upon that Vile Intention" (*BA* 1: 1046).[46] In Mather's way of thinking, any functional similarity between these instruments of divination was either purely accidental or intended to be deliberately obfuscating because the devil – craving adoration – aped God's institutions to mislead the faithful. This conventional explanation was prevalent among theologians of the day, and Mather was no exception (*BA* 1: 435–36).[47] If the correspondence between holy and pagan implements of worship pointed to their common origin, it was the wily serpent, the arch marplot of Eden, who mimicked the Lord. And if Israel's idolatrous neighbors practiced the same rites, then, in Mather's view, the envious pagans simply borrowed their

---

45 See also Jurieu (*Critical History* 1: 327–33, 339–40) and Gaffarel (146–56). In Ezekiel's vision (Ezek. 1:6–10; 10:1, 14–22), these cherubim are mixed creatures with four faces – man, lion, ox, and eagle – and thus explain the polymorphous cherubim in Solomon's temple (1 Kings 6:21–35, 7:25) and the presence of the twelve brazen oxen supporting the huge laver. On this, see Gaffarel (17–31, 68–75). The examination of Old Testament iconography climaxes in John Spencer's *De Legibus* (bk. 3, diss. 5–6, pp. 829–1037), which claims that the images of the man-shaped teraphim were widely used in Egypt and Chaldea, and are the same as the Mosaic Urim and Thummim used in divinatory rituals and kept in a pocket of Aaron's ephod or breastplate (Exod. 28:30). As if this bold claim were not enough, Spencer asserts in his *De Legibus* (bk. 3, diss. 5, cap. 4, sec. 1–4, pp. 857–62) that the polymorphous cherubim (human, leonine, bovine, and aquiline) were derived from the figures of Egyptian deities and by Moses adapted for pious use to accommodate the Israelites' desire for visible deities. Matthew Poole provides a useful summary of the controversy in his *Synopsis Criticorum* (1:446–47), on Exod. 25:18. Modern explications of the polymorphous cherubim essentially agree with those of Spencer that they were of pagan origin (*Anchor* 1: 899–90).
46 See Jurieu's *Critical History* (2: 100–01) and Marsham's *Chronicus* (bk. 2, secul. 9, pp. 149–50).
47 See especially *The Court of the Gentiles* (1672), by Theophilius Gale (1628–78), an ejected English nonconformist, whose huge work was designed to demonstrate that "the wisest of the Heathens stole their choicest Notions and Contemplations, both Philologic, and Philosophic, as wel Natural and Moral, as Divine, from the sacred Oracles" ("Advertisements" 2r-v).

ceremonies from God's chosen people. From our modern perspective, Spencer's massive expedition into comparative religion may have pointed in the right direction, but Mather and most of his contemporaries were unprepared and unwilling to accept the logical conclusion of their common origin. The Mosaic distinction between true and false worship, between sacred and profane, between monotheism and polytheism, was so ingrained in their theological perception of these matters that they rejected offhand any evidence to the contrary. Too much depended on defending the primacy of the Holy Scriptures.[48]

The same holds true for the alleged Egyptian origin of the cherubim which reappear not only on God's mercy seat on the Mosaic ark, but also as enormous statues in Solomon's temple and in Ezekiel's vision of God's merkabah. A quick glance at Matthew Poole's *Synopsis Criticorum* (1: 446–47) demonstrates that the opinions of the standard authorities on Exod. 25:18 disagreed widely on the physical appearance of the golden cherubim on the ark. Junius, Ainsworth, Piscator and Malvenda insisted they were of a human form; Munster, Menochius, Junius, and Piscator, agreeing with the standard rabbinic sources, thought they were in the shape of boys, because the Hebrew word for *cherub* כְּרוּב is derived from כְּמוֹ רַבְיָא *quasi puer* "like a boy." Drusius, however, deemed this bowdlerized derivation rather feeble.[49] Yet others pointed out that if they were boys, their arms would have interfered with their extended wings. Besides, interjected Oleaster, the "face of the cherub" (Ezek. 10) is distinguished from a "human face." To Grotius (*Annotationes* 55) and many others, the cherubim were in the μοσχόμορφοι (*formâ vitulorum*) "in the shape of calves," perhaps commemorating Joseph's dream vision of the seven fat and lean cows. And what in Ezek. 1:10 is called שׁוֹר [showr] "ox" is called כְּרוּב [keruwb] "cherub" in Ezek. 10:14, which to Grotius is the primary form of the living creature in Ezekiel's merkabah vision. And where Menochius points out that the cherubim were a composite of four animal species – "vultus hominis, alæ aquilinæ, leonis jubæ" – the face of a human, the wings of an eagle, the mane of a lion – in addition to the face of an ox, Grotius allegorizes them as symbols of God's qualities: "man a symbol of goodness, the eagle of swiftness, the lion of judgment, and the feet of the oxen slowness."[50] Mather's own commentary on the Mosaic cherubim bespeaks his

---

48 For a discussion of the Mosaic distinction and its significance in shaping the Judeo-Christian religions, see Assmann's *Moses the Egyptian* (1–8, 57–72) and *Of God and Gods* (3–4, 84–86).

49 In this, Drusius had the full support of John Calvin's *Commentaries on the Four Last Books of Moses*. Here, Calvin argues that "those who suppose the כ [kaph] to be a note of similitude, render it 'like a boy;' which in itself is forced, and besides it is refuted by the words of Ezekiel, (ch. i.10, and x. 1,) who calls the forms of a calf, a lion, and an eagle by this name, as well as the human form" (2: 157).

50 "Homo bonitatis symbolum; aquila, celeritatis; lëo, vindictæ; pedes bovini, tarditatis" (Poole 1: 446). Mather is not far behind and glosses, "*The first Face, was the Face of a Cherub*: That is to say, of an *Oxe*, or, a *Calf*: A Representation of great Account among the Jewes, for

indecision as he vacillates between their shape as polymorphous animals and as angelic creatures with a human body. With Jacques Saurin's *Discours Historiques, Critiques, Theologiques et Moraux* (1720) at his side, Mather acknowledges that the cherubim are *"Hieroglyphicks"* of angelic and celestial qualities frequently symbolizing "certain Mysteries of Religion and Morality." However, whether the shape of the Mosaic cherubim is the same as those in the visions of Ezekiel and of John in Revelation is a different matter. The question still remains whether the assorted animal faces merely signify "some *Likeness* to those Objects, and not the *Visage* of them" and whether they "had Four Heads, or but one, or even whether Four Half-Heads." Trying to find a satisfactory solution, Mather allows John Spencer to have his say that (based on Ezek. 10:14) the cherubim "had mostly, something of a *Bovine Figure* belonging to them," because the ancient Hebrew meaning of *cherub* was *"An Oxe"* with its related connotation in Arabic and Syriac "To *Plough*." Yet Mather appears to be still ill at ease with what amounts to an endorsement of the Egyptian bestiary on the sacred ark. At last, he cuts through this Gordian knot and invites Maimonides to settle the issue–at least for the time being: "Be the Figure what it will; it is evident, That the *Cherubims* which *Moses* made by the Order of GOD, were Emblems of ANGELS." For according to Maimonides, God's purpose "was to inculcate the Doctrine and Beleef of ANGELS" [*BA*, Exod. 25:18].[51]

If this conventional solution satisfied Mather for the moment, "Biblia Americana" purports to entertain his readers with anything but the worn and pedestrian. His synopsis of some hieroglyphic inscriptions on an Egyptian mummy, originating in Athanasius Kircher's 1676 *Sphinx Mystagoga, sive Diatribe Hieroglyphica de Mumiis* (pt. 2, chs. 2, 4, pp. 21–23, 29–35), is a case in point.[52] Mather extracts this curious passage at second hand from Herman Witsius's *Ægyptiaca* (bk. 1, ch. 9, p. 46) without mentioning Kircher. It illustrates just how far Mather was prepared to go: "The *Egyptians* had their God *Hempta*," the ram-headed god Khnum (Kneph), whom the Greeks called Jupiter Ammon. He is attended by certain guardian spirits (genii): the first is Horus, with "the Face of *a Boy*," the god of the sentient world; the second is the vigilant Anubis, with "the Face of a *Dog*," signifying the Hermetic economy; the third is Thaustus, with "the Face of an *Hawk*," representing the heat of the sun and source of the earth's fertility; finally, the fourth is the formidable deity Momphta, with "the Face of a *Lion*," presiding over the Hylean (or watery) world.

---

the sake of their *Joseph*. It is here intimated, That the Upper Part of the *Cherubims* Head, was distinguished, & remarkable, for Circumstances, that had something *Bovine* in them. *The Second Face, was the Face of a Man*; That is to say, The whole *Countenance* was *Humane*. The *Third, the Face of a Lion*; That is to say, The *Neck*, & the *Main*, was *Leonine*. The Fourth, the *Face of an Eagle*; This was in the *Wings* added unto their shoulders" [*BA*, Ezek. 10:14].

51   Maimonides (*Guide* 1.49.109–10; 2.6.262; 3.45.577).

52   On Kircher's interest in Egypt, see Stolzenberg's "Egypt" and "Ruins," and Findlen's "Introduction."

"Was not *Hempta*, the same with the God /אמת/ *Emet* [Truth], of the Israelites," whose throne is on the mercy seat of the ark of the covenant? "And were not the *Cherubim*, an Imitation of *Hempta*'s Attendents" with the face of a man, a lion, an ox, and an eagle? "God forbid, we should imagine so. We have no Proof of *Hempta*'s Antiquity. And neither the *Number* nor the *Figure* of his Attendents, was the same with the *Cherubim* in the Tabernacle" [*BA*, Lev. 27:34].[53] Mather clearly wrestles with the amazing similarities between divine and pagan emblems outlined by Kircher and here borrowed from Witsius (46). To him, the appalling implications about pagan idols resurfacing on the sacred ark of Moses even in Ezekiel's merkabah vision were just too much. Yet Mather was unwilling to let go. In his commentary on Acts, he revisits the topic once again in an excerpt from Archbishop Thomas Tenison's *Of Idolatry* (1678). Here Mather argues that the angelic cherubim resembled a part of God's Shechinah glory, which Aaron and the seventy elders had seen in their ascent on Mt. Horeb. Aaron modeled his golden calf on the attending angelic cherubim, who "appeared with Heads of a *Bovine* Aspect." The Hebrew word *cherub* signifies "*A Beef*; and it was derived from the Chaldee /כרב/ [keruwb] *He ploughed*." Ironically, in worshipping the figure of the bovine cherub, the wayward Israelites turned the Shechinah glory "into a *Similitude*" of God's presence and into "the Symbol of an *Angel*, which was not so much to the *Shechinah* of God, as one *Spoke* of a *Wheel* is to an Eastern Emperour in a triumphant Chariot." The Israelites in the wilderness fell to worshipping it even as they danced around

---

53 It is telling that Mather's strips the excerpted passage from Witsius's *Ægyptiaca* (46) of the references to the Egyptian Khnum (Kneph, Jupiter Ammon) Horus, Thaustus, and Momphta (which are here restored from Witsius). Mather's bowdlerized version reads as follows: "The *Egyptians* had their God *Hempta*; and he had certain *Genius*'s Attending him; One had the Face of *a Boy*; Another, the Face of a *Dog*; A Third, the Face of an *Hawk*; A Fourth, the Face of a *Lion*. Well; And now, was not *Hempta*, the same with the God /אמת/ *Emet*, of the *Israelites*? And were not the *Cherubim*, an Imitation of *Hempta*'s Attendents? God forbid, we should imagine so. We have no Proof of *Hempta*'s Antiquity; And neither the *Number* nor the *Figure* of his Attendents, was the same with the *Cherubim* in the Tabernacle" [*BA*, Lev. 27:34]. Witsius's source (46, 154) is Kircher's explication of the mystical numen Hempta (Emet, Kneph) as the supreme creator of the Egyptians (*Sphinx* 21, 22–23, 29, 52, 57, 66); attended by the boy-faced Horus, son of Isis and Osiris, who wards off evil (21, 23, 29, 31–32); the dog-(jackal) headed Anubis (the Egyptian Mercurius), custodian of the souls of the dead before the judge (49, 56, 61, 69); Thaustus (hawk-headed Horus) associated with Ammon and Osiris (23, 29, 51, 68); finally, Momphta (Mophta), guardian of the sacred Nile, who presides over the watery world (33 55, 68–69, 71). If Kircher's translations are no longer trustworthy, be it remembered that the Egyptian hieroglyphs were not deciphered until more than 140 years after Kircher's death. The English naturalist John Hutchinson (1647–1737) was equally attracted to these mysterious hieroglyphics and (like Mather) transcribes numerous passages from Witsius, Vossius, and Spencer, in his oft-reprinted *The Covenant of the Cherubim* (385–406) and compares them to Egyptian precedent. The shocking depiction of the ark of the covenant appears on the inside cover-page of Hutchinson's 1749 edition of his *Philosophical and Theological Works*, vol. 7, misnumbered as vol. 6.

Herman Witsius, *Ægyptiaca* (Amstelædami, 1696)

The Cherubim or Figure of the Great Ones.

Hebrew Writings Perfect.

The Christian Covenant in Hieroglyphicks.
and the Origin of all such among the Heathens.

John Hutchinson, *The Covenant in the Cherubim* (London, 1749)

their Apis or Mnevis bull, the idol of the Egyptians [*BA*, Acts 7:2].[54] In strip-
ping the cherubim of their bovine aspects, then, Mather turns the winged creatures once again into angels of human shape. In this as in many other instances,
Mather acknowledges Moses Maimonides as his master.[55] After all, the familiar
appearance of winged angels, as they could be seen in myriads of medieval and
renaissance paintings, inspired the beholder with assurance that comes with
faith in the reality of things not seen. These winged messengers ascended and
descended from God's throne. They instilled in the faithful the same awe and
wonder that Jacob must have felt when he beheld a ladder standing on earth and
reaching all the way to heaven (*BA* 1: 1018–19).[56]

Mather's frank denial notwithstanding, he seems simultaneously fascinated and troubled by the plentitude of new connections between rites sacred and
profane which Spencer's *De Legibus* opened up. If nothing else, his fascination
with the prominent use of images and statues in the Mosaic religion and in
Mather's iconoclastic age underscores the difficulty of drawing the line between
true and false. For who in the colors of the rainbow can tell apart the line between where the orange tinge begins and the violet ends?

No matter his fascination with Spencer, Mather's admiration could also
turn into downright hostility. A notable instance occurs in his annotations on
Numb. 10:36. Here, as in several other cases, Mather turns to parallel accounts
in "Pagan *Antiquitie*" to validate the Bible's primacy. He does Spencer the hon-
or of excerpting his evidence on Moloch's portable ark (Amos 5:25; Acts 7:43).
The Canaanites and many other heathen nations, Spencer insists, employed sacred arks in the worship of their god long before the Israelites adopted the like
custom under Moses (*De Legibus* bk. 3, diss. 1, ch. 3, sec. 2, pp. 673–75). It is
amusing to witness how Mather exploits Spencer's primary sources as if they
were Mather's own. In one instance, Spencer cites *Commentarii in Acta Apostolorum* (1616), by Gaspar Sanctius (1553–1628), a learned Jesuit professor of
theology at Alcala (Spain); in another, *Moses and Aaron, or the Civil and Ecclesiastical Rites used by the ancient Hebrews* (1678), by Dr. Thomas Godwin
(1587–1643), rector of Brightwell (Berkshire). Both sources pinpoint similarities between pagan and Mosaic rites, but ultimately insist that the pagans stole

---

54 See Tenison (337–38) and Calvin (3: 333–34).
55 For their contrasting assessments of the shape, function, and origin of cherubim, see
Spencer's *De Legibus* (bk. 3, diss. 5, chs. 3–10, pp. 844–89) and Maimonides's *Guide* (1.49.108–
10; 2.6.261–65; 3.45.577). Significantly, John Calvin – though agreeing that the cherubim's
polymorphous shape as described in Ezek. 1:10 and 10:1 is that of "a calf, a lion, and an eagle
by this name, as well as the human form" – ultimately sidesteps the issue by arguing that the
cherubim on the Mosaic ark were angels: "It is enough for me that the images were winged,
which represented angels" (2: 157).
56 The transformation of the pantheon of the pagans into Judeo-Christian saints is illustrated in Seznec's magnificent study. See also Manuel (esp. 15–53).

theirs from Moses.[57] With this evidence in place, Mather lashes out against Spencer:

> The learned Pen, of *Spencer,* would needs perswade us, *That the Tabernacle of Moloch, was the first Original of the Tabernacle of God*; and that it is a *Vulgar Error,* to think, *That the Divel Apes the Almighty.* But it is a wonderful Thing, that so Accomplished a Person [as Spencer], should pervert his Accomplishments, to mentain such monstrous Assertions. Hee will never bring so *Præposterious* a *Schæme* to bee embraced in the Church of God!" [*BA,* Numb. 10:36].[58]

But already in the next paragraph, Mather is forced to eat his own words: "'Tis true," Mather concedes, "Gods *Tabernacle* was portable; and so was *Molochs.* Gods Tabernacle had in it, his Ark & the Images of *Cherubims*: and *Molochs* had his Image in it. God, exhibited, by Audible answers, & otherwise, his peculiar Presence in His Tabernacle; and *Moloch* did the like in his. God appeared as a *King,* in the Circumstances of His *Tabernacle*; and *Moloch* in his, claimed a Name that signifies as much." "But," Mather asserted," it is far from True, That the Tabernacle of God, fetched its Pattern, from that of *Moloch*; or, that the Cursed *Fiend* is Imitated by the God of Heaven. The Figure, which wee call, *The Cart before the Horse,* runs thro' the Writings of some learned Authors. But, wee now add, that from the *Ark* in the Tabernacle, the Gentile Worshippers borrowed, the *Little Chests,* wherein they carried about their Gods" [*BA,* Numb. 10:36]. Mather's vociferous objection to Spencer's thesis belies how close he came to Spencer's historical-contextual approach in many places, and how much his intellectual curiosity was piqued by Spencer's evidence. Yet Mather's belief in the divine origin of the Judeo-Christian religions demanded that he rise in defense of the Bible's authority.

Just how compelling Mather found Spencer's research is especially evident in his commentary on Amos, where the argument from *De Legibus* once again proves irresistible. Here, Mather provides a detailed summary of Spencer's corroboration (bk. 3, diss. 1, ch. 3, sec. 1, 664–70) that confirms the prevalence of portable arks, shrines, and tabernacles employed by pagan neighbors and adapted by the Israelites for their own use. One of Mather's comments seems unique.

---

57 Mather's pragmatic use of his sources is intriguing. He translates Spencer's Latin citation of Sanctius (*Commentarii,* on Acts 7, note 94), but turns to his own copy of Godwin's *Moses and Aaron* (bk. 4, ch. 2, p. 149) either for accuracy or to spare himself the trouble of retranslating into English what Spencer had rendered into Latin (*De Legibus* 673).

58 In his commentary on the Prophet Amos, Mather revisits Spencer, Sanctius, Godwin on the likeness between Moloch's ark and tabernacle and that of Moses. This time, however, Mather seems much less provoked by Spencer's audacity: "To this Opinion [that the devil aped God's portable tabernacle] of *Sanctius,* of *Godwyn,* and others, I rather incline, than to that scandalous one of Dr. *Spencers,* that the *Mosaic Tabernacle* was made in Imitation of the like Sacred Fabricks, commonly used among the more ancient Pagans. And yett unto that learned Mans Lucubrations, I will be beholden, for some Illustrations of the Texts now before us" [*BA,* Amos 5:26].

In his gloss on Amos 5:26, Mather goes as far as to abet Spencer by encouraging readers to "Attend now to something of *Curiosity*!" as Mather explains why, in spite of the Second Commandment, the Israelites carried the effigies of their household gods Remphan and Chiun with them during their travels through the wilderness:

> These *Deities* were peculiarly accommodated unto the Condition of *Israel* in the Wilderness, according to the Notions of *Paganism* then prevailing. For *Osiris*, whom they considered in *Moloch* was accounted, according to *Mercurius Trismegistus*, *The Overseer of every* ones *Body* καὶ ἰχνος καὶ ῥωμης καθηγητης, *Virium et Roboris Ductor*. Now, a *Leader* giving Strength to *Travellers*, how agreeably did the Idolatry of weary Travellers pitch upon *him*, for an Object of their Adoration?"

In Mather's endorsement of Spencer's account, then, Moses accommodated the Israelites' idolatrous habits by allowing them to carry with them images of Chiun (Saturn, Jupiter), the patron god of prosperity and hospitality. For a traveler carrying such an image could not be refused hospitable reception, because "*Saturn* would avenge it, if it were denied him. The *Israelites* now being Afflicted *Strangers*, behold, what they have Recourse unto!" Thus until today, Mather claims, the rabbis have a particular regard for the planet Saturn and think of him "in the *Hospitality* of their *Sabbaths*" [*BA*, Amos 5:26].[59] Mather seems so drawn to *De Legibus*, as these passages make clear, that he frequently crosses over to Spencer's side. In penetrating the logic of Spencer's argument and in following his reasoning closely, he tends to be unaware at times how this line of reasoning relativizes the religion of Moses as just one among many ancient creeds vying for ascendancy.[60]

---

59 See Spencer (669–70).

60 Perhaps inspired by Spencer's allocation of proof, Mather adds to his own collection a passage extracted from the Spanish Jesuit José Acosta (1539–1600), whose 1604 *Naturall and Morall Historie of the East and West Indies* (bk. 7, chs. 4–7, pp. 504–14) proved irristible: "There is a strange Passage in *Acosta*, about the Indians, who came from far, to settle about *Mexico*," Mather quotes from the English translation of Acosta's contribution to the study of Native American religions in the Spanish colonies. "That the Divel, in their Idol, *Vitzlipultzli*, governed that mighty Nation, & commanded them to leave their Countrey, promising to make them Lords of all the Provinces, possessed by *Six* other Nations of Indians, and give them a Land, abounding with all precious Things. They went forth, carrying their Idol with them, in a Coffer of *Reeds*, supported by four of their papal *Priests*; with whom hee still discoursed, in secret; Revealing to them, the Successes, and Accidents, of their Way. Hee advised them, when to *march*, and where to *stay*, and without his Commandment, they moved not. The first Thing they did, wherever they came, was to erect a *Tabernacle*, for their False God; which they sett always, in the Midst of their Camp, and there placed the *Ark* upon an *Altar*. When they, tired with Pains, talked of, *Proceeding no further*, in their Journey, than a certain pleasant Stage, whereto they were arrived, the Divel, in one Night, horribly kill'd them, that had started this Talk, pulling out their Hearts. And so they passed on, till they came to *Mexico*" [*BA*, Numb. 10:36]. Obviously, Acosta's etiological myth to account for temples and

Was Mather fully cognizant of the implications of Spencer's radical thesis? His genuine admiration for Spencer's scholarship and his vociferous disapproval of Spencer's radicalism in places suggest that he was. What we can say with certainty, though, is that Mather's rationalist interest in the origin of the Mosaic rituals and their parallels in paganism is evident throughout "Biblia Americana." He was fascinated by the intellectual panorama of his age, but he was reluctant to embrace its vistas. Spencer's subversive *De Legibus* is a case in point. Although not the work of a Deist by any stretch of the imagination, Spencer's magisterial book was perhaps even more perilous than Charles Blount's *Great is Diana of the Ephesians* (1680), John Toland's *Letters to Serena* (1704), *Origines Judaicæ* (1709), *Clidophorus* (1720), and *Tetradymus* (1720), or ultimately, David Hume's *The Natural History of Religion* (1757) – an association Mather would have vehemently disavowed.[61] The aims of a Blount or Toland were all too obvious; but those of a Spencer, "our Spencer," as Mather calls him in moments of unrestrained admiration, were more ambiguous. Spencer's historical scholarship opened up hitherto unprecedented glimpses into the origin of religion that to a mind like Mather's were highly attractive. Whether he critiques the philological scholarship of a Hobbes, Spinoza, Simon, and LeClerc, or evaluates the accommodationist thesis of Maimonides and Spencer, Mather incorporates in his "Biblia Americana" the choice fruits of friend and foe alike. In his mind, they allowed him to plumb the depth of God's word and to make its rich mines of wisdom accessible to readers of his commentary.

The religion of Moses, then, did not emerge in complete isolation from its neighbors – as Jewish and Christian theologians of Mather's time insisted it did – but as an evolutionary process with strong roots in the customs, ceremonies, and cultic rites of Egypt and Chaldaea. To take Spencer's argument – and Mather's half-hearted assent – one step further, Christianity, then, as purported heir to Judaism equally derives its origin and legitimization from ritual and sacrificial practices with roots in paganism. But this conclusion did not become accepted until widely disseminated by German Higher Criticism in the nineteenth century. In some way, Mather must have been conscious that this new type of biblical criticism was very different from the partisan bickering of Protestant

---

rituals he witnessed among the Natives of Mesoamerica is viewed through the lens of its Old Testament precedent.

61   Justin Champion's *Pillars of Priestcraft* (esp. 133–69) and *Republican Learning* (esp. 167–212) provide excellent analyses of the subversive tendencies of the age. In his *Clidophorus* (1720), Toland specifically rejects the idea that the Egyptians received their wisdom from Moses: "But you will ask, from what Original did it [ancient philosophy] proceed? From the *Jews*, say some, who suppose that the ancient Barbaric Nations received all their Wisdom from *Moses* or *Abraham*. As for *Moses*, it appears from the Sacred Scriptures, that the *Egyptian* Wisdom was more ancient than his [Moses], and he was a Disciple rather than the Teacher of that learned Nation. ... Therefore the Wisdom of the Egyptians could not be first born with *Moses*; but we must trace its Original from a higher Spring" [Noah] (241, 243–46).

sectarianism. The stakes were much higher. Cotton Mather's "Biblia Americana," then, is a historical record of the Enlightenment debates that contributed to the breakdown of the old, established order, and to the destabilization of the Bible's authority. If nothing else, "Biblia Americana" reveals that in his embrace of Newtonian science as well as of philological and historical-contextual criticism, Mather had long transcended the regional scope of his *Magnalia Christi Americana* with its focus on New-England's place in providential history. In his "Biblia Americana," then, he carved out an intellectual space in which he could converse with his European colleagues on their terms.

Works Cited

Primary Sources

St. Augustine. *Letters of St. Augustine.* Trans. J.G. Cunningham. *Nicene and Post-Nicene Fathers.* Ed. Philip Schaff. Vol. 1. 1886. Peabody: Hendrickson Publ., 1999. 14 vols. 211–593.

Acosta, José. *The Naturall and Morall Historie of the East and West Indies.* Trans. Edward Grimston. London, 1604.

Bachya ben Asher. *Torah Commentary.* Trans. Eliyahu Munk. 7 vols. Jerusalem: Lambda Publ., 2003.

Basnage (de Beauval), Jacques. *The History of the Jews. From Jesus Christ to the Present Time.* Trans. John Taylor. London, 1708.

Bede. *Historia Ecclesiastica Gentis Anglorum. A History of the English Church and People.* Trans. Leo Sherley-Price. 1955. Rev. ed. Harmondsworth: Penguin, 1968.

Blount, Charles. *Great is Diana of the Ephesians. Or, The Original of Idolatry.* London, 1680.

Bochart, Samuel. *Hierozoicon Sive bipertitum opus De Animalibus Sacræ Scripturæ. Pars Prior. De Animalibus in genere. Et de Quadrupedibus viviparis et oviparis. Pars Posterior. De Avibus, Serpentibus, Insectis, Aquaticis, et Fabulosis Animalibus.* 2 vols. 1646. Londini, 1663.

Burnet, Thomas. *Archæologiæ Philosophicæ: Sive Doctrina Antiqua De Rerum Originibus. Libri Duo.* Londini, 1692.

–. *Doctrina Antiqua de Rerum Originibus: Or, an Inquiry into the Doctrine of the Philosophers of all Nations, Concerning the Original of the World.* Trans. Mr. Mead and Mr. Foxton. London, 1736.

Calmet, Augustin. *Dissertation sur l'Origine de l'Idolatrie des Israelites.* In *Discours et Dissertations sur tous les Livres de l'Ancient Testament.* Vol. 1. Paris, 1715. 3 Vols. 39–61, 599–616.

Calvin, John. *Commentaries on the Four Last Books of Moses arranged in the Form of a Harmony.* Trans. Charles William Bingham. In *Calvin's Commentaries.* 22 vols. Grand Rapids, MI: Baker Books, 2005.

Diodorus Siculus. *The Library of History.* Ed. Jeffrey Henderson. 12 vols. 1933. Cambridge: Harvard UP, 2004.

Edwards, John. *A Discourse Concerning the Authority, Stile, and Perfection of the Books of the Old and New Testament*. 3 vols. London, 1693–95.

–. ΠΟΛΥΠΟΙΚΙΛΟΣ ΣΟΦΙΑ [Polypoikilos Sophia]. *A Compleat History or Survey Of all the Dispensations and Methods of Religion, From the beginning of the World to the Consummation of all things*. London, 1699.

Eusebius of Caesarea. *The Proof of the Gospel*. Trans. W. J. Ferrar. 2 vols in 1. Eugene: Wipf and Stock, 2001.

Gaffarel, Jacques. *Curiositez inouyes sur la sculpture talismanique des Persans*. Paris, 1629. *Unheard-of Curiosities: Concerning the Talismanical Sculpture of the Persians; The Horoscope of the Patriarkes; And the Reading of the Stars*. Trans. Edmund Chilmead. London, 1650.

Gale, Theophilus. *The Court of the Gentiles: Or a Discourse touching the Original of Human Literature, both Philologie and Philosophie, From the Scriptures & Jewish Church*. 4 parts. The second edition revised and enlarged. Oxford, 1672–78.

Godwin, Thomas. *Moses and Aaron, or the Civil and Ecclesiastical Rites used by the ancient Hebrews*. 12th ed. London, 1685.

Grotius, Hugo. *Annotationes ad Vetus Testamentum*. In *Opera Omnia Theologica in Tres Tomos Divisa*. Vol. 1. Londini 1679. 1–800.

Huet, Pierre-Daniel. *Demonstratio Evangelica ad serenissimum Delphinum*. Parisiis, 1679. Tertia editio. Parisiis, 1694.

Hutchinson, John. *The Covenant in the Cherubim*. 1734. *The Philosophical and Theological Works of the Late Truly Learned John Hutchinson, Esq; In Twelve Volumes*. Vol. 6 [7]. London, 1749.

Ibn Ezra, Abraham. *Commentary on the Pentateuch: Exodus (Shemot)*. Trans. H. Norman Strickman and Arthur M. Silver. New York: Menorah, 1996.

Index librorum prohibitorum: 1600–1966. Montreal: Médiaspaul, 2002.

St. Irenaeus. *Against Heresies. Ante-Nicene Fathers*. Ed. Alexander Roberts and James Donaldson. Vol. 1. 1885. Peabody: Hendrickson, 1999. 10 vols. 309–567.

Jurieu, Pierre. *A Critical History of the Doctrines and Worships (Both Good and Evil) of the Church from Adam to our Saviour Jesus Christ*. 2 vols. London, 1705.

Kircher, Athanasius. *Oedipus Ægyptiacis. Hoc est universalis hieroglyphicæ veterum doctrinæ temporum inuria abolitæ instauratio*. Tomi tres. Romæ, 1652–54.

–. *Sphinx Mystagoga, sive diatribe hieroglyphica, qua mumiæ, ex Memphiticis pyramidium adytis erutæ*. Amstelodami, 1676.

Maimonides, Moses. *More Nebuchim. Doctor Perplexorum*. 1551. *The Guide of the Perplexed*. Trans. Shlomo Pines. 2 vols. Chicago: U of Chicago P, 1963.

–. *Rabbi Mosis Majemonidis Liber* מורה נבוכים *Doctor Perplexorum ... Translatus: ... in Linguam Latinam persicuè & fideliter Conversus, à Johanne Buxtorfio, Fil.* Basileæ, 1629.

Manetho. *Ægyptiaca. Manetho*. Trans. W. G. Waddell. Cambridge: Loeb Classical Library, 1940.

Marsham, Sir John. *Chronicus Canon Ægyptiacus Ebraicus Græcus & disquisitiones ... liber quartus*. Londini, 1672.

Mather, Cotton. *Biblia Americana*. Vol. 1. Ed. Reiner Smolinski. Tübingen and Grand Rapids: Mohr Siebeck and Baker Academic, 2010.

Moncaeus, Franciscus. *Aaron purgatus, sive de vitulo aureo libri duo, simul cheruborum Mosis, vitulorum Jeroboami, theraphorum Michæ formam et historiam, multaque pulcherrima alia eodem spectantia explicantes.* Arras, 1606. Rpt. in *Criticorum Sacrorum.* Vol. 1. Amstelædami, 1698. 9 vols. 86–192.

Nachmanides (Moshe ben Nachman). *Commentary on the Torah.* Trans. C. Chavel. 5 vols. Brooklyn: Shilo, 1973–99.

Newton, Sir Isaac. "Papers Relating to Chronology and 'Theologiæ Gentilis Origines Philosophicæ'" The Newton Project. Web. Dec. 12, 2009.

Parker, Samuel. *Reasons for Abrogating the Test, Imposed upon All Members of Parliament Anno 1678, Octob. 30.* London, 1688.

Patrick, Simon. *A Commentary upon the Historical Books of the Old Testament.* 3rd ed. 2 vols. London, 1727.

Pfaff, Christoph Matthäus. *"Dissertatio Præliminaris,"* in Spencer c–g.

Philo Judaeus. *De Vita Mosis. The Works of Philo.* Trans. C.D. Yonge. Peabody: Hendrickson Publ., 1993. 459–517.

Plutarch. *De Iside et Osiride. Plutarch's Moralia.* Vol. 5. Cambridge: Harvard UP, 1919. 1–191.

Poole, Matthew. *Synopsis Criticorum Aliorumque S. Scripturæ Interpretum.* 5 vols. Londini, 1669–76.

–. *The Works of the Reverend Matthew Poole: The Exegetical Labors of the Reverend Matthew Poole.* Trans. Steven Dilday. 5 vols. Culpeper: Master Poole Publishing, 2007–08.

Riboudealdus, Philippus. *Sacrum Dei Oraculum Urim & Thummim. A Variis D. Joh. Spenceri Theologi Cantabrigiensis excogitationibus liberum.* Genevæ, 1685.

Rufinus Aquileiensis. *Historia Ecclesiastica* (2.23). *Patrologiae Latinae Cursus Completus. Omnium SS. Patrum, Doctorum Scriptorum Ecclesiasticorum.* Ed. J. P. Migne. Vol. 21. Turnholti: Typographi Brepols Editores Pontificii, N.D.

Sanctius, Gaspar (Caspar Sanchez). *Commentarii in Acta Apostolorum.* Lugduni, 1616.

Selden, John. *De Diis Syris Syntagmata II.* Londini, 1617.

Simon, Richard. "Avertissement qui était à la tête de l'édition d'Elzevier" 1685. *Histoire.* 796–801.

–. *Histoire Critique du Vieux Testament suivi de Lettre sur l'inspiration.* 1685. Nouvelle édition annotée et introduite par Pierre Gibert. Montrouge: Bayard Éditions, 2008.

Soncino Midrash Rabbah. Brooklyn: Soncino, 1983.

Spencer, John. *De Legibus Hebræorum Ritualibus Earumque Rationibus. Libri Quatuor.* 1685. Tubingæ, 1732.

Stillingfleet, Edward. *Origines Sacræ. Or a Rational Account of the Grounds of Christian Faith, as to the Truth and Divine Authority of the Scriptures, And the matters therein contained.* 3rd. ed. cor. London, 1666.

Tacitus, Gaius Cornelius. *Tacitus. The Histories.* Trans. W.H. Fyfe. New York: Oxford UP, 1997.

Tenison, Thomas. *Of Idolatry: A Discourse, In which is endevoured A Declaration of, Its Distinction from Superstition.* London, 1678.

Tertullian. *Against Marcion.* Trans. Dr. Holmes. *Ante-Nicene Fathers.* Ed. Alexander Roberts and James Donaldson. Vol. 3. 1885. Peabody: Hendrickson Publ., 1999. 10 vols. 269–475.

Theodoret of Cyrus. *The Questions on the Octateuch.* Trans. Robert C. Hill. 2 vols. Washington: Catholic U of America P, 2007.

St. Thomas Aquinas. *Summa Theologica*. Trans. Fathers of the English Dominican Province. 5 vols. New York: Benziger Bros., 1948.

Toland, John. *Letters to Serena*. London, 1704.

—. *Adeisidæmon et Origines Judaicæ*. Comitis Hagæ, 1709.

—. *Clidophorus, Or, Of the Exoteric and Esoteric Philosophy; That is, Of the External and Internal Doctrine of the Ancients*. London, 1720.

—. *Tetradymus*. London, 1720.

Turretin, Francis. *Institutes of Elenctic Theology*. Trans. George Musgrave Giger. 3 vols. 1679–85. Phillipsburg: P&R Publishing, 1994.

Visorius, Robert. *Aaronis purgati, seu Pseudo-cherubi ex aureo vitulo recens conflati Destructio*. Parisiis, 1609.

Vossius, Gerardus Joannes (Gerhard Johannes Voss). *De Theologia Gentili, et Physiologia Christina, sive De Origine ac Progressu Idololatriæ. Libri IV*. Amsterdami, 1641.

Warburton, William. *The Divine Legation of Moses Demonstrated, on the Principles of a Religious Deist, from the Omission of a Doctrine of the Future State of Reward and Punishment in the Jewish Dispensation*. 2 vols. London, 1738–41.

Witsius, Hermann. *Ægyptiaca, et ΔΕΚΑΦΥΛΟΝ. Sive de Ægyptiacorum sacrorum cum Hebraicis collatione libri tres*. 1683. Amstelodami, 1696.

Woodward, John. *Of the Wisdom of the Antient Egyptians*. London, 1777.

Yaakov ben Rabbeinu Asher. *Tur on the Torah*. Trans. Eliyahu Munk. 4 vols. Jerusalem: Lambda, 2005.

Secondary Works

The Anchor Bible Dictionary. Ed. David Noel Freedman. 6 vols. New York: Doubleday, 1992.

Assmann, Jan. *Of God and Gods: Egypt, Israel, and the Rise of Monotheism*. Madison: U of Wisconsin P, 2008.

—. "The Mosaic Distinction: Israel, Egypt, and the Invention of Paganism." *Representations* 56 (Autumn, 1996): 48–67.

—. "Moses as Go-Between: John Spencer's Theory of Religious Translation." *Renaissance Go-Betweens: Cultural Exchange in Early Modern Europe*. Ed. Andreas Höfele and Werner von Koppenfels. Berlin: De Gruyter, 2005. 163–76.

—. *Moses the Egyptian: The Memory of Egypt in Western Monotheism*. Cambridge: Harvard UP, 1998.

—. *The Price of Monotheism*. Trans. Robert Savage. Stanford: Stanford UP, 2010.

Benin, Stephen D. *The Footprints of God: Divine Accommodation in Jewish and Christian Thought*. Albany: State U of New York P, 1993.

—. "The 'Cunning of God' and Divine Accommodation." *Journal of the History of Ideas* 45.2 (1984): 179–91.

Champion, Justin (J. A. I). *The Pillars of Priestcraft Shaken: The Church of England and its Enemies, 1660–1730*. Cambridge: Cambridge UP, 1992.

—. *Republican Learning: John Toland and the Crisis of Christian Culture, 1696–1722*. Manchester and New York: Manchester UP, 2003.

Copenhaver, Brian P. Ed. *Hermetica: The Greek Corpus Hermeticum and the Latin Asclepius*. 1992. Cambridge: Cambridge UP, 1995.

Dannenfeldt, Karl H. "Egypt and Egyptian Antiquities in the Renaissance." *Studies in the Renaissance* 6 (1959): 7–27.

Delitzsch, Friedrich. *Babel und Bibel. Ein Vortrag.* Leipzig: Hinrichs, 1902.

Elukin, Jonathan. "Maimonides and the Rise and Fall of the Sabians: Explaining Mosaic Laws and the Limits of Scholarship." *Journal of the History of Ideas* 63.4 (2002): 619–37.

Findlen, Paula. "Introduction." *Athanasius Kircher: The Last Man Who Knew Everything.* Ed. Paula Findlen. New York and London: Routledge, 2004. 1–48.

Frazer, Sir James George. *The Golden Bough.* Abr. ed. 1922; New York: Macmillan Publishing Co., 1963.

Freud, Sigmund. *Moses and Monotheism.* 1939; New York: Vintage Books, 1955.

–.   "Moses ein Ägypter." *Imago* 13.4 (1937): 387–419.

Friedländer, M. "Analysis of the Guide for the Perplexed." *The Guide for the Perplexed by Moses Maimonides.* Trans M. Friedländer. 2nd ed. rev. 1904. New York: Dover Publications, Inc., 1956. xxxix-lix.

Funkenstein, Amos. *Theology and the Scientific Imagination from the Middle Ages to the Seventeenth Century.* Princeton: Princeton UP, 1986.

Goldish, Matt. *The Sabbatean Prophets.* Cambridge: Harvard UP, 2004.

Grafton, Anthony T. "Joseph Scaliger and Historical Chronology: The Rise and Fall of a Discipline." *History and Theory* 14 (1975): 156–85.

Idel, Moshe. "Jewish Apocalypticism 670–1670." *The Encyclopedia of Apocalypticism.* Vol. 2. Ed. Bernard McGinn. New York: Continuum, 1998. 204–37.

Iversen, Erik. *The Myth of Egypt and Its Hieroglyphs in European Tradition.* 1961. Princeton: Princeton UP, 1993.

Katz, David S. and Richard H. Popkin. *Messianic Revolution. Radical Religious Politics to the End of the Second Millennium.* New York: Hill and Wang, 1999.

Lehmann, Reinhard C. *Friedrich Delitzsch und der Babel-Bibel-Streit.* Fribourg: Presses Universitaires, 1994.

Manuel, Frank E. *The Eighteenth Century Confronts the Gods.* 1959. New York: Atheneum, 1967.

Pines, Shlomo. "Translator's Introduction." In Moses Maimonides, *Guide* 1: lvii-cxxxiv.

Parente, Fausto. "Spencer, Maimonides, and the History of Religion." *History of Scholarship: A Selection of Papers from the Seminar on the History of Scholarship Held Annually at the Warburg Institute.* Ed. Christopher Ligota and Jean-Louis Quantin. Oxford: Oxford UP, 2006. 277–304.

Ravitzky, Aviezer. "The Messianism of Success in Contemporary Judaism." *The Encyclopedia of Apocalypticism.* Vol. 3. Ed. Stephen J. Stein. New York: Continuum P, 1998. 204–29.

Rossi, Paolo. *The Dark Abyss of Time: The History of the Earth and the History of Nature from Hooke to Vico.* Trans. Lydia G. Cochrane. 1979. Chicago & London: U of Chicago P, 1984.

Schmidt, Francis. "Polytheism: Degeneration or Progress?" *History and Anthropology: The Inconceivable Polytheism. Studies in Religious Historiography.* Eds. François Hartog et al. London: Harwood Academic Publishers, 1987. 9–60.

Scholem, Gershom. *Sabbatai Sevi: The Mystical Messiah.* Trans. R.J. Zwi Werblowsky. 1957. Princeton: Princeton UP, 1973.

Seznec, Jean. *The Survival of the Pagan Gods. The Mythological Tradition and Its Place in Renaissance Humanism and Art*. Trans. Barbara F. Sessions. 1953. Princeton: Princeton UP, 1972.

Sheehan, Jonathan. "Sacred and Profane: Idolatry, Antiquarianism and the Polemics of Distinction in the Seventeenth Century. *Past and Present* 192 (2006): 35–66.

Stolzenberg, Daniel. "Kircher Among the Ruins: Esoteric Knowledge and Universal History." *The Great Art of Knowing: The Baroque Encyclopedia of Athanasius Kircher*. Ed. Daniel Stolzenberg. Stanford: Stanford U Libraries, 2001. 127–39.

–. "Kircher's Egypt." *The Great Art of Knowing: The Baroque Encyclopedia of Athanasius Kircher*. Ed. Daniel Stolzenberg. Stanford: Stanford U Libraries, 2001. 115–25.

Stroumsa, Guy G. "John Spencer and the Roots of Idolatry." *History of Religions* 41.1 (2001): 1–23.

Sutcliffe, Adam. *Judaism and Enlightenment*. Cambridge: Cambridge UP, 2003.

Harry Clark Maddux

Euhemerism and Ancient Theology in Cotton Mather's "Biblia Americana"

Some readers of Cotton Mather's "Biblia Americana" are likely to be mystified by the presence of so many heathen gods and heroes. If titles are any indication of content, then we would have expected a study of the Holy Scriptures, not of the pagan pantheon, and so it might seem strange when Mather habitually links biblical figures, stories, and beliefs with those of classical mythology and other non-Christian traditions. Thus Mather, for instance, correlates Adam with Saturn and Chronos; Eve with Minerva; Noah, with Bacchus, Janus, or Prometheus; and Moses is transmuted into Apollo, Osiris, and Hermes Trismegistus. This curiosity for modern readers was actually a widely used approach in the biblical interpretation of Mather's time. When placed in its historical context, the "Biblia Americana" usually proves to be a broad and deep reflection on what the major thinkers – and Mather's reading is remarkably current for all the practical difficulties of being a colonial academic far removed from the metropolitan centers of learning – wrote in the various fields of early modern scholarship. Mather was certainly not alone in arguing that the Mosaic record and Hebrew religion were the sole origin of pagan wisdom (a view associated with the term *prisca theologia*, "ancient theology"), or in reading the actions of pagan gods and heroes as either allegories of natural phenomena or corrupted memories of actual events and persons recorded in the scriptures. This interpretative method is known as Euhemerism. Among Mather's most significant sources in this regard are John Selden (1584–1654), Gerhard Voss (1577–1649), Samuel Bochart (1599–1667), Pierre-Daniel Huet (1630–1721), and Pierre Jurieu (1637–1713). All these writers did not necessarily agree with one another, but Mather felt comfortable to pick and choose from them what he saw as most cogent and useful for his own argument.

The "Biblia" demonstrates that Mather did not shy away from the many uncomfortable questions that his contemporaries raised about the Bible as a divine revelation from God. Rather, he confronted them directly and expected his readers to do the same. If his response was ultimately orthodox, he was in good company among the leading minds of his generation that defended the biblical record. It is the purpose of this essay to examine Cotton Mather's theory about the origin of the pagan gods and pagan mythology, to explore his endeavor to associate the mythological heroes of ancient Greece and Rome with the patriarchs of the Bible, and to establish how far he was prepared to compromise the established Reformed position on these matters. In this effort, it is helpful, and will be the method of this essay, to examine Mather's Euhemeristic authorities in the order of their own lives. Mather's most venerated sources (which he often quotes at second hand) were in conversation with one another, and treating them chronologically rather than topically will help us to follow their individual rejoinders to and further developments of one another's arguments. Before we can fully appreciate Cotton Mather's contribution to this debate, however, we need to come to terms with the ancient concept of Euhemerism and its subsequent use during the seventeenth and early eighteenth centuries.

Euhemerus and his Reception in the Early Modern Period

The eponymous term Euhemerism refers to the writings of an ancient Greek historian, probably from Messene in what is now Sicily, though that place of origin is sometimes debated. The claim, for which his name would later become famous, that the gods originated in historical personages, appears in a text that most likely dates to the third century BCE, the *Hiera Anagraphe*. The entire text is lost, but the fragments that survived, in Ennius (239–169 BCE) and in the *Bibliothecae* of Diodorus Siculus (1st c. BCE), indicate that the *Hiera* of Euhemerus relates an imaginary voyage commissioned by the Macedonian King, Cassander (305–297 BCE), in which Euhemerus lands at an island called Panchaea.[1] There, he finds a remarkable monument that relates the supposed historical record of a ruler named Uranus, who gave birth to Chronos, who in turn sired Zeus and Hera and Poseidon (Brown 259–60).

As Truesdell Brown demonstrates in his important essay, "Euhemerus and the Historians," the type of imaginary history composed by Euhemerus already had a long history in the ancient near east before the *Hiera* was conceived (259). In one sense, Euhemerus merely recast existing traditions. Two particular themes in these traditions about how myths were literally brought down to earth were, first, that the gods and heroes of fables were either "poetic exaggeration or allegory" (263); second, that the misdeeds of the gods reported by Homer and others constituted corruptions of original, real, divine interventions (263). Both of these interpretations of the origins of later pagan mythol-

---

1 The most recent scholarly edition of the surviving fragments (entitled *Euhemeri Messenii reliquiae)* was undertaken by Marek Winiarczyk, whose study *Euhemeros von Messene: Leben, Werk und Nachwirkung* also offers the best current discussion of Euhemerus, the ancient concept of Euhemerism, and its early modern applications.

ogy filter into the "Biblia Americana" and the sources from which it was composed.

For a long time Euhemerus was available to the Western world mostly through the writings of the early Church Father Eusebius of Caesarea (c. 264 – c. 340 CE). His *Praeparatio evangelica*, a work written sometime after 313 CE, contains sizable portions of the *Bibliothecae* of Diodorus Siculus. During his lifetime, Diodorus had compiled a catalog of summarized books that was intended to link mythic history with the more recent chronicles of the campaigns of Alexander and of Julius Caesar. This catalogue survives only in fragments, and often what Diodorus wrote is only preserved by others. We learn from Eusebius's excerpt of Diodorus that Euhemerus was probably a historian who came across a stele or historical marker while travelling in Arabia. The stele's inscription revealed that Uranus had once been a beloved ruler in mythic times. He was

> a gentle and benevolent man, and learned in the motion of the stars, who also was the first to honour the celestial deities with sacrifices, on which account he was called Uranus. By his wife Ilestia he had sons Pan and Kronos, and daughters Rhea and Demeter: and after Uranus, Kronos became king and, having married Rhea, begat Zeus and Hera and Poseidon. And Zeus, having succeeded to the kingdom of Kronos, married Hera and Demeter and Themis, of whom he begat children, of the first the Curetes, of the second Persephone, and of the third Athena. (Eusebius, *Praeparatio Evangelica* 2.2)[2]

The writings of Euhemerus therefore bring together a whole complex of similar explanations of deified rulers whose apotheosis elevated their historical reign to a cosmic level. Throughout the period of the Roman Empire such "Euhemeristic" narratives had been a favorite instrument of skeptics. Cicero (106–43 BCE), for example, was among those who held that the gods must have been born of man. In his highly influential *De Natura Deorum* (44 BCE), Cicero claimed that the gods were entirely explicable in one of three ways: they had their beginning in fabulous, pre-historical times (Euhemerus), they were allegories and symbols of elementary and cosmic conflict, or they were personifications of some moral precept in fables (Seznec 4).

These main lines were adopted by Eusebius in his *Praeparatio*, but because the early Church Father from Caesarea wanted to demonstrate the absurdity of pagan belief, he viewed Euhemerism as indicative of the muddle-headedness of pagans. In book one, for instance, he notes that "it is reported ... that Phoenicians and Egyptians were the first of all mankind to declare the sun and moon and stars to be gods" (1.6). Eusebius's point here, of course, is not to condone the pagans' piety, but to mock their confusion. Another origin of pagan my-

---

2 Diodorus, according to Eusebius, elsewhere claims that Uranus was an earthly ruler, who married Ilestia (later deified as Ge) and had many children, some of whom also inspired the stories of the gods (*Praeparatio* 2.2).

thology is seen in those "tyrants, or even sorcerers and quacks, who after some falling off from holier ways had devised their evil arts" and tricked the multitude who sensed how far they had fallen from Eden, if they did not already know (2.5). This idea, that the pagan pantheon might have had its beginnings in deception, remained viable throughout the seventeenth century. One of Mather's favorite targets, Jean LeClerc (1657–1736) even held that Moses offered to the Jews in the desert a theology appropriate to their barbarism (Manuel 29). Mather himself appropriates this notion when he confronts the ancient religious beliefs of New England's indigenous tribes. Just as ancient magicians "in and for their Designs of Incantation, did use to call forth, *Leviathans* out of their Holes, and concern themselves with Terrible *Snakes*," so also, Mather claims in his commentary on, "our Indian *Powawes*, [were] frequently sending a *Divel* in a *Snake*, to kill their Neighbor"[*BA*, Job 3:8]. Such a comparison, he believed, provided a "Notable illustration" of how nature can be controlled and used to incite fear in the superstitious.[3]

As it was applied by most seventeenth and eighteenth-century writers, Euhemerism became a way to link pagan mythology to scripture. Though they sometimes adopted the Eusebian application of the old Democritan idea that the gods are born in fear inspired by a ruling class, as the passage from Mather's above-cited commentary demonstrates, Reformed writers of the period were more likely to consider the pagan pantheon simply as degeneration from the true religion given to Adam and corrupted over time. Seen from this perspective, pagan mythologies were little more than corrupted traditions of a true history that began with Adam and continued through Noah and his sons after the flood. This intellectual genealogy was offered to explain why virtually all peoples, even Native Americans, seemed to have concepts and stories similar to those of the Old Testament. After the confusion of the tongues, the various descendents of Shem, Ham, and Japheth corrupted the true religion they had inherited from Noah by adding their own interpretations over long periods of time. Thus, each nation had a residue of an ancient theology, which (in the case of Moses) could even have been derived from the Egyptians but restored to its original purity through the Mosaic laws. Daniel Walker astutely identifies this concept of ancient theology or *prisca theologia* as the belief in an aboriginal and pure doctrinal creed that could be traced back through the ages ultimately to Adam (1). At every turn, early modern reformers tried to show how the many pagan parallels to the Bible in fact proved that the pagans owed their religion to the patriarchs of Genesis and how pagan religious belief preserved a dim memorial of a pristine monotheism.

Scripturally grounded Euhemeristic readings of pagan mythology during the seventeenth and eighteenth centuries were also embedded in an emerging

---

3   Unless otherwise indicated, emphases are in the original texts.

debate over the issue of scriptural authority. Euhemerism in this sense was a countermove to attacks like those of Benedict Spinoza (1632–77) and Thomas Hobbes (1588–1679), which held that Moses could not have written the Pentateuch and that the books attributed to him were patently inconsistent. Mather demonstrates his own awareness of this connection by his extensive discussion of contemporary scholarly literature relating to the primacy and accuracy of the Pentateuch. Reiner Smolinski shows how Mather was able to adhere to the orthodox line that Moses was the author of at least the core of the first five books of the Bible while simultaneously asserting that the Pentateuch had obvious, if ultimately insignificant alterations, which showed the hand of at least one compiler ("Authority and Interpretation" 186). But Mather also knew that Euhemerism might demonstrate not reliance of pagan mythology on biblical history but the converse: a dependence of biblical narrative upon pagan originals. If Euhemerism highlighted, as Christian divines had argued since Eusebius, a habit of pagans to deify their ancestors, it also revealed their depraved desire to fashion idols and so, to refuse the right worship of God. As Jonathan Sheehan observes, this tendency might well imply that *all* worship carried in it the seeds of idolatry, which could be proved, among other things, by the Israelites of the Northern Kingdom erecting a golden calf at Bethel (44). Hobbes, like most educated men of the period, accepted that the "Gentiles" had worshipped idols, but he argued that they did so as a result of fear, not love. Therefore, if the pagans were so regularly idolatrous and so because of the operation of imagination, the same process might have led the Jews astray, as the biblical record showed it had. All worship could derive from demons or the simple way men had of erring from the truth. Hobbes's critique and others' like it could be troubling simply because they "pushed the Calvinist line to its logical limit and moved monotheism and idolatry into the same conceptual frame" (49). The effects were potentially devastating to any believer who accepted the primacy of biblical history.

Mather sought to answer critics by proving through his sources in the "Biblia Americana" how the mythologies of ancient cultures must have surely descended from the Hebrew patriarchs as those figures were recorded in the Bible. He believed that in pushing the initial corruption of the *prisca theologia* as far back as possible, he could refute the contradictory assertion that the Hebrews must have borrowed their faith from the Egyptians, Phoenicians, Greeks or Romans. In this manner, he hoped to demonstrate both how a pre-Hebraic worship of the God of the Bible might be verified through the putatively non-Judaic source of Job and how a true record of nations could be traced back to the table of the sons of Noah and their descendants recorded in Gen. 10. If the moment of spiritual and cultural rupture from the aboriginal monotheism was shown to be at or near the time that the tongues were confused at Babel, as Mather and his sources believed, then the most dangerous anti-scriptural explanation that Moses had gleaned his theology from the Egyptians could be deflated as unlikely at best. The Egyptians, after all, had already had a great deal of time to fall away from the beliefs of their forebear, Ham. And if the Egyptians did preserve a remnant of the *prisca theologia*, they could be compared to Job, who surely came before Moses and who also seemed to preserve certain ancient sacrificial rituals as burnt offerings and beliefs such as in the resurrection of the dead.

Behind these debates about the history of religions was a deep-seated anxiety over the priority and singularity of the Old Testament writings and, ultimately, over the authority of scripture in general. If the trustworthiness of the Old Testament as an accurate historical record was called into question, the status of the New would also have to be reconsidered. And despite the valiant efforts of orthodox apologists such as Mather this is exactly what happened. By the end of the eighteenth century, as Manuel and Rossi show, the Bible had irrevocably lost its status as an errorless record of God's revelation to man. Such eighteenth-century Deists as John Toland (1670–1722), Voltaire (1694–1778), and David Hume (1711–76) were perhaps not willing to dispense with God altogether, but this God certainly was not the Trinitarian being of the Nicene Creed, much less the God of Moses and Abraham. For the Deists, the interventionist and often wrathful God of the Judeo-Christian tradition was merely one of the countless mythic deities in the pantheon of mankind's many religions.

However, even in the later eighteenth century the radical intellectuals who shared such persuasion were still widely outnumbered by the defenders of scriptural authority. Though the camp of the faithful was sometimes rent by internal divisions, most agreed that Spinoza, Hobbes, Toland, and other detractors needed answering, and that right smartly. Euhemerism was one way in which Spinoza and those like him might be refuted. If it could be shown that the various pagan parallels to the stories in the Bible – the flood of Deucalion (aka. Noah) or the fables of Hercules (aka. Samson) – in fact owed their origins to the Hebrew scripture, then it would be reasonable to believe that the biblical account of the flood was the true original and Samson the source for Hercules. If that could be proven, then the whole diabolical edifice of the skeptics would collapse. Every extended apology for scripture that was prepared during the seventeenth and eighteenth centuries was written with this larger project in mind. The Italian historian Paolo Rossi, who has written a superb history of early modern science convincingly argues that the scientific forays into the origin and history of the earth need to be interpreted in light of contemporary defenses of the Bible's historical accuracy. In this context, Thomas Burnet's (1635–1715) *Telluris theoria sacra* (1689), which presents a mechanistic account of the flood of Noah (Rossi 34), is connected to Samuel Bochart's *Geographia Sacra* (1646), which seeks to show that the names of the pagan gods derive etymologically from the names of Noah's descendants (Rossi 153). Even though the Cartesian Burnet aims at providing a non-miraculous account of the flood, he does accept the flood as a true historical event. While Bochart wants to preserve the status of the Bible, he must account for the multitudes of pagan gods and goddesses worshipped by every ancient culture except that of the Hebrews. During the seventeenth and eighteenth centuries the history of the earth is therefore inseparable from the history of the nations (Rossi 4).

Euhemerism in the "Biblia Americana"

"Biblia Americana" evinces the extent to which this issue occupied the theologians of the seventeenth and eighteenth centuries. One of the earliest scholars to deploy Euhemerism in defense of scripture, and therefore one of Mather's most respected sources, was John Selden. A student of the ancient origins of the law, Selden also was a premier Orientalist of the seventeenth century. He was, as Frank Manuel notes, something of a transitional figure. His texts stand between medieval allegorical and demonological versions of Euhemerism and later Renaissance attempts to employ Euhemerism as a heuristic tool to explain the diversity of world religions in the service of demonstrating the exceptionality of Judeo-Christian revelation against the onslaught of historicist critics (29). Rather straightforwardly, Selden's *De Diis Syris Syntagmata* (1617) argues for a dependence of Syrian and Phoenician religious practices and deities on their supposed Hebrew originals. Still, Selden had a far-reaching influence over English writers who followed him.

Mather's sources in the "Biblia" prove the extent of Selden's impact. Even as Deistic attacks on scripture mounted, Mather's English scholars from the latter seventeenth century had frequent recourse to Selden's earlier works. Thus, often in the "Biblia" when Mather refers to Selden by name, this attribution is at second-hand and can have other, immediate purposes than the simple identification of Hebrew origins for pagan gods. For example, in identifying Moses with the Phoenician Moschus – a mystic who believed that the universe originated in a cosmic egg – Mather cites Selden indirectly from Edmund Dickinson's 1702 work, *Physica Vetus & Vera* (*BA* 1: 358).[4] An English physician and member of the Royal Society, Dickinson (1624–1707) turns to Selden because the *Physica* was intended to defend the corpuscular theory of the world. Moschus was sometimes believed to have originated the atomistic philosophy that Democritus later developed, and Moses was therefore seen as having adumbrated the Newtonian theories of corpuscular light.

---

4 Smolinski, who has assiduously identified Mather's sources in Genesis and who recognizes the ways in which Mather deployed Euhemerism, observes that Mather is quoting from the *Physica* (ch. 2, p. 11). Wherever Mather's commentaries on Genesis are discussed I am relying on Smolinski's notes.

Elsewhere, in defense of his idea that Job exemplifies a pure worship of God in the days before the law, Mather is careful to point out that "Mr. Selden observes" how "many of the Hebrew writers ... think that *Job* lived in the Dayes of *Isaac and Jacob* [*BA*, Job].[5] This conclusion, however, is drawn not from Selden directly, but from the Preface to Simon Patrick's popular *The Book of Job Paraphras'd* (1679). Patrick (1625–1707), the influential Bishop of Ely and frequent textual reference for Mather, asserted that Job must have lived before Isaac and Jacob. When Job therefore speaks of a bodily resurrection and prays to a righteous God, this action was taken as proof that the ancient theology antedates at least two of the patriarchs. Consequently, a pure body of doctrine was at least partially preserved by some of Noah's descendants despite the rise of idolatry amongst many other of his offspring.

Although Mather does not immediately identify his source, Patrick acknowledges Selden's 1640 *De Iure Naturali & Gentium* (bk. 2, ch. 11, pp. 834–35). Significantly, this historical placement of Job is presented in a book in which Selden argues that the Noachic covenant (cf. Gen. 8 f.) reflects the pure "natural law" of God. This idea had profound implications for Euhemeristic interpretations in the ancient theological vein, because it meant that long before Moses Noah was the guardian of the divine law, and thus Noah, rather than Moses, might be the source from which all the religions the world over derived their own creeds no matter how corrupted. There could still be an immediate dependence of the Greeks upon Moses (via Egypt), but the fountainhead of this inspiration was Noah. Pushing the date back in this way had the benefit of freeing Moses from any taint of Egyptian idolatry, and of accounting for the emergence of other beliefs through the migration of Noah's sons.

Others were quick to follow Selden, though they soon developed Euhemerism along lines different from those he had laid down. The Dutch Calvinist Gerhard Voss, or Vossius, was one of several scholars to do so. According to Paolo Rossi, Voss's 1642 *De Theologia et philosophia Christiana sive de origine et progressu idolatrae* is "a grandiose work, teeming with an endless quantity of gods" (153). Voss established a vast hierarchical system of classifications whereby pagan religions are studied in terms of their beliefs relating to "spiritual creatures, celestial bodies, elements meteors, men, quadrupeds, birds, fish, snakes, insects, fossils, plants, and symbols" (153).

Voss's originality lay in the way in which he traced many pagan gods back to a few Biblical heroes. Unlike Selden, whose aim was not polemical, Voss attempted to show how the Gentiles, in searching for God, had mistaken the creature for the creator, and had deified their Hebrew ancestors, and later, animals and the stars. In Voss's history, therefore, Moses became as important as

---

5   The quote comes from Mather's introduction to the Book of Job and therefore cannot be keyed to a specific scriptural verse.

he was among the Jews. Thus, in the religion of the Egyptians, Moses was identified as the Egyptian Thoth; among the Gauls, he became Teutates; among the Greek, Hermes, and among the Romans, Mercury. Likewise, "there were many Bacchus ... who is none other than Noah." Voss even identified the early Chinese emperors with the biblical patriarchs: Fohi is Adam, Xu-nung is Cain (Rossi 154).

Voss's linkage of biblical history to that of the Chinese was significant because their similarities posed an obvious threat to those who would claim that the scriptures were both more accurate and ancient than any other writing. Jesuit accounts like Martino Martini's *Sinicae Historiae Decas Prima res àgentis origine ad Christum natum in extrema Siae, sive magno Sinarum imperio gestas complexa* (1659) and Louis LeComte's *Nouveaux memoirs sur l'état présent de la Chine* (1697) did much to undermine the traditional belief in the Bible's inerrancy. China is never directly mentioned in scripture, but even to the biased eyes of the seventeenth century was obviously an ancient civilization. Euhemerism, however, provided a way out of this apparent bind: if the scriptural account could be defended as factual and accurate, then it was no great leap to conclude that the Chinese must have descended from one of the patriarchs, and their language, if not their religion, must retain some colors from its origins in Eden.

As he does with Selden, Mather typically draws on Voss indirectly, but with full awareness of the argument Voss is making. The disquisitions that owe themselves to Voss generally serve the function of demonstrating that pagan mythologies and the idolatry that goes with them are the logical, even inevitable, consequences of the first sin. Yet ancient humans still seemed to retain a shadowy memory of their origins in Eden. Voss and those who followed him thought both these assertions could be proved by analyzing the names of the gods and goddesses and showing how they might be etymologically rooted in the names of biblical figures.

For this reason, Mather asks an apparently unrelated question in his commentary on Gen. 2:25 ("The man and his wife were both naked, and they felt no shame"). The answer is a lengthy discourse on the etymology of the pagan pantheon:

> Q.   That the Pagans did under other Names, mention in their Stories, many of the Persons mentioned in the Scriptures, is very likely; but is it not as likely, that the *Gods* worshipped by the Pagans, were but some of the *Hero*'s in the Bible, disguised under other Denominations? v. 25.
> A.   Yes. The Book of *Genesis*, as *Edwards* truly observes, afforded unto the *Pagan* World, the greatest Part of their Ancient Gods and Goddesses.
> *Adam* [or, *Noah*, with whom the Pagans ignorantly confounded him] seems to have been the *Saturn*, descended, as the Poets tell us, of his Father *Cœlus*, and his Mother *Tellus*: under him, was the *Golden Age*, but hee was afterwards expelled from his Kingdome, & became the Author of *Agriculture*. This is *Adam* all over. Moreover, *Adam*, with whom was the Beginning of *Time*, is very fitly called Χρονος, or

Κϱονος, i.e. *Time*, which was the Name of *Saturn*. As for the Name of *Saturn*, it might bee given to *Adam*, from *Satar*, i.e. *Latere*; for hee *hid himself*. [Gen. 3.10.] *Saturnus* is therefore, as *Vossius* tells us, the same with *Latius*; and the Place which was once called *Saturnia*, was afterwards call'd, *Latium*, as *Virgil* testifies. (*BA* 1: 435–36)[6]

As his own attribution indicates, Mather here is directly copying from one of his favorite authors, the conservative English Calvinist John Edwards (1637–1716), who wrote a three-volume text entitled, *A Discourse Concerning the Authority, Stile, and Perfection of the Books of the Old and New Testament* (1693–95). It is noteworthy that Edward's approach is very different from Mather's. Edwards is writing a systematic, tightly structured defense of the Bible, and therefore *A Discourse* explicates in detail the topics outlined in its title: The first and lengthiest volume defends the authority of the Bible, the second and third more briefly treat the style and usefulness of scripture. Edwards's arguments are made even starker by Mather's method of weaving broad swaths of this carefully concentrated text into his own annotations of the Bible.

Mather selects this particular passage because Edwards's discussion – which in turn is culled from Voss's *De Theologia Gentili* (bk. 1, ch. 18, pp. 138–39) – interprets the nakedness of Adam and Eve metaphorically to signify "hidden" and "unknown." Adam was "naked" before God, but the truth of his life was "hidden" from the eyes of pagans. Mather adopts Voss's argument (via Edwards) and etymologically links the Latin signification of "hidden" ("satar") and "unknown" ("latere") with the Roman deity Saturn, whose name suggests these meanings. On this basis, Voss concluded that Saturn is associated with Latius, the ancient territory of the Latini. Smolinski in his edition of Mather's commentary on Genesis (*BA* 1: 436 n36) further notes that Voss's case was strengthened by Virgil, who tells how Saturn, fleeing from Olympus, found refuge in Latium, where he gave his laws to the people of the Golden Age (*Aeneid* 8.319–29). The condition of Adam and Eve, then, is emblematic of human history. At the same time that they became aware of their nakedness, the first couple made possible the shameful corruption of worship of the one true God. Paganism is the necessary corollary of original sin, even if the connections are often hidden, wrapped in what Mather elsewhere calls a "Book of *Mysteries*; it is very much a *Seal'd Book* unto us, until wee come at those *Mysteries*" [*BA*, Ezra 1:8]. The work of Voss and his contemporaries gave Mather a way to solve at least one of the scriptural mysteries: if scripture revealed that a divinely inspired religion had been available to our first parents and their descendants, and if the record contained in the Bible was accurate, then how come the errors of paganism perpetuated themselves so quickly and widely?

---

6 See *A Discourse* (vol. 1, ch. 5, pp. 204–05).

Nimrod as Orion

One likely person in the Bible who might have spawned these errors was a character whose name only occurs four times in Hebrew scriptures. Nimrod (cf. Gen. 10:8–9; 1 Chron. 1:10; Mic. 5:6), the son of Cush, the son of Ham, the son of Noah, is nevertheless often associated with two seminal scriptural events: the building of the tower of Babel and the founding of the Babylonian empire. It is perhaps not by chance that Nimrod's name has long been thought to mean "we shall rebel" (cf. Gen. 11:1–9). These identifications are as old as the Midrash (*Rab.* 23.7), and repeated by Josephus in his *Antiquities* (1.4), but Samuel Bochart, one of Voss's fellow antiquarians, did much to cement the notoriety of Nimrod in the early modern history of the pagan pantheon. In his two magisterial works, *Geographia Sacra* (1646) and *Hierozoicon* (1646), Bochart propounded hundreds of Euhemeristic histories that relied on perceived etymologies which were frequently based on little more than similarities of sound. The first work traced the dispersal of the peoples of the earth after the building of the tower of Babel; the second examined the various animals named in scripture and their mythological counterparts. Both texts were standard references in seventeenth-century universities, and Mather often turns directly to Bochart's writings when he wants to make a Euhemeristic connection for himself.

Mather's several entries on Nimrod, that "mighty hunter before the Lord" (Gen. 10:9), reveal the method of Bochart and those who followed his lead. In Genesis (*BA* 1: 727–28) Nimrod's strength initially makes him one of the "giants in the earth" (Gen. 6:4) in those days. His strength, however, is also a metaphor of his pride. The phrase, "mighty hunter before the Lord" was sometimes rendered "warrior against the Lord." From this vantage point, Nimrod is easily identified with those builders of Babel who sought to ascend to Heaven on their own power, motivated by their hubris. Ovid, of course, records a similar attack of Jove on heaven (*Metamorphoses* 1.151–62). All of these associations are proposed by Bochart in his first book of the *Geographia Sacra* (bk. 1, ch. 1, p. 13).

Nimrod, however, is rich with interpretive possibility, and so he ranges widely over the "Biblia." He appears toward the end of Genesis as the inspiration of the Phoenician Bel, Belus, or Baal. Mather here returns to Edwards and asserts that "Dr. *Edwards* thinks it probable, That *Idolatry* began first, with the Worshipping of *Bel*, or *Belus*, whom the Scripture calls *Nimrod*, the first King of *Assyria* after the Flood" (*BA* 1: 1058).[7] Identifying Nimrod as the original idolater was an important matter because another contender for that disgrace was Cain, who might have been the first to worship the sun as a substitute for his banishment from the presence of God. In his commentary on Gen. 4:3, Mather, cribbing from the two-volume *Commentary upon the Historical Books*

---

7   See Edwards, *A Discourse* (vol. 1, ch. 6, p. 203).

of the Old Testament (1727) by Simon Patrick (1625–1707), remarks that if, after the murder of Abel and subsequent punishment from God, Cain turned *"Idolater,* it is likely, he introduced the Worship of the *Sun,* (which was the most ancient *Idolatry*) and of the *Fire*; the best Resemblance he could find of the *Shechinah,* or, *The Glory of the Lord."*[8] Mather's own preference for Bochart's etymological methodology and obvious admiration for his learning, however, means that more often than not he accedes to Bochart's historical conclusions.

Remarkably, Nimrod rises again as the fabulous Greek hero Orion in the gloss on Job 38:31. Mather here reiterates not Borchart, but Voss's thesis that many Greek words are derived from Hebrew originals. The Septuagint by a kind of backward transliteration substitutes the Greek constellation Orion for the Hebrew word "Kesil."[9] Mather's (and Voss's) logic is evident in the "Biblia" entry:

> Q.   What Constellation is that which the Lord mentions unto *Job,* under the Name of *Cesil,* by us translated, *Orion?* v. 31.
> A.   The same, as you find in our Translation.
> You must know, that *Nimrod,* the *Mighty Hunter,* whom the Seventy Interpreters also call, *A Giant,* ... was in After Ages, Deified, or at least, advanced as High as the Starry Sphære; for hee was Eternized by the Designation of that Constellation, which wee now call by the Name of *Orion.* The Greeks confess this *Orion* to have been a *Mighty Hunter*; and the Astronomers of *Arabia* call him, *Algebar,* that is, *A Giant.* His posture in the Heavens, is with *Sword* and *Buckler*; & as an Intimation of his Huntsmanship, with the Skin of a Wild Beast in his hand. ...
>
> Now, this Constellation tis, that is here, & elsewhere called, *Cesil,* from the Great Inconstancy of the Weather, at the Astronomical Ascension thereof: and hence also the Month *Cislen.* ...
>
> The Chaldee paraphrase renders *Cesil* ... *A Giant*; which confirms the common opinion of Interpreters, for *Orion*; or, *Nimrod,* who was called *Orion,* because that is the Chaldee plural ... *Orin,* of ... *Or,* Light; for this Constellation has the most Conspicuous *Lights* of Heaven in it. [*BA,* Job 38:31][10]

This entry in Mather's "Biblia" again occurs in a crucial context: the lengthy reply of God to Job, in which Job is silenced and shown to be entirely out of his element in his pitiful attempt to understand the transcendent mind of the creator. Mather does not reproduce the question God poses to Job, but the identification of Nimrod with Kesil and with Orion makes little sense without it: God asks as one of a string of similarly impossible feats, if Job can "loose the bands of Orion" that hold him in the sky (Job 38:31). There Nimrod stands, remembered by the Greeks under a different name. Job cannot perform the impossible,

---

8   See Patrick, *Commentary* (1: 23, 26).
9   "Kesil," according to Strong's *Concordance,* means "large, fat, or burly."
10   For all of this information and the linguistic underpinnings of it, Mather depended not only on Voss, but also on Brian Walton's *Biblia Sacra Polyglotta* (2: 77), held in the Harvard Library during Mather's lifetime.

but, Mather implies, we can use Nimrod to remind us of just how far we have fallen that we should place our ancestors in the sky and worship them.

Noah, Moses, and the Ancient Theology

Edmund Dickinson's *Delphi Phoenicizantes* and its appended, but separately paginated, *Diatriba* (1655), which provided Mather with access to Vossius's *De Theologia Gentili*, also elucidated for him how the Greeks and Romans perhaps borrowed their religious practices *and* their gods from the Hebrews. Mainly, Dickinson tried to prove that the practices at Delphi preserved traditions from the age of the Judges (Momigliano 24). Along the way, however, he spun a narrative about Noah's wanderings that permitted Dickinson to identify Noah with numerous other deities (*Delphi Phoenicizantes*, ch. 9, pp. 75–91).

Mather extracts from these pages the substance of two long entries. One of these occurs in answer to the question of, "What became of *Noah* after the Flood? What Habitations did hee seek? and what Remembrances ha's hee left" (*BA* 1: 678). The other treats "the Rise of the several Nations in the World, and of their Scatterings" (*BA* 1: 693). Noah, "finding his Posterity so increase{d}, that *Palæstine*, could not hold them," he eventually "left *Shem* in *Syria*, hee sent *Cham* to *Egypt*, and went himself, with *Japhet*, into the Countrey that is now called *Italy*; where hee built a City, called *Chethim*, (afterwards *Volterra*) which, proving the Metropolis of *Tuscany*, all *Italy* was afterwards from thence denominated" (*BA* 1: 693). This convenient passage across the Mediterranean allows Mather to follow Dickinson in two important, related conclusions.

First, Noah becomes the original of numerous Latin gods and mythic heroes, among them Janus, Vadimon or Vertumnus, Ogyges, Deucalion, Sol and Coelum, and Saturn (*BA* 1: 679–84). Many of the same identifications occur briefly in the 1650 posthumous publication of Mathias Prideaux's (c. 1622–46) *An Easy and Compendious Introduction for Reading All Sorts of Histories* (bk. 1, ch. 1, pp. 4–5). Dickinson, however, exceeds Prideaux by providing a full etymology for each name as a buttress to his claim (*Diatriba* 1–4). The derivation of Saturn from Noah disagrees both with Edwards and Bochart, but Mather translates Dickinson's Latin without comment and so here has Saturn related to Noah by way of the Orphic Hymns, in which Saturn is euphemized as the "father of all" and the "begetter," as Noah himself begat the entire postdiluvian population of the earth.[11]

Second, and more importantly, Noah paves the way for removing the ancient theology from Egypt to Italy. For much of the period of the European

---

11   On the Orphic Hymns, see Walker (22–41).

Renaissance, a favorite pastime of scholars was demonstrating how the pagan world might have preserved some of the truth that was more fully contained in holy writ. One of the individuals commonly identified with this *prisca theologia* was the mythical Egyptian priest, and original of the god Thoth, Hermes Trismegistus (the thrice-great Hermes). Bishop Edward Stillingfleet (1635–1699), a contemporary of Mather and Dickinson, in his *Origines Sacrae* (1662), managed to summarize even as he critiqued the prevailing view of Hermes. Through a chain of classical sources, including Josephus's *Against Apion*, Hermes came to be identified with "the *first invention* of their [Egyptian] *learning*, and all excellent *Arts*, from him they *derive* their *history*; their famous *Historian Manetho*, professing to transcribe his *Dynastyes* from the pillars of *Hermes*" (bk. 1, ch. 2, p. 33). Hermes, it was believed, was either confused with Moses himself, or, more likely, an earlier Egyptian priest-king who wished to preserve the worship of God through the teachings of Ham, Noah's son, and whose cult then passed these teachings on to Moses, prince of Egypt, who subsequently conveyed them, along with God's law, to the people at Sinai. More remarkably, Pythagoras could have acquired the teachings of Hermes in Egypt and transmitted them to Plato, whom Eusebius styles "Moses speaking Attic Greek" (*Praeperatio* 11.10).

The problems with this narrative were manifold. Placing too much reliance on a Platonic *or* Egyptian transmission of divine truth seemed, among other things, to relativize the singular importance of scripture. Worse, hermeticism could even be taken as implying that Moses borrowed *his* religion from the Egyptians. Therefore, Stillingfleet emphasizes the dubious qualities of Manetho's history, which very much agrees with Josephus's attitude in *Against Apion*, where Manetho, a 3rd century BCE Egyptian historian, was among those writers who might level "reproaches … against us [the Jews] … and will not believe what I have written concerning the antiquity of our nation" (1.1.3). Stillingfleet, like the Cambridge Platonists, wanted to preserve some strand of Christian thought in pagan literature, but would not go so far as to assert that the influence was in any way doctrinally significant; as Sarah Hutton observes: "the main thrust of his argument is aimed at discrediting non-biblical testimony" (Hutton 71). While Stillingfleet sought to maintain biblical priority in antiquities, he was in no way shy of new ideas: as his *Discourse in Vindication of the Doctrine of the Trinity* shows, he was discriminating of the new directions of philosophy, locking horns on different occasions with both Spinoza and Locke – even to receive a response in "Mr. Locke's reply".

Like Stillingfleet, Mather and Dickinson do not follow Bochart, Edwards, and Voss who placed much reliance on the hermetic tradition as a forerunner of Christianity. Mather and Dickinson also went along with Stillingfleet in that they wanted at least to preserve the principle of the ancient theology. Unlike him, they saw the question of how this theology was maintained as crucial to a defense of scripture. Therefore, they traced the line of succession back several more generations, to Noah. In a long entry, Mather, copying Dickinson (*Delphi* ch. 9, pp. 75–91), remarks how in the *"Tuscan Antiquities ... we are there told, That the great Vandimon, or Noah"* in a speech to his "Offspring" laid out the history that was past and that which was to come. The prophecy in these texts is arresting from a Christian standpoint, particularly when Noah foresees a *"King, that shall deliver you from the power of another over you"* (*BA* 1: 694).

Smolinski notes how many of the same problems that mark the extant hermetic texts are also present in the *Etruscan Fragments* (*Ethruscarum Antiquitatum Fragmenta*) (1636), a forgery of the Italian Curzio Inghirami (1614–55), to which Mather and most of his contemporaries fell prey.[12] Although the *Etruscan Fragments* are now recognized as a fraud, it would be facile to accuse Mather or Dickinson of simple gullibility in this matter. There were many reasons that they relied upon this collection rather than upon the hermetic tradition; the *Fragments* were moreover accepted by many reputable authorities throughout Mather's life.

In the end, Mather very much emulates Stillingfleet. Mather was not willing to entirely dismiss a discernible origin of the ancient theology in the pagan world, but he ultimately opted for explanations that propounded a general rather than a particular influence of the Hebrews on the ancient world, especially upon the Greeks. There was, for Mather, an apparent, and orthodox, confirmation of the Noachide hypothesis in a book far removed from either Genesis or the *Fragments*. Like Noah, Job could be readily seen as cleaving to the *prisca theologia* and thus as also confirming that Plato's cosmology was indirectly derived from the ancients.

Mather was willing to agree with the Mosaic interpretation so far as to allow that the Jews transmitted their beliefs to Plato via Egypt in some unspecified way. In arguing this point, he draws on the 1720 English edition of *The Works of Plato Abridg'd* by André Dacier (1651–1722). In order to explain the appearance of Satan before God and the power that he is given over Job, Mather reproduces a remark from Dacier (vol. 1, p. 110) that notes

> ... a surprising passage of *Plato* [De Legib. L.10.Tom.2.]; *Seeing we are agreed* (sais he,) *that the Air is filled with Good and Bad Genii, which are entirely opposite unto each other, this occasions an Immortal Combate, & requires a Continual Attention on our Part; The Good Angels being ready to help us; For we are their Possession.* *Eusebius* is amaz'd at the Beauty of this Passage; and shows, that he must needs have it from the Book of *Job*; where the *Devil* appears before GOD, with the *Good Angels*.
>
> The amazing stroke that follows [in the Laws], about, *The Combate*, M. *Dacier* observes, Tis the very same, that is admirably explain'd by the Apostle *Paul*;

---

12   In the passage quoted above Mather specifically draws on bk. 3 (p. 174) of the *Fragments* (*BA* 1: 695 n4).

Eph. 6.12. *We wrestle against the Rulers of the Darkness of this world.* [*BA*, Job 1:6][13]

Significantly, neither Mather nor Dacier explain how Plato came by this knowledge. Mather, though, does suggest that Job had a more certain prophetic knowledge and therefore it was not unlikely that somewhere in history he or another pious saint might have influenced some devout pagan. This is why Mather follows elsewhere the lead of writers such as Pierre Jurieu and Thomas Sherlock (1678–1761). Jurieu's *A Critical History of the Doctrines & Worships (Both Good and Evil) of the Church from Adam to our Saviour Jesus Christ*, published in an English edition in 1705, supports Mather's placement of Job "doubtless long before the Time of *Moses*; For his Life Extended at least unto Two Hundred Years, & seems to have been in an Age before the Life of Mankind was brought down unto what it was in the Days of *Moses*." Job moreover participated in pre-Mosaic rituals and "offered *Sacrifices* in person, but also was Eminent for the Fear of GOD; whereas the Grace of GOD was more withdrawn from the Nations, after the Days of *Moses*." Jurieu can easily account for the use of Hebraic titles for God such as "JEHOVAH" because "He imagines, That *Solomon*, or some such person might be the Translator of the Book [of Job]; the memoirs thereof being taken from the Monuments of the *Chaldæans* and *Arabians*." Mather's conclusion about Job, however, is even more far-reaching than that of Jurieu. At the end of this annotation, Mather exclaims in a rare intrusion of his own voice,

> But now, in this Illustrious Book, Behold, The Divinity known and own'd by the Patriarchs, before the Days of *Moses*! *Behold, How much nearer it approach'd unto the Christian, than unto the Jewish Religion!* The Articles of the Faith embraced by the Ancient Church, here appear to be such, as cannot be read without astonishment. [*BA*, Job, emphasis added][14]

Earlier, Mather quotes at length from Thomas Sherlock's *The Use and Intent of Prophecy, in the several Ages of the World*. Sherlock's work was enormously popular, going through six editions by 1755, and so it is not surprising that Mather considered Sherlock's opinion worth reproducing. Mather and Sherlock assert that Job

> ... appears to be the Oldest Book in the World, and written before any of the Books of *Moses*; and it gives an Account of the State of Nature and Religion, in the World, before *Moses* had committed any thing to writing. To suppose it written for the sake of afflicted *Jews* (who were far from a *Righteous* People) without one single word of the *Mosaic* Law, or Allusion to any one Rite in it, or any one piece of *His-*

---

13   The idea, loosely translated by Dacier, can be found in Plato's *Laws* (10.906a). The remark of Eusebius is in *Preparatio Evangelica* (11.26).

14   This entry in the "Biblia" is a composite of quotes selected from the first volume of *A Critical History* (vol. 1, bk. 1, ch. 2, pp. 14–19). The comment is part of Mather's general introduction to the Book of Job, and hence not tied to a specific verse.

tory Later than *Moses*, or any Forms of the *Idolatry* for which they were punished; it would be much as if a Critick should suppose *Homers Iliad*, written to celebrate the Military Expeditions of the *Goths* and *Vandals*. [*BA*, Job]

Mather goes on to extract a sizable portion of the Appendix of Sherlock's *Use and Intent of Prophecy* (ch. 2, pp. 206–20) to reiterate in the end that Job anticipates the appearance and return of Christ, the creation, and man's fall – all well before Moses.

Whatever the origin of ancient theology, the descent from Noachide purity had been swift. Within two generations of Noah, according to Dickinson's *Delphi Phoenicizantes* (ch. 9, pp. 78–79), "a fearful Degeneracy overtook the Posterity of those that had been thus Instructed; they soon left and lost the Religion of their Fathers, and the very Name of that *Jehovah* who was the God of their Fathers, came to bee changed among them." Finally, "in that very Place, where *Dodanim*[15] had his Church, there succeeded the horrid Ceremonies & Superstitions, of the *Dodonæan* Oracles. Yea, all the Diabolical *Oracles* of *Greece*, were once the Schools of the True Religion" (*BA* 1: 695). The sad lesson of the ancient theology was that if "True Religion" was preserved, so was the habit of humanity to corrupt the right worship of God. This perversion of pure worship always happened and would not cease, until Christ returned to set mankind again on course.

Elsewhere, in his commentary on Gen. 2:25, Mather does seem to consider more seriously the possibility of a Mosaic influence upon the pagan world. However, within the larger framework of his selections from Edwards's *Discourse*, the revolutionary aspect of this position, drawn from a prominent ancient theologian of the Mosaic school, is hardly visible in comparison to Mather's more developed opinion in the notes on Gen. 10. Pierre-Daniel Huet published a work in 1679 which borrowed the title from Eusebius's own *Demonstratio Evangelica*, a text in its turn written to accompany the *Praeparatio Evangelica*. In Huet's *Demonstratio*, Mather observes through Edwards, "Monsieur *Huet*, showes, how *Moses* was also repræsented by *Apollo, Æsculapius, Pan, Priapus, Prometheus, Janus*, and by those Egyptian Deities, *Osiris, Apis, Serapis, Orus, Anubis*" (*BA* 1: 441). Daniel Walker astutely remarks how in identifying Moses with such a number of pagan gods, Huet went where even Voss was slow to tread (Walker 216). Though Huet accepted Voss's version of Chinese history, he radically simplified his Euhemerism and made virtually every god identical with Moses so that the divine lawmaker was forced to bear the burden of Prometheus (in bringing the law of God to man and being scorned for it by the Exodus tribes) as well as the trials of Priapus (in that Moses spread

15 Dodanim was, according to Masoretic texts, a son of Javan and grandson of Japhet. In Dickinson, Dodanim settled in Epirus where he erected a *"Temple*, wherein the People of {the} Neighbourhood, might Assemble to Seek the Face of God, and Hear the Præcepts of their Father *Noah* preach'd upon" (*BA* 1: 694).

his theological seed to the redeemed and the depraved alike). Mather, however, as already indicated, clearly leaned in the direction of Noah rather than Moses. Thus Mather's implicit criticism of Huet is either a hasty duplication of Edwards' argument (vol. 1, ch. 6, p. 219) or Mather's prudence coming to the fore. For although Mather traces the various names of Moses, it is finally Noah's children who bear the guilt for all the errors that followed upon the death of the last antediluvian.

This is why Mather and Dickinson (*Delphi Phoenicizantes*, ch. 9, pp. 90–91) are both explicit about the similarities between the descendants of Noah and those mildest of heretics, the Quakers. After the worship of Noah was corrupted, according to Dickinson, the oracle at Delphi came to sit "upon a *Tripos*, to receive the *Vapour*, or, if you will, the *Spirit*, of the Cave, over which, it was placed; the *Dæmon*, which the Scripture calls, *Ob*, entred into her." Consequently, the oracle "was then immediately taken with an extraordinary *Trembling* of her whole Body; shee *Quaked*, and shee *Foamed* horribly; and so there issued from her, the *Prophecies*, which enchanted all the World into a Veneration of them" (*BA* 1: 696). The issue is not simply academic when Mather finally says, "I'l Insist no further on this Matter; but only from the Passage last mentioned, putt you that Quæstion, *Whether you now think the QUAKERS, to* BEE SO NEW A SECT, *as they have commonly been accounted*" (*BA* 1: 696). If we are the responsive readers he hoped for, we already know the answer and indeed, the logic behind it.

The Hebrew Origins of Classical Literature in the "Biblia Americana"

The manifold Euhemeristic and ancient theological elements of the "Biblia" escape easy cataloguing. They are so numerous that any study is bound to be no more than a survey. There is one final source for Mather, however, that deserves mentioning. Nehemiah Grew, famous as a botanist, published his *Cosmologia Sacra* in 1701. Grew straightforwardly announces its polemical purpose in the Preface:

> The Many Leud Opinions, especially those of Antiscripturists, which have of late Years; by *Spinosa* [sic] and some others, in *Latin, Dutch*, and *English*; have been the Occasion of my Writing this Book. As seeing too well, that hereby, not only Men of Erudition, but the Citizens themselves, grown of late more Bookish, are very dangerously infected. In so much, that every Apprentice, who can but get a Play to his Tooth, Stuffed with Vice and Prophaneness; formeth all his Thoughts, Words, and Actions, by This, as his Bible. (Preface, n.p.).

The entry on Gen. 1:2, drawn from the fourth book of Grew's text, is instructive for understanding Mather's differing intents in his "Biblia." For two manuscript pages (*BA* 1: 332–37), Mather selectively quotes from Grew, but it is Mather's own question that frames the answer he provides: "The Sacred Oracles tell us, That *God made Man after His own Image*. May we not find that, and many other Passages of the Sacred Oracles, imitated in the Pagan Writers?" (*BA* 1: 332). The pronouncements of scripture are oracular, as Dickinson showed to Mather's satisfaction, but other oracles, other cryptic messages and hermetic knowledge, are echoed in pagan lore. Mather, through Grew, quickly leaps from man being made in God's image, to the "many other Passages" imitated in antiquity. Grew's original, by contrast, occurs not in the pointed context of explaining what the specific verse means, but in a sprawling chapter appropriately entitled "Of the TRUTH and EXCELLENCY of the *Hebrew Code*[.] And first as they appear from FOREIGN PROOF" (bk. 4, ch. 2, p. 144). Still, Grew's words conveniently fit Mather's distinct purpose and he copies them carefully: "The very Expressions of the Sacred Writers, are much imitated, both by Fabulous, and Philosophick Poets" (bk. 4, ch. 2, p. 153).

Neither Grew nor Mather begins with the fundamental author of the Greek world, but both of them rapidly proceed to compare scripture to the work of Homer. Both believe that "no Poet imitates the Scriptures more than *Homer*, who having been, as *Pausanias* tells us, an *Inquisitive Traveller into all Countreyes*, had no doubt, been among the Jewes" (*BA* 1: 333). Mather does not reproduce Grew's identification of the assertion of "*Pausanias* in his *Attica*," that Homer "travelled into all countries," but the conclusion remains Grew's that therefore Homer had been "doubtless among the *Jews*" (bk. 4, ch. 2, p. 153). The actual claim of Pausanias was far more circumspect: in his *Attica*, he only remarks on Homer having travelled into "far" countries (1.2.3).

This idea that Homer had sojourned among the Jews was commonplace in Euhemeristic histories. Mather's selections from Grew are more startling for their range and, it might be said, whimsy. Enoch, translated into heaven (Gen. 5:24), becomes Ganymede, taken up to heaven by Zeus in a whirlwind (*Iliad* 20.231–35). Similarly, "In Allusion to the Story of *Balaam*, he [Homer] will have *Xanthus*, the Horse of *Achilles*, upon his Career, to speak to him, and *Achilles* answer him" (*BA* 1: 334).[16] After a few more parallels, Mather concludes that he will

> from Dr. *Grew*, mention only Two more of this Poets Imitations; and they are pretty Remarkable ones. One of them is This.
> He transfers the Circumstances of the Transactions between the *Israelites* & the *Egyptians*, to that between *Penelope* and her Wooers. *Penelope* takes Presents of them, & this by the Advice of *Pallas*, before they were all Destroyed, even by *Ulysses*, who answers to *Moses*. ... The other of them is This. His *Twentieth Iliad* is wonderfully taken out of our *Eighteenth Psalm*. *David* makes a Triumphant sort of Descant upon his Deliverance from all his Enemies, & from *Saul*. Much of this the

16   See *Iliad* (19.392).

Poet borrowes, to express *Æneas*'s Præservation from *Achilles*. The Psalmist saies, *God Thundred with fiery Lightnings in the Heavens*. The Poet saies, *Jove Thundred terribly above*. The Psalmist saies, *Then the Earth Shook & Trembled*. The Poet saies, *Neptune shook the Earth on every Side*. (*BA*·1: 335)

The wrath of Odysseus wreaking his revenge on Penelope's suitors (*Odyssey* 22.1) Mather believes, here alludes to the wrathful Jehovah of Arms, whom David celebrates. God and Jove both thunder; the earth is shaken by God and Neptune. For Mather, the arguments for Euhemerism and the ancient theology, at least in broad outline, seem to mount until they might be denied in their specifics, but could not be refuted in the mass. If Balaam's ass might be found in the *Iliad* as Achille's steed, why might Moses or Noah not also hide in the guise of the gods? In almost every case, Mather seems to conclude that pagan myths plainly reflect a degeneration of scriptural narratives.

The persistent strangeness of God's interventions in human life after Adam do much to explain both Mather's interest in antiquity and his advertisement for it in *A New Offer to the Lovers of Religion and Learning* (1714). There, as the second of twelve purposes identified for the "Biblia," Mather advertises

A Rich Collection of ANTIQUITIES, which the Judicious Men in the later Ages, have recovered; for a sweet Reflection of *Light* from thence upon the Heavenly *Oracles*: Especially those wherein the *Idolatry*, the *Oeconomicks*, the *Politicks*, the *Agriculture*, the *Architecture*, the *Art of War*, the *Music*, the *Habits*, and the *Diets* in the former Ages, may be referr'd unto. (*New Offer* 11)

The derivations, corruptions, and miraculous preservations of divine truth in pagan culture are a reflection of the "Heavenly *Oracles*" contained in the Bible, as it had been carefully proven from the original languages by reformed divines. The pagan parallels to scripture were so many and so varied that collectively they seemed to stand as compelling evidence for the primacy of the scriptural record and the validity of its doctrines. They were like the mirror of nature, reflecting the mind of the creator, but they had the benefit of confirming Christianity and securing the faith. Idolatry was a negative proof, but ancient economics, politics, agriculture, architecture, war, culture, and customs – all demonstrated a debt to the history recorded in the Bible.

Another trope employed by Mather in *A New Offer* neatly encapsulates the sum and substance of his argument about the ancients. Writing to his European colleagues whom he tried to enlist as subscribers, he identifies the "Biblia" with a "*Tree*, that grew on the Western side of the *Atlantic*" (10). If that tree bore good "*Fruits* ... the *Seeds* that produced them, were most of them, Originally *Your own*: And it cannot but be *Pleasure*, if not a *Surprize* unto you, to find that so many of your *Best Things*, have passed over *the great and wide Sea* unto the *American Strand*" (10). The "Biblia," though, had even deeper roots. There was one tree from whence all others came, whose seeds had spread as far as America long before Mather, one tree with many branches and many fruits, some better formed than others, but all ripe for the harvest.

Works Cited

Primary Sources

Bochart, Samuel. *Geographia Sacra. Cujus Pars Prior: Phaleg De Dispersione gentium & terrarum divisione facta in ædificatione turris Babel; Pars Posterior: Chanaan De Colonijs & sermone Phoenicum.* 1646. 4th ed. Lugduni Batavorum, 1707.

–.   *Hierozoicon Sive birpertium opos De Animalibus Sacrae Scripturae.* 1646. 2 vols. Londini, 1663.

Dacier, André. *The Works of Plato Abridg'd: With an Account of his Life, Philosophy, Morals, and Politics.* Trans. from the French by Several Hands. 2nd ed. cor. 2 vols. London, 1720.

Dickinson, Edmund. *Delphi Phoenicizantes, sive, Tractatus, in quo Graecos, quicquid apud Delphos celebre erat. Appenditur Diatriba de Noa in Italiam adventu.* Oxoniae, 1655.

–.   *Physica Vetus & Vera: sive Tractatus De Naturali veritate hexaëmeri Mosaici. Per quem probatur in historia Creationis, tum Generationis universae methodum atque modum, tum verae Philosophiae principia, strictim atque breviter à Mose tradi.* Londini, 1702.

Edwards, John. *A Discourse Concerning the Authority, Stile, and Perfection of the Books of the Old and New Testament.* 3 vols. London, 1693–95.

Eusebius of Caesarea: *Praeparatio Evangelica.* Trans. E.H. Gifford. 4 vols. Oxford: Oxford UP, 1903.

Flavius, Josephus. *The Works of Flavius Josephus.* Trans. William Whiston. 1737. CD-ROM. Garland, TX: Galaxie Software, 2002.

Grew, Nehemiah. *Cosmologia Sacra: Or a Discourse of the Universe as it is the Creature and Kingdom of God.* London, 1701.

Homer. *The Iliad.* Trans. A.T. Murray. 2 vols. London: Heinemann, 1924.

–.   *The Odyssey.* Trans. A.T. Murray. 2 vols. London: Heinemann, 1919.

Inghirami, Curzio. *Ethruscarum Antiquitatum Fragmenta, quibus urbis Romae, aliarumque gentium primordia, mores, & res gestae indicantur A Curtio Inghiramio Reperta Scornelli propè Vulterram.* Francofurti, 1637.

Huet, Pierre-Daniel. *Demonstratio Evangelica ad serenissimum Delphinum.* 1679. 4th ed. Lipsiae, 1694.

Jurieu, Pierre. *A Critical History of the Doctrines & Worships (Both Good and Evil) of the Church from Adam to our Saviour Jesus Christ.* 2 vols. London, 1705.

Mather, Cotton. *Biblia Americana.* Ed. Reiner Smolinski. Vol. 1. Tübingen and Grand Rapids: Mohr Siebeck and Baker Academic, 2010.

–.   *A New Offer to the Lovers of Religion and Learning.* Boston, 1714.

Midrash Rabbah. Ed. H. Freedman and Maurice Simon. CD-ROM. New York: Soncino, 2000.

Ovid (Publius Ovidius Naso). *Metamorphoses.* Trans. Frank Justus Miller. 2 vols. London: Heinemann, 1916.

Patrick, Simon. *The Book of Job Paraphras'd.* 2nd ed. cor. London, 1685.

–.   *A Commentary upon the Historical Books of the Old Testament*. 3rd ed. cor. 2 vols. London, 1727.

Pausanias. *Description of Greece*. Trans. J. G. Frazer. 6 vols. London: Macmillan, 1913.

Plato. *Works*. Trans. R. G. Bury. 12 vols. Cambridge: Harvard UP, 1968.

Prideaux, Mathias. *An Easy and Compendious Introduction for Reading all Sorts of Histories*. Oxford, 1650.

Selden, John. *De Diis Syris Syntagmata II*. 1617. Amstelaedami, 1680–81.

–.   *De Iure Naturali & Gentium, Iuxta Disciplinam Ebraerum, Libri Septem*. Londini, 1640.

Sherlock, Thomas. *The Use and Intent of Prophecy, in the several Ages of the World. In Six Discourses, Delivered at the Temple Church, In April and May, 1724*. 6th ed. cor. London, 1755.

Vergil (Publius Vergilius Maro). *Aeneid*. Trans. Theodore C. Williams. Boston: Houghton Mifflin, 1910.

Vossius, Gerardus Ioannes (Gerhard Johannes Voss). *De theologia gentili et physiologia Christiana sive de origine ac progressu idololatriae ad veterum gesta ac rerum naturam reductae*. Amstelaedami, 1642.

Walton, Brian. *Biblia Sacra Polyglotta, Complectentia Textus Originales, Hebraicum, cum Pentateucho Samaritano, Chaldaicum, Graecum, Versionumque antiquarum, Samaritanae, Græcae LXXII Interp. Chaldaicae, Syriacae, Arabicae, Æthiopicae, Persicae, Vulg. Lat. Quicquid comparari poterat Cum Textuum, & Versionum Orientalium Translationibus Latinis*. 6 vols. Londini, 1653–57.

Winiarczyk, Marek, ed. *Euhemeri Messenii reliquiae*. Stuttgart: Teubner, 1991.

Secondary Sources

Brown, Truesdell S. "Euhemerus and the Historians." *Harvard Theological Review* 39.4 (1946): 259–74.

Hutton, Sarah. "Edward Stillingfleet, Henry More, and the Decline of *Moses Atticus*: A Note on Seventeenth-Century Anglican Apologetics." *Philosophy, Science, and Religion in England, 1640–1700*. Ed. Richard Kroll, Richard Ashcraft, Perez Zagorin. New York: Cambridge UP. 68–84.

Manuel, Frank E. *The Eighteenth Century Confronts the Gods*. 1959. New York: Atheneum, 1967.

McDermott, Gerald R. *Jonathan Edwards Confronts the Gods: Christian Theology, Enlightenment Religion, and Non-Christian Faiths*. New York: Oxford UP, 2000.

Momigliano, Arnaldo. *On Pagans, Jews, and Christians*. Repr. Middletown: Wesleyan UP, 1973.

Rossi, Paolo. *The Dark Abyss of Time: The History of the Earth and the History of Nations from Hooke to Vico*. Trans. Lydia G. Cochrane. Chicago: U of Chicago P, 1987.

Rubiés, Joan-Pau. "Theology, Ethnography, and the Historicization of Idolatry." *Journal of the History of Ideas* 67.4 (2006): 571–96.

Seznec, Jean. *The Survival of the Pagan Gods: The Mythological Tradition and Its Place in Renaissance Humanism and Art*. 1953. Princeton: Princeton UP, 1972.

Sheehan, Jonathan. "Sacred and Profane: Idolatry, Antiquarianism and the Polemics of Distinction in the Seventeenth Century." *Past and Present* 192 (2006): 35–66.

Smolinski, Reiner. "Authority and Interpretation: Cotton Mather's Response to the European Spinozists." *Shaping the Stuart World, 1603–1714: The Atlantic Connection.* Ed. Allan I. Macinnes and Arthur H. Williamson. Leiden: Brill, 2006. 175–203

Walker, Daniel P. *The Ancient Theology: Studies in Christian Platonism from the Fifteenth Century to the Eighteenth Century.* Ithaca: Cornell UP, 1972.

Winiarczyk, Marek: *Euhemeros von Messene: Leben, Werk und Nachwirkung.* München: Saur, 2002.

Section 5: Aspects of Scriptural Exegesis
in the "Biblia Americana"

Stephen J. Stein

Cotton Mather and Jonathan Edwards on the Epistle of James:
A Comparative Study

Contemporary scholars often recite ambiguities surrounding the Epistle of James in the New Testament, beginning with a debate concerning identification of its author, its place in the Christian canon, the judgment of some moderns who characterize its contents as more Jewish than Christian, and the challenge posed by Martin Luther who called it an "epistle of straw."[1] In this essay I will compare and contrast the commentary on the Epistle of James written by Cotton Mather in the "Biblia Americana" with that written by Jonathan Edwards in his general commentary called the "Blank Bible," also paying attention to the ways they addressed issues of continuing concern to interpreters of the epistle.[2] I regard this essay as simply opening a comparative conversation rather than providing the last word on these two American colonial exegetes. I am coming to this task having invested heavily in the biblical writings of Edwards but having worked much less on the "Biblia Americana."[3] Hence, my reading of Cotton Mather's commentary in particular should be understood as a tentative exploration rather than a final evaluation.

The Epistle of James is an especially interesting biblical text because it has divided many commentators. There is discussion among some about its very character, that is, whether it is a letter, or perhaps a homily. Nor does a consensus exist regarding the community to which it was addressed, whether it was a Palestinian church or not. Debate regarding the identification of James as the author also continues because that assignment was not made until the time of the Church Father Origen in the third century, and the epistle itself remained a disputed book late in the process of canon formation. The contents and the substance of the Epistle of James have also attracted controversy. The author of

---

1 For example, see Moo (1) and Jackson-McCabe (1–3). For a useful "Survey of the History of Interpretation of James," see Johnson (*Brother* 39–44). See also Johnson, "Letter of James."

2 The "Biblia Americana" (6 ms. vols. in folio) is located in the Massachusetts Historical Society in Boston, Massachusetts. The "Blank Bible" (ms.) is located at the Beinecke Rare Book and Manuscript Library, Yale University, in New Haven, Connecticut.

3 See my edition of Edwards's *Apocalyptic Writings* (Edwards, vol. 5), *Notes on Scripture* (Edwards, vol. 15), and *The Blank Bible* (Edwards, vol. 24), as well as my study "Edwards as Biblical Exegete."

the epistle asserts that belief must be evident in conduct; in the words of the King James Version, "so faith without works is dead" (Jas. 2:26). That affirmation concerning the critical importance of conduct resulted in a judgment by some that this epistle reflects the outlook of Hellenistic Judaism and that its contents stem from "a very early period in the life of the Church" (Elliott-Binns 1022).

Similar judgments concerning the essential role of human conduct or works in the salvation process are the basis for the perceived tension between the Epistle of James and the Pauline epistles which place a high priority on the redemptive role of faith instead of works. A key Pauline text in the Epistle to the Romans asserts, "The just shall live by faith" (Rom. 1:17). Another letter by the Apostle Paul, the Epistle to the Ephesians, states, "For by grace are ye saved through faith; and that not of yourselves: it is the gift of God: not of works, lest any man should boast" (Eph. 2:8–9).

The tension between the notion of faith alone as the basis for salvation and the judgment that good works retain an essential role in the salvific process divided Protestants and Catholics at the time of the Reformation.

> Although [Martin] Luther's 'discovery' of justification by faith took place in the struggle of his own conscience as it sought an answer to the question, 'How do I obtain a God who is gracious to me?' the doctrine of justification by faith was to become one that 'all churches reformed, with a sweet consent, applaud, and confess,' including those churches that opposed Luther on many other points. Thus the seventeenth-century Reformed followers of John Calvin knew that they disagreed with the followers of Luther on many questions, but they recognized that all of them agreed on this doctrine as the foundation of the entire Reformation, in fact, the chief doctrine of Christianity and the chief point of difference separating Protestantism from Roman Catholicism. (Pelikan 138–39)

The title of a 1554 book by the Swiss Reformed theologian Heinrich Bullinger summarized the two elements that continued to surface in the debates, *The Grace of God that Justifies Us for the Sake of Christ through Faith Alone, without Good Works, while Faith Meanwhile Abounds in Good Works* (qtd. in Pelikan 139)

It is therefore no surprise that the status and the interpretation of the Epistle of James were significant concerns for Protestant exegetes in eighteenth-century British America. The issue of justification by faith alone (*sola fide*) versus the necessary role of good works (*bona opera*) remained a focus in the commentaries of both Mather and Edwards.

This essay does not intend a final synthesis of the interpretations of the Epistle of James by Mather and Edwards. Such a synthesis is not possible if we use only these two commentaries. It would require systematic examination of multiple other manuscripts by Edwards with substantial exegetical content as well as scores of sermons by both Edwards and Mather.[4] There are, however, important points of similarity and contrast between the "Biblia Americana" and the "Blank Bible," and it is the pursuit of those two aspects of these commentaries that are the primary goal of this essay.

Before turning to the comparison of the two commentaries on the Epistle of James, a few preliminary remarks seem in order. Cotton Mather (1663–1728) and Jonathan Edwards (1703–58) did not only belong to different generations. They also carried out their professional responsibilities in sharply contrasting local circumstances, namely, the port city of Boston on the Atlantic coast with Harvard College almost within walking distance, and the inland town of Northampton on the Connecticut River in western frontier Massachusetts. Moreover, the careers of the two were affected by different historical circumstances: Mather's by a variety of colonial developments including the Indian offensive called King Philip's War, the Salem witchcraft trials, the royal imposition of a new charter for Massachusetts, and conflicts in the Atlantic world including King William's War and Queen Ann's War; Edwards's by the continuing imperial struggles, the evangelical revivals in the colonies – the so-called Great Awakening – and his life among Native Americans as a missionary in Stockbridge, Massachusetts. Both of these ministers also were tied directly by correspondence and by their publications to the larger North Atlantic religious world.[5]

In these diverse circumstances, both Mather and Edwards invested untiringly in the study of the Bible. The commentaries created by these Puritan ministers include a wide range of different materials. In 1710, hoping to attract a publisher for his ever-expanding "Biblia Americana," Cotton Mather crafted an advertisement, itemizing its contents. He declared that his reflections on "the glorious *Book of Truth and of Life*" included philological examination of the original texts, observations on life circumstances in ancient times, consideration of references to the natural order, chronology, geography, and history, as well as interpretation of materials dealing with ancient Israel, Jewish writers, and post-biblical Jewish history. The "Biblia Americana" also offered typological and prophetic readings, as well as practical advice on Christian ethics and devotion, together with all kinds of "Curious Notes." The whole of the commentary was in accord, wrote Mather, with "the *Principles of Religion*, Professed in the most *Reformed Churches*" (Mather, *Bonifacius* 200–06).

---

4 Twelve sermons preached by Edwards on the Epistle of James are listed in the inventory of sermons and sermon fragments included in the *Works*, vols. 10, 14, 17, 19, 22, and 25.

5 For major biographies of the two, see Silverman and Marsden. On Mather, see also S. Mather, Wendell, Boas, Middlekauff (189–367), and Levy. On Edwards, see also Hopkins, Winslow, Miller, Murray, and Smith. Autobiographical reflections include Mather's *Paterna* and Edwards's *Personal Narrative* (16: 790–804).

I know of no equivalent description by Jonathan Edwards of the contents of his general commentary. The "Blank Bible" also ranges widely, although at first glance the physical contrast with Mather's commentary is most striking. The massive size of the "Biblia Americana" comprised of the six manuscript volumes in folio, some 4,561 manuscript pages, makes the "Blank Bible" containing only 900 pages seem a modest endeavor. The contrasting size of these two manuscripts as a measure of the comparative investments in biblical exegesis by Mather and Edwards falls away, however, when we note that Edwards scattered his scriptural commentary in a number of other major manuscripts he compiled over his lifetime, including "Notes on Scripture," "Notes on the Apocalypse," the "Theological Miscellanies," "Prophecies of the Messiah," "History of the Work of Redemption," and "Harmony of the Old and New Testament."[6]

But size is not the only difference. The two commentaries are physically different in other ways. The "Blank Bible" is a "leather-bound, hard-covered, interleaved volume, booklike in external appearance" (Edwards 24: 84), measuring 24 x 18 cm. Bound into this volume is a small King James Version of the Bible comprising 796 pages interleaved between the 455 larger sheets of foolscap numbered as pages 1 to 904.[7] The physical presence of the printed version of the English text was a shaping force on Edwards's exegetical practice. Many of his entries in the "Blank Bible" were triggered directly by the King James Version of the biblical text printed on the interleaved pages.

There is another point of contrast between the two commentaries. Cotton Mather was responsible for the physical design and construction of the "Biblia Americana," but Jonathan Edwards did not design or construct the "Blank Bible." He came into possession of the leather-bound, booklike manuscript which was originally owned by Benjamin Pierpont, his wife's brother. Benjamin Pierpont, the son of the minister of the Congregational church in New Haven, signed the title page of the manuscript in 1728, but he ultimately failed as a ministerial candidate.[8] Edwards took possession of the manuscript in mid-1730. Some time later he wrote on the opening page the title, "Miscellaneous Observations on the Holy Scriptures." The "Blank Bible" contains 70 random entries by Pierpont; it contains some 5,500 entries by Edwards.[9]

---

6   These biblical manuscripts by Edwards have been published in the *Works*, vols. 5, 9, 13, 15, 18, 20, and 23.

7   For a detailed description of the "Blank Bible," see Edwards (24: 84–89). There are, in fact, 910 pages in the manuscript; some pages have been misnumbered.

8   See Stein, "The Biblical Notes of Benjamin Pierpont." This essay describes the short career of Pierpont, and it includes the text of his entries in the "Blank Bible."

9   One additional historical footnote regarding the "Blank Bible" needs to be in the record. Those of us who work with manuscripts from earlier times are very aware of the challenge such documents face, namely, preservation. The fact that the "Blank Bible" exists today in excellent condition at the Beinecke Library at Yale University is something of a miracle be-

As already stated, for many years Cotton Mather was hopeful that the "Biblia Americana" would not remain a private document, but rather that "some generous minds" might "appear as benefactors in the publishing of it."[10] His plan for the "Biblia Americana" was to produce a synoptical commentary that would simultaneously satisfy the demands of a transatlantic scholarly community and also appeal to a broader readership seeking guidance in their reading of the Bible as well as religious edification. The "Biblia Americana" was intended to combine the format of John Pearson's *Critici Sacri* (1660) or Matthew Poole's *Synopsis Criticorum* (1669–76) with the counsel and reflections of popular commentaries such as Matthew Henry's *Exposition of the Old and New Testament* (1708–10), while also including intermittent observations on the biblical texts drawn from various scientific discourses.[11] Many of the words Mather wrote on nearly every subject were, in fact, published, but this huge biblical commentary proved an exception.[12]

The "Blank Bible," by sharp contrast, was not compiled for potential publication. The manuscript was a personal professional tool developed for Edwards's own use. Many of the entries include cross-references to his other manuscripts. In that sense the "Blank Bible" functioned as an organizing, index-like tool for his theological and especially his biblical reflections. The fact that the "Blank Bible" was not intended for publication proved an interesting challenge when it was being published in the Yale Edition of *The Works of Jonathan Edwards*.[13]

Edwards did have plans for a major exegetical publication, but it was not to be the "Blank Bible." His letter to the Trustees of the College of New Jersey who had invited him to become the president of that college identified a future

---

cause in 1853 a young Scotsman named Alexander B. Grosart, in the employ of an Edinburgh publishing house, came to America to gather materials for an enlarged Scottish edition of Edwards's works. He came, took notes, and copied manuscripts. By the fall of 1854 he had returned to Scotland, carrying a variety of papers and manuscripts, including the "Blank Bible." More than a decade later Grosart published *Selections from the Unpublished Writings of Jonathan Edwards of America. Edited from the Original MSS, with Facsimiles and an Introduction* (1865), which included 324 entries from the "Blank Bible." The miracle is that four decades later the interleaved Bible and a few other manuscripts were returned to America, and eventually in 1900 the "Blank Bible," with some other papers, was given by the Edwards family to the Yale University Library where it safely resides at present.

10   Mather's letter to Dr. John Woodward, Nov. 17, 1712 (*Selected Letters* 112).

11   An example of a scientific publication with religious implications cited in Mather's commentary on James is Robert Boyle's *Some Physico-theological Considerations about the Possibility of the Resurrection* (1675).

12   Now, of course, such "generous" minds have appeared. An authoritative edition of Cotton Mather's "Biblia Americana" in ten volumes will be published by Mohr Siebeck and Baker Academic with Reiner Smolinski as the General Editor.

13   The printed edition of the "Blank Bible" in the *Works* (vol. 24) does not include the text of the King James Version of the Bible, a decision which was reached after considerable discussion.

exegetical publication he tentatively entitled "The Harmony of the Old and New Testament." But that project was not the "Blank Bible." Edwards's description of the proposed "Harmony" identified three potential parts: a section dealing with "prophecies of the Messiah" and their fulfillment focusing on the "correspondence between predictions and events"; another part dealing with "types of the Old Testament" and their "agreement" with "the great things of the gospel of Christ"; and a third section "considering the harmony of the Old and New Testament, as to doctrine and precept."[14] Edwards's death in 1758 as a result of a smallpox inoculation cut short his work on the "Harmony."

So much for the prolegomena. The following comparison of the contents of the two commentaries on James reveals a number of striking similarities and contrasts concerning methods and thematic concerns in the two documents. The "Biblia Americana" and the "Blank Bible" are similar in that the entries in both commentaries range across all five chapters of the Epistle of James. Mather's commentary on James is larger, containing a total of fifty-six entries on passages from the epistle. Individual entries in the "Biblia Americana" on James extend in size from as few as fifteen words (Jas. 3:8) to almost seven hundred words (Jas. 2:24). Edwards's commentary on James in the "Blank Bible" includes thirty-four entries, one comprising a mere cross reference embracing only three words (Jas. 2:19) while another is an exposition four hundred and forty words in length (Jas. 1:17). The entries by both Mather and Edwards display a concentrated focus of attention on chapters 1–3 in the epistle.[15]

The most striking point of contrast between the two commentaries is the format in which the two exegetes structured their comments on the text. The "Biblia Americana" employs a "Q" and "A" format, a question and answer structure. Sometimes the questions that open entries in the "Biblia Americana" are short and explicit. For example, with respect to Jas. 3:6 Mather asks, "Q. How is the *Tongue a World of Iniquity*?" The answer, by contrast, is not short; it is a twenty-two line entry that ranges from a discussion of the Greek word for "world," κόσμος, to a comment on a paraphrase of the text offered by Daniel Whitby [*BA*, Jas. 3:6]. Other times the question is longer and more detailed. The entry on Jas. 2:10, for example, begins, "Q. What might be the Special Rea-

---

14 Edwards to the Trustees of the College of New Jersey, Oct. 19, 1757 (Edwards 16: 728–29).

15 Mather's entries on James in the "Biblia Americana" address the following chapters and verses with multiple entries indicated in square brackets: Jas. 1:1 [3], 1:6, 1:10, 1:17 [3], 1:19 [3], 1:21 [3], 1:27, 2:1, 2:4, 2:5, 2:6, 2:10, 2:13 [2], 2:20, 2:24, 3:1, 3:2, 3:6 [5], 3:8, 3:9, 3:13, 3:17 [4], 3:18, 4:1, 4:2, 4:5, 4:5–6 [2], 4:8 [2], 4:11 [2], 4:15, 5:1, 5:3, 5:9, and 5:14 [3]. Edwards's entries on James in the "Blank Bible" address the following chapters and verses with multiple entries indicated in square brackets: Jas. 1:10–12, 1:14, 1:16, 1:17, 1:18, 1:19–21, 1:23–24, 1:25, 1:27, 2:2, 2:4, 2:5, 2:8, 2:13, 2:14–26, 2:19, 2:21 ff., 2:24, 2:25, 2:26, 3:2, 3:13–18, 3:14, 3:18, 4:5–6, 4:6, 4:8, 4:11, 4:14, 5:1–6, 5:9, 5:12, 5:16, and 5:17.

son of introducing that Admonition, *He who transgresses in one Point, is guilty of all.* v. 10" [*BA*, Jas. 2:10]. A long detailed answer follows. Another example of an explicit question opens Mather's entry on Jas. 1:17. "Q. What may be the distinction between, *A Good Gift*, and a *Perfect Gift*?" [*BA*, Jas. 1:17]. The answer fills two-thirds of a column on that manuscript page. Many times the "question" is not explicit, not even a question, though introduced by the letter "Q." Often in those cases the question is implicit. For example, the short entry on Jas 2:6 reads, "Q. The '*Rich Oppressors*' v. 6. A. They were the Persons, who appear most in opposing the Christian Religion" [*BA*, Jas. 2:6]. The implicit question is, "Who were the Rich Oppressors?" Mather's Q & A format functions in a useful way, focusing each entry.

The format for Edwards's entries in the "Blank Bible" is different and was developed by Benjamin Pierpont. It rests upon the fact that the blank sheets of foolscap are adjacent to printed pages of the interleaved King James text. Edwards wrote his entries on the blank sheets that are divided by a vertical line, creating two columns parallel to the columns of printed text on facing pages of the King James text. He situated his entries on the foolscap at analogous locations to the verses in question on the pages of the KJV.[16] If a section of the foolscap sheet where an entry was to be placed was filled, Edwards used symbols, including asterisks, other signs, or short notes, and sometimes page numbers, to identify the location where he wrote or completed the entry. There are scattered clusters of pages in the manuscript not facing printed pages which he filled with longer entries or with the continuation of entries begun elsewhere.

Edwards introduced his entries in diverse ways. A short entry on Jas. 2:8 illustrates one approach. The text of Jas. 2:8 was at hand, printed on the facing interleaved page. Edwards cited the number of the verse followed by three words from the text, "the royal law," which he set apart from what follows by a square bracket "]". His observation follows, "Probably so called because the law of love was by way of specialty the law of Christ, the king of the church" (24: 1171). The entry answers an implicit question, "Why is loving your neighbor called the 'royal law'?" Sometimes when an entry in the "Blank Bible" deals with an entire verse or multiple verses, there is no textual citation; the commentary simply follows the verse number or numbers and the square bracket "]". That is the case with his comment on Jas. 3:13–18, verses Edwards summarized as follows, "How meekness and peaceableness is a great part of true wisdom" (24: 1173).

Despite the differences that shaped these two commentaries, it is instructive to note the ways that Mather and Edwards on occasion came to strikingly similar judgments regarding particular texts in the Epistle of James. Their respective entries on Jas. 4:11 are evidence of the same. Mather's entry begins with

---

16   A photograph of entries on Jas. 3–4 in the "Blank Bible," illustrating the physical arrangement of the manuscript, is located in Edwards (24: 1174).

the question, "Why is it said, *He that Speaketh Evil of his Brother, & Judgeth his Brother, Speaketh Evil of the Law, & Judgeth the Law!*" Mather's answer then asserts, "On this Account; The *Law* expressly forbids us to *Speak Evil of our Brother & Judge him*. If we do it, we thereby reflect on this *Law*, as not *Holy & Just & Good*, & not worthy to be obey'd." Mather then goes on to add another reason for his judgment.

> Or, on this Account. Men did then *Speak Evil of their Brethren, & Judge them*, for though that God had left indifferent; they proceeded meerly, by their own Sense, & Will, & Humour, without any Warrant from the Word of God, in condemning one another. This now was to condemn the *Law*, as not perfect, not exact, but wanting to be peeced up with Institutions of our own. *To make more Sins than God ha's made is to Reproach the Law of God.* [*BA*, Jas. 4:11]

In other words, Mather rejected the notion that humans are to add to the law, for by so doing they are implying that God's law is not perfect and is in need of expansion.

Edwards comes to a somewhat similar interpretation of the prohibition contained in Jas. 4:11. He opens his entry with the assertion, "He that judgeth another don't act like 'a doer of the law,' or like one that is subject to law himself, but rather like a lawgiver and judge." In other words, he is presumptuous and "is not content to be a fellow servant. He refuses to own himself, so he casts off the yoke; he finds fault with it. He is not contented with it." For Edwards, this failure to be content with the law provides occasion to condemn the law and to reject the obligation to obey it. "In this sense he 'speaks evil of the law, and judges the law.' He withdraws himself from subjection to the law as a fellow servant, and so finds fault with it as his law, or a law by which he is obliged." Therefore the person that judges another by his actions rejects the notion that God is "the only judge, and himself a fellow subject" (24: 1175).

On other occasions, Mather and Edwards present contrasting judgments regarding the meaning of particular texts in the epistle, for example, the second clause in Jas. 1:21 which reads, "and receive with meekness the engrafted word, which is able to save your souls." Both exegetes turn to other commentators to support their interpretations of the key term, "the engrafted word." Mather, drawing on the exegetical reflections of Dr. John Edwards (1637–1716), an Anglican divine of Calvinist persuasion, writes, "I much incline to expound it, of our Blessed Lord Jesus Christ. ... Our Lord Jesus Christ is, *The Word of God Engrafted*. The Similitude of *Engrafted* very sweetly expresses, the Mystery of *God Manifest in Flesh*. ... Tis our Lords being *Such a Person*, that renders him able to *Save Souls*" [*BA*, Jas 1:21].[17] Jonathan Edwards comes to a different interpretation of the term "engrafted word" based on his reading in Philip Dod-

---

17   John Edwards was the author of *An enquiry into four remarkable texts of the New Testament which contain some difficulty in them, with a probable resolution of them* (1692).

dridge's *Family Expositor,* declaring, "That word which is implanted in our minds by the influence of divine grace." He continues, "The word of God is frequently compared to a seed or plant" which is said to be "engrafted or implanted" in the minds of believers (24: 1169).[18] In the case of Jas. 1:21, therefore, Mather and Edwards adopted alternative but very common meanings attached to the concept of the "word of God."

The views of Mather and Edwards on critical questions that surround the Epistle of James are instructive. For example, one such question is, "Who was the author of the epistle?" This question arises because there are several men named "James" in the New Testament – James, the elder brother of John and the son of Zebedee, one of three disciples within the inner circle surrounding Jesus, also called "James the Great"; James, the son of Alphaeus, again one of the twelve apostles, sometimes identified as "James the less"; and James, the "brother" of Jesus, another son of Mary and Joseph, also identified as "James, the Lord's brother."[19] That there has been confusion among commentators regarding these three figures is stated repeatedly in contemporary scholarship. Tradition ascribes the authorship of the epistle to James, the Lord's brother. But questions raised by that judgment are multiple.[20]

The issue of authorship does not seem to have been critical for either Mather or Edwards. Their references to James as the author seem unconcerned with possible confusion. There is, however, evidence that Edwards recognized the potential for confusion in biblical references. His entry on Heb. 13:7–8, verses which counsel readers to remember those who had spoken the word of God to them, cites Philip Doddridge's *Family Expositor* which references "James the Apostle" and "James, commonly called the first bishop of Jerusalem," both of whom were dead at the time the Epistle to the Hebrews was written. The Hebrews entry, of course, does not deal with the authorship of James, but it does acknowledge possible confusion in biblical references (24: 1164–65).[21] I have not discovered Mather addressing the question of the specific identity of James, the author of the epistle.

Another pair of longstanding questions related to the Epistle of James asks whether the letter was widely accepted by early Christians and what has been its status within the New Testament canon. These questions have surfaced repeatedly throughout Christian history and remain in conversation yet today. It is significant, in my judgment, that the first entry on the epistle in the "Biblia

---

18   Doddridge's six-volume commentary is *The Family Expositor: Or, A Paraphrase and Version of the New Testament: with Critical Notes; and a Practical Improvement of each Section* (1739–1756).
19   See, for example, "James, the son of Zebedee, and John his brother" (Mat. 4:21); "James the son of Alphaeus" (Mat. 10:3); and "James the Lord's brother" (Gal. 1:19).
20   For example, see the three entries on "James, St." and on "James, Epistle of St." in *The Oxford Dictionary of the Christian Church* (857–59).
21   The Doddridge source is *Family Expositor* (6: 145–46, n. f.).

Americana" documents Mather's engagement with these critical issues. The question he asks on Jas. 1:1 is, "What might be the Occasion of the Name, *Catholick Epistles?*" The term, "catholic epistles," was used for those New Testament letters, also called "general epistles," not addressed to specific churches or individuals. Mather's answer rejects the notion that the Epistle of James was received uniformly by all parties everywhere. He cites doubts expressed in "Testimonies" from Church Fathers including Origen, Eusebius, Amphilochius, and Jerome. Mather also repeats the judgment of Oecumenius, a sixth-century Greek commentator, who spoke of the Catholick Epistles as being written "to the faithful, or to the Jewes of the dispersion" [*BA*, Jas. 1:1]. That judgment seems to relegate the epistle to a lower status within the canon and lends support to a later time of composition than the lifetime of James the brother of Christ, who was put to death in 62 C.E.

Two other entries in the "Biblia Americana" on verse 1 in the opening chapter of James continue Mather's pursuit of the Jews who were "*Scattered Abroad,*" some he identifies as "*Infidel* Jews" and others as "*Believing* Jews." He cites ancient authors in support of his judgments, including Agrippa, Strabo, Philo, and Cicero. There is also commentary by Mather on the possibility that the Epistle of James was written by Jews for Jews, and therefore the Christian character of the epistle was acquired when this epistle was judged in the fourth century to be consistent with Christian teachings [*BA*, Jas.1:1]. Clearly Cotton Mather was aware of and engaged with critical issues surrounding the epistle, issues still present today in exegetical circles. I find no evidence that Edwards directly engaged these questions regarding authorship, time of composition, or reception within the Christian community.

One issue that does arise in the commentaries of both Mather and Edwards on James is the extent to which their entries give voice to anti-Jewish judgments. Mather has a focused anti-Jewish invective in his exegesis of Jas. 2:10. His opening question is, "What might be the Special Reason of introducing that Admonition, *He who transgresses in one Point, is guilty of all.*" His answer echoes sources he was reading. Mather writes,

> Dr. *Whitby* thinks, this passage may be directly levelled against that loose Doctrine of the Jewish Doctors, mentioned by Dr. *Pocock*; That *God gave so many Commandments to them, that by doing any of them, they might be Saved. ...* It was, it seems, a common Rule among them; *That Men should single out some one Commandment of the Law, & therein exercise themselves, that so they might make God their Friend by that, lest in others they should too much displease Him.* And we find this Rule by Dr. *Smith* cited from them; *He that observes any one Præcept, it shall be well with him and his Dayes shall be prolonged, and he shall possess the Earth.* And this Præcept, was with them usually, that of the *Sabbath,* of *Sacrifices,* or of *Tythes*; These they look'd on as the *Great Commandments of the Law.* [*BA*, Jas. 2:10][22]

---

22 This paragraph derives from Daniel Whitby's 1703, *A Paraphrase and Commentary on*

In other words, Mather viewed the Jewish understanding of the law – the commandments – as a flawed understanding of the will of God.

Mather also depicts the Jews as "*Contentious Spirits*: [Rom. 2.8] filled with *Wrath* against the Teachers of Christianity, and especially against those who denied the Necessity of *Circumcising the Gentiles*" [*BA*, Jas. 2:10]. In comments on Jas. 3:13, he responds to the question posed by the writer of the epistle, "Who is a Wise Man?" by answering, "The *Jewes* were great Pretenders to *Knowledge*" [*BA*, Jas. 3:13]. In his commentary on chapter 4, Mather asks the occasion of the exhortation in verse 8, "*Cleanse your Hands.*" His answer reads, "We learn from Josephus, That the Hands of the *Jewes*, and especially of the *Zealots* among them, were full of *Murders* and *Rapines*" [*BA*, Jas. 4:8]. With reference to Jas. 4:11, Mather asserts, "The unbeleeving *Jewes*, and the Judaizing *Beleevers*, were prejudized against the Beleeving *Gentiles*, That they *observed not their Feasts; & were not Circumcised.* For this Cause, they *Spoke Evil* of them, as differing little from the *Heathen Idolaters*" [*BA*, Jas. 4:11]. Commenting on the exhortation in Jas. 5:9, "Grudge not one against another," Mather cites the judgment of the early Church Father Justin Martyr that Gentile converts were "*Better Christians*" because Jewish converts were preoccupied with liberty from the Romans and the establishment of a temporal kingdom, and, he adds, "they were *no better than Heathen*, on this account" [*BA*, Jas. 5:9].

Edwards's commentary also contains what may be seen as anti-Jewish judgments. For example, his exposition of the admonition in Jas. 1:19, "Let every man be … slow to speak," draws directly on Philip Doddridge's *Family Expositor*. Edwards writes, "It is well known that the Jewish doctors were apt to contend very fiercely about their different opinions" (24: 1169; cf. Doddridge 6: 174–75). With respect to the exhortation in Jas. 5:9, "Grudge not one against another," Edwards cites approvingly Doddridge's judgment: "Justin Martyr represents the Jewish converts as the worst sort of Christians, who were apt to be impatient of the Gentile yoke, and to retain their attachment to the views of a temporal kingdom" (24: 1176; cf. Doddridge 6: 208, n.a.). Regarding Jas. 5:12 which reads, "But above all things, swear not," Edwards notes, "This the Jews were very apt to do upon trifling occasions" (24: 1176; cf. Doddridge 6: 209, n.d.). Again, drawing on Doddridge, Edwards seems to identify Jewish converts as the principal recipients of the letter because the opening verses of chapter 5 speak of the "miseries" that shall come upon them, perhaps referring to the future destruction of Jerusalem in 70 A.D (24: 1175–76; cf. Doddridge 6: 204–06, nn. b. and c.).

---

the New Testament. In two volumes (2: 143). Whitby references Edward Pococke (1604–91), an Orientalist who took part in the preparation of the London Polyglot Bible in 1657, and John Smith (1618–52) who published *Select discourses* (1660).

Edwards's heavy reliance on Doddridge's *Family Expositor* in his commentary on James provides an occasion to comment on the use of sources. Philip Doddridge, an English Nonconformist, published *The Family Expositor* in six volumes between 1739 and 1756. Edwards cited the work in eleven of the thirty-five entries on James. He referenced the *Family Expositor* more than 300 times throughout the "Blank Bible" (see Edwards 24: 60). Through his reading of Doddridge, Edwards accessed the judgments of earlier commentators, theologians, and religious figures on James including Josephus, Theodore Beza, Archbishop Tillotson, Lambert Bos, Jakob Elsner, Johann Christoph Wolf, and Ezekiel Hopkins. Edwards also cited other sources directly in his commentary on the epistle including Thomas Manton's *Practical Commentary on James*, John Glas's *Notes on Scripture-Texts*, and Tübingen's own Christoph Matthaeus Pfaff's *Institutiones theologicae dogmaticae et moralis*.[23]

Mather's commentary on James is even more heavily saturated with references to and quotations from his reading. In addition to those already mentioned, his citations include, amongst others, Agrippa, Philo, Josephus, Tacitus, Justin, Cicero, Hermas, Origen, Lactantius, Eusebius, Augustine, Maimonides, Grotius, Pococke, Bull, and Whitby – only to mention some of the authors he engaged.

Both Edwards and Mather, of course, drew on the work of predecessors in the field of biblical exegesis. I am, however, inclined to affirm that the two commentaries on James seem to indicate that Mather was more deeply immersed in the world of scholarship on the Bible. Mather's reading ranged more widely, especially in what appears to be first-hand engagement with ancient sources, sources very different from the synoptic commentaries such as Doddridge's *Family Expositor*. There may be multiple reasons why that was true. One reason may have been Mather's physical proximity of the Harvard College library. Edwards, by contrast, spent the 1750s in western Massachusetts at Stockbridge among the Indians.

Another point of comparison between the "Biblia Americana" and the "Blank Bible" involves the ways the two commentators engaged the Greek text of the epistle. At least three possibilities existed – little or no engagement, citation of judgments from other commentators, or direct engagement, translation, and interpretation of the Greek text.

Edwards's commentary on James is typical of the way that he referenced the Greek text most of the time in the "Blank Bible." Literally, all of his Greek citations in James are drawn from sources he was reading, again especially from Philip Doddridge. Ten entries contain Greek words or phrases. Many are single Greek terms. For example, the note on Jas. 1:17 includes the phrase, "every per-

---

23 See Edwards, "Blank Bible" (24: 111–12), for a table containing "Chronological Information" on a number of the principal sources Edwards cited in the "Blank Bible."

fect gift is from above." Edwards's comment reads, "It is said to be 'from above,' ἄνωθέν." Edwards copied this Greek term, ἄνωθέν, from Thomas Goodwin's *Works* (1681) which he cited immediately following this sentence (24: 1168).[24] Similarly, commenting on the phrase in Jas. 1:21, "receive with meekness the engrafted word, which is able to save your souls," he draws from Doddridge a sentence containing a key Greek term. It reads, in part, "The word of God is frequently compared to a seed or plant ... said to be ἔμφυτος, engrafted or implanted in their minds" (24: 1169; cf. Doddridge 6: 174–75, nn. d. and f.). A more complex interpretive issue is evident in Edwards's citation of a discussion of the Greek phrase κριταὶ διαλογισμῶν πονηρῶν in Jas. 2:4 copied from Thomas Manton's *Exposition on James*. The King James Version reads, "Are ye not then partial in yourselves, and are become judges of evil thoughts?" Manton argued that it should be translated, "You judge altogether perversely, according to the rule of your own corrupt thoughts," switching the onus of the passage (Edwards 24: 1170).[25] In all three cases cited, Edwards echoes the judgments of his sources.

In the "Biblia Americana" dealing with James, Mather has countless citations of the Greek text. We must remember, of course, that his commentary on James in the "Biblia Americana" is longer than Edwards's in the "Blank Bible." That alone might account for greater engagement with the Greek text. But there appears to be more to it than size. Mather's comment on Jas. 1:6 and 8 reads, "who is the ανηρ διψυχος και διακρινομενος, *the double-minded and wavering man*?" His long answer draws on Greek texts from Hermas, Barnabas, and Clement, in each case citing Greek excerpts [*BA*, Jas. 1:6 and 1:8]. Another example is Mather's short entry on Jas. 3:17, which opens with the "Q. The *Wisdom from Above, is full of Mercy?* v. 17." His answer reads, "A. *Josephus* tells us, *This, of all good Passions, was most lost among the Jewes.*" Then follow two lines of Greek Mather cites from Josephus's text on the "Jewish War" [*BA*, Jas. 3:17].

But it is not just Greek that is evident in Mather's entries on the epistle. His comment on Jas 3:13 opens with the question, "Who is the Wise Man and endued with knowledge among you?" Mather's answer includes, "The *Jewes were great Pretenders to Knowledge.* ... Hence their Divines are called, as *Buxtorf* tells us /חכמי הא מת/ *Wise Men as to Truth.*" [*BA*, Jas. 3:13]. It is, of course, no surprise that both Mather and Edwards were able to cite Hebrew, the other biblical language, in their commentaries, and they both do. It is perhaps more surprising to discover that Mather's comment on the phrase, "easy to be entreated," which occurs in Jas. 3:17, has the following entry: "A. The German

---

24 See *The Works of Thomas Goodwin* (vol. 1, pt. 1).

25 See Thomas Manton, *A Practical Commentary, or an Exposition with Notes on the Epistle of James. Delivered in sundry Weekly Lectures at Stoke-Newington in Middlesex, neer London* (1651).

Translation is a very Instructive one; Läßt ihr sagen, or, *patiens Admonitionis*, willing to take an Admonition" [*BA*, Jas. 3:17]. Mather's interest in and knowledge of foreign languages therefore included German. It seems clear that Cotton Mather was more engaged with foreign language materials and perhaps more comfortable in dealing directly with them than Jonathan Edwards.

Now to the theological issue that has occupied many commentaries on the Epistle of James, especially Protestant commentaries written in the post-Reformation centuries. Martin Luther's movement away from traditional Roman Catholic dogma culminated in his conviction that the essence of the Christian gospel was that faith alone without works justifies the sinner. That theological judgment became a cornerstone of the Protestant Reformation, a judgment shared by others, including John Calvin in Geneva. The scriptural base of that view of the gospel was Pauline, especially the epistles of Paul to the Romans and the Galatians. The English Puritan movement continued the Protestant emphasis on faith, but it also affirmed the necessity of an active Christian life.[26] Puritans in both Old England and New England vigorously asserted the role of both faith and works in the Christian life.

The English Puritan or Nonconformist world was the larger theological context for both Mather and Edwards in their study of the Bible. Both ministers were familiar with the publications of leading English exegetes who affirmed the necessity of moral activity – "works" – as part of the Christian life. Matthew Poole (1624–79), one of the most productive scriptural commentators, in addition to his multivolume *Synopsis Criticorum* (1669–76), also began the compilation of a popular biblical commentary, *Annotations upon the Holy Bible* (1683–85), a project embracing two folios which was completed after his death by interested ministers. The *Annotations* devotes nine columns of commentary to the second chapter of James, the portion of the epistle which affirms the critical role for "works" in the process of eternal salvation. In comments on verse 14, which address the claims of "Hypocritical Professors" who "boasted of their Faith as sufficient ... though they neglected the practice of Holiness and Righteousness," the *Annotations* declares that such claims are "empty and dead, *v. 26*, and unfruitful." With respect to verse 17 which reads, "Even so faith, if it hath not works, is dead, being alone," the *Annotations* asserts that such a faith is "Void of that Life, in which the every Essence of Faith consists, and which always discovers it self in Vital actings, and good Fruits." The second chapter of James closes on a comparative judgment, "For as the body without the spirit is dead, so faith without works is dead also." Therefore, the *Annotations* argues, a "lively Faith and Works" are "Inseparable."[27]

---

26 See Coolidge (99–140).
27 Matthew Poole, *Annotations upon the Holy Bible*, at Jas. 2:14, 17, and 26.

Mather and Edwards also knew the exegetical work of Matthew Henry (1662–1714), an English Presbyterian minister whose five-volume devotional commentary, *Exposition of the Old and New Testaments* (1708–10), embraced all of the Bible except the epistles and the Book of Revelation. Following Henry's death, thirteen Non-Conformist ministers prepared and published in 1721 a sixth volume in the commentary that dealt with the remaining books of the Bible. In the section on the exposition of the Epistle of James, this final volume addressed directly "how to reconcile Paul and James." The text boldly asserts, *"There is a very happy agreement between one part of scripture and another, notwithstanding seeming differences."* Both Paul and James "magnify the faith of the gospel"; the commentators declared that "there must be both faith in Jesus Christ and good works the fruit of faith." The two are therefore complementary. "Paul may be understood as speaking of that justification which is inchoate, James of that which is complete; it is by *faith* only that we are put into a justified state, but then good works come in for the completing of our justification at the last great day."[28]

In the "Biblia Americana," Cotton Mather also addressed directly the relationship between faith and works. One short comment on Jas. 2:20 states the relationship in almost poetic synoptic fashion. Mather writes, "Q. *Faith without works* is compared unto the *Body without the Spirit.* v. 20." The answer reads, "A. I rather choose to read it, *As the Body without Breathing* [χωρις πνευματος] *is dead* – So is *Faith* if it *Breaths* not in *Works*" [*BA*, Jas. 2:20]. On that same passage, Jas 2:20, in the "Blank Bible," Edwards asserted in short order – though not so poetically – the same critical relationship between faith and works. He wrote, "The apostle Paul, as well as James, held good works to be essential to true faith" (24: 1172).

Both Mather and Edwards, however, had much more to say about the issue. In the "Biblia Americana," the fullest discussion of the relationship between faith and works in the Christian life occurs in Mather's entry on Jas. 2:24, which opens with the question, "How Shall wee Reconcile these Words of James, *By Works a Man is justified & not by Faith only*: with the words of *Paul*, to the *Romans*, & the *Galatians*, *That a Man is not justified by the Works of the Law, but by the Faith of Jesus Christ*?" One might state Mather's question another way: Is the epistle of James fundamentally in tension with the Pauline corpus in the New Testament where the saving grace of faith – *sola fide* – is a dominant theme? Mather's answer reads,

> A. The Doctrine of *Paul* is, That a *Justifying Faith*, is a Receiving of, and a Relying, on the *Gift of Righteousness* from God, by the Lord Jesus Christ; or, the Consent of a *Distressed Soul*, to bee Justified by Gods graciously Imputing unto him, the Obedience, which the Lord Jesus Christ, as our *Surety*, yielded unto God, on the

---

28 Matthew Henry's *Commentary on the Whole Bible* (980–81).

behalf of His Elect. This *Faith*, does justify a Sinner, not as it is a *Work*, but only Relatively, & Instrumentally; in asmuch as it is, the Instrument, by which a Man apprehends the Righteousness of the Lord Jesus Christ, as freely tendred unto the Sinner in the Gospel; Tis only in this Regard, that Faith, and no Grace but This Faith, ha's the Honour to Justify us. [*BA*, Jas. 2:24]

For Mather, the apparent conflict between Paul and James stems from the fact that Paul focuses attention on the doctrine of justification which "does plainly assert that no man Living is Justified by *Works*, but *only by Faith. James* does nevertheless assert That a Man is Justified *by Works, and not by Faith only.*" But, Mather continues, "The appearance of Contradiction is easily Reconciled. *Paul* wrote of our *Justification* before *God*, and the Right unto Everlasting Life therein granted unto us: which is only by Faith in our Lord Jesus Christ. *James* treats of that which makes *manifest* the *Justification* unto *Men* that see and hear, our *Profession of our Faith*" [*BA*, Jas. 2:24]. In other words, Mather finds Paul and James consistent because they are speaking about different stages in the salvation process.

Edwards has a relevant entry on Jas. 2:14–26 in which he identified three errors of those opposing the writer of the Epistle of James. First, opponents of James misunderstood the nature of justifying faith, thinking it mere assent to the Christian doctrine of "one God" by contrast with "heathen infidelity." Second, they did not understand that "the working nature of faith was the life and soul" of "justifying faith." Third, they failed to "distinguish between the first and second justification," one being the imputation of righteousness "by faith alone," and the other "at judgment" when a person is "proved and declared righteous," which "is by works, and not by faith alone" (24: 1171).

Even more significant for Edwards's reconciliation of James and Paul is his commentary on Jas. 2:26. He opens that entry stating, "The working acting nature of anything is the life of it; that which makes men call anything alive is because they observe it has an active nature in it. ... Therefore 'as the body without the spirit is dead, so faith without' a working nature 'is dead also.' This working nature, or active fruitful spirit that there is in faith, is love, as the apostle Paul tells us." Edwards then cites two Pauline texts, Gal. 5:6 and 1 Cor. 13:2. His summary judgment reads, "So that love is included in the nature and essence of saving faith, yea, is the very life and soul of it, without which it is dead, as the body without the soul" (24: 1173).

This reconciliation of James and Paul appears to be the critical theological center of the two commentaries on the Epistle of James. Both Mather and Edwards are explicit in affirming that life actions are evidence of the "working nature" of "saving faith."

A natural question to ask of all biblical commentators is whether their exegesis of scripture speaks to particular problems or situations in the real world? Did the scriptural observations of Cotton Mather and Jonathan Edwards address directly any of the practical realities in colonial America during the first half of the eighteenth century? One issue both commentators addressed which had relevance for them and their contemporaries involved the presence of conflict, hostility, and warfare in their respective worlds. Both Mather and Edwards lived during more than one of the French and Indian wars between Great Britain and France which also involved the Native American allies of the two nations. The two ministers witnessed their fellow English colonists muster to launch assaults on French outposts and to defend against attacks during King William's War (1689–97), Queen Anne's War (1702–13), and King George's War (1744–48). They also knew the hardships and terror their fellow colonists experienced as a result of raids by hostile Native Americans. At times Mather and Edwards supported uncritically the participants in these conflicts. But there is evidence they also recognized another pastoral responsibility.

In the commentaries on the Epistle of James in the "Biblia Americana" and the "Blank Bible," both Mather and Edwards affirmed that the "working nature" of the Christian faith involved a responsibility for peacemaking. Their entries on Jas. 3:18 speak directly to the issue. Jas. 3:18 in the King James Version reads, "And the fruit of righteousness is sown in peace of them that make peace." Regarding that passage, Cotton Mather wrote, "Q. The *Fruit of Righteousness how is it sown in Peace, of* [or, for, or to,] *them that make Peace?* v. 18." Mather's answer reads,

> A. The *Reward* of *Righteousness*, to them who make it their Business, to live *peaceably* themselves, & incline others unto it, is here sown happily & quietly by the Preachers of the *Gospel, of Peace*, declaring it unto the World, and shall hereafter be assuredly Reaped by them.
> Or thus; These *Fruits of Righteousness*, now sown by the Christian endued with this Heavenly Wisdome, will yeeld an Happy Harvest, unto them who are Promoters of *Peace*. [*BA*, Jas. 3:18]

Of that same text, Jas. 3:18, Jonathan Edwards wrote,

> In these words the Apostle seems to have a plain reference to those words in Is. 32:17, "And the work of righteousness shall be peace; and the effect of righteousness quietness and assurance forever." The former part of the verse declares what is the genuine exercise or work of righteousness, viz. peaceableness or peacemaking. The latter part expresses the effect, consequence, and reward of righteousness to those who have it, in this its genuine nature, and who exercise it, in this its genuine work. (24: 1173)

Here Mather's and Edwards's understanding of the proper business of religion, or the working nature of saving faith, led them to a powerful witness to the work of peace.

Works Cited

Primary Sources

Boyle, Robert. *Some Physico-theological Considerations about the Possibility of the Resurrection.* London, 1675.

Critici Sacri, sive, Doctissimorum Virorum in SS. Biblia Annotationes & Tractatus. Ed. John Pearson, Anthony Scattergood, Francis Gouldman, and Richard Pearson. 9 vols. London, 1660.

Doddridge, Philip. *The Family Expositor: Or, A Paraphrase and Version of the New Testament: with Critical Notes; and a Practical Improvement of each Section.* 6 vols. London, 1739–56.

Edwards, John. *An enquiry into four remarkable texts of the New Testament which contain some difficulty in them, with a probable resolution of them.* Cambridge, 1692.

Edwards, Jonathan. *The Works of Jonathan Edwards. Apocalyptic Writings.* Ed. Stephen J. Stein. Vol. 5. New Haven: Yale UP, 1977.

–. *The Works of Jonathan Edwards. A History of the Work of Redemption.* Ed. John F. Wilson. Vol. 9. New Haven: Yale UP, 1989.

–. *The Works of Jonathan Edwards. Sermons and Discourses, 1720–1723.* Ed. Wilson H. Kimnach. Vol. 10. New Haven: Yale UP, 1992.

–. *The Works of Jonathan Edwards. "The Miscellanies," Entry Nos. a-z, aa-zz, 1–500.* Ed. Thomas A. Schafer. Vol. 13. New Haven: Yale UP, 1994.

–. *The Works of Jonathan Edwards. Sermons and Discourses, 1723–1729.* Ed. Kenneth P. Minkema. Vol. 14. New Haven: Yale UP, 1997.

–. *The Works of Jonathan Edwards. Notes on Scripture.* Ed. Stephen J. Stein. Vol. 15. New Haven: Yale UP, 1998.

–. *Personal Narrative. The Works of Jonathan Edwards. Letters and Personal Writings.* Ed. George S. Claghorn. Vol. 16. New Haven: Yale UP, 1998.

–. *The Works of Jonathan Edwards. Sermons and Discourses, 1730–1733.* Ed. Mark Valeri. Vol. 17. New Haven: Yale UP, 1999.

–. *The Works of Jonathan Edwards. "The Miscellanies," 501–832.* Ed. Ava Chamberlain. Vol. 18. New Haven: Yale UP, 2000.

–. *The Works of Jonathan Edwards. Sermons and Discourses, 1734–1738.* Ed. M. X. Lesser. Vol. 19. New Haven: Yale UP, 2001.

–. *The Works of Jonathan Edwards. "The Miscellanies," 833–1152.* Ed. Amy Plantinga Pauw. Vol. 20. New Haven: Yale UP, 2002.

–. *The Works of Jonathan Edwards. Sermons and Discourses, 1739–1742.* Ed. Harry S. Stout, Nathan O. Hatch, and Kyle P. Farley. Vol. 22. New Haven: Yale UP, 2003.

–. *The Works of Jonathan Edwards. "The Miscellanies," 1153–1360.* Ed. Douglas A. Sweeney. Vol. 23. New Haven: Yale UP, 2004.

–. *The Works of Jonathan Edwards. The Blank Bible.* Ed. Stephen J. Stein. Vol. 24. New Haven: Yale UP, 2006.

–. *The Works of Jonathan Edwards. Sermons and Discourses, 1743–1758.* Ed. Wilson H. Kimnach. Vol. 25. New Haven: Yale UP, 2006.

Glas, John. *Notes on Scripture-Texts.* Edinburgh, 1747.

Goodwin, Thomas. *The Works of Thomas Goodwin.* London, 1681.

Grosart, Alexander B. *Selections from the Unpublished Writings of Jonathan Edwards of America. Edited from the Original MSS, with Facsimiles and an Introduction.* Edinburgh, 1865.

Henry, Matthew. *An Exposition of All the Books of the Old and New Testaments: Wherein the Chapters are summ'd up in Contents; the Sacred Text inserted at large, in Paragraphs, or Verses; and each Paragraph, or Verse, reduc'd to its proper Heads: the Sense given, and largely illustrated, with Practical Remarks and Observations.* 6 vols. London, 1708–10.

–. *Matthew Henry's Commentary on the Whole Bible Wherein Each Chapter is Summed up in its Contents: The Sacred Text Inserted at Large in Distinct Paragraphs; Each Paragraph Reduced to its Proper Heads: The Sense Given, and Largely Illustrated with Practical Remarks and Observations.* Vol. 6. Old Tappan: Fleming H. Revell Company, 1970.

Hopkins, Samuel. *The Life and Character of the Late Reverend Mr. Jonathan Edwards, President of the College of New-Jersey.* Boston, 1765.

Manton, Thomas. *A Practical Commentary, or an Exposition with Notes on the Epistle of James. Delivered in sundry Weekly Lectures at Stoke-Newington in Middlesex, neer London.* London, 1651.

Mather, Cotton. *Bonifacius. An Essay Upon the Good, that is to be Devised and Designed, by those Who Desire to Answer the Great End of Life, and to Do Good While they Live.* Boston, 1710.

–. *Paterna: The Autobiography of Cotton Mather.* Ed. Ronald A. Bosco. Delmar, NY: Scholars' Facsimiles & Reprints, 1976.

–. *Selected Letters of Cotton Mather.* Ed. Kenneth Silverman. Baton Rouge: Louisiana State UP, 1971.

Mather, Samuel. *The Life of the Very Reverend and Learned Cotton Mather, D.D., F.R.S., Late Pastor of the North Church in Boston.* Boston, 1729.

Pearson, John. *Annotata ad Actus Apostolicos, epistolas & apocalypsin, sive Criticorum sacrorum: tomus VII.* London, 1660.

Pfaff, Christoph Matthaeus. *Institutiones theologicae dogmaticae et moralis.* Tubingae, 1720.

Poole, Matthew. *Annotations upon the Holy Bible. Wherein the Sacred Text is Inserted, and various Readings Annex'd together with Parallel Scriptures, the more difficult Terms in each Verse are Explained, seeming Contradictions Reconciled, Questions and Doubts Resolved, and the whole Text opened. By the Late Reverend and Learned Divine Mr. Matthew Poole.* 2 vols. London, 1683–85.

–. *Synopsis Criticorum Aliorumque S. Scripturæ Interpretum.* 5 vols. London, 1669–76.

Smith, John. *Select Discourses.* London, 1660.

Whitby, Daniel. *A Paraphrase and Commentary on the New Testament. In two volumes.* Vol. 2. London, 1703.

Secondary Sources

Boas, Ralph, and Louise Boas. *Cotton Mather: Keeper of the Puritan Conscience.* New York: Harper & Brothers, 1928.

Coolidge, John S. *The Pauline Renaissance in England: Puritanism and the Bible.* Oxford: Clarendon P, 1970.

Cross, F.L. and E.A. Livingstone, eds. *The Oxford Dictionary of the Christian Church.* 3rd ed. Oxford: Oxford UP, 1997.

Elliott-Binns, L.E. "James." *Peake's Commentary on the Bible.* Ed. Matthew Black. London: Nelson and Sons, 1962.

Jackson-McCabe, Matt A. *Logos and Law in the Letter of James: The Law of Nature, the Law of Moses, and the Law of Freedom.* Leiden: Brill, 2001.

Johnson, Luke Timothy. *Brother of Jesus, Friend of God: Studies in the Letter of James.* Grand Rapids: Eerdmans, 2004.

—. "The Letter of James: Introduction, Commentary, and Reflections." *The New Interpreter's Bible.* Ed. Leander E. Keck, et al. Vol. 12. Nashville: Abingdon Press, 1994. 175–225.

Levy, Babette May. *Cotton Mather.* Boston: Twayne Publishers, 1979.

Marsden, George M. *Jonathan Edwards: A Life.* New Haven: Yale UP, 2003.

Middlekauff, Robert. *The Mathers: Three Generations of Puritan Intellectuals, 1596–1728.* New York: Oxford UP, 1971.

Miller, Perry. *Jonathan Edwards.* New York: W. Sloane Associates, 1949.

Moo, Douglas J. *The Letter of James.* Grand Rapids: Eerdmans, 2000.

Murray, Iain H. *Jonathan Edwards: A New Biography.* Edinburgh: The Banner of Truth Trust, 1987.

Pelikan, Jaroslav. *Reformation of Church and Dogma (1300–1700). The Christian Tradition: A History of the Development of Doctrine.* Vol. 4. Chicago: U of Chicago P, 1984.

Silverman, Kenneth. *The Life and Times of Cotton Mather.* New York: Harper & Row, 1984.

Smith, John E. *Jonathan Edwards: Puritan, Preacher, Philosopher.* Notre Dame: U of Notre Dame P, 1992.

Stein, Stephen J. "The Biblical Notes of Benjamin Pierpont." *The Yale University Library Gazette* 50 (1976): 195–218.

—. "Edwards as Biblical Exegete." *The Cambridge Companion to Jonathan Edwards.* Ed. Stephan J. Stein. New York: Cambridge UP, 2007. 181–95.

Wendell, Barrett. *Cotton Mather: The Puritan Priest.* New York: Dodd, Mead and Company, 1891.

Winslow, Ola Elizabeth. *Jonathan Edwards, 1703–1758: A Biography.* New York: The Macmillan Company, 1940.

PAUL SILAS PETERSON

"The Perfection of Beauty": Cotton Mather's Christological Interpretation of the Shechinah Glory in the "Biblia Americana" and its Theological Contexts

> Every scribe which is instructed unto the kingdom of heaven is like unto a man that is an householder, which bringeth forth out of his treasure things new and old.
> Matt. 13:52

As is well known, Cotton Mather was no stranger to angelic beings in radiant glory visiting his study, especially when long bouts of fasting and fervent prayers rendered him susceptible to such ethereal manifestations.[1] One such event, sometime in 1685, was particularly memorable. Following intense religious devotions, the young Mather saw a radiant, winged angel in the shape of a "beardless" man, "whose face shone like the noonday sun," wearing a "splendid tiara" and "white and shining" robes down to his feet. A messenger from Jesus Christ, the angel prophesied to him a future of superlative productivity, like a *"Cedar in Lebanon with fair branches"* in Christ's kingdom and "in the revolutions that are now at hand." That the angel spoke to him "in the words of the prophet Ezekiel" (Ezek. 31:3–7, 9) is perhaps not surprising (*Diary* 1: 86–87; *Paterna* 112–13).[2] After all, Ezekiel's theophanic vision of the four living creatures "in the likeness of man" (1:5) typifies for Mather a manifestation of

---

1 I would like to thank Reiner Smolinski not only for access to his transcriptions of vol. 1 (Genesis) and 2 (Exodus, Leviticus, Numbers, Deuteronomy) of the "Biblia," but also for his helpful footnotes in those volumes, as well as a few helpful suggestions during the Tübingen conference. I would also like to thank Harry Clark Maddux for access to the transcriptions of vol. 4 (Ezra, Nehemiah, Job, Psalms), Rick Kennedy for vol. 8 (John, Historia Apostolica, Acts, Appendix to Acts), and Michael P. Clark for vol. 10 (Hebrews, James, 1–2 Peter, 1–3 John, Jude, Revelation, Coronis). Special thanks as well to Jason LaFountain for his suggested literature on the topic of *shining* in Mather. Finally, I would like to express my gratitude to Jan Stievermann for his helpful guidance both in the evolution of this paper and also within the Tübingen "Biblia"-team's shared undertaking of vol. 5 (Proverbs, Ecclesiastes, Canticles [The Messiah], Isaiah, Jeremiah). All translations in this essay are my own; all Bible citations are from the 1769 Oxford edition, Benjamin Blayney's revision of the 1611 *King James Version* of the English Bible. This essay is dedicated to my mother.
2 For the significance of Mather's angelic visions, see David Levin, "When did Cotton Mather See the Angel?" and his biography *Cotton Mather* (106–08, 200); Kenneth Silverman's review of *Paterna* and his biography *Life and Times* (127–30, 135–37, 311–12, 414). Mather also wrote about angels in his sermons *Coelestinus* and *Things for a Distress'd People*. For Increase Mather's interest in angels, see his *Angelographia* (1696).

Christ in his glorious reign. In the "Biblia Americana," this prefiguration of the glorious presence of Christ is usually referred to as the Shechinah, and it is one of the objects of Mather's insatiable curiosity throughout his commentary.

Mather's preoccupation with the ancient Jewish notion of Theophany is apparent in some of his earliest entries on Genesis. His aim is to show the presence of the second person of the Trinity in the Shechinah glory as a way to trace Christ's pre-incarnate existence in the Old Testament from the very beginning. "Entertain us, if you please, with a Jewish Curiosity, upon that Passage, *Lett there be Light*? [Gen. 1] v. 3." With this characteristic dialogue format, Mather begins to explore the issue. Dutifully answering his own request, he offers the following gloss taken from the rabbinic commentary of Isaac Abrabanel (1437–1508)[3]:

> *Abarbinel* (upon the XL of *Exodus*) takes this to be the SHECHINAH, the most excellent of all created Things, called in the Holy Scriptures, *The Glory of the Lord*; which God, saith he, sealed up in His Treasures, after the *Luminaries* were created, for to serve Him on special Occasions; (as, for instance, to lead the *Israelites* in the Wilderness, by a *Cloudy Pillar of Fire*,) when He would make Himself appear extraordinarily present. (*BA* 1: 320)

Abrabanel's explanation, however, does not fully satisfy Mather, for his interest in a Christological reading of the Old Testament governs his exegetical vision and selection criteria, one which the medieval rabbi is not prepared to supply:

> There may be Fancy enough, in this Notion; yett it is not altogether to be despised. There is a certain *Bright Cloud of Heaven*, of quite another Consistence than that which drops our ordinary Rain upon us; That *Cloud* filled with the *Light* and *Fire*, wherein the Son of God chose to lodge, as in His Covering, from the Beginning, that so He might therein exhibit Himself with an Agreeable *Majesty* unto His People: Tis the same that was called, The *Shechinah*; and it was of old seen by the People of God, on several great Occasions. The Great God ha's chosen, to dwell in this *Light, which no Man can approach unto*; and a special Remark, may be putt upon the *Goodness* of the *Light* in general, because unto the general Head of *Light* belongs that Illustrious & Cœlestial Matter, on which the God of Heaven ha's putt this peculiar Dignity. (*BA* 1: 320–21)

In Mather's understanding of the divine Shechinah as "a certain *Bright Cloud of Heaven*" where "the Son of God chose to lodge," the manifestation of God's glory simultaneously prefigures the second person of the Trinity: the yet unborn, but eternally existent Son, Christ, or the *Logos* pre-incarnate. In line with

---

3   Isaac Abrabanel [also Abarbanel, Abravanel] had a noted influence on early Protestantism: Calvin criticized his commentary on Daniel, and many exegetes of the Old Protestant orthodoxy read his Bible commentaries. The reception of Abrabanel in early Protestant theology has, however, not yet been fully researched. Hans Georg von Mutius has called Isaac Abrabanel "the most important Jewish Bible exegete and philosopher of religion at the end of the Middle Ages" ["der bedeutendste jüdische Bibelexeget und Religionsphilosoph am Ende des Mittelalters"] (Mutius 302).

a long patristic tradition, stemming itself from the New Testament, e.g. St. Paul (Col. 2:16),[4] the "Biblia" here appropriates the ancient Jewish notion of Theophany into a Christological framework of interpretation: Theophanies become Christophanies. This essay will argue that, far from being a "Jewish Curiosity" of mere antiquarian interest to the Puritan intellectual, this Christianized understanding of the Shechinah is indeed a central concept for Mather's theology that, like a symbol in a Persian rug, appears throughout the "Biblia" commentary. The concept of the Shechniah helped Mather to argue not only for the Christocentric unity of redemption history spanning both the Old and New covenants, but also to defend the organic wholeness and harmony of the scriptures against the rise of historical criticism by pointing to the interpretive center of the Old and New Testament.

As I will demonstrate, Mather's interpretation of the Shechinah can only be adequately understood in the context of an ongoing theological debate among early modern Christian Hebraists. After a brief look at the origins of the Hebrew neologism and its adoption into the English language, I will provide a survey of this theological debate, paying particular attention to Mather's main sources, John Stillingfleet (1630–87) and Thomas Tenison (1636–1715), as well as to the period's foremost critic of any hermeneutical approach that read Christ into the Hebrew Bible: Hugo Grotius (1583–1645). Following the analysis of Mather's contribution to the contemporary debate about the significance of Shechinahism, I will conclude with a short comparative glance at Jonathan Edwards (1703–58), his most important successor in the New England tradition.

The Biblical Background and Rabbinical Origins of the Neologism Shechinah and its Introduction into English

What exactly does the word *Shechinah* mean and where does it come from? *The Oxford English Dictionary*, with its emphasis on the etymological origins of words in English usage, is a helpful starting point. Here the word is explained as follows:

> The visible manifestation of the Divine Majesty, esp. when resting between the cherubim over the mercy-seat or in the temple of Solomon; a glory or refulgent light symbolizing the Divine Presence. ... In the Targums the word is used as a periphrasis to designate God when He is said to dwell among the cherubim, etc., so as to avoid any approach to anthropomorphic expressions. ("Shechinah")

---

4 Col. 2:16–17: "Let no man therefore judge you in meat, or in drink, or in respect of an holyday, or of the new moon, or of the sabbath days: Which are a shadow of things to come; but the body is of Christ."

The central notion of divine manifestation or indwelling, which the *Oxford English Dictionary* rightly indentifies as underlying the word *Shechinah*, is rooted in the biblical concept of God's glory, which is rendered in the Hebrew scriptures as כבוד יהוה (*kabod YHWH*). The Septuagint translates this phrase as ἡ δόξα τοῦ θεοῦ, which correlates with both *notion* as well as *brightness, radiance,* and *splendor.* The Vulgate provides *gloria Domini,* while Luther's Bible (1545) renders it as *die Herrlichkeit des HERRN* ("the glory [literally: 'lordliness'] of the Lord"); the *King James Version* (both 1611 and 1769) translates the phrase with the Latinized *the glory of the LORD,* as does the modern French (*Traduction Oecuménique de la Bible,* 1988): *la gloire du SEIGNEUR.* The Hebrew word *kabod* signifies *weightiness. Kabod* is however also related to the Greek δόξα (*brightness, radiance, splendor*) in that *kabod* is often associated with light, especially in Exod. 24:17 (Podella 1681).[5]

The term Shechinah itself, however, derives from another Hebrew word, this one being a verb, šākēn שכן, "to dwell," "remain," "inhabit" (Brown 1015). The substantive form of this verb is miskân משכן i.e., "tabernacle," "tent," or "dwelling place." In the Hebrew Bible this verb is linked with the above mentioned glory of the Lord. A famous example of this signification can be seen in Exod. 24:16: "And the glory of the LORD abode [וישכן כבוד־יהוה] upon mount Sinai, and the cloud covered it six days: and the seventh day he called unto Moses out of the midst of the cloud."[6] When early Jewish authors of the Targums, such as Onkelos or Pseudo-Jonathan, interpreted God's dwelling presence they often used the Hebraism *Shechinah* to speak of God's actual spatial presence on earth.[7] Although it was later used to avoid anthropomorphic reference to God (esp. with Moses Maimonides [1138–1204]), its earliest usage signified a specification of the way in which God was present (Goldberg 450, 535–36). The Hebrew neologism can be found in the Targums Onkelos and Pseudo-Jonathan.

As Arnold Goldberg has argued, in the early rabbinic literature Shechinah was not a *representative* of God, but the Divine Being *ad se ipsum:* "The term Shechinah must have originally identified the act of descent, the inhabitation or presence of the Godhead, and then the Godhead itself: how it is present at a

---

5 "And the sight of the glory of the LORD [כבוד יהוה] was like devouring fire on the top of the mount in the eyes of the children of Israel."

6 Another passage which speaks of this dwelling of God is Exod. 25:8: "And let them make me a sanctuary; that I may dwell among them." At this passage, as McClintock and Strong relay (9: 637–38) Onkelos has "I will make my Shechinah to dwell among them." At Ps. 74:2b, "this mount Zion, wherein thou hast dwelt," the Targum records: "Wherein thy Shechinah hath dwelt." At Isa. 6:5c, "for mine eyes have seen the King, the LORD of hosts," Jonathan has: "the glory of the Shechinah of the King of ages, the Lord of hosts." For further examples, see McClintock and Strong (9: 637–39); Schäfer (79–93); and for perhaps the most extensive list of the use of Shechinah in Rabbinic literature, see Goldberg (13–430).

7 How the term *originally* came about can only be conjectured (Goldberg 440).

particular place or reveals itself" (450).[8] He cites a passage from Targum Onkelos, at Deut. 33:16: דשכנתה בשמיא ועל משה אתגלי באסנא [whose Shechinah is in heaven, but who reveals himself to Moses in the thornbush] (440).[9] This strong account of immanence (almost suggesting a plurality) in the commentary was not left unchallenged.[10] Some rabbinical philosophers of the medieval period attempted to distance the Shechinah from God, as Peter Schäfer remarks,

> The most extreme step in distancing the Shekhinah from God was taken by the emerging Jewish philosophy of the early Middle Ages. Its representatives have been labeled "rationalistic," because one of their major concerns was to maintain – or rather restore – the integrity of the monotheistic and abstract concept of God. (103)

Schäfer shows that although some medieval Jewish philosophers, theologians, and poets – such as Saadia Gaon (892–942), Judah Ben Barzillai (c. 1035–1105), Judah Ha-Levi (before 1075–1141), and Maimonides – sought to interpret the Shechinah as created and thereby "'restore' a pure, non-anthropomorphic monotheism,"[11] in actuality the attempt was "quite alien to the much richer biblical and early postbiblical lore" (118). Rabbinical commentary and translation before this period never claimed that Shechinah was created (Schäfer 103).[12] Goldberg asserts that "it can be positively established that the Shechinah is not a middle being, and also cannot be, because the term *Shechinah* always indicates the unmediated presence of God" (535).[13] *Deus absconditus* is here revealed; Shechinah is nothing less than an explanation of the actual presence of God among us. With this background, we are now better prepared to appreciate how this new idiom entered the theological discourse of English and American scholars of the early modern period.

The birth of the Hebrew neologism Shechinah can be wonderfully illustrated by one of Cotton Mather's key study tomes. An often referenced text for many theologians and biblical scholars of the seventeenth century and later,

---

8   "Der Terminus Schekhinah muß ursprünglich den Akt der Herabkunft, der Einwohnung oder Gegenwart der Gottheit bezeichnet haben und dann die Gottheit selber, wie sie an einem bestimmten Ort gegenwärtig ist oder sich offenbart."

9   "dessen Schekhinah im Himmel ist, der sich aber Moses im Dornbusch offenbart."

10   Goldberg proposes the term *emanation* as a possible explanation of Shechinah. He has serious reservations about its helpfulness, however, if the term leads to a foreign concept of God as an *Urgrund*, as in Neoplatonism, and later Kabbalah – a concept foreign to the ancient rabbis (536).

11   As Goldberg argues, only in one case of his entire investigation was Shechinah presented as the "Angel of the Lord," from a late Midrash collection and an unknown source (470).

12   Goldberg demonstrates this point from his study of Targum Pseudo-Jonathan, Targum Onkelos, the Babylonian and Palestinian Midrash as well as the Tosephta, the Midrash Hagadol, Midrash Rabbah, and countless other sources, collections, and commentaries (535).

13   "es kann positiv festgestellt werden, daß die Schekhinah kein Mittelwesen ist und auch nicht sein kann, weil der Terminus Schekhinah immer den unmittelbar gegenwärtigen Gott bezeichnet."

Brian Walton's *Biblia Sacra Polyglotta* (1653–57) published the Targum of Pseudo-Jonathan. This Aramaic commentary records the following on Exod. 25:8:
ועשו ויעברון לשמי מוקרשא ואשרי שכינתי ביניהון; the Latin translation reads, "Et facient
nomini meo sanctuarium, & habitare faciam [שכינתי] divinam meam majestatem
inter eos" (Walton 4: 148), which can be rendered, "And they should make unto
my name a sanctuary, so that I will make שכינתי [my Shechinah / my divine majesty {or, grandeur}] to dwell with them." If the transliterated Hebraism is left
standing without explication of its meaning, the passage then reads, "And they
should make unto my name a sanctuary, so that I will make my *Shechinah* to
dwell with them." Interestingly, the Latin translators in Walton's edition of
Pseudo-Jonathan did not transliterate the term but elected to render its signification *meam majestatem*. At some point in the early English reception of these
texts, however, *majestas* no longer satisfied those who employed Walton's London Polyglot, either because theologians deemed the Latin interpretation inadequate or because they preferred to leave the genius of the Hebraism *Shechinah*
to stand as an unique idiom. An early example for the actual usage of the neologism within the theological discourse of the seventeenth century can be found
in Matthew Poole's *Synopsis Criticorum* (1669–76), one of the key sources for
the biblical humanists in Old and New England. Poole's *Synopsis* retains *Shechinah* in the Latin commentary on Ps. 17:15:

> R. Menachem ad Levit. 10. hæc habet, Nemo venire potest coram celsissimo &
> benedicto Rege sine Shecinah, (quod est Divina Majestas Dei in Christo;) ideóque
> dicitur, [nempe hoc loco,] In justitia videbo faciem tuam. (2: 637)
> [R. Menachem, at Lev. 10, has, 'no one can come into the presence of the most ce-
> lestial and blessed King without Shechinah (that is the Divine Majesty of God in
> Christ;) therefore it is said {truly in this place,}' 'in righteousness I will see thy
> face.']14

This passage is significant because Poole's rendition already inserts the Christological emphasis in his translation of the Hebraism: "(quod est Divina Majestas
Dei in Christo)", ["(that is 'the Divine Majesty of God in Christ')"]. Although
many English speaking theologians would have read such passages in Latin, the
first actual employment of the term in English, according to the *Oxford English
Dictionary*, was John Stillingfleet (1631–87) – the elder brother of Edward Stillingfleet (1635–99), bishop of Worcester, Latitudinarian theologian, and critic of
John Locke. This attribution seems to be correct, for his book titled *Shecinah,
or, A demonstration of the divine presence in the places of religious worship*
(1663) presents the term as a new-found jewel for theological reflection. Here,
John Stillingfleet appropriately introduces the term in its non-Christological
sense:

---

14 Ps. 16:15 in the *Vulgata*: "ego autem in iustitia apparebo conspectui tuo satiabor cum ap-
paruerit gloria tua" (Ps. 17:15 in the *KJV*).

God is said *to dwell between the Cherubims*, Because God had promised to be Present there, and from thence to give his answer to the People. Here the *Jews* placed the SHECINAH the *Majesty* of God and his *Glory* dwelling upon the *Ark*, for this was the usual terme to expresse Gods Majesty and Presence in his Church by. And the *Hebrews* by *Shecinah* are wont to note; that visible sign of the Lords Presence, whereby he signifyed to the *Jews*, that he would dwell and stay amongst them, and what the Jews are wont to call *Shecinah*, in the Scripture we may often find set out by *Gods Glory;* And the word Δόξα is frequently used both in the LXX and New Testament, in that sense. Now, because the Ark was counted the most holy type that the Jews had, and the most Principal evidence and Pledge of Gods Presence, hence God sanctified those Places where the Ark came, because of the solemnity of manifesting of his Presence. (70)[15]

Stillingfleet takes a rather standard interpretation here, but on the following page he introduces the Christological connection by arguing that the presence of the Shechinah in the sacrificial ritual at the altar is "not so much for the Types sake as for the thing Typifyed by all these, and that was *Christ*" (71). As will be shown in the following section, this Christological account of the Shechinah served as a theological tool, enabling not only John Stillingfleet but also Thomas Tenison to connect the Old and New covenants and thus, in a certain sense, emphasize a synthetic continuity of tradition.

The Role of Shechinah in the Contemporary Theological Debates in England

As is already partly clear from the justification given in the title of Stillingfleet's trailblazing book, which is *"to promote Piety, prevent Apostacy, and to reduce grosly deluded souls,"* the term *Shechinah* was employed from the beginning for apologetic and polemic purposes by English theologians. Stillingfleet sets out to present a true account of piety and Christian worship. The book actually received a heated response by William Smith (d. 1673), a Quaker, prolific defender of the free churchmen, and author of Quaker catechisms, in *A brief answer unto a book intituled SHETINAH* [sic], *or a demonstration* (1664). Smith claims that Stillingfleet "hath endeavored to cloud the sun on a clear day" (3) in his theological arguments against the Quakers. His short twenty-eight-page response takes the form of a point-counterpoint defense of Quaker piety and ecclesial polity against Stillingfleet's criticism. In his polemic against the

---

15 In the margin, Stillingfleet cites the French philologist Joannes Mercerus (Jean Mercier, * c. 1547), and his explanation of the Hebrew word: "Divinitas שכינה Gloria Divina inter homines habitans a שכן habitare. Hæbroram [sic] magistri vocant divinam Majestatem, Shecinah, quod suae ecclesiae habitet & adsit ubique locorum presentis [sic]. Merc. in Pagn." [Divinity שכינה Divine glory dwelling among mankind, from שכן to inhabit. The teachers of the Hebrews call divine majesty, Shechinah, because she {Shechinah is femine} would inhabit her assembly and be present wherever the place may be. Merc. in Pagn] (Stillingfleet 70).

Quaker doctrine of "the light within," Stillingfleet was keen to prove the necessity of public worship and to establish the correct use of the famous "light within," for as he argues at one point, the saints were *"panting after Gods presence in publick"* (from *The Contents*). Subsequently, Stillingfleet employs Shechinah as a confirmation that the presence of God is associated with orderly worship in an established format, not as a light within as the Quakers insisted. He continues to show how in the Old Testament the Temple, where the Shechinah dwelt, was a lawfully organized place of worship: *"A private Altar was not lawful to be erected but by a Prophet.* And the *Temple*, upon such accounts was a Part of the ceremonial Worship" (71). However, the Temple and its sacrifice, Stillingfleet argues, were only shadows of things to come that typified Christ:

> And they were to set their faces towards it, when they Prayed. And all this, not so much for the Types sake as for the thing Typifyed by all these, and that was *Christ*, through whom alone God accepts both of our Persons, Prayers, and all our Performances. (71)

Given Stillingfleet's anti-Quaker polemic, he carefully argues on the one hand for the importance of traditional worship and places of worship, while on the other, he maintains the fulfillment of the Old Testament-type in Christ as the New Testament-antitype, who abrogates the previous exclusivity of sacred places. He continues, "Therefore it follows that all that Legal and Ceremonial holiness of Places should quite vanish away with the Types, when Christ who is the substance, at which all there shadows Pointed is come" (71). The temple and Shechinah therein was fulfilled in Christ. It thus follows that he cannot adhere to a theology which prefers a certain holy place over another, one which would necessarily run counter to the radical message of Christ's universality. Stillingfleet justifies his interpretation as follows:

> Yet I have neither faith to beleeve, nor any reason to see, that there is in any such separated, I add, and consecrated Places for Divine Worship, any such Legal or Ceremonial kind of Holiness, which renders Duties performed there, more acceptable unto God, than if performed by the same Persons and in the like manner in any other Places. Which both in the Speculation, and in the Practice, smells too rank of down-right Popery. (71–72)

Stillingfleet walks a thin line between Catholic conceptions of holy places on the one hand and complete disregard of places of public worship on the other. We need not rehearse his argument here, but in brief, he draws upon the many passages of the Old and New Testament that speak of angels in relationship to religious gatherings as indication of a necessity for orderly worship (as St. Paul said, "because of the angels" 1 Cor. 11:10). The angels gather in particular places and aid the "heirs of salvation" – however, they are not to be worshiped. Following this excursus into angelology, Stillingfleet turns to the importance of the teaching and preaching of the word of God in the church service. He introduces the Hebraism at this critical point in his argument. The Old Testament account of the Shechinah confirms that God becomes present in a certain finite place. For Stillingfleet, there is a direct analogy between the Old Testament Shechinah in the temple and the New Testament presence of God in the church. God is present in both cases, and both entail certain expectations upon the particular place and form of worship, the house of worship, and the worshipers. The Shechinah thus secures his theological argument and enables him to construct a direct continuity between the two covenants. This integrated concept of redemption history, with its religious norms, was employed by Stillingfleet against what he saw as a radicalization of the religion in the Quaker's unconventional and unregulated worship style as well as their emphasis on the doctrine of the "inner light" centered in the individual.[16]

The reception of the Shechinah terminology was varied, but it quickly gained wider publicity and became a *terminus technicus* in the English theological world. Some fifteen years later, Thomas Tenison (1636–1715) draws upon the Hebraism in a more focused and comprehensive presentation of the theme in his *Of Idolatry* (1678), which employs a variety of different sources, including other rabbinical commentaries, such as Moses Maimonides (1135–1204) and Abrabanel, and Targums, such as Onkelos, as well as reference to the Swiss Hebraist Johann Buxtorf (1564–1629).[17] Tenison received his B.A. from Corpus Christi College, Cambridge, and as Edward Carpenter argues, was directly influenced by the Cambridge Platonist Ralph Cudworth (1617–88) (*Thomas Tenison* 7). Some of this influence can be detected in one of Tenison's earlier works, *The Creed of Mr. Hobbes Examined in a Feigned Conference between Him and a Student of Divinity* (1670), which made him a popular figure for his critique of the materialism of Thomas Hobbes (1588–1679). As Carpenter records, in 1694 Tenison was chosen over Stillingfleet to become the Archbishop of Canterbury, a position he held until his death (*Cantuar* 229). In his *Of Idolatry*, Tenison charts idolatry *ab antiquo* and then doubles back to show *"the Cure of Idolatry by the* Shechinah *of God"* at every step along the way. In the margin of his text, he begins his discourse on the Shechinah as follows: "Let this difficult Argument, about the Shechinah, be read with caution; even where I have not interspersed words of Caution" (315). His warning is merited, for his work is an adventurous claim that the light of God, the Shechinah, has been shining in many cultures and in many different lands, leading all mankind to

---

16 "The light of reason, the *inward light* of the mind, improved with rules of morality, may make us morally honest, but it is the Word of God that teaches us how to be truly gracious" (Stillingfleet 113).

17 Although Tenison was certainly familiar with Stillingfleet's polemic *Shecinah, or, A demonstration* (1663), the parish theologian appears to have investigated some primary sources as well; he writes at the end of the book, "the Argument is a beaten one; a subject handled by Maimonides, Viretus, Vossius, Reinolds, Selden, and many others of great Learning" (392).

the light of the truth in God. His first source is by Neoplatonist philosopher Iamblichus Chalcidensis (c. 245-c. 325), who "in his book of the Egyptian Mysteries," "setteth out by light, the Power, the Simplicity, the Penetration, the Ubiquity of God" (Tenison 315–16). From St. Basil to Albin Levita, from Chaldean Oracles to Origen, from Justin Martyr, to Jerome, Augustine, and Maximus the Confessor, and from Eusebius to Philo Judaeus, Tenison charts out in a "parti-coloured" fashion how the second person of the Trinity has been seen in the divine presence of the Shechinah, a *"super-cælestial star; the fountain of all the sensible Luminaries"* (Tenison 320) from days of yore, in theological conflict and theurgia. He then turns to the Bible itself charting his course in epochs: From Adam to Noah, Noah to Moses, Moses to the Captivity – and "therein largely of the Ark and Cherubims and Urim and Thummim" (Tenison, "Introduction") – and then finally from the Captivity to the Messiah. This elucidation leads him to a discourse on the cure of idolatry by the "image of God in Christ God-man," before closing with two sections and a summary on the utility and the propriety of God's Shechinah in his theological discourse.

It is fair to argue that Tenison's account builds upon the synthetic theology of Stillingfleet. Whereas Stillingfleet employed his interpretation of the term *Shechinah* to show the binding of the covenants and, accordingly, the subsequent modified continuity of norms for public worship, with Tenison, Shechinah is a code for understanding Christ's presence among the nations, that is, how God has vouchsafed "the World towards the cure of Idolatry" (311). Tenison thus incorporates Shechinah into a more specific theological argument against a variety of different schools of thought.[18] His main emphasis centered

---

18 Tenison's main arguments are as follows: A) An "Anthropomorphite" who could not conceive of God in "any natural colour or figure" stands refuted, Tenison states, because "God by his Logos using the ministry of inferiour creatures, hath condescended to a visible Shechinah" 379). B) Tenison then turns to what seems to be the Quakers: "those people who run into the other extream, the *Spiritualist* and *abstractive Familists*," who are concerned with the "light or love in their own breasts." They "may be induced to own the distinct substance of God, and the visible person of Christ" and not to "subtilize the Deity and its Persons, and all its appearances into a meer notion ... or habit of mans spirit; or to bow down to God no otherwise than as he is the pretended light or love in their own breasts" (379). C) Next, Tenison looks across to the Continent: the theological problems of the German Anabaptist (Cloppenburg) would have never been thought of if he and his followers had read the rabbis (379–80). D) Tenison then turns his attention to the early history of Christian doctrine and against the ancient Gnostic Valentinians who, had they understood the preexistence of the Logos in the *Shechinah*, would not have fallen into error (380). E). Furthermore, Tenison sees the Shechinah in a general sense as an aid to the unfolding of Scriptures, "which speak of the Præexistence of Christ before he was God-man" (380), against Laelius Socinus (1525–62) and the Socinian denial of the Trinity. F) He also perceives it as a weapon against the semi-Socinians such as Conrad Vorstius (1569–1622) and his disciples, who limit the ubiquity of the Divine, "confound the Immensity of the God-head, and the visible Glory of the Shechinah, which God hath pleased as it were to circumscribe. They will allow this King of the world no further room for his Immense substance than that which his especial Presence irradiates in his particular Palace. Which conceit though in part it be accommodable to the

on two aspects of Christology: preexistence and Logos (universality) and incarnation (particularity). With these, however, he saw in the Shechinah a key to a variety of theological problems and conflicts. Tenison ends his argument with words, which probably refer to the scholastic theology of Thomas Aquinas and the *visio beatifica*: "This Shechinah in milder, but most inexpressible luster, I suppose to be that which the Schools call the Beatifick Vision; and which the Scripture intendeth in the promise of seeing God face to face" (Tenison 378–9). That the force and "parti-coloured" nature of Tenison's argument was not universally appreciated by his critics can be seen in the works of those who resisted his expanded application of the term Shechinah. Although the Bishop of Ely Simon Patrick (1625–1707) adopted the rabbinic terminology, he does not seem to accept the Christology behind it. Significantly, Cotton Mather, who extracts much of Patrick's learned commentary, dismisses Patrick's reservation and chooses to follow Tenison's interpretation instead, one that endorses not only the orthodoxy of ancient theology but also the universality of the faith in an accelerating world of science and discovery.

Although Patrick was aware of Tenison and his Shechinah theology,[19] he carefully diverges from Tenison's Shechinah theology in explanation of the giving of the Law (Exod. 19:11):

> *For the third day the LORD will come down* ... Not from the Mount, but from Heaven upon Mount Sinai. On which the SCHECHINAH descended in a Cloud, which struck a great awe into them: For it was darker than the Pillar of the Cloud, by which they had been conducted hither; thro' which some rays, or glimpse of a glorious Majesty that was in it, broke forth upon them. (*Commentary upon the First Book of Moses* 350)

While Patrick includes Shechinah into his interpretive narrative, he does not speak of the second person of the Trinity nor Christ, nor of the Logos, as do Tenison (333–34), and, as I will demonstrate, Cotton Mather. Shechinah here is simply "a Token of God's special Presence" (Patrick, *Commentary upon the historical books* 49). This difference between Patrick and Tension (as well as Mather) should not be overemphasized. Patrick also has a Christology of preexistence. For example, in his commentary on Gen. 3:8 Patrick follows Tenison's reading of Onkelos but only insofar as to claim that the "Word of God, that is the Son of God," spoke to Adam and Eve in the Garden. For Patrick,

---

Shechinah; yet is it a presumptuous limitation of the great God, when it is applied to his substance which Heaven and Earth together cannot contain" (381). G) Then, Tenison addresses the "blindness of some of the modern Jews," who are against "Divine Statues and Images ... yet hope (some say) for an especial presence of God by furnishing with a Cheft and Roll of their Law, the place of their Religious Assemblies." H) Finally, Tenison examines the difficulty associated with the worship of angels, a problem that Stillingfleet also addresses.

19 Simon Patrick cites Tenison and *Of Idolatry* in his *Commentary upon the First Book of Moses* (61).

wherever there is a direct entrance to God's *speaking* the connection to the *Word* of God is made (see Gen. 1 ff., Exod. 13, 19–20, etc.). As a more reserved voice, Matthew Poole – in both his academic *Synopsis Criticorum* as well as the laymen's *Annotations* – appears to be nearly silent about the Shechinah, at least in the places where the others are vocal (see Gen. 3:8, 32:24; Exod. 3, 19–20; Josh. 5:13; Ez. 1; etc.). In the places where he interprets the Theophanies of the Hebrew Bible as manifestations of the Son, Poole does not use the Hebraism.[20]

Interestingly, Matthew Henry (1662–1714), the influential nonconformist pastor of Chester, follows Patrick's reception of Shechinah in his *Exposition of all the books of the Old and New Testament* (1708–10), a Calvinist commentary for laymen (Henry 336). Henry glosses on Num. 7:89, "Now when Moses went into the tent of meeting to speak with Him, he heard the voice speaking to him from above the mercy seat that was on the ark of the testimony, from between the two cherubim, so He spoke to him." Henry's remarks on this passage succinctly gather the vital emphasis of the Shechinah interpretation. In following Patrick at the outset, Henry goes on to introduce the specifically Christian theological language which, tellingly, Patrick leaves out:

> And here the excellent Bishop *Patrick* observes, that God's speaking to Moses thus by an audible articulate Voice, as if he had been cloth'd with a Body, might be look'd upon as an Earnest of the Incarnation of the Son of God in the Fulness of Time, when the Word should be *made Flesh*, and speak in the Language of the Sons of Men. For however God at sundry Times, and in divers Manners, spake unto the Fathers, he has in these last Days spoken unto us by his Son. And that he that now spake to *Moses*, as the *Shechinah* or Divine Majesty from between the Cherubims, was the Eternal Word, the second Person in the Trinity, was the pious Conjecture of many of the Ancients; for all God's Communion with Man is by his Son, by

---

20 In at least one place Poole's *Synopsis* employs the term Shechinah (2: 637), even translating it as above mentioned ("*quod est Divina Majestas Dei in Christo*"). Although he translates the term, the commentary and the term come originally from R. Menachem. However, Poole does not mention this citation, or Shechinah in his *Annotations* on the same passage (on Ps. 17:15). Poole clearly takes a Christological reading of the creation narrative, but he does not refer to the Shechinah in his commentary on Gen. 3:8, or elsewhere. Regarding the "Voice of the LORD God walking in the garden" (Gen. 3:8), Poole remains conservative: "Either God the Father, or rather God the Son, appearing in the shape of a man, as afterwards he frequently did, to give a foretaste of his incarnation" (*Annotations*, vol. 1, at Gen. 3:8). Concerning the descent of God onto Mt. Sinai (Exod. 19:18), Poole glosses, "And mount Sinai was altogether on a smoke, because the LORD descended upon it in fire: and the smoke thereof ascended as the smoke of a furnace, and the whole mount quaked greatly." Poole emphasizes that the spectacle was intended "For further terrour to obstinate Sinners. Hence the Law is called a fiery law, Deut. 33.2" (on Exod. 19:18). At the opening verses of the Decalogue, Poole expressly sides against any interpretive wish-wash: "Or, then, to wit, when Moses was returned into the Mount. Immediately, and not by an Angel. For though an Ambassadour or Messenger may act in the name of his Master, yet it is against the use of all Ages and Places for such to call themselves by his name" (on Exod. 20:1). See also his *Synopsis Criticorum* at Gen. 3:8 and esp. at Exod. 3:2 in determining the identity of the *Angelus Dei*: "*nempe, Christus*" ["certainly, Christ"] (1: 326).

whom he made the World, and rules the Church, and who is the same yesterday, to day, and for ever. (336)

Henry not only follows but also adds to Patrick's tentative modification of Tenison's interpretation, which itself builds on Stillingfleet's exegesis and the rabbinical tradition. When God spoke (interpreted as the "Word of God"), Patrick was happy to employ the Christological association as well as use the neologism as Tenison does. Poole, by contrast, does not seem to introduce the Hebraism into his commentary; he rather holds to a strict intertextual approach while simultaneously tending toward a scientific interpretation.

English Bible exegetes of Mather's period employed the interpretation of the Shechinah in different ways and with different emphases. Stillingfleet and Tenison drew upon the Shechinah in two common ways: on the one hand, they attempted to hold together the relative norms of worship in the two Testaments against Quakerism, a new non-traditional form of Christianity; on the other, they attempted to hold together the organic continuity of the Testaments against a new humanism which was calling this continuity into question.

The Humanist Critique of Christological Interpretation from the Sozzinis to Grotius

Standing against these Shechinah-interpretations and their entire Christological interpretive method is another exegetical tradition, which rejects these approaches as hermeneutically unscientific and inventive. This tradition has its nearest roots in the Reformation understanding of scripture, which itself can be traced back to Nicholas of Lyra (1270–1349). This approach finds the measure of exegesis in clear explanations of Holy Scripture: *claritus scripturae*. As Hans Frei has argued, Luther's words on Scripture

> represent his drastic alternative to the complex and long development of traditional theory of scriptural interpretation which had come to distinguish among literal, allegorical, anagogical, and tropical senses of the text. Against that multiplex view Luther's simplification meant drastic relief, affirming as it did that the literal or, as he preferred to call it, the grammatical or historical sense is the true sense. (19)[21]

Although both Luther and Calvin read the Old Testament by means of Christological typology, their emphasis on the *sensus litteralis*, at the cost of the other senses, had unexpected consequences. The Reformation and the broader movement of humanism stood at the same time both for and against one another

---

21 See also Frei's subsequent remarks: "Not very much of Protestant orthodoxy passed over into rationalist religious thought, but this one thing surely did: the antitraditionalism in scriptural interpretation of the one bolstered the antiauthoritarian stance in matters of religious meaning and truth of the other" (55).

(Kraus 28). Their point of contention is exemplified in Luther's conflict with
Erasmus, but their shared interests are best seen in the textually honest biblical
exegetes of humanism. Both Lelio Sozzini (aka. Laelius Socinus, 1525–62) and
his nephew Fausto Sozzini (aka. Faustus Socinus, 1539–62) have therefore a
complex but verifiable relation to Luther's bibliology. Sympathizers of the Reformation and the Sozzinis' cause have often put their theology in direct continuity with the Reformation; thus, in perpetuating the Reformation's mythic
battle against the Roman Antichrist, admirers often said of their theology: *Tota
ruit Babylon: tecta destruxit Lutherus, muros Calvinus, sed fundamenta Socinus.* [All of Babylon is destroyed: the roof by Luther, the walls by Calvin, but
the foundations by Socinus] (Urban 600). In Socinianism, as the movement was
named, the Old Testament is to be understood as a historical document. Here
Ps. 2 speaks only of David, and Ps. 22 of the calamities of Israel (Kraus 41).
Tenison objected to the Socinians in his *Of Idolatry*, because they challenged
the preexistence of Christ and the doctrine of the Trinity. If Luther wrestled the
Holy Scripture from the hands of the Magisterium, the Sozzinis wrestled it
from the hands of the dogmaticians. As Kraus argues, "the Sozzinis attempted
to loose the Holy Scripture from the bonds of dogmatic examination and to
carry through the humanistic norms" (43).[22] For the first time, the Old Testament becomes "*historically* detached from the New Testament"[23] (41, emphasis
in original). Kraus quotes H. E. Weber's analysis, claiming that Socinianism is a
knotting point in intellectual history, for it ties lines from the middle ages with
lines from the beginning of the modern age (41). Looking forward, the spirit of
humanism passes from the Sozzinis through Grotius to the age of the Enlightenment (43). In this regard, Grotius's *Annotata ad Vetus Testamentum* (1644;
Annotationes in subsequent editions) were carrying on the tradition of the
Sozzinis and, at the same time, present an entirely novel development. As Kraus
puts it,

> a question emerges in the Annotata which we already saw with the Sozzinis: *Gro-
> tius seeks out the profane historical background of the Old Testament testimonies,
> and searches, far from every aspect of salvation history, a pure historical explana-
> tion.* (Kraus 50–51, emphasis in original)[24]

Grotius's explication did not go without criticism; the Lutheran Abraham Calov
claimed that his *Annotata* was "an irrational mixture of pagan scriptures"

---

22 "die Sozinianer bemüht, die Heilige Schrift aus den Fesseln dogmatischer Betrachtung
zu lösen und die humanistischen Normen durchzusetzen" (Kraus 43).
23 "So wird das Alte Testament bei den Sozinianern zum erstenmal *historisch* vom Neuen
Testament abgehoben" (Kraus 41).
24 "Außerdem tritt in den Annotata eine Fragestellung hervor, die wir bei den Sozinianern
kennenlernten: *Grotius sucht den profangeschichtlichen Hintergrund der alttestamentlichen
Aussagen und erstrebt, fern von jedem heilsgeschichtlichen Aspekt, eine rein historische Erk-
lärung*" (Kraus 50–51).

(Kraus 53).[25] The conservative Lutheran theologian J. G. Carpzov, who speaks of the "profane intellect, to which nothing is beautiful except that drawn from the pools of the pagans," was even more outspoken in his criticism (Kraus 53).[26] It is in this context that Grotius emerges as a debate partner for Mather and his companions. Grotius bypasses Christological interpretations of the grand *fiat lux* (Gen. 1:3). For the great Dutch legal scholar and founder of historical criticism, there is no Christ, no *Logos*, and clearly no Shechinah in Gen. 1:3, but rather "three primal substances" (1:1).[27] Though certainly aware of them, Grotius also looks over any fanciful *pluralitatem & unitatem*-interpretations of נעשה *faciamus*, "let us make" (Gen. 1:26, so also אלהים, *Dii* "Gods" Gen. 1:1), which for other exegetes of the time provided an ideal entry point for a discussion of the Trinity.[28] Instead, these terms are for Grotius a "tradition of the Hebrews concerning God" (1: 1).[29]

Gen. 2:15 records, "And the LORD God took the man, and put him into the garden of Eden to dress it and to keep it." Mather, Patrick, and Tenison interpreted this so that it was the Shechinah that took the man and put him in the garden. By way of contrast, Grotius, following Rabbi Solomon, claims that one should understand it in the sense of *suasione*: God *recommends*, *persuades*, or *urges* him to go. Concerning Gen. 3:8 ("and they heard the voice of the LORD God walking in the garden in the cool of the day: and Adam and his wife hid themselves from the presence of the LORD God amongst the trees of the garden"), Grotius offers minimally: "with a certain unusual moving of the air, which is a sign of divine presence"[30] (1: 4) while no mention is made of *vocem Domini Dei*. There is also no reference to the "thick cloud" (Exod. 19:9). The opening words of Exod. 20, *locutus quoque est Dominus*, Grotius opines, refer *"Per Angelum"* (1: 33), provoking Poole's later criticism: "Immediately, and not by an Angel" (*Annotationes* [1683–85 ed.] on Exod. 20:1). In support of his argument, Grotius points out that "It is said of Josephus, that through the angels the law is given: Hebr. 1:1, 2:2" (1: 33).[31] The two aspects (Heb. 1:1 and 2:2) are negotiated and excused by Tenison (*Of Idolatry* 333–34) and later *ad verbum* by Mather [*BA*, Acts 7:2]. Interestingly, Grotius does not address the "glory of the Lord" which "filled the tabernacle" (Exod. 40). In fact, many of the major pas-

---

25 *"Ethnicorum scriptorum intempestive collatio"* (Kraus 53).

26 *"profanum ingenium, cui nihil pulchrum nisi ex gentilium lacunis haustum"* (Kraus 53).

27 *"tria prima corpora"* (Grotius 1: 1).

28 See for example, the gloss by Joannes Drusius (Johannes van den Driesche, 1550–1616) excerpted in Pearson's *Critici Sacri*: "Hic mysterium latere putant, pluralitatemque innui asserunt personarum ... Si singulariter, habetur sensus ratio, ut in, *creavit Deus*: si pluraliter, habetur ratio terminationis, ut in קדושים אלהים *Deus sanctus*." (1: col. 25).

29 "mos est Hebræis de Deo" (Grotius 1: 1).

30 "cum motu quodam aëris insolito, qui signum divinæ præsentiæ" (Grotius 1: 4).

31 "per Angelos data lex dicitur Iosepho: Hebr. I.1, II.2" (Grotius 1: 33).

sages addressing the visible presence of God in the Old Testament are either skipped over or addressed with exegetical precision.[32]

Regarding the oft-quoted Prov. 8:22 ("The LORD possessed me in the beginning of his way, before his works of old"), Grotius makes no mention of the Logos; he addresses, instead, the Chaldean version and the interesting use of ברא, as well as the LXX's ἔκτισέ[ν], both of which, as stand-alone words, implicitly challenge the preexistence theology. Nevertheless, *dubitando ad veritatem*, Grotius contends that "the sense is not bad, if *create* we take for *fashion in order to display*" (1: 249).[33] For Grotius, as Hubert Filser argues, *dogmata Christi* is not to be equaled with *omnia dogmata Christianismi* (222–23). The author of *Via ad Pacem Ecclesiasticam* (Grotius 3: 532) rather squares with certain fundamental aspects of Christology and other central doctrines.[34] Filser argues this constitutes his *regula fidei*. As Otto Ritschl summarizes the issue, this approach "requires no exact knowledge of the doctrines of the Trinity and the two natures of Christ" (284 f).[35] With Grotius, these traditional Christological entries into the Old Testament are read in a new historical way. Although Mather was well aware of these novel historical interpretations which viewed the Old Testament as a purely historical record, he carefully avoided them. He rather chose to preserve an older hermeneutical tradition in seeing Christ throughout salvation history, albeit with a newly available – and also, in another sense, historical – Rabbinic variation. Far from holding the traditional Christian position for tradition's sake, there is good reason to believe that Mather found this style of reading the Old Testament more profound and, indeed, more in accordance with the scholarly standards of divines. It is thus fully reasonable to argue that Mather's overlooking of Grotius's interpretation is linked to Mather's direct – or indirect (e.g., via Tenison, Patrick, et al.) – acquaintance with the explosion of Old Testament studies on the European continent, which began in the mid-sixteenth century at the outworking of the Reformation but blossomed in the seventeenth with the rise of the Christian Hebraists (Sebastian Münster [1489–1552], Johann Buxtorf, Samuel Bochart [1599–1667], and others).[36]

---

32 Grotius's methodology is prototypical of later Biblical scholars of the modern period, such as the founder of New Testament textual criticism, Johann Bengel (1687–1752), the influential literary historian Karl Lachmann (1793–1851), and the so-called founder of the modern historical critical method, Julius Wellhausen (1844–1918). Looking back before Grotius, we can already find pulses of this tradition in the Sozzinis, in John Colet's (c. 1467–1519) turn to the plain sense, and Martin Luther's (1483–1546) exclusion of the allegorical method, which followed Nicholas of Lyra's (c. 1270 – c. 1349) emphasis on the *sensus litteralis*.
33 "sensu non malo, si *creare* sumas pro *facere ut appareat*" (Grotius 1: 249).
34 "natum e virgine Spiritus sancri opera, judicem futurum viventium ac morentium, per eundem partam nostris peccatis veniam, Ecclesiamque ejus perpetuo duraturam" (Grotius 3: 752).
35 "Dagegen bedarf es dazu keiner genaueren Kenntnis der Lehren von der Trinität und den beiden Naturen Christi" (qtd. in Filser 224).
36 Mather's engagement with the Hebrew vowel signs controversy, in his master thesis, at-

Mather's Interpretation of the Shechinah in the "Biblia Americana"

Unlike the new humanist interpreters of the Old Testament, Mather sees passages such as Exod. 24,[37] which speak of the glory of God, as historical witnesses of Christ. With Mather, the glory of God or the presence of God in the Old Testament is often understood as Christ himself, the divine essence of Christ, or the second person of the Trinity before the incarnation. Mather thus incorporates a Christological account of Theophanies in the Old Testament and calls these, like Tenison, Shechinah. Mather understands both *glory* and *Shechinah* as mediators and direct agents of God as well as the physical and identifiable, indeed, personal, presence of God in the world. Whereas in the Old Testament the mediator of God, Christ, is present in the Shechinah, in the New Testament and the "most gracious *Dispensation*," this Mediator (μεσίτης, *mesites*, 1 Tim. 2:5[38]) took on flesh and "condescends unto the *Creatures*", as Mather writes in an Appendix to Rev. 17:

> The Divine Essence is also altogether *Incorporeal*, and *Invisible*; and utterly *Incomprehensible* by any Creature. How can what is *Finite*, comprehend what is *Infinite*?
>
> Wherefore, the Great God in the Communicating of Himself to the *Eye*, and the *Love* of any Finite Understanding, makes not the Communication, in the Way of meer *Intuition*, for no Creature can arise to *That*; nor does He make it by a meer *Intellectual Apprehension*; for *That* cannot be made without an *Idæa*. But He makes it by the Means of a certain *Oeconomy*, as the Ancients call it; a Voluntary Repræsentation and Exhibition; which may be called, The Divine *Shechinah*, or, Cohabitation.
>
> The Great GOD, in this most gracious *Dispensation*, condescends unto the *Creatures*, unto whom He will communicate Himself; They cannot otherwise Dispose or Conform themselves unto His Incomprehensible Majesty.

This identification threads through Mather's account of redemption history. As mentioned earlier, Mather here expands Abrabanel's identification of the Shechinah with the *"Glory of the Lord"* (Gen. 1:3) to encompass the locus where the "Son of God chose to lodge" (*BA* 1: 321). For his initial idea, Mather seems to have drawn on Patrick's commentary, for the bishop of Ely argues,

---

tests to an earlier, rather than later, interest in the European Hebraists (in this case, Ludwig Cappellus [1585–1658] and Johann Buxtorf the Younger [1599–1664]), their debates and theological orientations. On this, see Muller.

37 Exod. 24:15–18: "And Moses went up into the mount, and a cloud covered the mount. And the glory of the LORD abode upon mount Sinai, and the cloud covered it six days: and the seventh day he called unto Moses out of the midst of the cloud. And the sight of the glory of the LORD was like devouring fire on the top of the mount in the eyes of the children of Israel. And Moses went into the midst of the cloud, and gat him up into the mount: and Moses was in the mount forty days and forty nights."

38 1 Tim. 2:5 "For there is one God, and one mediator [μεσίτης] between God and men, the man Christ Jesus"

> Having spoken of the Creation of all things, now follows an account of their *Formation* out of that rude Matter which was at first *created*. And the first thing produced was *Light*. ... Abarbinel (upon the xlth of *Exodus*) takes this to be the *SHECHINAH*, the most excellent of all created things, called in Holy Scripture, *the Glory of the* Lord; which God, saith he, sealed up in his Treasures, after the *Luminaries* were created, to serve him upon special Occasions, (for instance, to lead the *Israelites* in the Wilderness, by cloudy Pillar of Fire) when he would make himself Present. ... But it seems to me most rational by this *Light* to understand those Particles of Matter, which we call *Fire*, (whose two Properties, every one knows, are *Light* and *Heat)* which the Almighty Spirit that formed all things, produced as the great Instrument, for the preparation and digestion of the rest of the Matter. (*Commentary upon the historical books* 3)

Significantly, Mather is less concerned with an atomistic or Cartesian explanation of this light (as Patrick ventures) but with a spatial identification of the Shechinah glory as the abode of Christ. Thus while Patrick's annotation reaches for a more scientific explanation of the universe- similar to Grotius's *tria prima corpora* explanation – Mather carries his high Christology forward in the creation account and synthetically encapsulates all of time and existence in Christ.[39] Here, Mather speaks of Christ's role in the creation of the world and his frequent appearances in history before the incarnation:

> Our Blessed *Mediator*, who was afterward, very frequently conversant on *Earth*, and appear'd in an *Humane Form* to the Patriarchs, & gave the *Law* in a *visible Glory*, and with an *audible Voice* on Mount *Sinai*, and guided the *Israelites* personally in a Pillar of *Fire* & *Cloud*, thro' the Wilderness, and inhabited between the *Cherubins* in the *Holy of Holies*, & took the peculiar Style, Titles, Attributes, Adoration, and Incommunicable Name of the God of *Israel*, and at last, was *Incarnate*, *Lived* a True Man among us, *Died* for us, and *Ascended* into Heaven, and still makes *Intercession* for us with the Father, and will come to *Judge the World in Righteousness* at the Last Day: That this very same Divine Person, was Actually & Visibly in an *Humane Shape*, conversant on *Earth*, and was really employ'd in this *Creation* of the World, (& particularly, in this peculiar Formation of *Man*,) so frequently ascribed unto him in the Holy Scriptures. (*BA* 1: 355)

In making this argument, Mather relies on many sources but Tenison is the primary influence. Published before Tenison became archbishop, *Of Idolatry* may very well have been a key source text for much of Mather's "Biblia Americana," which associates God's glory and many other supernatural occurrences in the Bible with the Shechinah. Mather draws from nearly every one of Tenison's epochs.

In addition to identifying God's eternal fiat "let there be light" with the Shechinah glory and Christ in his pre-incarnate existence, Mather also sees

---

39   On Gen. 1, *fiat lux:* "De his verbis vide Dionysii Longini locum, quem in dictis Annotatis protulimus ... tria prima corpora, terra, aër, ignis. Plut. & illa Parmenidis principia lucidum & tenebrosum" (Grotius 1: 1).

Christ in the splendor of God's glory appearing to our "First Parents" in Eden. At the fall of mankind, another aspect of this glory is seen. For Mather, Adam and Eve were not so foolish as to entertain conversation with the serpent in the garden. This manifestation of Satan was falsely portrayed as a vile serpent, Mather recalls, because Lucifer appeared in his true form as a glorious angel. Indeed, it was the angel's glorious splendor to which our parents were attracted in the first place, because they associated the angel's splendor with the Shechinah glory of the Logos [*BA*, Num. 21:9]. In like manner, Mather sees a Christophany in God's appearance to Adam and Eve after their fall. Mather asks,

> Q. What was the *Presence of the Lord*, from whence our Fallen Parents hid themselves? v. 8.
> A. The Son of God, now appeared in the very Glorious *Clouds*, or *Flames* of the *Shechinah*, with a most amazing Brightness. Probably, The *Shechinah* or the *Divine Majesty* appeared not now in so mild a Lustre, as when they were first acquainted with Him. No, but in a more terribly burning *Light*, which look'd as if it would consume them. So we know, He appeared, at the giving of the Law, upon Mount *Sinai* [Exod. 19.18. and Deut. 4.11] (*BA* 1: 483).

In this instance as in several others Mather relies on Tenison's reading of Theophilus of Antioch (later 2nd c.), an early Christian apologists. Tenison incorporates Theophilus's expansive history of the world as well as his early comparison of the Judeo-Christian and ancient Greek accounts of creation (*Autolykus*, esp. bk. 2). Theophilus's theology is thus interpreted to associate the Shechinah of the creation account (Gen. 1:3) with the one that cursed Adam and Eve (Gen. 3:8–19) as well as with the flaming Cherubim (Gen. 3:24) that stood guard at the entrance against their return. In addition to Bishop Theophilus of Antioch, Tenison also drew on the Targum Onkelos, medieval commentators such as Maimonides, and on Stillingfleet's careful analysis in *Shecinah*. The similarity between Mather's explication and that of Tenison is all too apparent in the following passage:

> And to Adam the Logos appeared, I know not whether I should say in the shape of man or in the way of a bright cloud moving in Paradise when the wind began to rise (a [Gen. 3.8–9]), and asking with a voice of Majesty, after his rebellious subject. And that this was the Son of God is insinuated by the *Targum* of *Onkelos* in the eighth verse of the third of *Genesis*. The Text of *Moses* is thus translated, *And when they* [our first Parents] *heard the voice of the Lord God*. But this is the sense of the words of *Onkelos*, *And they heard the voice of the Word of the Lord God*. (Tenison 321)

Mather was clearly persuaded by Tenison's interpretative stance regarding the Shechinah glory here, even if it went against the guidance of Patrick.[40] In Math-

---

40 Patrick – unlike Mather and Tenison – does not specify the Shechinah as the "Son of God," or the "Logos" here (Patrick, *Commentary* [1698 ed.] 68–69).

er's interpretation, then, the Son of God appears to our fallen progenitors not in the "mild Lustre" of the Shechinah of yore, but as a terrible burning light which threatens to consume them:

> [O]ne of the *Seraphim* (in *Moses*'s Age call'd *Cherubim,*) which alwayes attended the *Shechinah*, remained for a while there, darting out Flames on every Side of him, to terrify our First Parents from all Thoughts of being Re-admitted there. (*BA* 1: 500)

In synthetic fashion, then, Mather links the later account of the fall and expulsion in Gen. 3:24 with the Shechinahism in Gen. 1:3. However, in the former case, Mather does not explicitly link Christ with the command to leave the garden of Eden. It seems that the very nature of Christ as redeemer and reconciler would not fit comfortably, because the phrase *fiery swords* (as Dr. Nichols helps Mather to see) are perhaps better translated as *"Flame of Cutting,* or, a *Dividing Flame."* At any rate, Mather's conception of the Christophany was not set in stone, but remained flexible enough to explain the ungraspable, fearful, and attractive glory of God.

With Mather, the Shechinah as an interpretative device shows up in unexpected places. For instance, in the case of Cain's mark on his forehead, Mather reaches for new explanations: "Except we shall rather say, That the *Face* of *Cain*, was Blasted with Lightning from the *Shechinah*" (*BA* 1: 516–17). The Shechinah was involved not only with Cain but also with his brother Seth, who shared similar encounters: "But *Seth* is he, whom God from the *Shechinah*, Elected & Appointed, for the Second *Patriarch*, or *Emperour* of the World; the Successor to *Adam* in the Government of the World" (*BA* 1: 528). There are many other instances where Mather encounters the operation of the *Shechinah*. Following Tenison's precedent, he argues that the tower of Babel's "impious Design" was impeded by the Shechinah [*BA*, Acts 7:2]. Much later in his commentary on Acts 7, Mather carries out what amounts to a full account of salvation history by way of the Shechinah. Here, we learn that Abraham was visited several times by the Shechinah glory, that "God by such Appearances Encouraged Religion in the Holy Land" [*BA*, Acts 7:2]. Grounding his interpretation in Tenison's account of the Church Fathers, Mather maintains that "*Enoch* was Translated in some such visible Manner, as *Elijah* was afterwards, perhaps, with a glorious Appearance of the *Shechinah*" (*BA* 1: 538). Similarly, Mather incorporates Noah's ark in an interpretative framework that typifies the light of the church. There were holes in the ark to admit light, Mather remarks in his quest for allegorical parallels: "The *Church* is likewise a Place of *Light*; and from a Glorious Christ, that *Sun of Righteousness*, it fetches all its *Light*" (*BA* 1: 622). Not to leave anything out, Mather has the preachers, prophets, and patriarchs also enjoy this special encounter: "The Son of God, in the *Shechinah*, frequently made His Descent among them. ... *Cœlestial Apparitions* were very frequent among them. By the Inimitable *Glory* of the *Shechinah*, wherein the Son of God appeared" (*BA* 1: 561). Indeed, Mather discovers the Shechinah in places that a literal reading of the text might not necessarily permit.

Mather's reorientation of the messianic glory also helps us understand some of the specific theological nuances he introduces in his "Biblia Americana." The eponymous story of the burning bush is a notable example. Mather asks, "Is there any further, and higher Mystery, of the *Burning Bush*, to bee considered?" [*BA*, Exod. 3:2]. His answer reveals just how far he is prepared to deploy his Christological lens to detect evidence of the Shechinah in the Old Testament: "The Ancients considered, it, as a Figure of the *Messiah*, wherein the *Bush* of His *Humanity*, is possessed, & yett not consumed, by His *Divinity*, which is a *Consuming Fire*" [*BA*, Exod. 3:2]. From one major event to the next, Christ is present in the Shechinah and guides his people towards salvation at the parting of the Red Sea: "We are sure, the *Shechinah* was present; and the Divine Majesty employ'd His Angels in this Work" [*BA*, Exod. 14:21]. Whether surmounting the laws of nature or intercepting the enemies of Israel, the Shechinah is active in the history of redemption: "Probably, the *Cloudy* Part of the *Shechinah*, had been towards the *Egyptians* hitherto. It now turned the other side towards them; & the fiery Part appearing, both lett 'em see the Danger, into which they had thrown themselves, and by its amazing Brightness perfectly confounded them" [*BA*, Exod. 14:26]. This cloud was more than a natural cloud, Mather insists with the Torah commentary of the medieval Jewish philosopher Levi ben Gershom (1288–1344) at his side: "This *Cloud* was, (as R. *Levi ben Gersom* speaks,) An *Emanation* from God; and (as others of the *Jewes* express it,) a *Sign*, that God was Day & Night with them, to keep them from Evil" [*BA*, Exod. 13:21]. In such a fashion, Mather is able to reread difficult Bible passages in new ways. His annotations on Exod. 20:24 is another case in point. "In all places where I record my name I will come unto thee, and I will bless thee," Mather records the following gloss with the aid of the London Polyglot: "The *Chaldee* seems to have given us the True Intention. *In every Place where I shall make my Glory,* [that is, The SHECHINAH :] *to dwell, from thence I will bless thee*; that is, Hear thy Prayers."

This trend continues throughout the "Biblia." Apparently, the Shechinah became an essential interpretive key for Mather to unlock the hermeticism of many scriptural passages. Such is the case in a puzzling instance in Exodus where God did not strike down "the nobles of the children of Israel" even though "they saw God, and did eat and drink." Mather explains, "To sett this whole Matter, in its true *Light*, The *Shechinah*, of the *Divine Majesty*, surrounded with an Heavenly Host of *Angels*, was now seen by the *Elders* of Israel" [*BA*, Exod. 24:11]. Indeed, rather than casting them down as in St. Paul's case on the road to Damascus, the Shechinah "strengthened, & made [them] more Vigorous" [*BA*, Exod. 24:11]. This passage (and the events that follow) is a critical text in the history of Israel, for it climaxes in the giving of the law. In Mather's reading the cloud that enveloped Mt. Sinai was the Shechinah shining more glorious than the sun – as he comments on Exod. 24:16. It is interesting to note that Exod. 24:15–18 receives little attention in the massive volumes of the *Critici Sacri* (1660), where Hugo Grotius's apophatic remark resounds loudly: "this cloud signifies the weakness of our intellect concerning the divine."[41] Tellingly, Mather goes in the opposite direction with his interpretive key in his elucidation of the tabernacle and the "Holy of Holies," where he speaks of the *"Dwelling* of God." Again, his thematic reference becomes apparent: "Thus the Lord is *for a Sanctuary,* [Isa. 8.14.] when a *Stone of Stumbling, a Rock of Offence to both Houses of Israel.* More particularly, The *Tabernacle* signified, the *Humane Nature* of our Saviour; in which *there dwells the Fulness of the Godhead Bodily"* [*BA*, Exod. 25:40]. In this citation, Mather evinces yet again his awareness of the early church's Christological controversies. In this passage, he discovers not only a hidden allusion to Christ in the Old Testament but, more surprisingly, an allegory to the complex theology of Christ's two natures. At the mercy seat of God, Mather reasons, "Here was a *Cloud* filled with *Bright Rayes* of the Divine Majesty; the same that the Hebrewes call, The *Shechinah.* Intimating how there *Dwells* in our Lord, *the Fulness of the Godhead Bodily"* [*BA*, Exod. 25:40].

Legion are such instances in Mather's commentary on the Old Testament. At many of the meetings between God and Israel, Christ is present in the Shechinah, dwelling in magnificence as a token and sign of the mystery of the coming incarnation. If the glory of the Lord at Sinai "had no determinate *Form,* nor could ... be described by any *Art"* [*BA*, Exod. 24:11], Christ the Lord, the incarnate second person of the Trinity, is the concrete form of the glory of God. Christ is, as Mather remarks on Ps. 50:2, the "Perfection of Beauty" coming out of Zion:

Q. *Zion* here, why is it called, *The Perfection of Beauty?* v. 2.
A. According to the Chaldee, it is not *Zion,* but *God,* that is here called so; Namely, our Lord-Messiah, who is God. [*BA*, Ps. 50:2]

Christ is the specific form of glory – and the specific interpretative key for looking beyond the initial reading. In fact, this Christological specification is apparent throughout Mather's commentary on the Psalms. As if implying an analogical correspondence between the invisible glory of God and its physical manifestation in the glory of creation, Mather asks, in his gloss on Ps. 8,

Q. When was it that the Lord *sett His Glory above the Heavens?* v. 1.
A. It was done at the *Ascension* of our Lord JESUS CHRIST. This Text is to be

---

41 "Nubes hic significat imbecillitatem intellectus nostri circa Divina" (*Critici* 1: 615).

understood as intending that Illustrious Matter. And in this Hint, you have a *Key* to many more. [*BA*, Ps. 8:1][42]

To be sure, the glory of God Almighty is not *in* nature, but only beheld in and through Jesus Christ. Perhaps we should not push this point too far, but it seems that Mather does not intend to introduce an aesthetic of nature and of nature's beauty as the Romantics would do decades later. For Mather, the spiritual apprehension of this beauty occurs through the inner eye of the soul, but the visible composition of nature's beauty is habitually tied to a form, the figure of Christ. Again, Mather makes this point clear in his commentary on the Psalmist: "I will behold thy face in righteousness: I shall be satisfied, when I awake, with thy likeness" (Ps. 17:15). Mather asks, "What is that *Righteousness*, with which wee are to *behold the Face of God*?" Mather's response underscores his triumphant message: "Not one Word can I say, to withdraw you, from considering the Glorious Righteousness of the Lord Jesus Christ, as that by the Imputation whereof wee are fitted for our Appearance before God in Glory ... without which ... no man shall see the Lord" [*BA*, Ps. 17:15]. Christ is the mediator of God's glory and the most beautiful attraction that draws the elect unto God. Annotating Ps. 110:3 "Thy people shall be willing in the day of thy power, in the beauties of holiness from the womb of the morning: thou hast the dew of thy youth," Mather asks,

Q. What may be the *Beauties of Holiness*, here spoken of? v. 3.
A. Tis very sure, That the *Beauties* of the *Holy Jesus*, invite & allure His People, to become a *Willing People*; *Willing* to become *His People* [*BA*, Ps. 110:3].

The same son of God who confronted the sinful naked parents in the Garden of Eden as a terrifying burning light here shows the other side of the Shechinah glory: a magnetic beauty not to be enjoyed for its own sake but to attract the beholders with his alluring splendor "to become *His People*."

Another important moment in Mather's interpretation of the Shechinah can be found in his essay on Acts 7, which closely follows the path of Tenison's *Of Idolatry*. Acts 7 entails a long discourse on St. Stephen's beatific vision of Christ. The chapter is introduced with a description of the councilors sitting in Stephen's judgment: "And all that sat in the council, looking stedfastly on him, saw his face as it had been the face of an angel" (6:15). Stephen then relates his own salvation history, beginning with "the God of glory" that appeared to Abraham in his sojourn from Mesopotamia to Charran (Acts 7:2) and culminating

---

42 Mather's interpretation builds on the Psalmist's juxtaposition of the glory of God's creation and the divine charge of humanity to rule over the creation (see Gen. 1:26 f.; Ps. 8:6 f.): "O Lord our Lord, how excellent is thy name in all the earth! who hast set thy glory above the heavens. ... When I consider thy heavens, the work of thy fingers, the moon and the stars, which thou hast ordained; What is man, that thou art mindful of him? and the son of man, that thou visitest him?" (Ps. 8:1, 3–4).

in "the coming of the Just One" (Acts 7:52). Finally, pointing an accusing finger at his judges, the "betrayers and murderers" of Christ (Acts 7:52), Stephen is martyred even as he is "full of the Holy Ghost, looked up stedfastly into heaven, and saw the glory of God, and Jesus standing on the right hand of God, And said, Behold, I see the heavens opened, and the Son of man standing on the right hand of God" (Acts 7:55–56). Understandably, this story demanded Mather's full attention. If the glory of God appeared to the patriarchs in past epochs, this time, the Shechinah of the Lord is manifest *after* the death and resurrection of Christ. Mather's gloss on this chapter follows his source text closely as he draws a long ark from the Shechinah's first appearance in God's eternal *fiat* (Gen. 1:3) all the way to the Shechinah's presence in the celestial New Jerusalem at the end of the world. He speaks of it more specifically here:

> At this Time, The *Shechinah* will visit the World, with more Splendor than in the Ancient Generations, which is the Meaning of, *The Tabernacle of God with Men.* Christians also will no more Dy an untimely Death, but after a long Life, by a sleight Change, be translated into Everlasting Life. [*BA*, Appendix to Rev. 17][43]

For Mather, then, the Shechinah not only unifies the Old and New Testaments, but all of history and existence itself find themselves enveloped in this personalized glory of God.

A Brief Comparison of Mather's and Jonathan Edwards's Theological Aesthetics

Mather's Christological reading of the glory of God is in some ways different from the theological aesthetics of Edwards and his aesthetisized understanding of God's glory as beauty, excellency, and Christ, or the "beauty of Being itself," as Paul Ramsey calls it in his edition of Edwards's *Freedom of the Will* (Edwards 1: 51). Drawing on Poole's *Synopsis Criticorum*, Edwards occasionally employs the Christo-rabbinical interpretation of the Shechinah and clearly argues for a theology of preexistence and accounts of Christophanies.[44] For Edwards, however, Christology is not – as it is with Mather – the habitual center of his reflections on glory and beauty. If Mather personalizes and affixes glory to Christ, Edwards fastens glory to Christ *and* Plotinus's *impersonal prohodos*.[45] Edwards synthesizes these two accents and indeed emphasizes the per-

---

43   See Mather's long discussion of the glory of the celestial Jerusalem and its shining occupants, in *The Threefold Paradise* (245–67).
44   As Edwards remarks, "The saints in Israel looked on this person as their Mediator, through whom they had acceptance with God in heaven and the forgiveness of their sins, and trusted in him as such. Here see what Rabbi Menachem says of coming to God through the *shechinah*, in *Synopsis*, on Psalms 17:15" (21: 386).
45   A good example for this is the following passage from Edwards's "Miscellanies": "The

sonality of Shechinah as Christ.[46] Nonetheless, there is a very subtle shift of emphasis with Edwards, one that results in a minute but important difference in the contours of their aesthetics. With Mather, it is difficult to find passages with neoplatonic inflections like the ones in the following passage from Edwards's *Concerning the End for which God Created the World*:

> But he, from his goodness, as it were enlarges himself in a more excellent and divine manner. This is by communicating and diffusing himself; and so instead of finding, making objects of his benevolence: not by taking into himself what he finds distinct from himself, and so partaking of their good, and being happy in them; but by flowing forth, and expressing himself in them, and making them to partake of him, and rejoicing in himself expressed in them, and communicated to them. (8: 461–2)[47]

Edwards appears to synthesize Neoplatonism with Christian Hebraic commentary and Reformed theology. As he remarks in one of his "Miscellanies," "The flowing forth of the ineffably bright and sweet effulgence of the *shechinah* represented the flowing out and communicating of this, as well as the manifestation of his majesty and beauty" (20: 465). In contrast, the Shechinah glory with Mather appears, paradoxically, both nearer and at the same time further away. It is nearer because he refers to the Shechinah much more often and in places where one might not expect it; it is also nearer because the glory of God is usually clarified by the Shechinah and in most cases personalized by Christ, who endows her almost tangible personhood. In fact, the mystery of the Shechinah glory is often synonymous with Christ the Lord who, in Mather's reading, is indeed closer than expected. On the other hand, the Shechinah appears much more distant, because it also appears in cases where God meets out punishment to offenders. This, perhaps more sinister manifestation, can be seen in the mark

---

glory of the Lord in Scripture seems to signify the excellent brightness and fullness of God, and especially as spread abroad, diffused and as it were enlarged, or, in one word, the excellency of God flowing forth. This was represented in the *shechinah* of old. Here by "the excellency of God" I would be understood of everything in God in any respect excellent, all that is great and good in the Deity, including the excellent sweetness and blessedness that is in God, and the infinite fountain of happiness that the Deity is possessed of, that is called the fountain of life, the water of life, the river of God's pleasures, God's light, etc. The flowing forth of the ineffably bright and sweet effulgence of the *shechinah* represented the flowing out and communicating of this, as well as the manifestation of his majesty and beauty. Joy and happiness is represented in Scripture as often by light as by waters, fountains, streams, etc.; and the communication of God's happiness is represented by the flowing out of sweet light from the *shechinah*, as well as by the flowing forth [of] a stream of delights and the diffusing of the holy oil, called the fatness of God's house" (20: 465). Edwards's neoplatonic bend can be seen in his careful integration of the phrases "flowing forth," "emanation," "diffusing," "the excellency of God flowing forth," etc.

46 Edwards argues for a personal understanding of the Shechinah as Christ: "Christ, who is the essential glory of God and is that word, idea or essential character by which he is known to himself and his glory shines in his own eyes" (21: 380).

47 See also Munk's article on Edwards's interpretation of Shechinah.

of Cain that the Shechinah burns upon his countenance. In fact, Cain was actually "Blasted with Lightning from the *Shechinah*" (*BA* 1: 516). Mather's understanding of the glory of the Lord, then, is not yet infused with the aesthetization of Edwards's more generalized notion of glory. In this notion, beauty or excellency are inextricably bound together, reflecting the influence of the Cambridge Neoplatonists on Edwards. Glory with Mather, by contrast, is an extraordinary manifestation of the supernatural in the natural order, a discontinuity of unpredictable consequence. He does not understand glory as a static, passive essence of nature, or a subject of our artistic and humanistic appreciation. For Mather, it is not finally an object for human internalization, as becomes apparent in his comments on the cloud enveloping Mt. Sinai at the giving of the Law: "This Glorious Light, had no determinate *Form*, nor could ... be described by any *Art*" [*BA*, Exod. 24:11]. In Mather's view glory is also something unpredictable and even potentially dangerous. After all, its imitation enabled Satan to deceive our "First Parents" [*BA*, Num. 21:9]. Whereas Mather is thus still a far cry from what M. H. Abram's has called "natural supernaturalism" in the aesthetics of the Romantics, Edwards's theology seems to have moved a step in that direction.

Mather's Synthetic Theological Vision for Today

There are many more examples of Mather's Shechinah interpretation, as well as of his Christological theology of Glory in the "Biblia" and his other publications that deserve attention.[48] Likewise, a more thorough comparison of Mather's and Edwards's theologies of glory is clearly called for. For reasons of space, however, a brief return to Mather's *modus operandi* must suffice here. In his 1706 sermon *The Good Old Way*, he bemoans that

> The *Modern Christianity*, tis too generally, but a very *Spectre*, Scarce a *Shadow* of the *Ancient! Ah! Sinful Nation, Ah, Children that are corrupters*; What have your Hands done, to defile, and to deface, a *Jewel*, which Restored unto to its Native Lustre, would outshine the *Sun* in the Firmament! (3–4)

Perhaps there is something programmatically sentimental about Mather's theological vision; it is most certainly retrospective. Despite this obvious tendency, he does not appear to look back for the mere sake of looking back, as if the glory had departed and everything significant had happened in a distant past. Quite to the contrary! For Mather the truth of the faith is "yesterday, and to day, and for ever" (Heb. 13:8). In looking back *ad fontes*, he learns from the

---

48 Similar themes and a comparable Christological orientation can be found in many of Mather's shorter publications as well. See, for instance his *Christianus per Ignem* (esp. 53–60); *The Heavenly Conversation*; *Reason Satisfied*; *Thoughts for the Day of Rain*.

ancients, and in so doing, Mather attempts to restore a timeless truth and beauty so that it may be properly seen in its "Native Lustre." Indeed, he endeavors to show how God's glory is found, fulfilled, even subsumed, in the beauty of the Shechinah, which is all in all in Christ, "the Perfection of Beauty." Granted, there is something sentimental in Mather's theology, something that falls, perhaps, into Nietzsche's category of *monumentalische Historie* in one sense. Yet in another, Mather's theology offers a manifold Christological synthesis, according to which the eternal *forma Christi* constitutes the center of history.

The "Biblia Americana" is a theological work written by one who looked out onto the landscape of not only Newton and Grotius, but also Münster, Buxtorf, Bochart, and others. Mather attempts to harmonize and incorporate the innovations of his age while at the same time he carefully maneuvers through the humanist literature and attempts to avoid what he sees as its harmful tendencies. In this sense, Mather is an example of a mediator who stands between the polarities of what Hans Frei has called pre- and post-critical periods – if these categories are here applicable in the first place. Mather, then, does not neatly fit in either the pre-critical or the post-critical classification. As Reiner Smolinski claims regarding Mather's engagement with the European Spinozists,

> As if maintaining a double consciousness, he could comfortably employ Newtonian Science to celebrate the perfection of Nature's Laws even as he tacitly submitted to the existence of an invisible, moral entity that accomplished its grand purpose through secondary causes. (203)

The publication of the "Biblia Americana" calls for a rediscovery of – and a new critical engagement with – Cotton Mather as an unduly neglected patriarch of America's theological tradition. The breadth of his learning, polyglotism, wit, and omnivorous mind, and above all else, his realization that theology's end is the demonstration of the wonder and sentient mystery of the faith itself, is most apparent in this grand achievement of his life. As readers will find, this great inheritance from the New England colonial period easily fulfills its goal of presenting the relics and artifacts of faith in their "Native Lustre." Mather's incorporation of a rabbinic Hebraism in his Christological interpretation of the Old Testament is one example of the fruit of this synthetic theological vision.

Works Cited

Primary Sources

Critici Sacri, sive, Doctissimorum Virorum in SS. Biblia Annotationes & Tractatus. Eds. John Pearson, Anthony Scattergood, Francis Gouldman, and Richard Pearson. 9 vols. London, 1660.

Edwards, Jonathan. "Concerning the End for which God Created the World." *The Works of Jonathan Edwards. Ethical Writings*. Ed. Paul Ramsey. Vol. 8. New Haven: Yale UP, 1989.

–. *The Works of Jonathan Edwards. Freedom of the Will*. Ed. Paul Ramsey. Vol. 1. New Haven, Yale UP, 1957.

–. The *Works of Jonathan Edwards. The "Miscellanies," 833–1152*. Ed. Amy Plantinga Pauw. Vol. 20. New Haven: Yale UP, 2002.

–. *The Works of Jonathan Edwards. Writings on the Trinity, Grace, and Faith*. Ed. Sang Hyun Lee. Vol. 21. New Haven: Yale UP, 2003.

Grotius, Hugo. *Annotata Ad Vetus Testamentum*. Amsterdam, 1644.

–. *Opera Omnia Theologica, in tres tomos divisa, Operum theologicorum tomus primus, continens annotationes ad Vetus Testamentum*. 3 vols. London, 1679.

Henry, Matthew. *An Exposition of All the Books of the Old and New Testament*. 3rd ed. 6 vols. London, 1721–25.

Mather, Cotton. *Christianus per Ignem*. Boston, 1702.

–. *Coelestinus: A Conversation in Heaven*. Boston, 1723.

–. *Diary of Cotton Mather*. Ed. Worthington Chauncey Ford. 2 vols. Massachusetts Historical Society Collections 7th Series, Vol. VII–VIII). Boston: MHS, 1911–12.

–. *The Good Old Way. Or, Christianity Described, From the Glorious Lustre of It, Appearing in the Lives of the Primitive Christians. An Essay Tending, from Illustrious Examples of a Sober, & a Righteous, and a Godly Life, Occurring in the Ancient Church-History, to Revive the Languishing Interests of Genuine and Practical Christianity*. Boston, 1706.

–. *The Heavenly Conversation. An Essay Upon the Methods of Conversing with a Glorious Christ, In Every Step of Our Life. With Directions Upon that Case, How May the Consideration of Christ, Be Brought into All the Life of a Christian*. Boston, 1710.

–. *Paterna: The Autobiography of Cotton Mather*. Ed. Ronald A. Bosco. Delmar, NY: Scholar's Facsimiles & Reprints, 1976.

–. *Reason Satisfied: and Faith Established. The Resurrection of a Glorious Jesus Demonstrated by Many Infallible Proofs: and the Holy Religion of a Risen Jesus, Victorious Over All the Cavils of Its Blasphemous Adversaries*. Boston, 1712.

–. *Things for a Distress'd People to Think Upon*. Boston, 1696.

–. *Thoughts for the Day of Rain. In Two Essay's: I. The Gospel of the Rainbow. In the Meditations of Piety, on the Appearance of the Bright Clouds, with the Bow of God upon Them. II. The Saviour with His Rainbow. And the Covenant which God Will Remember to His People in the Cloudy Times that Are Passing Over Them*. Boston, 1712.

–. *The Threefold Paradise of Cotton Mather: An Edition of "Triparadisus."* Ed. Reiner Smolinski. Athens: U of Georgia P, 1995.

Mather, Increase. *Angelographia, Or a Discourse Concerning the Nature and Power of Holy Angels*. Boston, 1696.

Patrick, Simon. *A Commentary upon the First Book of Moses, called Genesis*. 2nd ed. London, 1698.

–. *A Commentary upon the historical books of the Old Testament*. 2 vols. London, 1697.

–. *A Commentary upon the historical books of the Old Testament*. 3rd ed. corr. 2 vols. London, 1727.

Poole, Matthew. *Annotations upon the Holy Bible. Wherein the Sacred Text is Inserted, and various Readings Annex'd together with Parallel Scriptures, the more difficult Terms in each Verse are Explained, seeming Contradictions Reconciled, Questions and Doubts Resolved, and the whole Text opened. By the Late Reverend and Learned Divine Mr. Matthew Poole.* 2 vols. London, 1683–85.

–. *Synopsis Criticorum Aliorumque S. Scripturæ Interpretum.* 5 vols. London, 1669–76.

Stillingfleet, John. *Shecinah: Or, a Demonstration of the Divine Presence In the places of Worship. Being An Essay, Tending to promote Piety, prevent Apostacy, and to reduce grosly deluded souls, first to their right wits, then to the right waies, of Gods Publick Instituted Worship.* London, 1663.

Tenison, Thomas. *Of Idolatry: A discourse in which is endeavoured a declaration of, Its Distinction from Superstition; Its Notion, Cause, Commencement and Progress; Its Practice Charged on Gentiles, Jews, Mahometans, Gnosticks, Manichees, Arians, Socinians, Romanist: As also, of the Means which God has vouchsafed toward the Cure of it by the Shechinah of His Son.* London, 1678.

Walton, Brian. *Biblia Sacra Polyglotta, Complectentia Textus Originales, Hebraicum, cum Pentateucho Samaritano, Chaldaicum, Graecum, Versionumque antiquarum, Samaritanae, Græcae LXXII Interp. Chaldaicae, Syriacae, Arabicae, Æthiopicae, Persicae, Vulg. Lat. Quicquid comparari poterat. Cum Textuum, & Versionum Orientalium Translationibus Latinis.* 6 vols. London, 1653–57.

Secondary Sources

Abrams, M. H. *Natural Supernaturalism: Tradition and Revolution in Romantic Literature.* London: Oxford UP, 1971.

Brown, Francis., S. R. Driver and Charles A. Briggs, eds. *A Hebrew and English Lexicon of the Old Testament.* Oxford: Clarendon Press, 1906.

Carpenter, Edward. *Cantuar. The Archbishops in their Office.* 3rd ed. London: Wellington House, 1997.

–. *Thomas Tenison, Archbishop of Canterbury. His Life and Times.* London: SPCK, 1948.

Filser, Hubert. *Dogma, Dogmen, Dogmatik: eine Untersuchung zur Begründung und zur Entstehungsgeschichte einer theologischen Disziplin von der Reformation bis zur Spätaufklärung.* Münster: LIT Verlag, 2001.

Frei, Hans W. *The Eclipse of Biblical Narrative: A Study in Eighteenth and Nineteenth-Century Hermeneutics.* New Haven: Yale UP, 1974.

Goldberg, Arnold. *Untersuchungen über die Vorstellungen von der Schekhina in der frühen rabbinischen Literatur, Talmud und Midrasch.* Studia Judaica. Bd. 5. Berlin: Walter De Gruyter, 1969.

Kraus, Hans-Joachim. *Geschichte der historisch-kritischen Erforschung des Alten Testaments.* 3rd ed. Neukirchen-Vluyn: Neukirchner Verlag, 1982.

Levin, David. *Cotton Mather: The Young Life of the Lord's Remembrancer 1663–1703.* Cambridge: Harvard UP, 1978.

–. "When Did Cotton Mather See the Angel?" *Early American Literature* 15.3 (1980/81): 271–75.

Muller, Richard A. "The Debate over the Vowel Points and the Crisis in Orthodox Hermeneutics." *Journal of Medieval and Renaissance Studies* 10 (1980): 53–72.

Munk, Linda. "His Dazzling Absence: The Shekinah in Jonathan Edwards." *Early American Literature* 27.1 (1992): 1–30.

Mutius, Hans Georg von. "Isaak Abrabanel." *Theologische Realenzyklopädie*. Eds. Gerhard Krause, Gerhard Müller, et al. Vol. 16. Berlin: De Gruyter, 1997–2007. 42 vols. 302–04.

Oxford English Dictionary Online. Oxford UP. Web. 10 Oct. 2009.

Podella, Thomas. "Herrlichkeit Gottes: I. Alter Orient und Altes Testament." *Religion in Geschichte und Gegenwart*. 4th ed. Ed. Hans Dieter Betz et al. Vol. 3. Tübingen: Mohr Siebeck, 1998–2007. 9 vols. 1681–82.

Ritschl, Otto. *Dogmengeschichte des Protestantismus: Grundlagen und Grundzüge der theologischen Gedanken- und Lehrbildung in den protestantischen Kirchen*. Bd. 4. Leipzig: Hinrichs, 1927.

Schäfer, Peter. *Mirror of His Beauty: Feminine Images of God from the Bible to the Early Kabbalah*. Princeton: Princeton UP, 2002.

"Shechinah." *Cyclopedia of Biblical, Theological and Ecclesiastical Literature*. Eds. John McClintock and James Strong. Vol. 9. Repr. Grand Rapids: Baker: 1981. 12 vols. 637–39.

Silverman, Kenneth. *The Life and Times of Cotton Mather*. New York: Harper & Row, 1984.

–. Rev. of *Paterna*, ed. by Ronald A. Bosco "With a Note on the Date of Cotton Mather's Visitations by an Angel." *Early American Literature* 15.1 (1980): 80–85.

Smolinski, Reiner. "Authority and Interpretation: Cotton Mather's Response to the European Spinozists." *Shaping the Stuart World 1603–1714: The Atlantic Connection*. Ed. Allan I. Macinnes, Arthur H. Williamson. Dortrecht and Boston: Brill, 2006. 175–203.

Urban, Wacław. "Sozzini/Sozinianer." *Theologische Realenzyklopädie*. Eds. Gerhard Krause, Gerhard Müller, et al. Vol. 31. Berlin: DeGruyter, 1997–2007. 42 vols. 598–604.

Michael P. Clark

The Eschatology of Signs in Cotton Mather's "Biblia Americana" and Jonathan Edwards's Case for the Legibility of Providence

Cotton Mather had a life-long interest in the nature of signs, particularly those that could be used to discern spiritual truths. That interest was based on a profound ambivalence about the capacity of material signs to lead us beyond knowledge of the visible world now that the time of miracles and direct revelation was past. For Mather and most other Puritans, human understanding never "starts" with revelation, and it cannot get there through reason and empirical observation. Suspended historically between medieval mysticism and the Deist rationalism of the Enlightenment, Puritanism was caught between the promise of faith and the limits of reason and the senses, and Mather faced an especially difficult struggle with this irremediable antinomy. As Reiner Smolinski has recently shown, Mather was strongly invested in scientific speculations about the natural causes behind miraculous or supernatural events described in Scripture ("Natural Science and Interpretation").[1] This fascination with the emergent empiricism of Newtonian science joined with Mather's exegetical interest in Euhemerist hermeneutics to produce naturalistic readings of scriptural events, starting with the Mosaic hexameron and looking forward to apocalyptical catastrophes.[2] His empiricism even invaded Mather's soteriology, as when he urges the Jews to make an "Experiment" of the salvific power of Christ: "He is THE *Saviour*. Oh! That you would at last make the happy Experiment! *Come*

---

1 On the more general issue of Mather's role in adapting European rationalism to the strong spiritual (not to say mystical) dimension of American Puritanism, see Smolinski, "Authority and Interpretation," and Solberg's introduction to his edition of Mather's *The Christian Philosopher*.

2 Euhemerism treated mythology as an allegorical account of actual historical events. Christian exegetes adopted the method to propose naturalistic explanations of what scripture presents as supernatural miracles (see Brown). On Mather's use of Euhemerism, see Maddux's essay in this volume. In "God's Responsibility," Maddux analyzes the relation between Mather's biographical interest in the natural events of human history and the narrative of God's providential plan. Rivers characterizes this synthetic impulse in Mather somewhat facilely as "an easy reconciliation between religion and science" (185), but she goes on to note that not all of Mather's Puritan colleagues shared his enthusiasm for joining religious and scientific topics. Samuel Sewall observed in his journal, "Dr. C. Mather preaches excellently from Ps. 37. Trust in the Lord &c. only spake of the Sun being in the centre of our System. I think it inconvenient to assert such problems" (Sewall 2: 779; qtd. in Rivers 186).

and See; see, see, whether you do not find Him so!" (*Things* 12). At the same time, Mather reported personal encounters with angels, believed in the revelation of "particular faiths" that guided his life, and solemnly wrote about witnessing spectral torments – including an actual levitation in the midst of a crowded room – and other pneumatological phenomena at a time when such mystical topics were beginning to disappear from learned discourse.[3]

Over the course of his career the discrepancy between these two exegetical proclivities led Mather to develop an extraordinary and idiosyncratic repertoire of mediatory concepts designed to join the material world of matter to the invisible world of spirit. Whereas the physico-theologians were intent on an epistemological demonstration of how we can know God's attributes from an analysis of natural events, Mather repeatedly interrogated the ontological relation between matter and spirit that would allow us to experience some bit of that spirit, however fragmented and degraded, within the corporeal limits of the material world.[4] So, in the *Angel of Bethesda* Mather proposes a "plastic spirit" and the "Nishmath Chajim" or "breath of life" as fungible forces capable of moving between, and so joining, matter and spirit to produce liminal phenomena that cannot be consigned entirely to either realm.[5] Such mediating concepts carry with them more than a whiff of philosophical desperation when encountered in Mather's work; Kenneth Silverman has characterized them as Mather's "unified field theory."[6] They would be little more than antiquarian curiosities if they were not closely related to Mather's much more profound and innovative investigations into the nature of signs. Commenting on Revelation in his "Biblia Americana," for example, Mather portrays the ontological paradox of spirit co-existing with flesh as what he calls an "Oeconomy" of representation:

> The Divine Essence is also altogether *Incorporeal*, and *Invisible*; and utterly *Incomprehensible* by any Creature. How can what is *Finite*, comprehend what is *Infinite*?
>
>   Wherefore, the Great God in the Communicating of Himself to the *Eye*, and the *Love* of any Finite Understanding, makes not the Communication, in the Way of meer *Intuition*, for no Creature can arise to *That*; nor does He make it by a meer

---

3   Mather reports the levitation in affidavits enclosed with his letter to Robert Calef of 15 Jan. 1693/4 commenting on the case of Margaret Rule. See Calef (60). On Mather's pneumatological research and his interest in angels, see Silverman, ch. 4.

4   Two of the most important works of physico-theology are Ray (whom Rivers characterizes as "the father of natural science in Britain" [187]) and Derham. Rivers claims that Derham "was one of the models for Mather's own work in the field of natural science" (187).

5   Wise's paper in this collection discusses the *Nishmath Chajim* as a mediating concept between the mystical and empirical strains in Mather's thought. See also Smolinski (*Triparadisus* 122–26) and Warner.

6   "The Nishmath-Chajim is his fullest elaboration, after years of pondering the notion, of the plastic spirit, an attempt to harmonize his scientific and religious ideas, his understanding of matter and of spirit, his natural philosophy and pneumatology, his vitalistic and mechanistic views of the universe – Mather's own unified field theory" (Silverman 408–09).

Intellectual Apprehension; for *That* cannot be made without an *Idæa*. But He makes it by the Means of a certain *Oeconomy*, as the Ancients call it; a Voluntary Repræsentation and Exhibition; which may be called, The Divine *Shechinah*, or, Cohabitation.

The Great GOD, in this most gracious *Dispensation*, condescends unto the *Creatures*, unto whom He will communicate Himself; They cannot otherwise Dispose or Conform themselves unto His Incomprehensible Majesty. [*BA*, Appendix to Rev. 17].[7]

Mather's place in intellectual history might be characterized in part by his attempt to work through the conflict between matter and spirit with a precise and highly articulated theory of signs – a new science that the main founder of the Royal Society, John Wilkins, coined as "semaeologia," or semiology, in 1641.[8] Wilkins was primarily interested in the correspondence between signs and the objects to which they referred, or what today would be called the signifier and its referent. The clarity and precision of the concept or meaning derived from that connection, i.e., what modern semiologists would call the "signified," depended on the stability of the referential bond. The ideal for Wilkins was a one-to-one correspondence between sign (or signifier) and its referent that would produce a semantically stable, universal language. At its best, the signifier simply substituted for the thing, a discursive convenience that saves us the time and energy of having to haul around a bagful of empirical objects to support our empirical claims.[9] For the Puritans, who were closely associated with the Royal Society, this theory of a scientific language model reinforced their iconoclastic distrust of material signs and rhetorical ornaments. Such flourishes reeked of popery and were thought to distract believers from the spiritual meaning conveyed. Self-consciously rhetorical language instilled a taste for the sauce rather than the meat of discourse, as Thomas Hooker put it when advocating a plain

---

7   Consideration of Mather's commentary on Revelation in the "Biblia Americana" was greatly facilitated by a draft transcription prepared by Reiner Smolinski and his team of graduate students.

8   The first appearance of "seimiology" listed by the *OED* is 1641 in John Wilkins's *Mercury*. *Mercury* was published anonymously as a cryptographic treatise intended to support the war effort. (Wilkins was married to Robina Cromwell, sister of Oliver Cromwell.) Wilkins (1614–72) was Bishop of Chester and became the first Secretary of the Royal Society in 1660. He is best known for a*n Essay towards a Real Character and a Philosophical Language* (1668).

9   Robert Markley describes these attempts to establish a universal language by Wilkins and other scientists "as failed efforts to idealize the material order of 'things,' a semiotics of the 'real,' that could serve as the basis of an authoritative rendering of the natural and political world." He goes on to argue that in such schemes "the interlocking discourses of theology, semiotics, and natural philosophy" converged to confront "the crisis of Baconianism in the late seventeenth century: the problems of practicing and defending natural philosophy without a theory, a metalanguage, to negotiate between a fallen nature and its divine Creator" (9–10). We may read "Biblia Americana" as Mather's effort to create just such a "metalanguage" by joining science and theology in the study of scriptural signs.

style of preaching.[10] Mather, of course, was famously eager to be counted among the Fellows of the Royal Society (and eventually was in 1713), and the topics and terminology of this new science of semiology exist in his work alongside more traditional hermeneutic techniques Mather found in biblical commentaries by Matthew Poole, Matthew Henry, Simon Patrick and other exegetes of his time.

This essay will argue that, as a consequence of the abovementioned tensions and conflicts, Mather developed what I will call an eschatological semiotics. Generally speaking, this semiotics was still rooted in a strictly dualistic ontology that made a sharp distinction between the world of nature and a higher realm of the spirit, and hence assumed that the spiritual significance of natural or historical referents could not be completely known to the finite mind of mortal man. More specifically, Mather thought that the full meaning of signs, including those given in the scriptures, would not be revealed on this side of the millennium. At the same time, his exegetical writings show how this rather pessimistic belief in the continuous temporal deferral of scriptural meaning was frequently counterbalanced by the hopeful expectation that, with the end-time approaching, more and more glimpses of divine truth could be caught through the disintegration of material signifiers. In his "Biblia Americana" – and especially in his commentary on Hebrews and Revelation – Mather thus sketches out a hermeneutics that seeks to look beyond the progressively disintegrating referents of the biblical texts and their *sensus literalis* in order to grasp their true significance. As I will suggest in my concluding remarks, this eschatological semiotics differs markedly from the more neoplatonic theory of signs which Mather's great successor in the New England tradition, Jonathan Edwards, embraced, and which gave him much more confidence in the legibility of the scriptures even before the end of days.

The simultaneous – or, more precisely, coterminous – existence of two or more levels of meaning in signs has a long history in Christian hermeneutics. It is evident as early as Philo of Judea in the first century C.E., continuing through Augustine and Aquinas, and persisting in Protestant interpretive practice despite the rejection of the four-fold hermeneutics of Scholastic theology.[11] In the

---

10   "As it is beyond my skill, so I professe it is beyond my care to please the nicenesse of mens palates, with any quaintnesse of language. They who covet more sauce then meat, they must provide cooks to their minde" ("Preface" to *A Survey of the Summe of Church-Discipline*). On the Puritans' ambivalence toward the power and danger of material signifiers, see Kibbey.

11   On the four-fold interpretation of scriptural signs, see Thomas Aquinas's *Summa Theologica* (1256–72), especially Part One, Question One, Article 10 (Ia.Q1.10). There Aquinas proposes four levels of meaning for scriptural signs: (1) historical and literal references; (2) allegorical (what Puritans would call typological) parallels between Old and New Testaments; (3) tropological or moral figuration of Christ as exemplum; and (4) the anagogical prolepsis that points from the mysteries of the present toward future revelations. Drawing on

hands of Reformers, Scholastic exegesis was often simplified into a two-fold interpretation of individual signs that distinguished more simply between literal or historical referents on the one hand and, on the other, spiritual or mystical meanings. As Mather puts it in his commentary on Revelation,

> Sometimes the Lord speaking of a *Spiritual* Thing, uses an Expression evidently allusive to some corporeal & material Thing heretofore occurring in the History. Thus, The New Condition of things, whereto our Lord brings His Church, is called, *A New Creation*; which intimates, that the first Chapter of *Genesis* had *Mystery* in it, as well as *History*. [*BA*, Rev. 2:1]

The spiritual continuity that held the four levels together in the Scholastic sign was rejected by Reformed theology, however, in favor of a purely symbolic or semiological association between the "History" and the "Mystery," i.e., between the material sign and its spiritual signified, a point illustrated in the Calvinist rejection of transubstantiation. Nevertheless, polysemantic interpretation persisted even in Reformed accounts of the figural dimension of scriptural language and of typological parallels between Old and New Testaments, which often resembled what Aquinas called the allegorical and anagogical levels of meaning. When those typological parallels were extended to link scriptural paradigms to natural or historical events up to the present time, as in Mather's *Magnalia Christi Americana*, typological interpretation was often indistinguishable from Aquinas's tropological or "moral" interest in aligning Old Testament figures or types with Christ as the antitype.[12]

After more than a half-century of relentless interrogation by scholars of American intellectual history, typology has become so closely identified with Puritan hermeneutics that it is difficult to remember, or even see on the page, the congeries of other methodological influences and exegetical practices that affected the way Puritans interpreted signs. Among those other attitudes toward scriptural interpretation was what Lisa Gordis describes as an "underlying ... distrust of human interpretive authority" that eroded confidence in the ability of readers – especially lay readers and untrained ministers – to perceive the connection between the literal and spiritual meanings of signs (2; see also 113–21 and 193–94). The problematic nature of interpretation was certainly not lost on Cotton Mather, whose insistence on the limits of human reason and corporeal vision was reinforced by his guarded interest in the historical-contextual critique of biblical authority that emerged in the second half of the seven-

---

Augustine's *On Christian Doctrine*, Aquinas claimed that the exegete's ability to negotiate through those levels depended on the state of one's soul, with natural man attaining "intellectual truths through sensible things" and those in a state of grace reading through those "things" to the spiritual meaning reflected in their own hearts (*Summa* Ia.Q1.9.). For a discussion of the four-fold hermeneutic and preaching in the Middle Ages, see Caplan.

12 On the distinction between typological and allegorical interpretation, and on the Platonic origins of the latter, see Lowance's "Images."

teenth century. Hobbes and especially Spinoza argued that associations between material signs and their purported spiritual significance might be arbitrary conventions, fanciful delusions, or even fraudulent mystifications. This
semiological skepticism undermined the divine authority of the scriptures and
opened up biblical interpretation to rational analysis and historical verification
by reference to the time and place at which a particular book was written.[13]
Smolinski argues that Mather cautiously responded to this hermeneutic "crisis
of certitude" in the "Biblia Americana," resisting the full-blown skepticism of
the historical critics. Mather acknowledged the complicated genealogy of scriptural texts and occasional anachronistic references, but he defended the latter as
merely rhetorical necessities required to update older accounts for later readers
(Smolinski, "Authority and Interpretation" 190). So, while Mather conceded
that "Revelation must be *local*, and be in a certain *Place*; because no Creature
can be every where" [*BA*, "Appendix" to Rev. 17:18], he claimed that historical
inconsistencies and textual variants were merely the accidents of transmission,
epiphenomena of the vagaries of human experience that had nothing to do with
the doctrinal truth that inspired them.[14] Nevertheless, getting at that inspired
truth remained problematic for Mather. Although saved from skepticism by
what Smolinski describes as a "practical certainty" in the experience of faith
("Authority and Interpretation" 201–03), Mather's certainty in faith stopped
well short of interpretive confidence in the spiritual significance of material
signs, even for the most saintly of worldly readers. He had none of the neoplatonic optimism in allegorical correspondence between nature and divinity that
would transform Puritan hermeneutics in the hands of Jonathan Edwards a few
years later.

Mather attempted to resolve this hermeneutic tension between skepticism
and faith through analysis of how semiotic properties of scriptural signs join
material things and images to the spiritual truths with which they are associated. In his commentary on Revelation, Mather proclaims his intention to "declare the *Lawes* of *Allegorical Expositions*" that should govern interpretation of

---

13   See Spinoza, ch. 6 et passim. In his discussion of Spinoza's influence on Mather, Smolinski points out that "to Spinoza, supernatural revelation is the least trustworthy of all forms of
human knowledge. Even the Bible demands confirmation by signs. Yet these signs and wonders were not uniformly accepted. ... [W]hatever the ancients could not explain, they esteemed a prodigy and a miracle, when in truth such signs were little more than natural phenomena of which the secondary causes were not easily understood" ("Authority and Interpretation" 196).

14   Mather did not hesitate to question and correct the language of scriptural text if it conflicted with his understanding of doctrine. Despite his strong philological interest in the etymology of scriptural terms and a comparative perspective that juxtaposed different translations of a particular passage in search of the most accurate rendering of the original, when a
clear answer was not evident Mather often relied on an experiential confirmation of theological doctrine as the ultimate test of his exegesis (Smolinski, "Authority and Interpretation"
202).

the Seven Epistles to the Seven Churches. He promises to "bring some Thoughts to maintain the meer *Historical Sense* of the *Seven Epistles*; that is to say, to argue for the *Literal* Accommodation of the *Epistles*, unto the Particular Churches whereto they were directed; but, by no means Exclude the Interests which the Faithful & the Churches of all Ages have therein." In such cases, Mather explains, the spiritual and historical meanings associated with scriptural signs act as interpretive limits that can be approached only as we understand those signs to be a conjunction of matter and spirit rather than one or the other. So, on the one hand,

> Men may not at their own meer Will and Pleasure, coin Expositions, which never were intended by the Spirit of God. The Curiosity of discovering *Allegories*, where they never were intended, may easily be carried farther than it should be; and we know how *Jerom* censured it unto the *Oneiracriticks*, wherein People interpreted the *Phantasms* of their strange Dreams. [*BA*, Rev. 2:1]

Conversely, just as men may not spin out allegorical fantasies from thin air, they are also forbidden to treat material things as if they embodied the mysteries that they signify. To reduce the spiritual significance of a sign to the material signifier was an error characteristic of idolaters who attribute divine properties to mere things in the guise of fetishes and relics, a practice he associates with the Church of Rome:

> The *Body* of CHRIST, they own the very *Sacrament* thereof to be *God*, the very *God*, and the Great Creator of the World. What a *Blasphemy*! while they make it also the true Substantial Body of CHRIST, and yett own, that it may be eaten by *Rats* as well as *Men*, and stol'n, or pawn'd, & carried about in the Pocket of a wretched *Sacrificer*. ... Yea, the very *Stocks* and *Stones* worshipped by the *Papists*, if they had *Ears to hear*, and *Eyes to see*, and *Mouthes to speak*, would complain, that they by their *Adorers* they were themselves *Blasphemed*: For, as hard as they are, they would not have so hard a Forehead, as knowingly to admit the Honours of their Great Creator. [*BA*, Rev. 17:18]

As we shall see, Mather himself was intensely interested in the role of Christ's flesh as a pathway to spirit, but here that path is blocked by a focus on the flesh as a material object, hard and opaque as the stones that would be embarrassed to be so honored by the Papists – *if* they possessed the animate spirit attributed to them by idolaters. In the Church of Rome, Mather says, every "*outward Act of Worship is Idolatrous*" precisely because it is entirely "outward," directed toward the material surface of the sign rather than to its spiritual meaning:

> Now tis Evident, They *bow*, they *kiss*, they burn *Incense*, they *kneel* before their *Images*; in that Posture of Address, they say their *Prayers* with their Eyes upon their *Images*; which to the Beholder looks as if they said their Prayers unto *them*. As to the *Outward Act*, they worship *them*, in these Addresses. Nay, they confess they do so; they Proclaim it, they Enact it, as a *Law*; they curse, & Persecute the Opposers of this Worship. [*BA*, Rev. 17–18]

Thus the entire authority of the Roman Church is imaginary, Mather claims: "The *Pope* is an *Image*, and not the Thing itself." His authority is mere illusion, sustained by a glittering surface of things without spiritual substance or meaning, and therefore vulnerable to simple verbal negation at the level of the sign itself, the mere word: "The *Roman Church* is an *Empire*. However, it is but an *Image* of an *Empire*; an *Imaginary Empire*; an *Empire* founded only in a Deceived *Imagination*. There needs no more, than for Men to say, NOT, and the *Empire* of *Antichrist* is destroy'd" [*BA*, Rev. 13:14–15].

Mather's economy of representation is intended to steer a safe course between oneiric fantasy and material idolatry in scriptural interpretation. His strategy is to approach signs within an eschatological framework linking the material dispensation of the universe, which separated matter and spirit at the moment of creation, to the resolution of that ontological opposition at the end of time. At its most general level, this eschatological semiotics simply reflects the proleptic thrust of all prophetic scripture, which describes a world in waiting, as it were, for the revelation of its true meaning. Thus Mather, in commenting on Dan. 12:4, quotes Burnet's *Essay on Scripture-Prophecy* to make the point that the referential connections of prophecy to the present (or past) world depend on future events for their complete meaning:

Q. A Remark on that, *Seal the Book, even to the time of the End*? v. 4.
A. The Book in the V. Chapter of the *Revelation*, is in all appearance, the same Book, in which *Daniel* is ordered, *To Shutt up the Words, and Seal the Book, even to the Time of the End*, when it was to be further explained by *John*, and *unsealed*, in order of Time, as the *Events* were to happen, which are the only compleat Interpreters of Prophecy; According to *Peters* Observation, *That no Prophecy of the Scripture, is its own Interpreter*.

If therefore, that *Time of the End* is not already come, it is in vain to attempt any Explanation of the Periods mentioned in the Chapter of *Daniel*: For *the Words are Closed up, & Sealed until the Time of the End*. But, when that *Time* comes, *Many shall be purified & made white, & tried, but the Wicked shall do wickedly, and none of the Wicked shall understand, but the Wise shall understand*. So that as certainly, as the Prophecy ought to be obscure, till that *Time*, it ought to be plain after it is come, to those who are meant by, *The Wise*. And if it can be shewn, what those Events are, which the Prophecy refers to, and that they are already happened, in order, as they are described by *Daniel*, and explained by *John*, Then it must be confessed, That the *Time* is come, and that *those who will not understand, are Wicked*: that is, Engaged in Interest to oppose the Truth; and will deserve to have applied unto them, what our Saviour on a like Occasion says of the Pharisees, *O Ye Hypocrites, Can Ye not discern the Signs of the Times*? [*BA*, Dan. 12:4][15]

15 William Burnet (1688–1729) published *An Essay* anonymously while he was governor of New York (1720–28). Reiner Smolinski provided a draft transcription of Mather's commentary on Daniel that first directed my attention to the passages quoted here.

An illustration of this temporal signifying can be found later in Mather's commentary on Daniel when he describes the way Christ used things of the present to represent his spiritual meaning, which would be unveiled in the apocalypse: "He makes the *Destruction* of the *Temple*, and Literal *Jerusalem*, a *Sign* of what was to befall *His own Church*, which was not so very *Near*, but of which other Events that were very *Near*, would be a *Sign*, and be a *Parable* for their Instruction" [*BA*, Dan. 12:12]. Lacking that omniscient perspective, Mather can do no more than anticipate that confirmation of spiritual signification by treating the signs of *our* time – the words of the scripture as well as the objects and events to which they refer – as an ontologically ambivalent realm. That ambivalence creates meaning by deferring reference from the visible, material world (subject to empirical description and, later, rational analysis) to the invisible, spiritual world (available only through mystical revelation and, hence, inaccessible to reason and the senses). Mather believed that understanding this deferral allows us some insight into the spiritual significance of material things by making it possible to foresee, in semiotic terms, the conjunction of matter and spirit at the end of time as believers experience that conjunction proleptically in the temporal disintegration of the material signifier. The referential status of signs thus serves as a precise measure of the interpreter's place in the eschatological scheme of time. That place was to be discovered through a close interrogation of the materiality of the sign itself in a method of interpretation that is more properly semiological than typological and that is informed as much by the inchoate empiricism of seventeenth-century scientific investigation as by Reformed hermeneutics and the more traditional exegetical controversies of the era.

A quick and dramatic illustration of Mather's semiotic hermeneutics can be found in his early work *Wonders of the Invisible World*.[16] In his infamous defense of the Salem witchcraft trials of 1692, Mather catalogs the many anomalous natural events that preceded the trials: comets, fires, and earthquakes being the most common. He describes their natural causes and distinguishes those causes carefully from the spiritual causes that resemble them. There is an ontological barrier between flesh and spirit in our time that protects the natural world from direct spiritual affliction, Mather says. However, as the end of time approaches that barrier will erode and natural causality will be replaced by direct spiritual intervention:

> One *Woe* that may be look'd for is, A frequent Repetition of *Earthquakes*, and this perhaps by the energy of the Devil in the *Earth*. The Devil will be clap't up, as a Prisoner in or near the Bowels of the earth, when once that *Conflagration* shall be dispatched, which will make, *The* New *Earth wherein shall dwell Righteousness;* and that *Conflagration* will doubtless be much promoted, by the Subterraneous *Fires*, which are a cause of the *Earthquakes*, in our Dayes. (26)

---

16 The following remarks on Mather's *Wonders* are based on an extended reading of that work in Clark (115–30).

Mather's point here is that we can determine our proximity to the end of time by the extent to which the spiritual significance of the event is joined to the material sign in either a metaphorical or literal way. If current events exceed what can be explained by natural causes, we must be approaching the end of time, when the distinctions between literal references to the visible world of matter and metaphorical references to the invisible world of spirit will collapse. If, as Mather fears, witchcraft has broken down the barrier between the visible world of nature and the invisible world of spirit, then the end of time is near, and the stench of fire and brimstone will no longer be merely an allegorical promise of spiritual tribulation; it will become a horribly literal torment: "Behold, sinners, Behold and *Wonder*, lest you *Perish*: the very *Devils* are Walking about our Streets, with Lengthened *Chains*, making a dreadful Noise in our Ears, and *Brimstone* even without a Metaphor, is making an Hellish and Horrid Stench in our Nostrils" (66).

A similar interest in the eschatological dimension of signs pervades Mather's commentary on The Epistle to the Hebrews in the "Biblia Americana." Hebrews is addressed to converted Jews in Israel or Judea who are a generation removed from the first Christians.[17] That means their experience of Christ's words and the time of "signs and wonders" is necessarily based on second-hand reports, "confirmed unto us by them that heard him" (Heb. 2:3–4). Hebrews is thus especially pertinent to Mather's eschatological semiology because the book focuses directly on the issue of revelation mediated by time. In Hebrews, that mediation is portrayed in such a way as to turn the readers' attention from the literal and historical referents of their past under the old law to the spiritual meaning signified by those referents and verified to us by Christ's "promise." Commenting on Heb. 12:2, in which the author of the epistle directs his readers to be "Looking unto Jesus," Mather notes that looking *to* Jesus requires that the Hebrews look *away* from the earlier objects of their devotion, i.e., the prophets of the Old Testament, and thereby make of themselves an "analogy" to Christ:

---

17   Like most commentators, Mather believed that the letter was addressed to the Hebrews "not only because the Name of *Jews*, was apace becoming odious but because hee would point out the *Jewes* which dwelt in the land of Israel" or Judea, as opposed to those Jews "which dwelt in foreign Countryes ... throughout the whole Dispersion" [*BA*, Intro. to Heb., "Who were, the *Hebrews*?"]. Attridge says most commentators agree the addressees were in Palestine or Jerusalem in particular; they were either Jewish Christians, Gentile Christians, or a mix of the two (10). More importantly, the community was at least second-generation Christians, and the author is concerned about apostasy, a threat of decline that similarly preoccupied many New Englanders at the time Mather wrote. The authorship of Hebrews is unknown. The book is usually considered among other Pauline epistles in the New Testament, and Mather refers to its author as "the Apostle." However, modern scholars tell us that Hebrews is almost certainly not by Paul. Despite speculations to that end by Clement and Origen, among others, linguistic evidence does not support that attribution. See Attridge (1–6) and Koester (42–46).

A.   A *Looking off* from others. Ἀφορῶντες is *Looking off*. Many & Famous Believers had been proposed for *Exemples*, unto the people of God. But, at last the
Spirit of God [*illeg.] Invites us, to *Look off* from all these unto an Incomparably
more perfect *Exemplar*, even, that of our Lord Jesus Christ. Unto this Blessed Jesus
wee are advised in the next Verse, to *Analogize* or Proportionate ourselves. [*BA*,
Heb. 12:2][18]

Mather's shift of emphasis here from "looking unto Jesus" to "looking off from
others" is indicative of the extent to which our relation to the spiritual significance of the sign – here described as the degree to which we *"Analogize* or Proportionate ourselves"* to Christ – depends on the negation of the literal and
historical referent. Mather makes a similar point in his commentary on Rev. 6,
where "looking off" from the material world is portrayed dramatically as a
physical blindness that leads to spiritual vision. Citing Lactantius's recently discovered books on *The Deaths of the Primitive Persecutors*, Mather tells the
story of Daia Maximinus, who fleeing pursuit by Licinius found himself
trapped.[19] Despairing of escape, Lactantius says, Daia Maximinus took some
poison that fails to kill him. Instead,

> The *Poyson* began now, to work violently on him; it burned his Vitals so much, that
> his unsufferable Pains threw him into a Phrensy; so that for Four Dayes Times, he
> Eat Earth, which he Dug up with his Hands, and Swallowed it up very greedily.
> The Rages of his Pain were so intolerable, that he run his Head against a Wall, with
> such force, that his Eyes started out of the Ey-holes. But as he lost the Sight of his
> Eyes, a *Vision* represented himself to his Imagination as Standing to be Judged by
> GOD, who seem'd to have Hosts of Ministers, about Him, all in white Garments.
> [qtd. in *BA*, Rev. 6:17]

Mather's interest in the story of Maximinus illustrates the extent to which
Mather's understanding of spiritual truth depends on the destruction of the
flesh for its visibility, whether in literal blindness or merely a "looking off" that
deflects the reader's attention from the material or historical referent. Later in
Mather's commentary on Hebrews we will see that deflection in the literal dis-

---

18   I'm indebted to Jason LaFountain for pointing out to me that Mather used the phrase
"looking off" to similar ends at least twice in print: "Thirdly. Excellent *Examples* of a WELL-
GOVERNED ANGER well *considered* with us, may be of use to save from the *Follies* of
UNGOVERNED ANGER. Bright *Examples* of *Meekness* have been set before us; Let us
observe the Examples, till we can *Follow* them. ... But after all, I will rather say *Run with
Patience, looking off unto JESUS,*; [sic] A JESUS, *Fairer than the Children of Men!"* (*Febrifugium* 33–35). "Be sure, that whatever you see *Great*, and *Good*, and *Bright*, in any Excellent
Person, whose *Life* you have in your Hands, you *look off* to the Glorious JESUS, as having in
HIM all these Excellencies after a Transcendent Manner, and as being the Author and Giver
of them to the *Distinguished Glowworm"* (*Manuductio* 67).
19   Lactantius (Lucius Caecilius Firmianus, c. 250–c.325) was known primarily as a teacher
of rhetoric under the Emperor Diocletian before Lactantius converted to Christianity around
A.D. 300. See ch. 49 of Lactantius's *A Relation of the Death of the Primitive Persecutors*
(1687).

memberment of the physical signifier always involves the temporal deferral of meaning to the future.

This temporal deferral of spiritual significance through the disintegration of the material signifier is evident in Mather's quarrel with the definition of faith in the English translation of Heb. 11:1: "Now faith is the substance of things hoped for, the evidence of things not seen." Rather than "substance," Mather says

> A. By υποστασις, wee may either understand *Expectation* … And if wee say, *Faith is the Expectation of things Hoped for*, it will sound better than our Translation, of *Substance*: or, wee may render it, *Confidence*, agreeably to the Import of the Word 2. Cor. 9.4. 2. Cor. 11.17. Heb. 3.14. Our Translation, *Substance*, is both dark, & harsh: wee had better say, *Confident Expectation. [BA*, Heb. 11:1][20]

For Mather, the temporal dimension of faith is inherent in, and necessary to, our ability to read the things of this present world as signs of things to come. Heb. 11:3 tells us that it is "Through faith we understand that the worlds were framed by the word of God," and that frame ensured a barrier between matter and spirit, "so that things which are seen were not made of things which do not appear." Following his substitution of "expectation" for "substance," Mather describes the faith that distinguishes between things seen and "things which do not appear" in terms of a temporal frame: "Now, whatever was done by *Faith*, our JESUS was the *Author* & the *Finisher* of it all" [*BA*, Heb. 11.1].

Mather's familiar characterization of Jesus as "Author" obviously alludes to the Logos, but here it also looks forward to Christ as a speaker in Heb. 12. There, the world of the present is portrayed as suspended in time between two performative speech-acts, the second of which will transcend the boundary that currently separates matter and spirit and thereby make the spiritual significance of this speech intelligible: "For if they escaped not who refused him that spake on earth, much more shall we not escape, if we turn away from him that speaketh from heaven: whose voice then shook the earth, but now he hath promised, saying, yet once more I shake not the earth only but also heaven" (Heb. 12:25–26). Mather's comment on this passage first identifies "Him that speaketh from Heaven" as Christ and "him that spake on earth" as Moses. Then, in a passage that recalls his remarks about earthquakes in *Wonders*, Mather proceeds to explain how the different sites of those two voices are joined in the rhetorical mode of Christ's promise to bring together heaven and earth in the future:

---

20 The difference here between expectant deferral on the one hand and, on the other, the immediate "substance" of "things not seen" reflects what commentators on Hebrews often characterize as tension between the Hebraic temporal understanding of spirituality and a Greek or Hellenistic "spatial" concept of the difference between material and spiritual experience. See Koester (59–63 and 98–100).

> It is very probable, that *Moses* is the Person here *Speaking on Earth*: For he alone is all along singly as a Lawgiver opposed unto the Son of God, thro' the whole Epistle. It is CHRIST then, who *is from Heaven* and *Speaks from Heaven*. [See Joh. iii.31, 32.] Now the *Voice* of Him who *Spake from heaven* in publishing the *Gospel*, was what *Shook the Earth* in publishing the *Law*. So then, it was CHRIST, who *Shook the Earth* and published the *Law*. But that very Person[21] who *Shook the Earth*, and *Speaketh from Heaven*, is He who has *promised, saying, yett once more I shake, not the Earth only, but also Heaven*. [*BA*, Heb. 12:25–26]

Just as natural causes give way to spiritual causes in Mather's interpretation of earthquakes, and substance yields to expectation in his commentary on faith, here God's voice first shakes only the earth but promises later to bridge the gap between matter and spirit to shake both earth and heaven together. The spiritual significance of Moses's speech and its true origin or author is heard as the temporal deferral in Christ's promise, and it is rendered legible here as the visible world is literally shaken apart, a point made explicitly in Heb. 12:27: "And this word, yet once more, signifieth the removing of those things that are shaken, as of things that are made, that those things which cannot be shaken may remain." The time of direct revelation having passed, the spiritual world to come is accessible to the present only in, or rather *as*, the destruction of material signs.[22]

The temporal deferral of spiritual significance thus has a crucial counterpart for Mather in the destruction of the material sign by which that significance is rendered legible in the present. That destruction enables us to treat visible things as signs, as Augustine would say; or, in Mather's terms, to look away from their literal and historical meanings and to look toward their spiritual significance. In his commentary on Hebrews, Mather consequently does not simply invoke typology to establish the anagogical significance of past events or characters from the Old Testament. He portrays that literal meaning as, literally, disintegrating, fading away under the pressure of time. Introducing

---

21 Mather originally wrote "Spirit" but changed it to "Person."

22 This association of signification with the destruction of the material signifier is a pervasive motif in Puritan poetry. In "What rocky heart is mine" (Meditation 1.36), which Edward Taylor wrote in preparation to celebrate the Lord's Supper, he portrays a similar situation in which the poet describes the human condition as so wrapped up in concerns about the present material world that there is no room to admit (in several senses) the millennial glory. Taylor's solution to this dilemma, like Mather's, is the destruction of the natural sign. That destruction is first portrayed as the revocation of the poet's inadequate language in a striking pun on the sacramental occasion of the poem ("I eate my Word. ... I now Unsay my Say") and then in an even more extraordinary invocation of Christ's wound as a break in the materiality of the present world that makes room for salvation in the present time: "Thy Argument is good, Lord point it, come/ Let't lance my heart, till True Loves Veane doth run./ But that there is a Crevice for one hope/ to Creep in, and the Message to Convay/ That I am thine, makes me refresh" (2: 71–75). For a complete reading of Taylor's poem and the importance of the motif in Puritan aesthetics, see Clark (98–101). See the use of Christ's wound for this same end in a sermon by John Donne (28n below).

the epistle, Mather say Hebrews may be read as a funeral sermon for the Old Law, figured in the decaying body of Moses:

> Q. What may one call, *The Epistle to the Hebrews*?
> A. Tis well expressed by Sr. Charles Wolseley; This Epistle is a *Funeral Sermon*, preached at the Interment of the *Law*: The Material Body of *Moses*, God Himself Buried, long before, and no Man ever knew the Place of his Sepulture; and now, his Mystical Body, his Doctrine, growing old & ready to vanish away, ripe for Aboli- tion, or rather Dissolution, not so much by being Repealed or Rescinded, but its Use ceasing, the End and Substance of it appearing, and its Glory being of course swallowed up into a greater Glory; the Holy Ghost Himself, by this Epistle layes it Honourably in the Grave; And so wee have the Sepulchre of this mystical Body of *Moses*, abiding with us to this day. [*BA*, Intro. to Heb.]

Here, as we would expect, Mather positions Hebrews as a typological gloss on relations between the Old and New Law. The typological significance of Moses and the superannuation of his doctrine are not, however, established through narrative parallels or doctrinal negation as we might expect. Instead, Mather portrays the literal referent – Moses's body – as missing, long buried in an un- known grave. He then portrays the mystical significance of that body – Moses's "mystical Body, his doctrine" – as similarly vulnerable to the ravages of time, "growing old & ready to vanish away, ripe for Abolition," its spiritual "End and Substance of it appearing" as it is "swallowed up into a greater Glory," the anti- type, "the Holy Ghost Himself." What is left, Mather concludes, is only "the Sepulchre of this mystical Body of *Moses*, abiding with us to this day."

The image of decaying bodies here illustrates – we might say prefigures – the waning influence of Mosaic law, and the image of bodily disintegration be- comes a crucial figure for the revelation of spiritual truth throughout Mather's commentary on Hebrews. At times Mather's use of this trope is suggested by the epistle itself: "For the word of God is quick, and powerful, and sharper than any two-edged sword, piercing even to the dividing asunder of soul and spirit, and of the joints and marrow, and is a discerner of the thoughts and intents of the heart" (Heb. 4:12). Mather's commentary on the passage, however, focuses obsessively on the image of grisly disembodiment as a path to truth and revela- tion, the destruction of the body as the avenue to spirit:

> The *Word of God is Living*; and Lives forever to Revenge the Contempt of His *promised Rest*.
>   And He *is powerful*; yea, *Sharper than any two-edged Sword*; which the Priest makes use of, to lay open the *Sacrifice*.
> – *Piercing, even to the Dividing asunder of Soul and Spirit*; Ransacking all the Se- cretest Parts of the Humane Composition, separating those that are most nearly connected; even, the *Soul* & and the *Spirit*. [See 1 Thess. v.23]
>   *And of the Joints*, or Nerves (by which other Parts are held together) *and Mar- row*; under which those Parts that lie hid, and are enclosed in others, are compre- hended.

> *And is a Discerner,* or, Judge of the *Thoughts & Intents of the Heart;* As the Priest sitts Judge of the Sacrifice thus laid open before him, whether entire & without Blemish, or no.
>
> And not only are *we* thus laid open before Him ... *but all things are naked & open before* the eyes of Him *with whom we have to do* ... *Naked & open* and as perfectly discovered unto Him, as the *Sacrifice* is unto the *Priest,* when it is flay'd & cutt down the Back, & laid open before him, in order for his passing a Judgement on the Soundness of it. [*BA,* Heb. 4:12]

(Interestingly, Mather's elaborate account of piercing, dividing asunder, ransacking and separating, flaying open and cutting down the body in pursuit of spiritual truth appears on a loose sheet inserted into the bound manuscript at a point where Mather also comments on the same verse on the fixed page. The comment on the bound page is very abstract and tame by comparison, citing authorities and referring only briefly to the violence inherent in this passage.[23])

In his commentary on Revelation, Mather makes explicit this methodological analogy between dismemberment and semiotic analysis by comparing the interpretation of scriptural tropes to anatomical dissection:

> Q. What may be the Special Intention and Emphasis of that Passage, *I am He that Searches the Reins?* v. 23.
> A. The Knowledge of the *Most Secret Things* in Man; is here challenged by our Lord. For, the *Reins* ly hid behind all the Bowels, and are the most secret of our Secret Parts. *Anatomy* itself comes not at them, without abundance of Difficulty, and until many Parts are first removed out of the Way. When they are come at, they are found covered with a Fatt, which still will not lett them easily come into the Sight of the Discoverer. A little *Anatomy* would notably illustrate the Expression of, *Searching the Reins.* [*BA,* Rev. 2:23]

It is not simply the methodological parallels between dissection and interpretation that drives Mather's interest in anatomy. Mather attends to the destruction of the flesh in the name of spirit throughout Hebrews, even when that attention contradicts the gist of the scriptural verse. Commenting on the author's rejection of bloody sacrifice as an opening to spirit – "For it is not possible that the blood of bulls and of goats should take away sins. Wherefore when he [Christ] cometh into the world, he saith, Sacrifice and offering thou wouldest not, but a body hast thou prepared me" (Heb. 10:1–5) – Mather turns that preparation into the mortification of the flesh as a sign of spiritual identification:

---

23 "And one of the Christian Ancients long since observed, how agreeable this is, to the Prophecies of *Isaiah* about the Messiah. *Origen* on *John* has a Passage of this Importance. "It is said in Isaiah [Ch. 49.2.] The Father hath *made His Mouth, like a Sharp Sword.* The *Mouth* of the Son of God is a *Sharp Sword ... The Word of God is Quick and Powerful, piercing even to the Dividing asunder of Soul and Spirit.* It comes not to *send Peace upon the Earth,* that is upon Corporeal and Sensible Things, but a *Sword;* cutting asunder the Hurtful Friendship between the Soul and Body, that the *Soul* permitting itself so the Spirit, that wars against the Flesh, might be at Friendship with God" [*BA,* Heb. 4:12].

Q. In Psal. 40.6. the Psalmist, in Type of our Saviour sais, *Mine Ears hast thou Opened*, or *Digged*; Why do's the Apostle, render it, *A Body hast thou prepared for mee?* v. 5.

A. Lett it bee considered, That the Hebrew Word, signifies, *To prepare*, as well as, *To pierce*. And lett it bee Remembred, That the *Boring of the Ear* with an Awl, was of *Mosaical* Institution, for such *Israelites*, who having served *Six* Years with their *Brethren-Masters*, were willing to continue in that State of Servitude, until Death Freed them. By which *Boring of an Ear*, the Servant as it were took on him a New political *Body*, whereof, being thus Inaugurated, hee could not bee divested, until hee Dy'd. Our Lord thus took on Him, the *Form of a Servant*. [*BA*, Heb. 10:5][24]

Throughout the epistle, Christ's incarnation and crucifixion are portrayed as efficacious anti-types of sacrifices under the Old Law. As suggested by these remarks on Heb. 10:5, however, Mather's commentary focuses less on the soteriological power of Christ's divinity than on the semiotic function of Christ's flesh. That body, "the *Form of a Servant*" here associated with the "*Boring of the Ear* with an Awl," will serve as a portal to the spirit, Mather says, but paradoxically only as a "veil" that must be "rent open," broken and bloodied, before its spiritual significance can be read.

Q. We read of, *A New and Living Way, consecrated for us, thro' the Vail, that is to say, the Flesh of our Lord.* How are we to understand it? v. 20.

A. The Way into the *Third Heaven*, was Αβατος (as *Josephus*[25] calls it,) *Unpassable*. There was no Entrance for us into it, until our *Fore-runner had entred* into it, & until He had *prepared* it for us, by His *Better Sacrifice*. This, as Dr *Whitby*[26] observes, was the Doctrine of all the primitive Christians; That our Saviour by His Death opened this *Veil* for the Just, that were from *Adam*, αποκεκλεισμενοι, (tis Old *Cyrils*[27] Word) *Excluded* from those Blessed Regions. Ηε διεσχισε πραγμον

---

24 Mather defends this reading by claiming that the Septuagint phrase "A body hast thou prepared" simply mistranslates the Hebrew words of the Psalmist to which the Apostle is referring: "when the Psalmist says, *Mine Ears hast thou bored*, he means, that He was to become the *perpetual Servant* of God. It is very normal & obvious to find a *Body prepared* here because the Body of the Servant was no longer his own, but his Masters: which was the very thing implied in the *Boring of the Ear*" [*BA*, Heb. 10:5]. For a brief contemporary analysis of the translations of this verse that supports Mather's reading, see Attridge (23).

25 Josephus (c. 37–100) was a Jewish historian also known as Titus Flavius Josephus and Yosef Ben Maitityahu (Joseph, son of Matthias). He described the destruction of Jerusalem in 70 A.D. See his *Antiquities of the Jews*, "Concerning the Tabernacle Which Moses Built in the Wilderness" (ch. 6). Mather is probably citing Josephus's *De bello Judaico* 4.7.

26 See Whitby (517–18). What follows, through "Sensitive world," quotes Whitby directly, with only a few minor and inconsequential departures from Whitby's text. The concluding typological interpretation of the passage is Mather's.

27 Cyril of Alexandria (c. 378–444) was named Pope of Alexandria in 412. See his *That Christ is One by way of dispute with Hermias*: "for it is written, *Having therefore, brethren, boldness to enter into the holy in the blood of Christ, which He inaugurated for us, a new and living way through the veil, that is, through His flesh.* Understand therefore how he says that His is the Blood and His the flesh, which he also calls *the veil*, and with good reason, in order that whatever in the temple the sacred veil used to effect, concealing full well the holy of holies, somewhat of the same might the flesh too of the Lord be conceived of as doing, not per-

τον εξ αιωνος μη σχισθεντα *rent open the Enclosure, which from the Beginning had not been Laid open.* ... The Flesh, or Body, of our Saviour, broken on the Cross, and so Letting out the Blood that procures our Entrance into the *Holy of Holies*, as the Blood, the High Priest carried with him, did procure this Entrance: This was the *Veil*, which till it was Rent, we could not Enter there. [*BA*, Heb. 10:20][28]

In this passage – which also appears on an inserted loose sheet as did the other extended reflection on dismemberment – the revelatory power of the crucifixion is portrayed in temporal terms as a connection to spirit that was, on the one hand, precluded from the present by past sins and, on the other, postponed in Christ's promise to the future for which it prepares us. Access to this Holy of Holies is thus literally a passage through time, prepared by the rending of the veil and the breaking of Christ's body on the cross.[29]

In Mather's commentary on Heb. 9:1, he describes this Holy of Holies as a "Second Tabernacle," of which the "First Tabernacle" is merely the "temporary" "Figure and a Shadow" of a "World to Come." The Apostle has shown us how "an End was putt unto the Jewish Constitutions" under the first covenant, Mather says, and

> he proceeds now to proove the same, from the Consideration of the *Tabernacle*, which was a *Shadow of Good Things to come.* And the Contexture of the Apostles

---

mitting the marvellous and choice Excellence and glory of God the Word to it united, to be seen by any bare so to say and unhidden" (297).

28 There is a long tradition of meditation on Christ's wounds that flourished in the middle ages and was adopted by Reformed theology. It became a recurrent motif in Protestant poetics (see Martz and Lewalski) and was also a popular device in sermons. Writing at the end of his career, for example, John Donne concludes his account of the Passion, entitled "Death's Duell," with an image of Christ on the Cross: "There now hanges that *sacred Body* upon the *Crosse, rebaptized* in his owne *teares* and *sweat*, and *embalmed* in his *own blood alive.* There are those *bowells of compassion*, which are so conspicuous, so manifested, as that you may *see them through his wounds.* ... There wee leave you in that *blessed dependancy*, to *hang* upon him that *hangs* upon the *Crosse*, there *bath* in his *teares*, there *suck* at his *woundes*, and *lye downe in peace* in his *grave*, till he vouchsafe you a *resurrection*, and an *ascension* into that *Kingdome*, which hee *hath purchas'd for you*, with the *inestimable price* of his *incorruptible blood*. AMEN" (10: 247–48).

29 In his commentary on Rev. 7:14, Mather noted the hermeneutic complications posed by the doctrinal use of blood as a material signifier for spiritual clensing, but he resolves the problem rhetorically rather than eschatologically. "We read of some, who have *Washed their Robes, made them White in the Blood of the Lamb.* Wee know, *Blood* will Spott and Stain that which is *White. Made White in Blood* seems truly but an Harsh Kind of a *Metaphor?*" The problem, Mather claims, derives from exegetes' confusion between two kinds of tropes: metaphors, which claim an equivalence between signifier and signified; and metonymies, which simply link attributes associated with the signifier and the signified – in this case, salvation. "The Short of it, is, That by Vertue of the *Blood* of the Lord Jesus Christ applied unto us, we are made *Priests* unto God, & capable of Wearing the *White Garments* of an Heavenly *Priesthood.* ... Wee come to have *White Garments*; How? The *Blood of the Lamb* ha's purchased this Dignity for us" [*BA*, Rev. 7:14]. The precision of Mather's tropological distinction here suggests how seriously Mather took the ontological implications of using material signs to represent spiritual signifieds in truly metaphorical (vs. metonymical) expressions in Scripture.

Argument, seems plainly to require this Reading. For, the *Tabernacle* consisting of Two Parts, an Outward House, called, *The Holy Place*, and an Inward House, called, *The Holy of Holies*, the Apostle here calls, the Outward House, the *First Tabernacle*; and then proceeds to the Inward House as the *Second Tabernacle*.

But why is the *First Tabernacle* called, *A Worldly Sanctuary*? Both the Jewes & the Fathers tell us, It was to represent this *Lower World*; the *Earth* & the *Sea*, saies Josephus. It was κοσμου του αισθητου συμβολον. Saies *Clemens Alexandrinus, A Symbol of the Sensitive World*.[30]

We may add, The Seat of the *Sanctuary* was in this *Present World*, & stood in Opposition to the *Sanctuary* of the *World to Come*, whereof it was a Figure and a Shadow. A *Worldly Sanctuary*, is as much as to say, *A Terrestrial & a Temporary*.[31] [*BA*, Heb. 9:1]

To that terrestrial and temporary tabernacle Mather contrasts the second tabernacle of the world to come, which "belongs not to the class of the Visible Creation. It is not to be reckoned in the Naming of the Visible Creatures" [*BA*, Heb. 9:11].

Throughout his commentary on Hebrews – and throughout the "Biblia Americana" – Mather insists on these distinctions between visible creatures and invisible spirit, and between the world to come versus the figures and shadows that constitute "evidence" of that world to an expectant faith. The significance of his insistence on such distinctions becomes evident in his portrayal of how different things will be at the end of time, when spirit will stalk this earth "even without Metaphor," as he warns us in *Wonders of the Invisible World*. Commenting on the apocalyptical "*City that has Foundations*" described in Heb. 11:10, Mather describes it as a millennial resolution of the ontological distinctions between matter and spirit. Those distinctions require the mediation of signs in our time, but that need will disappear as that time ends:

A. It is that Glorious and Cubic *City*, whereof we have a Description, in the *Twenty First* Chapter of the *Revelation*. The City will be Inhabited by the *Raised Saints*. The Raised Saints, with their *New Bodies* will Inhabit it. By Consequence, it will be a *Material City*. Tho' the *Matter* of it will be vastly more precious than the finest of our *Metals* or *Jewels*. Tis the same, that is called, *The Third Heaven*, and, *The Heaven of Heavens*; for the Singular Excellency of it. ... It shall be a *City with Foundations*, for *Bodies* to inhabit it. [*BA*, Heb. 11:10] ... we should consider the Holy *City of God*, in the *Clouds* of the *New Heavens*, as being peculiarly over the

---

30 Clement of Alexandria (150-c. 211), also known as Titus Flavius Clemens, was a member of the Church of Alexandria. He was teacher of Origen, who succeeded Clement as head of the Catechetical School of Alexandria.

31 The deferral of spiritual significance could occur forward in time or backward; either way, the point was to connect the material signifiers to a spiritual significance that was distant in time from the natural world. On this, see Mather's commentary on *Ezra*: "The *First Art* was made and consecrated by Divine Appointment, and was possessed of these Distinguishing Priviledges & Praerogatives: But the Second being made & substituted by man only, had none of them. The only use of it, was to represent the former, on the Great Day of Expiation (qtd. in Maddux, "God's Responsibility" 313).

Land of Promise, at the Time of the *Restitution*, and the *Land of Promise* having a peculiar Share above other Countryes, in the Visits, which the Raised Saints from time to time shall give unto the Lower World. [*BA*, Heb. 11:15][32]

These passages from the "Biblia Americana" can only suggest the consistency and precision with which Mather approached a fundamental paradox at the heart of Puritanism: in our time, material events, whether signs or speech, can function as evidence of spiritual meaning only through the dissolution of the very substance that made them visible in the first place. This paradox led, in its crudest form, to the iconoclastic destruction of images of faith in churches and a suspicion of representation in general, whether in the theater or on the page. In more subtle hands, such as those of Anne Bradstreet in "Contemplations" and Edward Taylor in *Meditations*, this suspicion of signs could generate its own aesthetic (see 22n above). For others, it would produce its own language, as Puritans in the Royal Society pursued a scientific style that would reduce words to things and do away with signification altogether in pursuit of a transparent empiricism. This latter interest in "semaeologia" provided Mather with a critical methodological link between his scientific interests in empirical description and the typological analysis of scriptural hermeneutics, and it underlies Mather's elaborate and insightful articulation of this paradox as an essential measure of humanity's place in the providential plan.

Mather's effort to reconcile the interpretation of natural signs with the scriptural bases of typological analysis also preoccupied his younger contemporary Jonathan Edwards, and a brief consideration of Edwards's remarks about the materiality of signs will help clarify Mather's complex place in this period of rapid change in biblical hermeneutics.[33] Scholars of Edwards's work

---

32 Mather's insistence on the millennial resolution of the opposition between matter and spirit also pervades his description of the New Jerusalem in *Triparadisus*: "It is a *Material City*. ... Tis a *City* to be inhabited by *Bodies*; The Inhabitants will be *Embodied Spirits*; The Glorious KING of the *City* Himself, will be so. But insist upon it if you please, that it be an *Ethereal City*. And Lett the *Matter* be so rich, & so fine, & so splendid, that our *Gold* and *Gems* are little better than *Shadows* of it. I object nothing to *That*. Spiritualize the Matter as much as You please; But if you think, a *Visible City*, of a *Cubical* Form is too *Corporeal* a Thing, yett you must allow, That there will be a *Place* of Reception for Bodies. ... Finally, *Spiritual Bodies*! Not ceasing to be *Bodies*, or turned into meer *Spirits*; They will be *Material* still; but highly *Spiritualized* (*Triparadisus* 244–45, 256).

33 Hans Frei claims that the early eighteenth century marks the end of typological or "precritical" interest in the real or historical referents of biblical narratives as figures of their spiritual meaning. The subsequent emergence of historical criticism shifted attention from the connection between material signs and their spiritual significance to questions related to the production of the biblical text itself as a linguistic and historical artifact. More recently, Gordis has argued that at the end of the seventeenth-century Puritan New England saw a notable "decline of a pure ideal of reading in the Spirit" to a "heightened emphasis on the minister's interpretative artistry" (215), and Markley claims that the period around 1700 saw even broader "crises of representation" in science, philosophy, and historiography as well as theology. For an extended analysis of Edwards's role in the conflict at this time between "or-

have differed significantly in their assessments of his relative interests in two radically different approaches toward the interpretation of signs, both of which are evident throughout Edwards's writings: (1) traditional forms of typological hermeneutics, with their focus on scriptural signs and the temporal deferral of spiritual significance beyond the world of time and matter; and (2) more modern interpretive methods based on Newtonian metaphysics and Lockean psychology that assumed an ontological continuity among scripture, nature, and God's divinity. The continuity is intelligible in the congruity between matter and spirit, which is Edwards's definition of beauty, and that notion of congruity contrasts markedly with Mather's emphasis on rotting flesh and flayed limbs as ideal standards for the material sign. Edwards believed that God is essentially a "communicative being"[34] and that this divine impulse to communicate was manifest in the beauty of the visible world:

> one thing which contributes to the beauty of the agreement and proportion of various things is their relation one to another, which connects them and introduces them together into view and consideration, and whereby one suggests the other to the mind, and the mind is led to compare them and so to expect and desire agreement. ... The reason, or at least one reason, why God has made this kind of mutual consent and agreement of things beautiful and grateful to those intelligent beings that perceive it probably is that there is in it some image of the true, spiritual original beauty, which has been spoken of: consisting in being's consent to being, or the union of minds or spiritual beings in a mutual propensity and affection of heart. The other is an image of this, because by that uniformity diverse things become as it were one, as it is in this cordial union. And it pleases God to observe analogy in his works, as is manifest in fact in innumerable instances. (Edwards 8: 563–64)

This emphasis on the congruity or agreement between the material sign and its spiritual significance is often taken as a measure of Edwards's modernity, whereas Mather's emphasis on typology as a historical metanarrative as late as the *Magnalia* is read as evidence of Mather's reactionary conservatism. As his "Biblia Americana" makes clear, however, Mather had an encyclopedic knowledge of secular as well as sacred interpretive methods of his time and was not

---

thodox exegesis of the types" and "scientific interest in the natural universe," see Lowance's *The Language of Canaan* (251). Lowance places Cotton Mather among "conservative theologians" of the time who experimented with newer exegetical methods during this period, and he claims that Edwards's reconciliation of typology and the interpretation of natural signs represented a profound epistemological break from traditional Puritan typology (*Canaan* 276). Conversely, Stein exempts Edwards from the shift described by Frei and portrays Edwards as a defender of typological interpretation, though he notes Edwards' decidedly nontypological confidence that signs could lead us to the spirit dwelling within them (119).

34   "The great and universal end of God's creating the world was to communicate himself. God is a communicative being. This communication is really only to intelligent beings: the communication of himself to their understandings is his glory, and the communication of himself with respect to their wills, the enjoying faculty, is their happiness" (Edwards 13: 410).

hesitant to use both for scriptural exegesis as well as scientific observation. Similarly, Perry Miller's celebration of Edwards as an early avatar of Transcendentalism has been largely discredited as scholars have established the extent to which Edwards reconciled more innovative interpretive methods derived from modern science with typological hermeneutics. The result was what Knight calls a "typologizing of nature" that was "the fruit of Edwards's larger project of joining the lessons of the new science and psychology to the verities of the old piety" (534–35).

The conjunction of typology and a more scientific or semiological hermeneutic led Edwards to treat nature and scripture alike as sign-systems open to interpretation. Edwards describes typology as a "certain sort of Language, as it were, in which God is wont to speak to us." Directly contradicting Mather's warning against "oneiracritics" whose interpretive fantasies exceeded scriptural authority, Edwards asserts the legibility of types in both scripture and nature for anyone who knows how to read the language:

> If we may use our own understandings and invention not at all in interpreting types, and must not conclude anything at all to be types but what is expressly said to be and explained in Scripture, then the church under the Old [Testament], when the types were given, were secluded from ever using their understanding to search into the meaning of the types given to 'em; for God did, when he gave 'em, give no interpretation.
>
> Types are a certain sort of language, as it were, in which God is wont to speak to us. And there is, as it were, a certain idiom in that language which is to be learnt the same that the idiom of any language is, viz. by good acquaintance with the language. ... I expect by very ridicule and contempt to be called a man of a very fruitful brain and copious fancy, but they are welcome to it. I am not ashamed to own that I believe that the whole universe, heaven and earth, air and seas, and the divine constitution and history of the holy Scriptures, be full of images of divine things, as full as a language is of words. (Edwards 11: 150–52)

These differences between Mather and Edwards may be most evident in their commentaries on the Epistle to the Hebrews in the "Biblia Americana" and Edwards's "Blank Bible." Given their interests in typological hermeneutics and the interpretation of natural signs, it is not surprising that they would both focus on the nature of signs and signification as they explicate the epistle's emphasis on the divinity of Christ and on the superiority of the New Law to the Old. Like Mather, Edwards immediately turns his attention to the epistle's portrayal of Christ's relation to God as "The express image of his person" (Heb. 1:3). Unlike Mather, however, who catalogs the various ways representations can differ from their originals before acknowledging the special adequacy of matter to spirit in the incarnation, Edwards stresses the exact equivalence between representations in general and what they represent: "But it may be observed that whatsoever is the express or exact image of a thing is, in the Apostle's sense, equivalent or of equal value with that thing, it having a full answerableness"

(Edwards 24: 1137). This emphasis on the ontological continuity or equivalence of image and original, signifier and signified, is repeated in Edwards's commentary on the word of God as a two-edged sword in Heb. 4:12, a passage that inspired one of Mather's most hyperbolic characterizations of signification as material disintegration. Edwards turns what Mather portrayed as a life and death struggle between flesh and spirit into a purely spiritual psychomachia within the soul itself, explicitly rejecting the materiality of the metaphor and, with it, the ontological conflict between flesh and spirit that informs Mather's account of the scriptural image. Edwards says of this verse

> It is not meant that the word pierces to the dividing the soul from the spirit, the joints from the marrow, as some have supposed, which is very unintelligible, but dividing asunder these things themselves. The word in its powerful efficacy in mortification and conversion, emptying the soul of itself, and parting it from sin, and weaning it from the world, and bringing to a thorough self-denial or self-renunciation, does as it were cut the soul asunder. (Edwards 24: 1143)

Such examples of Edwards's emphasis on the continuity between material signifier and spiritual signified could be multiplied almost endlessly in his commentary on Hebrews. His difference from Mather is evident in the smallest detail of translation, as in Heb. 11:1 ("faith is the substance of things hoped for, the evidence of things not seen"). Both Edwards and Mather reject the translation of υποστασις as "substance," but Edwards recommends "confidence" instead, whereas Mather suggests "expectation" or at best "confident expectation," a phrase that stresses the deferral of meaning rather than confidence in the evidence itself. Edward's difference from Mather is manifest as well in their diverging explanations of the "city which hath foundations" in Heb. 11:10. For Mather, that image evokes millennialist speculations about the refinement of matter and sprit at the end of time, but the phrase merely occasions an anthropological observation by Edwards: the tabernacle has no foundations, he says, "because 'tis a movable thing, and is designed for no settled abode, but is such as travelers are wont to lodge in. ... But the 'city that has foundations' is that wherein they shall dwell in a fixed manner as the proper citizens" (Edwards 24: 1158).

The test-case of Christ's crucifixion implied in Heb. 10.20 ("a new and living way, which he hath consecrated for us, through the veil, that is to say, his flesh") results in similarly discrepant accounts, moving Mather to meditate on Christ's broken body and bloody flesh, but eliciting nothing from Edwards more than a reference to his exegetical notebooks where Edwards observes that the veil over the temple (here in Matt. 27:51) was "typified by the flesh of Christ ... when his human nature died, then this veil was removed" (Edwards 15: 324–25). And at the largest possible scale, that of providential time, the difference between the ways Mather and Edwards treat material signs becomes most dramatic, as in their response to Heb. 2:5, "For unto the angels hath he not put in subjection the world to come." Mather turns immediately to the temporal deferral inherent in the promise: "It remains then, That the *World to come*, should be the State of Things during the Day of Judgment, or, after the Second Coming of the Lord Jesus Christ." Edwards, on the other hand, emphasizes the a-temporal continuity of the promise in that passage, and the continuity between this world and the next:

> The renewed state of things brought to pass by Christ, called 'the new heavens and new earth,' is here called 'the world to come,' although already come in its beginnings. Even as the blessings of Christ's kingdom and of this new creation are called 'good things to come,' ἀγαθά μέλλοντα (Heb. 9:11 and Heb. 10:1), though they were already come in their beginnings. (Edwards 24: 1138–39).

In these remarks on Christ's promise in this passage from Hebrews, we can see the balance between ontological continuity and typological history that characterizes his treatment of material signs and marks his place in the intellectual history of America. His interest in signification and typology as a language raises some of the same semiological issues that so interested Mather, but Edwards's confidence in the ultimate legibility of scripture and nature marks a dramatic shift from Mather's emphasis on the ontological *dis*continuity between material signs and their spiritual significance.

Mather's semiological analysis of signs in the "Biblia Americana" reflects some of the most innovative scientific theory of his age. He couches that analysis, however, within the more traditional eschatological framework of seventeenth-century Puritanism, which led him to equate signification with corporeal disintegration and the legibility of types with the progressive decay of their historical referents over time. Unlike Edwards, who looks *to* nature to read what God communicates of Himself to man, Mather is always "looking away" from nature, as he would put it, deferring the significance of the sign to an apocalyptic future in which the epistemological problems associated with scriptural exegesis will be resolved ontologically in the experience of a new bond between flesh and spirit.[35] The rhetoric of promise, a decaying corpse, the torn sinews and broken bodies of sacrifice – all of these images are Mather's attempt to represent a signifying process that will reveal, in the future, the mystical significance of the natural world but that is legible to us now only in, and as, the

---

35   In a brilliant analysis of the extent to which this notion of deferral informs Mather's sense of his role as author in the *Magnalia*, Jan Stievermann shows how Mather's chiliasm joins with his ideal of *copia* or "copius writing" to produce a rhetoric of literally infinite delay. Mather suspected "that the attainment of the ideal of *copia* would have to be deferred to the very end of history," Stievermann says. "Mather's Puritan eschatology also seems to inform his hope for the complete fulfillment of all the typological allegorizations of European texts that would simultaneously solve the problems of textual disintegration. ... He looked forward to the time when God would make all things new to vindicate his ambitious studies and reestablish a paradisiacal unity of *res* and *verba*" (286).

violence of interpretation. In this sense, then, we may read in Mather's extended meditations on the disintegration of material signs yet another manifestation of the tension between the inchoate empiricism of seventeenth-century science and Puritan insistence on the epistemological limits of that science, focused precisely on those points where human experience intersects with Providence in dramatic and terrifying ways.

Works Cited

Primary Sources

Aquinas, Thomas. "The Nature and Domain of Sacred Doctrine." In *Summa Theologica*. Trans. by Fathers of the English Dominican Province. 2nd Edition, 1920. *The Christian Classics Ethereal Library*. Web. 11 Nov. 2009.

Burnet, William. *An Essay on Scripture-Prophecy, Wherein It is Endeavoured to Explain the Three Periods Contain'd in the XII Chapter of the Prophet Daniel: With Some Arguments to Make it Probable that the First of the Periods Did Expire in the Year 1715*. New York, 1724

Calef, Robert. *More Wonders of the Invisible World*. London, 1700.

Cyril of Alexandria. *Quod unus sit Christus. That Christ is One by way of dispute with Hermia*. Trans. P.E. Pusey. *Library of Fathers of the Holy Catholic Church* [LFC] 47 (1881): 237–319. *Early Church Fathers*. Ed. Roger Pearse. Web. 11 Nov. 2009.

Derham, William. *Physico-Theology, or A Demonstration of the Being and Attributes of God, from His Works of Creation*. London, 1712.

Donne, John. *The Sermons of John Donne*. Ed. G.R. Potter and E.M. Simpson. 10 vols. Berkeley, CA: U of California P, 1953–62.

Edwards, Jonathan. *The Works of Jonathan Edwards. Ethical Writings*. Ed. Paul Ramsey. Vol. 8. New Haven: Yale UP, 1989.

–.   *The Works of Jonathan Edwards. Typological Writings*. Ed. Wallace E. Anderson, Mason I. Lowance, Jr., and David H. Watters. Vol. 11. New Haven: Yale UP, 1993.

–.   *The Works of Jonathan Edwards. "The Miscellanies," Entry Nos. a-z, aa-zz, 1–500*. Ed. Thomas A. Schafer. Vol. 13. New Haven: Yale UP, 1994.

–.   *The Works of Jonathan Edwards. Notes on Scripture*. Ed. Stephen J. Stein. Vol. 15. New Haven: Yale UP, 1998.

–.   *The Works of Jonathan Edwards. The Blank Bible*. Ed. Stephen J. Stein. Vol. 24. New Haven: Yale UP, 2006.

Henry, Matthew. *An Exposition of All the Books of the Old and New Testaments: Wherein the Chapters are summ'd up in Contents; the Sacred Text inserted at large, in Paragraphs, or Verses; and each Paragraph, or Verse, reduc'd to its proper Heads: the Sense given, and largely illustrated, with Practical Remarks and Observations*. 6 vols. London, 1708–10.

Hooker, Thomas. *A Survey of the Summe of Church-Discipline*. London, 1648.

Josephus, Flavius. *Flavii Iosephi Opera*. Ed. B. Niese. Berlin: Weidmann, 1895. *Perseus Digital Library*. Web. 11 Nov. 2009.

Lactantius. *Of the Manner in Which the Persecutors Died. The Ante-Nicene Fathers Translations of the Fathers down to A.D. 325*. Ed. Alexander Roberts and James

Donaldson. 1867–97. Vol. 7. *Christian Classics Ethereal Library.* Web. 11 Nov. 2009.

–. *A Relation of the Death of the Primitive Persecutors.* Amsterdam, 1687.

Mather, Cotton. *The Angel of Bethesda: An Essay Upon the Common Maladies of Mankind.* Ed. Gordon W. Jones, M.D. Barre: American Antiquarian Society and Barre Publishers, 1972.

–. *The Christian Philosopher.* Ed. Winton U. Solberg. Urbana: U of Illinois P, 1994.

–. *Febrifugium. An Essay for the Cure of Ungoverned Anger.* Boston, 1717.

–. *Manuductio ad Ministerium.* Boston, 1726.

–. *Things to be More Thought Upon.* Boston, 1713.

–. *The Threefold Paradise of Cotton Mather: An Edition of the "Triparadisus."* Ed. Reiner Smolinski. Athens and London: U of Georgia P, 1995.

–. *The Wonders of the Invisible World.* Boston, 1693.

Patrick, Simon. *A Commentary upon the Historical Books of the Old Testament.* 2 vols. 3rd ed. London, 1727.

Poole, Matthew. *Annotations upon the Holy Bible. Wherein the Sacred Text is Inserted, and various Readings Annex'd together with Parallel Scriptures, the more difficult Terms in each Verse are Explained, seeming Contradictions Reconciled, Questions and Doubts Resolved, and the whole Text opened. By the Late Reverend and Learned Divine Mr. Matthew Poole.* 2 vols. London, 1683–85.

–. *Synopsis Criticorum Aliorumque S. Scripturæ Interpretum.* 5 vols. London, 1669–76.

Ray, John. *The Wisdom of God Manifested in the Works of the Creation.* London, 1691.

Sewall, Samuel. *The Diary of Samuel Sewall 1674–1729.* Ed. M. Halsey Thomas. 2 vols. New York: Farrar, Straus and Giroux, 1973.

Spinoza, Benedict Baruch. *A Theological-Political Treatise.* 1670. New York: Dover, 1951.

Taylor, Edward. *The Poems of Edward Taylor.* Ed. Donald E. Stanford. U of North Carolina P, 1989.

Whitby, Daniel. *A Paraphrase and Commentary Upon all the Epistles of the New Testament.* London, 1700.

Wilkins, John. *An Essay towards a Real Character and a Philosophical Language.* London, 1668.

–. *Mercury; or the Secret and Swift Messenger.* London, 1641.

Secondary Sources

Attridge, Harold W. *The Epistle to the Hebrews. Hermeneia – A Critical and Historical Commentary on the Bible.* Philadelphia: Fortress P, 1989.

Brown, Truesdell S. "Euhemerism and the Historians." *Harvard Theological Review* 39.1 (1946): 259–74.

Caplan, Harry. "The Four Senses of Scriptural Interpretation and the Mediaeval Theory of Preaching." *Speculum* 4 (1929): 282–90.

Clark, Michael P. "'Even Without a Metaphor': The Poetics of Apocalypse in Puritan New England." *Millennial Thought in Historical Context.* Ed. Bernd Engler and Oliver Scheiding. Trier: WVT, 2002. 97–132.

Ellingworth, Paul. *The Epistle to the Hebrews: A Commentary on the Greek Text*. The New International Greek Testament Commentary. Grand Rapids: Eerdmans, 1993.

Frei, Hans. *The Eclipse of Biblical Narrative: A Study in Eighteenth and Nineteenth Century Hermeneutics*. New Haven: Yale UP, 1974.

Gordis, Lisa M. *Opening Scripture: Bible Reading and Interpretive Authority in Puritan New England*. Chicago: U of Chicago P, 2003.

Kibbey, Ann. *The Interpretation of Material Shapes in Puritanism: A Study of Rhetoric, Prejudice, and Violence*. New York: Cambridge UP, 1986.

Knight, Janice. "Learning the Language of God: Jonathan Edwards and the Typology of Nature." *William and Mary Quarterly*. Third Series. 48.4 (1991): 531–51.

Koester, Craig R. *Hebrews: A New Translation with Introduction and Commentary*. The Anchor Bible. New York: Doubleday, 2001.

Lewalski, Barbara Kiefer. *Protestant Poetics and the Seventeenth-Century Religious Lyric*. Princeton: Princeton UP, 1979.

Lowance, Mason I., Jr. "Images of Shadows of Divine Things: The Typology of Jonathan Edwards." *Early American Literature*. Special Typology Issue. 5.1, Part 1 (1970): 141–81.

–.   *The Language of Canaan: Metaphor and Symbol in New England from the Puritans to the Transcendentalists*. Cambridge: Harvard UP, 1980.

Maddux, Harry Clark. "God's Responsibility: Narrative Choice and Providential History in Mather's *Biblia Americana* Commentary on Ezra." *Early American Literature* 42.2 (2007): 305–21.

Markley, Robert. *Fallen Languages: Crises of Representation in Newtonian England, 1660–1740*. Ithaca, New York: Cornell UP, 1993.

Martz, Louis. *The Poetry of Meditation: A Study in English Religious Literature of the Seventeenth Century*. New Haven: Yale UP, 1954.

Rivers, Cheryl. "Cotton Mather's *Biblia Americana* Psalms and the Nature of Puritan Scholarship." Diss. Columbia U, 1977.

Silverman, Kenneth. *The Life and Times of Cotton Mather*. 1984. New York: Columbia UP, 1985.

Smolinski, Reiner. "Authority and Interpretation: Cotton Mather's Response to the European Spinozists." *Shaping the Stuart World, 1603–1714: The Atlantic Connection*. Ed. Allan I. Macinnes and Arthur H. Williamson. Leiden: Brill, 2006. 175–203.

–.   "How to Go to Heaven, or How Heaven Goes? Natural Science and Interpretation in Cotton Mather's 'Biblia Americana' (1693–1728)." *New England Quarterly* 81.2 (2008): 278–329.

Stein, Stephen J. "The Spirit and the Word: Jonathan Edwards and Scriptural Exegesis." *Jonathan Edwards and the American Experience*. Ed. Nathan O. Hatch and Harry S. Stout. New York: Oxford UP, 1988. 118–30.

Stievermann, Jan. "Writing 'To Conquer All Things': Cotton Mather's *Magnalia Christi Americana* and the Quandary of *Copia*." *Early American Literature* 39.2 (2004): 263–97.

Warner, Margaret Humphreys. "Vindicating the Minister's Medical Role: Cotton Mather's Concept of the Nishmath Chajim and the Spiritualization of Medicine." *Journal of the History of Medicine and Allied Sciences* 36.3 (1981): 278–95.

David Komline

The Controversy of the Present Time:
Arianism, William Whiston, and the Development
of Cotton Mather's Late Eschatology

One of the most engaging traits of the "Biblia Americana," as demonstrated by several other essays in this volume, is its reflection of Cotton Mather's often conflicted stance toward the modern theological developments taking shape around him. Sometimes Mather accommodated these new movements, and sometimes he rejected them. Perhaps more common, however, was the attempt to finesse their conclusions into an acceptable compromise. This paper specifically examines one such instance: Mather's move, late in his life, to adopt a preterite interpretation of several biblical prophecies that most of his contemporary millenarians believed remained to be fulfilled. While this transition in Mather's thought has previously been examined within the context of his larger theological environment,[1] this paper approaches the development from the angle of concrete events in Mather's life and in the Christian community in which he lived. In doing so, my investigation moves beyond the "Biblia Americana," drawing from the full spectrum of Mather's diverse writings. This added breadth not only serves to highlight and contextualize some of the specific hermeneutical changes Mather makes within his "Biblia Americana," but also provides a broader picture of the cultural and theological environment that birthed his *magnum opus*.

My main argument is that Mather's shift should be understood as part of a slow response to a conflict in England among the Dissenting churches over Arianism that erupted in the second decade of the eighteenth century. This conflict challenged Mather's conviction that the world would soon be entering a time of dramatic Christian reformation as a prelude to Christ's second coming. With this hope overturned, Mather slowly changed his mind not merely about the awaited reformation, but also about all the other signs – including the conversion of the Jews – that he had expected to occur before the coming of his Lord. Furthermore, William Whiston's prominent role both in initially reinforcing Mather's expectations of specific cataclysmic events to occur toward the end of the decade and then in smashing those very hopes underscores Mather's

---

1 See especially Smolinski's introduction to Mather's *Threefold Paradise*.

tumultuous intellectual environment, which was complicated by the Arian controversy. It is fair to say that Mather's changing eschatology is a microcosm of much of the transatlantic debate in theology then taking shape.

This paper begins by providing an introduction to Mather's early eschatology, paying special attention to the role of the Jewish people in the millennium. Next, I will discuss an important but temporary strand of Mather's eschatological thought: his expectation in the 1710s of a dramatic Christian reformation rooted in ecumenical union prior to Christ's second coming. In this context, I will consider how William Whiston's eschatological speculations encouraged Mather to expect this reformation to begin in or soon after 1716. On the basis of this overview, I will examine Mather's ecumenical activities within the context of his ministry. It will be shown that Mather's eschatologically motivated ecumenism continued apace through 1718, and then quickly evaporated. The English Arian controversy that culminated in a conference at Salters Hall (1719) appears to be one of the main reason for this quick shift in Mather's thought, leading him to abandon his hopes for an ecumenical union that would usher in the millennium and to embrace a preterite interpretation of several key prophecies. To help us appreciate Mather's changing position, I will provide a background sketch of the English Arian movement in the early 1700s and Whiston's leading role in fomenting the transatlantic controversy.[2] Finally, I will explore how his souring friendship with Whiston impacted Mather's annotations in his "Biblia Americana."

Mather's Early Eschatology

Interest in Cotton Mather's eschatology has seen a considerable rise in the last couple of decades. Although a number of scholars have previously examined his millennialism,[3] Mather's eschatology finally emerged on the scholarly scene full-force in the 1990s, first as the subject of a monograph (Erwin), and then in the publications of two previously unpublished Mather manuscripts on eschatology: "Triparadisus" and "Problema Theologicum." Both of these projects inspired the current endeavor to edit Mather's "Biblia Americana." Eschatological themes pervade almost every aspect of Mather's thought and appear in many of his writings. Given the complex and sometimes changing nature of Mather's ideas concerning the end times, I will introduce them through the lens of a single work of Mather's, his 1703 treatise "Problema Theologicum." This early work provides a solid foundation for later discussion of Mather's shifting views.

---

2   For an older but still valuable account of Mather's relationship to Whiston, see Tuttle.
3   For a short bibliographical introduction, see Mares (355).

"Problema Theologicum," like all Christian millennial thought of Mather's era, is rooted in the basic assumption that the Bible offers signs indicating how the world's end-times will unfold. Based on prophecies found in the biblical books of Daniel and Revelation especially, along with supplemental biblical passages such as Rom. 11 and 2 Pet. 3, Mather believed Christians could construct a general timeframe for the world's eschatological events. According to Mather, and many others like him, it was even possible to recognize recently fulfilled prophecies from these books. These prophecies could provide clues as to when later prophecies might be fulfilled. For instance, Mather believed that the "Second Woe," which is described in Rev. 11:14, could be identified with the defeat of the Turkish empire in 1697 ("Problema" 401–04). The same passage then indicates that a third woe would quickly follow. This third woe, however, is not explicitly named in Revelation. Mather reasons that by this woe is to be understood precisely what occurs next in the narrative: a seventh angel sounds a trumpet, the kingdom of Christ on earth is announced, and the dead are judged (Rev. 11:15, 18). Mather speculates that this confluence of events would coincide with Christ's second coming. Obviously, it was his hope, then, that, because the world has just witnessed the passing of the second woe, Christ's return, like the third woe, was imminent.

According to Mather, Christ's physical return would inaugurate his thousand-year reign on earth. This opinion sets Mather in a broad camp of eschatological thought termed "pre-millennialism." The larger motivation of "Problema Theologicum" is to support Mather's own pre-millennialist stance. He summarizes this argument clearly at the beginning of his essay: "the Second Coming of our Lord JESUS CHRIST, will be at the Beginning of the Happy State, which, according to his Word, we Expect for his Church, upon Earth, in the Latter Days" (368).

Mather never strayed from this broadly pre-millennial position. His interpretation of specific aspects of it, however, did shift as Mather grew older. Most prominent among these changes is the role that the Jewish people play in the millennium.[4] In "Problema Theologicum" Mather argues that a conversion of the Jewish nation predicted in Rom. 11 would occur at the beginning of the thousand-year-reign of Christ. The first of Mather's six arguments in support of his overall thesis concerns this Jewish conversion (382–91). Because this anticipated sign remained yet to be fulfilled, he asserts, "Therefore. – Wee Look for a *Conversion* of the *Jewish* Nation" (382).

Several questions about the timing of Mather's eschatology remain. As explicated in "Problema Theologicum," both Christ's return and the conversion

---

4 One other significant point on which Mather changed his mind relates to a conflagration that 2 Pet. 3 predicts. For more information on this shift, and particularly on how it relates to his shift on the conversion of the Jews, see Smolinski's introduction (38–44) and Mather's own discussion of this issue (295–319), both in *Triparadisus*.

of the Jews would occur "at the beginning" of the millennial kingdom. Mather leaves it unclear, however, if these two events would take place simultaneously or consecutively, and if the latter, in which order. This ambiguity is significant. For instance, if the conversion of the Jews were to occur as a precondition for Christ's return, then Mather would have a strong incentive to work towards this goal.[5] But if the Jewish conversion were sparked by Christ's return, occurring either with it or after it, any personal efforts to engage in their national conversion prior to the second coming would be uncalled for.

While composing "Problema Theologicum" in the closing years of the seventeenth century, Mather was apparently still undecided on this point. First Mather argues that the conversion would precede Christ's return, basing his argument on a reading of Acts 3:19: "Repent, and be converted, to the blotting out of your Sins, so that the Times of Refreshing may Come from the Presence of the Lord" (386–87). Later, however, Mather allows for a simultaneous prophetic fulfillment. He recognizes his contradiction, but ultimately lets it stand: "I confess, there is a Difficulty in it, which I am willing to leave *Undecided*" (389). Still, despite the space Mather allowed for both interpretations within "Problema Theologicum," his own actions seem to imply that he leaned towards a pre-appearance conversion of the Jews.[6]

One more problem plagued Mather's early eschatological speculations with regards to the signs of the millennial times and their chronology. Several biblical passages (in the synoptic gospels, Mat. 24, Mark 13, and Luke 21; elsewhere Joel and 2 Pet. 3) seem to foretell disaster and ruin in the last days before the millennium. This dark scenario involved the condition of the church as well, Mather believed, because the "Happy State" of the church would be postponed and kept "in feeble, narrow, Difficult, yea *Defective* Circumstances" (370) until the Jewish nation as a whole had embraced Christianity. As Mather applied the prophecy of Miriam's leprosy (Num. 12), "The Church of God must be retarded in its progress, towards its *Happy State*, until Excluded *Israel* be restored" (384). In fact, the conversion of the Jews "will be one of the first things, to come to pass at the arrival of that *Happy State* which we expect for the Church upon Earth. It cannot be Imagined that the *Happy State* which we Expect for the Church can arrive, and the Jewish Nation long remain in its *Tribulation*" (384).[7] To support his speculations, Mather simply read the signs of the time in

---

5   In this case the millennial kingdom would have begun to break into the world before Christ's actual return. Holding to this interpretation does not necessarily disqualify one from a place in the broad "pre-millennialist" camp referred to above. The key consideration is that Christ would still return at the beginning of the millennium, and not at its end.
6   Though it is outdated in several respects, Friedman offers a brief overview of Mather's personal dealings with Jews. For more on Mather's evangelism of the Jews, see chapter two of Smolinski's introduction to Mather, *Triparadisus* (28–31).
7   Richard Lovelace takes a slightly different approach to this theme in Mather's thought. Asserting that Mather looked for signs of a "preparatory revival" and not actually the begin-

the European world. More often than not, he concluded that *"Common sense might have taught all Good men, That the Church of God has never yet seen the Happy State intended for it"* (379). Periods of intermittent discouragements were frequently offset by positive news to the contrary as Mather scanned the horizon for pregnant signs of the pending millennium. His unfinished "Biblia Americana" manuscript, a synoptic commentary on the Bible, testifies to his unfolding eschatological theories.

Mather and Whiston in the "Biblia Americana"

Much like Matthew Poole's famous *Synopsis Criticorum* (1669–76), Cotton Mather's "Biblia Americana" synopsizes his predecessors' theological debate on specific biblical passages. Mather's own interpretive position is often elusive when he withholds his opinion as he presents his colleagues' arguments. What makes reading "Biblia" challenging to modern scholars is that Mather did not compose his entries in chronological order but recorded his thoughts and excerpts as the works of his colleagues fell into his hands. This process took more than thirty years (1693–1728) and, as a result, distracts from the unity of the work even as it contributes to its eclectic and comprehensive appearance. Furthermore, because Mather was unable to publish his "Biblia Americana," he kept adding to and revising his *magnum opus* until the end of his life.

Of particular interest for my argument is a portion of the "Biblia" that Mather entitled "Coronis." This section is tacked on at the end of Mather's whole manuscript, as a sort of appendix to his commentary on Revelation. In it he summarizes and evaluates William Whiston's *Essay on Revelation*, which was published in 1706. The fact that Mather's entry in "Coronis" is a block summary of Whiston's interpretation of Revelation separates it from most of the other entries in Mather's "Biblia" and indicates an approximate date for its composition. In 1706 Mather fell seriously ill and, fearing that he would be unable to finish the "Biblia," applied immense effort to the task of bringing it to completion. In May he came to believe that he had, indeed, finished it and later that year he sent off advertisements to England seeking subscribers for its publication (Silverman 236). That he did not receive a copy of Whiston's *Essay* until sometime after Mather had sent off his advertisements is apparent in his "Coronis." Mather here speaks of "concluding" the "Biblia" with a discussion of Whiston's work and thanks God for sending it, presumably in the knick of time, just before the "Biblia's" hoped-for publication [*BA*, "Coronis"]. While he went

---

nings of the kingdom of God itself, Lovelace argues that at different times in Mather's life, he thought positive signs concerning the state of the church indicated Christ's imminent return (20, 66, 72, 247).

back and later edited the entry – in a manner to be discussed later in this essay – the initial rhetorical emphases in the "Coronis" point to an authorship around 1706.[8]

When Mather first wrote his "Coronis," he was enamored with Whiston's eschatological theories. Mather believed that "the Accurate *Whiston*, after Laborious Researches into the Matter," has found considerable support for determining distinct dates in the millennial timeline, like the previously mentioned 1697, on which the prophecy of the Turkish Woe was fulfilled [*BA*, "Coronis"]. With these dates fixed, and with the help of other interpretive moves, Whiston settles on 1716 as the next significant juncture.[9] The commentary goes through Whiston's work point by point, lists the events that can be expected around that time period, and praises Whiston for his perceptive insights: "To Conclude, our Mr. *Whiston* having advanced such Assurances for the Year 1716; we cannot but ask, What *Great Mutations* are to be expected, at that *Grand Period*?" Whiston's speculations were so convincing to Mather that he thought they were "no longer *Conjectures*, but irrefragable & incontestable *Demonstrations*, on many things which have appeared heretofore something *Dubious*" [*BA*, "Coronis"]. Reading Whiston's *Essay on Revelation* thus enticed Mather to search for specific signs of the coming millennium sometime in the middle of the second decade of the eighteenth century – signs that might be fulfilled in widespread revivals among the Protestant churches. Mather quotes Whiston approvingly: "That it should now be the Attempt of Good Men, with a Peculiar Vigour, to Revive and Reserve *Primitive Christianity*; For so to do, would be a Sweet Compliance with the Divine Providence, & with the Promises, which now point at a Sudden Exaltation to the Kingdome of our glorious LORD" [*BA*, "Coronis"]. Encouraged by such hopeful expectations, Mather began a campaign for ecumenical unity among the worldwide Protestant churches, an endeavor that – if blessed – might pave the way for Christ's kingdom on earth.

Mather's Eschatological Ecumenism

It is not immediately obvious how Mather might have thought that a campaign for ecumenical unity would help to foster the millennium, especially

---

8   Richard Lovelace argues that "by 1713" Mather "had reached the last book of the Bible" (67). Lovelace, however, does not account for Mather's editorial remarks in the "Coronis" manuscript, which suggest a composition date of sometime before 1711.

9   Whiston was not the first to posit 1716 as a significant date for the millennium; before him Joseph Mede had done the same, and Whiston explicitly acknowledged his debt to Mede's work. Mather also cites Mede frequently in the "Biblia Americana," but it seems that it was Whiston who finally convinced Mather of the importance of 1716. For general background on the millenarianism of the time, see Smolinski, "Apocalypticism" (37–48). For Whiston's reliance on Joseph Mede, see Jue (171–73).

given his early eschatological assumptions outlined in "Problema Theologicum." Even early in the 1710s, Mather still spoke in pessimistic tones about the world's imminent doom. For instance, on October 12, 1712, he worried, "There is a dismal Prospect before us. And God knows, what share this poor Country may have, in the Calamities, which threaten to overwhelm a Wicked world" (*Diary* 2: 84). On February 1, 1713, he prayed for Christ's speedy arrival: "Lord, Let a Glorious CHRIST return, Like the *Sun*, to a Miserable World, and bring a *New Face* upon it; Produce upon it a New Creation, and fill it with the Fruits of Righteousness" (*Diary* 2: 124).

Slowly, however, a new tone of optimism begins breaking through in the *Diary*, becoming more and more pronounced until around 1716, when Mather expresses confident hope that positive signs do indeed indicate the imminence of Christ's return as predicted by William Whiston. Now, Mather's hope seemed to center on a particular biblical passage that did not play any significant role in "Problema Theologicum." The famous prophecy of the stone cut out of the mountain and filling the entire earth (Dan. 2:31–35) symbolized to many millenarians of the day the miraculous spread of evangelical Christianity throughout the world.[10] This idea is key to understanding Mather's commitment to ecumenism, which led him to reach out to like minds in Europe. Mather references Dan. 2 frequently in these years, often with allusions to international revival and often with eschatological overtones. In February of 1710, for instance, he mentions two essays on "Methods of *Piety*" that he hopes will "contribute unto the Shaping of that People" who "are shortly to be the *Stone cutt out of the Mountain*." Furthermore, he sent his essays to August Hermann Francke of Halle to enlist the support of the German Pietists in his worldwide revival, which he thought corresponded with the stone's expanse and offered hope of Christ's imminent return (*Diary* 2: 23). In July of 1712, Mather prayed to God that he might help him to "understand the uniting Principles and Properties of that People, who are to be the Stone Cut out of the Mountain; and be improved in the Shaping and Serving of that Holy People, for the Grand Revolution that is now Coming on" (*Diary* 2: 50). His 1712 tract *Thoughts for the Day of Rain* mentions "A *Spirit of Association* for Noble & Pious Purposes" that "has of late begun Strangely to Visit the World." This has been witnessed "as far off as in Switzerland," and it "*annunciate[s] a more Illustrious State of the Church of God, that is to be Expected, in the Conversion of Jews and Gentiles*" (qtd. in Lovelace 224). In the same year he also joined an international prayer campaign, specifically petitioning Christ for his return. As it was advertised in an anonymous pamphlet that Mather valued highly enough to actually stitch into his

---

10 Mather's interpretation of this text is laid out clearly in his commentary on this passage in the "Biblia Americana," where he argues that "By that *Stone*, wee may understand, the *Church*" [*BA*, Dan. 2] He particularly argues against Iranaeus's idea that the stone actually represents Christ.

Diary, the campaign organizers hoped that these *"United Prayers* of the Faithful, may be followed with *Voices, and Thundrings and Lightnings, and Earthquakes,* and the sound of the *Trumpet,* which will bring on the Time when the *Kingdomes of this World, shall become the Kingdoms of our Lord"* (*Diary 1712* 117). Mather particularly valued the international ecclesial scope of this effort: "By such an Exercise," he recorded, he would "prove [himself] a Living Member in the Body of our Saviour" (*Diary 1712* 87). Furthermore, he believed the prayer campaign would be effective. While participating in it he was "filled with Unutterable Groans, for the Day to Come on, when Mankind Shall more generally see and become the Kingdom of God." Indeed, he was convinced that "Some Great Thing is at the Door!" (*Diary 1712* 114).

Mather soon began to do more than simply pray for Christ's return as he saw more and more signs of an international revival on the horizon. As epitomized in the "admirable Piety, shining among the Professors of modern Pietism" in Germany, Mather began to "look on the Strains of Piety conspicuous in them, as notable Dawns of the Kingdome of God among the Children of Men." Encouraged specifically by their work, Mather himself resolved to "seek a particular preparation for Services which [he] may do, in the coming on of the Kingdome of God" (*Diary* 2: 193). Two weeks after recording these thoughts in his *Diary*, Mather seemed to have lit upon the means by which this worldwide revival might be effected. Noting the "mighty Tendency to Reformation," he hoped that the essence of the Christian faith – if distilled into a few Pietist maxims – might overcome widespread sectarianism among the churches. These ideological divisions among Protestants, Mather thought, were some of the principal obstacles to be removed before the millennium could begin. He therefore set out "to publish unto the World, the Maxims, which are to unite the People that the glorious God will form for Himself, and that will quickly be the Stone growing into a great Mountain, which the whole Earth shall be filled withal." These maxims might just be what it takes to "bring on the Kingdome of God" (*Diary* 2: 196–97). To this end, he sent his tract *Things to Be More Thought Upon* to the publisher in 1713.

Things to Be More Thought Upon represents Mather's first significant activist stance to prepare for the millennium on an international scale. Among other things, the tract outlines fourteen "Maxims of Piety" upon which he hoped Christians the world over might unite. These Maxims became a substantial part of Mather's ecumenical repertoire during this time; he wrote about them repeatedly in his *Diary*,[11] in his correspondence,[12] and in other

---

11 For additional references not specifically mentioned in this paper see (2: 200, 201, 202, 213, 220, 277, and 468). Also, it should be noted that Mather had a blueprint of these maxims, though without their eschatological baggage, up and running long before he first published them. Before 1713, then, Mather's *Diary* also makes references to "Maxims of Piety."

12 See for instance his letters to Robert Woodrow, professor at the University of Glasgow,

tracts.[13] Furthermore, as time advanced, Mather grew bolder in his claims for these maxims. In fact, he came to believe that a union of churches based on his maxims was actually a precondition to, and would bring about, the kingdom of God. A 1716 letter to Anthony William Boehm – Mather's correspondent in London – makes this link clear: "it is vital Piety embracing the Maxims of the everlasting Gospel ... which must unite the People of God. And a more explicit union being produced on those Maxims, the Papal Empire will fall before it, and the Kingdome of God will come on" (*Diary* 2: 406–07). As the time for the expected millennium drew closer, Mather supplemented his frequent allusions to Dan. 2 with a second biblical prophecy (Joel 2:28) in which God promised to pour out his spirit upon all people to precipitate the hoped-for event.[14] Mather believed that this prophecy was about "to receive its full Accomplishment" (*Diary* 2: 329) in part through the ecumenical union he had advocated through his maxims of piety. Just as the spirit had watered the seeds of the apostolic church, Mather believed, so it would now revive the church: Heavenly angels would descend to the earth and "possess and inspire Instruments to serve the Kingdome of God, and spread the maxims of the everlasting Gospel into the World" (*Diary* 2: 376, 387, 396). Through the outpouring of the spirit the church would attain harmony among its ranks, and through this concord the kingdom of God would arrive on earth.[15]

The *annus mirabilis* 1716 came and went, but the prayed-for cataclysm failed to materialize. The only significant sign of God's looming judgment occurred in Versailles, where the aged Louis XIV, that "Old French Leviathan," died on 1 September 1715. Far from being discouraged, Mather continued to express strong eschatological hopes tied to his expectation of the imminent fulfillment of the prophecies in Daniel and Joel through 1718. After all, only God knew the precise moment in time when the millennium would commence like a thief in the night (Matt. 24:44; 1 Thess. 5:4, 9–10). Meanwhile, it was incumbent upon Mather and his fellow millenarians to press on. Although Mather never surrendered his lifelong belief in the nearness of millennium, an unexpected development occurred in England that would make him change his mind on how God might effect his plans.

---

and Anthony William Boehm, a German Pietist at the royal court in England, in Mather (*Diary* 2: 329, 333). He also wrote about his maxims to Francke, as well as to two Halle missionaries stationed in Tranquebar (Ceylon). For information on the Francke letter, see Lovelace (34); for information on the letter to Tranquebar, see Benz (44).

13   Mather republished all fourteen Maxims in his 1716 *Stone Cut out of the Mountain*, and then condensed these fourteen maxims to three christologically centered principles in his 1717 *Malachi*. In addition, they appear to have been a part of his now lost sermon *Boanerges. The Work of the Day* (*Diary* 2: 381). Mather's son, Samuel, gives some insight into the contents of this work in his biography of his father (72).

14   For additional references to this passage, see *Diary* (2: 387, 397, 460, 463, and 469).

15   Mather makes this connection explicitly again in *Diary* (2: 454).

Arianism in England

On 24 February 1719 a group of Dissenting ministers met in London's Salters Hall to respond to an urgent plea for advice from a group of their fellow ministers in Exeter. The Exeter clergy had recently been confronted with the impending ordination of a known Arian sympathizer – one Herbert Sogdon – to the ministry in a neighboring community. Suspecting that the Rev. Joseph Hallett and James Peirce had supported Sogdon's candidacy, the Dissenting ministers wrote to a group of London clergy for advice.[16] In deliberating over their response, the London ministers debated whether the Exeter clergy should be required to subscribe to the Trinity. Ultimately they agreed that the only test of orthodoxy that should be demanded was an adherence to scripture as the perfect and only rule of faith. Furthermore, the Salters Hall convention specifically voted that the Exeter ministers should not compel their colleagues to subscribe to the Trinity. This vote was highly controversial, passing by only a 57–53 margin; it revealed just how far the Dissenters were divided on this issue. Several days later the London ministers resumed their discussion, but a group of disgruntled ministers demanded that the assembly itself affirm several statements supporting the Trinity. No consensus could be reached, and after several heated debates, one clergyman held a scroll up into the air, stormed out of the meeting, and called on others to join him in subscribing to the proposed statements.[17] Ultimately, neither side was satisfied, and the disputants subsequently engaged in a pamphlet war that attests to the significance of the Salters Hall debate. Between 1719 and 1721, publishers released a flood of treatises on Arianism, in which combatants on both sides side jockeyed for high moral grounds.[18]

Although this controversy erupted in England, its tremors soon reached the shores of New England. Predictably, Mather was alarmed by this news from abroad. Granted, Arianism had reared its ugly head before in the 1690s, but this time, the controversy was much more volatile. In the 1690s, powered by the twin engines of rationalism and toleration, antitrinitarianism and particularly Socinianism flourished in England. Even though the storm lost its strength around 1697 (Sullivan 264), the two trends driving its growth persisted; it took only a little more than a decade for a milder and more acceptable brand of antitrinitarianism to emerge: Arianism.[19] Two figures are at the center of the early

---

16   Hallett, the leader of this group, read and corresponded with Whiston while a student at Exeter's Dissenting Academy in 1710 (Duffy 137).

17   In providing the background on the Salters Hall controversy, I have chiefly relied on Thomas.

18   For a summary of these treatises, see section III, "The Debate in Public," in Thomas (175–79).

19   John Locke's treatises *The Reasonableness of Christianity as Delivered in the Scriptures* (1695) and *A Letter Concerning Toleration* (1689) testify to the temper of the time. Locke

eighteenth-century Arian movement: William Whiston and Samuel Clarke. Both of these men were personal friends of Sir Isaac Newton, who was anxious to keep his own Arian beliefs out of the public limelight. But while Newton discouraged his friends from publicizing their Arian views, both Whiston and Clarke did collaborate in their philological investigation of St. Athanasius's alleged textual interpolations in the Bible. According to Whiston, Clarke instigated Whiston's search into ante-Nicene doctrine in 1705 when he relayed to him his suspicion that the Athanasian doctrine of the Trinity was not actually held by early Christian authors. By 1707 Whiston was fully persuaded that Christ himself was an Arian.[20]

The next stage in Whiston's developing Arian persuasion occurred in July 1708 when he perused the *Apostolic Constitutions*, which supplied him with the firm evidence he was looking for. Convinced that this fourth-century Arian document was "plainly sacred, and belonging to the Companions of the Apostles, if not to the Apostles themselves," Whiston arrived at his mature Arianism (Duffy 134).[21] He began propagating his newfound notions in Cambridge and, predictably, came under fire. When he proclaimed his views in his *Sermons and Essays* in 1709, he drew the ire of his Trinitarian colleagues who forcefully removed him from the Lucasian chair of mathematics at Cambridge, previously occupied by Sir Isaac. If anything, such opposition by men of the cloth spurred Whiston on to publish his four-volume *Primitive Christianity Revived* (1711), an edition of original documents and philological proof that the doctrine of the Trinity was based on a fourth-century forgery. No wonder that Whiston was charged with heresy as the Convocation of Bishops proceeded against him.[22] If that were not enough, Whiston's fellow Arian Samuel Clarke went public with his *Scripture-Doctrine of the Trinity* (1712), arguing that the Bible represents the Father alone as the supreme deity; while the Son and Holy Spirit are co-eternal, they are subordinate to and without union with the Father.[23]

---

argued for toleration of all creeds (except atheism), but the Members of the House of Lords were unprepared to go that far and sought to halt the spread of antitrinitarianism by passing the Blasphemy Act of 1698. The space allotted to my paper does not allow me to explore the extent to which eighteenth-century "Arians" actually were Arians. Many who were accused of Arianism rejected or at least qualified the term. When used in my essay, the term "Arian" signifies the belief in Jesus's divinity, but not his consubstantiality with the Father.

20 For Whiston's account, see his *Historical Memoirs*.
21 For more on the shape of Whiston's Arian thought, see Wiles (93–110) and Force (17–20).
22 The best treatment of this investigation is Duffy.
23 For a fuller treatment of Clarke's theology, see Wiles (110–34).

Mather's Reaction to English Arianism

Cotton Mather had long admired the scholarship of William Whiston, his friend and correspondent. However, when in September of 1711 Mather "received an Account of [Whiston's] Proceedings" from the author (probably outlining Whiston's argument in *Primitive Christianity Revived*), Mather feared that Whiston would "raise a prodigious Dust in the world, by reviving the *Arian* Opinions." That same day Mather resolved "to explain and maintain the glorious Doctrine of the *Trinity*" (*Diary* 2: 106–07) and called on influential colleagues to rise up in defense of the Trinity. His *Diary* twice records intentions to petition William Jameson, a professor at the University of Glasgow, to refute Whiston and his representation of early Christian doctrine (2: 73, 205). Still not satisfied, Mather composed (in May of 1713) an epistolary discourse against Arianism. Unfortunately, Mather's *Goliathus Detruncatus* never saw the light of print because the London publisher died unexpectedly and the manuscript was irretrievably lost.[24]

Mather contributed one more piece of work to his short-lived anti-Arian crusade in the second decade of the eighteenth century. This treatise, interestingly enough, was *Things to Be More Thought Upon*, the same piece that was supposed to launch Mather's campaign to unite the Christian world on the basis of his "Maxims of Piety." The second and longest of the three sections in this essay is devoted to combating Arianism and singles out Whiston for particular reproach. As Mather put it in his *Diary*, the treatise was designed "as an Antidote against the wretched Poison, wherewith *Whiston* is endeavouring to corrupt the Church of God" (2: 186). In addition to laying out the Augustinian doctrine of the Trinity and Christology, Mather specifically attacks as a "wicked forgery" the *Apostolical Constitutions* that Whiston deemed genuine (*Things* 52–55). After this brief flurry of anti-Arian commotion in the early 1710s, Mather put the issue aside. Perhaps he no longer considered it a significant threat, or he simply considered other issues more important, for instance the burgeoning ecumenical revival. It was not until Mather first began to get wind of an Arian threat among his fellow Dissenters in England that he returned to this issue full force.

---

24 The full title of the epistolary discourse is *GOLIATHUS DETRUNCATUS. The Trinity of Persons, in the One most Blessed and Glorious God; and the Eternal Godhead of our Great Saviour; briefly asserted and clearly explained, and victoriously defended; both by the Infallible Scriptures, and by the Antenicene Fathers. In an American Letter to the Learned Mr. William Whiston.* Mather's son and biographer apparently thought highly of this book, finding it important enough to merit a place in his list of "great performances," a list that included such major works as "Angel of Bethesda," "Triparadisus," and "Biblia Americana" – all of which remained unpublished during Mather's lifetime. See S. Mather (73) and Silverman (328–32).

The Salters Hall controversy was actually not the first indication Mather received of an incipient Arian menace lurking among his brethren across the ocean. The episode at Salters Hall was only the climax of a controversy that had been brewing for several years. Mather appears to have first been apprised of potential Arian threats in Exeter sometime in 1717. In December of that year he composed a letter to John Stirling, principle of the college at Glasgow, relating how "an eminent person in the west of England"[25] lately wrote [him] bitter lamentations that the Whistonian Arianism had begun to infect not only the Church of England, but also the young Dissenting ministers in those parts of the country." As usual, Mather took immediate action: he entreated Stirling to reprint the portion of his 1713 *Things to Be More Thought Upon* that explicitly addressed Arianism.[26] At this early point the Arian threat did not preoccupy Mather as yet, but over the next year it continued to peck at his conscience. In October of 1718, for instance, he recorded writing again to one of his English correspondents to spur the publication of his tract against Arianism (*Diary* 2: 563).

Sometime around 1719 Mather received the first news of the actual meeting at Salters Hall. Soon after being appraised of the events he complained to Governor Gurdon Saltonstall of Connecticut that Salters Hall was "the most grievous tidings that ever came over the Atlantic unto us" (*Selected Letters* 289). Mather quickly sent off a wave of other correspondence on the issue and in the process raised not a small amount of opposition. Indeed, in the early 1720s the fallout of the Salters Hall conference was "the chief, passionate" concern of many of his letters (*Selected Letters* 278). Nor did he limit his communication to simple correspondence.[27] Cotton and Increase Mather joined the pamphlet

---

25   "West of England" may seem a vague phrase, but it clearly refers to Exeter. Mather uses the same designation to refer to Exeter in the letter in which he relates hearing the first news about Salters Hall. See Mather, *Selected Letters* (289).

26   Mather, *Selected Letters* (245). Mather does not explicitly name the article he hoped to reprint, but his request that the phrase "*The Father be the Foundation of the Deity*" be changed into "*The Father be the Fountain in the Deity*" confirms that Mather is referring to *Things to Be More Thought Upon*. This phrase appears on page 30 of the original publication.

27   The Arian controversy also makes a direct appearance in Mather's "Biblia Americana" in his commentary on 1 John 5:7–8. This text, which in the King James Version reads: "For there are three that bear record in heaven, the Father, the Word, and the Holy Ghost: and these three are one. And there are three that bear witness in earth, the spirit, and the water, and the blood: and these three agree in one" was the *locus classicus* for proofs of the Trinity. However, as almost all modern scholars agree, the key phrase "in heaven, the Father, the Word, and the Holy Ghost; and these three are one" (dubbed the 'Johannine Comma') is an interpolation that was not written by the epistle's original author. In Mather's time, the authenticity of this text was only beginning to be questioned (for more information, see Bludau). Mather's initial commentary on this text completely passed over its trinitarian nature, but at some point he went back and inserted another page with a strongly worded rebuke to those who argued that it was an interpolation. This page was almost certainly inserted sometime after 1713 because

war in England with their own piece entitled *Three Letters from New-England, Relating to the Controversy of the Present Time* (1721).

While Cotton insisted over and over again that Arianism cut at the heart of the gospel and thus could not be tolerated, his fellow combatants retorted that his inflexibility undermined his own efforts on behalf of ecumenical union. Mather himself was not very receptive to this critique. In one letter, he asserted simply that it was "to be pitied rather than answered" (*Selected Letters* 303). It is important to recognize, however, that, as his earlier *Things to Be More Thought Upon* demonstrates, Mather's position on ecumenism was ultimately consistent. From his very first activist treatise in favor of ecumenism, Mather emphasized certain minimal, but key, doctrinal standards: orthodox Christology was nonnegotiable. Mather's ecumenical efforts were never grounded in simple Pietism, as modern scholars have occasionally implied.[28] Rather, his ecumenism is rooted in Christocentric piety. Indeed, the first three of Mather's fourteen original Maxims are entirely doctrinal (*Things* 88–89).

Moreover, when examined in light of his whole career, Mather's ecumenical efforts demonstrate the importance of doctrine, specifically the doctrine of Jesus Christ. Mather's first substantial publication on Christological ecumenism was his essay *Blessed Unions* (1692). This tract is based on two sermons that he had preached in 1692 in support of an ecumenical union that his father, Increase, had recently helped negotiate among the United Brethren in England. Mather chose for his text John 18:21 – "That they all may be ONE, as Thou, Father, art in me, and I in Thee, That they also may be ONE in Us." In the first sermon, Mather addresses the union of the believer with Christ, which he grounds in two preconditions:

> (1) The whole Undivided Adorable Trinity is concerned in the *Union* which Believers have with the Lord Jesus Christ.
> (2) It is more *peculiarly* the Lord Jesus *Christ* with whom all Believers have their *Union*. It is the Lord Jesus Christ, as GOD MAN, who is, *The Head of the Church;* and in that capacity we have our *Union* with Him. Indeed, the *Personal Union* of the Two Natures in our Lord, is that upon the account whereof He is an Object admirably Fitted for an *Union* with us. (*Blessed Union* 5–6)

In these two preliminary statements, Mather places a classically creedal understanding of the Trinity and Christology at the center of his exposition of the Christian's union with the redeemer. The sermon expounds the nature of this union and urges such a union upon its hearers. It is only in the second sermon that Mather addresses the first half of the Johannine verse: "that they all may be one." Mather predicates his second sermon upon the first; he implores his pa-

---

he refers readers to another, unnamed, piece in which he has defended the text. This piece is in all likelihood *Things to Be More Thought Upon*, where he discusses this text on p. 35.
28   See, for instance, Lovelace (265).

rishioners to become *"One*, with the Lord Jesus Christ, [that] you may *also*, and *therefore*, become *One* among yourselves" (40). Mather never wavered on this high Christology, and his efforts for ecumenical union must always be considered in light of it.[29] Consequently, when Arianism reared its head again in the second decade of the eighteenth century, and hence at the height of Mather's ecumenical activism, his strong response was to be expected.

One more note about Mather's *Blessed Unions* bears mention in this context. As previously suggested, this sermon specifically recognized the ecumenical union that his father helped to negotiate in England. On the basis of the *Heads of Agreement*, a coauthored document in which Increase Mather traced the history of the Presbyterians and Independents in England, these two denominations joined to form the United Brethren, a merger that came to be known in England as the "Happy Union" (Thomas 167).[30] This association quickly deteriorated in London but persisted for some time in Exeter, where the Dissenters retained the name United Brethren (Thomas 167). Thus when Arianism threatened the unity of this body, it threatened not only Mather's more general hopes for an ecumenical union across the whole Christian church, but more concretely, it demonstrated the frailty of even a unity among Mather's own distinct sect within it. Mather was hit particularly hard by this unexpected development. In fact, Arianism quickly became his principal concern and crushed his hopes for a worldwide union of all Protestant churches on the basis of his maxims. Instead of sounding his call for ecumenism in preparation for the millennium, he was now struggling to defend his most basic theological tenets.

Mather's Eschatological Shift

Mather did not immediately put an end to all efforts toward ecumenical union, nor did he cease to campaign for union on the basis of his maxims.[31] He also did not stop looking for signs of the millennium.[32] He did, however, cease to link ecumenical unity with the eschaton. It is fair to argue that at the height of the Arian controversy, Mather did not mention any positive signs of a larger

---

29 Mather also explicitly links Christology and ecumenism in his *Piety and Equity United* (1717), in which he insists that "'tis in a Glorious CHRIST, that all Good men are *United*" (26).

30 For more background, see Miller (217–18).

31 The Maxims reappear, for instance, in Mather, *Genuine Christianity*. In 1721 he reported entertaining "a Purpose, of writing in the Latin Tongue, a Discourse about the Union of *Lutherans* and *Calvinists*, on the Basis of PIETY." It does not appear, however, that such a work was published (*Diary* 2: 663).

32 Mather even helped lead a *"Conference on the Sacred Prophecies concerning the Coming and Kingdome of our Saviour"* in 1722 (*Diary* 2: 685).

revival that might portent the imminent arrival of the kingdom of God.[33] Indeed, references to his ecumenical hopes began to disappear from his publications as the Arian menace took center stage in his thought. His ordination sermon for a Boston Baptist minister in 1718 is among the few public discourses in which Mather continued to sing to the old tune.[34] But it was not until Mather was apprised of Salters Hall that Arianism extinguished the flame of his ecumenical optimism. By 1724 Mather not only had given up his hopes for a worldwide revival of the Church, but also had become positively pessimistic about the church's condition: The church was "now generally slumbering and sleeping" (*Diary* 2: 726). More importantly, Mather now arrived at the conclusion that the church's lukewarm complacency at this juncture of the eschatological timetable was actually one of the portents of the pending millennium: "The world [is] fearfully Ripening for such a Revolution," Mather warned in a letter to Governor Saltonstall (3 August 1724). "And the Sleep of Midnight [is] growing into the deepest Lethargy, among the professors of our Holy Religion; which has now in a manner everywhere almost given up the ghost" (*Diary* 2: 804). Mather's disappointment was evidently so profound that he interpreted the present lukewarm condition of the church as the last sign to be given before Christ's return. In fact, no further precondition – such as the long hoped-for conversion of the Jews – needed to be fulfilled, and nothing stood in the way of the sudden arrival of the millennium. Mather's new conviction evidently acquired solidity sometime in June of 1724, as we learn from his *Diary*:

> The glorious Lord has led me into fuller Views than I have ever yet had, and such as I have exceedingly longed for and asked for, of what shall be the true State of Things in His Kingdome. And I am now satisfied, that there is nothing to hinder the immediate Coming of our Saviour, in these Flames, that shall bring an horrible Destruction on this present and wicked World, and bring on the new Heaven, and the new Earth, wherein shall dwell Righteousness. I purpose quickly to write on these things. (2: 733)

---

33 One notable exception is his tract *India Christiana*, which was published in 1721. However, this tract was originally written four years earlier, on December 31, 1717.

34 Lovelace has pinpointed Mather's "last public utterance of the imminent revival" in Mather's January 1718 tract reporting the conversion of three Jewish girls in Berlin (250). While Lovelace correctly discerns that some doubt is beginning to creep into Mather's mind by this time, this doubt has not yet overcome Mather, nor is this the last hurrah for his hopes. Further evidence of Mather's hope can be found in *Brethren Dwelling Together in Unity* (1718), where his eschatological themes continue to resound: "Since you are such *United Brethren*, why should you not *Unite* in *Projections* to advance the Kingdom of GOD? ... Instead of contriving every one to enlarge his own *Little Party*, would *Good Men Unite* in promoting that PIETY which all *Good Men* in *every Party* confess to be the *main Interest*, the World would soon feel the Blessed Effects of such *Associations*. Yea, that cry so long hoped for, *Babylon is fallen, is fallen!* would soon be heard upon them" (16–17). Mather's *Diary* records that he saw "the Kingdome of God opening" in this ecumenical partnership (2: 531).

Mather did quickly move to write about these things, in the manuscript that represents his mature eschatology, *Triparadisus*.[35] Here Mather accommodated his belief that nothing would now hinder Christ's immediate return. In fact, he argued that the conversion of the Jews had taken place long ago in the first two or three centuries after Christ's ascension. St. Paul's prophecy in Rom. 11 was therefore no longer applicable to the still unconverted Jews, but to the body of the spiritual Israelites, the church, from which the wall of separation between Jews and Gentiles had been completely removed.[36] Thus this prophecy had already been fulfilled long ago. Mather also changed his interpretation of the prophecies in Joel and Daniel that had played such a large role in his thought only a decade earlier. While Mather earlier had explicitly said that the prophecy in Joel remained yet to be fulfilled, in *Triparadisus* he changes his mind, saying rather that this prophecy applies to how "the *Gospel* was to be *preached throughout the whole World*, before the Destruction of *Jerusalem*" in 70 AD (206). Regarding Dan. 2, *Triparadisus* does not opt for a preterite fulfillment, but rather pushes its fulfillment back to after Christ's return and the worldwide conflagration wrought in Christ's path (319–320).

Despite Mather's clear statement that he attained his new understanding of the prophecies in 1724, his change of mind should not be seen as a sudden event but as a slow and arduous process fostered by the Arian controversy of his time as well as his thwarted hopes for a worldwide ecumenical union.[37] The controversy served as the catalyst, which forced Mather to reassess his assumptions about the condition of the church and the signs of Christ's imminent return. Indeed, the Arian controversy continued to haunt Mather for the remaining years of his life.[38] In at least three separate places Mather explicitly links the infiltration of Arianism into the church of English Dissenters with a broader spiritual decline throughout the world.[39] In the first two instances, he expresses his fears that the United Brethren would unknowingly be caught up in the ter-

---

35   This holograph manuscript was edited and published in *The Threefold Paradise of Cotton Mather* (1995).

36   For more background, see especially "The 'New' Hermeneutics and the Jewish Nation in Cotton Mather's Eschatology," chapter 2 in Smolinski's introduction to *The Threefold Paradise* (21–37). Section xi of Mather's "Third Paradise" defends his shift (295–318).

37   Several scholars have commented on Mather's change of mind and listed 1720 as the actual date for this sudden rupture (see, for example, Middlekauff 322). Smolinski seems ambiguous on the date, in one place listing 1720 and in another the traditional 1724 (General Introduction xxi, *Threefold Paradise* 32). Instead of settling on either an early or a late date, however, Mather's conversion is best viewed as a slow development, the beginning of which can be traced to his exposure to the Arian controversy.

38   In addition to the three instances listed here, Arianism makes its ways into Mather's writings in several other negative ways during his last three years; his *Paterna*, *Diary*, and his *Manuductio* further illustrate the extent to which Arianism was still on his mind (Lovelace 94).

39   For the first two of these, see Mather's letter to Thomas Bradbury (22 April 1724) and Mather's *Diary* entry for June 1724 (2: 796–97, 738).

rible events of the unfolding cataclysm. Two years before his death, Mather had become so disillusioned that he believed the inroads of Arianism among his fellow Dissenters in England would actually help to precipitate the coming calamity. This is what he confesses in a letter to his friend and fellow millenarian in Boston, Thomas Prince (24 January 1726):

> For my own part, I Look on the part which our Brethren, (I will not now say, *United Brethren*,) have taken in Countenancing the Conspiracy to dethrone and degrade and ungod the Eternal SON of GOD, as having a deep share in preparing the world for that *Catastrophe*, which my *Diluvium Ignes* warns you of. (*Diary* 2: 817)

Looking back over the course of his ministry, Mather mourns the loss of the ecclesial unity he first celebrated in his 1692 *Blessed Unions* and blames Arianism as the source of this disillusionment. Despite this shift in emphasis, however, Mather holds fast to his belief that Christ is coming soon.

My primary argument is that Cotton Mather's conversion regarding the signs that remained to be fulfilled before Christ's return (the preterite interpretation of Rom. 11, Joel 2, and the postponement of Dan. 2 until after Christ's return) is best understood as a long process whose roots are to be found in Mather's reaction to the Arian controversy of his day. My examination of this issue pinpoints several ironic turns in the course of Mather's thought. The most prominent of these is the twin role that William Whiston played in Mather's eschatological conjecture. Whiston first encouraged Mather's firm belief in the apocalyptic events that would occur in the year 1716. In fact, Mather recites Whiston's argument in the "Biblia Americana" and intersperses his commentary with high praises for Whiston and his work. However, when Mather discovered Whiston's Arian proclivities, he revised his long excerpt of Whiston ("Coronis") and struck from "Biblia Americana" all words of praise for Whiston, replacing such terms of endearment as "my *Whiston*" with the more objective "Mr. Whiston." At least in one case, after crossing out "our" and other positive adjectives preceding Whiston's name, Mather lamented, "Oh! had he continued ours!" [*BA*, "Coronis"].

Mather did not stop at editing out adjectives, however. Among other substantial changes, Mather also struck from the "Coronis" a reference to "the Restoration of the *Jewes*" from a list of seven events to be expected in 1716. This emendation is particularly interesting, because Mather never got around to removing all pertinent references to the hoped-for national conversion of the Jews. Further, when Mather made these alterations, likely towards the end of his life, it was manifestly obvious that this was not the only detail in the "Coronis" that was problematic. The whole scheme centered on 1716 was obviously false, and furthermore, Mather had elsewhere decried its chief advocate, Whiston as a "grand satanic tool of [Arian] mischief" (*Selected Letters* 289). Whiston's "Primitive Christianity," which Mather extolled in the "Coronis," had actually led to the demise of Mather's own ecumenical dreams. And yet Mather allowed the substance of Whiston's argument to stand, making only minor adjustments by inserting and removing some phrases here and there.

In considering the implicit irony in Mather's engagement with Whiston, we need to look at the whole scope of "Biblia Americana." Although the "Coronis" is a dramatic example, it is not the only section of the "Biblia" in which Mather allows seemingly contradictory statements to stand side-by-side with his own views. Perhaps the incongruity of such pairings demonstrates just how much Mather tried to establish his own ground in the controversy of his own time. The "Biblia Americana" testifies to this struggle as he incorporated the opposing views of fellow theologians in his synoptic commentary. His commentary on the Bible emerged in an age in which rapidly advancing scientific discoveries and traditional Christianity maintained an ambivalent relationship, sometimes supporting and sometimes undercutting each other. William Whiston's own publications illustrate this point well: despite pushing the boundaries of orthodoxy by advocating his Arian Christology, his desire to defend the traditional authority of the Bible motivated him to delve into the interpretation of scriptural prophecies. Significantly, both of these strains of his thought can be traced to his own "Newtonian" leanings.[40] Cotton Mather's "Biblia Americana" therefore not only illustrates Mather's evolving thought, but also stands as a monument to the conflicting challenges of the early Enlightenment that Mather embodies.

Works Cited

Primary Sources

Clarke, Samuel. *The Scripture-Doctrine of the Trinity. In Three Parts. Wherein All the Texts in the New Testament Relating to that Doctrine and the Principal Passages in the Liturgy of the Church of England are Collected, Compared, and Explained.* London, 1712.

Maimbourg, Louis, Bernard Lamy, and W. Webster. *The History of Arianism.* 2 vols. London, 1728.

Mather, Cotton. *Blessed Unions.* Boston, 1692.

–.   *Brethren Dwelling Together in Unity.* Boston, 1718.

–.   "Cotton Mather's 'Problema Theologicum': An Authoritative Edition." Ed. Jeffrey Scott Mares. *Proceedings of the American Antiquarian Society* 104 (1995): 333–440.

---

40   For more on Whiston's "Newtonianism," see Force.

–. *Diary of Cotton Mather.* Ed. Worthington Chaucey Ford. 2 vols. Massachusetts Historical Society Collections. 7th Series, Vol. VII–VIII. Boston: MHS, 1911–12.

–. *The Diary of Cotton Mather, D.D., F.R.S. for the Year 1712.* Ed. William R. Manierre II. Charlottesville: UP of Virginia, 1964.

–. *Genuine Christianity.* Boston, 1721.

–. *India Christiana.* Boston, 1721.

–. *Malachi. Or, the Everlasting Gospel, Preached unto the Nations.* Boston, 1717.

–. *Paterna: The Autobiography of Cotton Mather.* Ed. Ronald A. Bosco. Delmar: Scholars' Facsimiles & Reprints, 1976.

–. *Piety and Equity United.* Boston, 1717.

–. *Selected Letters of Cotton Mather.* Ed. Kenneth Silverman. Baton Rouge: Louisiana State UP, 1971.

–. *The Stone Cut Out of the Mountain.* Boston, 1716.

–. *Things to Be More Thought Upon.* Boston, 1713.

–. *The Threefold Paradise of Cotton Mather: An Edition of "Triparadisus."* Ed. Reiner Smolinski. Athens: U of Georgia P, 1995.

Mather, Cotton, and Increase Mather. *Three Letters from New-England, Relating to the Controversy of the Present Time.* London, 1721.

Mather, Samuel. *The Life of the Very Reverend and Learned Cotton Mather, D.D. & F.R.S.* Boston, 1729.

Whiston, William. *An Essay on the Revelation of Saint John So far as Concerns the Past and Present Times.* Cambridge, 1706.

–. *Historical Memoirs of the Life of Dr. Samuel Clarke. Being a supplement to Dr. Sykes's and Bishop Hoadley's Accounts. Including Certain Memoirs of Several of Dr. Clarke's Friends.* 2nd Ed. London, 1730.

–. *Primitive Christianity Reviv'd in Four Volumes. Vol. 1. Containing the Epistles of Ignatius. Vol. II. The Apostolical Constitutions in Greek and English. Vol. III. An Essay on those Apostolical Constitutions. Vol. IV. An Account of the Primitive Faith Concerning the Trinity and Incarnation.* London, 1711.

–. *Sermons and Essays upon Several Subjects.* London, 1709.

Secondary Sources

Benz, Ernst. "Pietist and Puritan Sources of Early Protestant World Missions (Cotton Mather and A.H. Francke)." *Church History* 20.2 (1951): 28–55.

Bludau, August. "The Comma Johanneum in the Writings of English Critics of the Eighteenth Century." *Irish Theological Quarterly* 17 and 18 (1922): 128–39, 201–18.

Duffy, Eamon. "Whiston's Affair: The Trials of a Primitive Christian, 1709–1714." *Journal of Ecclesiastical History* 27.2 (1976): 129–50.

Erwin, John. *The Millennialism of Cotton Mather: An Historical and Theological Analysis.* Studies in American Religion. Vol. 45. Lewiston: Edwin Mellon P, 1990.

Force, James E. *William Whiston: Honest Newtonian.* New York: Cambridge UP, 1985.

Friedman, Lee M. "Cotton Mather and the Jews." *Publications of the American Jewish Historical Society* 26 (1918): 201–10.

Jue, Jeffrey K. *Heaven Upon Earth: Joseph Mede (1586–1638) and the Legacy of Millenarianism.* Dordrecht: Springer, 2006.

Lovelace, Richard F. *The American Pietism of Cotton Mather: Origins of American Evangelicalism.* Grand Rapids: Christian UP, 1979.

Middlekauff, Robert. *The Mathers: Three Generations of Puritan Intellectuals 1596–1728.* New York: Oxford UP, 1971.

Miller, Perry. *The New England Mind: From Colony to Province.* Cambridge: Harvard UP, 1953.

Silverman, Kenneth. *The Life and Times of Cotton Mather.* New York: Harper & Row, 1984.

Smolinski, Reiner. "Apocalypticism in Colonial North America." *The Encyclopedia of Apocalypticism.* Vol. 3. Ed. Stephen J. Stein. New York: Continuum, 1998: 36–71.

–. General Introduction. *The Kingdom, the Power, & the Glory: The Millennial Impulse in Early American Literature.* Ed. Reiner Smolinski. Dubuque: Kendall/Hunt, 1998. viii-xlvi.

–. Introduction. *The Threefold Paradise of Cotton Mather: An Edition of* "Triparadisus," Ed. Reiner Smolinski. Athens: U of Georgia P, 1995. 3–86.

Sullivan, Robert E. *John Toland and the Deist Controversy: A Study in Adaptations.* Cambridge: Harvard UP, 1982.

Thomas, Roger. "The Non-Subscription Controversy amongst Dissenters in 1719: The Salters' Hall Debate." *Journal of Ecclesiastical History* 4.2 (1953): 162–86.

Tuttle, Julius H. "William Whiston and Cotton Mather." *Publications of the Colonial Society of Massachusetts* 13 (1912): 197–204.

Wiles, Maurice. *Archetypal Heresy: Arianism Through the Centuries.* Oxford: Oxford UP, 1996.

Section 6: Gender, Race, and Slavery
in the "Biblia Americana"

Helen K. Gelinas

Regaining Paradise: Cotton Mather's "Biblia Americana" and the Daughters of Eve

My dove, my undefiled, is but one; she is the only one of her mother, she is the choice one of her that bare her.
Canticles 6:9a
Many daughters have done virtuously, but thou excellest them all.
Proverbs 31: 29

His popular image as a misogynist witch-hunter notwithstanding, Cotton Mather's special concern for female piety as well as for the role of women in New England society has long been noted. Scholars of the colonial period have drawn attention to the complex and highly ambiguous conceptualization of gender roles underlying Mather's numerous tracts and sermons on the subject of women. On the one hand, Mather upheld a traditionalist understanding of women's subordinate position in the social and ecclesiastical order which excluded them from political or economic realms and confined them to a domestic realm under male authority. On the other hand, while Mather's respective writings thus propagated submission and "invisibility to the temporal world" as female virtues, he was an unusually outspoken champion of spiritual equality between the sexes, who, as Pattie Cowell notes, frequently exalted women's "secret glory in their piety." Unlike most of his male contemporaries and ministerial colleagues, he also emphasized women's equal "capacity for intellectual pursuits" (Cowell xiv), and strongly supported female scholarship. Best-known of Mather's works written specifically for women is *Ornaments for the Daughters of Zion, or, The Character and Happiness of a Virtuous Woman* (1692). Primarily a work on female conduct and devotion, *Ornaments* vigorously defended womankind against the opinions of men who had too long denigrated them as "not being rational creatures" (46). What is more, Mather's tract made a passionate case for wider access of women to higher learning, and hailed their great potential as writers from whose pious labors of the pen the church and society might greatly profit. It has also been shown that in the immediate environment of his congregation and household Mather practiced what he preached; nearly half of his published funeral sermons were written for women (Cowell xvii), and as a father, he nurtured and educated his own daughters in a surprisingly egalitarian manner for his time (*Diary* 2: 112; *Angel of Bethesda* 228–29).

So far, critics have had difficulties explaining what seems to be a contradictory stance. How did Mather, despite his conservative opinions on social hierarchy and on women's "proper place," come to his extraordinary investment in the notion of women's spiritual and intellectual equality as well as to his commitment to the full development of their capacities through education? Drawing on the hitherto untapped resource of his "Biblia Americana," this essay will argue that the complexities of Mather's conceptualization of gender roles can properly be understood only within the larger framework of his biblical theology. More specifically, I will explore the complex ways in which Mather's views on women are tied into his interpretation of redemption history and the history of the church. After a short historical background section, I will begin my investigation by showing from the commentaries on Genesis how his understanding of women's capacities and their place in society is directly related to his in many ways innovative interpretation of mankind's creation and of the original fall. Of special interest will be Mather's commentaries on Eve's role in the fall and in the future atonement of human sin through Christ. As a second step, the interdependencies between Mather's gender-ideology and his ecclesiology will be examined, particularly in the context of his glosses on Canticles. Finally, consideration will be given to the important influence which his millennialist eschatology had on the endorsement of female learning and on the reformist activities which he directed towards women.

Mather's Publicized Views on Spiritual and Intellectual Equality in Historical Context

To appreciate what was specific or new about Mather's views on the spiritual *and* intellectual equality of women, one needs to take into account the predominant concept of the Puritan Goodwife in early New England and its religious foundation. Due in part to the importance of female labor in a pre-industrial farming economy, Puritan women of the seventeenth century, when compared to later periods, held an "integral and essential part" in community life although not in public life. A woman's responsibilities were defined by "a series of discreet duties rather than by a self-consistent and all-embracing 'sphere'" (Ulrich, *Good Wives* 8).[1] Yet, while she may have functioned "simul-

---

1 A wife's "place" in Puritan New England was not necessarily confined to housework and childrearing; her duties might well include farming, dairying, and "almost any task as long as it furthered the good of the family and was acceptable to her husband" (Ulrich, *Good Wives* 36–8). Because numerous tasks "overlapped" in male and female "space," and because colonial wives often fulfilled the role of deputy-husband when their spouses were away, the married couple functioned not only as equals in covenant, but also in partnership (Chamberlain 334). It is in this same sense that the commendatory remarks by Anne Bradstreet's brother-in-law in *The Tenth Muse* praise the author for "her exact diligence in her place" even though

taneously as a housewife, a deputy husband, a consort and a mother" among other roles such as neighbor and mistress over servants, she could neither "own nor acquire property ... enter into a contract [n]or write a will" unless she had attained legal permission signed by her husband prior to her marriage (Ulrich, *Good Wives* 7). Likewise, in their lives as Christians, Puritan women played a vital part in the religious activities of their congregations, but were not allowed to assume official functions, nor were they given a public voice in the affairs of the church.

A woman's proper place was at home with her family for whose physical and spiritual well-being she had primary care. Her role was to be a helpmeet for her husband who held authority over her, but in turn was under obligation to treat his wife with love and respect. Thus, that help which was "meet" for seventeenth and early eighteenth century Puritans in New England was based on a complex system of beliefs in temporal subordination and bonds of mutual affection within a hierarchy meant to mirror the mystical union of Christ and his church.[2] One of the hallmarks of a truly godly marital relationship was the demonstrated conduct of a wife who obediently submitted to her husband. This subordination had been established by God as the direct punishment of Eve's transgression for which the Bible recorded the judgment: "Thy desire shall be to thy husband and he shall rule over thee" (Gen. 3:16).

Of course, it was always understood that women were included in Christ's redemptive promise to those who put their trust in him and that their immortal souls were as valuable to God as those of men. At the same time, however, women were widely deemed to be inferior in their capacities for reason and moral self-government, weaknesses traceable to Eve's lapse in paradise. Her transgression, the result of the serpent's beguiling, was considered to be "an inevitable consequence of her nature" which was "weak, unstable, susceptible to suggestion" (Ulrich 97). While both sexes were considered to be liable to the entire panoply of sins, "as the 'weaker sex,' women ... ran the risk of ... leaving the path of morality, reason and propriety" more easily and frequently than men (Klaiber 306). Therefore, it was thought, women's naturally inferior powers of reason and intellectual capabilities made them more vulnerable to temptations, creating the perceived need for male guidance and supervision. The Puritan pursuit of creating a truly godly commonwealth thus translated into a rigid system of rules enforcing female piety and moral conformity.[3]

---

she had written a book of poetry (Bradstreet A3). Although somewhat dated, E.S. Morgan's *Puritan Family* (esp. chs. 2–4) is still a very useful book on the relationships between husband and wife, parents and children, and on education in Puritan New England.

2 The Puritan view of affectionate marriage was sometimes tainted, however, by an undercurrent of presumed inferiority among theologians and ministers. For example, in his *Commentary Upon the First Three Chapters of Genesis* (1656), John White cautioned men that the wife should remember "that though she be a helper, yet she is but a helper" (87).

3 As Amanda Porterfield explains, the guarding of female piety was perceived as being of

Women's alleged intellectual inferiority was sometimes cited as the reason that female education, beyond the necessary literacy for bible study and devotional reading (which Puritans deemed essential for everyone), was not only a usually fruitless endeavour, but even a potentially dangerous one. Just as Eve had been led into ruin by her desire for knowledge outside of her grasp, postlapsarian women were seen as liable to transgress God's laws in pursuit of higher learning which might expose them to ideas and bring them under influences that they might find impossible to control. Such a view was (in)famously expressed by John Winthrop, who recorded his admonishment of the husband of Ann Yale Hopkins for allowing his wife the liberty to give "herself wholly to reading and writing." Winthrop attributed Ann's loss of sanity to the fact that she *had* given herself to study, thereby attempting to exceed her God-given capabilities: "[If] she had attended her household affairs and such things as belong to women, and not gone out of her way and calling to meddle in such things as are proper for men, whose minds are stronger, etc.," he wrote, "she had kept her wits and might have improved them usefully and honourably in the place God had set her" (Winthrop 272). In a world in which hierarchical order and the keeping to one's "place" were essential to godliness, Ann Hopkins clearly had stepped out of her role.

Thus, in Puritanism, women were expected to find personal fulfilment and blessing under the temporal subjection which was known to be a "woman's place." The ideal Goodwife was to be gentle, humble, quiet in her manner, and of few words. She was to be receptive to her husband, virtuous in her behavior, and faithful above all things. Her meekness contrasted sharply and plainly with the manner of the loud, unruly wife, who did not hesitate to make her opinions known. Contentious women sacrificed honor to self-will when pressing for self-expression and by so doing ventured flagrantly beyond the bounds of proper place. In Puritan society such attitudes conveyed rebellion. According to many commentators, Eve disobeyed by leaving Adam's side, and her daughters ever since had been prone to the same disobedience. A woman who refused her role in her proper place was not a virtuous woman at all, but one revealing herself to be a "strange woman," a potential outcast who teetered dangerously on the precipice which divided the merely sinful from the demonic; witchcraft, as all knew, was by biblical definition the ultimate form of rebellion.[4]

---

utmost importance in New England: "Enforcing conformity to relatively rigid norms of personal morality was especially important in Puritan culture, which was dedicated to promoting individual responsibility for social order, and women were especially vulnerable to moral criticism because of their role as symbols of the moral purity and integrity of their culture. ... No group's behavior was more important in Puritan culture than that of young women" (149). See also Morgan (ch. 4).

4   "For rebellion is as the sin of witchcraft, and stubbornness is as iniquity and idolatry" (1 Sam. 15:23).

As in so many other respects, Cotton Mather was simultaneously a guardian of orthodoxy and an innovator when it came to the role of women. The sense of proper place plainly divided along gender lines was just as much an incontestable component of normative and acceptable social behavior to him as it had been to his forebears. However, with regard to the question as to whether females could or should be offered more than a basic education and what part intellectually gifted women who were pious ought to play in the reformation of church and society, he differed sharply from the majority of earlier Puritan ministers. There are certainly many reasons for Mather's departure from previously held views on women.[5] While changes in theology and scriptural interpretation – changes undergone partly in response to new theological trends in the Atlantic world, especially to Pietism – seem to have been the most decisive factor, dramatic transformations in the social and ecclesiastical fabric of New England certainly also contributed.

Mather's re-evaluation of female education and its benefits was born out of a profound sense of crisis. By the time he published *Ornaments*, his first significant work on the subject, the days of the Puritan theocracy in Massachusetts were gone for good, and the uproar in Salem had dangerously blurred the lines between true virtue and hypocrisy by calling into question the lives of many respectable matrons who had been known for their piety.[6] Just how much the events of Salem account for Mather's interest in redefining female virtue and widening the parameters of woman's place is open to debate. But it is certainly no coincidence that both *Ornaments* and *Wonders of the Invisible World* were

---

5   A notable exception to the nearly universal tendency among theologians to dismiss formal education as unimportant for girls is the Catholic François Fénelon, Archbishop of Cambray (1651–1715), whose *Instructions for the Education of a Daughter* (*Traite de l'education des filles*) appeared in 1686/87. Although not published in America until 1847, English translations as early as 1707 were in circulation. Mather, who was familiar with Fénelon's works, and who published several sermons in French, may well have had access to it in either language. While his advocacy of female education was progressive and unique for his time, Fénelon's motivation, unlike Mather's, derives primarily from his observations of women's influences on society rather than from a regard for the value of God-given, regenerated female intellect. Even as he campaigned for formal learning for daughters as well as for sons, he cautioned against making women "ridiculous by making them learned," due to their natural intellectual weakness (Fénelon 2). This was an assessment with which Mather did not concur. "'Tis certain," Fénelon maintained, "that the bad education of women, doth generally even more mischief than that of men; since the vices of men often proceed, from the ill education which they received at first of their mothers, or else from the passions which other women inspire into them in a riper age" (Fénelon 4). The notion of educating girls partly because they would be future mothers, and thus, teachers of children, is, however, reflected in Mather's explication of 1 Tim.2:12–15 in the "Biblia Americana," in which he notes that the Greek word for childbearing implies the bringing up, as well as the bring forth, of children.
6   Despite the ongoing furor over his public role in the aftermath of the Salem debacle, *Ornaments* was a well-received, instant success. So popular was it, in fact, that the book went through three printings, the last of which, issued posthumously, was brought out in a new edition at the height of the revivals in 1741.

written in 1692/93, the same year that Mather also began work on the "Biblia Americana." Thus, the two published works might be viewed as a closely interrelated endeavour,[7] demonstrating to New England's women the extremes of following either the virtuous or the wicked course, while the unpublished "Biblia" served as the theological laboratory in which Mather developed his theories.

As in all of his later publications on female piety and education, in *Ornaments* Mather sought to inculcate the traditional virtues of submissiveness, humility, and domesticity, thereby in many ways affirming the gender roles defined by early New England culture. More specifically, Mather maintained that women from less privileged ranks of the colony needed guidance from those who had been educated in the ways of godliness, not the least of which was to quell resentments based on incongruities between economic and social status which may have been the true motive for many of the accusations of the young women in the colony against their elders and "betters."[8] But he also warned that many of the worldly distractions which came with prosperity such as romance novels, too-fine clothing, and the temptations of dancing were filtering into the households of many "women of quality" and undermining their piety. Thus, the tract sketched out patterns of pious devotion and comportment for women at all stages and of various social ranks, patterns that Mather hoped would help to maintain the established social hierarchy.

Yet *Ornaments*, as suggested above, was not merely a rehearsal of a familiar litany of proscriptions for pious women. It declared women's general capacity for reason and higher learning, advocated study for women as a means of forwarding religious reformation, and in fact, strongly exhorted the pious women of New England to trust in their intelligence and to take up their pens. Mather's stance was certainly bold for his time and one for which he anticipated criticism. In defense of his argument he not only pointed to the fact that God had inspired several women to write passages of the Bible, but he also referred to women of antiquity, to women of New England's glorious past (there is a thinly veiled reference to Anne Bradstreet in his catalogue) as well as to women of recent European Pietism who had served God with their intellectual and literary tal-

---

7   It should be kept in mind that Mather's exhortations toward literary and intellectual pursuits were extended to pious women who could be trusted to use their gifts for the support and furtherance of Christ's kingdom, a kingdom which in New England had suffered a severe blow. The foundations of the New England errand had been threatened in the events in Salem by a blurring of the lines between good and evil and by an attack mounted by evil toward a reversal of "right order" (Kamensky 152). Thus, Mather may have written *Ornaments* partly as an attempt to restore that order on the heels of Salem, for as Jane Kamensky tells us, "the witch was not merely the lapsed version of the Puritan matron, but her inverse" (Kamensky 152).
8   On this, see Karlsen (226–229 and passim).

ents.[9] "As one *Woman* was the *Mother* of him who is the *Essential Word* of God, so diverse *Women* have been the *Writers* of his *Declarative Word*," he proclaimed. "They to whom the common use of *Swords* is neither Decent nor Lawful, have made a most Laudable use of *Pens*, and ... have with much *Praise* done the Part of *Scholars* in the World" (4). The long list of learned as well as godly women Mather then recites in *Ornaments* is obviously intended to corroborate his claim that intellectually, women could certainly be men's equals.[10] If so many females had demonstrated talents against the prevailing resistance of their societies, how much more could be expected from women when allowed sanctioned access to higher learning? But to achieve this, Mather knew, the prejudices of men had to be overcome. Hence, *Ornaments* attacked wide-spread notions about women's inherent weaknesses as the unjustified and distorted views of "froward and morose Men," who

> treated the *Female Sex* with very great Indignities; *Blades*, I guess, whose *Mothers* had undutiful *Children*, or whose *Wives* have had but cruel *Masters*. I am lothe to shew my Catalogue, nevertheless whole *Volumns* have been written to disgrace that *Sex*, as if it were ... *The meer Confusion of Mankind*. (*Ornaments* 46)

Given the chance, Mather argued, women could be powerful instruments in building the kingdom of God not through their pious behaviors alone, but also through religious writing, a form of expression that would allow them to participate in the public realm without leaving their proper place or violating the codes of decency. Just how radical these opinions were in their contemporary context is underscored by Mather's repeated references to Anna Maria van Schurman (1607–78) as a model of female learning.[11] The first woman to attend

9 Mather's own family was related by marriage to the poet Anne Bradstreet, also called "The Tenth Muse," who was highly esteemed for her virtue and faith in New England, further bolstering his opinion that women could be a formidable power for good in the world, and that history revealed that many of them had wielded pens.

10 "If the *Philosopher* may challenge the *Praise* of *Wisdom*, doubtless those were wise Women who were *Tutoresses*, if I may call them so, to the old famous Professors of all *Philosophy*. The Daughter of *Pythagorus* who made Comments on her Father's Books, was a *wise Woman*; and so *Hippatia* formerly, who taught the Liberal Arts, and wrote some Treatises of *Astrology;* and so *Sarrocha* more lately, who was ordinarily Moderatrix in the Disputations of the learned Men of *Rome*. The three *Corinnae* which equall'd, if not excell'd the most celebrated *Poets* of their Times, were *wise*; and such Ladies as *Olympias*, or *Trota*, whose Physical Skill, was the wonder of the Universe. The Empress *Eudocia*, who compos'd Poetical Paraphrases on divers Parts of the Bible, was a *wise Woman*; so was *Rosuida*, who compil'd the *Lives* of Holy Men, and *Pamphilia* who penn'd no despicable Histories; and the French Lady, who a while since, publish'd Homilies on the Epistle to the *Hebrews*; and thus was the Lady *Jane Grey*, who so admirably could read the Word of God in its *Originals*. There is *Wisdom* in these Things; and the Women which have had it, are therefore to be *praised*" (*Ornaments* 36–7).

11 While it is obvious that Mather supported higher education for women through private tutoring, it is not clear whether he would have approved of gifted female scholars attending university in the way van Schurman did. Van Schurman, after intense private tutoring, stud-

a Dutch university, the Pietist van Schurman was a *cause célèbre* in the Atlantic world although her praise from men in effect maligned women as a whole by considering her to be an anomaly.[12]

As the first public attempt to establish guidelines for women and to propagate their education, *Ornaments* was certainly a reaction to recent experiences of sinful backsliding in New England, particularly to the destabilizing events of Salem, as well as to the perceived need to instigate godly reformation of the people by means other than state-enforced conformity. At the same time, however, the ideas put forth in Mather's book developed directly from the scriptural exegesis he was pursuing in the "Biblia Americana." Indeed, the theological basis for Mather's position on the untapped potential of women lies in his interpretation of Eve, which has been hitherto hidden in the unpublished commentaries he wrote on Genesis.[13]

---

ied under the auspices of her mentor, Gisbertus Voetius, rector of the University of Utrecht. In spite of the fact that she was obliged to sit behind a curtain in an alcove so that she would not be visible to male students, van Schurman excelled in languages at Utrecht, where she mastered Greek and Hebrew in addition to the Latin she had been taught in her earlier years. She became adept at Ethiopian, Chaldean, Syriac and Arabic, all of which she used in biblical exegesis. Her exercise in logic, published as her dissertation, argued on the point of whether women should be educated. A devoted Calvinist, she longed for a Christian community which would incorporate practical charity with a sense of family devotion. Later she became a follower of the radical Pietist, Jean Labadie, whose teaching stressed heart religion over intellectual doctrine. Unlike the Quakers, however, who often placed the enlightening of the Holy Spirit above the word, Labadists insisted that revelation must be in agreement with the Bible in order to be valid. Mather's references to van Schurman, upon whom he had lavished praise for her writings which he used as an example to all women, calling her "that most accomplished lady ... [who] has in our Age addressed the World withal," is both notable and strategic in light of the fact that at the age of fifty she had relinquished all of her previously acquired academic notoriety upon her conversion to a vital Christian faith and employed her talents in the service of Pietism for the remainder of her days. Her conversion was a wonderful boon to the Pietistic cause. Interestingly, van Schurman was also acquainted with Madame de Gournay, author of *L'Égalité des hommes et les femmes* (1622), another woman often cited by Mather. On this, see Irwin. Mather lavishly praised van Schurman's talent in *Ornaments*, in the *Magnalia*, in reference to Anne Bradstreet, and in his private letters.

12 As Sylvia Brown points out, "Even the men who praised her called her a '*miraculum seu naturae monstrum*' a miracle or a prodigy of nature-with the implication, of course, that she had nothing to do with the rest of womankind" (197). Significantly, Mather showed no investment in making a similar claim.

13 A tremendous debt of gratitude is owed to Reiner Smolinski not only for giving me access to his impeccable transcriptions of Mather's commentaries on Genesis, but also for his thoroughly expounded and extremely enlightening annotations, on which I have relied throughout.

Mather's Interpretation of Eve's Role in the Original Fall

As he had promised in his advertisements for the "Biblia," Mather's schol-arship had procured "gems" that would shed new light on many aspects of even the most well-known passages in the Bible.[14] Every child in New England could have related the events of how Adam and Eve had come to forfeit paradise and knew that in that loss they had accrued suffering and death. But Mather had studied, sifted, parsed, and compared the writings of early Church Fathers, rab-binical scholars, and contemporary exegetes to produce new insights on ancient suppositions. In this fashion his interpretation of the original fall tackles the three assumptions that lay at the very heart of traditional anti-female suspicion in the Christian church: Eve's (morally) inferior nature even before the fall, which made her more susceptible to evil, her special culpability in bringing about the expulsion from paradise, and her particularly severe punishment, in-volving a greater diminishment of reason than for Adam.

Eve had always been the target of a host of blasting and malicious criticisms as the source of all evil perpetrated by women and as the original pattern of feminine wiles and temptations, weaknesses, deceits, and darkness throughout history. One of the most pronounced and influential among biblical interpret-ers in this respect was Tertullian, who in his *On the Apparel of Women* (ca. 202 CE) infamously accosted the female Christians of his time:

> And do you not know that you are (each) an Eve? The sentence of God on this sex of yours lives in this age; the guilt must of necessity live too. You are the devil's gateway; you are the unsealer of that (forbidden) tree; you are the first deserter of the divine law; you are she who persuaded him whom the devil was not valiant enough to attack. You destroyed so God's image, man. On account of your desert-that is, death-even the Son of God had to die. (1.1) [15]

---

14 Mather describes his work on the "Biblia" in an advertisement in *Bonifacius* in these words: "No little part of what has been written on the great intention of illustrating the divine Oracles, has been perused. Some hundreds of the latest, as well as of the oldest writers, that had anything looking that way, have been consulted. Many thousands of their finest thoughts have been found out, extracted and digested. The eye of the author's industry, has not yet seen every precious thing; yet it has often ... visited the place of sapphires, and found the dust of gold, which is here exposed unto the refined part of mankind, when it shall see cause to accept thereof ..." (*Bonifacius* 160).

15 Significantly Mather, who had not only read and relied upon Tertullian for countless references in the "Biblia," also quoted the final statement of this very passage as an epigraph for *Ornaments*: "Go ye forth now array'd with such Ornaments as the Apostles have pro-vided for you: cloath your selves with the Silk of Piety, the Sattin of Sanctity, the Purple of Modesty; so the Almighty God will be a Lover of you." It is an obvious example of Mather's method of choosing what he deemed to be correct and rejecting the unacceptable from among the works of his predecessors. Later in *Ornaments*, without naming the author, Mather re-futes Tertullian's scathing reduction of all women as being "each an Eve": "It is indeed a Piece of great Injustice, that every Women should be so far an *Eve*, as that *her* Depravation should be imputed unto *all* the Sex" (54).

Over the course of the centuries, many Christian women had come to accept their hereditary evil as a given and had become accustomed to viewing themselves through the lens of learned social misogyny: "We of the weaker sex have a hereditary evil from our Grandmother, Eve," wrote Elizabeth Warren in her 1647 tract, *Spiritual Thrift* (81). Since the inception of the Christian church, it had been a widely-accepted belief that Eve had been inferior to Adam from the moment of her creation. Seventeenth-century English congregations were well acquainted with the concept that women were born with a greater natural propensity for sin. Frequently, the scriptural account of Eve's creation from Adam's rib was taken as a "proof" for this belief.

While some exegetes expounded upon Eve's creation from Adam's side as a representation of love and intimacy between a man and a woman, more frequently the rib was imbued with negative connotations. In some cases the fact that the rib is a "crooked" bone was the explanation given for woman's "crooked nature" (Almond 147). There had been disputes about whether the rib had come from Adam's right side, or from his left. The latter assumption, of course, was meant to allude to the supposed "sinister" aspects in women, as illustrated by John Milton's rendering in *Paradise Lost* (10.884–6). Mather, by way of contrast, denies any special significance to the former position of the bone.[16] Building on the ancient *Quæstiones in Scripturam Sacram*, a work ascribed to Athanasius (c. 296–373 CE), he categorically rejects other theories, several of which implied that Eve's was an inferior creation, taken as she had been from an already existent being rather than having been formed from the dust as Adam had been. Instead, Mather suggests that God had designed woman's creation specifically to circumvent the possibility of future arguments in favor of male superiority on the basis of creation, such as the claim "that *Adam* was formed from one sort of *Dust*, and *Eve* from another; and that the Dust of *Adam*, was more excellent than that of *Eve*; & that the Offspring accordingly took their Good Tempers from *Adam*, & their Ill from *Eve*" (*BA* 1: 429).[17] Indeed, in Mather's commentaries on Genesis Eve is as rational a creature as Adam. "Our *First Parents*," he writes, "when they first came into the World, were undoubtedly furnished with the strongest Powers of *Reason*, as well as the most Regular Dispositions of *Will* to be always led by the Dictates of *Reason*" (*BA* 1: 503).

In accordance with the belief in her inherent "crookedness," many biblical interpreters also subscribed to the view that Eve had been primarily responsible for the fall. Because of her weak and rebellious nature she had wandered off from Adam's side and thus from his wiser guidance, thereby virtually inviting

---

16   Mather, in fact, makes the case that the bone was not a rib at all but, more likely, the spine (*BA* 1: 427).
17   According to Smolinski, Mather's gloss here is a free translation from Athanasius of Alexandria's *Quaestiones in Scripturam Sacram* [PG 28.732–733, lines 55–56].

her temptation by the serpent.[18] In his *Annotations upon the Holy Bible* (1683–85) Matthew Poole, for instance, faults Eve on her waywardness which had created the conditions for the fall: "[Eve] had upon some occasion retired from her husband for a season; an advantage which the crafty serpent quickly espieth, and greedily embraceth, and assaulted her when she wanted the help of her Husband" (on Gen. 3:5). Matthew Henry's *An Exposition of All the Books of the Old and New Testaments* (1708–10) agreed: "Had [Eve] kept close to the side out of which she had lately been taken, she had not been so much expos'd [to Temptation]. [Satan] took Advantage by finding her near the forbidden Tree, and probably gazing upon the fruit of it, only to satisfy her Curiosity" (1: 13).

Significantly, Mather's commentary strongly relies on the work of one of the few contemporary exegetes who abstained from such judgments: Simon Patrick's *A Commentary upon the First Book of Moses, called Genesis* (1695). As he does so often throughout the "Biblia" Mather's interpretation of the fall follows Patrick's observations, which here offer no conjecture as to Eve's distance from Adam, nor do they portray her as aimlessly gazing upon the forbidden fruit. Rather, Patrick (and Mather after him) presents an Eve who is captivated by what she believed to be an angelic presence. While neither of the two exegetes undertakes an outright defense of Eve's motives, they offer mitigating explanations for her error: "Probably the *Divel* used some such *Serpent*, (but of a more surpassing *Brightness*, than any now extant)," Mather writes, "that he might resemble one of the most Illustrious *Angels*, as near as might be. *Eve* might the more easily hearken to the *Serpent*, when she took him, for one of the *Seraphim*; which herself had seen in such splendid Circumstances attending upon the Divine Majesty; for the *Angels* always made a Part of the *Shechinah*" (*BA* 1: 479). In other words, Eve fell first not because hers was an inferior or more rebellious nature than Adam's, but because of the devil's superior, supernatural powers of deception, whose disguise as a messenger of God, we might assume, would have fooled her husband as well.

Mather also chooses to follow Patrick in his departure from the traditional assumption that Eve's motives for giving in to the serpent's temptation had been morally base (lust, ambition, etc.), an assumption which, of course, was intimately tied to the belief in her particular culpability. "The Woman being deceive'd by the tempter's Artful management," Matthew Henry writes in a fashion representative of many other commentaries, "was Ring-leader in the Transgression. She was First in the Fault, and it was the Result of her Consid-

---

18 Gen. 3:6 reads: "And when the woman saw that the tree was good for food, and that it was pleasant to the eyes, and a tree to be desired to make one wise, she took of the fruit thereof, and did eat, and gave also unto her husband *with her*, and he did eat." (Italics added.) As William Scheick points out, according to traditional readings of Genesis "the mother of mankind was not only created from Adam's rib on second thought (as it were), but through a weakness of mind she ruined paradise and engendered mortality" (Scheick 7).

eration, or rather, her Inconsideration." (1: 18). But in the "Biblia" we find this evaluation of Eve's character and the underlying motives leading to the fall:

> Q. It seems much, that *Eve* should so easily take up, with the Account, which the Divel gave, of the *Forbidden Fruit?* v.5.
> A. Dr. *Patrick* saies, He can give no Account of it, but this: That when we are searching after the Reasons of Things, (as *Eve* doubtless was, after the Reason of the Lords *Forbidding* that *Fruit*,) and cannot find it; if one be suggested unto us, which never came into our Mind before, tho' in itself most unlikely, we readily catch at it, & are pleased with it. When the Mind is weary with enquiring, it will take up with a *False Reason*, rather than with None at all. The Promise also of *Knowledge*, especially of such Knowledge, as would advance her to a more Noble Condition, was very Tempting. And it is likely, she thought an Heavenly Minister might understand the Meaning of God, better than herself. (*BA* 1: 480)

Mather thus not only endorses the notion that Eve's fall was due to mistaking the devil for God's messenger, possibly even for the Son of God himself, arrayed as he was in a disguise of shining light in imitation of the angels she had seen in the presence of God; he also agrees with Patrick (and thereby disagrees with a long line of exegetes) that the motivation for tasting the forbidden fruit was not lust, rebelliousness, or ambition for power, but the search for knowledge stemming from the wish to obey God more perfectly. According to Mather, then, Eve's grievous error was born of a desire in a "Noble Condition" to hearken to an angelic being who, she thought, would "understand the Meaning of God better than herself." Unaware of imposters, in her innocence she could not have perceived the possibility of a devious plot to overthrow her. Too much zeal, according to Mather, had left Eve's mind grasping for and accepting answers which were false rather than contenting itself to remain unsatisfied. It is interesting to note that, in spite of the fact that Mather quotes Patrick's account of the fall verbatim and in its near entirety, he deliberately omits the following passage in a clear rejection of Patrick's consent to the popular belief that Eve was the more guilty of the two: "Next to the Serpent, the Woman receives her Sentence," Patrick writes, "because she was more in the fault than Adam: Being guilty ... both of her own personal sin, and of her Husband's also" (76). No such verdict can be found in the "Biblia." Mather's divergence from the received opinion is all the more surprising since the assumption of Eve's particular if not sole responsibility is voiced in passages of the New Testament (e.g. 1 Tim. 2:14) and had repeatedly been affirmed by Church Fathers such as Tertullian.

Tellingly, the "Biblia" passes over the question of Eve's particular guilt entirely. In one passage Mather summarizes the fall conclusively and succinctly with a quotation from history which uses the masculine gender to connote both sexes: "Man being tempted unto Disobedience, did actually Disobey his Maker; and thereby forfeit all Title unto Happiness, and unto Life itself: And God thereupon judged him, and the Deceiver likewise under the Form of a *Serpent*"

(*BA* 1: 495).[19] Mather chooses to explain Eve's susceptibility to the devil's guileful temptation by a holy desire for greater knowledge and righteousness that bespeaks her inherent intellectual equality to Adam. Departing from both the tone and the substance of the majority of his contemporaries, Mather portrays Eve's central weakness to consist of a benign naiveté which the devil used to overthrow her in her very resolve to obey God. The commonly held interpretation that feminine pride, rebellious ambition, and lust had predisposed Eve to be an easy target for enticement gives way to what Mather describes as "a Mind weary with Enquiring." It was that very hunger to know more from God and about God which had caused her to accept false information from a questionable source. This unaddressed hunger which had "wearied her mind" was Eve's central "weakness," her point of vulnerability which the devil had been able to exploit, according to the "Biblia."

Equally revealing are Mather's explanations of the penalties God inflicted on the first couple and their offspring. On the gender-specific penalties outlined in the scriptural text (the lifelong punishments of work for men, subjection, and painful childbirth for women, and physical death for all), Mather has little to say, remarking simply, "The *Punishments* inflicted on the *Man* & the *Woman*, are all intelligible enough" (*BA* 1: 495). Hence, he obviously agreed with tradition that woman's temporal subordination to male authority was a consequence of the fall. But he clearly finds fault with the traditional assumption that as a punishment for her particular guilt Eve's faculty of reason had been more severely impaired than Adam's.

The springboard for Mather's deliberations on this topic is the seemingly inconspicuous issue of Adam and Eve's nakedness after the fall. Mather departs from popular understanding such as that offered by Matthew Poole, who claimed that the very realization of the first couple's fallen state had come by way of a change in their perception: "[T]hey knew they were naked because of sinful concupiscence working in them" (*Annotations* on Gen. 3). By contrast, when the "Biblia's" interlocutor asks, "What is meant by their knowing themselves to be Naked?" Mather, again following Patrick, gives as an answer: "Dr. *Patrick* summs up all the Senses of it, thus; A *cold Shivering* siezed on them: They perceived also that they were stript of their Intellectual Ornaments; (as *Athanasius* expounds it;) and blush'd also at their Bodily Nakedness" (*BA* 1: 482).

Inspired by Patrick's scholarly exploration of the passage, which draws on Athanasius of Alexandria among others as a source,[20] Mather thus reads the

---

19 Smolinski explains that the passage quoted by Mather "is a rhetorical reconstruction of Sanchoniathon's history and appears in Sherlock's *Use and Intent*." (*BA* 1: 495, n49). The *New England Primer* also famously places the responsibility for the fall on the *male*: "In Adam's fall/ We sinned All."

20 In interpreting "naked" as "wise," Patrick here harks back to Athanasius of Alexandria's *Against the Heathen* (3.4.5).

couple's sad realization of their bodily nakedness as secondary to the more
dreadful awareness that their faculties of reason had lost much of their original
brightness. Unlike the gender-specific penalties God had pronounced upon
Adam and Eve, this punishment, in Mather's commentary, affected them both
in equal measure; an interpretation that clearly runs counter to the widespread
prejudice that women had weaker minds as a consequence of the fall, and hence
less capacity for moral self-government than men. By insisting that the first
couple together with both their male and female offspring had suffered the same
diminution of their "intellectual ornaments," Mather suggests the possibility
that custom, not creation, had denied women the possibility of unfolding their
potential for learning to the same degree as men. Here, then, we find the theological basis for Mather's startling pronouncements on the capacities of women
in *Ornaments*. Just as men and women were subject to the same diminishment
of their faculties in the postlapsarian world, their intellectual "ornaments"
would be equally restored to both male and female saints with regeneration.
Thus he offers the following corollary in Genesis: "But as the Enemy had by *Sin*
subdued them, *he* should be subdued by a Return of *Righteousness*; And this
must be followed with a Recovery of the Blessings which they had forfeited"
(*BA* 1: 497). Just how Mather imagined a final restoration, which would also
redeem men from laboring for a living and women from the penalty of temporal
subordination, will be discussed in due course. For the moment, it is important
to note that Mather's commentaries on Eve's role in the fall and its aftermath
enable us to understand the theological basis for his championship of female
intellectual capabilities.

Additionally, Mather's examination of Eve's character and of her motivation for disobedience demonstrate that he sought scriptural support for his dissent from the common assumptions of earlier generations which regarded scholarship in women to be a dangerous expression of the innately rebellious ambition of stepping out of divinely preordained place. Such a view stands in notable
contrast even to that of most of Mather's contemporary exegetes, including
Matthew Henry who blamed Eve for wanting "knowledge," assessing her curiosity as frivolous: "See here how the Affectation of Unnecessary Knowledge,
under the mistaken Notion of Wisdom, proves harmful and destructive to
many" (1: 14). Mather deemed knowledge in women to be neither an affectation
nor an unnecessary risk. On the contrary, he insisted on it as essential to their
own spiritual benefit as well as for that of church and society, given, of course,
that it was the right kind of knowledge from trustworthy sources. Implicit in
Mather's commentary on Eve's temptation was the notion that danger lurked
where intelligent minds were left idle and unfulfilled. Perhaps using the thrust
of other commentators' own premises against them, Mather argues *sotto voce*
that unless women in their thirst for knowledge again and again be deceived by
the tempter, they should be allowed to utilize their capacities for study, combin-

ing broad learning with piety. To be sure, the gaining of religious knowledge, from the perspective of Reformed orthodoxy, could save neither man nor woman. But from Mather's perspective it could help to prepare hearts and minds for God's saving grace through faith in Christ. It could also aid in creating a godlier society and a purer church, one more deserving of the promised bliss of Christ's millennial reign. Mather's estimation of the contribution of female intellect to the work of God is evidenced by the comment in his *Diary* recorded on the subject of his daughter Katy's exercises in writing: "Who can tell, of what use these Essays may prove, to the Interests [of] Religion?" (2: 84).

Mather's insistence on the spiritual and intellectual equality of women was, of course, difficult to reconcile with the scriptural precepts (especially those in the Pauline letters) which not only demanded the temporal subordination of women, but also prohibited their full participation in the public realm, precepts which Mather clearly wished to honor. The compromise which emerges from his printed works is one in which women of privilege would enjoy a private rather than an institutional education, but which clearly included the opportunity to express religious sentiment in writing as a form of "public" communication that would not violate Paul's stricture that women should keep silence in the church (1 Tim. 2:12). After all, Mather writes in *Ornaments*, "our God has employ'd man[y] *Women* to *Write* for the *Church*, & *Inspir'd* some of them for the Writing of *Scriptures*" (3). To back up this point, he reminds his readers that Bathsheba, the alleged authoress of Prov. 31, was once guilty of execrable sin. Even so, she was found worthy to pen the portion of scripture which defined the characteristics of "the virtuous woman." His underlying message implied that if even the most recalcitrant sinner might, like Bathsheba, become "a very eminent Saint, yea, a *Prophetess* of the Lord" (*Ornaments* 5), what might be the benefits to the church from the written records of faithful women in an age of grace?

Mather's Ecclesiological Interpretations of Eve and Her Daughters

Mather's representation of Eve and his affirmation of feminine intellect in both the "Biblia" and in *Ornaments* might seem surprisingly progressive to us. Yet they appear to conflict with passages on women which appear in his other writings as late as 1724. For instance, while in *Ornaments* Mather had maintained that "[i]t is indeed a Piece of great Injustice, that every Woman should be so far an *Eve*, as that *her* Depravation should be imputed unto *all* the Sex" (54), in *Angel of Bethesda*, composed thirty years later, we find the following advice for women concerning "feminine diseases":

> Poor Daughters of *Eve*, Languishing under your *Special Maladies, Look back* on your *Mother*, the *Woman*, who *being Deceived*, was first *in the Transgression*, that has brought in upon us, *all our Maladies.* Beholding your *Affliction* and your *Misery*, in the midst of your *Lamentations* under it, *Remember that Wormwood and Gall* of the Forbidden Fruit: Lett your *Soul have them still in Remembrance*, and *be humbled in you.* Under all your Ails, think, *The sin of my Mother, which is also my Sin, has brought all this upon me!* (233)[21]

Here again the "Biblia" provides the key which reconciles such seeming disparities that have long vexed scholars of Mather's work. Essential to his thinking was, as we have seen, the distinction between the temporal subordination of women, which accompanied gender-specific punishments for original sin (the "*Special Maladies*" which Mather related to the female reproductive organs), and their spiritual as well as intellectual equality. This "distinction," which would be transcended only during Christ's millennial reign on earth, had its parallel in, and was reflected by, his twofold concept of the church. Spiritually, Mather understood "Eve" as a type of the glorious "church invisible" or eternal, whereas the postlapsarian "woman" in Mather's lexicon represented the "church congregational" or "visible," which was subject to impurity, suffering, and persecution.

Mather founded this theological argument on the insight that Eve was the mother, not simply of "mere mankind," but also of Christ incarnate and his faithful flock. In his commentary on Gen. 3 Mather reads the faithful church, redeemed and restored through Christ, in the "Seed of the Woman." He therefore presents Eve as the "Mother of All Living," which in his interpretation is the Mother of all who will be saved:

> A Glorious CHRIST is now exhibited unto us. *Eve* is called, The *Mother of all the Living Seed.* Why was not she so called, before the *Promise*? Meer *Natural Life* is not all that is intended in it. It was from her apprehending of this *Promise*, that she obtained the Name. The *Living Seed* implies, both the, *Enlivening Seed*, and the *Enlivened Seed*; the *Sanctifying* and the *Sanctified.* [Compare, Heb. 2.11.] It is the *Messiah* that is the *Enlivening Seed* ... In and by the *Messiah*, shee is the *Mother of All Living*, who, brought into this World else none but Sinners, and such as without *Him*, are *Dead in Trespasses & Sins.* (*BA* 1: 488, 492)

For Mather, who read the Book of Genesis believing that "the Design lay deeper," Eve represented not just the aboriginal mother of "meer mortals" who are more properly, "the *Seed of the Man*" (273), but what he termed the "Prot-Evan-

---

21 Mather refers to the "Special Maladies" of womankind in another passage with darker implications as an explanation for the scourge of demonic torment which seemed to afflict more women than men. See *Another Brand Pluck'd Out of the Burning* (32). In both cases, while his conclusions are frightful, they are offered in sincerity and with the objective of being helpful. Note the use of plural pronouns. Though women's suffering is described, Mather's use of "our" and "us" connotes empathy and sharing in the fallen state of the human race rather than accusation.

gelium." By apprehending and believing in the future promise of Christ long before his birth to her descendant Mary, Eve becomes the type of the true church which contains in itself all of the regenerate men and women who would populate the earth in subsequent generations. Consequently, Mather interprets Eve's name-change symbolically as well, designating her as matriarch in a process reminiscent of the patriarchy conferred upon Abram/Abraham and on the same basis; she is no longer called by the name Adam had given her, *Ishah*, ("woman"), but according to Mather (273), she "obtained" her new name, *"Chavah"* ("Eve"), through her faith in the promised redeemer (276).[22] For Mather, Eve's descendants are spiritual descendants who have believed, as she had believed, in the (then, coming) savior.

Precisely because Mather interprets Eve to be a type of the true church, he seeks to explain her susceptibility to the serpent's temptations in terms of a genuinely noble, but tragically misguided, desire to obey God and to know him better. These are characteristics which he associated with the members of the true and universal church, who, though redeemed through faith in the atonement of Christ, were nonetheless subject to human frailties and the temptations of sin. Within the true or invisible church as the communion of Christ's faithful across all times, there are no distinctions before God between men and women. However, within the "church congregational," and the social order built around it, women continued under their gender-specific punishments, just as did men. In line with a long tradition that is rooted in the Bible itself Mather thus allegorized the temporal church as a woman. Like postlapsarian women the church had been suppressed and persecuted throughout its history; like the female body it was vulnerable to suffering and susceptible to the devil's deception.[23] Therefore, to Mather it was of utmost importance that "she" be filled with spiritual knowledge and thereby kept from the dangers of doctrinal error.

The significant interdependencies between Mather's interpretation of gender-roles and his ecclesiology can readily be observed in his commentaries on

---

22 Eve's faith follows what Mather calls the *"Prot-Evangelium"*: *"I will putt Enmity between thee and the Woman, and between thy Seed and her Seed; It shall bruise thy Head, & thou shalt bruise His Heel"* (Gen. 3:15). "It was from her apprehending this *Promise*," he explained in the "Biblia," "that she obtained the Name." The use of the verb "obtained" connotes an active decision on the part of the woman; it also is associated with one of the best-known passages in the Bible, the eleventh chapter of Hebrews, the great roster of faith, in which the verb "obtained" is used three times to convey the action of faith in the procuring of promises.

23 "The Malignant Vapours and Humours of our Diseased Bodies may be used by Devils, thereinto insinuating an engine of the Execution of their Malice upon those Bodies; and perhaps for this Reason one Sex may suffer more Troubles of some kinds from the Invisible World than the other, as well as for that reason for which the Old Serpent made where he did his first address." This explanation had been offered by Mather earlier when searching for a physical reason for fits suffered by some who were considered to be possessed (*Another Brand* 32).

Canticles. As had so many Christian exegetes before him, Mather allegorizes the love relationship between bridegroom and bride represented as the relationship between Christ and the church. Marriage itself becomes the symbol of the mystical union binding together Christ and his faithful in mutual love. "It would not seem strange to any one," Mather writes

> that *Messiah, the Prince,* is compared unto a *Bridegroom,* and His Church unto a *Bride*; which does but reflect on the XLV Psalm; and but observe how *Solomon* doth only follow the Metaphor, wherein his Father *David* had represented this Mystery; and observe withal, the common Language of the Prophets; who speak of the *Virgin Daughter of Zion,* whom God but Espoused unto Himself. We may add, That the profoundest of the Hebrew Divines, had such a Notion as this among them; *That sensible things are but an Imitation of things above.* And, that for instance, there was an original Pattern of that Love and Union, which is between a Man and His Wife, here in this World. [*BA*, Cant. 1.][24]

Such a reading was very much in agreement with an orthodox covenant theology, often expounded in terms of a marriage contract as well as with the traditional Puritan model of conjugal relationships. In Puritanism marriage was intended to reflect the essential union between Christ and his covenanted people, a relationship in which reciprocity and fidelity were paramount. This two-sided bond in marriage, every bit as sacred as the covenant between God and the Israelites, and Christ and his church, reinforced notions of friendship, parity and oneness between man and woman in the Puritan paradigm of married life. In the theocracy, every husband was commanded to love his wife as Christ loved the church and gave himself for it; indeed, he was to cherish his wife as his own body. To this loving authority the wife was expected to submit not only in humility, but in joy. Like his forebears, Mather's ecclesiology therefore reinforced the female virtues of subordination and obedience to male authority; however, unlike his forbears, his hermeneutical understanding actually liberated the intellectual talents of godly women among them, even while it preserved the requisite vertical hierarchy.

In many ways, Mather thus maintained in his commentary on Canticles what the Christian church had always maintained, that "immediately after the Fabrick of the World was reared, *Matrimony* followed" [*BA*, Cant.1] as part of the postlapsarian order which involved temporal inequality and social hierarchy. At the same time, Reformed Christian theology had also held marriage "as an Emblem of God's Great Love, to those that should beleeve on Him." Fur-

---

24 "This, by the way", writes Mather in the "Biblia," "gives a plain Account, why *John* the Baptist, uses the Word *Christ,* and *Bridegroom,* as if they were in a Manner Synonymous, & of-the-Same importance.-[John III:28,29] and why Our Saviour compares the Affaires of His Heavenly Kingdome, (called by the People, Mar. XI:10, *The Kingdome of Our Father, David*) unto a *Marriage,* or a *Marriage Feast,* which a King made for his Son [Matth. XXII:2]" [*BA*, Cant. 1].

thermore, the prophetic scriptures taught that the culmination of time will end as it had begun, with a marriage. "[S]o this World," in Mather's words, "shall end in *Marriage*. All the Mysteries of the Holy Scripture, are shutt up, with these Words in the *Revelation*, Rev. 19:7. *Lett us be Glad & Rejoice, for the Marriage of the Lamb is come, and his Wife ha's made herself ready*" [*BA*, Cant.1]. Thus conjugal relations interconnect the spiritual with the earthly, and marriage marks both the beginning and the end of redemption history. In both cases, the "faithful" from among mankind are cast in the symbolically feminine role as "bride," a long-held and cherished tradition among believers.

If the feminization of the church and its relationship to Christ were nothing new, Mather's emphasis on the other side of the allegorical equation was. More strongly than other commentators, he stressed the close identification of women with the church.[25] In his readings, what is required of women is required for the church and, inversely, that what is destined for the church becomes, in essence, prophecy for redeemed womankind. Consequently, Mather's search for the qualities Eve had lost reveals his true concern which was in seeing those blessings restored and applied to the universal bride of Christ. Similarly, Mather looked to Eve's losses for clues as to what God intended and intends for the church of Christ, whose visible saints, of course, included both men and women, if not in equal measure.

Indeed, Mather's close identification of women with the church also had an experiential and practical dimension. From his own congregation he knew that women made up the greater part of the membership, outnumbering converted men in New England's churches at a ratio of three to one. In *Ornaments* he remarks on this:

> [T]is plain that as there were three *Maries* to one *John*, standing under the Cross of our dying Lord, so still there are far more *godly Women* in the World, than there are *godly Men*; and our *Church Communions* give us a little Demonstration of it. I have seen it without going a mile from home, that in a Church of, between *three* or *four* Hundred *Communicants*, there are but few more than *one* Hundred Men; all the rest are *Women*, of whom *Charity* will *think no Evil*. (48)

Construing a gender-specific version of the *felix culpa*, Mather deduced that the greater propensity for conversion in women was a kind of providential compensation for the particular punishments inflicted on Eve and on her daughters.

---

25 Mather finds further affirmation for the identification of "woman" with "the church" in the writings of the Hebrew Divines on the subject of the "original Pattern of Love and Union which is between a Man and Wife, here in this World": "This they expressed by the Kindness of *Tipheret* unto *Malcuth*; which are the Names they give unto the Invisible *Bridegroom* and *Bride* in the Upper World. This *Tipheret* (or Beauty) they call also by the Name of, the *Adam on high*, and the *Great Adam*; in opposition to the earthly & little *Adam* here below. This *Malcuth* (or, Kingdome) they also call by the Name of *Cheneseth Israel*, or, *The Congregation of Israel*; who is united, they say, unto the *Cœlestial Adam*, as *Eve* was to the *Terrestrial*" [*BA*, Cant.1].

Female piety, he reasoned, was due in large measure to the physical risks of childbirth which, through fear of impending death, caused women to be more often confronted with mortality and thus more frequently concerned with the state of their souls than men. But he also found the penalty of subjection to contribute to womankind's heightened spirituality, recognizing it as a trial at least as difficult as childbirth. In a passage he repeats in *Ornaments*, in the "Biblia," and in *The Angel of Bethesda*, Mather argued, "[I]t seems that the *Curse* in the Difficulties both of *Subjection* and of *Childbearing*, which the *Female Sex* is doom'd unto, has been turn'd into a *Blessing*, by the *free Grace* of our most gracious God. God sanctifies the *Chains*, the *Pains*, the *Deaths* which they meet withal; and furthermore, makes the *Tenderness* of their Disposition, a further Occasion of serious Devotion in them" (*Ornaments* 48–49; *BA*, Eccles. 7:28; *Angel of Bethesda* 236). For Mather, then, pious women stood as exemplars for the church whose piety could be emulated by men and women alike. Thus, the undercurrent of his support of women's exemplary virtue contained the radical directive that men could learn by means of women's writings how better to imitate female humility and the virtues of obedience to Christ as their spiritual spouse.

In Mather's understanding of redemption history as a history of the church, virtuous female behavior within the conjugal relationship thus both symbolized and practically contributed to the outworking of the great drama of restoring Christ's people to himself. In Mather's ecclesiology the whole of human history was cast into two camps symbolized by the bride of Christ on the one hand (the redeemed who are obediently awaiting his return) and the "strange woman" or harlot church on the other, signifying a religion given over to idolatry: "One Argument of this being a very Ancient Notion," glosses Mather in Canticles, "is; That *Idolatry* and *False-Worship*, in the Church, is constantly exemplified in the Scriptures, under the Notion of a *Spiritual Fornication*; a going a Whoring from God*; whom therefore the Church was to look upon as *her Husband*. See Isa. LIV:5, LXII:4,5; Jer, III:4, 20; XXXI:32; Hos. II:2, 7" [*BA*, Cant.1].[26]

Just as throughout history the true church had been persecuted by the religion of the harlot (Babylon) and remained "hidden," so too women as the emblem of that church were to be hidden, submissive, and invisible in the temporal world of men's affairs. Like the true church, the righteous would be revealed, rendered openly "visible" at Christ's appearing and given equal participation in his glorious reign. But until that time, the virtuous woman Mather patterned in his ecclesiology would be content to remain hidden. It was the "lewd woman"

---

26   In his commentary on Canticles, the woman veiled is the hidden church. "And", adds Mather, "it may not be amiss to Conceive, that *Solomon* in his Book of *Proverbs* also, under the Name of a *Wise Woman*, intends the *Church of God*, but under the Name of a *Strange Woman*, the *Church of Rome*" [*BA*, Cant. Messiah].

who would refuse her role as subordinate helpmeet and the harlot who sought to stand out in the public realm; the virtuous woman was content to remain in her God-given place and to express herself in writing. Hence, while the bodies and outward existences of women in the temporal remained under the curse which fell upon Eve, the spirit of the converted woman, including her intellect, was redeemed and could flourish, silently but productively, in the kingdom of God. The inherent equality of her soul did not procure temporal equality with men in the present world just as it could not liberate her from physical exigencies. Yet Mather's insistence on the equality of female intellect and his unswerving support for female scholarship despite a life of obscurity and of bodily subjection were radical leaps forward for his time. On the basis of this duality Mather advocated study for women and particularly championed allowing pious and gifted women to pursue scholarly ambitions.

The Role of Women in Mather's Eschatology

Virtually every aspect of Mather's thinking contained an eschatological dimension which must be taken into consideration in order fully to appreciate the meaning and implications of his ideas. In his millennialist speculations Mather frequently spoke of the glory to which the redeemed would be restored in the latter days. By this glory he meant the original likeness to God possessed by Adam and Eve in their prelapsarian state, giving their entire bodies a supernatural radiance. In his commentary on Genesis he describes the loss of this condition as one of the consequences of the fall:

> There was a *Luminous Garment*, which the Lord putt upon our First Parents, as a Pledge of, & of their Protection under the *Shechinah* of the Son of God. When our First Parents Revolted from God, that *Luminous Garment* was taken from them, & they were left in a grievous Confusion, *Ashamed* to appear in the New *Nakedness* before the Son of God in the *Shechinah*. ... *And the Eyes of both of them were opened, for they found, that the Bright Garment, with which they had been created, was gone from them.* ... This *Garment* was their *Glory.* (*BA* 1: 474)

As an outward mark of their respective punishments the first couple had thus forfeited its glorious halo. Hence, the temporal subordination and invisibility of women in postlapsarian society was one aspect of a larger loss of the outward glory which Eve had once shared with Adam in equal measure. This notion is significant for our purposes here because in his writings about women Mather frequently referred to the "hidden glory" of the female members of the church, who lived pious lives of quiet obedience to Christ. This theme is especially pervasive in his 1722 tract *Bethia*, in which Mather, in reference to Ps. 45, writes: "To be a *King's Daughter*, and *all Glorious within*, is the blessed Condition of a

Soul *espoused* unto our SAVIOUR." Yet, Mather did not leave it there, but tied the concept of "hidden glory" into his theological vision of the end-times.

While in *Ornaments* he had touched on the subject of secret glory but stressed literary and intellectual pursuits, in the nearly thirty-year interim between the two works he had clearly shifted his emphasis towards eschatology. Fired by the feverish expectation of the millennium that characterizes so many of Mather's later works, *Bethia* holds up to regenerate women the promise of an imminent restoration to outward or visible glory. He again mentions the advantages of writing as well as of reading for women[27]: "It would be an uncommon *Glory* unto our *Daughters*, if they would more curiously and copiously *handle the Pen of the Writer* as well as the *Needle* and the Distaff," (59) but in his later tract for women Mather is decidedly caught up with a far more visionary aspect of the church. Perhaps hoping to induce many more women to seek conversion, he not only paints the portrait of the now visibly glorious woman in extravagant and dazzling rhetoric, but uses the full power of espousal imagery in order to win over his audience:

> It was a Sight once wondred at. *There appeared a great Wonder in Heaven, a Woman cloathed with the Sun.* O *Daughter* of the Lord, While thou art yet upon the *Earth* here below, thou shalt be that *Woman. Cloathed* with the *Righteousness* of a CHRIST, and by *Faith* entitled unto it, as unto thy *Inheritance*, thou art *Cloathed with the Sun*: thou hast *put on the CHRIST* who is *the Sun of Righteousness*. But Oh! How *Glorious* is the *Kings Daughter*, appearing in such *Robes* before her Everlasting *Father!* Our SAVIOUR, in what He was, and in what He did, *fulfilling all Righteousness*, produced the most Glorious *Righteousness*, that ever the Eyes of Heaven look'd upon. The *Law* of our GOD was never so *magnified*, and never so *Honourable*, as in the *Respects* paid unto it, by the *Holy, Harmless, Undefiled One*. The *Righteousness* of the best *Angels* in Heaven, tho' they are all array'd in *Garments of Light*, is infinitely short of that *Righteousness* which our SAVIOUR has prepared for, and has conferred on, the *Daughters* of GOD. (*Bethia* 37–38)

Mather's promise to the women in his congregation, "While thou art yet upon the *Earth*, thou shalt be that *Woman Cloathed* with the *Righteousness* of a CHRIST," must not be read as mere rhetorical flourish, but understood quite literally. In the *Triparadisus*, his final, posthumously published work on the millennium, Mather describes in great detail the glorious existence of the saints on the New Earth after the conflagration and the first resurrection. Under the rule of Christ they would reap their long-awaited rewards and once again shine forth as Adam and Eve had "in the *Terrestrial Paradise*, before they Rebelled

---

27 Mather's exhortations that women should write are all the more radical if considered in cultural context. While children in the colonial period were generally taught to read by their mothers, girls only rarely were taught to write. Literacy and writing were more common in urban areas such as Boston, but "women in general continued to be taught reading alone long after writing had become a primary part of male instruction" (Scheick 17). See also Ulrich, *Good Wives* (43–44), and Morgan (67) on the customary practices of education for girls.

against their *Maker*, and before they Sinned away those *Garments of Light*, the Loss of which *Defence* & *Beauty* made them *Ashamed* of appearing before their *Judge* ..." (*Triparadisus* 273). While on earth, under temporal bonds, the saints' glory is imputed unto them and compared to a garment "put on" but belonging to Christ, as Mather describes it in *Bethia*: "The *Glory* which is to set off the *Daughters* of GOD, lies very much in that *glorious Garment* which is put upon them, when the *Righteousness* of their SAVIOUR is imputed unto them ..." (*Bethia* 37). But at the second coming, female saints would undergo an additional, supernatural transformation. In their deathless, angelic existence women would also be freed from their "female maladies" as well as from the burden of temporal subordination, and reinstalled in their original equality.

Yet even on this side of the millennium, a foretaste of that future glory could be had. Regenerate women, Mather writes, would increasingly make their inward faith and virtue shine to the world even as they humbly resigned themselves to their place:

> But something of that *Glory* is now going to be declared. ... *Children*, your *Glory* must lie in that *Wisdom*, which is in the most *hidden Recess* of the Soul; that which is called *The hidden Man of the Heart* ... *Soul*, Having the Spotless *Righteousness* of thy SAVIOUR put upon thee, thou wilt then be all *Glorious*. (*Bethia* 32, 33, 36–37)

The "glory" of the converted woman before the millennium is her redeemed condition, veiled as it were, in submission, yet displaying in that very submission the "wisdom" which is the hidden man of the heart, or Christ. She would nurture that wisdom and allow it to well up within her, expressing its overflow through her pen. The very act of writing, then, becomes a further sign of her submission, but it is a submission filled and fuelled by spiritual grace and "glory." According to Mather, the truly pious woman is not compelled to draw attention to herself in respect of her spiritual understanding; she is content to wait and trust for that proper time when God shall decree that she be revealed as the saint she truly is. While in this world and while in her present state, she concedes her understanding of this by her acquiescence to God's will.

Thus, in *Bethia*, pious women are described as "People who make no Noise at all in the World ... and under all the Covert imaginable" (34–35). But in the *Triparadisus* it is revealed that the "Covert," which serves to hide virtuous women, is a "*Covert-femme*" or the female body! Once again drawing the distinction between the female body and the redeemed spirit, or "inner man," Mather argues that in the Third Paradise, which is the time of the New Jerusalem, both males who compose the true church and all godly women who had been held under submission to men in the bonds of their "*Covert-femme*" will be revealed as the glorious reigning brides of Christ that both are; and that as the angels, they will be neither male nor female:

> But, the *Different Sexes*!- No; There will be no *Different Sexes* in the *Holy City*. ... The Spirits, which once were in *Bodies*, kept under a *Covert-femme*, and could not move in any Higher Sphere, than to *Marry*, & *bear Children*, & *guide the House*: being exemplary in their PIETY, & having been of Old time, the *Holy Women, who trusted in GOD, and adorned themselves with such things as are of great Price in the Sight of GOD*; These will doubtless now have their Part in the Employments of the *Holy City*. ... Even while the *Curse* upon the *Sex* in the Third Chapter of *Genesis* is yett unremoved, we have seen other Ladies, beside the brave Jewess of *Palmyra*, at the Head of Mighty Empires. But, in the World, where there will be *no more Curse*, who can tell, what the *Daughters*, as well as the *Sons, of the Almighty*, may be advanced unto! Certainly, they will be *Equal to the Males*, who are made *Equal to the Angels*. ... They will so *Putt on CHRIST*, that there will be *neither Male nor Female*, nor any more Difference, between them, than between *Jew* and *Greek*, in the *Heavenly Places*.[28] (*Triparadisus* 264–65)

Difficult as it is from a modern perspective to view this eschatological promise of equality as anything less than a hypocritical, self-serving construct for keeping women content in their subordinate place, it must be remembered that Mather firmly believed that the time was very close at hand for Christ's appearing (he had expected it to occur during his own life time), and thus it would not be long for women to remain "under all the covert imaginable." Until then, his chief interest *was* in keeping New England's women closely and concertedly engaged in piety and in fostering female conversion. While Christians, male and female, would by virtue of their new natures in Christ exemplify the attributes of the submissive bride of Christ spiritually, it was the female sex which was called upon to exhibit those attributes both spiritually and temporally, until the time of the church's "unveiling" when the Bridegroom would appear.

Hence, Mather's eschatology, like his ecclesiology, elevated women to new importance and dignity at the same time that it essentially re-affirmed the traditional Christian model of female subordination. For Mather the very Hebrew word *Almah*, meaning virgin or young woman, connotes a covering, or an aspect of being hidden, a fact which he explains in his commentary on Canticles and to which he refers in *Bethia*: "Thus it must be enough to you, if your *Glory* be *hid*, as that of our Glorious CHRIST was in the Days of his Humiliation here, and none but the Invisible GOD look upon it. The Name for you in the Original of the Bible, signifies, *Hidden ones*" (*Bethia* 32). In accordance with this explanation, Mather often addressed the female sex as "Hidden ones," as

---

28 Mather does not elaborate on how or whether males will be changed, but implies the notion, shared commonly among thinkers of his era, that the male is the fully developed of the two sexes; that femininity was the result of remaining static at a certain point in development. Hence, women were considered to be permanently childlike, in contrast with men who were fully adult. For a discussion of this topic, see Lombard (10). It is also interesting to note that Mather comes close to Anne Hutchinson's argument here that there would be no gender distinctions in the resurrection, an opinion which contributed to her excommunication. This is noticed by Amanda Porterfield as well, in *Female Piety* (26).

"people who make no noise in the world," and urged women to accept this ig-
nominy even as he persuaded them to write for the church. *"Children*, Be
concern'd for, and be content with, an *Hidden Glory*; count it enough to be
Glorious before GOD, though you should be *hidden* from all the World"
(*Bethia* 32). Thus there appear to be two competing notions in Mather's exhortations for women; one, urging them to be glad to remain "invisible," and the
other, declaring to them, "But behold, how you may recover your impaired
Reputation! The *fear of God* will soon make it evident, that you are among *the
excellent in the Earth"* (*Ornaments* 46).

Mather's Interpretation of Female Prophecy

As he saw the time approaching for Christ's return and read the symbolic
directive for the true church to "rise up" as in Canticles, Mather was faced with
a dilemma. The churches were comprised mostly of women, who were forbidden to speak, yet Mather was becoming more and more concerned with the
end-time promise of the gift of prophecy. The restitution of lost blessings was
limited to those which Mather could justify within his theological framework.
How then were the handmaids to prophesy as described in Joel 2: 28–29 without breaking Paul's commandment forbidding speech? When Cotton Mather
ascended the pulpit to deliver the sermon for his eighteen year old daughter's
funeral in December, 1717, he was armed with an answer to that paradox. His
beloved daughter Katharin's dying request had been that her father would
preach on the pleasantness she had found in piety. Furthermore, she had supplied the text in her own words.[29]

Katharin had been a young woman not only of admirable piety but also of
remarkable intelligence. Instructed by her father, she had excelled in subjects
not usually taught to young women, including medicine. "As a *promising Soul*,
and a Good and Ingenious Disposition are polished and perfected by a good
Education," said Mather at her funeral, "so this Young Gentlewoman was happy in an Education, that was polite and agreeable to the Circumstances of a
Gentlewoman. Her proficiency in the Qualifications, which render such an one
accomplished in the esteem of the more Genteel part of the World, was not Inconsiderable." Among those accomplishments he named

> [H]er Accuracy at her Needle; her Dexterity at her *Pen*; her Knowledge of what
> concerns the *Table*; her Skill in *Musick*, both *Vocal* and *Instrumental*. To which she
> added this, that she became in her Childhood, a Mistress of the *Hebrew Tongue*.
> She had also attained to a considerable Knowledge in the Sacred *Geography*. And
> what added a Lustre to all the rest, was, that she never in the least affected *Ostenta-*

---

29 Mather used both spellings of his daughter's name, Katharin or Katharine.

tion. Her *Humility* was an agreeable and lovely shade to set off her Valuable Accomplishments. (*Victorina* 50)[30]

In his encomium he praised the selfless nature which had prompted her quietly to visit the unfortunate and socially outcast in prison as well as her surrender to God's will in her last illness. Katharin was "lodged in the *Paradise* of GOD" wrote Mather, from whence Christ would bring her with Him "at and for the *Resurrection* of the Dead" (*Victorina* A3). But on this particular day, Katharin, who never had spoken in church, would be among those pious daughters who "outlive their Funeral in the Perpetual Usefulness of their preserved *Speeches* and *Patterns* unto the Living" (*Victorina* A3-A4). [31]

---

30 Among the subjects of Katharin's education, but not mentioned in her funeral sermon perhaps because it was too controversial, was the instruction she received from her father in medicine. Not only did Mather approve of young women learning, he also prepared his daughters to earn a living through such knowledge, should it become necessary. In his *Diary* Mather records his decision in 1711 to begin instructing his three eldest daughters: "It is time for me to fix my three elder Daughters in the opificial and beneficial Mysteries, wherein they should be well-instructed; that they may do good unto others; and if they should be reduced into Necessities, unto themselves also. For Katy, I determine, Knowledge in Physic, and the Preparation, and the Dispensation of noble Medicines. For Nibby, and Nancy, I will consult their Inclinations" (2: 112). Even in 1724, some seven years after Katy's death, Mather continued to defend his position on the subject of females as practicing physicians against the rampantly vitupertive opposition of some males. In his *Angel of Bethesda* he writes, "I am well aware, What sharp *Satyrs* [satires] have been written against WOMEN pretending to practice *Physick*: The *Hae Galeni*, [female Galens] say, Master *Whitlock!-Nam Genus Variant.*–[for the sexes change]. The Quacking *Hermaphrodites*; the *Physican* and *Physic*, both *Simples*, compounding the destruction of the Patient: Applying their *Medicines* (as the *Athenians* their Altar *unto an unknown God*) unto an unknown Disease. ... But yet after all, In the most Ancient Writers, we find *Women* celebrated as Eminent in the *Art of Healing.* Homer in his Eleventh *Iliad*, mentions *Agamede*, in Terms almost like what we read of *Solomon: 'She that all Simples Healing Vertues knew,/ And Every Herb that drinks the Morning Dew.'* And in his *Odysses*, he mentions *Polydamne* as Excelling in this Way of usefulness. I call to mind also Mr. *George Herberts* Advice, That the *Wife* of the *Countrey-Minister*, should have Some Skill and Will to *help the Sick* ... For *Salves*, his *Wife* seeks not the City but prefers her Gardens and Fields before all outlandish Gums ... We will then venture to proceed, and say, it would be a Laudable Thing for our *Gentlewomen* to have their Closetts furnished with several Harmless, and Useful, (and Especially *External*) Remedies, for the Help of their poor Neighbours on Several Occasions Continually Calling for them ... and Several of the Remedies, mention'd in several of the former *Capsula's* Take your Choice, *Ladies!*" (288–89). It should be noted that Mather distinguishes between the external preparations of the "Countrey-Wife" and the internal remedies of the physician. He had been teaching his daughter the more complex of the two. It is open to speculation as to how advanced Katharin Mather may have become in the same discipline.

31 Ulrich explores the paradox that a woman's words could be heard in church only after she was dead in "Vertuous Women Found." She illustrates Mather's eagerness to include their words in their funerals, when at last it was sanctioned. That Mather wished his congregations to learn from the experiences of pious women is exhibited by the fact that, as Ulrich tells us, he "made much of the fact that Abiel Goodwin, a little damsel half his age, had taught him much of salvation, and in her funeral sermon he expressed pleasure that she could finally 'without any Disorder' speak in the church" (34).

According to Mather, Katharin's testimony of conversion, written in her own hand and read aloud to the church at Boston, would make her comparable to the four daughters of Philip the Evangelist, who had prophesied (and that, after the Apostolic Age, noted Mather defensively): "Certainly Such an One, is Qualified now, to be brought in as a Competent Witness, to testify unto the Pleasures in the Ways of Piety," for, as he assured his listeners,

> *Piety* is a brighter thing than *Prophecy*; and the *Exemplifying* of Real, Vital, Solid *Piety*, to the World, is on some accounts the most noble sort of *Prophesying*. TO SPEAK FOR GOD, is in the most proper Signification of the Term, *To Prophesy*. And this way of *Speaking in the Church* is allow'd even to the *Female Sex*, yea, attained by it sometimes when got not far out of *Infancy*. (*Victorina* A4)

Mather's innovation instructed the women in his congregation that the means of fulfilling Joel 2 was through a life lived in utmost piety. Yet, in describing the personal attributes of his own daughter, Mather was also extolling the virtues and characteristics of all virtuous women and, indeed, of the invisible church, consisting of the truly redeemed:

> She indeed even to a Fault affected *Obscurity*. *Retirement* was her delight, and the Noise and Encumbrances of the World were no way agreeable unto her. She was one of those, that could say, *They were least alone, when most alone*; Her mind in these grateful *Sequestrations*, these Pleasant *Solitudes*, being employed upon the most noble Subjects, and set upon the higher Things of another Life. (*Victorina* 51)

While Katharin's voice had never been heard in the public congregation, her own words were to ring out at her funeral evangelizing the youth of Boston. While she had inhabited her body, her life had "spoken for God" if not her voice. Now the words of the young prophetess, having conquered the last enemy by a joyful and victorious death, could be read aloud from the pulpit. Mather, speaking for his daughter to the Boston congregation, pled with words he would later include in *Bethia*: "On the behalf of this *Young Witness*, O our Young People, you are now Earnestly call'd into them. The *Voice of the Dove* is heard so calling upon you; A *Dove*, that has the *Sun of Righteouness* now, with what *Glory*! – Shining on her, *Wings covered with Silver*, and *Feathers with Yellow Gold*" (*Victorina* 45). Mather then read his daughter's account of her conversion, her written profession of faith, declared, as it were, from beyond the grave. "[I]t is not every Day," he said, "that we shall see one more worthy to be *Embalmed*, and to have her Name preserved to Posterity, than a Young Gentlewoman in this Neighbourhood, who has lately Exchanged this Life for a better" (*Victorina* 48–49). Mather freely related to the church that Katharin had received a direct word from the Lord, assuring her that, contrary to her family's exhortations that she would live until the Sabbath: "Oh! how she hoped, That she should have her *Sabbath* in the *Paradise* of GOD! In the *Evening*, when she was told, it was thought she might Live another Day; She replied with Rapture, *No, I have received other Advice; It has been said unto me,* This Night thou shalt be with Me in Paradise! And so it prov'd" (*Victorina* 45).[32]

But Mather had an even stronger point to make. After reading Katharin's profession he added the following: "One thing of Special Use to her was this: There was one Mrs. *Chandler,* a pious Gracious, Ingenious Woman at *Woodstock,* whose Custom it was to retire every Night, when all the Family-Business was over, and Write down a brief *Meditation of Piety,* which also she sometimes Versified ..." (*Victorina* 58). Mather spoke glowingly of the influences the older woman's writings had produced in young Katharin, who had copied many of Mrs. Chandler's poems and essays into her own notebooks:

> This *Fine Work* of PIETY, thus drawn by a *Female Pen,* pleased her mightily; And she exactly *Copied* it. She employed her *Pen,* to transcribe and preserve, in Blank Books, for her Closet, such Things as appeared Singular *Treasures* unto her. And Especially such Things as she proposed, for the *Moulds* whereunto she would have her Soul to be cast, and by being cast into such *Moulds,* to have the *Evident Tokens of Salvation* upon her. Many Fine Things had she done in *Wax Work,* when she was a Child. But these *Moulds* were of infinitely more worth and use unto her. ... (*Victorina* 59–60)

On a practical level, Mather both wanted and needed women to write their testimonies and their religious sentiments and experiences in the prayer closet for the purpose of inspiring others, particularly the young, thus increasing the general piety which could only serve to hasten the Lord's appearing. Mrs. Chandler had fulfilled precisely the role Mather had envisioned for godly women when he had written *Ornaments.* Having left a written legacy of her virtue, the record of her pious thoughts thus inscribed served as a spiritual "mould" for the shaping of the qualities of inner virtue in younger women. Earlier, in *Ornaments,* Mather had pressed home the example of the Hebrew daughters learning the alphabet by copying the text of Prov. 31 (*Ornaments* 7); now, he was harvesting the fruit of his teaching in his congregation in which his own daughter had been the beneficiary. Further scattering the seed of that harvest, Mather published a number of Mrs. Chandler's works of meditation and piety along with his daughter's written testimony: "*Examples* do most strangely charm us into *Imitation.*" Added Mather,

> And there is scarce any thing in the World has a greater Tendency to promote *Vital Piety,* and *Religion in Earnest* among Christians, than an Exhibition of it in the Holy *Lives,* and Joyful *Deaths* of some of the Servants of God. Nor have *Essays* of this Nature been without their desirable Effects and Consequences ... and therein

---

32 It should be remembered that Anne Hutchinson, only three generations earlier, had scandalized her examiners by declaring that she had heard from God "by an immediate voice" (Hall 337).

... recommend a *Life of Piety* with its Charms and Glories, to the Practice of Young People, that shall be the Readers of it. (*Victorina* 47–48)

Thus the words of the living Mrs. Chandler and the deceased Katharin Mather fulfilled the pattern Mather had envisioned for pious women. Vital piety as evidenced by holy lives and victorious deaths breathed power into the written word and infused it with new authority when given utterance from beyond the grave. In such a manner, the secret pennings of the pious among women could be transformed into the "*Voice of the Dove.*" The act of writing left not only a pattern of virtue which could be communicated to others while remaining within the literal confines of Paul's injunction that women may not teach in the church; it also served as the very sign and seal of the piety individual women professed. Women who were to be emulated as spiritual models were those who exhibited their submission in the act of writing rather than in attempting to "usurp authority" by speaking, thereby demonstrating virtue as well as "spiritual power through such submission" (Marsden 249).

Cotton Mather's views on the importance of pious and learned women for the advancement of the church in the last age was an important legacy which he bequeathed to the next generation of ministers and parishioners who participated in the Great Awakening. Significantly, women's testimonies were among the earliest declarations of the moves of the Spirit in the revivals beginning in the mid-1730s. Like Cotton Mather, Jonathan Edwards would continue to promote female scholarship and education for young women in New England. Beyond the basics of reading, spelling and arithmetic, he advocated that girls "with the best genius should be encouraged to go on" (Marsden 390). While a relatively small number of genteel women, primarily the daughters of learned ministers and magistrates such as Esther Stoddard Edwards, had enjoyed a modicum of private education and cultivation, equipping them to read the works in their fathers' libraries, to keep small schoolrooms and to carry on intelligent correspondence, their experiences were more a reflection of the privileges of class and of the vagaries of circumstance than of conviction. Cotton Mather was the first to promote the value of education for pious women, claiming reason and intellectual capability for women on the basis of orthodox theology and scriptural exegesis within the established Reformed tradition. Although his theological constructs, as recorded in the "Biblia Americana," ascribing intellectual equality and moral self-governance to godly women as the rightful inheritance of regenerate women were never published, his sermons and public writings promoted the value of female scholarship and his persistent exhortations established and sanctioned the tradition of writing as an important means by which women could contribute to the kingdom of God.

Written accounts of extraordinary manifestations experienced by women proliferated during the revivals under Edwards. Narratives such as those reported by Sarah Edwards brought attention to the awakening along with the numerous testimonies by women and girls published by Jonathan Edwards throughout its course. Edwards, too, would ponder the reason for the heightened spirituality of the female members of the churches and of their greater receptivity to the Spirit of God. Like Mather, he concluded that it was the habit of submitting which had rendered women more virtuous and thus more receptive to the move of the Spirit, a state which he envied and which he strove to imitate in his own relationship with God.

While Mather's enthusiastic support for the literary endeavors of pious females demonstrated his belief that men could learn from women (even as it circumvented the proscription that women should not teach them), Edwards, affected by the events of Northampton, ventured a step further when he admitted that he was inclined to believe that under "extraordinary circumstances" women could actually teach men (Marsden 553 n11).[33] In contrast to the specter of the clamorous "strange woman" verbally and thus publicly challenging authority, which continued to hover over Massachusetts congregational life and to rankle in the collective memory of the New England ministers, Sarah's ecstasies, Edwards asserted, were a sign of her submission (Marsden 243). Thus, in the time of the Great Awakening, with vertical relationships intact in a system of paternal hierarchy, women continued more often to "attain the requisite submission" that allowed the indwelling move of the Holy Spirit, and to experience those ecstasies more frequently than did men. Women's spiritual narratives in turn became all the more valued and necessary for their "usefulness" in the church. Begotten in the obscurity of the closet, the written testimonies of women became sermons which at times transcended those of the pulpit.

It will surely be argued that, even so, female texts remained firmly under the control of males throughout the colonial period and beyond. Moreover, progressive as they were for their times, both Mather and Edwards managed and manipulated female texts whether by rendering them through the male "voice" or by determining their worthiness for publication. While these are valid observations, it must not be forgotten that Mather's full exegesis on the restoration of female intellectual "ornaments" as developed in the "Biblia Americana" never entered the arena of theological debate in America. Neither should it be discounted that in his era, Cotton Mather's contribution to women in his elevation of Eve ratified woman's intellect and dignified her position as a rational, intelligent being to a degree which the daughters of Eve had never before been granted. Yet, paradoxically, it was female submission particularly as

---

33 In one incident Sarah Edwards witnessed to members of the congregation about her experiences for three hours – but only after the service had officially ended (Marsden 249).

evidenced by written records of piety, which continued to be the pathway which established spirituality as belonging to the domain of women into the eighteenth century (Marsden 242–49; Porterfield 156).

Works Cited

Primary Sources

Bradstreet, Anne. *The Tenth Muse.* Ann Arbor: Scholars' Facsimiles and Reprints, 1965.

Fénelon, François. *Instructions for the Education of a Daughter.* Trans. and rev. George Hickes, D.D. Dublin, 1753.

Henry, Matthew. *An Exposition of All the Books of the Old and New Testament.* 6 vols. London, 1721–25.

Mather, Cotton. *The Angel of Bethesda: An Essay upon the Common Maladies of Mankind.* Ed. Gordon W. Jones. Barre: American Antiquarian Society, 1972.

–. "Another Brand Pluckt Out of the Burning." *More Wonders of the Invisible World.* Robert Calef. New York: Franklin, 1970.

–. *Bethia. The Glory Which Adorns the Daughters of God. And the Piety, Wherewith Zion wishes to see her Daughters Glorious.* Boston, 1722.

–. *Biblia Americana.* Ed. Reiner Smolinski. Vol. 1. Tübingen and Grand Rapids: Mohr Siebeck, Baker Academic, 2010.

–. *Bonifacius: An Essay upon the Good.* Ed. David Levin. Cambridge: Harvard UP, 1966.

–. *Diary of Cotton Mather.* Ed. Worthington Chauncey Ford. 2 vols. Massachusetts Historical Society Collections Seventh Series, Vol. VII–VIII. Boston: MHS, 1911–12.

–. *Ornaments for the Daughters of Zion. Or, the Character and Happiness of a Virtuous Woman.* New York: Scholars' Facsimiles and Reprints, 1978.

–. *The Threefold Paradise of Cotton Mather: An Edition of "Triparadisus."* Ed. Reiner Smolinski. Athens: U of Georgia P, 1995.

–. *Victorina: A Sermon Preach'd On the Decease and At the Desire of Mrs. Katharin Mather, By her Father. Whereunto there is added, A further Account of that Young Gentlewoman, By another Hand.* Boston, 1717.

Milton, John. *Paradise Lost.* Ed. Alistair Fowler. London: Longman, 1977.

Patrick, Simon. *A Commentary Upon the First Book of Moses, Called Genesis.* London, 1698.

Poole, Matthew. *Annotations upon the Holy Bible. Wherein the Sacred Text is Inserted, and various Readings Annex'd together with Parallel Scriptures, the more difficult Terms in each Verse are Explained, seeming Contradictions Reconciled, Questions and Doubts Resolved, and the whole Text opened. By the Late Reverend and Learned Divine Mr. Matthew Poole.* 2 vols. London, 1683–85.

Tertullian. "On the Apparel of Women." Trans. Rev. S. Thelwall. *Early Christian Writings Online.* Web. 6 June 2009.

Warren, Elizabeth. *Spiritual Thrift. Or, Meditations Wherein humble Christians (as in a Mirrour) may view the verity of their saving Graces, and may see how to make a*

Spirituall improvement of all opportunities and advantages of a pious proficiencie (or a holy Growth) in Grace and goodnesse. And wherein is layd open many errours incident to these declining times. London, 1647.

White, John. *A commentary upon the three first chapters of the first book of Moses called Genesis.* London, 1656.

Winthrop, John. *The Journal of John Winthrop.* Ed. Richard S. Dunn and Laetitia Yeandle. Cambridge: Harvard UP, 1996.

Secondary Sources

Almond, Philip. *Adam and Eve in Seventeenth-Century Thought.* Cambridge: Cambridge UP, 1999.

Brown, Sylvia. "The Eloquence of the Word and the Spirit: The Place of Puritan Women's Writing in Old and New England." *Women and Religion in Old and New Worlds.* Ed. Susan E. Dinan and Debra Meyers. New York: Routledge, 2001. 187–211.

Chamberlain, Ava. "Edwards and Social Issues." *The Cambridge Companion to Jonathan Edwards.* Ed. Stephen J. Stein. Cambridge: Cambridge UP, 2007. 325–44.

Cowell, Patti. Introduction. *Ornaments for the Daughters of Zion.* By Cotton Mather. Delmar: Scholars' Facsimiles & Reprints, 1978. v–xx.

Hall, David D., Ed. *The Antinomian Controversy, 1636–1638: A Documentary History.* Durham: Duke UP, 1990.

Irwin, Joyce L. Introduction. *Whether a Christian Woman Should Be Educated and Other Writings from her Intellectual Circle.* By Anna Maria van Schurman. Ed. Joyce L. Irwin. Chicago: Chicago UP, 1998.

Kamensky, Jane. *Governing the Tongue: The Politics of Speech in Early New England.* New York: Oxford UP, 1997.

Karlsen, Carol F. *Devil in the Shape of a Woman: Witchcraft in Colonial New England.* New York: Norton, 1998.

Klaiber, Isabell. "Women's Roles in American Society: Differences, Separateness, and Equality." *A Companion to American Cultural History: From the Colonial Period to the End of the 19th Century.* Eds. Bernd Engler and Oliver Scheiding. Trier: Wissenschaftlicher Verlag Trier, 2009. 303–330.

Lombard, Ann S. *Making Manhood: Growing up Male in Colonial New England.* Cambridge: Harvard UP, 2003.

Marsden, George. *Jonathan Edwards: A Life.* New Haven: Yale UP, 2003.

Morgan, Edmund S. *The Puritan Family: Religion and Domestic Relations in Seventeenth-Century New England.* 1944. New York: Harper & Row, 1966.

Porterfield, Amanda. *Female Piety in New England: The Emergence of Religious Humanism.* New York: Oxford UP, 1992.

Scheick, William J. *Authority and Female Authorship in Colonial America.* Lexington: U of Kentucky P, 1998.

Ulrich, Laurel Thatcher. *Good Wives: Image and Reality in the Lives of Women in Northern New England 1650–1750.* New York: Vintage Books, 1982.

–. "Vertuous Women Found: New England Ministerial Literature, 1668–1735." *American Quarterly* 28.1 (1976): 20–40.

Robert E. Brown

Hair Down to There: Nature, Culture, and Gender in Cotton Mather's Social Theology

When Cotton Mather sat for his portrait with Peter Pelham, he wore a wig.[1] This in itself doesn't strike the contemporary viewer as unusual – many social elites posed in wigs and, of course, wore them in daily life. Since the wig represents a conscious choice in apparel, however, it is at least worth asking what Mather might have intended to communicate by wearing it. The answer to this question touches upon a number of theological, philosophical, and hermeneutical issues that Mather confronted in the "wig" as a cultural artifact, issues which he attempted to resolve (with the help of his sources) in the "Biblia Americana." His solutions to them reveal an interpretive strategy that was decidedly progressive (in a self-interested sort of way), one that reflects his desire to bring to bear the intellectual achievements of his era upon the understanding of sacred writ – in this case the discoveries of history, natural science, and the emerging humanistic study of culture, what we might call a kind of ethnology *avant la lettre*.

One of the markers of early modern biblical interpretation is its unsettling awareness of cultural distance.[2] The traditional or mythic reading of the Bible tended to collapse or compress that distance, to regard past and present as somewhat interchangeable – to read the past into the present, and the present into the past. The recognition of the disjunction between them required early modern interpreters to pay closer attention to the historical, linguistic, and intellectual contexts in which the biblical authors wrote. This heightened sensitivity to context resulted in a new anthropological interest in ancient cultures, fueled in no small part by post-Columbian European contact with new and strange peoples. Biblical interpretation often merged with this rudimentary "science of man," as evidenced in the ethnographic work of figures such as Jean Bodin, Bernard de Fontenelle, and Jean LeClerc.[3]

---

1 The painting appears to have been executed relatively close to the end of Mather's life. Shortly after his death, Pelham produced what is thought to be the first mezzotint engraving in colonial America, which was based on the portrait. Prints were made available to the public later that year. On this, see Oliver.

2 On the emergence of this awareness, see, among others, Frei, Reventlow, Thiselton, *The Two Horizons*, and more recently, Preus, as well as Sheehan.

3 On the development of this interest in the systematic appraisal of culture, see Hodgen and Wolff.

"Biblia Americana" shows many of the signs of this sensitivity to cultural context, and Mather displays a penchant for anthropological explanation. His rather pronounced Christian Hebraism is one example of this: the decidedly Jewish origins of the doctrine and practice of the primitive church is an important interpretive tool in his commentary. The same can be said for his frequent recourse to the influence of first-century Greek and Roman culture on the religious understanding of the New Testament authors. Mather mined his classical and contemporary sources for any information on the practices of the world's cultures that might help to explain those found in the Bible. This element of Mather's interpretive strategy was, I believe, a part of his broader effort to expand Protestant biblical interpretation in a modernized fashion. His "Biblia" was the primary venue for exploring this intersection between sacred text and erudition, and its potential impact on the religious practices of his parishioners. His interpretive modernism enabled him to push back against the primitivist hermeneutic of his Puritan heritage and to transcend what he considered to be some if its more parochial applications.[4]

Perhaps no issue in the New Testament seems more patently conventional than the Apostle Paul's treatment of the religious significance of hair in 1 Cor. 11, made precisely difficult by the fact that Paul roots his judgments in notions of natural law. In broad outline, Paul addresses a problem concerning the liturgical practices of the church at Corinth: women are praying and prophesying in public assemblies without head coverings, or, possibly, with unkempt hair. Paul urges them to observe the tradition of head covering for several reasons: the uncovered head dishonors the created hierarchical structure of the male-female relationship; due consideration must be given to angelic beings; the natural order of things must be respected – in this case in the way nature distinguishes the sexes with regard to hair length. At the same time, Paul explores the mutuality of the sexes in light of the incarnation: women may actively participate in the Christian public; they exercise spiritual gifts; men and women are mutually dependent upon one another in Christ. There are of course notorious interpretive problems with this passage, which make its meaning ambiguous at best as well as controversial.[5] Mather and other early modern interpreters were well aware of these issues. But they also worked within the context of a long-standing tradition of Christian interpretation of the passage, which rested on three premises: that women must cover their heads in some manner, that hair (length) was a natural sexual distinction, and that this distinction served as a sign of a divinely instituted sexual hierarchy.

One of the most notable aspects of Mather's commentary on this passage is his deep immersion in questions regarding the social and religious practices of

---

4   On the primitivist dimensions of Puritan biblical interpretation, see Bozeman.
5   On the textual difficulties of this passage, see Thiselton, *The First Epistle*.

first-century Greek, Roman, and Jewish communities. His sources for these practices include the paraphrastic commentaries of Daniel Whitby, John Locke (a "Late, Nameless Writer"), and John Lightfoot.[6] The most important of these, however, is the commentary of the Anglican cleric and polemicist John Edwards, found in his *Enquiry into ... the New Testament* (Mather maintained a correspondence with Edwards as well as with the Dutch Reformed theologian, Hermann Wits).[7] A second notable characteristic of Mather's commentary is its shift in emphasis from Paul's primary concern with liturgical issues to a concern for secular social politics, from the conduct of women to the conduct of men, from the issue of head covering to the issue of hair fashions. Fully one half of his commentary is taken up with these issues.

Mather discusses a wide range of head and hair customs of the ancient world, and their historical significance for Christian practice. While Jewish men covered their heads in worship, Greek men did not. Both Greek and Roman men of rank kept their heads bare in public as a sign of their status as free men (see Witsius). Greek women, on the other hand, worshipped with their heads covered, except perhaps when uttering ecstatic or prophetic speech (see Locke), while Jewish women prayed unveiled (see Lightfoot).[8] In many ancient cultures, men also wore long hair to indicate high status, including the Romans, Greeks, Lycians, Portuguese, Gauls, Persians, Indians, Parthians, Germans, Scythians, Tartars, Chinese, and Koreans ("Coræans"), as well as pre-Colum-

6 Mather frequently cites Daniel Whitby's *A Paraphrase and Commentary on the New Testament* (1706), John Locke's *A Paraphrase and Notes on the Epistles of St. Paul* (1707), John Lightfoot's *Horae Hebraicae Et Talmudicae* (1675–79) – the volume on 1 Corinthians first appeared in 1664. Mather also cites Hermann Wits(ius) (probably his *Miscellanea sacra*, 1692–1700), Sir Norton Knatchbull (probably his 1659 *Animadversiones in libros Novi Testamenti*, which appeared in English in 1693 as *Annotations upon some Difficult Texts in All the Books of the New Testament*), Robert Sharrock's *Hypothesis ethike* (1660), John Viccars's *Decapla in Psalmos* (1639), and Sir Matthew Hale's *Primitive Origination of Mankind* (1677).

7 John Edwards, *Enquiry into Four Remarkable Texts of the New Testament* (1692); Mather cites this work as Edwards's "Lucubration." On his correspondence and interactions with Edwards, see his *Selected Letters* (128, 135, 150, 245). On his correspondence with Hermann Wits(ius), see his *Diary* (1: 549–50).

8 Although there is no definitive consensus on these practices, archaeological and textual evidence suggests that Mather's sources, with some exceptions, were generally correct on these variant practices. Greek men did pray uncovered (though Roman men covered their heads in worship). Evidence for the liturgical practice of Jewish men in the first century is either absent or inconclusive, but most likely did not include the later traditions of a shawl or cap that Mather's sources seem to assume. This question is obviated, of course, if "covering" here actually refers to long hair on men. But if this were so, the controversial sexual implications would remain. There is strong evidence in both Jewish (e.g. Philo) and classical (e.g. Pseudo-Phocylides) literature that long hair often served as a "homosexual semiotic" in the first century, as it did in Mather's era. Greek women typically covered their heads in worship, with the (controversial) exception of some cults (e.g. Bacchus). However, Jewish women, *contra* Mather and his sources, seem to have been covered in public at all times, including worship. On this, see Thiselton, *First Corinthians* (823–33), and Derrett.

bian "Mexican Priests" (see Edwards). In these cultures short (or shaved) hair was a sign of humiliation, for instance in mourning, in war, or as a token of enslavement.

These practices were not universal or static, however. Some cultures made long hair on men a sign of exceptional dedication: the Nazarite vow of the Jews, for example. Egyptian rituals of mourning were known to utilize both long and shaved hair. Greek warriors generally cut their hair to prevent it being grasped by the enemy, yet Macedonian soldiers used long hair to terrorize their enemies on the battlefield. Some of the cultures that originally esteemed long hair (Greek, Roman) came to embrace shorter hair as a sign of civilization. To quote Edwards, "the less Barbarous they were, the more they affected an Hair but of a Moderate Growth." This shorter, civilizing hair style was embraced by the primitive church. It was expected of priests; penitents and monks were shorn upon their induction. Hermits who expressed their mortification with floor-length hair were condemned by the church, as were nuns who shaved their heads. This normative practice had been interrupted only with the fall of the Roman Empire, by the incursion of "Long-Hair'd Barbarians" such as the Goths and Vandals, subsequently emulated by British Saxons, Picts, and the "Wild Irish" (Edwards 61, 67).

In his commentary on 1 Cor. 11 Mather devoted considerable effort to discovering the history of male hair fashions, treatments which go well beyond the rather limited parameters of Paul's liturgical discussion. Evidence suggests that his interests were not simply contextual-exegetical in nature, but in fact reflected a broad and intense conflict over changing cultural signifiers of sexuality in the seventeenth century. As Susan Niditch has observed, "hair plays an integral and intricate role in the way human beings represent themselves. It is related to natural and cultural identity, to personal and group anxieties, and to private and public aspirations" (5), and serves as an important means for enforcing social control, as well as expressing attitudes towards social authorities.[9] The early modern context offers a potent illustration of the complex nature of the religious and social meaning of hair, and helps to explain the shaping of Mather's interpretive strategy, and its decided ethnological orientation.

Since at least the late sixteenth century, Europeans had been locked in an intransigent debate over the religious and social significance of hair. Ostensibly the debate centered on appearance, first as to length: men had begun to grow out their hair as a sign of prestige and status, something which had fallen somewhat out of favor among the English elite during the reign of Henry I (1100–35).[10] As John Edwards noted, long hair had once again become "Modish" in

---

9   For theoretical interpretations of the significance of hair in the western cultural milieu, see Berg, Firth, (262–98), Myerowitz Levine, and D'Angelo.

10   The king and his court were wearers of long hair, as were other French nobility, but he

England, the nobility having imported this "Evil Practice" from France in the early seventeenth century [qtd. in *BA*, 1 Cor. 11]. Equally the dispute focused on style, and the inordinate attention paid to the crisping, curling, and arranging of hair. As wigs came increasingly into vogue in the late seventeenth century, they became an extension of the concerns expressed over both length and style. Hundreds of treatises, sermons, tracts, poems, marriage manuals, satires, and graphic editorials poured forth to address it: in most all of them, 1 Cor. 11 served as the rhetorical starting point of the debate.[11] In an era marked by violent conflict, it is no surprise that we should find this debate characterized in martial language. It was without too much hyperbole that some named it the *bellum capillare* – the "hairy war."[12]

It was a conflict with political dimensions. "Roundhead," after all, was a tonsorial pejorative; Royalists were similarly derided as "shaggeheaded Cavaliers" (Fisher 143). It had an ecclesiastical dimension as well. It internally divided the French Catholic clerical establishment as well as the Dutch Reformed church. It pitted Anglicans against Anglicans, Anglicans against dissenters of all stripes, and dissenters amongst themselves. Church edicts were issued and countermanded. Clerics who lost their livings over the issue under one bishop could find reinstatement under a more sympathetic one. Offending (wig-wearing) priests were not infrequently accosted as they attempted to conduct the liturgy (Corson 216–20). At times the language could be exceedingly sharp: the Dutch pastor-theologian Godefrid Udemans (a.k.a. Poimenander), for one, stating that to "wear the Hair below the Ears is a Sin, which deserves Eternal Death."[13]

---

responded to the criticism of this courtly fashion by French bishops by issuing an edict against it (see Woodforde). On the cultural backdrop for the early modern era, see Bartlett.

11 The classic English text on this issue is William Prynne's *Unlovelinesse of Lovelockes* (1628), which encompasses all of the fundamental evidentiary and argumentative lines of analysis. Prynne was a lawyer by profession, whose contrarian nature and puritanical assault on the stage *Histrio-Mastix* (1632) landed him in the Tower of London for life, with ears cropped, for sedition. He subsequently came to oppose the Interregnum and supported Charles II's restoration. Examples of the largely commentarial polemic on hair after Prynne can be found in the anonymous *Seasonable Advice from the Ancient Separation to All* (1650), Thomas Hall's *Loathsomnesse of Long Hair* (1654), *The Hairy Comet* (anon., 1674), the Quaker Richard Richardson's *Declaration Against Wigs or Periwigs* (1682), Vincent Alsop's *What distance ought we to keep, in following the strange Fashions of Apparel which come up in the day wherein we live?* (1683), *England's Vanity or the Voice of God against the Sin of Pride in Dress and Apparell* (anon., 1683), Thomas Wall's *Spiritual Armour to Defend the Head from the Superfluity of Naughtinness* (1688), and *God's Holy Order in Nature* (1690).

12 A conflict that, John Edwards lamented, "might easily [have been] decided by sober Minds" [qtd. in *BA*, 1 Cor. 11].

13 This formulation from Poimenander's *Absalom's Hair* (1643) is cited by Edwards (80). Claude Saumaise, a French classicist settled at Leyden, wrote a lengthy (750-page) defense of wigs, the *Epistola ad Andream Colvium super Cap. XI Primae ad Corinth. Epist.* (1644) as a rebuttal (he would write an apology for Charles I, *Defensio Regia*, in 1649). Jacques de Reves,

Developments in New England closely paralleled those in Europe. Court records, for example, reveal a man fined for long hair in 1637. In 1649, the General Court expressed its "detestation against the wearing of such long hair, as against a thing uncivil and unmanly, whereby men doe deforme themselves." In 1655 Harvard banned long hair for students, as Cambridge and Oxford had done twenty years before – though as late as 1672 John Eliot was still petitioning to have it enforced. In the wake of King Philip's War (1675), the Court again came out against long hair, as "manifest pride openly appearing amongst us, in that long haire, like weomen's haire, is worne by some men, either their oune or others haire made into periwiggs." The allusion here to transvestism is significant and part of a larger concern: on several occasions in the late seventeenth century women were fined for wearing men's clothing, and on at least one occasion a man was so fined; a law banning cross-dressing was enacted in 1695.[14]

Social paragons such as Eliot conducted a sustained jeremiad against changing hair fashions and the corruption of primitive church order and purity that they represented. It was the focal instruction of Charles Chauncy's 1655 commencement address (*God's Mercy*) to students who had been vocal in disputing his rationale against long hair. Michael Wigglesworth, Nathaniel Ward, and others condemned long hair in print, seeing in it, among other things, a reversion to the barbarism of Native Americans, who so maintained their hair (Koehler 43; Godbeer, "Perversions" 7–10). In his *Diary*, the magistrate Samuel Sewall recorded dozens of encounters, over a period of three decades, with council members, military officers, governors, clergy, and parishioners who had donned the wig, his disgust often issuing forth in a frank rebuke of the offender. Upon learning of the death of Boston's revered schoolmaster, Ezekiel Cheever, Sewall eulogized him as one who "abominated Perriwigs" (1: 600). Solomon Stoddard convened ministers in Northampton (c. 1701), which resulted in the condemnation of wigs; a topic he addressed later in his *Cases of Conscience* (1711), in which he allowed for some leeway (Godbeer, "Perversion" 10).

Increase Mather himself identified the rising tide of fashionable self-indulgence as a cause for divine displeasure. In his post-war jeremiad, *Exhortation to the Inhabitants of New-England* (1676), he notes the appearance of "strange Apparel" as a symbol of condemnable pride: pride in the poor, for dressing above their station; pride in the rich, for indulging in luxury. And "what shall we say when men are seen in the Streets with monstrous and horrid Perriwigs,

---

a theologian at Leyden, refuted Udemans in his *Libertas, Christiana circa usum capillitii Defensa* (1647). On this, see Fisher (145–50).

14   On this, see Koehler, Godbeer ("Perversions" 7–9), and Ford. On the broader dynamics of sexual mores in colonial New England, see Godbeer's *Sexual Revolution in Early America*.

and Women with their Borders and False Locks and such like whorish Fashions, whereby the anger of the Lord is kindled against this sinful Land!" (7).

Why did the subject of men's hair provoke such vigorous interest as an issue of religious concern? Some of the concern was obviously class-related, but it also reflected an anxiety over the kind of individualism or autonomy ("singularitie") that rising commercial affluence produced. Moreover, English Protestants were wary of the implications of foreign influence, attributing long hair and wigs to the influence of French and Spanish Catholic culture.[15] Furthermore, having had an association with paganism in Europe, long hair in the colonial context was associated with Indians and signified the demonic. According to William Prynne, the English had been inspired most recently to adopt long hair by their encounter with the "Heathenish and Idolatrous Virginians, who took their patterne from their Devill-god Ockeus" (Prynne, *Unlovelinesse of Lovelockes* 4–6).[16]

Even more important, at least according to anti-hair polemicists, was the unnaturalness of these fashions. "False hair," for example, obscured the effects of aging and so represented a form of deception, an attempt to appear younger and more virile. Wigs thus implied dissatisfaction with God's handiwork: those who wear them "taxe and censure God" as an "Imperfect, Bungling, or Unskilfull Workeman," and "labour to correct, and change his Worke" (Prynne, *Unlovelinesse of Lovelockes* 2, 16). The most frequently expressed concern about violations of nature, however, had to do with the threat to sexual identity that long hair and wigs represented. Men who changed their appearance in this way, according to William Prynne, take on the properties of the female: they become "effeminate," "unmanly," "humourous," "womanish," and "androginous" (Prynne, *Unlovelinesse of Lovelockes* 3, 49–50).

Prynne and his co-religionists used these terms quite literally. They shared an understanding of the body that made sexual identity relatively plastic and unstable. Mediated by the authority of Galen, European medical culture had adopted the anatomical theories of Aristotle. This system presupposed a singular sexual model of humanity, which found its perfect expression in the male. Females, according to this model, were deficient males, lacking sufficient potency or heat to generate full sexual completion – their genitalia in this case

---

15 As Godbeer ("Perversions" 3–6) notes, changing hair and apparel fashions signaled a rejection of the Puritan primitivist valorization of restraint and simplicity. It also undermined the class system, of which outward appearance served as an important indicator. Wigs, for example, allowed men of low status to obscure their social origins, and "pass" in more elite circles. Along with increasing geographic mobility, the loss of assigned appearance distinctions allowed for greater social anonymity. At the same time, as royal influence in New England increased in the late seventeenth century, these fashions potentially signaled one's loyalty to the new regime, along with its crypto-Catholic elements.

16 It is not incidental that Indian Christian conversion required the cutting of long hair; on the association of changing English hair styles with Indian barbarism, see Axtell (174–77).

being nothing more than inverted or incomplete male sex organs. As such women innately desired to become men and would be morally, psychologically, and even biologically inclined to achieve sexual completion.

This model of sexuality was made additionally unstable by the traditional Hippocratic theory of human physiology, which was based on the concept of bodily humors. When stimulated by the imagination or desire, unbalanced humors could transform the body's physical makeup toward "unnatural" states of sexual identity. Dramatic confirmation of this view was found in notorious cases of spontaneous sex change, in which individuals identified as females at birth would manifest male sex organs (as well as secondary sexual characteristics) in adolescence or early adulthood. Other stories in the medical literature told of women who became men by aping them: Taking on male work or clothing, they were stimulated physiologically to the point of anatomical metamorphosis.[17]

The instability and mutability attributed to female sexual identity held for men as well, though to a lesser degree. Fears of male-to-female transformations were not so forthcoming, but fears of emasculation to the point of femininity were, which raised the specter of homosexual behavior. The wearing of long hair, wigs, and other female accoutrements (makeup, lace, etc.) could just as easily stimulate or transfer feminine physiological and psychological qualities to men. As Richard Godbeer writes, "to look like a woman was to become a woman-like being" ("Perversions" 17).

This paradigm of human anatomy and physiology helps to explain why gender conventions such as hair and clothing were so vigorously contested. Nature and culture, sex and gender shared a significant degree of interchangeability. How the body was fashioned, what came into contact with it, and what the wearer imagined or desired his or her appearance to provoke could direct the transformation of the body. Such a prospect was destabilizing to the entire social fabric, premised as it was on the hierarchy of men. In the absence of notions of an anatomically permanent sexual distinctiveness, gender-coded norms such as hair and clothing were vital for stabilizing sexual identity, both physically and socially.

Mather's foray into his exposition of 1 Cor. 11, therefore, was heavily freighted with ideological controversy and that close at hand. The principle design of his anthropological investigations, I believe, was to relativize the social

---

17   On this, see Laqueur (124–42), Maclean (8–28), Fisher (15), and Godbeer ("Perversions" 6–15). There was at least one public instance of sexual ambiguity and transformation in the colonies as well: the now well-known case of Thomas/Thomasine, an indentured servant living in Virginia in the early seventeenth century, whose identity as both man and woman fluctuated to such a degree that a local court mandated his/her simultaneous wearing of men's and women's clothing. Whether Mather would have known of this case or others like it is unknown. On Thomas/Thomasine, see Brown (183–97).

and religious meaning of hair. Mather marshaled evidence which suggested that men's (and women's) hair styles differed between cultures, differed within cultures over time, and was altered by contextual considerations such as class, occupation, emotional states, and ritual settings. From this he constructed an argument that Paul's concerns and instructions for the Corinthians were cultural, particular, and temporally restricted, rather than doctrinal, universal, and indifferent to time or place.

For example, on the question of head coverings, Mather argues that the Corinthians had abandoned their native Greek customs in favor of Jewish practice, that they had "Judaized," a view derived from John Lightfoot [*BA*, 1 Cor. 11]. This had the potential to offend their pagan neighbors, whose men only covered their heads when engaged in polluting activities, or as a sign of humiliation (slavery, mourning). Thus Paul was concerned that they not implicitly communicate that Christian worship was a shameful activity. His advice, then, is conditioned by context: he "præscribes not a Rule necessary every where to be observed; but accommodates himself, unto the Custome, then observed among the *Corinthians*." Had he been speaking to Christians in Jerusalem or Arabia or Egypt, he would not have given them these directions, for they were "otherwise accustomed." Christians have historically adopted Paul's rule for men, not because the uncovered head itself is an intrinsic sign of reverence to God – for in "a very great Part of the World, it is not so to this Day" – but because it is in keeping with Christian liberty from Jewish custom and law [*BA*, 1 Cor. 11].

So much for men praying with heads uncovered. But what of the far more pressing problem of long hair? How then to understand Paul's assertion that hair length was rooted in the design of nature itself and thus seemingly beyond the vagaries of mere social convention? Much of this dimension of the argument was of course premised on what constituted "long" hair. For early polemicists such as Udemans, hair that was not closely cropped was by definition unacceptably long. One can see an example of this interpretation in the woodcut portrait of Richard Mather. But for many advocates of "moderate" hair, shoulder-length locks were acceptably short, on the grounds that hair could only fulfill its God-given utility for protection from inclement weather at this length – one thinks here of Increase Mather's early portrait done in London. This would apply to shoulder-length wigs as well, as in the case of Cotton Mather himself. For Mather, "long" hair would have meant well below the shoulder, a style that many colonials chose to embrace.

Still, whatever length was ultimately judged to be effeminately inappropriate, the interpreter must come to terms with Paul's argument from natural theology. Drawing on Edwards, Mather argues that the term "nature" (*phusis*) can be understood in any (and perhaps all) of three senses. First, and perhaps most strikingly, Paul's use of the term nature may actually mean custom itself. For

"Custome is a Second Nature" and thus "we may consider ... what Custome teaches" on this matter. Custom or culture arises out of human nature and thus is divinely (naturally) instituted as it were.[18] History teaches us that the custom of long hair has been prevalent across culture and time and is even religiously appropriate at times (mourning, vows), suggesting that it is not inherently against (human) nature. At the same time, however, the arc of human culture is, as it were, naturally bent toward the more civilizing effect of "moderate" hair lengths for men [*BA*, 1 Cor. 11]. Thus the weight of human custom, as an expression of the gradually refined principles of human nature, inclines one to the conclusion that relatively shorter hair on men is in keeping with nature and ought to carry with it a sense of the imperative.

Second, Paul may be referring here to the "Dictates of Reason, in the Breast of a Man" – natural because "they are Born with him." Rational reflection tells us that nature has enabled men as well as women to grow long hair, and so it cannot be intrinsically evil. But reflection also teaches us that the most sober thinkers and societies have perceived long hair to be contrary to "natural" decency. For example, long hair is often the mark of the criminal element, of "Ruffians," who represent a corruption of nature or reason. Worse still, long hair may quickly become a "Point of Effæminacy," as it apparently had for "the young Villains of *Corinth*" who were "Devoted unto Purposes filthily and horribly Sodomitical" [*BA*, 1 Cor. 11:14]. Ignoring the ill effects of long hair requires one to ignore one's rational faculties and thus to act against human nature.

Finally, by "nature" Paul may have been referring to that specific "Law of Nature," or dictate of reason, which insists that a distinction between the sexes must be maintained. When men wear their hair too long, that distinction is imperiled. But more to the point, it is not so much the length of hair that marks this confusion, but the manner in which it is maintained. If men adorn their hair in laces and ribbons, crimp it and curl it, pile it high on top of the head, or otherwise maintain it in the fashion of women, then sexual distinctiveness becomes increasingly problematic.

The logic of this assessment of long hair extends to wigs as well. Wigs were open to all the same criticisms of long hair, but particularly its "unnatural" and feminizing aspects. The borrowing of a woman's hair – for this was what men's wigs were made of – inclined men to become "Luxurious and Womanish" by literally placing themselves "under" the influence of the feminine. The longer and more sumptuous wigs are, the more they appear to be the fruit of an "Un-

---

18 Mather's source for the bulk of the remaining argument here is John Edwards. Edwards's source for the culture-nature equivalence is Calvin, and the scholastic exegetical-theological tradition whose understanding of nature and convention ultimately traces back to Aristotle. See Calvin's *Commentary on the Epistles of Paul the Apostle to the Corinthians* (362). On this, see Porter (77–85).

manly Vanity," indicative of a womanly intellect. Experience shows wig-wearing to be plagued with irrational impracticalities: This "Troublesome Tackle" impedes the simplest tasks, such as eating and drinking, not to mention military combat [*BA*, 1 Cor. 11].

Mather's commentary would seem to build a *prima facie* case against the modish hair styles that he himself had embraced. But in point of fact his selective use of sources contains a subtle but consistent emphasis on the conventional nature of the meanings assigned to hair and thus of its somewhat plastic coding for gender identity. Hair means what a given culture determines it to mean, within the broader natural consensus of moderation and gender distinction. Since custom is a "second nature," anthropological study can provide not only a guide for common socio-religious mores, but also a means to more reliably understand the meaning of scripture, and to distinguish its abiding principles from its transitory injunctions. In Mather's analysis, nature is also a second form of custom. Each of the three meanings of "nature" ultimately resolves into a form of social convention: whether in the historical practices of human societies, or in a shared sense of appropriateness, or in attitudes about gender distinction. In each case, standards dictated by "nature" can vary over time and place, even if their overall thrust is toward consensus. Thus even wigs themselves can meet the test of "nature" in this regard. Provided it maintains a distinction of the sexes, in keeping with accepted social conventions by being neither too long nor too effeminate in appearance, "Borrowed Hair may be Lawful for them whose Occasions call for it" [*BA*, 1 Cor. 11].[19]

What led Mather to subvert the gendered notion of hair so widely embedded and vehemently embraced within his close network of political, clerical, and social confederates as a social expression of religious orthodoxy and the standing order? To begin with, we need to recognize the force of modernizing elements in Mather's commentary, his embrace of a historically contextualized method of interpretation. It is apparent throughout his "Biblia" that Mather

---

19 Two other biblical passages relating to men's hair length figured prominently in seventeenth-century polemics: the story of Samson (Judg. 13) and the story of Absalom (2 Sam. 18). The story of Samson gave ammunition to those who favored longer hair, while the story of Absalom provided a cautionary tale for those opposed to long hair. Mather does not directly tie his comments on either story to contemporary debates about hair. However, in both instances his notes lend themselves to a sympathetic attitude toward unconventional fashions. Regarding Samson, Mather devotes attention to the dignified purposes attending his primping: "The *Nazarites* did not lett their Hair hang loose, but curled it up in Locks, or plaited it, and braided it; after the manner of a Chain." Samson wrapped his seven locks "about a Weaver's Beam ... to weave them one within another, so that they should be but one Lock ... [that] they might keep right, and not be Loosed" [*BA*, Judg. 13]. As to Absalom's unfortunate fate, Mather simply denies that his long hair was the cause of his being caught in the tree: "Dr. Patrick sees no Colour, for their Opinion, who think, he hung by his *Hair*, which being very long, was wrapt about the Boughs of the Tree; Nor is it probable, that he was without an *Helmett*, which covered his Hair" [*BA*, 2 Sam. 18:9].

understands ancient culture, including ancient biblical culture, to be precisely that: the artificial constructs of a given society, limited by time and place. Thus all manner of mannerisms in the Bible were open to historical investigation and interpretation – speech patterns, customs of dress, food, marriage, and the like. It was through historical contextualization that the true significance of a given passage could be elucidated. Distinguishing the historical and cultural from the underlying moral or theological principle made the passage applicable to modern readers.[20]

More so than any other of his colonial contemporaries, Mather was demonstrably committed to the notion that biblical interpretation would benefit from the gains of intellectual modernity. In one of his earliest descriptions of the "Biblia," which appeared in his *Diary* (1697) and again in the preface to the *Magnalia* (1702), he asserts that "all the *Improvements*, which the *later Ages* have made in the Sciences, might bee also, with an inexpressible Pleasure, call'd in, to assist the *Illustration* of the *Holy Oracles*" (*Diary* 1: 231). In the *New Offer to Lovers of Religion and Learning* (1714), Mather characterizes "Biblia Americana" as a work that would observe "all the Solid Discoveries in *Philosophy*, all the Curious Researches of *Antiquity*, or [what] has occur'd in *Physick*, or in *Law*, relating to the *Sacred Scriptures*, and appl[y] it all with a signal *Dexterity* to the *Illustration* thereof."[21] In keeping with a spirit of erudition, his "Biblia" would be a conduit for the free exchange of ideas, ones that his readers might find controversial, ones that he himself may not endorse. Mather sought to expose his readers to the relatively undigested opinions of a range of biblical scholars, whose interpretations he did not necessarily share: "If I *do*, you must not expect, that I declare myself, how far *I* concurr, with every Point, that shall be offered. And I will also leave *you* to the same Liberty that I take *myself*" (*BA* 1: 338).

His anthropological treatment of hair should be understood in this context. What for Prynne and others served as evidence of the pagan or even demonic origins of long hair is for Mather evidence of the variability of culture stemming from human nature. The meaning of these fashions is thus relative to time and place. Paul contextualizes his advice to the (largely Greek) Corinthians, but would have given decidedly different advice to Jewish Christians living in Judea, or to Gentile Christians living in Egypt. Mather worked from a different set of interpretive goals than many of his interlocutors, one that sought to bring together the collective learning of the day as a means of deciphering the ancient texts and resolving their critical difficulties. His approach to such prob-

---

20 On these problems of hermeneutics in "Biblia Americana," see Smolinski.
21 "Not only the *Rare Thoughts* of the more Illustrious *Literators*, who are known for *Stars of the first Magnitude* in the Catalogue of them that have *handled the Pen of the Writer*, but also the *Hints* occurring in Books that have made no Profession of serving this Cause, and many of them very *unsuspected ones*, have been seized for it" (Mather, *A New Offer* 2, 3, 5).

lems is relatively conciliatory, catholic, and cosmopolitan. Departing from the hermeneutic of his Puritan heritage, he was no longer wedded to an ideological primitivism. What is original to Christianity may be precedential, but it can and in many cases must be altered or added to, as the achievements of modernity may dictate.

Along these lines, we cannot discount what Mather's considerable interest and literacy in medicine may have contributed to his views on sex and gender. While he accepted the standard humoral theory of human physiology, Mather was also aware that Galen's anatomical authority was being supplanted by modern empirical studies of the body.[22] As Ian Maclean has observed, in the early eighteenth century an emerging medical consensus was coalescing around the notion that the female sex was not "the imperfect and incomplete version" of the male. "Indeed, far from being described as an inferior organ, the uterus now evokes admiration and eulogy for its remarkable role in procreation" (33). Women were coming to be described as functionally "perfect in their sex" – sexually distinct from the male, even if still physiologically destined to be inferior to men (27–45).

Mather does not comment on sexual or gender differences between men and women in either his posthumously published medical handbook *The Angel of Bethesda* or in *The Christian Philosopher*, although in the former he does have sections on menstruation, pregnancy, and venereal disease. But it is clear that his views of the body were decidedly mechanical in orientation, rooted in a more deterministic understanding of biology: In *The Christian Philosopher*, for example, he describes the body as "a Machine of a most astonishing Workmanship and Contrivance!" Thus it may be that he viewed sexual identity as more fixed and gender identities as more stable than was popularly understood. In this sense he may turn out to represent a kind of transitional thinking toward the more dichotomized views of sex and gender (nature and culture) that developed later in the eighteenth century.[23]

Some indication of this perhaps can be seen in his treatment of the phenomenon of male lactation in *The Christian Philosopher*. Medical literature of the time included the case of a Danish man, who, "upon the death of his Wife, suckled the Infant himself." Anatomists such as Marcello Malpighi had discovered that males possess mammary glands in their breasts. Since even "the *Paps* in Men ... sometimes contain *Milk*," they were clearly designed, in emergencies, for the suckling of infants (240).[24] A phenomenon which might have been inter-

---

22   On this, see Beall and Shyrock (24–26) as well as Mather's *The Christian Philosopher* (247).

23   On the increasingly fixed understanding of sexual difference in the eighteenth century, see Jordanova.

24   Mather's source is the Danish anatomist Thomas Bartholin (1616–1680), author of the *Historarium anatomicarum* (1654–1661). Malpighi (1628–1694) was a celebrated anatomist

preted under the "one sex"-model as indicative of sexual mutability, and thus a threat to gender order, appears to Mather as a teleological and providential phenomenon, something to be celebrated. Perhaps because he understands human anatomy and physiology to possess a more fixed character, such phenomena do not represent a threat to sexual identity or hierarchy – an understanding consistent with his relatively lax attitude toward long hair and wigs.

Mather understands hair in a similarly mechanistic and utilitarian fashion and uses his medical knowledge to polemical advantage. As its Latin name *capillus* implied, hair was thought to have the function of drawing off excess moisture from the brain, which is encased in fluid.[25] Domenico de Marchetti (*Anatomia*, 1652) discovered that this fluid is absent at times in the (deceased) aged. Mather adopts his conclusion that baldness is a result of the brain drying out, wherein the capillary function of hair would cease. Small wonder then that men should be so eager to replace this fading "graceful Ornament" with wigs, which represent in this case a *return* to nature rather than a *departure* from it and, from a medical perspective, a device that signals health and virility, rather than effeminacy (Mather, *The Christian Philosopher* 250, 423).[26]

Finally, we should not underestimate the influence of Mather's cosmopolitan aspirations upon his interpretive strategy, a fact that suggests a more pedestrian or mundane element to Mather's hermeneutic, one that demonstrates the importance of ideological self-interest for his biblical interpretation. As much as any other colonial, Mather desired to be a part of the greater European republic of letters and manners, and he also held the conviction that a distinctly American contribution could be made to it, whether in history, musicology, medicine, natural philosophy, and of course, biblical interpretation. His support for the royal charter negotiated by his father, his ecumenical efforts in the 1690's, his latitudinarian alterations of Puritan ecclesiastical polity, his transactions with and eventual membership in the Royal Society, and his pleasure at rubbing shoulders with English high society all point to the fact, as Kenneth Silverman has observed, that Mather held a "lively sympathy with new fashions and ideas," and "in many ways enjoyed the more various and cosmopolitan

---

who discovered the phenomenon of microscopic vesicles across animal species. He was the first Italian member of the Royal Society (1668) and physician to Pope Innocent XI. See Mather's *The Christian Philosopher* (383, 423).

25   Mather operates here on the (Galenic) belief that men are naturally "dry" and "hot" in humor, while women are "moist" and "cold." Hair serves to keep them masculine by preventing fluid buildup in the brain. Why the long hair of women would not equally serve to undermine their femininity is not considered, though perhaps the excess of fluid surrounding the female brain maintains some kind of equilibrium.

26   One wonders whether such a view might not also have served to advance the cause of wigs as a health aid to those who "voluntarily" wore them while shaving their heads, as a means to draw off fluid in the brain case.

world" emerging in New England after the accession of William and Mary (145).

It can hardly be a coincidence, for example, that the earliest recorded instance of his defense of wigs came at the height of his fame and influence as a political activist during his father's mission in England, amidst the growing influence of English affluent and aristocratic society. As Samuel Sewall records it in his *Diary* on March 19, 1691, Mather publicly declaimed from the pulpit that it was a sign of hypocrisy to "be zealous against an innocent fashion, taken up and used by the best of men" while ignoring more pressing moral lapses. "'Tis supposed [he] means [the] wearing of Perriwigs ... I suppose [he] was fain to wear a Perriwig for his health. I expected not to hear a vindication of Perriwigs in [a] Boston Pulpit by Mr. Mather" (1: 276).[27]

Even Increase Mather managed to trim his sails on the matter of wigs in the wake of this new cosmopolitanism. In *Burnings Bewailed* (1711), a minor jeremiad preached on the occasion of a house fire, he once again took the opportunity to identify the sins of the community that provoked the "blameable Causes of this Calamity." Among these, haughty apparel once again makes the list, but in this case it is primarily an offense of the poor, for whom it represents "inestimable Pride." But for those who are "Men of Estates, and such as are in Place and Dignity above others," it is meet "to be distinguished by the Costliness of their Apparel. ... If they wear Silk, and Satten, and Velvet, and Purple, and Silver & Gold, there is no Offence to Heaven in it." Furthermore, it is "Lawful for men to comply with any Fashion ... once it is become the Custom of the Place where they Live." It is only "Novelty and Singularity" which carry the "Badge of a Vain Mind." Mather's softening on fashion extended to hair as well: "a man who has lost his Hair by Sickness, or by Age; or if his Health require it, may as Lawfully make use of a Modest Wig or Border, as of a Cap or Hat." With a bit of sophisticated casuistry, he reinterprets his remarks about wigs made some four decades earlier: "I have never said or thought otherwise: But I have said, and do say, That such *Monstrous* Periwigs as some ... indulge themselves in the wearing of, which make them resemble the Locusts that come out of the Bottomless Pit, are a Badge of Pride" (21–23, emphasis added).[28]

---

27 Advocates of wigs often used health as a primary argument for them, in that they provided warmth and protection from the weather in the wake of baldness. In addition, men tended to wash their hair infrequently and often resorted to substances such as grease to manage it – both of which resulted in pests and dirt invading the scalp; shaving the head and wearing a wig could be seen as a form of good hygiene. Sewall's principled refusal to wear wigs himself, against the whelming tide of fashion in Boston high society, cost him the favors of at least one prospective bride. On this, see LaPlante (246–50) and Godbeer ("Perversions" 3–10). Mather's long and complicated relationship with Sewall is discussed in Silverman (149, 227, 314–19, 385).

28 Mather's reference is to Rev. 9:7–8 ("whose Faces were as the Faces of Men, and they had Hair as the Hair of Women"), an analogy drawn from William Prynne.

Further evidence of Cotton Mather's urbane manners regarding wigs can be seen in his treatment of John Eliot in the *Magnalia* (1702). Eliot was, he writes, "in all regards a Nazarite indeed; unless in this one, that long hair was always very loathsome to him; he was an acute *Ramist*, but yet he professed himself a lover of a *Trichotomy*." Many contemporary readers of the *Magnalia* would have recognized the witticism in this seemingly obscure reference to Peter Ramus, whose system of dichotomous logic had been so important to Puritan pedagogy. The preface of Thomas Hall's *Loathsomeness of Long Hair* (1654) contains a satirical poem in which a wearer of long hair acknowledges his departure from the Ramist philosophy by embracing a "*Trichotomy*" – the marrying of a "female head to a male face" – becoming, in effect, a third (or hermaphroditic) sex (n.pag.). Mather inverts Hall's satire to his own rhetorical ends. It is Eliot, the otherwise acute Ramist, who had become the "lover of a Trichotomy" – existing in Eliot's embracing a Samsonesque asceticism while rejecting long hair, resulting in an anomalous "third" religious category of the "shaven Nazarite":

> Thus Mr. Eliot thought that for men to wear their hair with a luxurious, delicate, faeminine prolixity; or for them to preserve no plain distinction of their sex by the hair of their head and face; and much more for men thus to disfigure themselves with hair that is *none of their own*; and most of all, for ministers of the gospel to ruffle it in excesses of this kind; may prove more than we are well aware displeasing to the Holy Spirit of God. The hair of them that professed religion, long before his death, grew too long for him to swallow; and he would express himself continually with a boiling zeal concerning it, until at last he gave over, with some regret complaining, "The lust is become insuperable!" (*Magnalia*, vol. 1, bk. 3, pp. 540)

Mather treats Eliot's views on the matter charitably, even condescendingly, as those indicative of a bygone era. Perhaps this patriarch's concerns were in fact merely hygienic, his criticisms elicited by a phenomenon known in the day as the "Polish plait" (*Plica Polonica*), a serumous scalp infection which resulted from a long, matted, unkempt wearing of the hair (rather than the "sweeter, neater, but prolix locks" worn in New England). Eliot "was indeed one *priscis moribus* [of primitive manners] as well as *antiqua fide* [ancient fidelity]; and he might be allowed somewhat even of *severity* in this matter on that account."[29] Nonetheless, Mather explicitly rejects Eliot's views. "Doubtless, it may be lawful for us to accommodate the length of our hair unto the modest customs which vary in the Churches of God." Under appropriate circumstances, "it may be lawful for them that have not enough of their own hair for their health, to supply themselves according to the sober modes of the places they live." Mather then invokes the reasoning also developed in his "Biblia." While it may be true

---

29 Clearly a familiar work to Mather, Hall in his preface also mentions the *plica polonica* as a disease of modernity, arising out "moderne luxury and excess," and one resulting in blindness and madness.

that "the apostle tells us, 'Nature teaches us that if a man have long hair, 'tis a shame to him,'" the use of the term nature can mean "no other than the *difference of sex*, as the word elsewhere is used" (*Magnalia*, vol. 1, bk. 3, pp. 540).

Mather's use of humor here – important to polemicists on both sides of the issue – also appears in his Corinthian commentary. There he mentions "a Reverend Old Gentleman of my Acquaintance" – not doubt Eliot – "who was very Zealous for Short Hair," basing his argument on Paul's injunction. "It was answered" – no doubt by Mather himself – that "all Nations in all Ages have counted their Long Hair their Glory; and therefore the Text here, of what Nature teaches, must bee taken in another Sense, than what you putt upon it." The old man replied: "Nature taught those People this Lesson, but their Ears were so Covered with their Locks, that they could not hear it" [*BA*, 1 Cor. 11].

Sermonic literature has long been appreciated as a source for studying the lived religion of early America. The significant body of American biblical commentary, in contrast, has long suffered from relative neglect. One hopes that further investigation into this literature will encourage scholars interested in American religion to consider the ways in which Americans of all periods have read their religious hopes and concerns into and out of their fundamental sacred text. Mather's "Biblia Americana" provides an ample and important resource for such investigation. The present study suggests just how important biblical interpretation was in the tangible spiritual concerns of Mather and his parishioners.

The problem of culture was particularly nettlesome in the early modern interpretation of biblical texts, whose religious authority traditionally had been extended to the ancient social, moral, and cosmological patterns of thought found in sacred writ. As interpreters became increasingly disenchanted with such a hermeneutic, they pursued a range of interpretive strategies to account for this disjunction between past and present, including appeals to a kind of cultural relativism. Mather's commentary shows evidence of this manner of thinking. As made evident by other essays in the present volume, intellectual modernity, while it presented real challenges to the more traditional elements of his interpretation of the Bible, ultimately expanded Mather's hermeneutic vision and enabled him to consider a broader range of factors in reaching his interpretive conclusions. In the case of Paul's advice to the Corinthians, he emphasizes the conventional nature of certain biblical precepts – in this instance the arbitrary nature of the coding of hair for gender identity – and the need for interpretive subtlety and sophistication in determining their import for orthodox belief and practice. Cultural mores can be specific to time and place, while at the same time the history of social practices can yield something about the abiding elements, or rationality, of the divinely constituted human nature. Such customs are revealing of the dynamics of human nature, and so anthropological study can provide a guide for assessing socio-religious mores as well as a means to interpret scripture. In Mather's analysis, even "nature" itself can be conceived at times as a culturally determined concept.

Works Cited

Primary Sources

Alsop, Vincent. *What distance ought we to keep, in following the strange Fashions of Apparel which come up in the day wherein we live?* London, 1683.
Calvin, John. *Commentary on the Epistles of Paul the Apostle to the Corinthians.* Grand Rapids: Eerdmans, 1989.
de Reves, Jacques. *Libertas, Christiana circa usum capillitii Defensa.* Leiden, 1647.
Edwards, John. *Enquiry into Four Remarkable Texts of the New Testament.* London, 1692.
England's Vanity or the Voice of God against the Sin of Pride in Dress and Apparell. London, 1683.
Hale, Matthew. *The Primitive Origination of Mankind.* London, 1677.
Hall, Thomas. *The Loathsomnesse of Long Hair.* London, 1654.
The Hairy Comet. London, 1674.
Knatchbull, Norton. *Annotations upon some Difficult Texts in All the Books of the New Testament.* London, 1693.
Lightfoot, John. *Horae Hebraicae Et Talmudicae.* London, 1675–79.
Locke, John. *A Paraphrase and Notes on the Epistles of St. Paul.* London, 1707.
Mather, Cotton. *The Angel of Bethesda: An Essay Upon the Common Maladies of Mankind.* Ed. Gordon W. Jones. Barre: American Antiquarian Society and Barre Publishers, 1972.
Biblia Americana. Ed. Reiner Smolinski. Vol. 1. Tübingen: Mohr Siebeck, 2010; Grand Rapids: Baker Academic, 2010.
–. *The Christian Philosopher.* 1721. Ed. Winton U. Solberg. Urbana: U of Illinois P, 1994.
–. *Diary of Cotton Mather.* Ed. Worthington C. Ford. Collections of the Massachusetts Historical Society 7th series. Vols. 7–8. Boston: MHS, 1911–12.
–. *Magnalia Christi Americana: Or, The Ecclesiastical History of New England.* 1702. New York: Arno Press, 1972.
–. *A New Offer to the Lovers of Religion and Learning.* Boston, 1714.
–. *Selected Letters of Cotton Mather.* Ed. by Kenneth Silvermann. Baton Rouge: Louisiana State UP, 1971.
Mather, Increase. *Burnings Bewailed.* Boston, 1711.
–. *Exhortation to the Inhabitants of New-England.* Boston, 1676.
Prynne, William. *Histrio-Mastix.* London, 1632.
–. *The Unlovelinesse of Lovelockes.* London, 1628.
Richardson, Richard. *Declaration Against Wigs or Periwigs.* London, 1682.
Saumaise, Claude. *Epistola ad Andream Colvium super Cap. XI Primae ad Corinth. Epist.* Leiden, 1644.
Seasonable Advice from the Ancient Separation to All. London, 1650.
Sewall, Samuel. *The Diary of Samuel Sewall 1674–1729.* Ed. M. Halsey Thomas. 2 vols. New York: Farrar, Straus, and Giroux, 1973.

Sharrock, Robert. *Hypothesis Ethike*. London, 1660.

Viccars, John. *Decapla in Psalmos*. London, 1639.

Wall, Thomas. *God's Holy Order in Nature*. London, 1690.

–. *Spiritual Armour to Defend the Head from the Superfluity of Naughtinness*. London, 1688.

Whitby, Daniel. *A Paraphrase and Commentary on the New Testament*. London, 1706.

Wits(ius), Hermann. *Miscellanea sacra*. Utrecht, 1692–1700.

Secondary Sources

Axtell, James. *The Invasion Within: The Contest of Cultures in Colonial North America*. New York: Oxford UP, 1985.

Bartlett, Robert. "Symbolic Meanings of Hair in the Middle Ages." *Transactions of the Royal Historical Society* 44 (1994): 43–60.

Beall, Jr., Otho T., and Richard H. Shyrock. *Cotton Mather: The First Significant Figure in American Medicine*. Baltimore: Johns Hopkins UP, 1954.

Berg, Charles. *The Unconscious Significance of Hair*. London: Allen and Unwin, 1951.

Bozeman, Theodore Dwight. *To Live Ancient Lives: the Primitivist Dimension in Puritanism*. Chapel Hill: U of North Carolina P, 1988.

Brown, Kathleen. "'Changed ... into the Fashion of Man': The Politics of Sexual Difference in a Seventeenth-Century Anglo-American Settlement." *Journal of the History of Sexuality* 6.2 (1995): 171–93.

Corson, Richard. *Fashions in Hair: the First Five Thousand Years*. London: Peter Owen Ltd., 1965.

D'Angelo, Mary Rose. "Veils, Virgins, and the Tongues of Men and Angels." *Off With Her Head! The Denial of Women's Identity in Myth, Religion, and Culture*. Ed. Howard Eilberg-Schwartz and Wendy Doniger. Berkeley: U of California P, 1995. 131–64.

Derrett, J. Duncan M. "Religious Hair." *Man* 8.1 (1973): 100–03.

Firth, Raymond. *Symbols Public and Private*. Ithaca: Cornell UP, 1973.

Fisher, Will. *Materializing Gender in Early Modern English Literature and Culture*. Cambridge: Cambridge UP, 2006.

Ford, Worthington C. "Samuel Sewall and Nicholas Noyes on Wigs." *Publications of the Colonial Society of Massachusetts* 20 (1920): 109–27.

Frei, Hans W. *The Eclipse of Biblical Narrative: A Study in Eighteenth and Nineteenth Century Hermeneutics*. New Haven: Yale UP, 1974.

Godbeer, Richard. "Perversions of Anatomy, Anatomies of Perversion: The Periwig Controversy in Colonial Massachusetts." *Proceedings of the Massachusetts Historical Society* 109 (1998): 1–23.

–. *Sexual Revolution in Early America*. Baltimore: Johns Hopkins UP, 2002.

Hodgen, Margaret T. *Early Anthropology in the Sixteenth and Seventeenth Centuries*. Philadelphia: U of Pennsylvania P, 1964.

Jordanova, Ludmilla. *Sexual Visions: Images of Gender in Science and Medicine Between the Eighteenth and Twentieth Centuries*. Madison: U of Wisconsin P, 1989.

Koehler, Lyle. *A Search for Power: the "Weaker Sex" in Seventeenth-Century New England*. Urbana: U of Illinois P, 1980.

LaPlante, Eve. *Salem Witch Judge: The Life and Repentance of Samuel Sewall*. New York: HarperOne, 2007.

Laqueur, Thomas. *Making Sex: Body and Gender from the Greeks to Freud*. Cambridge: Harvard UP, 1990.

Levine, Molly Myerowitz. "The Gendered Grammar of Ancient Mediterranean Hair." *Off With Her Head! The Denial of Women's Identity in Myth, Religion, and Culture*. Ed. Howard Eilberg-Schwartz and Wendy Doniger. Berkeley: U of California P, 1995. 76–130.

Maclean, Ian. *The Renaissance Notion of Woman: A Study in the Fortunes of Scholasticism and Medical Science in European Intellectual Life*. Cambridge: UP, 1980.

Niditch, Susan. *"My Brother Esau Is a Hairy Man": Hair and Identity in Ancient Israel*. Oxford: Oxford UP, 2008.

Norton, Mary Beth. *Founding Mothers and Fathers: Gendered Power and the Forming of American Society*. New York: Knopf, 1996.

Oliver, Andrew. "Peter Pelham (c. 1697–1751), Sometime Printmaker of Boston." *Boston Prints and Printmakers 1670–1775. Publications of the Colonial Society of Massachusetts* 46 (1973): 133–73.

Porter, Jean. *Natural and Divine Law*. Grand Rapids: Eerdmans, 1999.

Preus, J. Samuel. *Spinoza and the Irrelevance of Biblical Authority*. Cambridge: Cambridge UP, 2001.

Reventlow, Henning Graf. *The Authority of the Bible and the Rise of the Modern World*. Trans. John Bowden. Philadelphia: Fortress Press, 1985.

Sheehan, Jonathan. *The Enlightenment Bible: Translation, Scholarship, Culture*. Princeton: Princeton UP, 2005.

Silverman, Kenneth. *The Life and Times of Cotton Mather*. New York: Harper & Row, 1984.

Smolinski, Reiner. "How to Go to Heaven, or How Heaven Goes? Natural Science and Interpretation in Cotton Mather's 'Biblia Americana' (1693–1728)." *New England Quarterly*. 81. 2 (2008): 278–329.

Thiselton, Anthony C. *The First Epistle to the Corinthians*. Grand Rapids: Eerdmans, 2000.

–. *The Two Horizons: New Testament Hermeneutics and Philosophical Description*. Grand Rapids: Eerdmans, 1980.

Wolff, Larry. "Discovering Cultural Perspective: The Intellectual History of Anthropological Thought in the Age of Enlightenment." *The Anthropology of the Enlightenment*. Ed. Larry Wolff and Marco Cipolloni. Stanford: Stanford UP, 2007. 11–31.

Woodforde, John. *The Strange Story of False Hair*. New York: Routledge and Kegan Paul, 1972.

Jan Stievermann

The Genealogy of Races and the Problem of Slavery in Cotton Mather's "Biblia Americana"

As with so many other facets of his life and work, Cotton Mather's reputation is ambiguous when it comes to what we, today, call race matters. Indeed, many scholars have deemed his attitudes and actions towards Africans and Native Americans to be contradictory, or even outright hypocritical. On the one hand, he has been seen by some as an exceptionally outspoken advocate of spiritual equality, who believed the elect could be found among all peoples, and who therefore insisted that slaves and Indians "should receive a Christian education and be allowed to join the church." On the other hand, it is widely believed that "he shared the racial prejudices of his fellow whites" (Elliott 274) and theologically justified the dispossession, oppression, and permanent bondage of these potential brethren in Christ on account of their supposed inherent inferiority. Historians of colonialism have pointed to a number of passages in Mather's writings where he literally demonizes native cultures, passages which are taken to demonstrate that, for all his talk on spiritual equality, the American Indians were, for Mather, "little better than animals, incapable of reason and [irredeemably] enslaved by the most brutal passions" (Axtell 133). Similarly, Mather's defense of the scriptural nature of slavery in *The Negro Christianized* (1706), together with the fact that he accepted black bondservants in his own household, have been cited as proof that he considered Africans inferior and natural-born servants and proof, therefore, of his implication in the anti-black racism of the day.[1]

---

1 Elliott's above-cited opinion, which attributes the tensions and inconsistencies in Mather's views on African slavery and "Indian affairs" to an inveterate racism trumping his belief in spiritual equality, has a very long scholarly tradition. It goes back at least as far as Greene's *The Negro in Colonial New England* (1942). While applauding him for his views on spiritual equality (264–67), Greene simultaneously made Mather a prime example for what he called "the racial philosophy of the Puritans, [according to which] Negroes and Indians were an inferior race whom God had given them as part of their inheritance" (285–86). Winthrop Jordan's very influential study *White Over Black* (1968) basically followed this interpretation. Jordan asserted that despite his insistence on the religious insignificance of skin color, Mather could not escape the deeply embedded "psychological mechanisms" (187, 200–01, 275) of racial prejudice. A similar view was taken by McManus (1973), who wrote that Mather's "racial views were more enlightened" than those held by many of his fellow New Englanders. At the same time, he cites Mather as an example of a specifically Puritan form of theologically inflected color prejudice that "gave the Calvinist doctrine of election a sociobiologi-

While there is certainly much to be said about Mather's conflicted views on African slavery and Anglo-Indian relations, I will argue that racism, in the modern sense, is not the interpretative framework that allows us to adequately understand them.[2] Indeed, the prevailing opinion of Mather as someone who, in some ways, was "ahead of his time," but who ultimately remained unable to break free from the all-determining logic of race, appears problematically presentist. There is now a growing revisionist consensus in early American scholarship that neither the concept of race nor the ideology of racism assume a recognizably modern meaning or level of importance before the middle or even the end of the eighteenth century, after going through a very slow and contested cultural evolution. This new understanding has also created a critical awareness that our contemporary scale of measuring progressive or reactionary thinking on racial issues is inadequate for the early modern period. In this spirit, we should no longer take it for granted that race, as we understand it today, constituted a key element of Mather's theology (or that of his fellow Puritan clergymen, for that matter), or that racial prejudices were a motivating force behind his writings and social practices.[3] Conversely, we should not assume that those

---

cal interpretation and argued that Negroes were an accursed people condemned by God to serve the whites" (64–65). In some of the standard histories of American racism, Mather has even been assigned a less ambiguous, much more sinister role. For Gossett the "idea expressed by Cotton Mather in the seventeenth century that the Indians were the devil's minions, damned from birth by God and incapable of redemption" paved the way for the nineteenth-century "conviction that the Indians were damned by biology – that they were incapable of taking the first step towards civilization" (229). Similarly, Vaughan, in *Roots of American Racism* (1995), read Mather's writings on Indians as heralding the advent of modern American racism (24). In so doing, Vaughan fell in line with critics of his earlier studies that had been accused of downplaying, in the customary fashion of traditional Puritan studies, the colonists' racial bias against Indians. Such criticism had been voiced, for instance, by Thomas, for whom Mather's *Magnalia* served as the main source of evidence for his argument against the traditionalist view of the rather benign nature of early Anglo-Indian relations in New England. By contrast, Thomas and other revisionists like Axtell held that "the Puritan belief that Indians were a fallen race led to an increasing conviction that Indians were an irredeemable race apart, regardless of the apparent Christianity of a few individuals" (Thomas 10).

2 Among the many definitions of racism that are being debated amongst scholars, I find the one offered by Frederickson very helpful. Constructed around the two components "*difference*" and "*power*," this definition distinguishes racism from other ideologies of "Othering" as follows: "It [racism] originates from a mindset that regards 'them' as different from 'us' in ways that are permanent and unbridgeable. This sense of difference provides a motive or rationale for using our power advantage to treat the ethnoracial Other in ways that we would regard as cruel or unjust if applied to members of our own group. ... In all manifestations of racism from the mildest to the most severe, what is being denied is the possibility that the racializers and the racialized can coexist in the same society, except perhaps on the basis of domination and subordination. Also rejected is any notion that individuals can obliterate ethnoracial difference by changing their identities" (9).

3 A notable recent exception to the scholarly consensus on Mather's inveterate racism is Margot Minardi's study of the Boston inoculation controversy of 1720–21. The controversy revolved around Mather's propagation of inoculation against small pox; for the effectiveness of this new technique he relied on the testimony of his black slave Onesimus, who had told his

few individuals in colonial British America who, unlike Mather, openly challenged the institution of slavery did so because they held less racist or anti-racist
opinions. This assumption, of course, informed many readings of early antislavery documents such as George Keith's (1639–1716) *An Exhortation and
Caution to Friends concerning Buying or Keeping of Negroes* (1693) and Samuel
Sewall's (1652–1730) *The Selling of Joseph. A Memorial* (1700), to which Mather's *The Negro Christianized* was often unfavorably compared (see, for instance,
Kaplan 34, 56).

There is, moreover, a questionable tendency in the predominant interpretation of Mather's stance on these matters, wherein his theological reasoning and
scriptural exegesis is regarded as being of secondary importance or even as epi-
phenomenal in nature. In other words, racism, in combination with other deeper motives such as economical interests or power politics, is taken to be the
primary reason behind Mather's writings and actions, just like his thinking is
assumed to have been informed by pre-existing racial categories of non-theo-
logical origin. Consequently, his religious arguments and interpretations of the
Bible appear as either convenient *a posteriori* justifications for existing attitudes
and interests or, where they collided with these attitudes and interests, as evidence for his ultimate inability to overwrite deeply entrenched prejudices.
However, given the discursive centrality of theology during the period and considering what we now know about the slow development of modern racial
thinking, such an approach seems anachronistic and out of step with recent
trends in the study of the early modern Atlantic world and its intellectual history.

After a long period of relative neglect, the biblical texts and their ever-
growing bodies of commentaries are now receiving renewed attention as a primary framework in which the changing concepts of race were being constructed and contested during the early modern era and beyond.[4] As such a primary

---

master about the successful application of this practice in his African homeland. Mather's
opponents, most prominently the physician and anticlerical polemicist William Douglass,
attacked Mather for practicing dangerous quackery and for crediting the stories of a "Negro."
Reading the debate over the testimony of Onesimus as part of the ongoing construction of
race in the British colonies, Minardi concludes that Mather certainly adhered to a highly
conservative understanding of "social hierarchies on earth" and "sought to integrate slavery
into a divinely ordained model of social relations," but resisted any notions of a natural superiority of white people over people of color. While Mather's writings consistently "down-
played the significance of innate physical difference" (67) between black and white, Douglass's disparagements of Onesimus show a "conception of human difference [that indeed] was
a nod towards the scientific racism of the later period, though it lacked the coherence of a
fully formed racial ideology" (72).

4 Of course, there have always been scholars who, in the words of Jordan, recognized that
"the Bible is the single most important historical source for an intellectual background of the
development of attitudes towards Negroes [or Indians] in early America" (597). Yet, until
quite recently, few systematic and comprehensive studies were undertaken in this area. For a
discussion of this *desideratum*, see Braude's "Primary Colors." Haynes and Johnson have

and overarching framework of interpretation scriptural exegesis certainly cannot be said to have worked in one way only, let alone in a way that we could neatly characterize as racist or anti-racist. Readings of the Bible were, without question, absolutely "central to the process of *racializing* peoples – to imposing categories of racial hierarchies upon groups of humanity or other societies" (Harvey 14). At the same time, the universalist vision of human origin and destiny, present in many parts of the scriptures, also inhibited the formation of racial prejudices, and theological arguments were employed to combat notions of an inherent inequality between the races. The ongoing exegetical battles over the book of Genesis were of special importance in what Kidd calls the "forging of races." From an early modern biblicistic viewpoint, which assumed that the scriptures contain a truthful and complete history of the world, the genealogical account in Genesis, "which sets out the families of the sons of Noah and claims that 'by these were the nations divided in the earth after the Flood,'" provided the very basis "for understanding the races, linguistic groups, ethnicities and nations of the world" (Kidd 20–21). Additionally, Genesis contains stories, most importantly of Noah's curse of Ham and the account of the marking of Cain, which were common reference points in the era's expanding arguments about the meaning of skin color. Together with a number of passages from Deuteronomy, Leviticus, Acts, and the Pauline letters, these stories constituted the central touchstones in early modern discussions over the biblical justification of slavery.

For the most part, Mather's precise role in these debates of his time has not yet been determined. Because his texts have too often been read through modern assumptions about racism and its sinister alliance with religion, relatively little is known about the ways in which he, as an academic theologian, actually interpreted humanity's diversity and thereby defined the spiritual, social, and legal significance (or insignificance) of color. Also, most assessments of Mather's record on race matters rest on a very slim textual basis – *The Negro Christianized* and parts of *Magnalia Christi Americana* (1702) are the most often cited works in this context – while much of his pertinent biblical scholarship remains neglected. With the publication of the "Biblia Americana" (1693–1728), the work which Mather considered the crowning achievement of his lifelong study of the scriptures, we are now able, for the first time, to assess fully how he

---

since shed much new light on the biblical justification of American slavery and the centrality of the curse of Noah or myth of Ham in this context, while Goldenberg places these findings in a comparative historical perspective. Whitford's in-depth study focuses on how during the Reformation period the story of the curse of Noah was being interpreted in new ways that provided justification for the radpidly expanding slave trade. In his superb *The Forging of Races* (2006), Kidd provides a much-needed survey on the changing and conflicted scriptural interpretations of race between 1600–2000. Even though it doesn't mention Mather at all, Kidd's book has been an invaluable help for me and provides a framework of reference throughout this study.

positioned himself on all the key exegetical issues relating to race and slavery.[5] His extensive commentaries on Genesis, in which he enters into a dialogue with a host of earlier interpreters, allow us to see in great detail how he explained the origin of humanity's dispersal into diverse peoples and what meanings he gave to phenotypical differences.

The Mather who emerges from these until now unpublished manuscript pages is a staunch champion of the orthodox belief in humanity's common origin, universal consanguinity, and spiritual unity in Christ. He defends this position against both the older theories of polygenesis and against a new kind of racial thinking that began to emerge out of developments in early Enlightenment natural philosophy as well as in response to decades of Indian warfare and the burgeoning slave trade. More surprisingly even, Mather, whose theology generally tends towards a heightened supernaturalism, rejects wholesale what George Fredrickson, in his history of racist ideologies, describes as the widespread supernatural proto-racism of the early modern period (42–52). In other words, Mather rejects any theological theories or popular myths such as Noah's curse in which biblical stories are taken as proof that Africans or Native Americans, because of the moral failure of their supposed ancestors, have been expelled from the community of God's children or relegated to perpetual social subordination and now carry their supernaturally transformed complexion as a visible mark of condemnation.

Although Mather himself was by no means free from pernicious prejudices against Africans and Native Americans, his biblical scholarship helps us to understand that these attitudes are not expressions of racism in a modern sense. In the "Biblia" he consistently reasons that the perceived varieties in appearance among the various groups of people are indeed only skin-deep and do not carry spiritual or moral significance. Nor does he understand them to mark innate and irredeemable differences in temperament or intellectual abilities. Instead, the Otherness and perceived inferiority of Africans and Native Americans is measured by standards of religion and civility and, therefore, conceived of as something that could be overcome. As Mather's thoughts on the origin and destiny of humankind reveal, these convictions generally translated into a strong sense of commitment to the conversion, Christian education, and charitable treatment of all human beings, even if this commitment did not make him question the standing social order which included various forms of oppression and dispossession.

---

5   In his commentary on Proverbs through Jeremiah, which I am editing for the series (*Biblia*, vol. 5), Mather has little to say on the topics addressed in this essay. Hence, I'm relying throughout on the transcriptions of my fellow editors. I'm especially indebted to Reiner Smolinski's volume on Genesis with its extensive and erudite notes. These notes have guided me throughout in positioning Mather within the theological debates of his time.

With regard to his concrete social agendas, the "Biblia" provides valuable new insights – often opening up fresh perspectives on familiar texts – into the sincerity and scriptural motivation of Mather's support for the flagging Indian mission in New England. Furthermore, his commentaries shed more light on his increasingly complicated and critical engagement with American slavery. While he maintained until the end of his life that enslaving criminals or non-Christian prisoners of war was, in principal, in agreement with scriptural precepts, sometime in the late 1690s he began to argue that the slave trade and the prevalent mistreatment of black slaves in the colonies systematically violated Christian law.[6] In the "Biblia," he argues that the capturing and disenfranchisement of innocent Africans on no other grounds than their skin color was by no means justifiable through scripture and constituted the deadly sin of "mansteal-ing." As I will propose, his condemnation of the slave trade and his defense of the institution slavery are both direct outgrowths of Mather's conservative theology and biblical literalism. The manifest tensions between his growing awareness that, even by his own standards, most slaves were unlawfully brought to the colonies, and his refusal to challenge the legal status of slaves already in the colonies cannot be adequately explained in terms of Mather's racist attitudes or his vested interests as an owner of black servants. While his cultural arrogance towards Africans and his concerns over valuable property were certainly factors contributing to Mather's inner conflicts, these conflicts primarily reflect an impasse into which he was led by his radical scripturalism, his closely related social conservativism, and his millennialist expectations.

Race as a Theological Problem in the "Biblia Americana": Mather's Defense of Monogenesis and the Noachic Descent of all Men

Before entering into a detailed discussion of Mather's biblical scholarship, I want to give brief consideration to why most recent studies in the field warn against projecting modern, biologically inflected notions of race and racist thinking back onto the diverse cultures of British North America. Generally speaking, these studies all show how varied, inconsistent, and contradictory race relations really were throughout the colonial period. By the turn of the eighteenth century, race, a multivalent category of common descent, had not assumed the determinate and determining meaning it would later carry in his-

---

6   As is true for most other Puritan clergymen of his generation, Mather's exact stance on slavery and the slave trade have never been studied in depth. Indeed, "[v]ery little has been written on the specifically local development of opposition to slavery in the American colonies before the mid-eighteenth century. Typically, scholars studying antislavery thought during this time have limited their attention to the important work of the Quakers and to the publication of Samuel Sewall" (Minkema, "Edwards's Defense" 23).

tory. It signified various, competing notions of kinship and peoplehood, most often defined through family lineage, sometimes through common regional origin or language and, beginning in the eighteenth century, also through complexion. At this time race was, therefore, not at all clearly distinguished from the neighboring categories of family, nation, or what is now termed ethnicity.[7]

Only towards the end of the century were the older familial or dynastic notions beginning to be systematically displaced by a new, much more comprehensive, and at the same time much more rigid understanding of race. This new understanding separated mankind into a small number of population groups distinguished and hierarchized by their physical appearances. By then, varieties of skin color, facial features, and hair texture were also firmly associated with temperamental, moral, or intellectual attributes. Even at the end of Mather's lifetime, however, race was still a relatively fluid category, and color was only just becoming a crucial marker of social identity as the institutionalization of slavery and the ongoing Indian wars deepened divisions along the color-line. "Well into the eighteenth century," writes Benjamin Braude, "the English, like other western Europeans, [primarily] classified and ranked human beings on the basis of culture, not color ..." ("Primary Colors" 742). Depending on the context, the English demarcated the diverse people with whom they interacted by multiple criteria comprised of, most of all, religion, civility, language, and class as well as commerce and technological or artistic skills. Complexion was one criterion, but by no means the most important one for much of the early modern period.[8]

This does not mean, of course, that biases against Africans or Indians did not exist or were not acted upon with detrimental effects. Whether or not we find it useful to talk about forms of proto-racism, there can be no doubt that throughout the colonial era differences in complexion were, in certain contexts,

---

7 For instance, this distinction is reflected in Nathan Bailey's *Dictionarium Britannicum* (1730), which defined "race" as follows: "RACE [Razza, Ital. of Radix, L. a Root] L'neage, or Generation proceeding from Father to Son; a Family; also a Root of Ginger."

8 Important revisionists studies on the evolution of race and racism in the second half of the eighteenth century are Schiebinger, Hannaford, Hudson, Smedley, and Wheeler. It should be noted, however, that the emerging "revisionist consensus" about the relatively recent origin of genuinely racist ideologies continues to be challenged by a number of historians, including Vaughan, who in my view makes the most convincing case that anti-black racism did not just evolve at the end of the eighteenth century in response to the growing numbers of enslaved Africans. Instead, he argues that prejudices were already well in place at the beginning of the early modern period and constituted one of the driving forces behind the development of American slavery from the very beginning. While, to a certain extent, I accept Vaughan's critique of the current tendency to push back the origins of racism into the late eighteenth and early nineteenth centuries, I still believe that the revisionists are basically right to insist that during these period we see the emergence of a new form of racist thinking that is not only gradually, but qualitatively different, and that does not develop from existing prejudices as a matter of necessity. For a very helpful discussion of these debates see Davis's introductory essay "Constructing Race: A Reflection."

interpreted as a badge of cultural or social inferiority and used as a reason for subordination, exclusion, displacement, and enslavement. This is especially true with regard to the growing numbers of Africans enslaved and brought to the colonies.[9] Even at the beginning of the seventeenth century, the English "had developed thoroughgoing ideas of an African distinctiveness and inferiority, drawing on preconceptions rooted in images of blackness and behavioral and physical differences" (Bruce 2; for detailed discussion see Vaughan 136–77; Davis, *Inhuman Bondage* 48–77). Even though these biases certainly existed and formed, among other things, an important precondition for the rise of American slavery, they did not amount to fully articulated theories of hereditary differences that would have systematically equated phenotypical appearances with inward characteristics. It was not until the beginning of the nineteenth century that racism, in the sense of biological determinism, emerged as a coherent and central discursive formation that organized and controlled other discourses by naturalizing race, making it an essential aspect of being and an all-important marker of difference. Before that "racial thinking had no coherent existence, let alone any independent ability to determine people's belief and actions" (Silver xxi).

Just as racial attitudes were still fluctuating in the early 1700s, the social and legal status of Native Americans and African slaves varied considerably from one British colony to another. The social and legal status of Native Americans and African slaves were also marked by significant internal tensions within a colony. Massachusetts' 1641 "Body of Liberties" (subsequently incorporated into the Articles of the New England Confederation) had reserved "Bond-slavery" for infidels captured in lawful wars or criminals who had forfeited their rights as punishment for crimes, but did not clearly distinguish this form of bondage from other kinds of unfree labour such as indentured servitude. Through the first decades of the colony's existence there were very few African slaves in Massachusetts anyway (less than two hundred in 1680), and a substantial part of these eventually gained freedom. Nevertheless, "the hereditation of slave status" (McManus 59) was legalized in 1670. Then, around the turn of the century the situation changed dramatically when the monopoly of the Royal African Company ended in 1696 (see Berlin 81–88; Twombley and Moore).

The opening up of the slave trade brought rising numbers of black slaves to Massachusetts, a development that, together with the ongoing Indian wars,

9 It is now widely accepted that notions about the physical distinctness of Native Americans as a separate "red race" emerged considerably later than in the case of Africans. Before the French and Indian Wars, the Otherness of the native tribes was primarily conceptualized in cultural terms, and the shift to a more racialized view of their distinctness in the second half of the eighteenth century evolved partly in response to the anti-white sentiments informing the Indian revitalization movements of the period. See Richter, Merritt, and Silver.

caused a rapid hardening of racial boundaries. Now, "old ambiguities in the legal and social status of black servants were being quickly and decisively resolved away from the indenture model towards slavery" (Von Frank 258). At the same time, an expanding body of legislation curtailed the civil liberties and enforced the social discrimination of all Africans and Native Americans, although even slaves continued to have access to courts and were generally protected by the law (MacManus 62–72). With African slaves still living side-by-side with free black servants, and with some free blacks even owning property and businesses, there was as yet no rigidly fixed equation between blackness and slavery in Mather's immediate environment. This said, Massachusetts was certainly not isolated from the general development in contemporary British America, where color was becoming an ever-more decisive marker of social identity and a crucial criterion in the accelerating exclusion from basic rights.

Many of Mather's own writings directly comment on or indirectly reflect these developments. Particular consideration is given to the growth of African slavery and the accompanying rise of anti-black prejudices in *The Negro Christianized*. Here Mather talks about how the blackness of African slaves "is made an Argument, why nothing should be done for them," while whiteness had, in the eyes of many colonials, become a sign of natural superiority. Whiteness, Mather says, was even turned by some into a prerequisite for being a true Christian. He criticizes such discriminations, but he nevertheless accepts and employs for his counter-argument (and does so on other occasions) such color-based classifications as "blacks," "whites," and "tawnies." This is evident, for example, when he writes, "As if the great God went by the *Complexion* of Men, in His Favours to them! As if none but *Whites* might hope to be Favoured and Accepted with God! Whereas it is well known, That the *Whites*, are the least part of Mankind" (*The Negro Christianized* 24). Though he was, in this way, unable fully to extricate his thinking and writing from the new modes of racial categorization, Mather, in *The Negro Christianized* and elsewhere, insists that the Bible is, in effect, color-blind and does not give any importance to physical appearances.

As a matter of fact, the "Biblia" clearly shows that as a biblical scholar, Mather was interested in refuting the emerging concept of race as a category of natural difference, or at least in circumventing the troubling religious implications of this concept. What many cultural historians have failed to see is that for Mather, as for many of his clerical colleagues, the increasing racialization of society and cultural discourse in the Atlantic world at the turn of eighteenth century posited a major theological problem. The question whether black slaves could "be of the elect" (Rosenthal 63) was only part of this larger problem. Generally speaking, the notion of humanity's separation into separate races constituted a challenge to the authority of the scriptures and the received interpretation of a unitary history of salvation.[10] More specifically, Mather was worried about the way in which this new kind of racial thinking drew on and thereby gave fresh currency to heterodox teachings, which claimed that some of the non-European peoples were either of pre-Adamic origin or not part of the Noachic pedigree.

On the whole, then, Mather's engagement with the concept of race was defensive. He sought to assert an understanding of peoplehood primarily hierarchized by religion, and secondarily by criteria of civility, custom, and language; an understanding which safeguarded the orthodox reading of the biblical narrative. According to this reading, human diversity came about as the consequence of the postdiluvian branching out of one family tree, rooted in the patriarch Noah. These efforts, however, were only partly an expression of Mather's concern over the human consequences of an emerging racism. His concern was primarily theological, and these efforts must be seen as part of his overall apologetics for the received (Reformed) theology. Like the majority of theologians at the time, Mather regarded the unity of the human race as fundamental to Christian belief.

In his commentary on Gen. 2, Mather explicitly states that the central tenets of Christian doctrine are all predicated on a common Adamic origin of humanity. Addressing the initial question of his rhetorical interlocutor, "wherein *Adam*, was a *Type* of the Lord Jesus Christ," he provides the following explanation:

> *Adam*, was a *Parent* of all the World. Wee read [1. Cor. 15.45.] Hee was *the First Man*; and, [Gen. 2.5.] when hee was first made, there was *No Man* else. *Præadamism* is by the Apostle condemned as *Hæresy*. Thus, our Lord Jesus Christ is the *Parent*, of all true Beleevers; they are [Isa. 53.10.] *His Seed*.
>   *Adam* was an *Agent* for all the World. The *Covenant* with him, was with all his Posterity, in him, as their Grand Repræsentative. When *hee* sinned [Rom. 5.12.] *All* sinned. When *hee* Dy'd [Gen. 3.19.] there t'was *Appointed unto all Men, once to Dy*. Thus our Lord Jesus Christ, is the *Agent* for all true Beleevers. Tis our *Union* with Him [2. Cor. 5.21.] that makes all that *Hee* had done, reckoned *Ours*. (*BA* 1: 501)

Here Mather's typological readings demonstrate how the orthodox understanding of a unitary redemption history rests upon Adam being both "a Parent of all the World" and "an Agent for all the World," in whose fall, to cite the famous verse from the *New England Primer*, "we sinned all." From a literalist viewpoint, only the common descent of humankind could guarantee that the he-

---

10   Thus, Mather's engagement with the problem of race is of a piece with his overall exegetical approach in the "Biblia," which was to tackle head on all the critical issues raised by the emerging biblical criticism (Grotius, Hobbes, Spinoza etc.) of the period in order ultimately to safeguard the infallible authority of the scriptures. For an insightful study of this issue, see Smolinski ("Authority and Interpretation").

reditary transmission of original sin from Adam had indeed corrupted the whole human race and thereby created a common, universal need for salvation. At the same time, only the assumption of such a common descent made it possible for Christ's redemptive work to have universal reach, so that the promise of regeneration through faith in the new Adam could extend to all parts of the human family, even though, of course, only a limited number of individuals from these groups were preordained to be "true Beleevers." One of the strongest expressions of Mather's belief in spiritual equality can be found in his posthumously published *Triparadisus* (written 1726/27), where, referencing Gal. 3:26–29, he writes, "That *the Righteousness of GOD, which is by the Faith of JESUS CHRIST, is unto all & upon all them that Beleeve*, in every Nation; *for there is no Difference*. But *Shiloh* is come, and now all Occasion for the *Distinction* is forever taken away." As the typological fulfillment of God's first chosen people, the New Israel of Christ's saints during the millennium would therefore transcend all national or social distinctions, and "[t]he *Carnal Children of Israelites, are to our Holy One of Israel*, no better than *Children of Ethiopians*" (312).[11]

In defense of this universalist vision, Mather, in his commentaries on Genesis, seeks to refute any polygenist accounts of humanity's diversity, in particular what he calls, in the passage above, the *"Hæresy"* of *"Præadamism,"* which, as he notes, contradicts the Apostle Paul's assertion that God "hath made of one blood all nations of men" (Acts 17:26). Earlier versions of the idea that humans existed before Adam had been formulated by Paracelsus (1493–1541) and Giordano Bruno (1548–1600), among others.[12] The most famous or notorious representative of pre-Adamism was, of course, the French theologian Isaac de la Peyrère (c.1594–1676). Mather repeatedly targets La Peyrère's writings in the "Biblia." In his *Prae-Adamitae* and *Systema theologica ex praeadamitarum hypothesi pars prima* (1655), La Peyrère argued that there had been two separate

---

11   The text continues, "*Now*, One found in the Sultry Regions of *Africa*, or, among the *Tranquebarians* in the Eastern *India*, or the *Massachusettsians* in the Western, that shall thro' the *Faith* of the Gospel, be by the SON of GOD made one of His *Members*, and by the SPIRIT of GOD made one of *Temples*, is as much valued by God, as ever any *Simeon* or *Levi*, that could show their Descent from the Good Man, who struggled with an *Angel*, & gott a *Blessing* from Him. To imagine, That the Glorious GOD *of the Spirits of all Flesh*, has a *Distinguishing* Regard for the Offspring of the *Flesh*, of One Ancestor more than another; 'tis an Imagination very Derogatory to the *Glory* of our GOD; very Contradictory to the *Language* of our *Gospel*" (312–13). If one considers this universalist conceptualisation of the typological New Israel, it becomes obvious that Mather did not assign any special role or privileges to New England in his vision of the coming millennium, as generations of Americanists under the influence of Perry Miller and Sacvan Bercovitch were wont to argue. His real concern was with whether or not the Puritan colonies would be part of Christ's global kingdom of saints to be established during the millennium, a kingdom which would have its center in ancient Judea. See Smolinski (*"Israel Redivivus"*; "Apocalypticism") and Stievermann.

12   For pre-Adamite theorists before La Peyrère, see Allen (132–33) and Huddleston (9–12, 138).

creations, first of the lawless gentiles before Adam (Gen. 1:27) and then of Adam and Eve (Gen 2:7–25), whom he considered to be the progenitors of the Jewish people and their Christian descendants, but not of humanity in general.[13] Even though its original impetus had been to rescue the biblical narrative in the face of newly discovered lands and peoples not mentioned in the scriptural account, La Peyrère's polygenist anthropology ultimately led him to question the overall textual accuracy, integrity, and, therefore, the authority of the Old Testament as a universal history of humanity. For La Peyrère, the Hebrew Bible was coherent only as a chronicle of the Jewish people (see Almond; Popkin, *Isaac La Peyrère*; Grafton). In England, much to the horror of Anglican and Puritan orthodoxy, some radical freethinkers took up these notions, including the Deist Charles Blount (1654–93), who propagated them in his *Oracles of Reason* (1693).

If Mather joined the European chorus of anti-pre-Adamite polemicists, he did so because he strongly felt that the notion of humanity's multiple racial origins undermined the very essence of Christianity. Following the major English authorities who had written on the issue, among them Edward Stillingfleet (1635–99) in his *Origines Sacrae* (1662) and Sir Mathew Hale (1609–76) in his *The Primitive Origination of Mankind, Considered and Examined, According to the Light of Nature* (1677), Mather blasted La Peyrère's interpretation of the pre-Adamite origins of gentile cultures because it threatened the authority of the scriptures and put into question the universality of original sin as well as the gospel promise of its atonement.[14]

---

13   La Peyrère's works appeared in an English translation as *A Theological Systeme upon that Presupposition, That Men were before Adam* (1655) and *Men before Adam* (1656), of which Mather had a copy in his personal library. In his *The Birth of Modern Critical Theology*, Klaus Scholder illuminates the larger significance of La Peyrère works and the reason for the violent reactions against them. The pre-Adamite theory, Scholder explains, was a reaction to the startling scientific and geographic discoveries since the late fifteenth century, which not only suggested that the world was far older than the orthodox reading of the biblical narrative allowed, but had also confronted Europeans with a whole New World inhabited by numerous peoples of which the scriptures gave no account. Like so many other theologians of the period, La Peyrère actually sought to reconcile these findings with the traditional biblical world picture and the scriptural account of creation, but found that he was unable to do so without introducing his controversial assumptions about the existence of men before Adam, who subsequently had survived in the farther regions of the earth supposedly unaffected by the Flood (67). *Pre-Adamites* should therefore be understood as "a summary and critical evaluation of the problems, questions and doubts which had accumulated over a century and a half," and which put increasing pressure on the credibility of the "biblical picture of universal history" (82–83). In their attacks on La Peyrère clergymen all over Europe and America indirectly acknowledged how serious they took these questions and problems, at the same time that they used his texts as a negative foil for their attempts to devise explanations that were consistent with the biblical worldview.

14   What was at stake for the defenders of orthodoxy in the debates over pre-Adamites and polygenism is strikingly expressed in Stillingfleet's *Origines Sacrae*. Here, the Bishop of Worcester argued that "the peopling of the world from Adam ... is of great consequence for us to understand, not only for the satisfaction of our curiosity as to the true origin of nations,

In defense of monogenism, Mather employs the full set of exegetical methods he uses throughout the "Biblia." These include traditional ones such as typology, but also advanced forms of textual and philological criticism, and extensive historical contextualization. Moreover, he draws on his wide-ranging knowledge in the various branches of early modern para-theology, such as sacred history and geography. Mather's variable methods and orthodox intentions are showcased in his reading of Gen. 4:15–17, an essential passage for La Peyrère revisionist interpretation. These verses tell the story of how God, after the murder of Abel, "set a mark upon Cain" and Cain "went out of the presence of the Lord, and dwelt in the land of Nod, on the East of Eden. And Cain knew his wife; and she conceived, and bare Enoch: and he builded a city, and called the name of the city after the name of his son, Enoch." For believers in the literal truth of the Bible, this skeletal narrative raises a number of perplexing questions: Where did Cain's wife come from, and who were the people helping him to build the city of Enoch if they did not belong to the family of Adam and Eve? According to La Peyrère and his Deist followers in England, the only plausible answer to this question was that the land of Nod had already been populated by gentile pre-Adamites.[15]

As usual, Mather lets his skeptical interlocutor raise the potentially dangerous issue only to have it then defused by the answering champion of orthodoxy:

Q. The silly & profane Deist cavils, that here must needs bee *Prae-adamites*; because wee find *Cain*, so early retiring to a *Land of Nod*? v. 16.

A. The Word *Nod*, does not necessarily signify, a Countrey; it may signify, *A Fugitive*: so that the Sense may bee, *Hee lived a Fugitive or a Vagabond, in the Land*.[16]

And there might bee a considerable Number of Men then in the World. The Murder of *Abel* probably happened in the 129 Year of *Adam*. It is not likely, that *Adam* had no Children all this Time. According to the Proportion of *Israels* multiplying in *Egypt*, *Adam* now might have his Offspring multiplied into one hundred thousand. (*BA* 1: 517)

Thus, Mather seeks to prove that by the time Cain murdered his brother, the land east of Eden could have very well been densely populated by descendants

---

but also in order to our believing in the truth of the scriptures, and the universal effects of the fall of man. Neither of which can be sufficiently cleared without this. For as it is hard to conceive of how the effects of man's fall should extend to all mankind, unless all mankind were propagated from Adam; so it is inconceivable how the account of things given in the scriptures should be true, if there were persons existent in the world before Adam was ..." (534).

15 This argument became an important basis for nineteenth century, Darwinistically-inflected theories of polygenism and modern racist ideologies. See Popkin's "The Philosophical Bases of Modern Racism," and ch. 7 in Kidd.

16 In his reflections on the alternative meanings of the word *"Nod"* Mather mainly relies on Ibn Ezra's gloss on Gen. 4:12 in his *Commentary on The Pentateuch* (1: 84).

of Adam and Eve. For this purpose, he provides detailed calculations on human reproduction in the antediluvian period, drawing on a wide range of international scholarship, including *Sacred Theory of the Earth* (1684, 1691) by Thomas Burnet (1635–1715) and *Dissertationes Historiques, Chronologiques, Geographiques et Critiques Sur la Bible* (1711) by Louis Ellies Du Pin (1657–1719).[17] Of course, this meant that the sons of Adam must have married their sisters and nieces, but Mather, like the exegetes he cites, was prepared to allow for this, arguing that under the given circumstances, intermarriage could not have been regarded by God as a sin, but constituted a necessity.

Mather's commentary on Gen. 4 is also pertinent to our topic because he, almost in passing, explains another scriptural conundrum, which had already been charged with racial meaning by some early modern exegetes, and would later become an important reference point for scripture-based racist ideologies (Goldenberg 178–82): What was the mark left upon Cain as the outward sign of his curse? None lesser than William Whiston (1667–1752), a leading Newtonian mathematician and controversial biblical exegete, had written an essay in 1725 entitled "An exposition of the curse upon Cain and Lamech: shewing that the present Africans and Indians are their posterity."[18] Whiston argued that the non-white races were not Noachids, but the descendants of Cain and Lamech, who had survived the deluge in Africa and the Americas. God had cursed these peoples, Whiston thought, for the sin of their progenitors, and their complexion was the outward mark of their exclusion from the grace of God, which would only be repealed at the end of history through the grace of Christ. Feeling that sciences could not satisfactorily explain the origin of racial diversity, Whiston, like others before and after him, thus made phenotypical differences the direct result of providential intervention in sacred history. According to this interpretation, biological differences, even though not significant in themselves, were expressive of a "deeper spiritual reality" and constituted "a mark of religious and moral failings" (Kidd 70).

For Mather, Whiston's exegesis and other similar theories were anathema. Insisting on the universality of the flood (which had also been questioned by La Peyrère), Mather's "Biblia" traces all of present humanity back to Noah and his family, the sole survivors of the catastrophe that covered the earth.[19] To the question posed by his skeptical interlocutor, "What was the *Mark*, which the *Lord sett upon Cain*?" he gives as the two most likely answers that, in witness-

---

17   For the details of Mather's calculations about human reproduction after Adam and Eve and the sources for these calculations, see *BA* 1: 514–19 and the accompanying footnotes by Smolinski.

18   The essay was appended to his 1725 *Supplement to the Literal Accomplishment of Scripture Prophecies* (106–34).

19   For Mather's contestation of Whiston's theory about the limitations of the flood, see Smolinski ("Natural Science and Interpretation").

ing the miraculous manifestation of God's power, either "the *Face* of *Cain*, was Blasted with Lightning from the *Shechinah*," or that maybe it was enough to simply say, "GOD secured *Cain* from being killed, as much as if He had sett a *Mark* upon his Face, for every one to know him" (*BA* 1: 517). In none of these scenarios is the mark of Cain passed on as a hereditary racial trait to his descendants, whose lineage would end with the deluge anyway.

Throughout his commentaries on Genesis, then, Mather rejects any suggestions that God either created separate races, whose natural distinctions in appearance would have mirrored their separate destinies in providential history, or that mankind underwent a racial division through supernatural causes. For him, all men were part of the same blood family begun by Adam and Eve, and all were descendants of Noah. In the older sense of kinship, the whole of humanity belonged to the same race. Whatever varieties in religion, culture, and appearances existed in the world were the long-term results of the dispersal of Noah's family into the different parts of the globe after God confused their tongues for building the tower of Babel. Wherever Mather speaks about different human races in the plural (which, in fact, he rarely does, preferring the terms nations or peoples, which were, for him, largely synonymous), he refers to the various lineages or branches of the Noachic family tree originating in Noah's three sons Japhet, Shem, and Ham.

If all were thus of one origin, how did Mather explain the diversity of human skin-color, built, facial features, and hair texture? Answering in a way that fit into the biblical narrative and squared with the tenets of (Puritan) orthodoxy demanded tackling issues to which the scriptures apparently provided no clue. What did Adam look like? When, how, and (most importantly) why did variations in complexion take effect amongst his posterity? The relevant manuscript pages of the "Biblia" show how deeply these questions concerned Mather and how, over the years, he contemplated different answers. All of them, however, remained within the realm of natural causes or general providence.

While working on his interpretation of the curse of Noah in Gen. 9:18–27, he approvingly nodded at older theories that saw "[t]he True Cause of their [i.e. the Africans'] *Blackness*" in a combination of climatic conditions and cultural practices which then permanently changed peoples' appearances. It may very well be, he writes, that they

> were made very *Brown*, by the *Hott Sun* striking upon them. They disliked this *Colour*. With proper *Juices* and *Unguents*, it was their Custome, to change their *Brown* into *Black*; and, *Versa est posteà Ars in Naturam*: *Nature* itself by Degrees conform'd, unto what had been by *Art* a long while Introducing. *Vossius* observes, That the Figure of the *Noses*, among the *Moors*, and other Nations, was by Degrees at length confirmed from *Artificial* into what is now *Natural* among them. (*BA* 1: 673–75)[20]

20 Mather's immediate source here is the Isaac Vossius's (1618–89) *Observationes ad Pom-*

Significantly, the original phenotypical differences between Europeans and Africans are, here, reduced to mere brown pigmentation brought about by permanent heat. Everything else, facial features, hair texture, and even the deeply back skin of many African peoples, is claimed to be the result of self-induced "cosmetic changes" which, over generations, eventually became innate characteristics. Behind these efforts to diminish the natural differences between the modern races as much as possible is, of course, the urge to demonstrate the scientific plausibility of mankind's universal consanguinity. In Mather's rendering it is implied that the members of Noah's family still looked very much alike and that the chromatic differentiations amongst the descendants of Japhet, Shem, and Ham only began much later due to the "bounds of habitation" God had had determined for them (Acts 17:26).

While Mather maintained this basic opinion throughout the decades he was working on the "Biblia," he apparently was not entirely content with Vossius's elucidation. Thus, when writing his commentaries on the table of nations (Gen. 10), Mather came back to the issue. The question with which he opens his renewed discussion of mankind's diversity clearly shows how crucial the whole matter was for him. "According to the *Mosaic* Account," his ever-probing interlocutor states, "We find all Nations of Men here descended from One Man; and the Account is unquæstionably True. Yett, you know, some have doubted, how tis possible for *Blacks*, and *Whites*, to be the Children of One Man." In his orthodox rejoinder Mather again lambastes polygenist theorists, who argued that, given their widely different looks, Europeans and Africans could not be of common descent. If phenotypical variations in humans made it necessary for us to assume different antediluvian progenitors, his argument goes, we would need not one parent before or besides Adam, but countless ones. "If we must have one *Adam* for *Whites*, and another for *Blacks*, must we not have a Third for *Tawnies*? If one for White, & another for Black *Skins*, why not one for White, and another for Black *Hair*? and another for *Red*?" Mather quips. "And were it not as necessary to have original Standards of Dimensions, as well as of Colours? One for the gigantic Breed of *Asia*, and another for the Dwarfs of *Lapland*?" (*BA* 1: 697–99) Yet, underneath this almost jovial tone we can feel genuine worry.

Writing at the beginning of the eighteenth century with an acute sense of the dramatic changes going on in the intellectual world, Mather clearly feared that traditional theories such as Vossius's would not withstand the scrutiny of the new sciences. He feared these new sciences might soon tear holes in the theory that hereditary blackness was the long-term effect of dyes. "Tis true," he

---

ponium Melam (1658), which argued that the Africans' black skin color and facial features had originally been introduced by cosmetic practices such as ungents, but that "art was afterwards turned into nature (304–5). For early modern climate theories, see Frederickson and Augstein.

conceded," "Living and Breeding within the *Torrid Zone*, or without it, is not enough alone, to produce this Difference. For the *Ethiopians*, and the *Malabars*, tho' in Part æqually distant from the Line, yett these are no more than *Duskish*, those are *Cole-black*. And it is said, That all over *America*, there are no Blacks, but only at *Quaveca*." To his great relief, however, Mather had found a representative of the new sciences who had just published a proto-hereditary theory about racial diversification that supported Mather's view of mankind's universal kindship. Mather's champion is Nehemiah Grew (1641–1712), fellow of the Royal College of Physicians and plant anatomist, who in his *Cosmologia Sacra* (1701) demonstrated "that the Climate may co-operate with the *Native Causes*," by which he meant certain anatomical variations. Of these native causes he held three mainly responsible for the distinct complexion of Africans. As Mather summarizes,

> First, *The Distribution of the Capillary Arteries more numerously into the outer Part of the Skin*. Secondly, *A less Proportion of Capillary Veins, to return the Blood from thence*. Thirdly, *The extream Thinness of the Cuticle*. Hereby some smaller Part of the Blood becoming stagnant there, it, like any other Blood when it is Dry, or upon a Bruise, turneth *Black*. And therefore, even among the *Ethiopians*, there is a Sort of Breed, which is neither Black, nor White, nor Tawny; but, as tis likely from the *Make* of their Skin, of a *Pale*, and a *Dead*, Complexion. In *Blacks* themselves, the Palms of their *Hands*, and the Soles of their *Feet*, where the *Cuticle* is much Thicker, and into which the Capillary Arteries do shoot more sparingly, are of a *Whitish Red*. Where these then, and it may be some other, Native Causes, meet with a suitable Climate, we may suppose they never fail to produce a Black Breed. So, in Part of the Province of *Quantung* in *China*, the People who are near the *Torrid Zone*, are Black; but in that of *Peking*, the most Northerly, they are *White*. And some Climates may be fitter to breed *Blacks*, than others; which, tho' of the same Latitude, yett may not be so Hott; or, the Heavens or the Earth, may be different on some other Accounts. Every *Florist* can tell, how great an Alteration, the Transplanting of some Flowers, only from the Field, into a Garden, will make in their Colours. And every good *Herbalist*, can tell, the Difference in Plants of the same Kind, growing in several Parts of the World, yea, tho' in the same Latitude. Nor is the *Woolly Hair* of the Blacks, any stranger, than for a Naked Dog, when brought from an Hott to a Cold Climate, to become Hairy. ... Properties, which in a Breed of Parents, alwayes in the same Climate, & both of the same Colour, would be as constant in the *Hair*, as in the *Skin*. (*BA* 1: 698–99)[21]

The language of plant anatomy, which Mather cites here from Grew, with its talk of species variations and traits passed on by different "Breed[s] of Parents," clearly announces the advent of the new anthropological and biological theories of race that the Enlightenment was about to introduce. After all, when Mather died in 1728, the first edition of *Systema Naturae* (1735), by Carl Linnaeus

---

21 Mather's here quotes and summarizes *Cosmologia Sacra* (bk. 4, ch. 4, par. 10, pp. 186–87).

(1707–78), was only seven years away. But if Mather, towards the end of his career, began to think about phenotypical differences in more naturalistic terms than preceding scholars such as Vossius, he (like Grew) did so in defense of monogenism. Also, in contrast to the coming generations of naturalists and anthropologists, such as Linnaeus or Johann Friedrich Blumenbach (1752–1840), he did not derive any kind of racial hierarchy from the differences in human physique, color, or visage.[22]

At some point early in the new century, Mather thus arrived at what he thought was a satisfactory explanation for the successive transformations of physical appearances among the descendants of Noah, resulting in humanity's present chromatic gradations. But what color had man been at his creation? It was only logical that Mather did concern himself with the complexion of Adam in his commentary on Genesis because the plausibility of any monogenist solution to the theological problem of racial diversity crucially depended on the point of departure (see Kidd 29). Most ordinary English people and many biblical scholars at the time no doubt believed that Adam had been light-skinned like themselves. Since the divine likeness had presumably been strongest in Adam, who was, as the prelapsarian man, not deformed by sin and thus the closest to God in all of human history, a superiority of white over black and brown could be derived from this belief about the protoplast's original color. Thus the English poet Thomas Peyton wrote in 1620 that in contrast to the "black deformed Elfe[s]," as he degoratorily described Africans, the "Northern people" were "white like unto God himselfe" (qtd. in Vaughan 6). Hence, interpreting darker skin colors as the result of a degeneration from an original state of whiteness and, hence, as a sign of deformity, was a way of defining a hierarchy of races without challenging orthodox monogenism.

Tellingly, Mather had no interest in privileging white people in this way. He thought, rather, that a gradual transformation from aboriginal whiteness all the way into blackness was not the most probable hypothesis in support of monogenism. Building on an etymology of Adam (meaning "man") as a derivation from the Hebrew word *"Adamah*, a Red, Rich, Rosie, and *Shining* Sort of Earth," he instead argues in the "Biblia" that mankind's first parent was created with a glowing, a ruby-red skin-color, a reflection of God's own glory. As a next step he then argues that "the *Body* of *Adam*, did by his Fall, unhappily lose much of the *Primitive Glory*, wherein it shone like the *Ruby*," which implies that the color of the postlapsarian Adam and his immediate descendants would

---

22   Linnaeus would include *homo sapiens* amongst the other species of nature and subdivide the human species into four different racial varieties or breeds: *Africanus, Americanus, Asiaticus,* and *Europeanus.* In the second edition of his *General System of Nature* (1740), he attributed different abilities and character traits (phlegmatic, choleric etc.) to these races, which strongly suggest the superiority of European peoples. Through his taxonomy he prepared the ground for the next generation racial theorists such as Blumenbach.

have been something like a reddish brown, or what Mather's contemporaries called tawny (*BA* 1: 374–75).[23]

From Mather's perspective, this account of Adam's appearance harmonized best with the current knowledge about the racial composition of the world's population, which, in *The Negro Christianized*, he throws into the face of those who foolishly held that "none but *Whites* might hope to be Favoured and Accepted with God!" "Whereas it is well known that the *Whites*, are the least part of Mankind. The biggest part of Mankind, perhaps, are *Copper-Coloured*; a sort of *Tawnies*" (24). This made the Native Americans, whom Mather, in contrast to the popular perception that was emerging in the second half of the eighteenth century, never describes as red, but variously as tawny, (reddish) brown or olive, closer to Adam in color than the European colonists.[24] In Mather's view, whiteness was therefore neither the original human norm, from which other racial identities deviated, nor did it or any other skin-colors carry deeper meaning. Instead, whiteness, just as blackness, was a mutation of brown or copper-colored skin-pigmentation and, like other phenotypical differences such as hair, presumably resulted from slight anatomic variations, environmental factors, and possibly certain cultural practices. Mather thus anticipates lines of reasoning very similar to those later developed by antislavery writers such as Thomas Clarkson (1760–1846) and Olaudah Equiano (1745?-1797) or Indian rights activists such as William Apess (1798–1839) in their fight against white

---

23 Mather's etymology runs as follows: "The Import of the Hebrew Word, *Adam*, is not only, *Rubuit*, Hee was *Red*; (and so *Adam* is as much as *Edom*, which was the Name of *Esau*, for his *Ruddy* Complexion, Gen. 25.25.) but it is of a larger Signification, and is as much as to say, *Splenduit*, Hee *Shone*. Thus the Word, *Adamdameth* (Lev. 13.19.) is to be rendred, *Shining*, or *Glistering*. Sometimes *Adam* is as much as, *Formosus fuit*. Thus of the Healthy *Nazarites*, wee read, Lam. 4.7. *Nitidi fuere*. It is noted of *David*, That hee was *Admoni* (1. Sam. 16.12.) *Ruddy*, that is to say, *Beautiful*. Compare Cant. 5.10" (*BA* 1: 425).

24 In his *India Christiana* (1721), Mather speaks about Indians as America's native "inhabitants of that Olive *Complexion*, which, they say, the *Biggest Part of Mankind* is Colored with" (22). With his hypothesis of an intermediary tawny Adam, Mather assumed very much a minority opinion in the eighteenth-century debates about racial diversity. Kidd mentions only two figures in the English speaking world who challenged the notion of a common white ancestor in similar ways: In 1743 the British physician John Mitchell (1690?-1768), who lived in Virginia between 1735 and 1746, sent his tract "An Essay upon the Causes of the Different Colors of People in Different Climates" to the Royal Society in which he argued that the tawny skin-color of the American Indians had been the "primitive and original complexion" of mankind. And in 1808 the Manchester physician Thomas Jerold (1770–1853) published his *Anthropologia: or Dissertation on the Form and Color of Man*, in which he proposed a similar view (Kidd 30–31, 90).

racism.[25] Mather does so, however, only partly for philanthropic purposes.[26] To his mind it was most of all more convincing (and put his overall understanding of orthodox theology on safer ground) to believe that a tawny Adam stood at the head of all progressive transformations among descendants spanning a wide chromatic spectrum between the extreme poles of white and black.[27]

To shore up the belief in the common descent and shared genealogy of humankind, Mather, as a next step, needed to trace all modern nations or peoples back to Noah's three sons. Naturally, his efforts are most concentrated in his observations on Gen. 10, which, in Mather's own words, gives an account of "[t]he Rise of the several Nations in the World, and of their Scatterings thro' the World ..." (*BA* 1: 693). It would exceed the confines of this paper to give a detailed analysis of Mather's explanations on the so-called "table of nations,"

---

25 In his famous *The Interesting Narrative* (1789), Equiano, for instance, attacks anti-black prejudices and racist justifications of the slave trade by employing a combination of theological and scientific arguments almost identical to those found in Mather's writings. After making a case for the common descent of Europeans and Africans from the Noachic family tree (he delineates the Africans from Afer and Afra, the descendants of Abraham's wife Keturah), Equiano proceeds to explain the phenotypical differences between the races by a theory of epidermal mutation induced mostly by climatic causes. For this theory he heavily draws on Clarkson's *Essay on the Slavery and Commerce of the Human Species* (1786), as well as on John Mitchell's essay (see above) and its notion of an intermediary tawny Adam. By demonstrating with the help of these authorities "how the complexions of the same persons vary in different climates," he hopes "to remove the prejudice that some conceive against the natives of Africa on account of their color." Insisting that the "apparent inferiority" of Africans was solely a matter of their lack of true religion and certain accomplishments of European civility, he then proclaims, "Let the polished and haughty European recollect that his ancestors were once, like the Africans, uncivilized, and even barbarous. Did nature make them inferior to their sons? And should they too have been made slaves? Every rational mind answers, No. Let such reflections as these melt the pride of white superiority into sympathy for the wants and miseries of their sable brethren, and compel them to acknowledge, that understanding is not confined to feature or color" (44–45).

26 In his autobiography *A Son of the Forest* (1831), Apess implies the notion of a "Red Adam" when he insists that the indigenous tribes should be called "natives" not only because they were the original inhabitants of the American continent, but also because they are closest to the original humans: "I humbly conceive that the natives of this country are the only people under heaven who have a just title to the name, inasmuch as we are the only people who retain the original complexion of our father Adam." And in "An Indian's Looking-Glass for the White Man" (1833), Apess challenges the racial prejudices of his readers by making a demographical argument similar to Mather's: "If black or read skins or any other skin of color is disgraceful to God, it appears that he has disgraced himself a great deal – for he has made fifteen colored people to one white and placed them here upon the earth" (Apess 10, 157).

27 In *The Negro Christianized*, Mather in fact argues that light-skinned Europeans are progressively and permanently darkening when living in a Southern climate: "And our *English* that inhabit some Climates, do seem growing apace to be not much unlike unto them [black Africans]. As if, because a people, from the long force of the African *Sun & Soil* upon them (improved perhaps, to further degrees by maternal Imaginations, and other accidents,) are come at length to have the small *Fibres* of their *Veins*, and the Blood in them, a little more Interspersed thro their Skin than other people, this must render them less valuable to heaven then the rest of Mankind?" (24).

which extends over dozens of manuscript pages. Suffice it to say that, for the
most parts, he follows the predominant understanding of early modern Protestant theology. "[F]inding his Posterity so increase{d}, that *Palæstine*, could not
hold them," as Mather narrates the beginning of the earth's peopling, Noah
"left *Shem* in *Syria*[;] hee sent *Cham* to *Egypt*, and went himself, with *Japhet*,
into the Countrey that is now called *Italy*" (*BA* 1: 693). From this starting point,
Mather draws a detailed population map, which, in its basic geography, follows
the traditional tripartite division that had been established by the leading early
modern authorities in sacred geography and history, most prominently Samuel
Bochart (1599–1667).[28] First there is "JAPHET, the eldest Son of *Noah*, had
Seven Sons, who peopled *Europe*, and Part of *Asia* the Less"; second there is
"SHEM, the middle Son of *Noah*; in the Division of the Earth, [he] had *Palæstine*, and all the Eastern Part of *Asia*." And thirdly there is "CHAM, the young-
est Son of *Noah*, [who] had *Africa*, from whence his Posterity made some Ex-
cursion into *Syria*, and *Arabia*." To understand his refutation of Noah's curse
(see below) it is important to note here Mather's explanation "that *Cush*, the
eldest Son of *Cham*, was the Father of the *Ethiopians*" (*BA* 1: 719), a nation from
which he believed all modern day dark-skinned Africans descended.[29]

What I cannot adequately convey here is the extreme lengths to which
Mather goes in his explications of Genesis to demonstrate that this part of "*Mosaic* History," which he calls the "choice Monument of *Antiquity*," is not only a
historically accurate, but also a comprehensive narrative of humanity's common origins and the early period of its cultural, religious, as well as linguistic
evolution after the dispersal. This argument forces him to integrate into the
biblical table of nations not only all of the nations mentioned in the historical
and ethnographic works of classical antiquity, but also those peoples with whom
Europeans came into contact in later centuries such as the Chinese and the Native Americans.[30] In order to do so, he has to connect the origins of every single

28 In this part of his commentary Mather mainly relies on Bochart's *Geographia Sacra*
(1646), but also on older sources such as the *Jewish Antiquities*, by Flavius Josephus (37?-100).
For an erudite and insightful survey over the changing interpretations of the table of nations
up until the early modern period see Braude ("Sons of Noah").

29 For the most part, Mather was apparently well satisfied with the conventional Protestant
readings of the respective blessings of Shem and Japhet, which need no detailed discussion
here. While the former signifies the special relation of the Jewish people with Jehovah and
intimates the birth of the messiah amongst them, the latter foretells the widespread expansion
of the Japhites, the ascendancy of the Roman Empire, and its Christian successors. "The
Blessing of *Japheth* was to bee *Enlarged*; his Posterity was to occupy the *Largest* Portion of
the Habitable World [,]" he writes. "But the Blessing {of} *Shem* was, the *Dwelling of God in
his Tents*: his Posterity was to enjoy the most notable and singular Tokens of the Divine Presence among them" (*BA* 1: 672).

30 Likewise, Mather has to claim that all of the world's languages developed from those
miraculously created through the confusion of tongues at the tower of Babel. Mather admits
that it was impossible to determine just how many of these original tongues God's intervention created among the Noachides, but insists that every existing language had to be related,

one of the known ethnic groups of the world with one of Noah's descendants. This is a cumbersome and often awkward task, which Mather accomplishes by employing a good deal of creative etymology in correlating the names of peoples, places, or cities. He is forced to explain numerous historiographic and ethnographic discordances between the literatures of Greece or Rome, for example, and the Christian tradition. What is more, he has to account for the very existence of these pagan civilization, which rose to power and cultural prominence long before and in ignorance of the Christian revelation and which worshipped multiple deities utterly different to the one God of Noah.[31]

Engaging with a multiplicity of ancient authors, Mather specifically attempts to refute all the pagan myths of origins that were known to him and which might imply that their respective people had developed independently from the lineages of Japhet, Shem, or Ham, whose descendents dispersed after the collapse of the tower of Babel. Mather provides detailed timetables, synchronizing scriptural chronology with dates given by non-biblical sources in order to disprove what he calls "all the Fabulous, and *Egyptian*, or *Græcian* Shams of Antiquity" (*BA* 1: 693). By these "Shams" he meant the far-reaching claims to antiquity made by these nations, claims that stretched back to before the time allowed by the orthodox limits of biblical chronology. According to the orthodox account and the widely accepted calculations in James Ussher's (1581–1656) *Annals of the World* (1658), none of these civilizations could have dated back to before 4004 BC. With the help of Euhemeristic methods of interpretation and what might be called a Christocentric proto-form of comparative religion, Mather also seeks to demonstrate that none of the Gentile cultures were or are genuinely autochthonous. Like Judaism and later on Christianity, all pagan religious beliefs and practices in the world, Mather argues, derive from Noah's faith. In other words, they are more or less depraved corruptions of the original, monotheistic religion established by the patriarch after the flood. Indeed, many of the deities – in so far as they were not actually demonic in nature – worshipped by the gentiles are interpreted by Mather as merely mythologized versions of Noah or his descendants, who once founded these civilizations.

In this context, Mather also tackles a problem that had concerned many intellectuals of the period, including Gottfried Wilhelm Leibniz (1646–1716). How was it possible to rectify the growing knowledge of China's apparently

---

however remotely, to that group of languages which were spoken by the other modern descendants of their respective common ancestor: "But now, if we come to that Quæstion, How many Languages are to be accounted *Originals*, or, may be supposed for to have been produced by the *Miraculous Touch* of God upon the Minds of Men at the Building of *Babel*; This is not *easy*, or perhaps *possible*, to be determined. But this may be said; The *Dispersion* soon following the *Confusion*, it is probable, that the Tribes which settled nearest unto one another, did retain most of Affinity in their different Languages" (*BA* 1: 813).

31 The studies of Manuel, Pailin, Grafton, and Rossi survey the discursive contexts in which Mather undertook these efforts.

very ancient civilization, which Jesuit missionaries brought back to Europe, with the orthodox understanding of the postdiluvian peopling of the world? In basic agreement with Leibniz's *Discourse on the Natural Theology of the Chinese* (1716), but also with Samuel Shuckford's *Sacred and Prophane History of the World Connected* (1728–37), which appeared in the very year Mather died, the "Biblia" defuses the explosive problem by claiming that *"Fohi,* the founder of the *Chinese* Monarchy, was the same with *Noah"* (*BA* 1: 279),[32] who had wandered eastward to China after leaving the domain of his son Japhet.

Mather's Commentaries on the Origin and Destiny of the American Indians

One other region of the earth not mentioned in the Bible was, of course, the New World. The Americas caused early modern theologians even more worries than China because, in contrast to the Asian continent, they were separated by a vast ocean from the Old World, and hence from the supposed regions where Japhet, Shem, and Ham had originally settled.[33] To discredit any heretical notions that the Native Americans were a separate branch of humanity, one had to clarify their Noachic pedigree and account for the ways in which they had reached and peopled the Western continent after the flood. For Mather, this was a vital issue in more ways than one. Not only did his overall understanding of redemption history depend on the common origins of all mankind, but also, the very legitimacy and the success of the "Puritan Experiment," in his conservative understanding of New England's divine mission, crucially depended on successfully "gospellizing" the Natives. This, of course, would have proven a vain endeavor had the American Indians, in fact, been separately created as an ultimately irredeemable people, or if they were, as a number of early modern theologians had claimed, including the English divines Nicholas Fuller (1557?-1626) and Joseph Mede (1586–1638), the minions of the devil.

---

32 Mather's reasoning on this issue continues as follows: "The *Chinois* tell us, he had no Father; no doubt the Memory of his Father was lost in the Deluge. They tell us, his Mother conceived him, as she was encompassed with a *Rain-bow;* which seems a cloudy Remembrance of the *Rain-bow* first appearing after the Flood. The *Character* of *Fohi* among the *Chinois,* agrees mighty well, with what the Scriptures relate of *Noah. Fohi* (they say) *carefully bred up seven sorts of Creatures, which he used to sacrifice, to the Supreme Spirit of Heaven & Earth. For this reason some called him,* Paohi, *that is, Oblation"* (*BA* 1: 279). The Chinese tradition which Mather cites here is taken from Louis Le Compte (Le Comte) (1655–1728), whose *Nouveaux memoirs sur l'état present de la Chine* was translated into English in 1693 as *Memoirs and Observations* (1696). For the larger context of this debate over a Chinese Noah, see Mungello and Kidd (36).

33 For the early modern discussion over the origins of the American Indians, see Huddleston. The evolution of the ten lost tribes-theory is surveyed by Parfitt. Cogley offers a very helpful analysis of the specific debate in mid-seventeenth-century England.

It is thus not altogether surprising to find Mather vehemently rejecting in the "Biblia" any polygenist speculations about the origin of the American Indians such as those by the Newtonian Thomas Burnet who, following Paracelsus and La Peyrère,[34] had argued in his *Sacred Theory of the Earth* (1693–95) that the inhabitants of the New World were of Pre-Adamic provenance. "Lett those two Fools *Paracelsus* and *Peyrerius* pretend what they will," Mather states in his gloss on Gen. 11, there could be no doubt "that the *Americans*, are of the *Noetic Original*" (BA 1: 825). For all his expressed certainty, however, Mather seems not to have reached a final, unequivocal conclusion concerning from which precise part of the patriarch's posterity the indigenous tribes descended.[35] In his commentary on Gen. 10, he explained at some length what seemed to him the most probable and secure solution of all: the Native Americans were the remote posterity of those descendants of Japhet – very likely the line originating in his son Magog – who had moved into Northeastern Asia, and which had been called the Scythians in classical antiquity.[36] That a group of Scythians at some point migrated to North America, in Mather's eyes, also constituted a wonderful fulfillment of the blessing of Japhet which promised his enlargement:

> God ha's remarkably fulfill'd it; in that unto *Japhets* Portion pertains all *Europe*, (so full of People,) *Asia* the Less, and *Media*, and Part of *Armenia*, and *Iberia*, and *Albania*, and those vast Northern Regions, inhabited once by the *Scythians*, and now by the *Tartars*; To say nothing, of *America*, which is likely, was much peopled by *Scythians*. (BA 1: 752–53)[37]

---

34 For La Peyrère's speculations on the pre-Adamite origin of Native Americans, see his *Theological Systeme* (bk. 3, ch. 13, pp. 276–81).

35 See also his *India Christiana* (1721) where he cites his own comments from the "Biblia" "that the Americans are of the *Noetic Original*" (23). In this very tract he publicly declared that the way in which the New World was peopled would probably be never be determined with certitude because too little evidence remained. "It is utterly Unknown unto us, *How* and *When* it was, that AMERICA came to be first *Peopled* ..." (22).

36 "*Magog*. From him were the *Scythians*, who dwelt on the East, and North-East, of the *Euxine* Sea: for, *Pliny* saies, that *Scythopolis*, and *Hierapolis*, which the *Scythians* took, when they conquered *Syria*, were ever after called, *Magog*. And it is granted by *Ptolomy*, that the proper Name of that Place was *Magog*. *Josephus* confirms this, when hee saies, That the *Scythians* were called *Magogæ* by the *Græcians*, & thence infers, that the *Scythians* had their Original of *Magog*, the Son of *Japheth*" (BA 1: 713). The other solution admitted as being not entirely unreasonable (if much more unlikely) was that "*America* [belonged] unto the Offspring of *Shem*; and particularly to the Descendents of *Jobab* and *Ophir*, the Sons of *Joctan*. This is the Sense of *Arias Montanus*, in his *Phaleg*; and *Vatablus* in his *Scholia* on the first Book of *Kings*" (BA 1: 825). The references are to the Spanish Orientalist Arias Montanus (1527–98) who argued for the Semitic origin of the Native Americans in his *Phaleg; sive, De gentium sedibus primis, orbisque terrae situ liber* (1572), and to the French Orientalist Franciscus Vatablus who had made a similar claim in his *Adnotationes in Sacra Biblia, et Scholia* (1546).

37 According to Hudleston (60–80), the Spanish Father Gregorio Garcia was the first to postulate the Scythian origin of the Native Americans, in his *Origen de los indios de el nuevo mundo, e Indias occidentales* (1607). It is interesting to note that Cotton Mather's son Samuel (1706–85) made his own contribution to the ongoing debate over the origins of the American

This solution doubtlessly also appealed to Mather because it implied that, genealogically speaking, America had already been a European plantation, which only had been forgotten long ago, and providentially kept hidden just until the time of the Reformation so that it could be re-colonized by the English standard bearers of the true Christian faith.

Mather found a possible key to unlock the mystery of how the Scythians might have made their way across the Atlantic in the *Enquiries Touching the Diversity of Languages* (1614), by Edward Brerewood (c. 1565–1613), a professor of astronomy at Gresham College, who argued that there must somewhere be an undiscovered isthmus between Asia and America (see also *India Christiana* 23). Otherwise, Noah's descendants and the wild animals released from the Ark would not have been able to cross over.[38] More importantly, by making a case for Japhet and against Shem as the forefather of the American Indians, Mather simultaneously reveals more of the scholarly reasons for his well-known rejection of the theory that they were the descendants of the ten lost tribes of Israel.

Already in his hagiography of John Eliot, *The Triumphs of the Reformed Religion in America* (1691), and again later in *Magnalia Christi Americana* and the *India Christiana*, Mather had dismissed as wishful thinking the supposed resemblances in language and customs between the New England tribes and the ancient Hebrew people, resemblances on which Eliot, Roger Williams, but also some of his contemporaries, including Samuel Sewall, built their hopes that the Americas were indeed home to the lost tribes whose conversion, according to their reading of certain scripture prophecies, would precede the onset of the

Indians in 1773 with his *An Attempt to Shew That America Must Be Known to the Ancients*. In this tract Samuel Mather advanced many arguments similar to those outlined by his father in the "Biblia". See esp. 14–16, where the language is particularly close to the "Biblia"-manuscript. So it is not unlikely that Samuel used the manuscript as a source.

38 See Mather's commentary on Gen. 11: "There is a great Probability of what is affirmed by *Acosta* and *Brierwood*; That *Asia* and *America* are contiguous. Besides this, the *Phœnicians* were great Sailors, and sometimes took long Voyages, by which, and by various Accidents, People might be carried over the *Atlantic* into *America*. Yea; the *Divine Providence* ha's ordered, that the Countreyes which have *huge Sea*'s between them, yett generally meet somewhere, with an *Isthmus*, or some small passable Distance of Water. An *Isthmus* unites *Asia* and *Africa*. The *Mexican* and *Peruvian* Divisions of *America*, are united by an *Isthmus*. There are but *Narrow Streights* between *Africa* and *Europe*; and *Europe* is very sufficiently joined unto *Asia*. If there be any Streights of *Anian*, between *Asia* and *America*, they may be produced in later Ages; possibly they were not from the Beginning ... *Shemites* might pass into *America* out of *Asia*; and so might *Japhetites* too, from *Tartary*. And why not *Europæans*? *Norway* is not far from *Iseland*; *Iseland* is but a little Way from *Groenland*; From *Groenland* we soon pass into the *Mexican America*" (*BA* 1: 826). Mather here summarizes Brerewood's *Enquiries* ch. 13. The other reference is to the Spanish Friar José Acosta who argued in his *Naturall and Moral Historie* (1604) that since Noah's Flood was universal, America was repeopled either by navigation or by a land bridge. But since wild animals are not likely to have been carried over in ships, Asia and America must be contiguous (bk. 1, chs. 19–21, pp. 61–71; bk. 7, chs. 2–3, pp. 497–503).

millennium.[39] The "Biblia" dutifully re-examines, but finds faulty all the alleged evidences concerning the Judaic origin of America's indigenous population.[40] The present-day descendants of the ten tribes, Mather opined in his gloss

---

39 In the *Magnalia* Mather writes on Eliot's belief in the Judaic origins of the American Indians with gracious irony: "I confess, that was one, I cannot call it so much *guess* as *wish*, wherein he was willing a little to indulge himself; and that was, *That our* Indians *are the Posterity of the dispersed and rejected* Israelites, *concerning* whom our God has promised that they shall yet *be saved, by the Deliverer coming to turn away Ungodliness from them.* He saw the *Indians* using many *Parables* in their Discourses; much given to anointing of their *Heads*; much delighted in *Dancing*, especially after Victories, computing their Times by *Nights* and *Months*; giving *Dowries* for Wives, and causing their Women to *dwell by themselves*, at certain Seasons, for secret Causes; and accustoming themselves to grievous *Mournings* and *Yellings* for the Dead; all which were usual things among the *Israelites.* ... He also saw some learned Men, looking for the lost *Israelites* among the *Indians* in *America*, and counting that they had *thorow-good* Reasons for doing so. And a few small *Arguments*, or indeed but *Conjectures*, meeting with a favourable Disposition in the Hearer, will carry some Conviction with them; especially, if a Report of a *Menasseh ben Israel* be to back them" (bk. 3, ch. 3, p. 192). In this commentary Mather mentions in passing two of the chief propagators of the ten lost tribes-theory during the seventeenth century against whom he positions his own argument. With his pun *"thorow-good* Reasons" he refers to Eliot's correspondent and supporter Thomas Thorowgood (c. 1595–1669), whose *Iewes in America; or, Probabilities that the Americans are of that Race* (1650) did much to popularize in the English speaking world existing speculations about the Hebraic pedigree of the American Indians, which had been advanced by earlier Spanish writers such as Diego Durán (1537–88) and Antonio Vásquez de Espinosa (d. 1630) but also by Jewish scholars such as Antonio de Montezino (Aaron Levi) or the Dutch Rabbi Manesseh ben Israel (1604–57). Mather alludes to the English translation of ben Israel's *Esperanza de Israel, The Hope of Israel* (1650), which greatly fired up the hope of English millennarians such as Eliot, Thorowgood, and John Dury (c. 1595–1680), who in 1650 wrote his *Epistolicall Discourse ... that the Americans are descended from the Israelites.* Eliot's "Indian Tracts," along with letters to Thorowgood and Richard Baxter, are now accessible in an excellent new edition by Michael P. Clark. For Williams' speculations about the Judaic origins of the American Indians, see especially the preface of his *A Key into the Language of America* (1643). For Sewall, see his *Phaenomena* (29–47).

  In rejecting the ten lost tribes-theory, so dear to many of his fellow Puritans, Mather found himself in undesirable company. Although Mather never mentions the name, his own arguments are in many respects reminiscent of those put forth by the Anglican Royalist Hamon L'Estrange (1605–60). In his *Americans no Iewes; or, Improbabilities that the Americans are of that Race* (1651), L'Estrange argued that many of their supposed similarities were not peculiar to the Jews or to the Indians, thereby stressing the fancifulness of Thorowgood's theory. Other similarities, L'Estrange argued, such as legends of the creation and the flood, could have been transported by a colony from the tower of Babel.

40 Mather explicitly dismisses the supposed similarities between ancient Hebrew and the languages of the Native American tribes on which proponents of the ten lost tribe-theory had built their arguments. See ben Israel's *Hope of Israel* (4–15) and Thorowgood's *Iewes in America* (ch. 5, pp. 14–16). In Mather's view, the American languages had to be related to those tongues spoken by the other descendants of Japhet. However, whether the Japhites had just one or several original languages when they dispersed after the tower of Babel was (yet) unknown: "The Sons of *Japhet* moved, we know, to the *West* and *North. Junius* ha's proved that the *Gothic* and *Græcian* Languages, are Dialects growing upon one Root. And all the Learned confess the *Latin* to be a Daughter of the *Græcian*. But whether all the dispersed Colonies of the *Japhettic Family*, had but One Tongue, is an Uncertainty." Mather hoped that future linguistic studies might be able to determine to which European tongues the Native

on 2 Kings 17:41, probably resided in Assyria and Media, Ethiopia, and India, but not in the New World. If at all, as he would put it in his *Triparadisus*, "some of their [the Israelites'] blood passing from Scythia may be found among the *Indians* of *North America*" (298).

Mather's rejection of the ten lost tribes-theory must be understood in the context of his millennialist theology. As descendants of Japhet the Native Americans would not hold an eschatological key-position in the way Eliot or Mather's friend Sewall expected them to do. Although Mather by all means considered the evangelization of the Indians an imperative duty of New England Christians and Mather expected the number of converts to increase as the millennium advanced – his last calculations pointed to the year 1736 (Smolinski, "Introduction" 64) – he got rid of the anxiety of looking for the wholesale conversion of the native population as a prerequisite for the coming of Christ's earthly reign. He expected that a number of saints would be found among the indigenous tribes, as with any other people, but did not have to believe in either the possibility or the necessity of their collective restoration.

At the same time, Mather, in the "Biblia's" commentary on Rev. 20, aggressively tackles the influential millennialist speculations of Nicholas Fuller and especially Joseph Mede,[41] who similarly assumed that Magog was the progenitor of the American Indians, but drew very different and, from an American perspective, very troubling conclusions from this pedigree. In agreement with Fuller's suggestions, Mede had conjectured that Christ's thousand-year reign on earth would only encompass the territory of Daniel's four empires, Babylon, Medo-Persia, Greece, and Rome (Dan. 2:31–45), making the Old World sole "partaker of the promised instauration" (Mede n.p.). Specifically, Mede, as

American languages were related. So far, he admitted "[t]he *American* Languages, can as yett have but little Account given of them" (*BA* 1: 812).

41 Nicholas Fuller's thoughts on the place of America in the Christianography of the millennial kingdom appear in his *Miscellaneorum Sacrum libri duo* (1622). Much more influential were the speculations on this topic made by Mede in an appendix to the enlarged edition of his *Key to the Revelation* (1650, orig. *Clavis Apocalyptica*, 1629), entitled "A Conjecture Concerning *Gog* and *Magog* in Revelation." All quotes by Mede are taken from this appendix which is without pagination.

At least for four generations of New England theologians, from the Mathers to Jonathan Edwards, would struggle in their commentaries on the Apocalypse to refute Mede's widely received arguments which in effect put the entire New World beyond the saving influence of Christ. Cotton Mather attacked Mede's theory on many occasions, including the opening chapter of the *Magnalia Christi Americana*, his "Problema Theologicum" (1703), *Theopolis Americana* (1710), and the posthumously published *Triparadisus*. In the "Biblia's" commentary on Rev. 20, he frankly states his reasons for attacking Mede: "I that am an *American*, and at work upon BIBLIA AMERICANA, must needs be lothe, to allow all *America* still unto the *Divels Possession*, when our Lord shall possess all the rest of the World ..." [*BA*, Rev.20]. See also his lengthy discussion of this issue in the *Triparadisus* (289–94). The reception and contestation of Mede in New England theology is discussed in depth by Smolinski ("Apocalypticism").

Mather paraphrases the English theologian, argued that the entire *"American Hæmisphere"* could not partake "in the Blessedness of the *Thousand Years*" [*BA*, Rev. 20]. According to Mede, America was the place from where the armies of Antichrist – designated as God and Magog by the Revelation of St. John (20:8–9) in a reference to the seat of Israel's enemy Gog (Ezek. 38–39) – would once more rise and attack the saints at the end of the millennium. Bringing his reasoning full circle, Mede had contested that the "nations &c., which are spiritually called *Gog* and *Magog*" by the prophet, were literally the native "inhabitants of the land of *America*, both Northern and Southern," since these peoples genealogically descended from "Colonies of the nation of *Magog*" (Mede n.p.).

In line with his own understanding of their Japhite lineage, Mather concedes in his commentary that "if they [the American Indians] were originally *Scythians*, [they] may well enough be called *Gog* and *Magog*" [*BA*, Rev. 20] in a historical or geographical sense. However, this did not imply that the inhabitants of American had to be identified as St. John's Gog and Magog, and hence be interpreted in a spiritual or prophetic sense as the deceived nations who would engage the saints in the final battle at the end of the millennium. There was simply no way of knowing, Mather proclaimed, exactly where the latter-day antitypes of the enemies of God's people would come from, since the scriptures said they "are in the four quarters of the earth." Thus, Mather rejected it as unscriptural and unreasonable to exclude, collectively, all Americans, either natives or colonists, from the camp of the saints, and condemn them to the outer darkness at the end of time.[42]

If Mather disowned the idea that the American Indians had any special part (either positive or negative) to play in the events leading up to and following the millennium, his biblical ethnography simultaneously asserted their full humanity as well as their inclusion in the gospel promise in no uncertain terms. Indeed, by arguing for their Japhite lineage he made the genealogical relationship of Native Americans to the European colonists a relatively close one. In so doing, he confirmed the orthodox opinion held by most first and second generation Puritan leaders, who did not conceptualize American Indians as a race

---

42 In his *Triparadisus* Mather also attacks Fuller and Mede on this issue. Here he writes: "One thing which does a little to *Encumber* us, [But may it not also a little *Enlighten* us!] about *Gog* and *Magog*, is, That the *Gog* and *Magog* of *Ezekiel*, & the *Gog* and *Magog* of *John*, do not appear to be the same *Gog* and *Magog*, but there is the Distance of a *Thousand Years* between them." The Gog and Magog of Revelation are spiritual antiytpes of the historical enemies of ancient Israel and hence should be understood as the armies of *"Antichrist* persecuting the true *Israel* of GOD, & at last perishing in the *Conflagration*, [which] will be an admirable Fulfilment of *Ezekiels* Prophecy" (291). In a separate essay "Where to find *Gog* and *Magog*," which Mather added to the *Triparadisus*, he once again asserted that one couldn't be certain about where exactly the apocalyptical minions of Satan will come from, but that most likely they the would be the spirits of the damned literally raised from hell to attack the camp of saints (292–94). On Sewall's engagement with the same problems in his *Phaenomena*, see Scheiding.

apart, or even as being significantly different in color from themselves.[43] Most early New England colonist conceived of the natives as a primitive Europeans, who by civilizing influences and the missionary efforts of the colonist could be made into Christian Englishmen. As Vaughan and, more recently, Richter, Merritt, and Silver have demonstrated, this view gave way to an increasingly racialized enemy image as English frustration grew over Indian resistance to Christianity and civility, the pressure on tribal territories grew, and armed conflict with colonists became an almost permanent condition in the decades following King Philip's War. Beginning in the early eighteenth century, Indians began to be perceived as belonging to the inferior darker races, and eventually – in line with the new naturalistic proto-theories of heredity – as constituting a separate "red race," whose differences in appearance reflected "primordial racial short-comings ... impervious to education or missionizing" (Vaughan 33).[44]

Finishing college in 1681, Mather thus came of age right at a time when an earlier, pejorative, but also paternalistic view of Native cultures and religions began to change into a widespread and indiscriminate hatred for "the Indian." As suggested above, some scholars have cited Mather's writings as illustrations of this paradigm-shift in Puritan thinking (e.g. Vaughan 24; Axtell 133; Thomas 10). It is easy to see why. If one primarily focuses on the rhetoric mobilized in some of Mather's texts without closely examining the underlying theological assumptions, this interpretation seems obvious. Especially in some of his early wartime sermons and pamphlets, Mather launches himself into such an excessive language of Indian-hating that to our modern ears he indeed sounds like someone calling for genocide. We find it difficult not to think about nineteenth-century anti-Indian racist propaganda when reading his invectives against "those Tawny Pagans, than which there are not worse Divels Incarnate upon Earth" (*Fair Weather* 86), or his advice to local militia men to "pursue them vigorously; *Turn not back* till they are *consumed. ... Beat* them small as the *Dust before the Wind, ... Sacrifice them to the Ghost of Christians whom they have Murdered*" (*Souldiers Counselled*).[45] Mather's biblical commentaries upon the

---

43 The surviving evidence suggest that, even though the natives were almost universally regarded as uncivilized heathens, initially most New Englanders did not perceive them as significantly different in color from themselves. Many writers of the period even explicitly expressed the opinion that the natives were naturally white or light brown, and that their skin-color darkened only with age through exposure to the sun and as an effect of certain ceremonial practices involving the application of dyes (Vaughan 3–34).

44 "By 1700, the Puritans had begun to regard the Indians as a race apart. An emerging racism, based on the fear of the Indian and a suspicion that he would never accept Christianity or English ways, seemed to justify a more callous treatment of the native tribes" (Bremer 205).

45 The quotes are from *Fair Weather: or, Considerations to Dispel the Clouds, and Allay the Storms of Discontent* (1692) and *Souldiers Counselled and Comforted: A Discourse Delivered unto Some Part of the Forces Engaged in the Just War of New England against the Northern and Eastern Indians* (1689), both of which were written in the context of King William's War.

genealogy of races, however, serve as an important caveat in this context that racism, here, is not a satisfactory explanation and, in fact, is rather misleading. The conflict is still primarily understood as a clash between Christians and hostile heathens, and the justification for an all-out fight against the Indian troops (not the tribes as a whole) draws on the Christian(ized) tradition of the *bellum justum* and the biblical notion of the holy war against the enemies of God. Similar justifications are invoked by Mather against Catholic Nouvelle France, an opponent who was likewise decried as being in league with the devil. Though he did not perceive the natives as naturally white in the way earlier Puritans did, he does not legitimize the killing or even mistreatment of Indians on account of their racial identity and does not suggest that their "tawny" skin-color was a badge of an incurable moral or spiritual corruption that warranted their extermination.

There can be no mistake that Mather was deeply prejudiced against Native Americans, whom he in the *Magnalia* calls "the veriest *Ruines* of Mankind, which are to be found any where upon the Face of the Earth" (bk. 3, ch. 3, p. 191). Yet, for him, their perceived savagery was not a matter of nature, but a result of history.[46] In the tradition of his forbears, he thus continued to conceptualize the Otherness of the Indians primarily in religious as well as in cultural terms. Although Mather was far less optimistic about the actual prospects for missionary work among the Northeastern tribes than either Eliot or Williams, he essentially upheld their core belief in the common descent of Old and New World people, as well as in the capacity of Indians for spiritual and cultural redemption. If he thought that the early Puritan apostles amongst the Indians had seriously underestimated the tenaciousness of the devil and hence the difficulty of bringing the light of the gospel to the American Gentiles, he nevertheless still agreed in principle with Eliot that the natives could and indeed should be first "*civilized*" and then "Christianized" (192).

His heavy investment in monogenism did not keep Mather from preaching that unconverted natives were abject devil-worshippers who, when rejecting conversion and acting openly hostile against God's people, were to be regarded as enemies of God and fought against without mercy. But monogenism cer-

---

[46] From his perspective, the "forlorn Indians," were the most "doleful creatures" because their forebears, like those of the Old World's gentiles, had quite literally been seduced by the devil, who had corrupted their religion from the primitive monotheism of Noah's family into the "most Explicit sort of Devil-Worship," and thereby also made their entire "way of living" "infinitely barbarous" (*Magnalia* bk. 3, ch. 3, p. 191; bk. 7, ch. 6, p. 44). Having been geographically cut off from the redeeming influence of true Christianity until the arrival of the English in the New World, Mather thought it only natural that the diabolic influence among the natives was still very strong and expected that it would not be entirely overcome until the onset of the millennium. Yet, a number of his writings report on the progress that, despite all difficulties and setbacks, he thought had been made in Christianizing and civilizing the New England tribes. See, for instance the Appendix to *Bonifacius* (153–57).

tainly did much to keep him from following the emerging trend among his fellow colonists who more and more collectively construed Native Americans as a naturally inferior and, hence, separate strand of mankind doomed to enslavement or extirpation. Mather's convictions about the common descent and spiritual unity of mankind help us to understand an attitude that otherwise would remain an inexplicable contradiction to his, in so many regards, inimical views on Indian people: Why was it that through decades of Indian warfare, which almost brought existing evangelizing efforts to a standstill and dramatically decreased the number of Praying Indians, Mather sustained his genuine dedication to the missionary cause as well as to a variety of related philanthropic efforts on behalf of the suffering converts? Because every single one of them was a potential brother in Christ, he regarded "[t]he work of Gospellizing the Aboriginal Natives of this Countrey" as one of the holiest duties and, were it to succeed, "one of *New Englands* peculiar Glories" (*Diary* 2: 808).[47]

In 1698, at the end of King William's War (1689–97), during which Mather had repeatedly animated Boston's soldiers from the pulpit to fight against hostile heathens in league with the French, he also became a highly active commissioner of the New England Company, a position which he would hold for thirty years.[48] One of the few detailed investigations into his respective activities, which cannot be discussed here at length, comes to the conclusion that after the death of Eliot, who had founded the missionary organization, "no person in New England, with the possible exception of Sewall, could match Mather's record of effort for the New England mission" (Rooy 252). Almost every year after 1698 he published a related work (mostly catechisms in the native languages or tracts in support of the cause), organized funds and evening schools, and also personally attended to several communities of Christianized Indians. To support local work, Mather, through his contacts in London, organized ecumenical cooperation with the Society for Promoting Christian Knowledge and

---

47 After all, the Christian imperative to spread the gospel amongst the gentiles encapsulated in Acts 16:9 "Come over and help us," had been made the very motto of the Massachusetts Bay Company's seal. And its original charter made it an official goal of the commonwealth to "win and incite the Natives ... [to] the only true God and Savior of Mankind" (qtd. in Bremer 199).

48 Founded in 1649 the New England Company (called the Society for the Propagation of the Gospel in New England until the Restoration) was the oldest Protestant missionary organization. As Lovelace has observed, Mather's early writings on Indian mission frequently link the call to convert the natives with the promise of their pacification. In his related publications after the turn of the century "there is a perceptible shift away from the pragmatic motive of protecting the colonists ... toward a pure and outspoken concern for their [the Indians'] spiritual welfare as they became less of an immediate threat" (Lovelace 280). This shift has also to do with the fact that Mather increasingly came under the influence of the Pietist ideal of a world mission and began to view the work amongst the Native Americans within the framework of a global evangelical effort that reached from Halle, Saxony, to the East Indian mission at Malabar. On Mather's growing investment in the notion of world mission, see Benz.

later on with the Society for the Propagation of the Gospel in Foreign Parts. When he realized towards the end of his life that, to quote from his *India Christiana* (1721), despite all the efforts to convert the remaining indigenous people, "Religion, ... is under a Decay among them: their *Good Order* languishing ..." (40), as Anglo-Indian relations deteriorated, it was a source of great frustration for him, even despair.[49] Indeed, the apparent standstill in spreading the gospel was an important, but rarely acknowledged, reason for his well-known anxiety over the spiritual decline and millennial fate of New England.

Mather's Refutation of Noah's Curse and the Problem of Slavery

Besides the languishing state of New England's mission to the American Indians, there was another closely related issue that weighed heavily on Mather's heart towards the end of his life. If the prayers and practical efforts of the righteous few were to win the hearts of more people "for the Propagating of a *Religion*, which Glorifies Him, and Recovers Mankind unto Felicity," he wrote in his *India Christiana*, "[t]hen we [should] see the *Africans* no longer treated like meer *Beast of Burden*, as they are in the Plantations of cruel *Americans*," and the "Charitable Design of *Christianizing* the *Negro's* [sic]" (47) would be successful. Instead of seeing these hopes fulfilled, the aging Mather witnessed the rapid expansion of a new form of slavery in the context of an emerging plantation economy, which systematically brutalized Africans while making their Christianization virtually impossible. These developments caused Mather grave concern, not least with a view to the providential implications they might have for his beloved New England.

Similar to other early British advocates of slave conversion such as Richard Baxter and Morgan Godwyn Mather's quarrel with the behavior of American slave owners was rooted in his uncompromising belief in the Adamic sameness

---

49 His *India Christiana* shows the great pride Mather took in the missionary work of his forebears. "We may truly say, The *First Planters* of NEW-ENGLAND, are the *First Preachers* of the Pure Gospel to the *Americans*" (27), he boasts and also applauds the continuation of the "Good Work" amongst his generation. But then proceeds "to *Confess* and *Bewail*, the Clouds which we see this *Good Work* encumbered withal" (37). "The Indians," he writes, "are not yet improved so far into *English* Civility, and Industry, and Husbandry, as were to be desired, and as a due Improvement in *Christianity* would oblige them to" (40). While Mather in part attributes this decline to Indian aggression and obstinacy, he also puts considerable blame on English settlers, who look at the Natives not as potential brethren in Christ, but as an inferior, irredeemable race which they have a right to exploit and displace. "[I]nstead of giving them Assistance and Encouragements," Mather complains, the English cheat and mistreat the Indians, sell alcohol to them and force them into indentured servitude. With a view to the advancing millennium Mather thus expresses the sincere hope "that the *Good Work* may not be lost, but be *Revived in the midst of the Years*, wherein we see so many Discouragements upon it" (41).

and spiritual unity of all mankind.[50] As such, this advocacy is not a new disclosure because he publicized his basic position in the well-known and frequently reprinted *The Negro Christianized*. Here, he plainly rejects any notion that Africans are a separate race shut off from the redemptive promise of Christ.[51] Many readers of the tract have rightly pointed out that this belief in the common origin and spiritual equality of Africans did not give Mather any respect for their native cultures, customs, religions, or languages. No less Christo- and ethnocentric than most of his contemporaries, Mather does, in fact, speak about the stupidity and superstitiousness of the illiterate slaves in the colonies. What needs emphasis, however, and what has not always been seen clearly enough, is that he does not ascribe these deficits to nature, but nurture. Similar to the perceived savagery of Native Americans, he rather regards the slaves' ignorance and irrationality as remediable symptoms of an African paganism and lack of civility.[52]

---

50 Mather's advocacy of slave conversion in many follows the lead of Richard Baxter, who in the chapter "Direction to those Master in foreign Plantations who have Negro's and other Slaves ..." of his *A Christian Directory* (1673) condemned the illegitimate enslaving of innocent Africans and called upon American slave owners to remember that their slaves "are of as good a kind as you; that is, They are reasonable Creatures, as well as you; and born to as much natural liberty. ... Remember that they have immortal souls, and are equally capable of salvation as yourselves" (pt. 3, ch. 14, p. 557). In his critical engagement with the theological rationales used by slave owners to justify their treatment of Africans Mather is also very close to Morgan Godwyn's *The Negro's & Indians Advocate* (1680). Godwyn was an Anglican minister who worked as a missionary both in Virginia and Barbados. In his tract he records and attacks the widespread currency of the pre-Adamite heresy and the curse of Noah-myth amongst plantation owners who had a vested interest in denying full humanity to their slaves or in representing the enslavement of Africans as being providentially preordained. Against such beliefs Godwyn insisted that black Africans have the same physical and intellectual capacities as white Europeans and that the differences between them are not innate, but rather the product of their religion and culture (see 12–41 and 114–20). Like Mather, Baxter and Morgan did not hold slavery as such to be incompatible with Christianity and did not demand the liberation of those who had already been enslaved. Although they criticized the ongoing slave trade, their main concern was the conversion and humane treatment of the slaves already in the colonies. For an insightful account of Godwyn's life and writing, see Vaughan (55–81).

51 The "Negroes in their households," he told slaveholders, must not be treated as beast of burden, but "as the *Children of Adam*" and hence "our *Brethren*" who descended from the same family and stood "on the same level with us in the expectation of a blessed Immortality, thro' the *Second Adam*" (*The Negro Christianized* 28).

52 Already in his 1689 tract *Small Offers towards the Tabernacle in the Wilderness* Mather complains that "poor Negro's are kept Strangers to the way of Life" on account of their masters' "pretense" that they were "dull." "They are kept only as Horses or Oxen, to do our Drudgeries," he writes, "but their Souls which are as white and good as those of other Nations, their Souls are not look'd after, but are destroyed for lack of Knowledge. This is desperate Wickedness. But are they dull? Then instruct them the rather; That is the way to sharpen them" (58). For a very similar argument on the educability of the African slave, see Godwyn (34–37).

After castigating those who question "[w]hether the *Negroes* have *Rational Souls*," Mather emphatically asserts the full humanity of Africans and, with this assertion, gives us a sense of the new mentality he was up against: "They are *Men*, and not *Beast* that you have bought, and they must be used accordingly." This rhetorical exclamation is followed by a historical comparison, which gains additional significance in the light of the genealogical discussions outlined above. "'Tis True; They are *Barbarous*, But so were our own *Ancestors*. The *Britons* were in many things as Barbarous, but little before our Saviours Nativity, as the *Negroes* are at this day if there be any Credit in *Caesars Commentaries*. *Christianity* will be the best cure for this *Barbarity*" (*The Negro Christianized* 23). From these premises Mather, like Baxter and Morgan before him, deduces the need for the education, Christianization, and charitable treatment of slaves.[53] At a time when blackness was increasingly defined as an outward sign of the natural inferiority of Africans, making them ultimately unconvertible and unredeemable, Mather thus insists "that [t]he God who *looks on the Heart*, is not moved by the colour of the *Skin*; is not more propitious to one *Colour* than another" (*The Negro Christianized* 24–25).

While his overall opinion on the spiritual insignificance of color is thus clearly expressed in *The Negro Christianized*, this text – probably because of its immediate strategic aim to promote slave conversion – does not tell us anything about Mather's views on the legitimacy of making racial difference a criterion for earthly inequality, or as a justification for slavery. Because the tract remains silent on the slave trade and argues that servitude for life is, in principle, in agreement with Christianity, most historians have deduced that in Mather's view the Bible condoned the specific kind of race slavery practiced in the Americas. More particularly, *The Negro Christianized*, as a practically oriented text, does not enter into any detailed theological engagement with the scripture-based, supernatural racism by which African slavery was frequently justified in the Atlantic world. The "Biblia" does much to clarify Mather's actual opinions on these issues and simultaneously complicates our understanding of his stance. Except for the question of a necessary nexus between baptism and emancipation, he was, in fact, much closer than has been hitherto understood to the position taken by Sewall in *The Selling of Joseph*.[54] However, the reason why Mather (who on this issue followed the predominant opinion of English theologians at the time, including Baxter and Godwyn) and Sewall were split over this crucial question appears not to have been a more or less pronounced racism, but their diverging scriptural interpretations of Christian freedom and charity.

---

53   Mather's *Bonicafius: An Essay Upon the Good* (1710) also contains an emphatic plea for a Christian treatment and education of slaves (53–55).

54   For accounts of the historical, social and biographical context in which Sewall wrote *The Selling of Joseph*, see Kaplan, Francis (221–39), and LaPlante (223–33).

Mather's commentaries on Gen. 9:22–27 undertake a detailed refutation of the racial interpretation of the curse of Noah, which was the most widespread and powerful (pseudo-) scriptural rationale for enslaving Africans without having to challenge openly the orthodox dogma of monogenesis.[55] Not only on in popular myth, but also, even if less frequently, in serious theological discourse, the story of the patriarch's curse was used to explain the blackness of Africans as the hereditary sign of a people eternally degraded for the gross disobedience of their supposed progenitor, Ham, against the patriarch Noah, who condemned Ham's son Canaan to become "a servant of servants ... unto his brethren" (v. 26). As the English clergyman R. Wilkinson expounded the myth in a 1607 sermon entitled *Lot's Wife*, "the accursed seed of Cham ... had for a stamp [of] their fathers sinne, the colour of hell set upon their faces" (qtd. in Vaughan 6), marking them off as the natural-born slaves of the descendants of Shem and Japhet. In *The Negro Christianized*, Mather's remark on the subject is both brief and somewhat equivocal. It reads, "Suppose these Wretched *Negroes*, to be the offspring of *Cham* (which yet is not so very certain,) yet let us make a Trial, Whether the CHRIST who dwelt in the *Tents of Shem*, have not some of His Chosen among them" (2).[56] Thanks to the "Biblia," we now have access to Mather's final thoughts on the question whether – to quote a formulation from Sewall's *The Selling of Joseph* – the "*Blackamores are of the Posterity of Cham, and therefore are under the Curse of Slavery ...*" (2).

In several manuscript pages, apparently written at different times, Mather wrestles with a number of perplexing exegetical questions that arise from the highly fragmentary and obscure narrative in Genesis and that had occupied interpreters for centuries (see Haynes 23–41). For reasons of space, I will pass over all of these questions (e.g., what was the exact nature of the offence com-

---

55 Godwyn's *The Negro's & Indians Advocate* gives us a good sense how popular the curse of Noah already was as a justification of race slavery in the late seventeenth century (43–56). It speaks for itself that this myth is also given extensive treatment in Sir Thomas Browne's 1646 *Pseudodoxia epidemica*, a collection of essays dealing with popular errors and prejudices. Unfortunately, Browne's essay "Of the Blackness of Negroes" seems to have inadvertently contributed to the further spread of an already popular myth which it criticizes as superstitious nonsense (Kidd 67). For a survey on the early modern debates about the curse of Noah and the ancient sources of these debates see Haynes (23–41).

56 As we can learn from his commentaries on Gen. 9: 28–29 in the "Biblia," Mather, like many interpreters before him, interpreted Noah's prophecy about the dwelling of God in the "tents of Shem" in typological terms. Hence, it is understood to signify the future birth of Christ amongst the descendants of Shem, i.e. the people of Israel. In his gloss, Mather also asserts that "[t]he *Sons of Cham* are not in the *Noetic Prophecy*, excluded from the *Tents of Shem*" (*BA* 1: 677). This helps us to grasp the full meaning behind the proposition from *The Negro Christianized* that it was a Christian duty to find out "[w]hether the CHRIST who dwelt in the *Tents of Shem*, have not some of His Chosen among them [i.e. African slaves]." For Mather any number of the elect could potentially be found amongst the descendants of Ham, to which many defenders of slavery denied the ability even to comprehend the meaning of Christianity.

mitted against Noah? what were the roles of Ham and Canaan in this offence?)
and skip Mather's elaborate answers to them, except for one absolutely crucial
question: Who is really the subject of Noah's curse and what are the precise
implications of the malediction? "[I]t is a Mistake in any," Mather writes in
answer to this question, "to imagine, That the *Blackness* of the *Ethiopians* &
other Children of *Cham*, arises from the Curse of *Noah* upon him." Nor could
the curse serve to justify the assumption that black people were born to be the
servants, as was claimed by even such serious biblical scholars of the period as
Augustin Calmet (1682–1757).[57] Mather's rejection of this notion is made explicit in the following exchange between the skeptical interlocutor and the orthodox apologist:

> Q. The Curse upon *Cham*, does it not Justify our Enslaving the Negro's, wher-
> ever we can find them?
> A. The whole Family of *Cham* was not concern'd in that *Curse*. None but *Ca-
> naan*, the youngest Son of *Cham*, is mentioned; and he is Thrice mentioned. The
> *Negroes* are not the Posterity of *Canaan*. The Imprecation of the *Patriarch*, seems
> to be little more than a Prophecy, of the *Canaanites* Overthrow & Reduction, un-
> der the Power of the *Israelites*, who were the Posterity of *Shem*. (*BA* 1: 672)

According to Mather, then, Noah's curse pertained only to Ham's son Canaan
and had to be read prophetically, but in a very precise historical fashion. It
merely foreshadowed the conquest of the Canaanites under Moses and Joshua,
in which the Canaanites effectively became subservient to the descendants of
Shem.[58] When *The Negro Christianized* was published in 1706, Mather was apparently still undecided on the question whether Africans belonged to the posterity of Ham or not. At some later stage, however, he seems to have firmly

---

57 The revised 1728 edition of Calmet's *Dictionnaire Historique, Critique, Chronologigue,
Géographique, et Littéral de la Bible* (first publ. 1722), translated into English in 1797, went
through multiple editions both in Britain and America. It was amongst the first and most influential theological works of the modern period to make a detailed academic argument that
connected Ham with blackness and slavery. See Haynes (38–39) and Peterson (43–44).

58 In refuting the curse of Noah as a chimera, Mather goes beyond the efforts made by Sewall. Mather approaches the issue very much in the manner of a biblical scholar by discussing
a wide range of historical and linguistic problems raised by the narrative in Genesis. Both his
methods and many of his results are comparable to those found in Godwyn's *The Negro's &
Indians Advocate* (43–56) or Pierre Bayle's landmark *Dictionaire Historique et Critique*
(1697), both of which argued in great detail that the curse was nothing more than a prophecy
of Hebrew victories under Joshua. See Haynes (37–38). Sewall, by contrast, was satisfied with
a brief reference to the authority of David Pareus's (1548–1635) *In Genesin Mosis Commentarius* (1609) to shore up his claim that "it is possible that by cursory reading, this Text [Gen
9:22–27] may have been mistaken. For *Canaan* is the Person Cursed three times over, without
the mentioning of *Cham*. Good Expositors suppose the Curse entailed on him, and that this
Prophesie was accomplished in the Extirpation of the *Canaanites*, and in the Servitude of the
Gibeanites. *Vide Pareum.* Whereas the Blackamores are not descended of *Canaan*, but of
Cush" (*Selling* 2). Interestingly, the radical antislavery pamphlet by George Keith does not
engage with the curse of Noah at all.

embraced the validity of this traditional claim. As we have seen, in the "Biblia" he firmly settled on the opinion that the immediate progenitor of the Ethiopians was actually Cush, the first son of Ham. Hence, the curse of Noah, Mather argued in full accordance with Morgan as well as Sewall, had no relevance whatsoever for modern Africans.[59]

In maintaining that "our Enslaving the Negros, wherever we can find them" was a practice for which neither this nor any other part of the scriptures provided justification, Mather, in a somewhat oblique way, questions the legitimacy of the Atlantic slave trade. If the Africans were not excluded from their "full membership" in the family of Adam by any supernatural causes, enslavement solely on account of their racial identity constituted a violation of the Mosaic law against manstealing (Exod. 21:16). In his commentary on this verse, Mather explains how the kidnapping and selling of an innocent person was treated by the ancient Israelites:

Q. Why so Severe a Law, against him who *Stole a Man, & Sold* him? v. 16.
A. No *Israelite* would buy him: And therefore such *Plagiaries* sold him to Men of other Nations. This made the Crime to be punished with Death; because it was a Cruel Thing, not only to take away his Liberty, but also to make him a Slave to Strangers. [*BA*, Exod. 21:16]

Given his Puritan assumption that the Mosaic laws ought to provide the basis for the constitutions of modern Christian commonwealths,[60] Mather here indi-

---

59 Greene erroneously assumed that Mather, like other Puritans, subscribed to the curse of Noah as a justification for race slavery. He wrote, "The Puritans also justified slavery upon the highest spiritual grounds. ... Were not Negroes and Infidels, outside the pale of civil and spiritual rights – heathen people whose souls were doomed to eternal perdition? Were thy not an accursed people, the descendants of Ham or 'Cham' whom 'it was quite proper to destroy or enslave?'" (Greene 61). Without pointing at any particular part of the text, Greene cited *The Negro Christianized* as the main reference for the last of these vicious beliefs he ascribed to the Puritans. Only much later in the book does he reveal his mistaken justification for doing so. In his tract, Greene argues, "Mather taught the Negroes that they were enslaved because they had sinned against God and that God, not their masters had enslaved them" (286). Here Greene seems to refer to the first and third item of the slave catechism attached to *The Negro Christianized* which reads, "*That by their sin against God, they are fallen into a dreadful condition. ... That if they Serve God patiently and cheerfully in the Condition which he orders for them, their condition will very quickly be infinitely mended, in Eternal Happiness.*" Yet, the first item of Mather's catechism has nothing to do with the belief in any particular curse against Africans, but refers to the doctrine of total depravity, according to which every human being inherits the sin of Adam which puts them into the "dreadful condition" of sinfulness from which they can only be redeemed by Christ. The third item is an expression of the Calvinist doctrine of predestination, according to which all aspects of human life, including one's social condition, have been preordained by God and therefore have to be accepted by the believer. Again, this article of faith is not related to any form of supernatural racism such as the curse of Noah.
60 In his unconditional condemnation of manstealing as a capital crime Mather also looks back to the first generation of Puritan settlers who apparently held similar views. In 1646 Massachusetts magistrates passed a sentence on several New Englanders for having commit-

rectly asserts that kidnapping and selling innocent human beings, regardless of their skin color, constituted a capital crime in which no Christian ought to be involved in any way. Merely by buying unlawfully enslaved bondsmen, masters might thus participate in a very grave sin. In his condemnation of manstealing Mather was in agreement with many leading British theologians of the seventeenth and early eighteenth centuries, for whom Exod. 21:16 served as a central reference point. Similar interpretations of the Hebrew law can be found in the writings of English Puritans, including William Perkins and Richard Baxter, but also in the publications of other contemporary representatives of New England Puritan orthodoxy such as Samuel Willard. On this issue there is also no principal difference to Sewall and even to the schismatic Quaker Keith.[61]

Mather's mature views on arbitrary enslavement are made more explicit in a highly unusual reflection on Gen. 47:13–26, which he added to the manuscript sometime after 1720. These verses give an account of the position that Joseph, as an official of Pharaoh, takes towards the Egyptian people to whom he in his youth had been sold as a slave. Interestingly enough, Mather departs from the vast majority of earlier Christian commentators and follows the exceptional interpretation of Jacques Saurin (1677–1730), which he had just read. According to Saurin, the policy of Joseph during the famine, forcing the people to sell their land and even their own persons in exchange for food, had to be understood as the imposition of bond-slavery upon innocent people.[62] In answer to the question "What is to be thought of *Josephs* Conduct, in enslaving the *Egyptians*? v. 23," he thus admits that, notwithstanding the patriarch's generally godly and admirable character, "his Conduct was not managed by the Rules of Goodness; and that *Joseph* did really strip the *Egyptians* of those *Rights*, which all the Innocent Part of Mankind have a Natural Claim to ..." (*BA* 1: 1111–13).

What Mather is saying here is in effect very similar to the argument made at the very beginning of *The Selling of Joseph*: Since "all Men, as they are the Sons of Adam, are coheirs; and have equal Rights unto Liberty, and all other outward Comforts of Life," it follows, writes Sewall, that "Originally, and Naturally, there is no such thing as Slavery" (1). Just like Joseph's brothers did not have any legal authority to sell him to a slave trader, no other human being can

---

ted the "haynous and crying sinn of mann stealing" when abducting two Africans by treachery and violence in order to sell them in the colony. By order of the general Court the two were returned to their native land (Jordan 69–71).

61 For the positions of Perkins and Baxter on manstealing, see his *Works* (3: 698) and Baxter (pt. 3, ch. 14, p. 559). For Willard see his *Compleat Body of Divinity* (613–16). Commenting on Exod. 21:16, Sewall writes, "This Law being of Everlasting Equity, wherein Man Stealing is ranked amongst the most atrocious of Capital Crimes: What louder Cry can there be made of that Celebrated Warning, CAVEAT EMPTOR" (*Selling* 1). See also Keith (601).

62 Mather read Saurin's *Discours Historiques* (1720), which appeared within the same year in an English translation. The discussion of Joseph's tyrannical policy towards the Egyptians can be found in Diss. 41 (1: 302–44).

rightfully enslave any other human beings, if they have not forfeited their original and natural rights. Ironically, then, a reflection upon the same biblical figure leads Mather to almost the same conclusion as Sewall, only that it is not the selling of young Joseph into slavery which serves as the occasion for his declaration of man's natural rights, but Joseph's own later practice of buying starving Egyptians as slaves.

However, to argue that slavery was not part of the natural order, as some of the philosophers of classical antiquity (most importantly Aristotle) had maintained, did by no means amount to calling into question slavery's legitimacy. In fact, it was a long established compromise position among Christians of all stripes to regard the institution of slavery not as a product of nature, but as one of the doleful consequences of man's fall. Both Catholic and Protestant divines had long conceived of bonded labor and slavery as something that "was contrary to the ideal realm of nature, but was a necessary part of the world of sin" (Davis, *The Problem of Slavery* 165), in which a rigidly stratified social hierarchy of masters and servants, and rich and poor would always exist. The Puritan orthodoxy on both sides of the Atlantic basically adopted this compromise position, and theologians such as Perkins, Baxter, and Willard all affirmed "that in this life Christian liberty extended only to the spirit ..." (Davis, *The Problem of Slavery* 200) and did not in principle forbid perpetual servitude.

Notwithstanding his belief then that all men, even in their fallen state, were endowed by their creator with certain inalienable rights, Mather also understood slavery, *per se*, to be a lawful institution that was condoned by God for the postlapsarian world, as was documented in both the Old and the New Testament. In fact, this was a conclusion hard to deny for any believer in the literal truth of the Bible, and Sewall likewise did not think that the scriptures forbade slavery as such. In his observations on the Pentateuch, Mather repeatedly touches upon the subject of slavery, which he interprets, historically correctly, as an accepted part of ancient Jewish culture.[63] He points out that while the enslavement of Jews was strictly regulated and always limited to a set period of time, the Israelites, in accordance with customary law, kept "gentiles" (especially Canaanites), who were usually prisoners of war, in lifelong bondage (Davis, *Inhuman Bondage* 38–40). While it was true, as Mather notes, that the Mosaic books made frequent admonishments to treat such slaves well, they were regarded as persons who had permanently lost their natural right to liberty and whose unfree status was passed on to their children. These "*Slaves* (which always were *Gentiles*,) in the Possession of the *Hebrewes*," Mather explains in his gloss on Lev. 27:29, "were the property of their masters and in their Power, as much as

---

63 A succinct survey of the contemporary scholarly knowledge about the historical realities underlying the discussions of slavery in the Hebrew and Christian Bibles is provided by the entries "Slavery in the ancient Near East" and "Slavery in the New Testament," in the HarperCollins *Bible Dictionary* (1029–31).

their *Beasts*, to give or to sell. But to take away their Life, or give them to be slain, was not in their Power ..." [*BA*, Lev. 27:29]. The "Biblia" thus indirectly provides a justification for holding non-Christians as perpetual slaves in God's New Israel.

Sewall's *The Selling of Joseph* also acknowledges the acceptance of gentile slaves in the society of the ancient Israelites.[64] The tract, however, infers from Eph. 2:19 that Christians ought to end the distinctions between their own people and gentiles. Without calling slavery as such incompatible with Christian law, Sewall nevertheless implies that Christians are now, therefore, to refrain from holding anyone in perpetual bondage (indentured servitude, of course, was a different matter) because they "*should* be of a more Ingenuous and benign frame of spirit [and] carry it to all the world as the Israelites were to carry it one toward another" (3, emphasis added). For Mather, no such clear-cut ethical obligation towards gentiles could be derived from the New Testament. Hence, with regard to the institution of slavery, the difference between Mather and Sewall is less about its general legality either under scriptural law or the *ius gentium*. Rather, the two diverged in how much emphasis they put on the necessity to "thrust [slavery] quite out of doors" (*Selling* 2) because of its inevitable conflicts with Christian ethics.

To argue directly that slavery and the laws of Christ were irreconcilable, as George Keith did, was a truly exceptional position in the early eighteenth cen-

---

64 It is often, but falsely assumed that Sewall principally condemned the institution of slavery as illegal. In fact, *The Selling of Joseph* opens with a translated quote from William Ames's (1576–1633) *De conscientia, et eius iure, vel casibus* (1623), which argues that no one should be (permanently) deprived of their liberty, "*but* upon most mature Consideration" (*Selling* 1, emphasis added). In *De conscientia* (bk.5, ch. 23, p. 3) Ames wrote: "2.2. Perfect servitude, so it be voluntary, is on the patients part often lawfull betweene Christian and Christian, because indeed it is necessary: but on the Masters part who is agent, in procuring and exercising the authority, it is scarce lawfull; in respect, it thwarts that generall Canon, *What you would have men doe unto you, even so doe unto them; Matth. 17.12.* 3.3. Perfect servitude, by way of punishment, can have no place by right, unlesse for some heinous offence, which might deserve the severest punishment, to wit, death: because our liberty in the natural account, is the very next thing to life itselfe" (translated in *Conscience with the Power and Cases thereof*, bk. 5, 160). Following Ames, Sewall's tract therefore does not attack the institution of slavery as such, but seeks to demonstrate that the "Foundation" for the specific form of slavery practiced in the American colonies was not "firmly and well laid" (1), mainly because the vast majority of slaves were very likely innocent persons who had been illegally kidnapped, a crime for which there was no religious justification. This does not mean, however, that Sewall held permanent servitude by indenture, or the enslavement of war captives or criminals to be illegal or unscriptural. Nowhere in the tract does he call for the immediate abolition of the institution of slavery. Worried about the spiritual costs and the social ramifications, he rather urges Massachusetts to live up to the demands of Christian charity, to end its involvement with the slave trade, and thereby eventually to eliminate African slavery in the colony.

tury.[65] In *An Exhortation*, Keith maintained that Christ's teachings on the true meaning of love, mercy, and freedom from the world had abrogated the old law where it condoned "outward Bondage, Slavery, or Misery." Instead, Christ commanded his followers "to ease and deliver the Oppressed and Distressed, and bring into *Liberty both inward and outward*" (600, emphasis added). Keith's radicalism brings into view a major problem of orthodox and socially conservative clergymen like Sewall and Mather. Regardless of how much they wanted to curb African slavery for moral and other reasons, as members of the establishment they had no intentions of propagating a notion of Christian liberty that, as a consequence, might call into question the entire social hierarchy by implying that all men should be outwardly free. While Sewall thought it appropriate to have recourse to Christian charity and the golden rule in his attack on African slavery (*Selling* 3), he simultaneously was quite ambiguous and attempted to hedge in the egalitarian implications of his argument, asserting the desirability of bringing more "White servants" (2) to America. Tellingly, he was called out for this inconsistency almost immediately by John Saffin (1632–1710), a Boston merchant and apologist of slavery, who disingenuously demanded to know whether Sewall was ready to take his argument all the way by supporting the complete abolition of servitude, if it was indeed unbecoming of Christians to make use of bonded labor. "If it should be unlawful to deprive them that are lawful captives, or Bondmen of their Liberty for life being Heathens" Saffin slyly asked Sewall in his public rejoinder to *The Selling of Joseph*, "it seems to be more unlawful to deprive our Brethren, of our own or their Christian Nations of the Liberty, (though but for a time) by binding them to Serve some Seven, ten, Fifteen, and some Twenty Years, which oft times proves for their whole Life ..." (653).[66]

---

65   Another radical antislavery protest which has come down to us from Mather's time is the *Petition of the Germantown Quakers* penned by a group of German Quakers and Mennonites around Francis Daniel Pastorius (1651–1720). Like Keith's *An Exhortation*, the *Petition* makes the claim that Christian liberty should be interpreted not only as an inward, but also an outward condition, demanding that in the new American Philadelphia there should be "liberty of conscience" as well as "liberty of the body, except for evil-doers, which is another case" (727). Such a revolutionary position, which ultimately challenged the entire standing order, was very rare at the time. Indeed, prior to the last third of the eighteenth century, almost all antislavery protest argued from the wickedness of the slave trade, while the institution "was usually accepted as one of the long-familiar statuses of the social and economic structure that formed the hierarchy of society. All recorded history, including the Bible, recognized the existence of slavery, and while some people called for the amelioration of the conditions of the enslaved, very few people imagined that slavery could, or perhaps even should, be eradicated" (Carretta 2–3).

66   In his *A Brief and Candid Answer to a Late Printed Sheet, Entituled, The Selling of Jospeh* (1701), Saffin argues that Sewall's plea to abolish African slavery ultimately threatens "to invert the Order that God hath set in the World, who hath Ordained different degrees and orders of men, some to be High and Honourable, some to be Low and Despicable; some to be Monarchs, Kings, Princes and Gouvernours, Masters and Commanders, others to be Sub-

Mather made every effort to avoid such treacherous grounds by keeping inward and outward liberty strictly separate in his interpretation the New Testament. In so doing, he basically affirmed the traditional Christian position according to which servants were spiritually the equal to masters, but outwardly completely subject as long as that did not interfere with a servant's relationship and obligations to God (see Davis, *The Problem of Slavery* 165–66). For Mather, Christian charity also did not translate into a moral imperative to eradicate earthly inequality, but only to mitigate its hardships.[67] He argued that Jesus's teachings never explicitly abrogated the Hebrew laws with regard to servitude or bonded labor. Nor did Mather think that the writings of Jesus's immediate followers contained any fundamental objections to the established practices of slavery among either Jews or within the Roman Empire. Especially when the "Biblia" deals with the Pauline letters, Mather finds opportunity to point out that primitive Christianity took the existence of slaves for granted. While demanding an alleviation of the state of servants and help for the poor in the name of charity, the apostle's interpretation of Christ's revelations, in Mather's orthodox reading, nowhere calls for an overthrow of the standing order. Mather reads in the letters an affirmation of the spiritual freedom proclaimed by Christ, but emphasized that the principle "neither slave nor free" (1 Cor. 12:13; Gal 3:28) does not imply the imperative to level the difference between these conditions in this world. Instead, he interprets it in the sense that faith in Christ was freely given to the elect, irrespective of their station in life, and, soteriologically speaking, gives them freedom from the law. This spiritual freedom in Christ ultimately abolished the significance of earthly inequality and bondage, putting believers *en par* in their relationship with God and establishing bonds of love between them regardless of their different stations in life.

That the order of society was inherently unequal and was comprised of different estates with different liberties, privileges and duties had, in Mather's

---

jects, and to be Commanded; Servants of sundry sorts and degrees, bound to obey, yea, some to be born Slaves, and so to remain during their lives, as hath been proved. Otherwise there would be a meer parity among men, contrary to that of the Apostle I *Cor.* 12 *from the 13 to the 26 verse*, where he sets forth (by way of comparison) the different sorts and offices of the Member of the Body, indigitating that they are all of use, but not equal, and of like dignity" (653). For the Sewall-Saffin debate, see Towner "The Sewall-Saffin Dialogue on Slavery," Rosenthal, and Von Frank.

67 In *The Negro Christianized* Mather does speak about the law of charity and the golden rule. Significantly, however, he does not interpret them as demanding the abolition of social inequality or bonded labor, but as an obligation to care for the physical and, most importantly, the spiritual well-being of one's fellow man: "*Thou shalt Love thy Neighbour as thy self.* Man. Thy *Negro* is thy *Neighbour.* 'T'were an Ignorance, unworthy of a *Man*, to imagine otherwise. ... Now canst thou *Love* thy *Negro*, and be willing to see him ly under the Rage of Sin, and the Warth of God? Canst thou *Love* him, and yet refuse to do any thing, that his miserable Soul may be rescued from Eternal miseries. Oh! Let thy *Love* to that Poor *Soul*, appear in thy concern, to make it, if thou canst, as happy as thy own!" (5–6).

traditionalist view, to be accepted as part of humanity's earthly lot, which it brought upon itself through the fall. Far from pushing for the eradication of the temporal differences between masters and servants, rulers and subjects, he understood Christianity to affirm the postlapsarian necessity of social hierarchies for the benefit of the whole, where those who were in power acted in accordance with the demands of their duties, caring both for the spiritual and the temporal welfare of those under their charge by God.[68] Conversely, Mather often represents the acceptance of their station, submission, and faithful service as the duties of those born into the lower estates and those who had rightfully lost their natural liberties (see Towner "'A Fondness for Freedom'"). From his perspective, African slavery did not, in principle, differ from other forms of servitude and was defined by the same mutual obligations, which are described in much detail in publications such as *A Good Master Well Served* (1696), *A Family Well Ordered* (1699), and the third chapter of *Bonifacius*. Ideally, Christian charity would make bondage "a reciprocal relationship between loving master and loyal servant, instituted by God for the better ordering of a sinful world, but limited by the rationale terms of the social covenant" (Davis, *The Problem of Slavery* 201).

In the "Biblia," these principles of Mather's scripture-based social conservatism are explicated, for instance, in his gloss on Eph. 6, where he speaks at length about what he calls the "Conscientious Discharge of Relative Duties" according to people's different stations in life. In Mather's view, Christianity demanded of its followers to remain content in the place to which God had providentially assigned them. In the tradition of Paul and Luther, he thus strictly distinguished between the inward and outward freedom of Christians and could thus reason that a spiritual regeneration through faith had no affect on a person's legal status. From this interpretation of Christian freedom, he arrived at the conclusion that he puts forward in *The Negro Christianized*: the conversion and baptism of slaves did not necessarily entail emancipation or even morally compel masters to free their bondservants.[69] Herein lies the crucial difference between Mather and his friend Sewall. Sewall passed over the issue in *The Selling of Joseph*, but in his 1705 Boston reprint of John Dunton's *The Athenian Oracle* (1704) he made it known that, in his understanding, conversion not only

---

68 The classical Puritan expression of such a hierarchical and paternalistic model of society can be found in John Winthrop's "Modell of Christian Charity," which takes it for granted that "in all times some must be rich some poore, some highe and eminent in power and dignitie; others meane and in subjection," but demands that all stations of society should be "knit … together in the bond of brotherly affection" (282–83).

69 Drawing on a long tradition of interpretation, including Luther's *On the Freedom of a Christian* (1520), Mather explicitly argues in *The Negro Christianized*: "*That he is the Lord's Free-man*, tho' he continues a *Slave*. It supposes, (Col. 3.11.) That there are *Bond* as well as *Free*, among those who that have been *Renewed in the Knowledge and Image of Jesus Christ*" (26–27).

introduced slaves into the spiritual freedom of Christ, but also put them "under the same Law with other Christians" (3) who, at least according to Dunton's understanding of English law, were not subject to possible permanent and inheritable bondage.[70] At the time, the opinions of Dunton and Sewall were truly exceptional and the vast majority of British Protestants, including professional theologians, denied that there was a necessary connection between conversion and emancipation. As Davis has shown, this was the official position of the Church of England and the SPG, and it was also the position that was translated into new legislation both in England (where the Attorney General ruled in 1729 that baptism did not automatically alter the legal status of slaves) and many of the British colonies (Davis, *The Problem of Slavery* 209–10).

Like most of his contemporaries, Mather did not share the view of Dunton and Sewall. He was convinced of the compatibility of temporal bondage and spiritual freedom. Thus, he reasoned that in principle "the *Law of Christianity* ... allows of *Slavery*" (*The Negro Christianized* 6), but only under certain conditions. First of all, he limited the circumstances under which persons might be permanently deprived of their natural liberty. In this respect, the "Biblia's" commentaries on Deuteronomy and Leviticus essentially confirm the prevalent opinion of early modern European theologians that slavery should be restricted to exceptional cases of individuals "voluntarily" entering into perpetual servitude for economic reasons, to infidel prisoners of lawful wars, or to perpetrators of capital crimes who were to be sold into foreign slavery.[71] Following this

---

70   As a matter of fact, the legality of slavery in England had long been in dispute, but it was not until the famous Manfield ruling of 1772 (which basically decided that slaves were free as soon as they stepped on English soil) that it was definitely outlawed. See Cotter and Drescher (25–49). The decisive passage of Dunton's text reads: "The Law of our Land is so far from allowing it [slavery]; that if an Infidel be brought into this Kingdom, as soon as he can give an Account of the Christian Faith and desires to be Baptized; any Charitable lawful Minister may do it and then he is under the same Law with other Christians ..." (3). Baxter also urged masters to release infidel slaves after their conversion (559), even if he didn't see manumission as a quasi-legal necessity like Dunton or Sewall do. Similarly to Mather, Godwyn's *The Negro's & Indians Advocate* denied any necessary nexus between baptism and manumission (30 ff.).

71   For the attitude of the Christian church towards slavery in the early modern period, see Davis (*Inhuman Bondage* 54–56). Baxter's *A Christian Directory* gives us a good idea of the prevailing view on legitimate forms of slavery amongst the Puritan community on both sides of the Atlantic. According to Baxter, there are three forms of lawful slavery: "a necessitated slavery by Contract or Consent through poverty," by which he meant permanent indentured servitude; slavery "by just penalty" and the enslavement of infidel "*Captives in a lawful War*" (559). This had also been the general position adopted in Article 91 of Massachusetts's *Body of Liberties* (1641). Referencing the Hebrew laws on slavery and manstealing from Exodus and Leviticus, this statue had principally allowed of slavery, but outlawed the importation of kidnapped slaves by stipulating that "there shall never be any Bond-slavery, Villenage or Captivitie amonst us, unless it be lawful Captives taken in just Wars, and such strangers as willingly sell themselves, or are sold to us, and such shall have the Liberties and Christian usages which the Law of God established in Israel concerning such persons doth morally require;

opinion, Mather also condoned the enslavement of captured Native Americans during the Indian wars in New England.[72] Of course, such a definition of lawful slavery can be called a form of indirect racial discrimination since it excluded Europeans (who were at least nominal Christians) from the most common type of enslavement as captives, and mainly, if not exclusively, applied to Africans or American Indians. At the same time, Mather's gloss on Gen. 9:22-2 explicitly rejects race as a legitimate reason for enslavement and considers manstealing a capital crime when it is perpetrated against innocent persons, regardless of their complexion.

Furthermore, Mather, both in his published works and in the "Biblia," declares that slavery, like other forms of servitude, is only admissible if managed according to the law of charity, which demanded the moderation of hardships, and that slaves be made members of the household.[73] With reference to Col. 4: 1, *"Masters, give unto your Servants, that which is Just & Equal, knowing that ye also have a Master in Heaven,"* Mather, in *The Negro Christianized*, spells out some of the basic obligations of slave owners as he derives them from "the Christian Law": "As it is *Just & Equal*, that your *Servants* be not *Over-wrought*, and that while they *Work* for you, you should *Feed* them, and *Cloath* them, and afford convenient *Rest* unto them, and make their lives comfortable" (4–5). Most importantly, in Mather's view, it was imperative for masters "that you should Acquaint them, as far as you can, with the way to Salvation by JESUS CHRIST" (5).[74] While the tract for strategic reasons politely pleads with his target-audience to follow these obligations, the gloss on Col. 4:1 in the "Biblia" takes a different approach to the subject:

Provided this exempts none from servitude who shall be judged thereto by Authority" (Ward 196–97). While Article 91 thus acknowledges the legitimacy of "Bond-slavery" under very specific conditions, it does not (as Von Frank convincingly argues) clearly distinguish slavery from the other forms of unfree labor it mentions (259–61). Significantly, "penal slavery" for white criminals seems to have been no longer practiced in the colony of Massachusetts after the mid-seventeenth century (Jordan 68).

72 See Mather's comments in the *Magnalia* (bk. 7, ch. 6) on Indian captives sold into slavery in the wake of the Pequot and King Philip's War ("Arma virosque Cano: Or, The Troubles Which the Churches of New-England Have Undergone in the Wars, Which the People of That Country Have Had with the Indian Salvages"). In July 1681 Mather records in his *Diary* that he purchased a *"Spanish Indian,* and bestowed him for a *Servant,* on my Father" (1: 22). Mather himself was given a *"Spanish Indian"*-servant by Governor Sir William Phips in 1693, whom he allowed to go to sea and then, upon his return in 1696, liberated (1: 203).

73 In this regard the "Biblia's" gloss on Eph. 6:9 is very telling: "Knowing that your Master also is in Heaven. It is usual for Powers on Earth, sinfully, to overlook, and not punish, the unjust and cruel Dealings of Masters towards their Servants; But the Sins by Men most connived at, will by God have a most Severe Notice taken of them. God will call Masters to an Account, how they carry towards their Servants."

74 Specific guidelines for the Christian education of servants are given in Mather's *Bonifacius* (54–55).

Q. Do you *Allow* the Translation? *Master, give unto your Servants, that which is Just and Equal?* v. 1.
A. No, such Things must not be reckoned *Gifts*. They are the *Dues* of Servants, and they have a *Right* unto them. Wherefore, I concur with him, who writes, *The Negro's and Indians Advocate*, that the Word, παρέχετε, had better be rendred, *Allow*, than, *Give*. [*BA*, Col. 4:1][75]

Following Morgan Godwyn, Mather thus describes a "Just and Equal" treatment (in the sense defined above) not as a concession of good will to be made by their masters, but as the God-given rights of slaves, which they retained despite their permanent loss of liberty. Conversely, a systematic violation of these rights made slavery unchristian in Mather's understanding.

This is not the place to go into a detailed analysis of Mather's practical work as a propagator of slave conversion, or to give an assessment of his personal record as the owner of at least three different domestic slaves, all of whom he eventually freed; the last in his will.[76] Generally speaking, he seemed to have lived up to his own demands for the religious education and humane handling of these slaves as well as the numerous long- and short-term servants (male and female, white, Indian, and black) who worked in his household over the years.

---

75 Mather directly quotes Godwyn here, who wrote in *The Negro's and Indians Advocate*: "The like must also *St. Paul's* Exhortation (or rather Precept) to his *Colossians* be, Chap. 6. 1 *Masters* [παρεχετε] *allow* (not give) *your Servants ... that which is just and equal*; such things not to be reckoned Gifts, which are our *due*, and to which we have a *just Right*" (66).
76 We only have more detailed information on one of these slaves who was given to Mather as a gift by his congregation in 1706. This man he named Onesimus after the runaway slave who joined St. Paul in Rome and became a fellow-Christian as well as a close friend. Eventually Paul sent Onesimus back to his Christian owner Philemon in Colossus along with a letter (which later became part of the New Testament canon) intended to reconcile master and slave in the spirit of mutual love without challenging the institution of slavery. In many respects, then, the name Mather chose for this particular slave was programmatic for his attitude he took towards slavery in general. On his treatment of Onesimus Silverman writes, "Since for Mather and other Puritans, servants were to be treated as family members – as persons, that is, for whose salvation the householder was obliged to be deeply concerned – he labored with a combination of piety and contempt for Onesimus' conversion. Consistent with his belief that blacks did not differ from the rest of humanity in their capacity for salvation, he found Onesimus governed best by 'the Principles of Reason, agreeably offered unto him,' encouraged him to read and write every day, and allowed him to marry. (Whether Onesimus' wife joined the Mather household is unclear; the couple had a son, who dies, however, in 1714.) He also permitted Onesimus to work outside the house and gain an independent income, charging him to keep the rules of honesty and to devote part of his income to pious purposes. For all that, Mather did not differ from most Puritans in regarding blacks as alien and untrustworthy." "Around 1716 Mather allowed him to purchase his release, by putting up money toward buying a black youth to serve in his stead ... whom he named Obadiah" (264–65 and 290). In her article on Mather's relationship with Onesimus, Kathryn S. Koo suggests that Mather dismissed the slave from his household because he did not succeed in converting him to Christianity. This failure, according to Koo, created a more general awareness on Mather's part of the impracticability of his ideal of the Christian servant. Recently, Onesimus has also attracted considerable scholarly attention because of his role in the so-called inoculation controversy of 1721–22. See Minardi and Herzogenrath.

He taught those who lived under his roof to read and write, alongside the fundamentals of the Christian faith. In addition to publishing several treatises and catechisms for the education and evangelization of Africans and Indians, he also established an evening charity school for them, which he ran at his own expense, despite his deteriorating financial situation (Rooy 245). In 1693, he helped to organize the Religious Society for Negroes, a neighborhood prayer society for slaves and free blacks of his parish, which later held meetings in Mather's house. These few surviving pieces of evidence about his own social practices are certainly important because they give us a better sense of the kind of slavery he regarded as being compatible with Christianity. It is more pertinent to emphasize, though, that his writings clearly demonstrate how conscious he was of the stark discrepancy between his Christian model of legitimate bond-servitude and the form that slavery had generally assumed in contemporary British America, especially in the West Indian and Southern colonies. Indeed, some of his later texts suggest increasing doubts about whether this discrepancy could be reconciled at all through the reform measures he supported. At the heart of Mather's increasing uneasiness with American slavery were the undeniable contradictions he perceived between the demands of Christian service both to God and man and the ways in which the ancient institution was organized in the New World.

Ultimately, the kind of slavery Mather thought consistent with Christianity was only possible with a relatively small number of bondservants living, working, and practicing their religion as members of the general household. During his lifetime this kind of domestic slavery was disappearing even in New England, not to speak of the Chesapeake or the West Indies where the plantation revolution introduced what would later be known as cattle slavery. Regional differences notwithstanding, then, slavery in the American colonies around the turn of the century was generally practiced in a way that involved the brutal physical exploitation and systematic mistreatment of bondsmen, but also the widespread neglect of their spiritual well-being. Reformers like Mather faced everywhere a staunch and very successful opposition of owners to the Christianization of their slaves,[77] which exposed the sheer hypocrisy of the argument that African slavery was a means to spread the gospel.

---

77 When Mather grew up African slaves had been a minor appendage to a mixed labour force in Massachusetts. Between 1680 and 1700, their numbers quadrupled from roughly 200 to about 800 persons, and in 1720 there were already more than 2,000. As in the rest of New England, these bondsmen toiled under deteriorating circumstances, and, like the remaining free blacks, became legally and socially ever more separated from the rest of the population, including white indentured servants. During the same period the slave population in Britain's West Indian and Southern colonies virtually exploded despite the appalling mortality rates on the new staple crop plantations, where excruciating physical labor, malnutrition, poor housing, and sanitary conditions were the norm. The last decades of the seventeenth century and the early decades of the eighteenth century also saw the introduction of slave codes every-

Mather was not blind to how widely his scripture-based ideal of domestic servitude differed from the realities of American slavery, as his frequent complaints about the inhuman, beast-like treatment of Africans attest. Like many of his clerical colleagues, though, he was most of all worried about the ways in which the multiplying numbers of slaves were being obtained. There was an increasing awareness that the majority of Africans brought to the New World were not lawful captives of war, even though apologists of the slave trade, such as Sewall's infamous public opponent John Saffin, still had recourse to this fiction.[78] To put it in modern terms, then, there was a growing realization among New England's Puritan elite that slavery in the Americas had, in fact, become a racial form of bondage with the justification for enslavement ultimately resting on the skin-color of those taken into bondage.

With Mather this awareness resulted in a very conflicted attitude. As Mark A. Peterson has recently noted, sometime around the turn of the century Mather joined the ranks of those Puritan clergymen who sought to end New England's involvement in the slave trade. Economical, social, and military considerations might also have played a part in the emergence of an antislavery sentiment in Massachusetts,[79] but the main reason, on Mather's part at least, was

---

where in the South, which gave masters complete rights over their "property," including the right to kill slaves in punishment. For a survey on how the slave trade and slavery developed in the Americas during Mather's lifetime, see Berlin (51–97). Despite the efforts of missionary society and individual clergymen such as Mather, the number of slaves converted in the early eighteenth century was miniscule in the South and also remained quite low in New England. See Raboteau (120–30) Greene (285), and Piersen (77).

78   On this issue Sewall writes, "For ought is known, their Wars are much such as were between *Jacob's* Sons and their Brother *Joseph*. If they be between Town and Town; Provincial, or National: Every War is upon one side Unjust. An Unlawful War can't make lawful Captives. And by Receiving, we are in danger to promote, and partake in their Barbarous Cruelties" (*Selling* 3). For George Keith there was no question that commonly "the Negroes that are sold to white Men, are either stolen away or robbed from their Kindred ..." (*Exhortation* 600).

79   James J. Allegro has rightly pointed out that the emerging anti-slavery sentiment amongst parts of New England's elite was by no means exclusively motivated by conscientious objections. Many also viewed slavery as hurtful to provincial finances and generally detrimental to the stability and safety of the colonies since the law did not allow slaves to serve in the militia and even free Africans were deemed to be incapable of full integration into society. All of these arguments are rehearsed by Sewall who writes, "And all things considered, it would conduce more to the welfare of the Province, to have White Servants for a term of Years, than to have Slaves for Life. Few can endure to hear of a Negro's being made free; and indeed they can seldom use their freedom well; yet their continued aspiring after their forbidden Liberty, renders them Unwilling Servants. ... As many Negro men as there are among us, so many empty places there are in our Train Bands, and the places taken up of Men that might make Husbands for our Daughters" (*Selling* 2). In combination these mixed motives led to series of acts passed between 1705 and 1728 by the Massachusetts General court to inhibit African slavery through heavy fines and promote white indentured labor. While these acts failed to stop African slavery in the colony, they provided an important basis for the post-revolutionary abolitionist movement in Massachusetts.

that, given the nature of the slave trade, there was no way to avoid complicity in the crime of manstealing. Moreover, in all his publications on the subject Mather "constructed a consistent argument characterizing the cruelty and inhumanity of slavery as an impediment to the expansion of true Christianity and therefore an obstacle in the ongoing war against popery and the anti-Christ" (Peterson 11). In *Theopolis Americana* (1710) – a text which Mather had preached as a sermon before the Massachusetts General Court a year before, and then published with a dedication to Sewall – he made it known, quoting Richard Baxter, that those who "go as *Pirates*, and Catch up poor *Negroes* ... that have never forfeited *Life* or *Liberty*, and to make them Slaves, and Sell them" were perpetrating "one of the worst kinds of Thievery in the World; and such persons are to be taken for the common Enemies of Mankind." What is more, he explicitly castigated all colonists who "buy them, and use them as *Beasts*, for their meer Commodity, and betray, or destroy, or neglect their Souls, are fitter to be called, *Incarnate Devils*, than *Christians*, tho' they be no *Christians* whom the so Abuse" (21–22).[80] To those who heard these words at the time and knew that Mather was describing the rule rather than the exception, there could be little doubt that, in the long run, he indeed wished to root out African slavery altogether from New England because it evidently corrupted the souls of those involved. Although I found no hard evidence, it is more than likely that he, like his friend Sewall, took a part in the repeated campaigns between 1700 and 1728, which urged the Massachusetts General Court to introduce new duties on the importation of black bondsmen which would promote the importation of white indentured servants and eventually phase out African slavery.[81]

Mather thus considered "the *slave-trade* ... a spectacle that shocks humanity" (*Bonifacius* 54),[82] and clearly wished for it to end. But for all his abhorrence of the evils involved in the trafficking of souls and the commodification of human beings, he never called for the abolition of slavery as an institution. As suggested above, he did not believe that the scriptures provided justification for,

---

80 Mather quotes these sentences from Baxter's *Christian Directory* (pt 3, ch. 14, p. 559).

81 In June 1700 Sewall's *Diary* mentions a motion by a "Boston Comitte to get a Law that all Importers of Negros shall pay 40s p head, to discourage the bringing of them. And Mr. C. Mather resolves to publish a sheet to exhort Masters to labour their Conversion." One year later Sewall writes about another such motion which apparently proved abortive as well: "The Representatives [to the Great and General Court] are further desired To Promote the Encourageing the bringing of white servt[s] and to put a Period to negros being Slaves" (qtd. in Kaplan 33–34, 45). Given Mather's sentiment about the slave trade, and the fact that Sewall mentions his plans for *The Negro Christianized* in one breath with the first legislative motion, it seems quite likely to me (contrary to Kaplan's assessment) that Mather was in favor of these initiatives too.

82 To illustrate the shocking nature of the slave-trade Mather here quotes Daniel Defoes's 1702 poem *Reformation of Manners, a Satyr*: "*The harmless natives basely they trepan,/And barter baubles for the souls of men./The wretches they to Christian climes bring o'er/To serve worse heathens than they did before*" (*Bonifacius* 54).

or indeed demanded, such a dramatic change of the social order. While he desired to put a stop to the slave trade, he also did not think of calling into question the legal status of bondsmen already in the colony. Instead, his concern was
with reforming the practice of slavery and fostering conversion at least in New
England where the number of African bondmen was still relatively low and
would hopefully remain so. "[W]hen we have Slaves in our Houses," he argues
in *Theopolis Americana*, there was no obligation to let them go, but "we are to
treat them with *Humanity*; we are to treat them that their *Slavery* may really be
their *Happineß*; Yea, in our treating of them, there must be nothing but what
the Law of CHRIST will Justify" (22). Because the spiritual freedom found in
Christ did not translate into outward liberty, as Mather assured slave owners,
they need not to be worried about losing their property as a consequence of
having their slaves educated and baptized. Knowing that this fear was a major
obstacle to slave conversion, Mather even banded together with a number of
clergymen, who in 1693 unsuccessfully petitioned for legislation that would
give slave owners legal security in this regard (Greene 267).

Even if we try not to impose our standards of morality and make a genuine
attempt to assume Mather's own perspective, there are undeniable incongruities
in this stance. After all, he was ultimately condoning the permanent bondage of
people whom he recognized as fellow human beings endowed with the same
natural rights and whom he knew had quite likely been captured illegally, according to the standards of legality he himself defined. Theoretically, none of
the theological axioms he subscribed to should have made it impossible to reason along the lines of Baxter who wrote in his *Christian Directory*:

> But what if men buy Negro's or other slaves of such as we have just cause to believe
> did steal them by Piracy, or buy them of those that have no power to sell them, ... nor
> take them Captives in a lawful War, what must they do with them afterward? Answ.
> 1. It is their heinous sin to buy them, unless it be in charity to deliver them. 2. Hav-
> ing done it, undoubtedly they are presently bound to deliver them: because by right
> the man is his own and therefore no man else can have a just title to him. (pt. 3,
> ch.14, p. 559)[83]

No such demand from Mather to liberate unlawfully captured Africans is on
record. Yet, I think that in light of what has been said so far, racism is not a satisfactory explanation for Mather's hesitance to take this stance.[84] Baxter's argu-

---

83   Keith makes a similar argument that "as we are not to buy stolen Goods, (but if at una-
wares it should happen through Ignorance, we are to restore them to the Owners, and seek
our remedy of the thief) no more are we to buy stolen Slaves; neither should such as have them
keep and their Posterity in perpetual bondage and Slavery ..." (*Exhortation* 601).

84   It should be noted that Sewall's plea to "thrust [African slavery] quite out of doors" contains more openly racist arguments than any of Mather's writings. In order to underscore his
argument that a large number of freed Africans could not be successfully integrated into colonial society Sewall, for instance, writes the following: "And there is such disparity in their
Conditions. Color & Hair, that they can never embody with us, and grow up into orderly

ment for delivering "stolen men" certainly was consistent and compelling, but it was one thing to be uncompromising about this issue as an Englishman, living in a society were foreign slaves did not play a significant role, and another for a colonial living in the context of the early 1700s. To take an uncompromising position on the obligation to free "stolen men" would have been tantamount to calling for the immediate abolition of slavery as such. Mather was not prepared to do this because, as indicated earlier, he wished to preserve a social hierarchy that included, and indeed crucially depended on, unfree labor. He very likely feared that in calling for the abrogation of one form of servitude, he would undermine the whole standing order.[85] In other words, Mather's reluctance to speak out more strongly about the illegality of the ways in which most slaves had been obtained was intimately connected with his abhorrence of the leveling tendencies inherent in the abolitionism represented by someone like Keith. To link the inward liberty of faith to outward liberty not only made the cause for slave conversion very vulnerable, as Saffin's attacks on Sewall proved, in Mather's own mind, it also meant opening a Pandora's box of potentially revolutionary ideas threatening to throw the "body politick" into turmoil.

Maybe even more importantly, however, his hesitance to call for an end to the institution of slavery as such reflects an impasse into which he was led by his strict scripturalism, the priority of which was to prove the literal truthfulness of the Bible as a coherent whole and its reliability as a guide to social practice. As shown above, his hyperliteralist readings of Genesis made him oppose race as a category of significant difference and a justification for enslavement. Yet, the same approach to other parts of the Hebrew Bible and the Pauline letters, where slavery was accepted under certain conditions, also made it impossible for him to think that the institution was in principle irreconcilable with Christianity or that Christian law demanded the freeing of converted bondsmen. From Mather's point of view as a biblical scholar, doing so would have raised very troubling and dangerous exegetical issues, not least the question whether there might be fundamental contradictions between Christ's teachings on charity and freedom and the interpretation of these teachings by his apostles, who accepted slavery as a given. In a situation where American slavery had, in fact, become racial in nature, he did not find a way out of this conundrum that seemed acceptable to him.

Families, to the Peopling of the Land: but still remain in our Body Politick as a kind of extravasat Blood" (*Selling* 2). This suggests, I think, that the difference between Mather and Sewall on the abolition of slavery is not motivated by a higher or lower degree of racism.

85   In this respect Mather represents a position that was widely held amongst contemporary members of the English elite on both sides of the Atlantic: "Associating slavery with the image of a stable Christian household ruled by the Bible and right reason, these British Protestants exhorted all bondsmen to revere their masters and to be patient, obedient, and diligent. If a servant were allowed to question his fate, he would undermine they very foundation of social order" (Davis, *The Problem of Slavery* 200).

Very likely, he also thought that openly promoting the abolition of African slavery, as Sewall had done, would damage the great cause of bringing the gospel to the infidels at a critical moment in history when the millennium was only years away. In fact, Mather's premillennialist belief in the imminence of a global conflagration, which would purge the world of all iniquities before Christ's return to earth, and from which only the saints would be saved through the rapture, is a very important but almost entirely overlooked context that helps to explain his inconsistent engagement with slavery. For someone who was convinced that most of the bondsmen in the colonies would live to see the end of the existing world order and would have to face the apocalyptical day of judgment along with everyone else, it was not simply a self-serving choice to prioritize the conversion of slaves over their release.[86] While advocating the justness of the latter demand was unlikely to move owners to part with their property, it was almost certain to make them even more opposed to allowing missionaries access to their slaves.

To be sure, Mather's anxiety over the many unconverted and brutalized African slaves in the colonies was not only motivated by his concern for the future state of their souls come the conflagration. Mather was also worried as least as much about the role of his beloved New England in the unfolding millennium. In his final years, Mather became ever more certain that the West Indian and Southern colonies would be consumed in the flames. "Amongst the Instances, wherein *Iniquity does abound* amongst the Nations of the *Earth*," he wrote with reference to Rev 18:5 in his *Triparadisus*, "most certainly the *Slave-trade*, and the Usage of *Slaves*, almost every where, but very conspicuously in You, o *Carribee*-Islands, it calls for a *Judgment without Mercy*, on *Men* becoming worse than *Wolves* to one another" (236).[87] To avoid this fate, then, New England had to extricate itself from the trafficking of humans. What mattered most to Mather was that those slaves whom God's providence had brought into New England and, as he explained to the audience of *The Negro Christianized*, "cast under your Government and Protection" (3), be given the "just and equal"

---

86 If read in the context of Mather's millennialism many passages of *The Negro Christianized* assume a different meaning. Especially the attached catechism is full of formulations emphasizing the shortness of time until the liberation of the slavery either through death or the arrival of Christ.

87 In a letter to his German Pietist correspondent in London, Anton Wilhelm Böhme, dating August 6, 1716 Mather answered the latter's inquiries "after the history of the introduction of Christianity into the other English plantations of America" "with a short and melancholy answer" that indicates his concerning the future fate of the southern colonies. Not only was religion life in these colonies characterized by "High Church follies" and a lack of true piety so that it mostly consisted "in lifeless forms and ceremonies expiating for a vicious life." Mather also thought that this viciousness of the southern lifestyle was inherent in the basic structure of the colonies' economy: "And how inhumane the way of their subsistence, on the sweat and blood of slaves treated with infinite barbarities!" (*Selected Letters* 215).

treatment and made acquainted with Christ like other servants.[88] As cynical as this may sound to our ears, Mather was doubtlessly sincere in arguing that, especially with the millennium fast approaching, "[t]he greatest *Kindness* that can be done to any Man is to make a *Christian* of him (9). In performing this kindness and caring for the well-being of their slaves, householders could presumably atone for the guilt involved in the purchase and therefore look with more confidence to the not too distant time when "you and they come at length to be together in the *Heavenly City*," (20) where the old differences in earthly station would be abolished.[89]

That most of the slaves remained strangers to Christ and were in fact regarded as expendable tools rather than human beings was, in Mather's view, one of the main reasons why God was angry with New England and punishing it with mounting afflictions. His trepidations about these providential signs of God's wrath are forcefully expressed in the surviving notes for a sermon or memorial he held in response to a series of arsons committed by slaves in Boston in June 1723. According to this manuscript, he urged his audience to consider "whether our conduct with relation to our African slaves be not one thing for which our God may have controversy with us." Are they, he asked in a rhetorical manner, "treated as those that are of one blood with us, and those that have immortal souls in them, and are not mere beasts of burden!" (*Selected Letters* 368). However, by the 1720s, the days of the Puritan theocracy had passed for good, and the jeremiads of a Mather no longer carried enough weight in the colony to affect such a far-reaching reform. Indeed, the futility of Mather's immediate efforts to stop the importation of "stolen men" and promote slave conversion fit into Von Frank's revisionist argument that "[s]lavery and the racism in which apologists sought to lay its foundation flourished in Massachusetts almost directly in proportion to the decline in the influence of Puritanism" (266).

In sum, the "Biblia" shows Mather as an apologist of orthodoxy who makes every effort to affirm not only the unitary origin of all mankind in Adam, but also the direct ties of kinship that connected all parts of humanity to different branches of the Noachic pedigree. Keenly, and indeed anxiously aware of the

---

88 In *Bonifacius* Mather calls for an influential "servant of God," who "may be so honored by Him, as to be made the successful instrument, of obtaining from a British Parliament, *an act for the Christianizing of the slaves in the Plantations*; then it may be hoped, something more may be done, than has yet been done, that the *blood of souls* may not be found in the *skirts* of our nation: a *controversy* of Heaven with our Colonies may be removed, and *prosperity* may be restored ..." (53).

89 Mather's reminder must be read as a response to the well-documented attitude of many slave holders who denied the possibility that they would have to face their slaves on equal terms in heaven. The missionary Francis Le Jau, for instance, recorded the query of a South Carolina lady who opposed any efforts to Christianize her slaves with the comment: "Is it possible any of my slaves should go to heaven, & must I see them there?" (qtd in Bruce 13).

increasing racialization of colonial society, Mather does engage with the emerging discourse that constructs race in terms of essential differences, but he consistently reintegrates his reasoning about the natural causes for phenotypical diversity into the essentially pre-modern biblical concept of race as lineage, which ultimately rendered racial Otherness "as a type of cousinage or remote kinship," however distant from the Japhetite branch (Kidd 21). For him, humankind's universal consanguinity was a necessary foundation for the doctrines of Calvinist Christianity. Conversely, the teaching of universal depravity was, to borrow a phrase from Rachel Wheeler, "the guarantor of spiritual equality" (206) of all people, who stood on equal terms in their need of divine grace through Christ's salvific work. In my opinion, Mather thus exemplifies how, in the area of race, religious conservatism *could* also work in what we now would describe as a progressive direction. To a certain extent at least, its totalizing view of humanity and its redemptive history inhibited or circumscribed the emerging tendencies towards a modern type of racial essentialism that sought to naturalize social and legal distinctions.

As far as race is concerned, then, Mather's theological project, for all its eagerness to accommodate the new sciences, clearly runs counter to the evolving naturalistic anthropology of the Enlightenment that divided humanity into a hierarchy of different racial groups inherently unequal in their abilities and capacities. There is no doubt that he would have crusaded against those radical philosophers who, like Voltaire (1694–1778) or Lord Kames (1696–1782), transformed earlier polygenist speculations into (pseudo-)scientific theories. He also would have opposed the new ideas of racial degeneracy from a white norm that, in the second half of the century, were embraced by many representatives of a more moderate Christian Enlightenment who wished to uphold the belief in monogenesis. To Mather the infamous "suspicion" advanced by Thomas Jefferson (1743–1826) in his *Notes on the State of Virginia* (1787) "that the blacks, whether originally a distinct race, or made distinct by time and circumstance, are inferior to the whites in the endowment both of body and of mind" (636) would have been totally unacceptable either way.[90] If we look ahead into the second half of the eighteenth century, the rhetoric in which Mather couched his orthodox dogmas indeed adumbrates the emphatic universalism of evangelical discourse that resisted this new kind of classificatory thinking and therefore proved so attractive to the poor, racially marginalized, and enslaved.

Like Jonathan Edwards two decades later, Mather strongly emphasized that Christ's elect were to be found in all social ranks and all the nations of the earth to which the gospel had to be brought. However, Mather also inherited from his Puritan ancestors and bequeathed to his evangelical heirs a strong dis-

---

90   For the development of modern (pseudo-)scientific racism in the second half of the eighteenth century, see Frederickson (49–97) and Kidd (79–121).

dain for non-Christian religions as well as an inveterate belief in the superiority of European civilization. Consequently, to our eyes his legacy as an advocate of missionary work among the Indians must necessarily appear mixed. As commissioner of the New England Company, which would later also employ Edwards in Stockbridge, he dedicated much ink, time, and money to converting Indians and to relieving the suffering of those who had converted. Even though Mather could be highly critical of the English failures in the behavior towards the Indians, he, like his New Light successors, generally exhibited the kind of ethnocentrism and Christian paternalism characteristic of missionary ideology. He was also unable to recognize any such thing as Indian rights to cultural or territorial autonomy, oblivious to the catastrophic loss of tribal traditions, and indifferent to the sufferings of those natives who resisted assimilation.

Similarly equivocal is Mather's theological legacy to the later antislavery movement. Like Edwards and George Whitefield after him, he shied away from drawing the ultimate conclusion of a wholesale condemnation of the African slave trade.[91] With his campaign to encourage slave conversions, he, in fact, helped to remove "the final Christian barrier to slavery" (Towner, "The Sewall-Saffin Dialogue on Slavery" 52) by assuring owners that the inward freedom in Christ attained through baptism did not necessarily translate into outward freedom.[92] Measured against the standard of the very few exceptional voices such as the radical George Keith, who called for an immediate abolition, Mather certainly fell short of what was possible even in his own age, even if his failure was not caused by racism.

On the other hand, Mather went much further in his criticism of American slavery than the vast majority of colonial ministers. Moreover, with the benefit of hindsight, we might say that the "egalitarian tendencies [inherent] in the missionaries' efforts" undertaken by advocates of slave conversion like him are undeniable, even though they themselves insisted on keeping inward and outward liberty strictly separate. In the long run, as Bruce has remarked, the idea of spiritual equality underlying the evangelical campaigns for slave conversion would show its full potential "to challenge the very fabric of slavery itself ..."(13).[93] And measured against the dominant cultural trend in British America

---

91 Jonathan Edwards's criticism of the slave trade and his defense of the institution of slavery are discussed in Minkema ("Slavery" and "Defense").
92 During Mather's lifetime most of the British colonies enacted new laws that put an end to the lingering debate over the legal effects of conversion by stipulating that baptism did not entail manumission (Kolchin 15). Even if its original intention was primarily to overcome resistance to slave conversion, Mather's *The Negro Christianized* thus lend ideological support to this development.
93 This idea of spiritual equality shows in a small episode reported by Morgan Godwyn in his *The Negro's & Indians Advocate*. Here Morgan narrates how he was challenged by a West Indian slaveholders, who complained that if "those black Dogs" should be made Christians, they should also "be like us" (Godwyn 61).

it was certainly of no small merit to promote this idea as powerfully as Mather did. Passed on through the generation of Edwards, it would prove to be the seed for the radical abolitionism of New Light Calvinists such as Samuel Hopkins, who also shared Mather's anxiety over the apocalyptical ramifications of slavery for New England (see Minkema and Stout).

Works Cited

Primary Sources

Aben Ezra. [Abraham ibn Ezra]. *Ibn Ezra's Commentary on the Pentateuch: Volume 1: Genesis.* Trans. H. Norman Strickman and Arthur M. Silver. New York: Menorah, 1988.

Acosta, José. *The Naturall and Morall Historie of the East and West Indies.* 1590. Trans. Edward Grimston. London, 1604.

Ames, William. *Conscience with the Power and Cases thereof.* London, 1643.

Apess, William. *On Our Own Ground: The Complete Writing of William Apess, a Pequot.* Ed. Barry O'Connell. Amherst: The U of Massachusetts P, 1992.

Arias Montanus, Benedictus. *Phaleg; sive, De gentium sedibus primis, orbisque terrae situ liber.* Antverpiae, 1572.

Bailey, Nathan. *Dictionarium Britannicum.* 1730. Hildesheim: Georg Olms Verlag, 1969.

Baxter, Richard. *A Christian Directory: Or, a Summ of Practical Theologie, and Cases of Conscience. In Four Parts.* London, 1673.

Bayle, Pierre. *General Dictionary, Historical and Critical, in which A New and Accurate Translation of that Celebrated Mr. Bayle with the Corrections and Observations printed in the late Edition at Paris, is included.* 1697. 10 vols. London, 1734–1740.

Blount, Charles. *Oracles of Reason.* London, 1693.

Bochart, Samuel. *Geographia Sacra. Cujus Pars Prior: Phaleg De Dispersione gentium & terrarum divisione facta in ædificatione turris Babel; Pars Posterior: Chanaan De Colonijs & sermone Phoenicum.* Caen, 1646.

Brerewood, Edward. *Enquiries Touching the Diversity of Languages, and Religion through the cheife Parts of the World.* London, 1614.

Browne, Thomas. *Pseudodoxia Epidemica: Or, Enquiries into very many Received Tenents, And commonly Presumed Truths.* 7th ed. London, 1669.

Burnet, Thomas. *Sacred Theory of the Earth.* 2nd ed. London, 1691.

Calmet, Augustin *Calmet's Great Dictionary of the Holy Bible: Historical, Critical, Geographical, and Etymological.* 1722. 4 vols. London, 1797.

Dunton, John. *The Athenian Oracle.* 1703. 3rd ed. Boston, 1705.

Du Pin, Louis Ellies. *Dissertationes Historiques, Chronologiques, Geographiques et Critiques Sur la Bible.* Paris, 1711.

Dury, John. *An Epistolicall Discourse of Mr. John Dury to Mr. Thorowgood. Concerning his conjecture that the Americans are descended from the Israelites.* London, 1650.

Eliot, John. *The Eliot Tracts: With Letters from Eliot to Thomas Thorowgood and Richard Baxter.* Ed. Michael P. Clark. Westport: Praeger, 2003.

Equiano, Olaudah. *The Interesting Narrative and Other Writings.* Ed. Vincent Carretta. London: Penguin, 1995.

Fuller, Nicholas. *Miscellaneorum Sacrum libri duo.* Leiden, 1622.

Godwyn, Morgan. *The Negro's & Indians Advocate, Suing for their Admission into the Church, Or a Persuasive to the Instructing and Baptizing of the Negro's and Indians in our Plantations.* London, 1680.

Hale, Sir Matthew. *The Primitive Origination of Mankind, Considered and Examined according to the Light of Nature.* London, 1677.

Jefferson, Thomas. *The Complete Jefferson.* Ed. Saul. K. Padover. New York: Tudor, 1943.

La Peyrère, Isaac. [*Prae-Adamitae*] *A Theological Systeme upon that Presupposition, That Men were before Adam.* London, 1655.

–. *Men before Adam.* London, 1656.

L'Estrange, Hamon. *Americans no Iewes; or, Improbabilities that the Americans are of that Race.* London, 1651.

Keith, George. *An Exhortation And Caution to Friends Concerning Buying Or Keeping of Negroes.* 1693. *Early American Writings.* Ed. Carla Mulford. New York: Oxford UP, 2002. 600–03.

Manasseh ben Israel. *The Hope of Israel.* 2nd. ed. London, 1650.

Mather, Cotton. *Biblia Americana.* Ed. Reiner Smolinski. Vol. 1. Tübingen and Grand Rapids: Mohr Siebeck and Baker Academic, 2010.

–. *Bonifacius: An Essay Upon the Good.* 1710. Ed. David Levin. Cambridge: Harvard UP, 1966.

–. *Diary of Cotton Mather.* Ed. Worthington C. Ford. Collections of the Massachusetts Historical Society 7th series. Vols. 7–8. Boston: MHS, 1911–12.

–. *Fair Weather: or, Considerations to Dispel the Clouds, and Allay the Storms of Discontent.* Boston, 1692.

–. *The Negro Christianized. An Essay to Excite and Assist that Good Work, The Instruction of Negroe-Servants in Christianity.* Boston, 1706.

–. *India Christiana: A Discourse, delivered unto the Commissioners, for the Propagation of the Gospel among the American Indians. ...* Boston, 1721.

–. *Magnalia Christi Americana: Or, The Ecclesiastical History of New England.* 1702. New York: Arno Press, 1972.

–. *Selected Letters of Cotton Mather.* Ed. Kenneth Silvermann. Baton Rouge: Louisiana State UP, 1971.

–. *Small Offers towards the Tabernacle in the Wilderness.* Boston, 1689.

–. *Souldiers Counselled and Comforted: A Discourse Delivered unto Some Part of the Forces Engaged in the Just War of New England against the Northern and Eastern Indians.* Boston, 1689.

–. *The Threefold Paradise of Cotton Mather: And Edition of "Triparadisus."* Ed. Reiner Smolinski. Athens: The U of Georgia P, 1995.

–. *The Triumphs of the Reformed Religion in America: The Life of the Renowned John Eliot.* London, 1691.

Mather, Samuel. *An Attempt To Shew That America Must Be Known to the Ancients.* Boston, 1773.

Mede, Joseph. "A Conjecture Concerning Gog and Magog in the Revelation." Appendix to *The Key of the Revelation, Searched and Demonstrated out of the Naturall and*

Proper Characters of the Visions. Translated into English by Richard More. 2ⁿᵈ ed. London, 1650. n.p.

Pastorius, Francis Daniel et al. "Petition of the Germantown Quakers, Reasons Why We Are against the Traffic of Menbody." 1688. *Early American Writings.* Ed. Carla Mulford. New York: Oxford UP, 2002. 727–28.

Perkins, William. *The Works of That Famous Divine and Worthy Minister of Christ in the Universitie of Cambridge, Mr. W. Perkins.* Cambridge, 1618.

Saffin, John. *A Brief and Candid Answer to a Late Printed Sheet, Entituled, The Selling of Joseph.* ... 1701. *Early American Writings.* Ed. Carla Mulford. New York: Oxford UP, 2002. 652–55.

Saurin, Jacques. *Discours Historiques, Critiques, Theologiques et Moraux.* 2 vols. Amsterdam, 1720 and 1728.

–. *Dissertations, Historical, Critical, Theological and Moral, On the most Memorable Events of the Old and New Testaments.* Trans. John Chamberlayne. 2 vols. London, 1720.

Shuckford, Samuel. *The Sacred and Prophane History of the World Connected.* ... 3 vols. London, 1728–37.

Sewall, Samuel. *The Selling of Joseph: A Memorial.* Boston, 1700.

Stillingfleet, Edward. *Origines Sacrae Or A Rational Account of the Grounds of Christian Faith, As to the Truth and Divine Authority of the Scriptures.* 1662. 3ʳᵈ ed. London, 1666.

Thorowgood, Thomas. *Iewes in America; or, Probabilities that the Americans are of that Race.* London, 1650.

Ussher, James. *Annals of the World.* London, 1658.

Vatablus, Franciscus. *Adnotationes in Sacra Biblia, et Scholia.* Parisii, 1546.

Vossius, Isaac. *Observationes ad Pomponium Melam. De situ orbis, Ipse Mela longè quam antehac emendatior praemittitur.* Hagae-Comitis, 1658.

Willard, Samuel. *Compleat Body of Divinity in Two Hundred and Fifty Expository Lectures on the Assembly's Shorter Catechism.* Boston, 1726.

Whiston, William. *A New Theory of the Earth, From its Original, To the Consummation of all Things.* ... London, 1696.

–. *Supplement to the Literal Accomplishment of Scripture Prophecies.* 1725.

Williams, Roger. *A Key into the Language of America.* London, 1643.

Winthrop, John. "Modell of Christian Charity." *Winthrop Papers.* Vol. 2. Boston: MHS, 1931. 282–95.

Secondary Sources

Allegro, James J. "'Increasing and Strengthening the Country': Law, Politics, and the Antislavery Movement in Early-Eighteenth-Century Massachusetts Bay." *New England Quarterly* 75.1 (2002): 5–23.

Allen, Don Cameron. *The Legend of Noah: Renaissance Rationalism in Art, Science, and Letters.* Urbana: U of Illinois P, 1963.

Almond, Philip. *Adam and Eve in Seventeenth-Century Thought.* Cambridge: Cambridge UP, 1999.

Aptheker, Herbert. *Anti-Racism in U.S. History: The First Two Hundred Years.* Westport: Greenwood P, 1993.

Axtell, James. *The Invasion Within: The Contest of Cultures in Colonial North America.* New York: Oxford UP, 1985.

Augstein, Hannah, ed. *Race: The Origins of an Idea, 1750–1850.* Bristol: Thoemmes Continuum, 1996.

Banton, M. *Racial Theories.* 2nd ed. Cambridge: Cambridge UP, 1998.

Benz, Ernst. "Pietist and Puritan Sources of Early Protestant World Missions." *Church History* 20.2 (1951): 28–55.

Berlin, Ira. *Generations of Captivity: A History of African-American Slaves.* Cambridge: Harvard UP, 2003.

Bremer, Francis J. *The Puritan Experiment: New England Society from Bradford to Edwards.* Rev. ed. Hanover: UP of New England, 1995.

Braude, Benjamin. "Primary Colors: Review of *The Complexion of Race: Categories of Difference in Eighteenth-Century British Culture* by Roxann Wheeler." *William and Mary Quarterly.* Third Series. 59.3 (2002): 742–46.

–. "The Sons of Noah and the Construction of Ethnic and Geographical Identities in the Medieval and Early Modern Periods." *William and Mary Quarterly.* Third Series. 54.1 (1997): 103–42.

Bruce, Dickson D. Jr. *The Origins of African American Literature, 1680–1865.* Charlottesville: U of Virginia P, 2001.

Burnside, Madeline. *Spirits of the Passage: The Transatlantic Slave Trade in the Seventeenth Century.* New York: Simon and Schuster Editions, 1997.

Carretta, Vincent. Introduction. *Unchained Voices: An Anthology of Black Authors in the English-Speaking World of the Eighteenth Century.* Ed. Vincent Carretta. Lexington: UP of Kentucky, 1996.

Cogley, Richard W. "'Some Other Kind of Being and Condition': The Controversy in Mid-Seventeenth-Century England over the Peopling of America." *Journal of the History of Ideas* 68.1 (2007): 35–57.

Cotter, William R. "The Somerset Case and the Abolition of Slavery in England." *History* 79 (1994): 31–56.

Davis, David Brion. "Constructing Race: A Reflection." *William and Mary Quarterly.* Third Series. 54.1 (1997): 7–18.

–. *Inhuman Bondage: The Rise and Fall of Slavery in the New World.* New York: Oxford UP, 2006.

–. *The Problem of Slavery in Western Culture.* Ithaca: Cornell UP, 1966.

Drescher, Seymour. *Capitalism and Antislavery: British Mobilization in Comparative Perspective.* London: Macmillan P, 1986.

Elliott, Emory. "New England Puritan Literature." *The Cambridge History of American Literature.* Gen. Ed. Sacvan Bercovitch. Vol. 1: 1590–1820. Cambridge: Cambridge UP, 1994. 169–307.

Eze, Emanuel C., ed. *Race and the Enlightenment: A Reader.* Cambridge: Cambridge UP, 1997.

Francis, Richard. *Judge Sewall's Apology: The Salem Witch Trials and the Forming of an American Conscience.* New York: HarperCollins, 2005.

Frederickson, George. *Racism: A Short History.* Princeton: Princeton UP, 2002.

Goldenberg, David M. *The Curse of Ham: Race and Slavery in Early Judaism, Christianity, and Islam.* Princeton: Princeton UP, 2003.

Gossett, Thomas F. *Race: The History of an Idea in America.* New York: Schocken Books, 1963.

Grafton, Anthony *New Worlds, Ancient Texts: The Power of Tradition and the Shock of Discovery*. Cambridge: Cambridge UP, 1992.

Greene, Lorenzo Johnston. *The Negro in Colonial New England, 1620–1776*. New York: Columbia UP, 1942.

HarperCollins Bible Dictionary. Gen. Ed. Paul J. Achtelmeier. San Francisco: Harper, 1996.

Harvey, Paul. "'A Servant of Servants Shall He Be': The Construction of Race in American Religious Mythologies." *Religion and the Creation of Race and Ethnicity*. Ed. Craig R. Prentiss. New York: New York UP, 2003. 12–27

Haynes, Stephen R. *Noah's Curse: The Biblical Justification of American Slavery*. New York: Oxford UP, 2002.

Herzogenrath, Bernd. "The Angel and the Animalculae: Cotton Mather and Inoculation." *Transatlantic Negotiations*. Ed. Christa Buschendorf and Astrid Franke. Heidelberg: Universitätsverlag Winter, 2007. 13–25.

Horton, James Oliver and Lois E. Horton, *In Hope of Liberty: Culture, Community and Protest Among Northern Free Blacks, 1700–1860*. New York: Oxford UP, 1997.

Huddleston, Lee Eldridge. *Origins of the American Indians: European Concepts, 1492–1729*. Austin: U of Texas P, 1967.

Hudson, Nicholas. "From 'Nation' to 'Race': The Origin of Racial Classification in Eighteenth-Century Thought." *Eighteenth-Century Studies* 29.3 (1996): 247–64.

Johnson, Sylvester. *The Myth of Ham in Nineteenth-Century American Christianity: Race, Heathens, and the People of God*. New York: Palgrave Macmillan, 2004.

Jordan, Winthrop D. *White Over Black: American Attitudes Toward the Negro, 1550–1812*. U of North Carolina P, 1968.

Kaplan, Sidney. "'The Selling of Joseph': Samuel Sewall and the Iniquity of Slavery." Samuel Sewall. *The Selling of Joseph: A Memorial*. Ed. Sidney Kaplan. Boston, The U of Massachusetts P, 1969. 27–54.

Keith, Thomas. *Man and the Natural World: Changing Attitudes in England, 1500–1800*. London: Penguin, 1984.

Kidd, Colin. *The Forging of Races: Race and Scripture in the Protestant Atlantic World, 1600–2000*. Cambridge: Cambridge UP, 2006.

Kolchin, Peter. *American Slavery, 1619–1877*. New York: Hill and Wong, 1993.

Koo, Kathryn S. "Strangers in the House of God': Cotton Mather, Onesimus, and an Experiment in Christian Slaveholding." *Proceedings of the American Antiquarian Society: A Journal of American History and Culture* 117.1 (2007): 143–76.

LaPlante, Eve. *Salem Witch Judge: The Life and Repentance of Samuel Sewall*. New York: HarperOne, 2007.

Lepore, Jill. *The Name of War: King Philip's War and the Origins of American Identity*. New York: Vintage, 1998.

Lovelace, Richard. *The American Pietism of Cotton Mather: Origins of American Evangelicalism*. Grand Rapids: Christian UP, 1979.

Manuel, Frank. *The Eighteenth Century Confronts the Gods*. Cambridge: Harvard UP, 1959.

McManus, Edgar. *Black Bondage in the North*. Syracuse: Syracuse UP, 1973.

Merritt, Jane T. *At the Crossroads: Indians and Empires on a Mid-Atlantic Frontier, 1700–1763*. Chapel Hill: U of North Carolina P, 2003.

Minardi, Margot. "The Boston Inoculation Controversy of 1721–1722: An Incident in the History of Race." *William and Mary Quarterly*. Third Series. 61.1 (2004): 47–76.

Minkema, Kenneth P. and Harry S. Stout. "The Edwardsean Tradition and the Antislavery Debate, 1740–1865." *Journal of American History* 92.1 (2005): 47–75.

–. "Jonathan Edwards on Slavery and the Slave Trade." *William and Mary Quarterly*. Third Series. 54.1 (1997): 823–34.

–. "Jonathan Edwards's Defense of Slavery." *Massachusetts Historical Review* 4 (2002): 23–61.

Mungello, D. E. *Curious Land: Jesuit Accommodation and the Origins of Sinology*. Studia Leibnitiana supplementa 25. Stuttgart: Steiner, 1985.

Pailin, David. *Attitudes to Other Religions: Comparative Religion in Seventeenth-Century and Eighteenth-Century Britain*. Manchester: Manchester UP, 1984.

Parfitt, Tudor. *The Lost Tribes of Israel: The History of a Myth*. London: Weidefeld & Nichols, 2002.

Peterson, Mark. A. "The Selling of Joseph: Bostonians, Antislavery, and the Protestant International." *Massachusetts Historical Review* 4 (2002): 1–23.

Peterson, Thomas V. *Ham and Japhet in America: They Mythic World of Whites in the Antebellum South*. Metuchen: American Theological Library Association, 1978.

Piersen, William D. *Black Yankees. The Development of an Afro-American Subculture in Eighteenth-Century New England*. Amherst: U of Massachusetts P, 1988.

Popkin, Richard.H. *Isaac La Peyrère (1596–1676)*. Leiden: Brill, 1987.

–. "The Philosophical Bases of Modern Racism." *The High Road to Pyrrhonism*. Ed. Richard H. Popkin and Richard A. Watson. San Diego: Austin Hill Press, 1980.

Raboteau, Albert J. *Slave Religion: The 'Invisible Institution' in the Antebellum South*. New York: Oxford UP, 1978.

Richter, Daniel K. *Facing East from Indian Country: A Native History of Early America*. Cambridge: Harvard UP, 2001.

Rosenthal, Bernard. "Puritan Conscience and New England Slavery." *New England Quarterly* 46.1 (1973): 62–81.

Rossi, P. *The Dark Abyss of Time*. Trans. L. Cochrane. Chicago: U of Chicago P, 1984.

Rooy, Sidney H. *The Theology of Missions in the Puritan Tradition: A Study of Representative Puritans: Richard Sibbes, Richard Baxter, John Eliot, Cotton Mather, and Jonathan Edwards*. Delft: Meinema, 1965.

Scheiding, Oliver. "Samuel Sewall and the Americanization of the Millennium." *Millennial Thought in America: Historical and Intellectual Contexts, 1630–1860*. Ed. Bernd Engler, Joerg O. Fichte, and Oliver Scheiding. Trier: WVT, 2002. 165–87.

Schiebinger, Londa. "The Anatomy of Difference: Race and Sex in Eighteenth-Century Science." *Eighteenth-Century Studies* 23 (1990): 387–405.

Scholder, Klaus. *The Birth of Modern Critical Theology: Origins and Problems of Biblical Criticism in the Seventeenth Century*. Trans. John Bowden. London, SCM Pres, 1990.

Silver, Peter. *Our Savage Neighbors: How Indian War Transformed Early America*. New York: Norton, 2008.

Silverman, Kenneth. *The Life and Times of Cotton Mather*. New York: Harper & Row, 1984.

Smedley, A. *Race in North America: Origin and Evolution of a Worldview*. 3rd ed. Boulder: Westview Press, 2007.

Smolinski, Reiner. "Apocalypticism in Colonial North America." *The Encyclopedia of Apocalypticism*. Vol. 3: *Apocalypticism in the Modern Period and the Contemporary Age*. Ed. Stephen J. Stein. New York: Continuum, 1998. 36–72.

–. "Authority and Interpretation: Cotton Mather's Response to the European Spinozists." *Shaping the Stuart World 1603–1714: The Atlantic Connection*. Ed. Alain I. Macinnes and Arthur H. Williamson. Leiden: Brill, 2006. 175–207.

–. "How to Go to Heaven, or How Heaven Goes? Natural Sciences and Interpretation in Cotton Mather's 'Biblia Americana' (1693–1728)." *New England Quarterly* 81.2 (2008): 278–329.

–. Introduction. *The Threefold Paradise of Cotton Mather: And Edition of "Triparadisus."* Athens and London: U of Georgia P, 1995. 3–79.

–. "*Israel Redivivus*: The Eschatological Limits of Puritan Typology in New England." *New England Quarterly* 63.3 (1990): 357–92.

Soderlund, Jean R. *Quakers and Slavery: A Divided Spirit*. Princeton: Princeton UP, 1985.

Stievermann, Jan. "Interpreting the Role of America in New England Millennialism, 1640 to 1800." *A Companion to American Cultural History: From the Colonial Period to the End of the Nineteenth Century*. Ed. Bernd Engler and Oliver Scheiding. Trier: WVT, 2009. 121–63.

Thomas, G. E. "Puritans, Indians, and the Concept of Race." *New England Quarterly* 48.1 (1975): 3–27.

Towner, Lawrence. "'A Fondness for Freedom': Servant Protest in Puritan Society." *William and Mary Quarterly*. Third Series. 19.2 (1962): 201–19.

–. "The Sewall-Saffin Dialogue on Slavery." *William and Mary Quarterly*. Third Series. 21.1 (1964): 40–52.

Twombley, Robert C. and Robert H. Moore. "Black Puritan: The Negro in Seventeenth-Century Massachusetts." *William and Mary Quarterly*. Third Series. 24.2 (1967): 224–42.

Von Frank, Albert J. "John Saffin: Slavery and Racism in Colonial Massachusetts." *Early American Literature* 29.3 (1994): 254–72.

Vaughan, Alden T. *Roots of American Racism: Essays on the Colonial Experience*. Oxford: Oxford UP, 1995.

Ward, Nathaniel. "The Massachusetts Body of Liberties." *Puritan Political Ideas: 1558–1794*. Ed. Edmund S. Morgan. Indianapolis: Bobbs-Merrill, 1965. 177–203.

Wheeler, Rachel M. "Edwards as Missionary." *The Cambridge Companion to Jonathan Edwards*. Ed. Stephen J. Stein. Cambridge: Cambridge UP, 2007. 196–217.

Wheeler, Roxann. *The Complexions of Race: Categories of Difference in Eighteenth-Century British Culture*. Philadelphia: U of Pennsylvania P, 2000.

Whitford, David M. *The Curse of Ham in the Early Modern Era: The Bible and the Justification for Slavery*. Farnham: Ashgate, 2009.

Contributors

Francis J. Bremer is Professor of History at Millersville University of Pennsylvania. He is interested in transatlantic Puritanism of the seventeenth century and has published more than fourteen books. He is the author of *Puritanism: A Very Short Introduction* (2009) and is completing a full-length biography of the Puritan divine John Davenport.

Robert E. Brown is Assistant Professor of Religious Studies at James Madison University, in Harrisonburg, Virginia. His research focuses on religion in early America. He has written on Jonathan Edwards and is currently working on the intellectual life of Ezra Stiles. Moreover, he is a contributor to *The Blackwell Companion to Religion in America* and editor of vol. 9 (Rom. through Philem.) of *Biblia Americana*.

Michael P. Clark is Professor of English and Vice Provost for Academic Planning at the University of California, Irvine. Research interests include early America, the history of literary theory, and contemporary U.S. fiction. His most recent book is an edition of *The Eliot Tracts*, a collection of religious books and pamphlets written by and about colonial Puritan missionaries and their work with Native Americans in seventeenth- and eighteenth-century New England. His other publications include articles on early American literature, witchcraft, and millennialism; books and articles on Jacques Lacan, Michel Foucault, literary theory, and on the Vietnam War and the representation of violence in contemporary US society. He is the editor of vol. 10 (Heb. through Rev.) of *Biblia Americana*.

Michael Dopffel recently finished his M.A. in American Studies at the University of Tübingen, where he will also pursue a Ph.D. He works as an assistant editor for vol. 5 (Prov. through Isa.) of *Biblia Americana*.

Helen K. Gelinas holds an M.A. in American Studies from the University of Tübingen and is currently working on her dissertation project, "Feminine Typology in Cotton Mather's 'Biblia Americana'" She is interested in all aspects of colonial history and literature and has published on Jonathan Edwards's eschatology. She also works as an assisytant editor for vol. 5 (Prov. through Isa.) of *Biblia Americana*.

E. Brooks Holifield is the Charles Howard Candler Professor of American Church History at Emory University in Atlanta, Georgia. His current interest is the comparison of religious developments in the United States and Europe. His *Theology in America: Christian Thought from the Age of the Puritans to the Civil War* (2003) won the Outler Prize of the American Society of Church History, and his *God's Ambassadors: A History of the Christian Clergy in America* (2007) won the Book of the Year Award from the American Association of Parish Clergy. He was named the Emory University Scholar-Teacher of the Year in 2010.

Rick Kennedy is Professor of History at Point Loma Nazarene University, San Diego, California, where he teaches early American and ancient history. He is the author of *A History of Reasonableness: Testimony and Authority in the Art of Thinking* (2004) and various works on textbooks and logic at Harvard College during the colonial period. He is the editor of vol. 8 (John through Acts) of *Biblia Americana*.

David Komline is a doctoral student in history at the University of Notre Dame, Indiana. His research examines nineteenth-century American religion in the context of international and especially German developments and has recently been supported by grants from the Deutsche Akademische Austausch Dienst (DAAD) and the Institute for the Study of American Evangelicals.

Harry Clark Maddux is Assistant Professor of English at Austin Peay State University in Clarksville, Tennessee. He received his PhD in American Studies from Purdue University in 2001, and since then has published on both Edward Taylor and Cotton Mather in several journals and essay collections, most recently in *Early American Literature*. He has held a summer stipend from the National Endowment for the Humanities (NEH) and has been a research fellow at the Huntington Library in San Marino, California, the Beinecke Library at Yale, and the Herzog August Bibliothek in Wolfenbüttel, Germany. Dr. Maddux is editing vol. 4 (Ezra through Ps.) of the *Biblia Americana* and assisting Rick Kennedy with his volume.

Kenneth P. Minkema is the Executive Editor of *The Works of Jonathan Edwards* and of the Jonathan Edwards Center & Online Archive at Yale University, New Haven, Connecticut, with a Research Faculty appointment at Yale Divinity School. His research focuses on early American and early modern religious history. He has edited vol. 14 in the *Works of Jonathan Edwards, Ser-*

mons and Discourses: 1723–1729, co-edited *A Jonathan Edwards Reader, The Sermons of Jonathan Edwards: A Reader*, as well as *Jonathan Edwards at 300: Essays on the Tercentennial of His Birth*, and *Jonathan Edwards's "Sinners in the Hands of an Angry God": A Casebook*. He has also co-edited *The Sermon Notebook of Samuel Parris, 1689–1694*, dealing with the Salem Witchcraft crisis, and *The Colonial Church Records of Reading and Rumney Marsh, Massachusetts*. Dr. Minkema is also editing vol. 3 (Josh. through Chron.) of the *Biblia Americana*.

ADRIAAN C. NEELE is Assistant Editor of *The Works of Jonathan Edwards*, Research Scholar at Yale Divinity School, New Haven, Connecticut, and Professor Extraordinary at the University of the Free State, Bloemfontein, South Africa. His research interests include Post-reformation studies and Early American history. Most recently, he published *Petrus van Mastricht (1630–1706): Reformed Orthodoxy, Method and Piety* (2009).

PAUL SILAS PETERSON is in the process of finishing his doctoral degree in theology at the University of Tübingen. He is interested in Biblical, systematic and historical theology as well as theological ethics; he earned an MA from Western Seminary and a MTh from the University of Edinburgh. He works as an assistant editor for vol. 5 (Prov. through Isa.) of *Biblia Americana*.

OLIVER SCHEIDING is Professor and Chair of American Literature at the University of Mainz, Germany. His main research areas are colonial literature and Early American Studies. He is co-editor of *Key Concepts in American Cultural History* (2007) and of the forthcoming *American Literature: An Introduction*.

REINER SMOLINSKI is Professor of American Literature at Georgia State University, Atlanta, and the General Editor of Cotton Mather's "Biblia Americana" holograph manuscript. He has published on a wide variety of Matheriana, on millennialism, typology, Salem witchcraft, and Spinozism, on John Cotton, Roger Williams, Poe, and Hawthorne, but most recently on Cotton Mather and Newtonian science. He has published the first volume of *Biblia Americana: Genesis* (2010) and has now turned to vols. 2 (Exod. through Deut.) and 7 (Matt. through Luke) in the same series.

WINTON U. SOLBERG is Professor Emeritus of History at the University of Illinois, Urbana-Champaign. His research interests focus on American intellectual and cultural history, with an emphasis on religion, science, legal and constitutional issues, and higher education. Most recently, he published *Reforming Medical Education: The University of Illinois College of Medicine, 1880–1920* (2009).

STEPHEN J. STEIN is Chancellor's Professor of Religious Studies, Emeritus, at Indiana University, Bloomington. He is the editor of three volumes of biblical manuscripts in the Yale Edition of *The Works of Jonathan Edwards*. His research interests include eighteenth-century religious history as well as the study of new religious movements in the United States. He is currently serving as the General Editor of the forthcoming three-volume *Cambridge History of Religions in America*.

JAN STIEVERMANN is Junior Professor of American Studies at the University of Tübingen. He has published on a broad range of topics in the fields of American religious history, culture, and literature, including articles for *Early American Literature* and *William and Mary Quarterly*. His first book is a comprehensive study of Ralph Waldo Emerson's religious thought and aesthetics. He is currently at work on his second book project on religion in contemporary ethnic minority literatures. Concurrently, he is editing vol. 5 (Prov. through Isa.) of Cotton Mather's *Biblia Americana*. For this project he also serves as executive editor.

HARRY S. STOUT is Jonathan Edwards Professor of American Christianity at Yale University and General Editor of *The Works of Jonathan Edwards*. He is coeditor of vol. 22 entitled *Sermons and Discourses 1739–1742* and of *A Jonathan Edwards Reader*. He is the author of *The New England Soul: Preaching and Religious Culture in Colonial New England* and of *The Divine Dramatist: George Whitefield and the Rise of Modern Evangelicalism*.

WILLIAM VAN ARRAGON is Assistant Professor of History at The King's University College in Edmonton, Alberta, Canada. His research interests include the history of New England Puritanism, American religion, and critical theory. He is working on revising his doctoral dissertation, "Cotton Mather in American Cultural Memory," for publication with Indiana University Press.

PAUL M. WISE is Assistant Professor of English as South Georgia College, in Douglas. His research interests include early American and early modern European folk culture and witchcraft, Native American shamanism, and ethno-botanical religious customs. Currently, Dr. Wise is implementing "The Big Read" at SGC, a National Endowment for the Arts grant (NEH), and is revising his critical edition of Cotton Mather's *Wonders of the Invisible World* for publication.

General Index

see also Angels; Ark of the Covenant; Cherubim; Idolatry; Moses; John Spencer

Callenberg, Johann Heinrich (Halle Pietist) 36, 133, 137, 138, 139, 140, 141, 142, 144, 145, 146
– establishes *Institutum Judaicum* in Halle 140, 141, 142
– and *Narratio Epistolica* 138, 140, 143, 144, 149–62
    see also August Hermann Francke; Cotton Mather; Society for Promoting Christian Knowledge (SPCK)

Calmet, Augustin 4, 48, 298, 330, 550, 570

Calvin, John 83, 84, 114, 115, 171, 172, 277, 291, 321, 326, 330, 364, 376, 384, 395, 396, 504, 512

Calvinism 15, 30, 62, 83, 84, 85, 86, 88, 89, 93, 99, 115, 118, 129, 131, 132, 133, 135, 147, 148, 179, 229, 244, 256, 293, 304, 341, 394, 417, 453, 515, 551, 568, 570

Cartesianism 8, 125, 169, 170, 177, 186, 190, 225, 231, 240, 266, 275, 343, 400

Cartwright, Thomas 115, 129

The Case of a Troubled Mind (1717) 93

Cassiodorus 269, 272, 274

Chauncy, Charles 93, 95, 105, 500

Cherubim 41, 300, 311–12, 314, 318–23, 325–26, 327, 331, 385, 389, 392, 394, 401–02
    see also Angels; Calf worship; Idolatry

Chilmead, Edmund 312, 331

Christian Hebraists 9, 44, 169, 296, 303, 385, 398, 407

The Christian Philosopher (1721) 3, 19, 32, 37, 39, 48, 53, 85, 90, 107, 109, 113, 125, 128, 130, 148, 169, 172–73, 176, 178, 179, 183, 193, 194, 196, 197, 198, 205, 216, 224, 225, 231, 240, 255, 264, 270, 274, 413, 437, 507, 508, 512

Christianus per Ignem (1702) 408, 410

Cicero, Marcus Tullius (Tully) 265, 271, 317, 339, 372, 374

Clarke, Samuel 185, 190, 197, 200, 265, 275, 449, 457, 458

Clarkson, Thomas 533, 534

Clement Alexandrinus 270, 271, 272, 274, 275, 375, 422, 430

Coelestinus: A Conversation in Heaven (1723) 86, 107, 232, 255, 383, 410

Coheleth (1720) 146, 240, 255

Collins, Anthony 9, 37, 192, 197, 200

Collins, William 85, 107

Colman, Benjamin 65, 66, 67, 68, 70, 71, 74, 78, 80, 167

Comenius, Jan Amos 118, 120, 123, 124

A Conquest over the Grand Excuse of Sinfulness (1703) 84, 107

The Converted Sinner (1724) 84, 107

Copernicus, Nicolaus 8, 170, 183, 210, 213, 214

Corderius Americanus (1708) 92

Cotton, John 3, 75, 116, 119, 120, 121, 127, 229, 579

Cotton, Josiah 65, 67, 80

Cranmer, Thomas 114, 115, 129

Critici Sacri 4, 27, 367, 380, 397, 404, 409
    see also "Biblia Americana"; John Pearson; Cotton Mather; *Biblia Sacra Polyglotta*; *Synopsis Criticorum*; Matthew Poole, Brian Walton

Crocker, Hannah Mather 90

Cudworth, Ralph 190, 197, 200, 391

"Curiosa Americana" (1712–24) 38, 183, 203, 204, 205, 206, 210, 211, 215, 216, 217, 218, 220, 221, 224

Cyril of Alexandria 158, 235, 428, 436

Dacier, André 351, 352, 357

Davenport, John 36, 116, 117, 119, 120, 121, 122, 123, 124, 125, 127, 577

De La Mothe, C.G. 195–96, 198

Delitzsch, Friedrich 295, 334

Demos, John Putnam 14, 50, 229, 256

Descartes, René *See* Cartesianism

The Diary of Cotton Mather (1910–11, 1964) 3, 4, 13, 16, 17, 26, 27, 48, 69, 74, 75, 77, 94, 96, 107, 135, 136, 139, 140, 145, 146, 148, 149, 151, 158, 163, 184, 185, 193, 194, 198, 227, 230, 231, 232, 233, 255, 261, 263, 274, 286, 292,

383, 410, 445–47, 450, 451, 453, 454–
55, 456, 458, 463, 477, 488, 493, 497,
500, 506, 509, 512, 545, 559, 571
Dickinson, Edmund 20, 87, 93, 105, 343,
349, 350, 351, 353, 354, 355, 357
Diodorus Siculus 319, 330, 338, 339
Doddridge, Philip 371, 373, 374, 375, 380
Douglass, William 15, 517
Drake, Samuel G. 97, 99, 105
Du Pin, Louis Ellis 528, 570
Dury, John 117, 118, 119, 120, 121, 122,
123, 124, 125, 127, 129, 540, 570

Earbery, Matthias 191, 197, 200
Ecumenism *See* Cotton Mather
Edwards, George (ornithologist) 211,
212, 224
Edwards, John 9, 23, 234, 235, 255, 299,
302, 316, 317, 331, 345, 346, 347, 349,
350, 353, 354, 357, 370, 497, 498, 499,
503, 504, 512
Edwards, Jonathan 11, 16, 17, 30, 31, 32,
42, 43, 44, 50, 51, 52, 53, 85, 87, 88,
89, 93, 99, 105, 106, 107, 129, 167, 177,
178, 179, 180, 278, 291, 358, 363–82,
385, 406, 407, 408, 410, 412, 491, 492,
494, 520, 541, 568, 569, 570, 573, 575,
576, 577, 578, 579, 580
–   and Cotton Mather 363–79, 406–
08, 413–38
Eichhorn, Johann Gottfried 11, 296
Eliot, John 49, 90, 122, 127, 131, 500, 510,
511, 539, 540, 541, 544, 545, 570, 571,
575, 577
Enlightenment 18, 19, 22, 29, 31, 37, 39,
44, 47, 53, 54, 85, 88, 130, 147, 183,
185–88, 193, 196, 199, 200, 201, 205,
208, 209, 225, 228, 242, 243, 280, 283,
293, 294, 304, 330, 335, 358, 396, 413,
457, 514, 519, 531, 568, 573
see also "Biblia Americana"; Cotton
Mather
Emerson, Joseph 91, 102, 106
Emerson, Ralph Waldo 19, 20, 23, 579
Emmons, Nathaniel 88, 108
Epicurean 241, 268
Epicurus *See* Epicurean

Equiano, Olaudah (Gustavus Vassa) 533,
534, 571
Eschatology *See* Millennialism; Cotton
Mather
Eusebius of Caesarea 24, 271, 272, 274,
275, 310, 331, 339, 341, 350, 351, 352,
353, 357, 372, 374, 392
Evangelicalism 19, 22, 28, 29, 30, 31, 32,
35, 36, 51, 52, 53, 87, 92, 117, 131, 134,
137, 139, 141, 142, 144, 147, 153–56,
158–59, 160, 161, 166, 278, 293, 331,
339, 365, 442, 445, 459, 489, 541, 545,
561, 568, 569

*Fair Weather: or, Considerations to Dispel
the Clouds* (1692) 543, 571
Family Religion, Excited and Assisted
(1707) 92
*Febrifugium. An Essay for the Cure of
Ungoverned Anger* (1717) 423, 437
Felker, Christopher D. 16, 18, 50, 95, 99,
109
Fisher, Samuel 187, 499
Fisher, Will 500, 502, 513
Flavius, Josephus *See* Josephus Flavius
Francke, August Hermann (Halle
Pietist) 10, 23, 25, 36, 48, 49, 85, 127,
128, 163, 164, 165, 166, 175, 176, 445,
447
–   and Correspondence with Cotton
Mather 131–62
–   *Manuductio ad Lectionem* 10, 48,
148, 151
–   Maxims of Piety of, 132
–   *Orphanotropheo* 136, 138, 150, 152
–   *Pietas Hallensis* 135, 137, 138, 140,
142
–   *Segensvolle Fußstapfen* 134, 141
See also Anton Wilhelm Böhme;
Johann Heinrich Callenberg;
Cotton Mather and Pietism; Society
for Promoting Christian Knowledge
(SPCK)
Francke, Gotthilf August (son of A.H.
Francke) 142
Francke, Kuno 132, 134, 135, 136, 138,
164